GUARDI
OF THE GALAXY

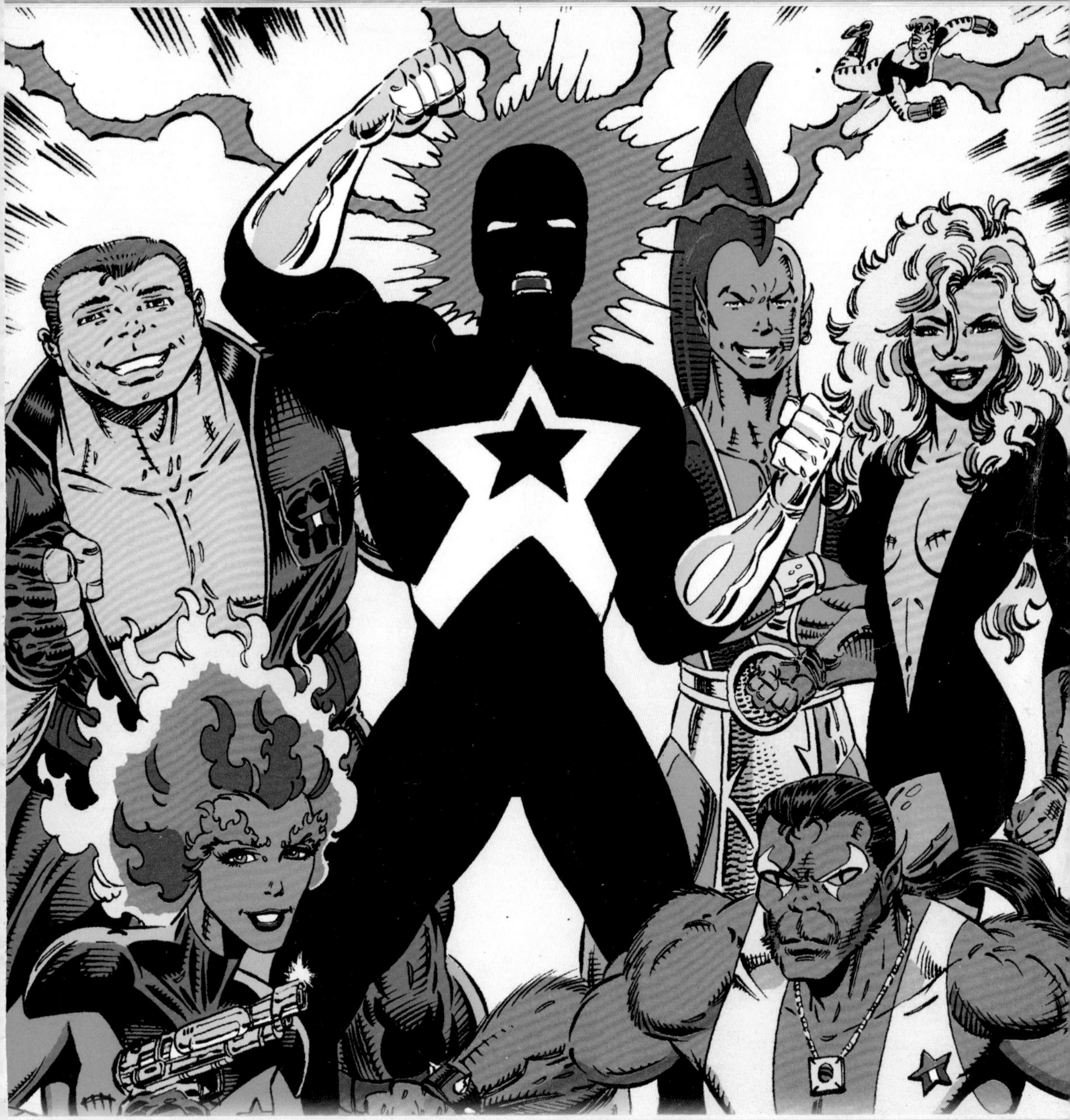

FRONT COVER ARTISTS: Kevin West, Steve Montano & Veronica Gandini
BACK COVER ARTIST: Kevin West

RESEARCH & LAYOUT: Jeph York
PRODUCTION: ColorTek, Romie Jeffers & Ryan Devall

COLLECTION EDITOR: Mark D. Beazley
ASSOCIATE EDITOR: Sarah Brunstad
ASSOCIATE MANAGER, DIGITAL ASSETS: Joe Hochstein
SENIOR EDITOR, SPECIAL PROJECTS: Jennifer Grunwald
VP, PRODUCTION & SPECIAL PROJECTS: Jeff Youngquist
SVP PRINT, SALES & MARKETING: David Gabriel

EDITOR IN CHIEF: Axel Alonso
CHIEF CREATIVE OFFICER: Joe Quesada
PUBLISHER: Dan Buckley
EXECUTIVE PRODUCER: Alan Fine

GUARDIANS OF THE GALAXY CLASSIC: IN THE YEAR 3000 VOL. 2. Contains material originally published in magazine form as GUARDIANS OF THE GALAXY #40-50 and ANNUAL #4, and GALACTIC GUARDIANS #1-4. First printing 2016. ISBN# 978-1-302-90214-8. Published by MARVEL WORLDWIDE, INC., a subsidiary of MARVEL ENTERTAINMENT, LLC. OFFICE OF PUBLICATION: 135 West 50th Street, New York, NY 10020. Copyright © 2016 MARVEL No similarity between any of the names, characters, persons, and/or institutions in this magazine with those of any living or dead person or institution is intended, and any such similarity which may exist is purely coincidental. **Printed in Canada.** ALAN FINE, President, Marvel Entertainment; DAN BUCKLEY, President, TV, Publishing & Brand Management; JOE QUESADA, Chief Creative Officer; TOM BREVOORT, SVP of Publishing; DAVID BOGART, SVP of Business Affairs & Operations, Publishing & Partnership; C.B. CEBULSKI, VP of Brand Management & Development, Asia; DAVID GABRIEL, SVP of Sales & Marketing, Publishing; JEFF YOUNGQUIST, VP of Production & Special Projects; DAN CARR, Executive Director of Publishing Technology; ALEX MORALES, Director of Publishing Operations; SUSAN CRESPI, Production Manager; STAN LEE, Chairman Emeritus. For information regarding advertising in Marvel Comics or on Marvel.com, please contact Vit DeBellis, Integrated Sales Manager, at vdebellis@marvel.com. For Marvel subscription inquiries, please call 888-511-5480. **Manufactured between 7/8/2016 and 8/15/2016 by SOLISCO PRINTERS, SCOTT, QC, CANADA.**

10 9 8 7 6 5 4 3 2 1

GUARDIANS OF THE GALAXY

IN THE YEAR 3000

WRITER
MICHAEL GALLAGHER

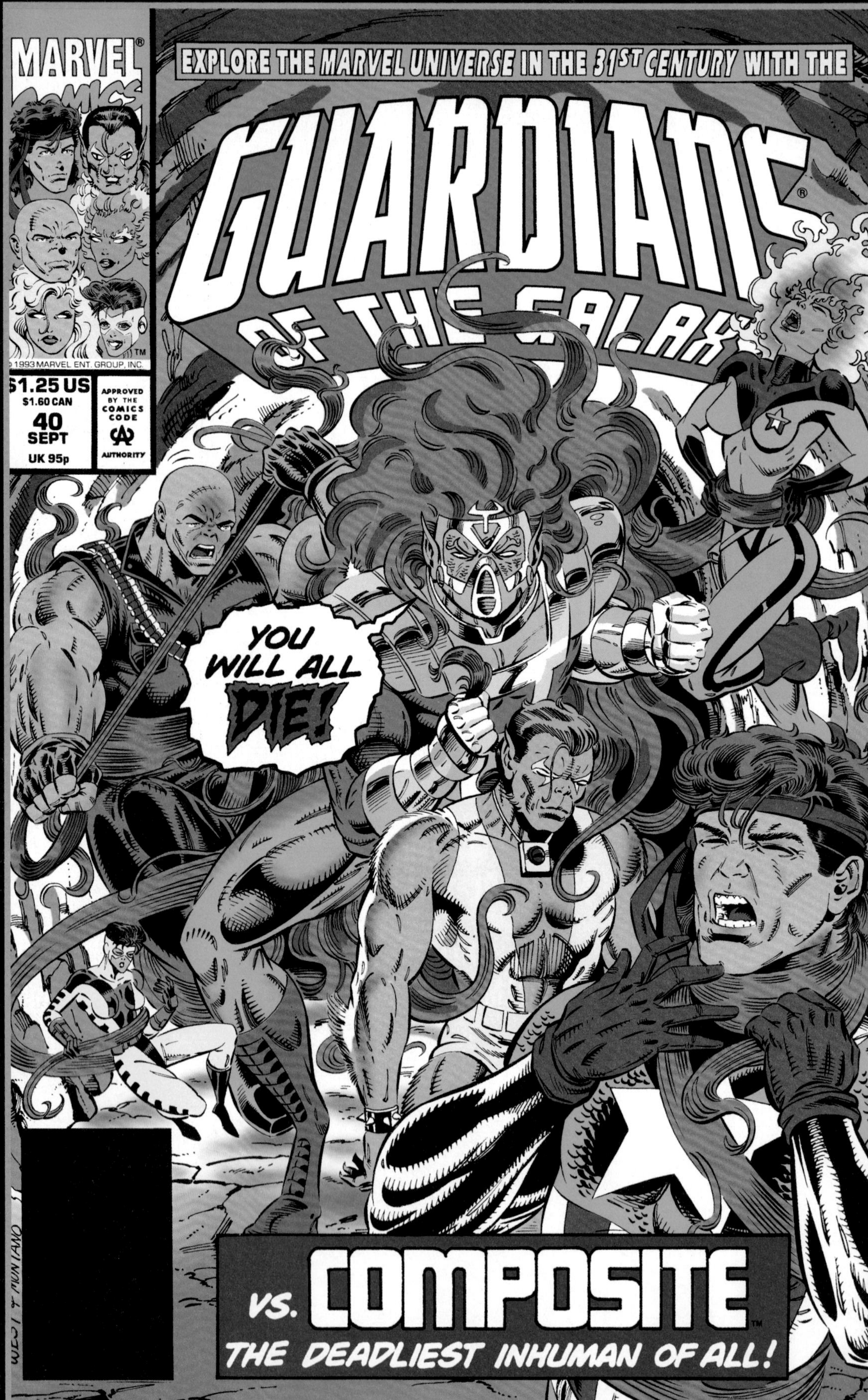
MARVEL COMICS
EXPLORE THE MARVEL UNIVERSE IN THE 31ST CENTURY WITH THE
GUARDIANS
OF THE GALAX
© 1993 MARVEL ENT. GROUP, INC.
$1.25 US
$1.60 CAN
40
SEPT
UK 95p
APPROVED BY THE COMICS CODE AUTHORITY
YOU WILL ALL DIE!
VS. COMPOSITE
THE DEADLIEST INHUMAN OF ALL!

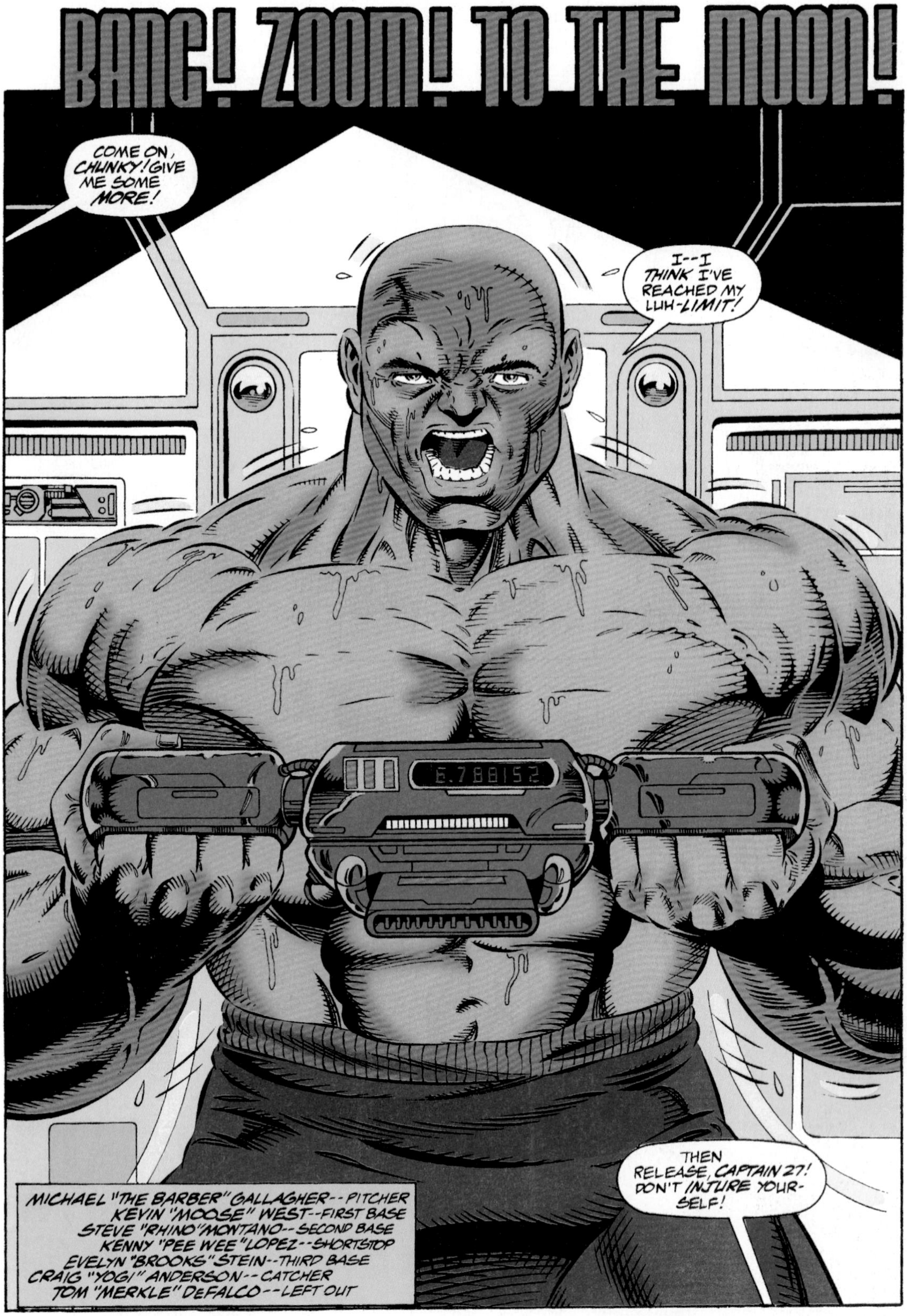
BANG! ZOOM! TO THE MOON!
COME ON, CHUNKY! GIVE ME SOME MORE!
I--I THINK I'VE REACHED MY LUH-LIMIT!
THEN RELEASE, CAPTAIN 27! DON'T INJURE YOURSELF!
MICHAEL "THE BARBER" GALLAGHER--PITCHER
KEVIN "MOOSE" WEST--FIRST BASE
STEVE "RHINO" MONTANO--SECOND BASE
KENNY "PEE WEE" LOPEZ--SHORTSTOP
EVELYN "BROOKS" STEIN--THIRD BASE
CRAIG "YOGI" ANDERSON--CATCHER
TOM "MERKLE" DeFALCO--LEFT OUT

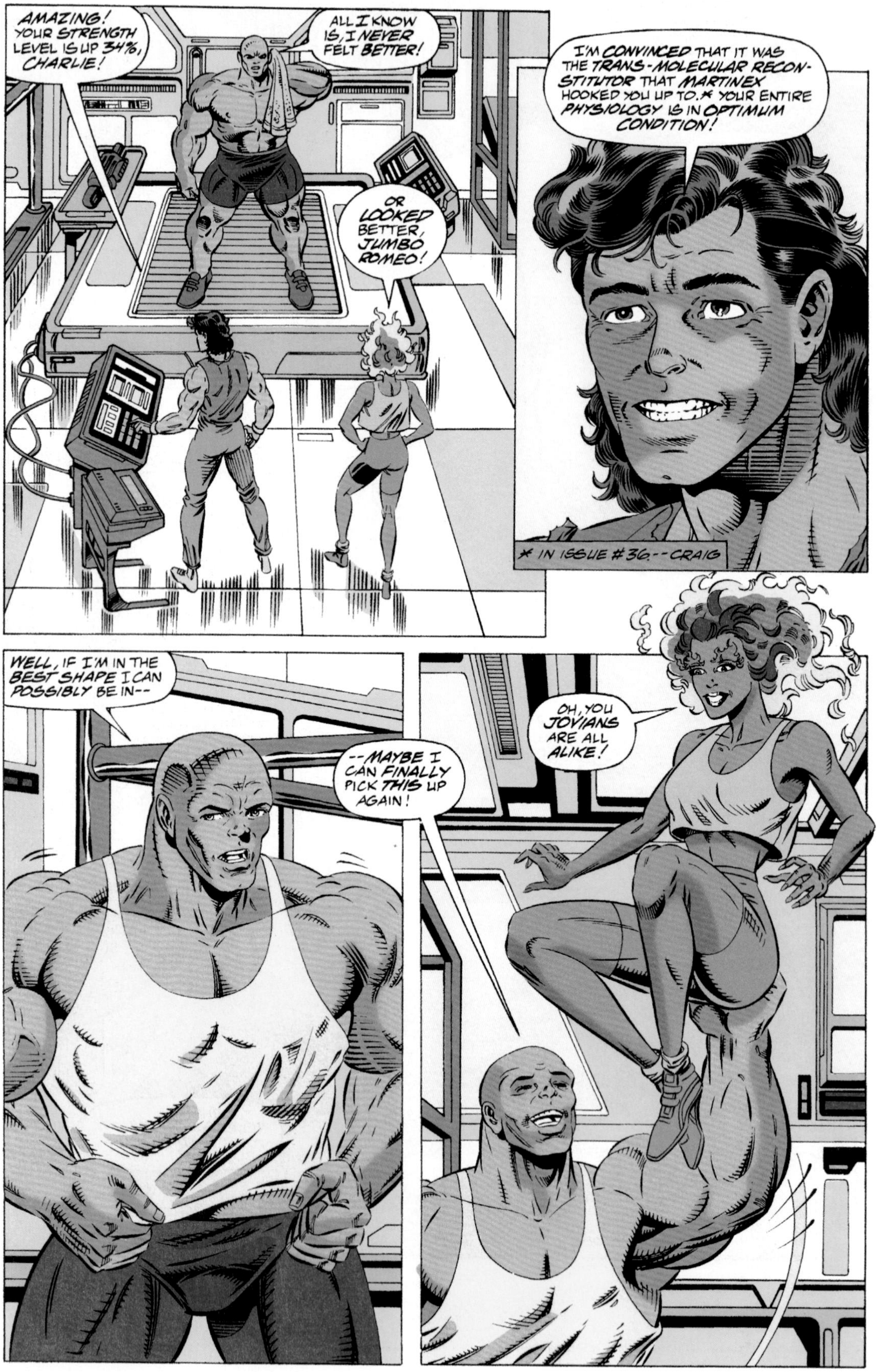
AMAZING! YOUR STRENGTH LEVEL IS UP 34%, CHARLIE!
ALL I KNOW IS, I NEVER FELT BETTER!
OR LOOKED BETTER, JUMBO ROMEO!
I'M CONVINCED THAT IT WAS THE TRANS-MOLECULAR RECONSTITUTOR THAT MARTINEX HOOKED YOU UP TO.* YOUR ENTIRE PHYSIOLOGY IS IN OPTIMUM CONDITION!
* IN ISSUE #36.--CRAIG
WELL, IF I'M IN THE BEST SHAPE I CAN POSSIBLY BE IN--
--MAYBE I CAN FINALLY PICK THIS UP AGAIN!
OH, YOU JOVIANS ARE ALL ALIKE!

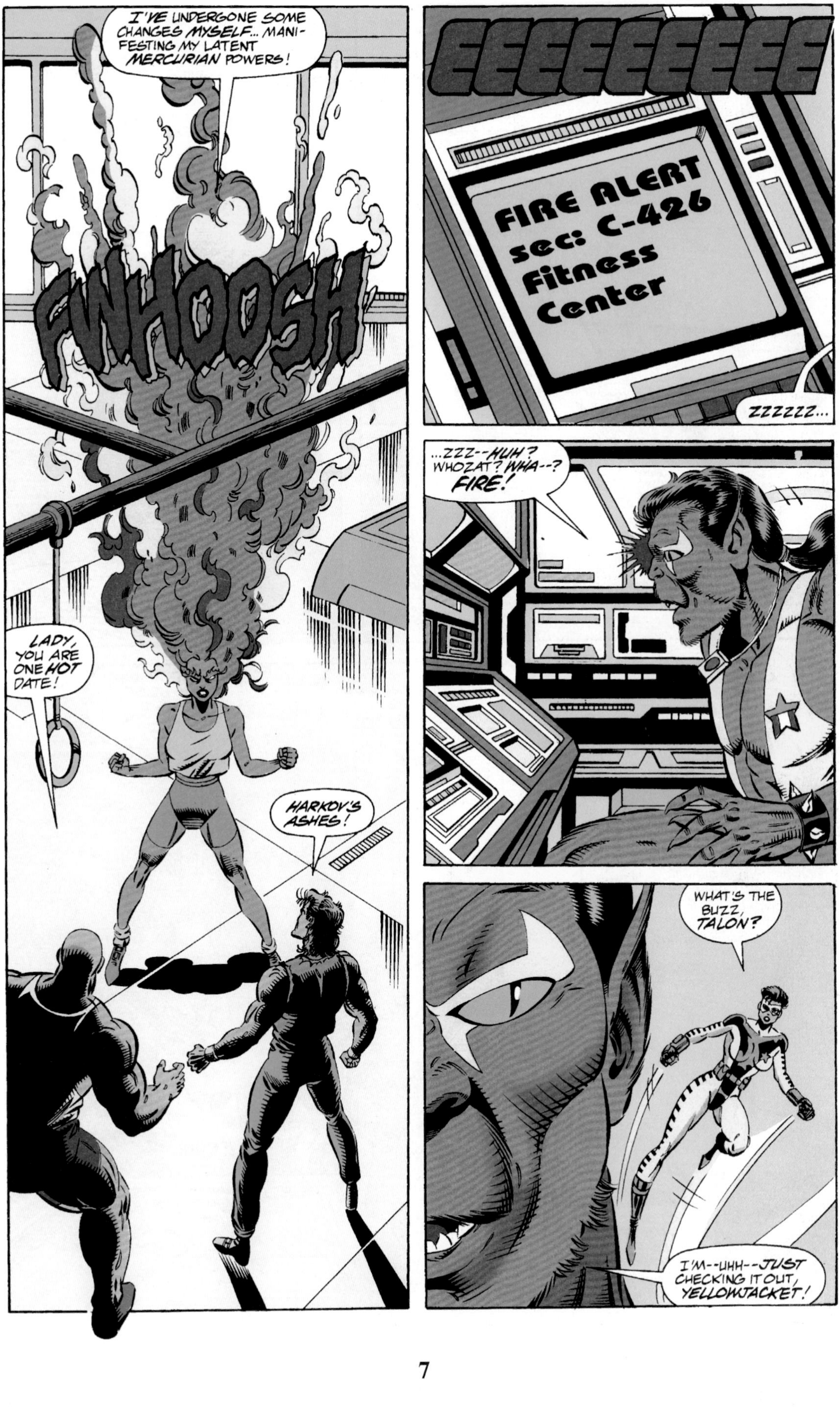
I'VE UNDERGONE SOME CHANGES MYSELF... MANI-FESTING MY LATENT MERCURIAN POWERS!
FWHOOSH
LADY, YOU ARE ONE HOT DATE!
HARKOV'S ASHES!
EEEEEEEEEE
FIRE ALERT
sec: C-426
Fitness
Center
ZZZZZZ...
...ZZZ--HUH? WHOZAT? WHA--? FIRE!
WHAT'S THE BUZZ, TALON?
I'M--UHH--JUST CHECKING IT OUT, YELLOWJACKET!

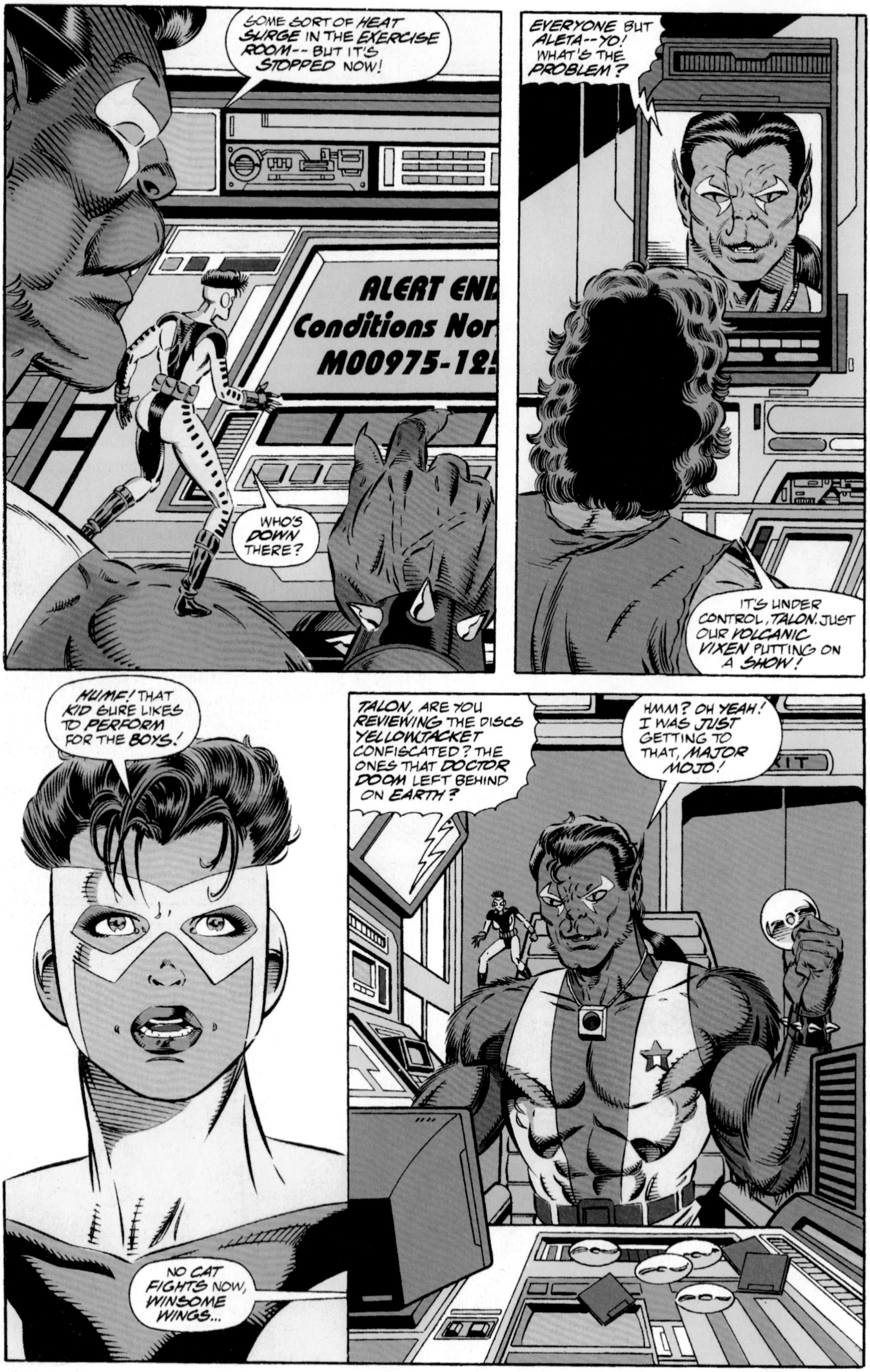
SOME SORT OF HEAT SURGE IN THE EXERCISE ROOM-- BUT IT'S STOPPED NOW!
ALERT END
Conditions Nor
M00975-125
WHO'S DOWN THERE?
EVERYONE BUT ALETA--YO! WHAT'S THE PROBLEM?
IT'S UNDER CONTROL, TALON. JUST OUR VOLCANIC VIXEN PUTTING ON A SHOW!
HUMF! THAT KID SURE LIKES TO PERFORM FOR THE BOYS!
NO CAT FIGHTS NOW, WINSOME WINGS...
TALON, ARE YOU REVIEWING THE DISCS YELLOWJACKET CONFISCATED? THE ONES THAT DOCTOR DOOM LEFT BEHIND ON EARTH?
HMM? OH YEAH! I WAS JUST GETTING TO THAT, MAJOR MOJO!

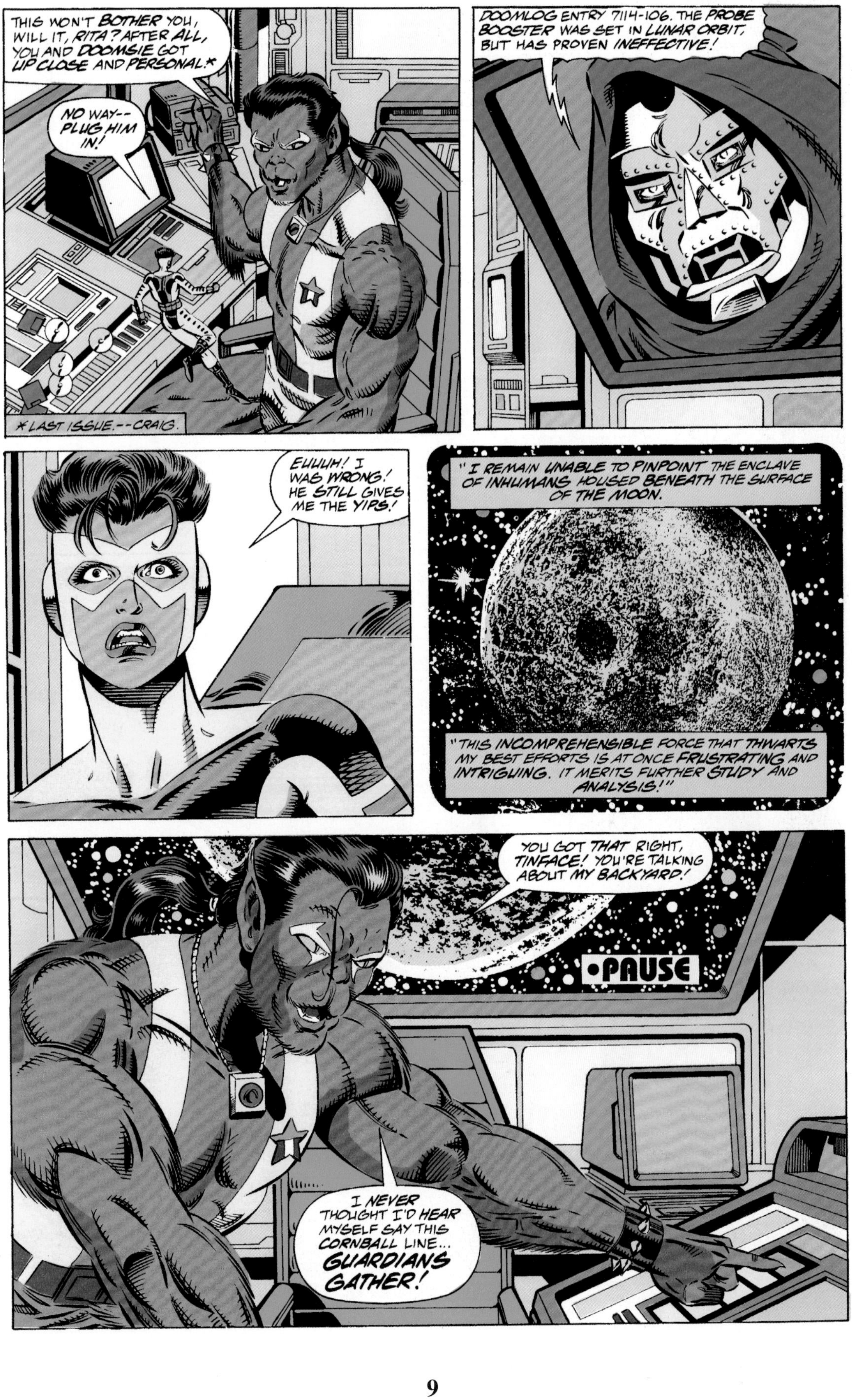
THIS WON'T BOTHER YOU, WILL IT, RITA? AFTER ALL, YOU AND DOOMSIE GOT UP CLOSE AND PERSONAL.*
NO WAY-- PLUG HIM IN!
*LAST ISSUE.--CRAIG.
DOOMLOG ENTRY 7114-106. THE PROBE BOOSTER WAS SET IN LUNAR ORBIT, BUT HAS PROVEN INEFFECTIVE!
EUUUH! I WAS WRONG! HE STILL GIVES ME THE YIPS!
"I REMAIN UNABLE TO PINPOINT THE ENCLAVE OF INHUMANS HOUSED BENEATH THE SURFACE OF THE MOON.
"THIS INCOMPREHENSIBLE FORCE THAT THWARTS MY BEST EFFORTS IS AT ONCE FRUSTRATING AND INTRIGUING. IT MERITS FURTHER STUDY AND ANALYSIS!"
YOU GOT THAT RIGHT, TINFACE! YOU'RE TALKING ABOUT MY BACKYARD!
•PAUSE
I NEVER THOUGHT I'D HEAR MYSELF SAY THIS CORNBALL LINE... GUARDIANS GATHER!

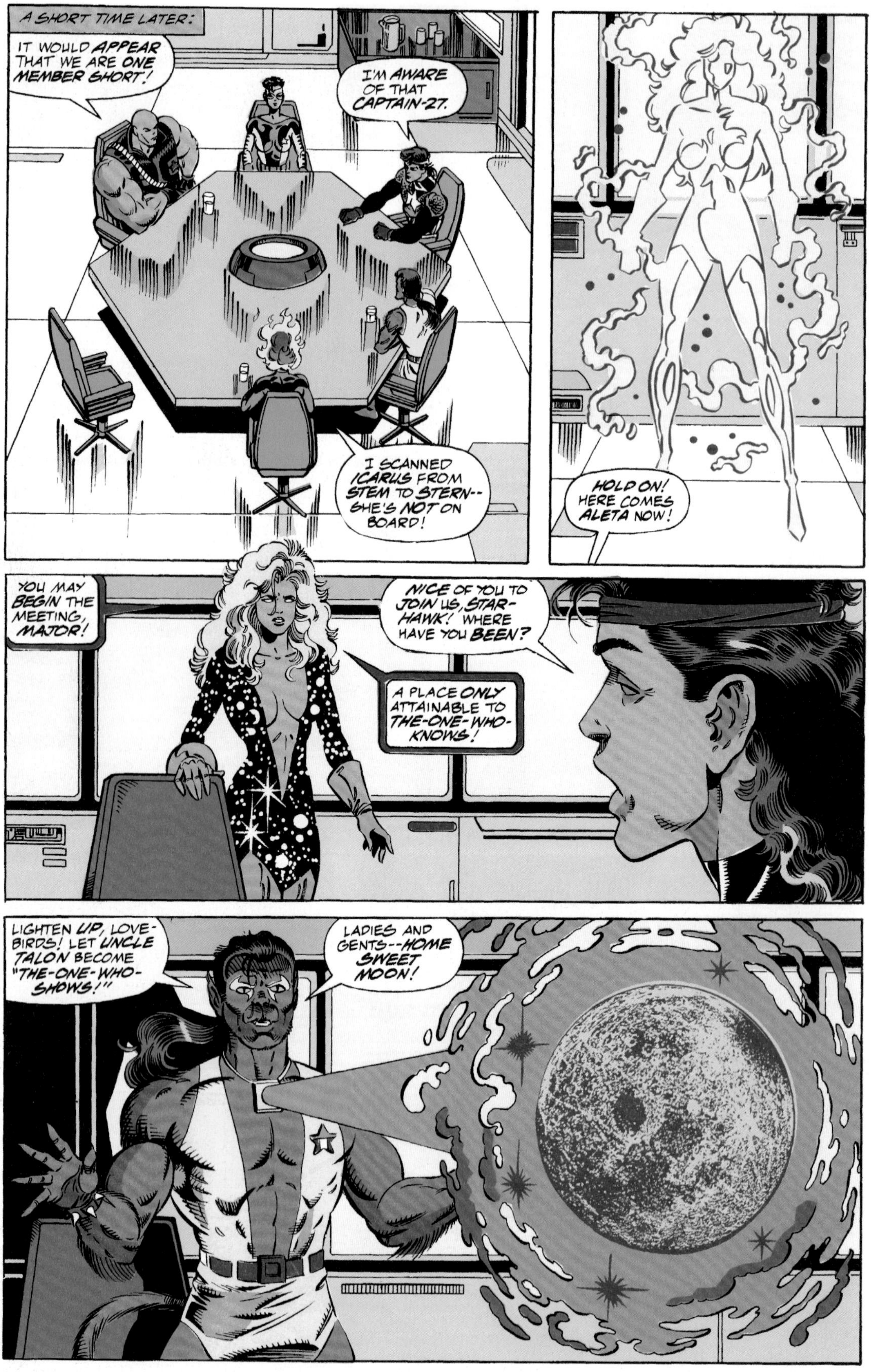
A SHORT TIME LATER:
IT WOULD APPEAR THAT WE ARE ONE MEMBER SHORT!
I'M AWARE OF THAT CAPTAIN-27.
I SCANNED ICARUS FROM STEM TO STERN-- SHE'S NOT ON BOARD!
HOLD ON! HERE COMES ALETA NOW!
YOU MAY BEGIN THE MEETING, MAJOR!
NICE OF YOU TO JOIN US, STAR-HAWK! WHERE HAVE YOU BEEN?
A PLACE ONLY ATTAINABLE TO THE-ONE-WHO-KNOWS!
LIGHTEN UP, LOVE-BIRDS! LET UNCLE TALON BECOME "THE-ONE-WHO-SHOWS!"
LADIES AND GENTS--HOME SWEET MOON!

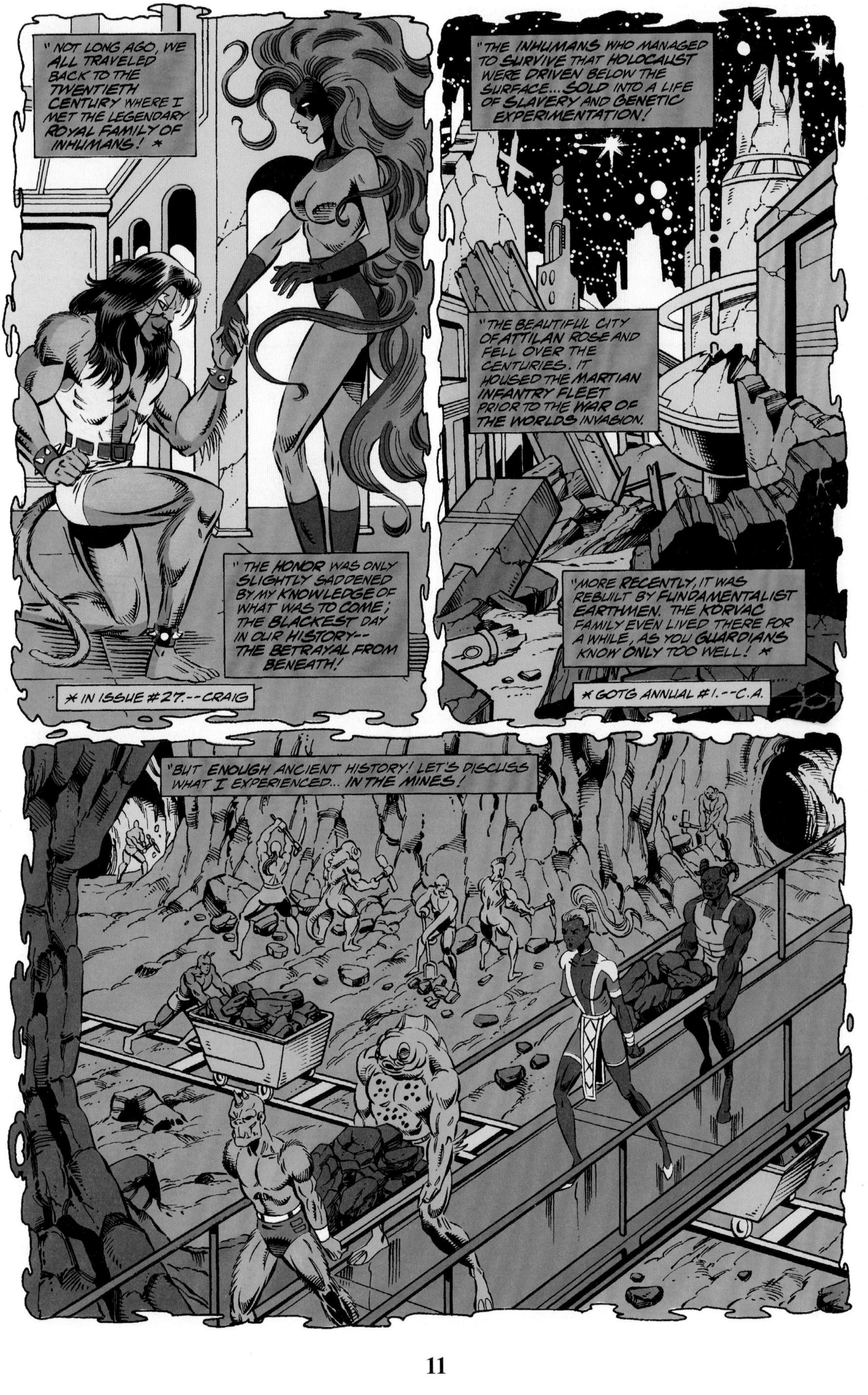
"NOT LONG AGO, WE ALL TRAVELED BACK TO THE TWENTIETH CENTURY WHERE I MET THE LEGENDARY ROYAL FAMILY OF INHUMANS! *
"THE HONOR WAS ONLY SLIGHTLY SADDENED BY MY KNOWLEDGE OF WHAT WAS TO COME; THE BLACKEST DAY IN OUR HISTORY-- THE BETRAYAL FROM BENEATH!
* IN ISSUE #27.--CRAIG
"THE INHUMANS WHO MANAGED TO SURVIVE THAT HOLOCAUST WERE DRIVEN BELOW THE SURFACE... SOLD INTO A LIFE OF SLAVERY AND GENETIC EXPERIMENTATION!
"THE BEAUTIFUL CITY OF ATTILAN ROSE AND FELL OVER THE CENTURIES. IT HOUSED THE MARTIAN INFANTRY FLEET PRIOR TO THE WAR OF THE WORLDS INVASION.
"MORE RECENTLY, IT WAS REBUILT BY FUNDAMENTALIST EARTHMEN. THE KORVAC FAMILY EVEN LIVED THERE FOR A WHILE, AS YOU GUARDIANS KNOW ONLY TOO WELL! *
* GOTG ANNUAL #1.--C.A.
"BUT ENOUGH ANCIENT HISTORY! LET'S DISCUSS WHAT I EXPERIENCED... IN THE MINES!

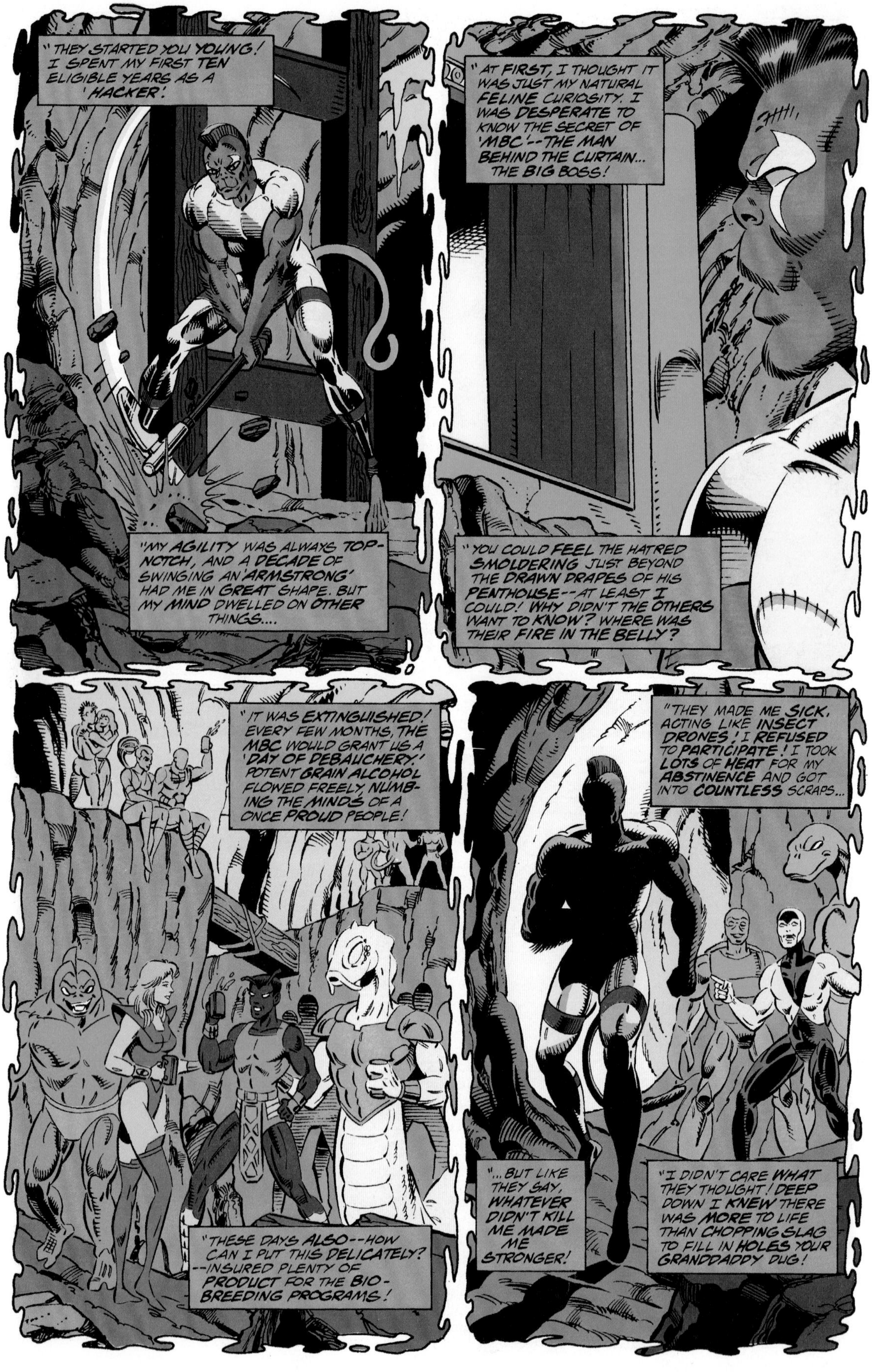
"THEY STARTED YOU YOUNG! I SPENT MY FIRST TEN ELIGIBLE YEARS AS A 'HACKER'.
"MY AGILITY WAS ALWAYS TOP-NOTCH, AND A DECADE OF SWINGING AN 'ARMSTRONG' HAD ME IN GREAT SHAPE. BUT MY MIND DWELLED ON OTHER THINGS....
"AT FIRST, I THOUGHT IT WAS JUST MY NATURAL FELINE CURIOSITY. I WAS DESPERATE TO KNOW THE SECRET OF 'MBC'--THE MAN BEHIND THE CURTAIN... THE BIG BOSS!
"YOU COULD FEEL THE HATRED SMOLDERING JUST BEYOND THE DRAWN DRAPES OF HIS PENTHOUSE--AT LEAST I COULD! WHY DIDN'T THE OTHERS WANT TO KNOW? WHERE WAS THEIR FIRE IN THE BELLY?
"IT WAS EXTINGUISHED! EVERY FEW MONTHS, THE MBC WOULD GRANT US A 'DAY OF DEBAUCHERY.' POTENT GRAIN ALCOHOL FLOWED FREELY, NUMBING THE MINDS OF A ONCE PROUD PEOPLE!
"THESE DAYS ALSO--HOW CAN I PUT THIS DELICATELY? --INSURED PLENTY OF PRODUCT FOR THE BIO-BREEDING PROGRAMS!
"THEY MADE ME SICK, ACTING LIKE INSECT DRONES! I REFUSED TO PARTICIPATE! I TOOK LOTS OF HEAT FOR MY ABSTINENCE AND GOT INTO COUNTLESS SCRAPS...
"...BUT LIKE THEY SAY, WHATEVER DIDN'T KILL ME MADE ME STRONGER!
"I DIDN'T CARE WHAT THEY THOUGHT! DEEP DOWN I KNEW THERE WAS MORE TO LIFE THAN CHOPPING SLAG TO FILL IN HOLES YOUR GRANDDADDY DUG!

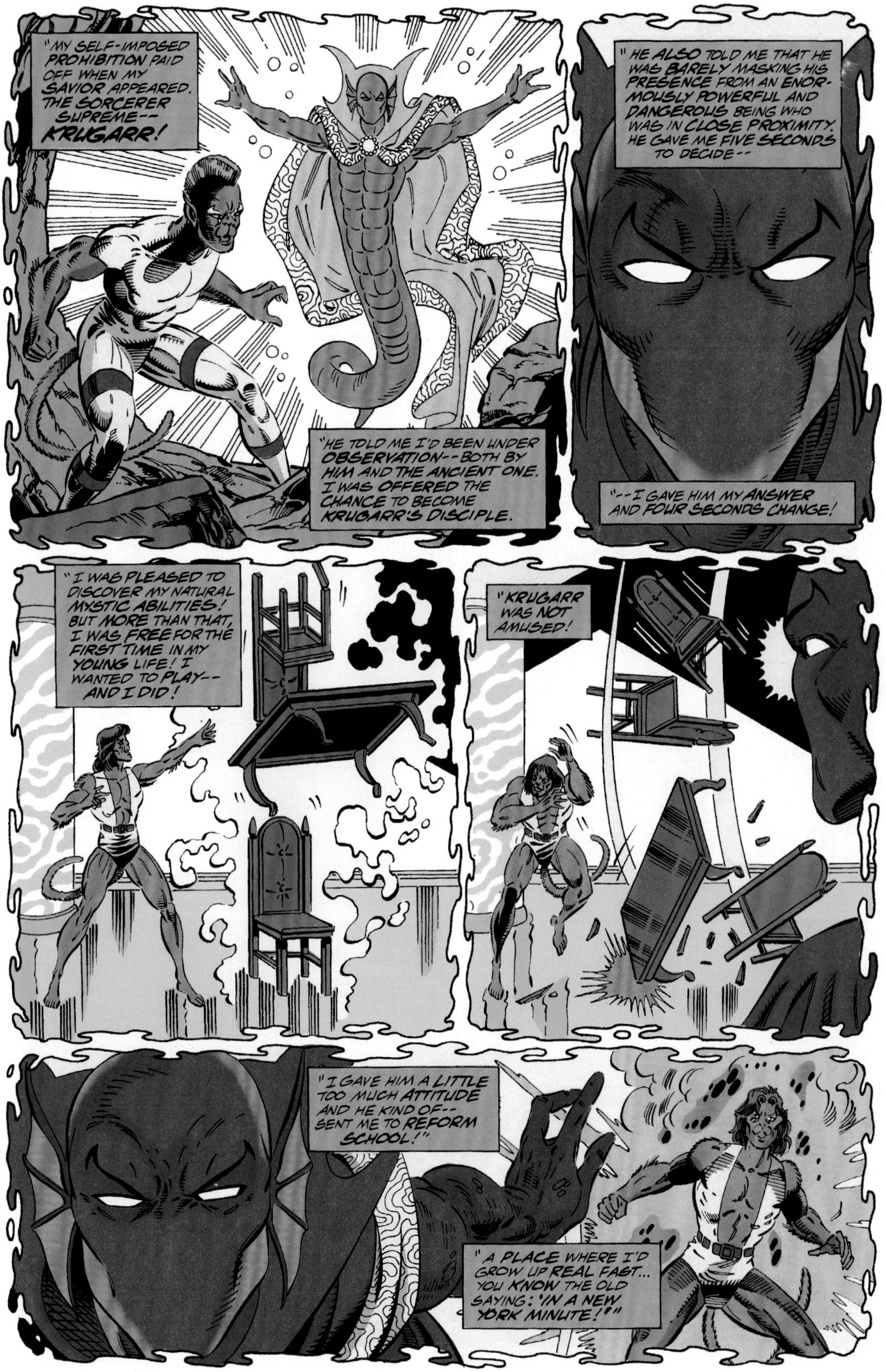
"MY SELF-IMPOSED PROHIBITION PAID OFF WHEN MY SAVIOR APPEARED. THE SORCERER SUPREME-- KRUGARR!
"HE TOLD ME I'D BEEN UNDER OBSERVATION--BOTH BY HIM AND THE ANCIENT ONE. I WAS OFFERED THE CHANCE TO BECOME KRUGARR'S DISCIPLE.
"HE ALSO TOLD ME THAT HE WAS BARELY MASKING HIS PRESENCE FROM AN ENORMOUSLY POWERFUL AND DANGEROUS BEING WHO WAS IN CLOSE PROXIMITY. HE GAVE ME FIVE SECONDS TO DECIDE--
"--I GAVE HIM MY ANSWER AND FOUR SECONDS CHANGE!
"I WAS PLEASED TO DISCOVER MY NATURAL MYSTIC ABILITIES! BUT MORE THAN THAT, I WAS FREE FOR THE FIRST TIME IN MY YOUNG LIFE! I WANTED TO PLAY-- AND I DID!
"KRUGARR WAS NOT AMUSED!
"I GAVE HIM A LITTLE TOO MUCH ATTITUDE AND HE KIND OF-- SENT ME TO REFORM SCHOOL!"
"A PLACE WHERE I'D GROW UP REAL FAST... YOU KNOW THE OLD SAYING: 'IN A NEW YORK MINUTE!'"

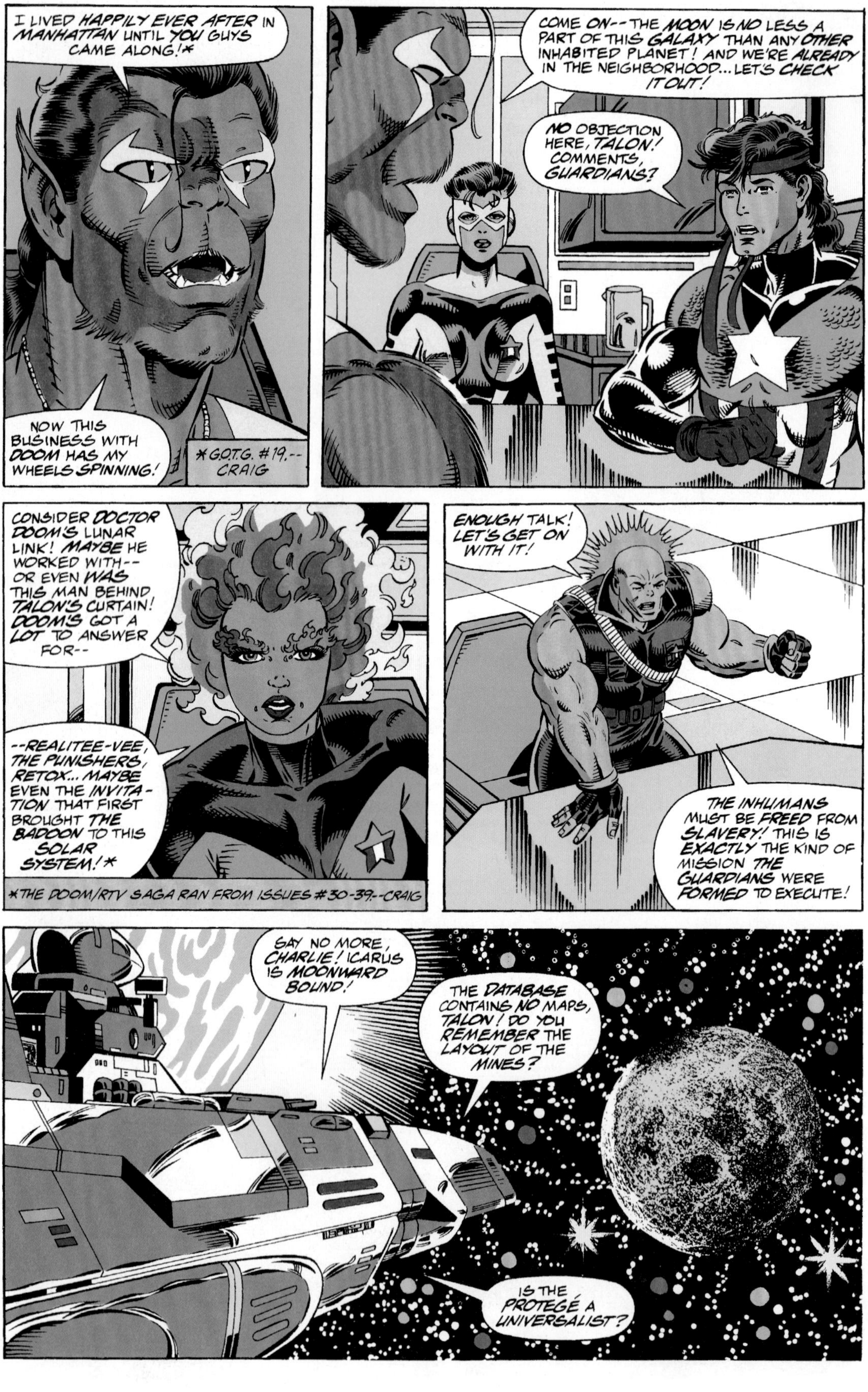
I LIVED HAPPILY EVER AFTER IN MANHATTAN UNTIL YOU GUYS CAME ALONG!*
NOW THIS BUSINESS WITH DOOM HAS MY WHEELS SPINNING!
*G.O.T.G. #19.--CRAIG
COME ON--THE MOON IS NO LESS A PART OF THIS GALAXY THAN ANY OTHER INHABITED PLANET! AND WE'RE ALREADY IN THE NEIGHBORHOOD... LET'S CHECK IT OUT!
NO OBJECTION HERE, TALON! COMMENTS, GUARDIANS?
CONSIDER DOCTOR DOOM'S LUNAR LINK! MAYBE HE WORKED WITH--OR EVEN WAS THIS MAN BEHIND TALON'S CURTAIN! DOOM'S GOT A LOT TO ANSWER FOR--
--REALITEE-VEE, THE PUNISHERS, RETOX... MAYBE EVEN THE INVITATION THAT FIRST BROUGHT THE BADOON TO THIS SOLAR SYSTEM!*
*THE DOOM/RTV SAGA RAN FROM ISSUES #30-39.--CRAIG
ENOUGH TALK! LET'S GET ON WITH IT!
THE INHUMANS MUST BE FREED FROM SLAVERY! THIS IS EXACTLY THE KIND OF MISSION THE GUARDIANS WERE FORMED TO EXECUTE!
SAY NO MORE, CHARLIE! ICARUS IS MOONWARD BOUND!
THE DATABASE CONTAINS NO MAPS, TALON! DO YOU REMEMBER THE LAYOUT OF THE MINES?
IS THE PROTEGÉ A UNIVERSALIST?

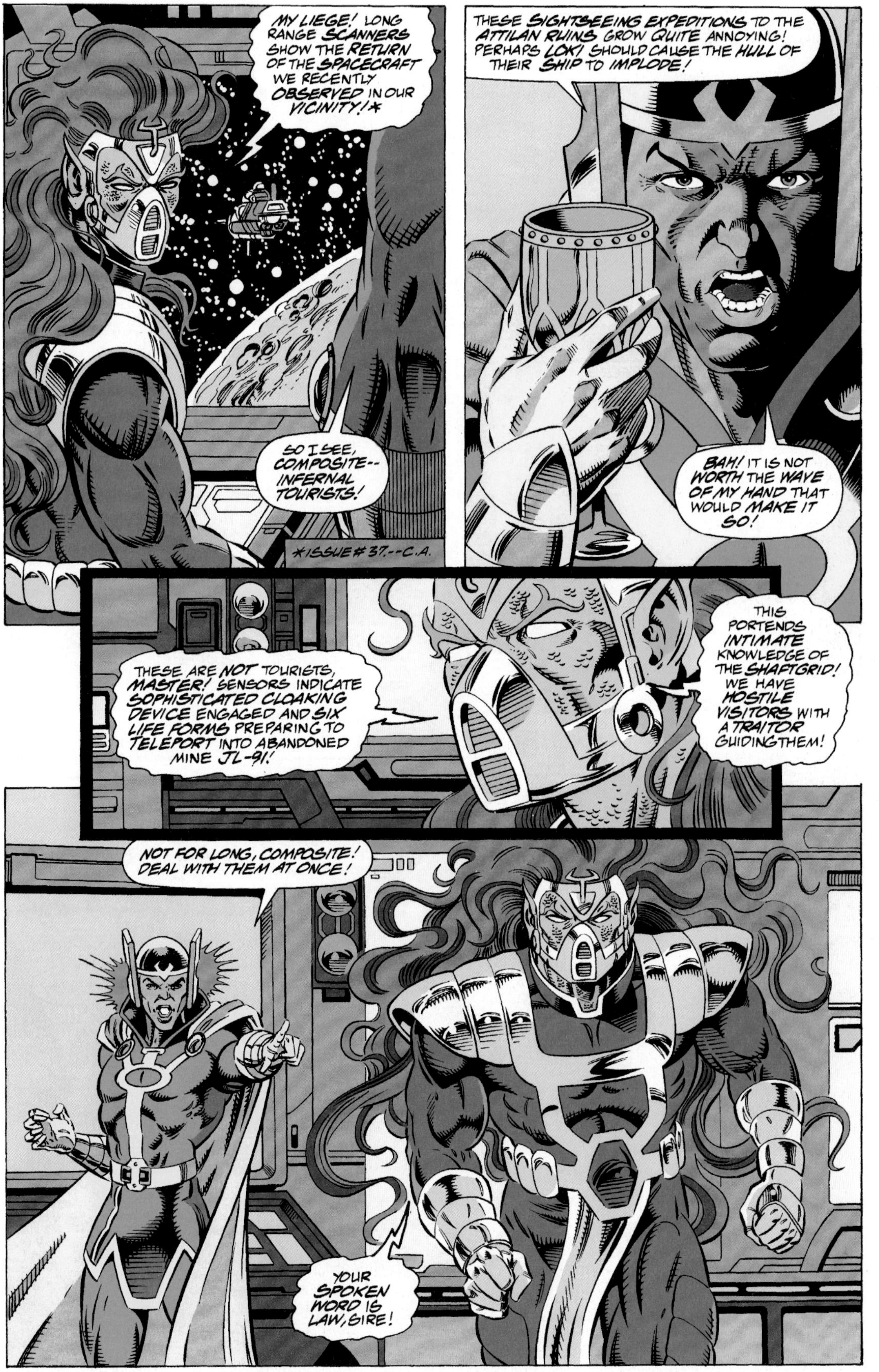

MY LIEGE! LONG RANGE SCANNERS SHOW THE RETURN OF THE SPACECRAFT WE RECENTLY OBSERVED IN OUR VICINITY!*
SO I SEE, COMPOSITE-- INFERNAL TOURISTS!
*ISSUE #37.--C.A.
THESE SIGHTSEEING EXPEDITIONS TO THE ATTILAN RUINS GROW QUITE ANNOYING! PERHAPS LOKI SHOULD CAUSE THE HULL OF THEIR SHIP TO IMPLODE!
BAH! IT IS NOT WORTH THE WAVE OF MY HAND THAT WOULD MAKE IT SO!
THESE ARE NOT TOURISTS, MASTER! SENSORS INDICATE SOPHISTICATED CLOAKING DEVICE ENGAGED AND SIX LIFE FORMS PREPARING TO TELEPORT INTO ABANDONED MINE JL-91!
THIS PORTENDS INTIMATE KNOWLEDGE OF THE SHAFTGRID! WE HAVE HOSTILE VISITORS WITH A TRAITOR GUIDING THEM!
NOT FOR LONG, COMPOSITE! DEAL WITH THEM AT ONCE!
YOUR SPOKEN WORD IS LAW, SIRE!

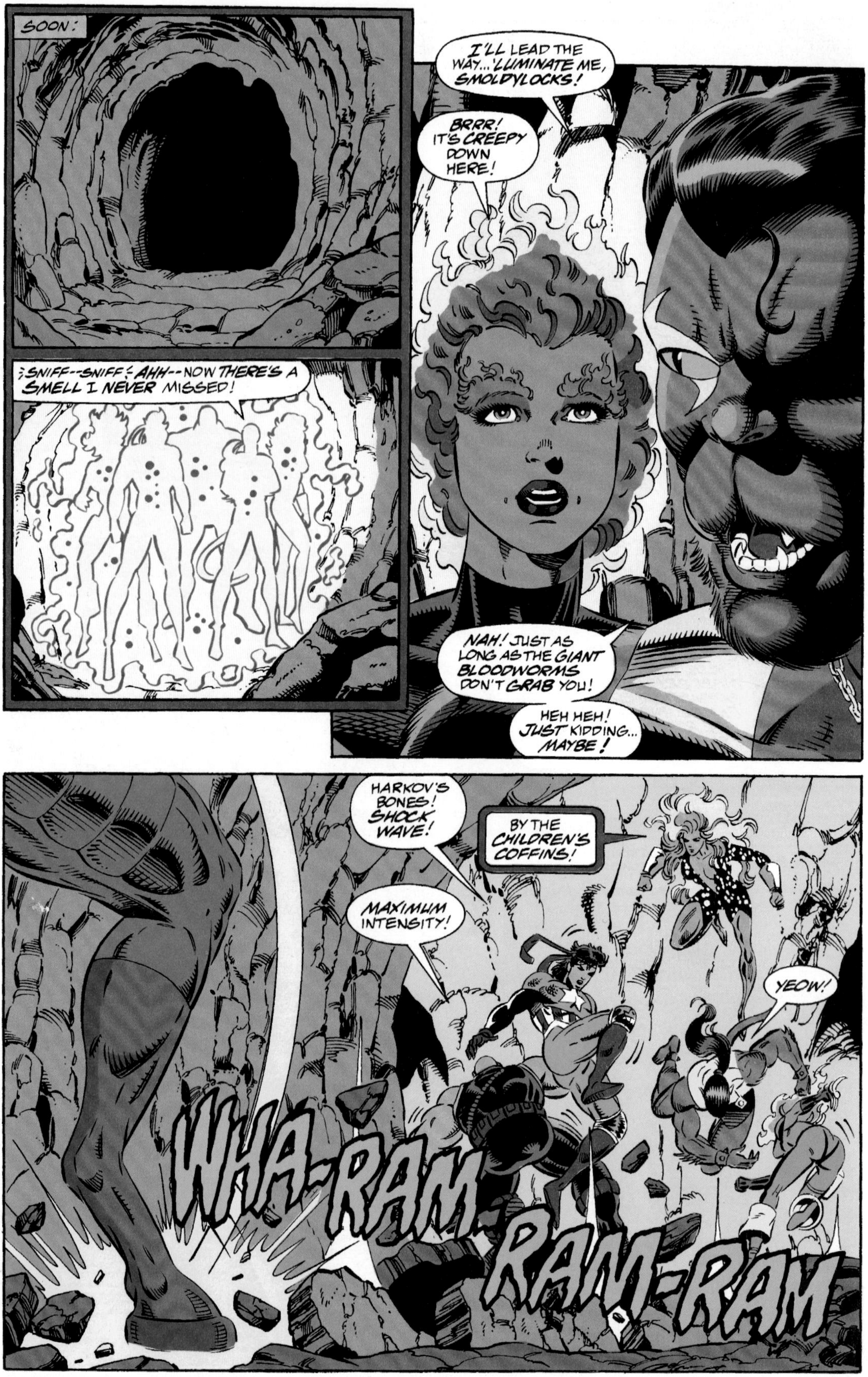
SOON:
I'LL LEAD THE WAY... 'LUMINATE ME, SMOLDYLOCKS!
BRRR! IT'S CREEPY DOWN HERE!
SNIFF--SNIFF-- AHH-- NOW THERE'S A SMELL I NEVER MISSED!
NAH! JUST AS LONG AS THE GIANT BLOODWORMS DON'T GRAB YOU!
HEH HEH! JUST KIDDING... MAYBE!
HARKOV'S BONES! SHOCK WAVE!
BY THE CHILDREN'S COFFINS!
MAXIMUM INTENSITY!
YEOW!
WHA-RAM RAM-RAM

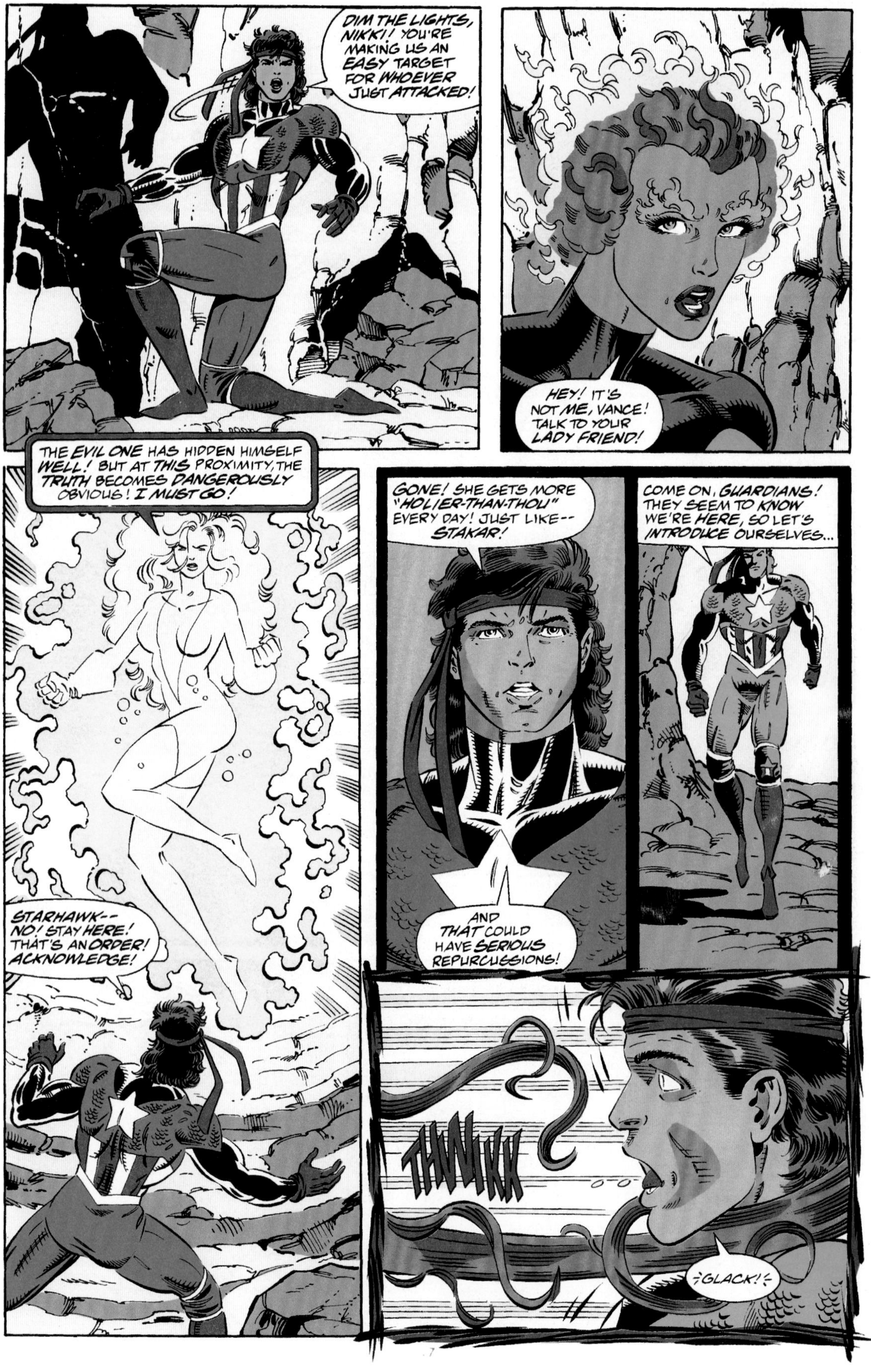

DIM THE LIGHTS, NIKKI! YOU'RE MAKING US AN EASY TARGET FOR WHOEVER JUST ATTACKED!
HEY! IT'S NOT ME, VANCE! TALK TO YOUR LADY FRIEND!
THE EVIL ONE HAS HIDDEN HIMSELF WELL! BUT AT THIS PROXIMITY, THE TRUTH BECOMES DANGEROUSLY OBVIOUS! I MUST GO!
STARHAWK-- NO! STAY HERE! THAT'S AN ORDER! ACKNOWLEDGE!
GONE! SHE GETS MORE "HOLIER-THAN-THOU" EVERY DAY! JUST LIKE-- STAKAR!
AND THAT COULD HAVE SERIOUS REPURCUSSIONS!
COME ON, GUARDIANS! THEY SEEM TO KNOW WE'RE HERE, SO LET'S INTRODUCE OURSELVES...
THWIKK
GLACK!

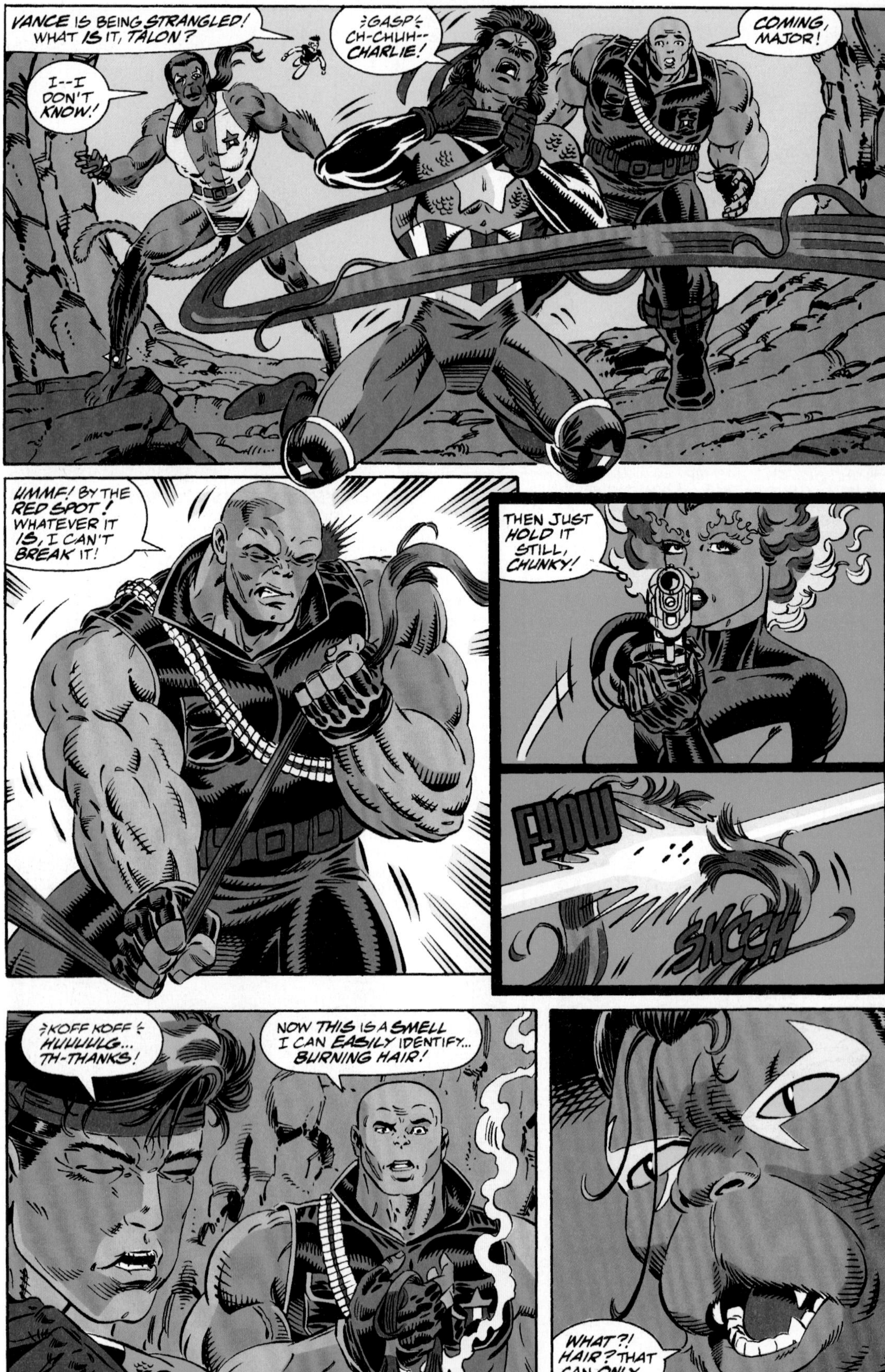

VANCE IS BEING STRANGLED! WHAT IS IT, TALON?
I--I DON'T KNOW!
GASP CH-CHUH-- CHARLIE!
COMING, MAJOR!
UMMF! BY THE RED SPOT! WHATEVER IT IS, I CAN'T BREAK IT!
THEN JUST HOLD IT STILL, CHUNKY!
FYOW
SKCCH
KOFF KOFF HUUUULG... TH-THANKS!
NOW THIS IS A SMELL I CAN EASILY IDENTIFY... BURNING HAIR!
WHAT?! HAIR? THAT CAN ONLY MEAN--

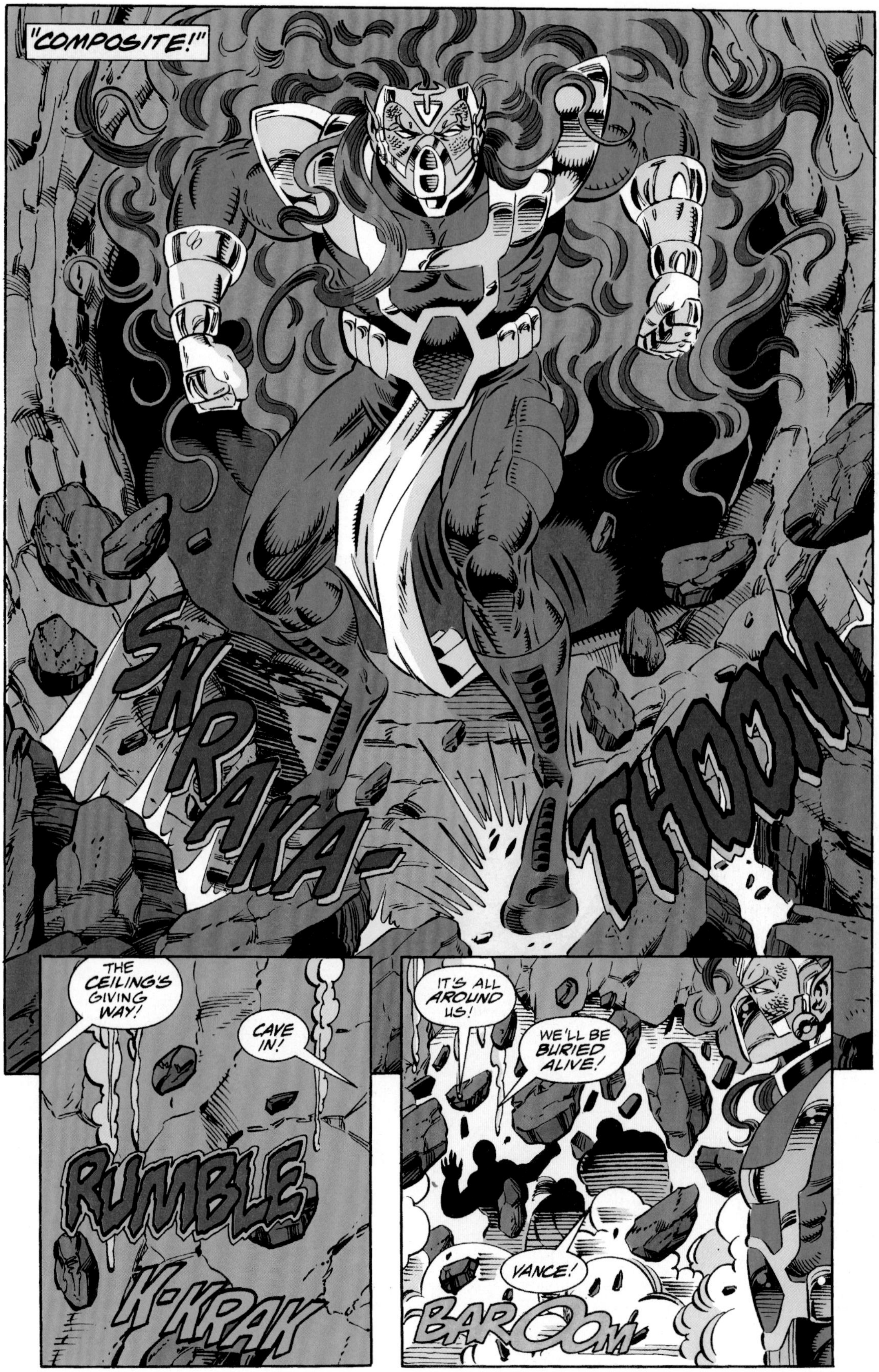
"COMPOSITE!"
SKRAKA-THOOM
THE CEILING'S GIVING WAY!
CAVE IN!
RUMBLE
K-KRAK
IT'S ALL AROUND US!
WE'LL BE BURIED ALIVE!
VANCE!
BAROOM

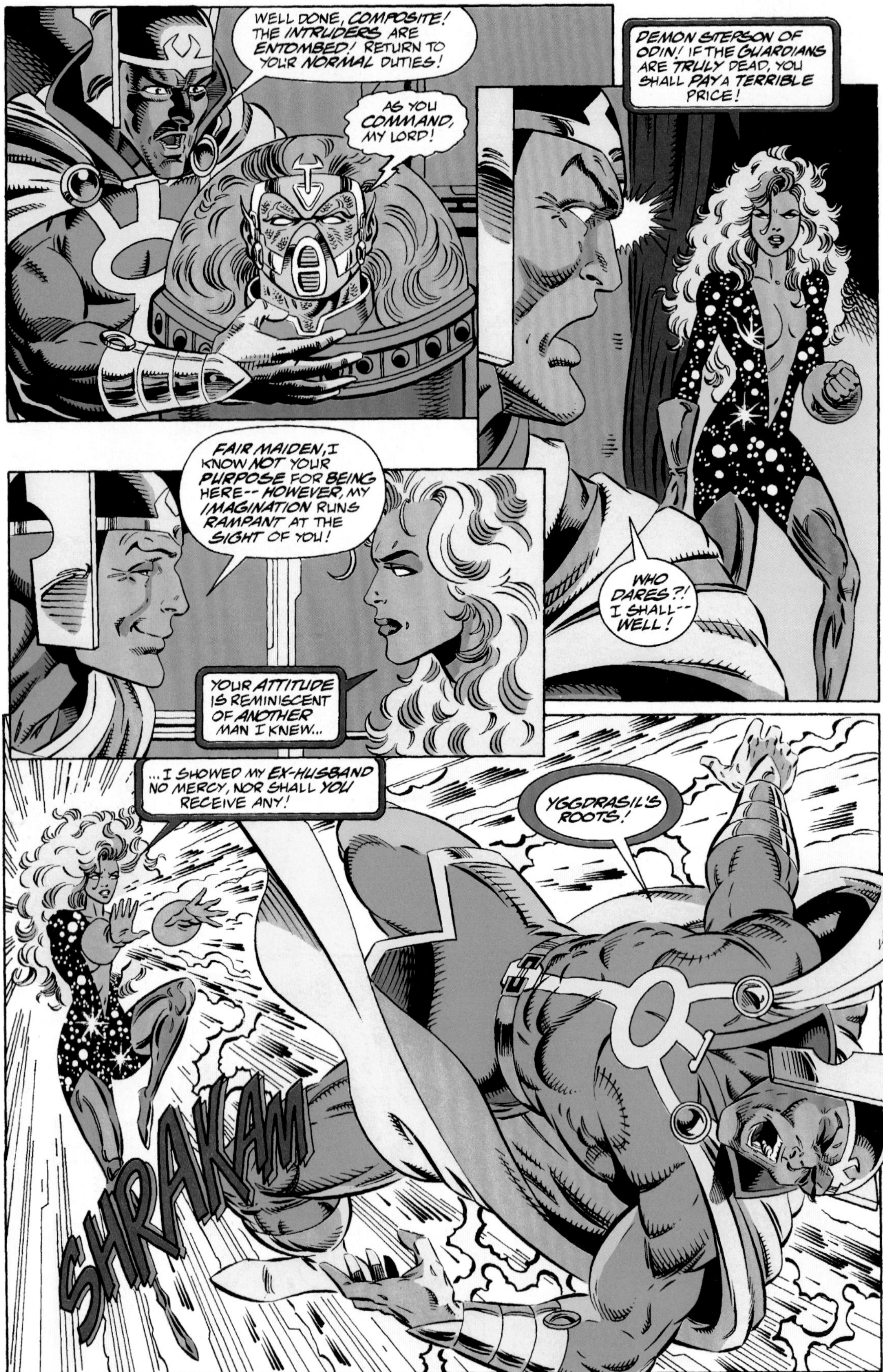

WELL DONE, COMPOSITE! THE INTRUDERS ARE ENTOMBED! RETURN TO YOUR NORMAL DUTIES!
AS YOU COMMAND, MY LORD!
DEMON STEPSON OF ODIN! IF THE GUARDIANS ARE TRULY DEAD, YOU SHALL PAY A TERRIBLE PRICE!
WHO DARES?! I SHALL-- WELL!
FAIR MAIDEN, I KNOW NOT YOUR PURPOSE FOR BEING HERE-- HOWEVER, MY IMAGINATION RUNS RAMPANT AT THE SIGHT OF YOU!
YOUR ATTITUDE IS REMINISCENT OF ANOTHER MAN I KNEW...
...I SHOWED MY EX-HUSBAND NO MERCY, NOR SHALL YOU RECEIVE ANY!
YGGDRASIL'S ROOTS!
SHRAKAM

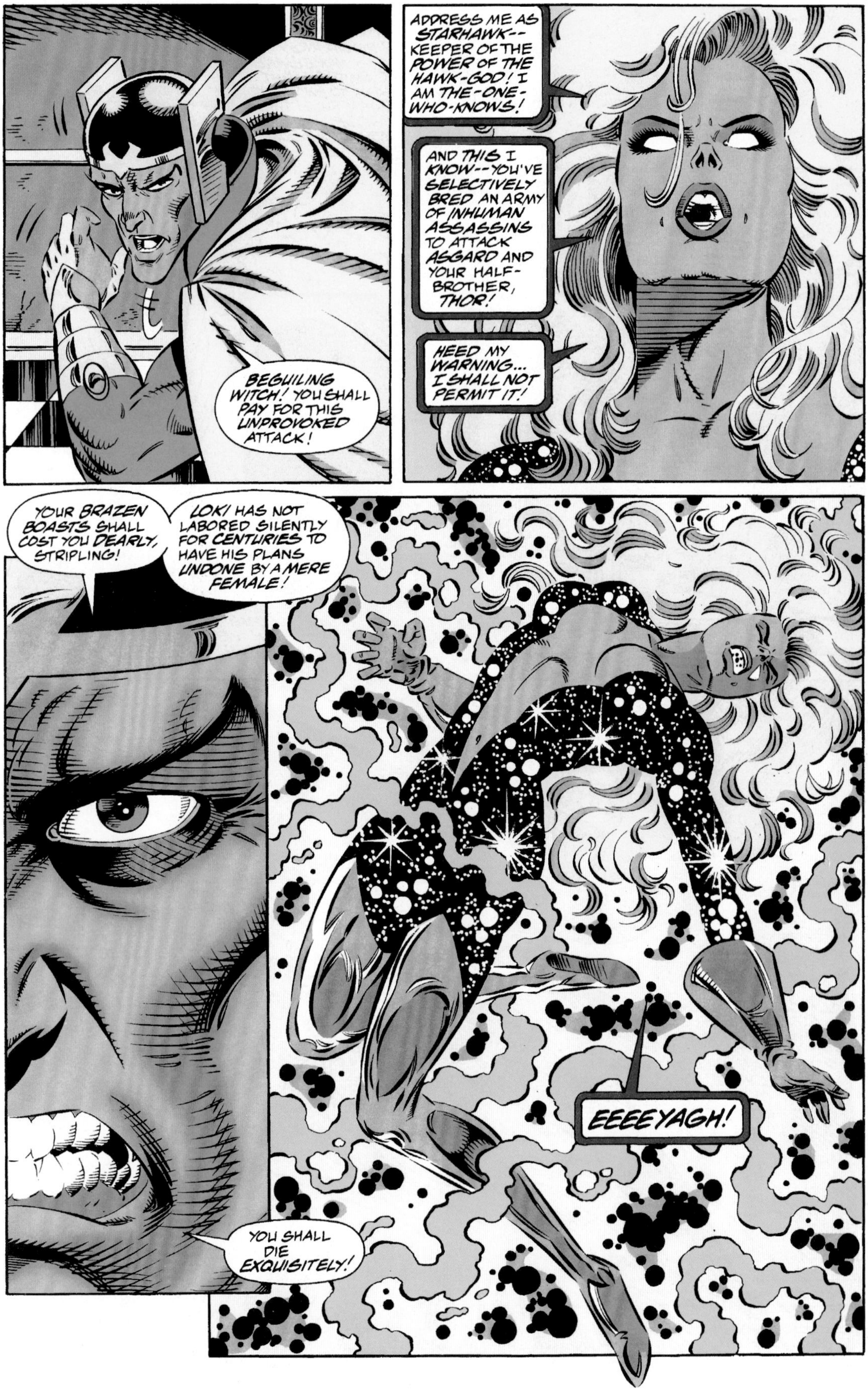
ADDRESS ME AS STARHAWK--KEEPER OF THE POWER OF THE HAWK-GOD! I AM THE-ONE-WHO-KNOWS!
AND THIS I KNOW--YOU'VE SELECTIVELY BRED AN ARMY OF INHUMAN ASSASSINS TO ATTACK ASGARD AND YOUR HALF-BROTHER, THOR!
HEED MY WARNING... I SHALL NOT PERMIT IT!
BEGUILING WITCH! YOU SHALL PAY FOR THIS UNPROVOKED ATTACK!
YOUR BRAZEN BOASTS SHALL COST YOU DEARLY, STRIPLING!
LOKI HAS NOT LABORED SILENTLY FOR CENTURIES TO HAVE HIS PLANS UNDONE BY A MERE FEMALE!
EEEEYAGH!
YOU SHALL DIE EXQUISITELY!

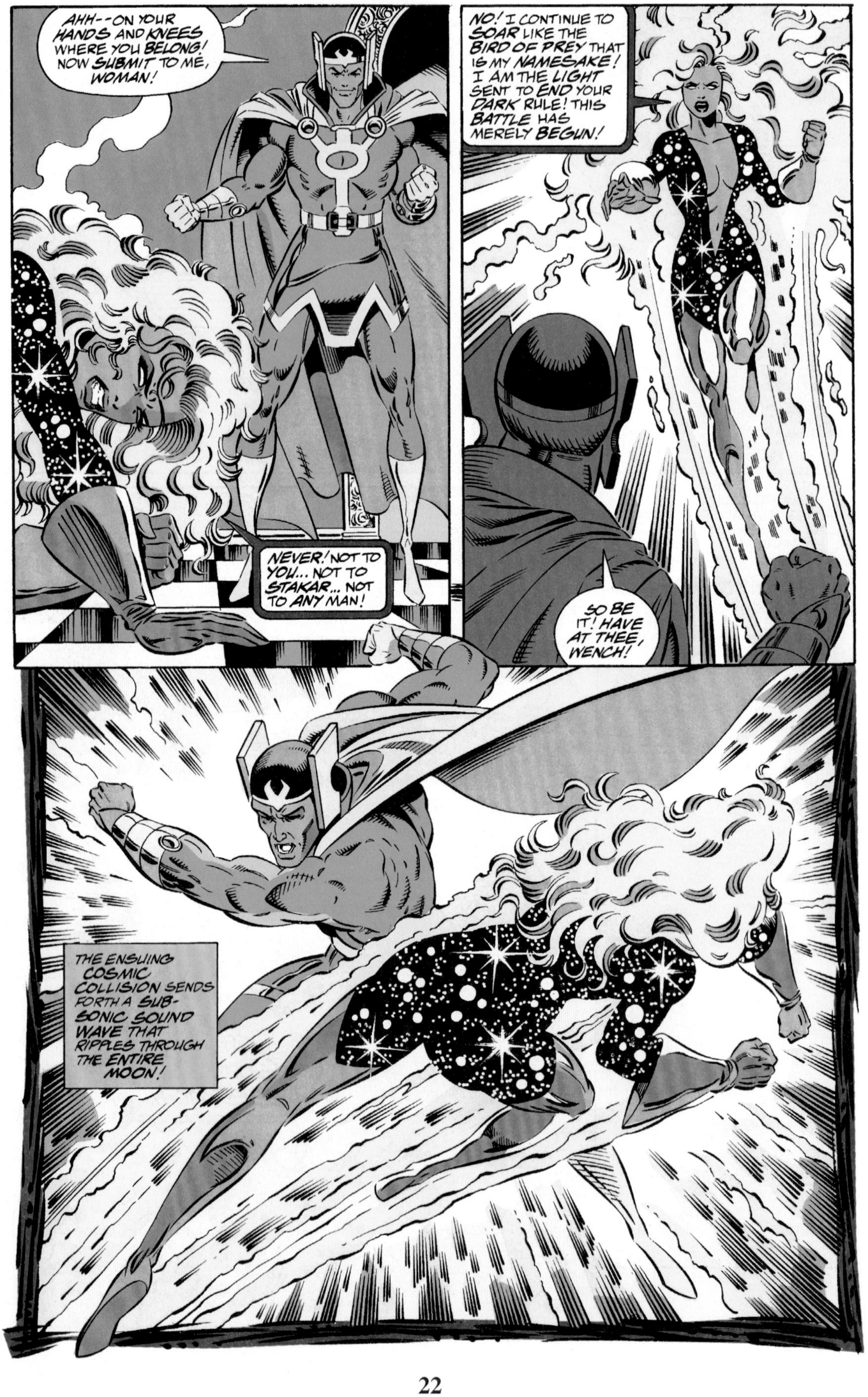
AHH--ON YOUR HANDS AND KNEES WHERE YOU BELONG! NOW SUBMIT TO ME, WOMAN!
NEVER! NOT TO YOU... NOT TO STAKAR... NOT TO ANY MAN!
NO! I CONTINUE TO SOAR LIKE THE BIRD OF PREY THAT IS MY NAMESAKE! I AM THE LIGHT SENT TO END YOUR DARK RULE! THIS BATTLE HAS MERELY BEGUN!
SO BE IT! HAVE AT THEE, WENCH!
THE ENSUING COSMIC COLLISION SENDS FORTH A SUB-SONIC SOUND WAVE THAT RIPPLES THROUGH THE ENTIRE MOON!

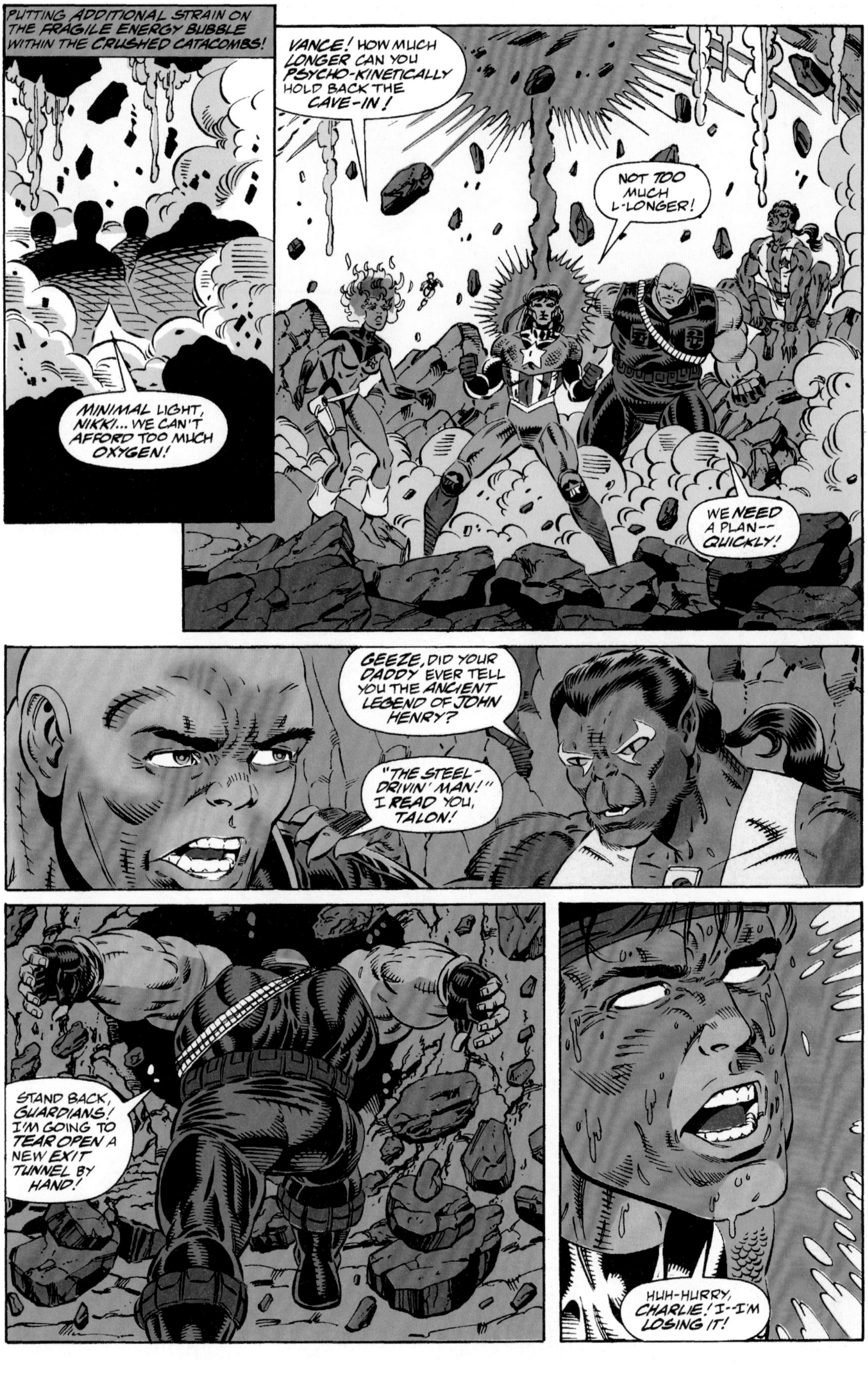
PUTTING ADDITIONAL STRAIN ON THE FRAGILE ENERGY BUBBLE WITHIN THE CRUSHED CATACOMBS!
MINIMAL LIGHT, NIKKI... WE CAN'T AFFORD TOO MUCH OXYGEN!
VANCE! HOW MUCH LONGER CAN YOU PSYCHO-KINETICALLY HOLD BACK THE CAVE-IN!
NOT TOO MUCH L-LONGER!
WE NEED A PLAN-- QUICKLY!
GEEZE, DID YOUR DADDY EVER TELL YOU THE ANCIENT LEGEND OF JOHN HENRY?
"THE STEEL-DRIVIN' MAN!" I READ YOU, TALON!
STAND BACK, GUARDIANS! I'M GOING TO TEAR OPEN A NEW EXIT TUNNEL BY HAND!
HUH-HURRY, CHARLIE! I--I'M LOSING IT!

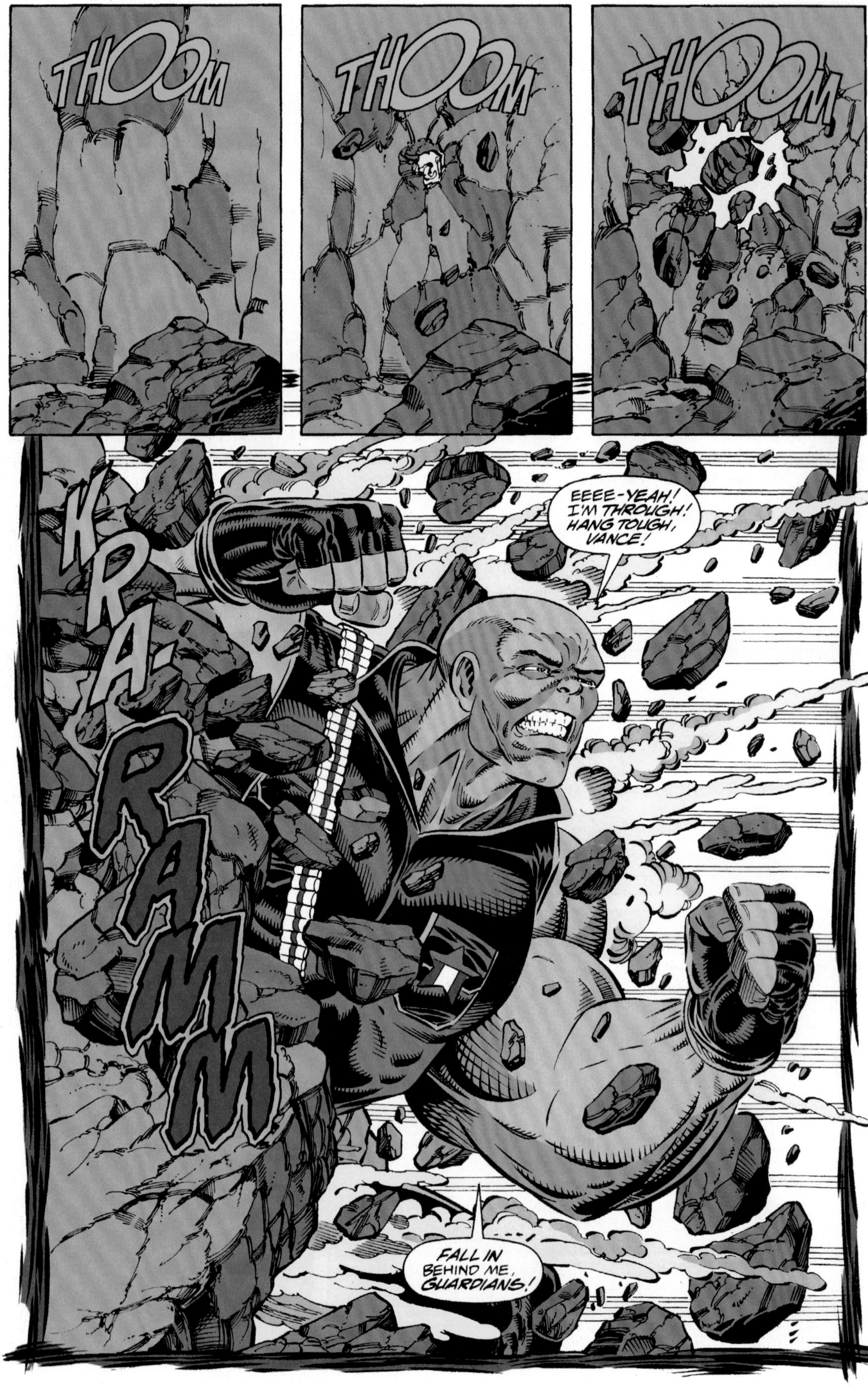
THOOM
THOOM
THOOM
KRAAARAMM
EEEE-YEAH! I'M THROUGH! HANG TOUGH, VANCE!
FALL IN BEHIND ME, GUARDIANS!

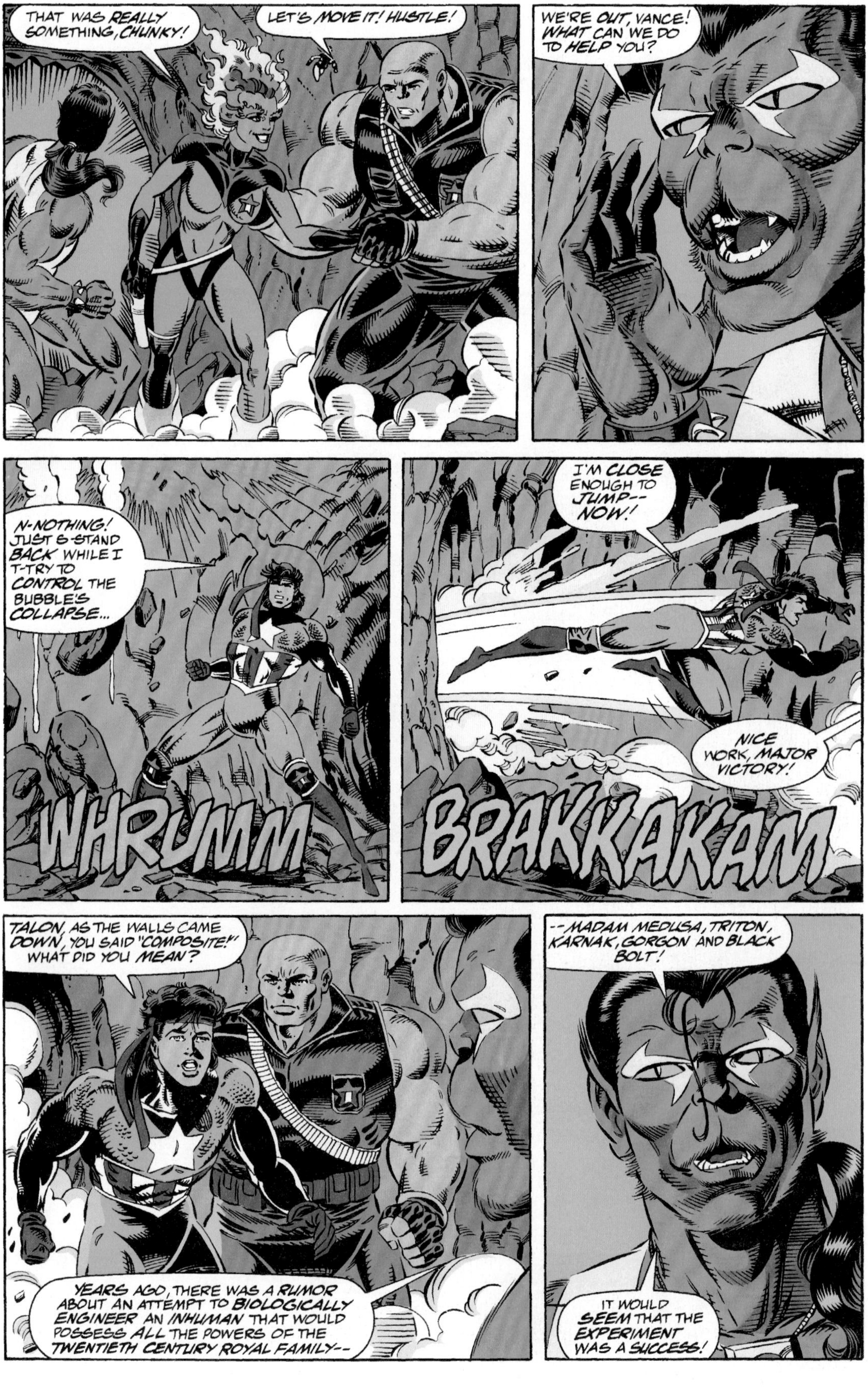
THAT WAS REALLY SOMETHING, CHUNKY!
LET'S MOVE IT! HUSTLE!
WE'RE OUT, VANCE! WHAT CAN WE DO TO HELP YOU?
N-NOTHING! JUST S-STAND BACK WHILE I T-TRY TO CONTROL THE BUBBLE'S COLLAPSE...
WHRUMM
I'M CLOSE ENOUGH TO JUMP-- NOW!
NICE WORK, MAJOR VICTORY!
BRAKKAKAM
TALON, AS THE WALLS CAME DOWN, YOU SAID "COMPOSITE!" WHAT DID YOU MEAN?
YEARS AGO, THERE WAS A RUMOR ABOUT AN ATTEMPT TO BIOLOGICALLY ENGINEER AN INHUMAN THAT WOULD POSSESS ALL THE POWERS OF THE TWENTIETH CENTURY ROYAL FAMILY--
--MADAM MEDUSA, TRITON, KARNAK, GORGON AND BLACK BOLT!
IT WOULD SEEM THAT THE EXPERIMENT WAS A SUCCESS!

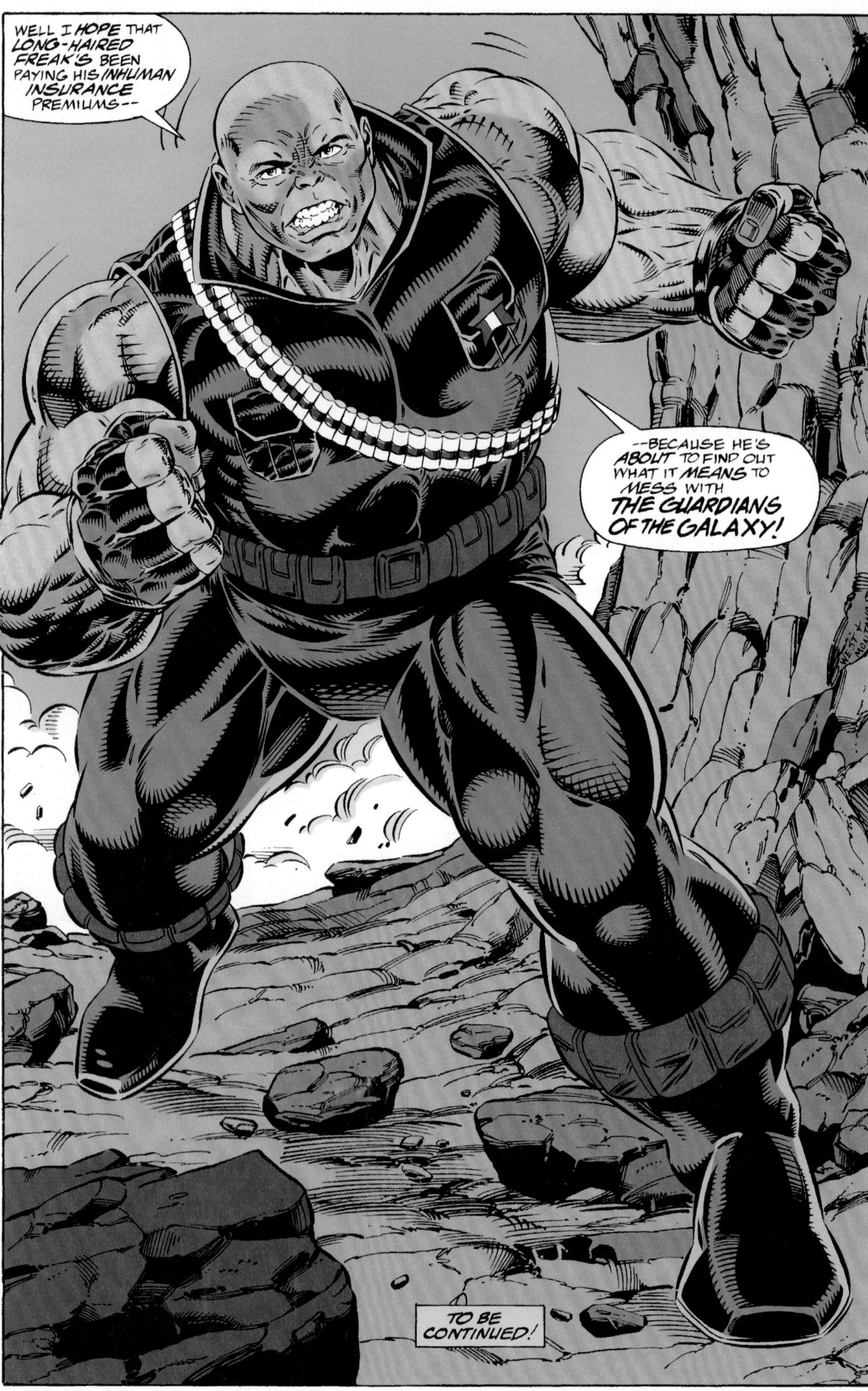
WELL I HOPE THAT LONG-HAIRED FREAK'S BEEN PAYING HIS INHUMAN INSURANCE PREMIUMS--
--BECAUSE HE'S ABOUT TO FIND OUT WHAT IT MEANS TO MESS WITH THE GUARDIANS OF THE GALAXY!
TO BE CONTINUED!

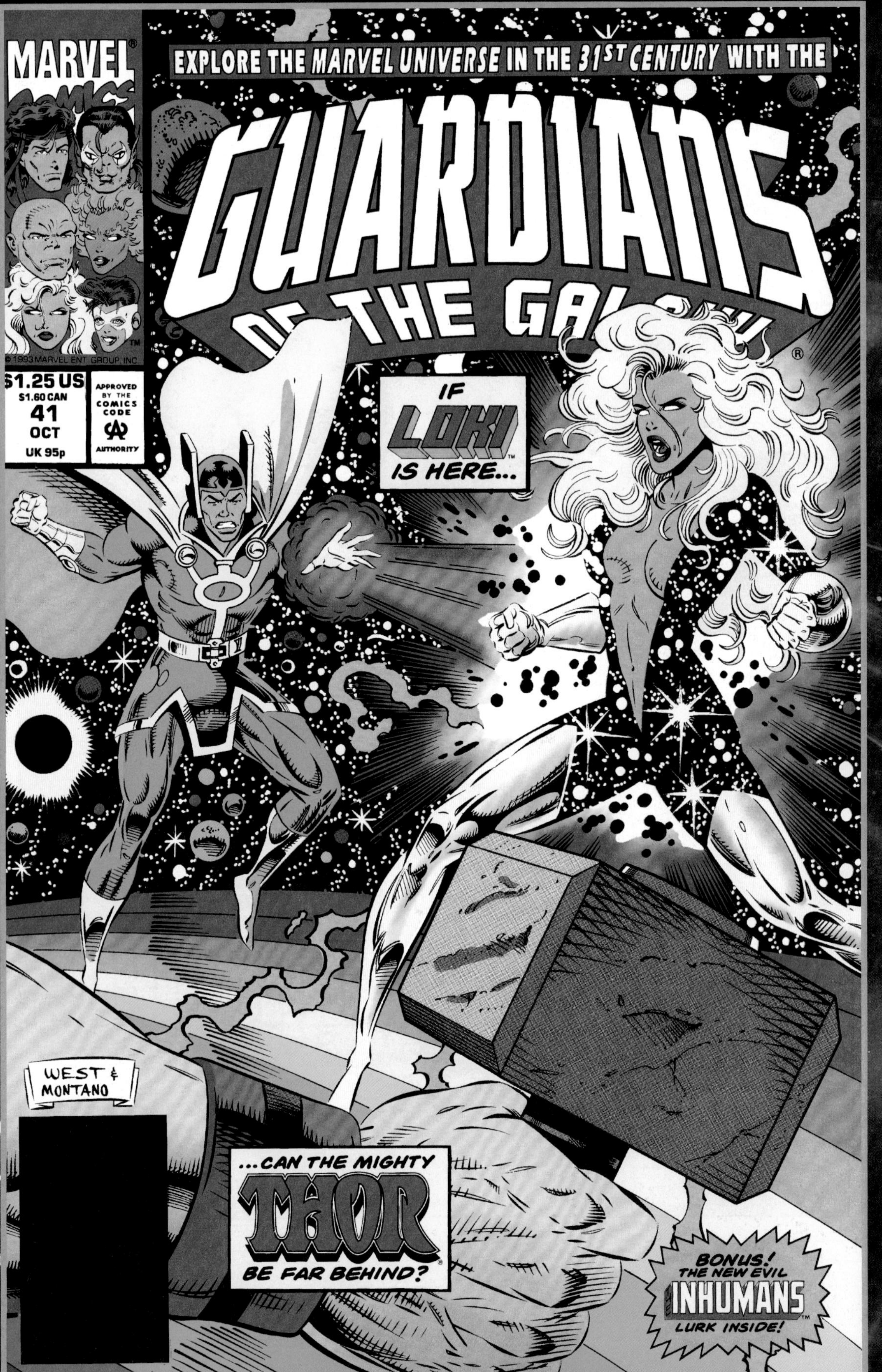
MARVEL COMICS
EXPLORE THE MARVEL UNIVERSE IN THE 31ST CENTURY WITH THE
GUARDIANS
OF THE GA
© 1993 MARVEL ENT. GROUP, INC.
$1.25 US
$1.60 CAN
41
OCT
UK 95p
APPROVED BY THE COMICS CODE AUTHORITY
IF LOKI IS HERE...
WEST & MONTANO
...CAN THE MIGHTY THOR BE FAR BEHIND?
BONUS! THE NEW EVIL INHUMANS LURK INSIDE!

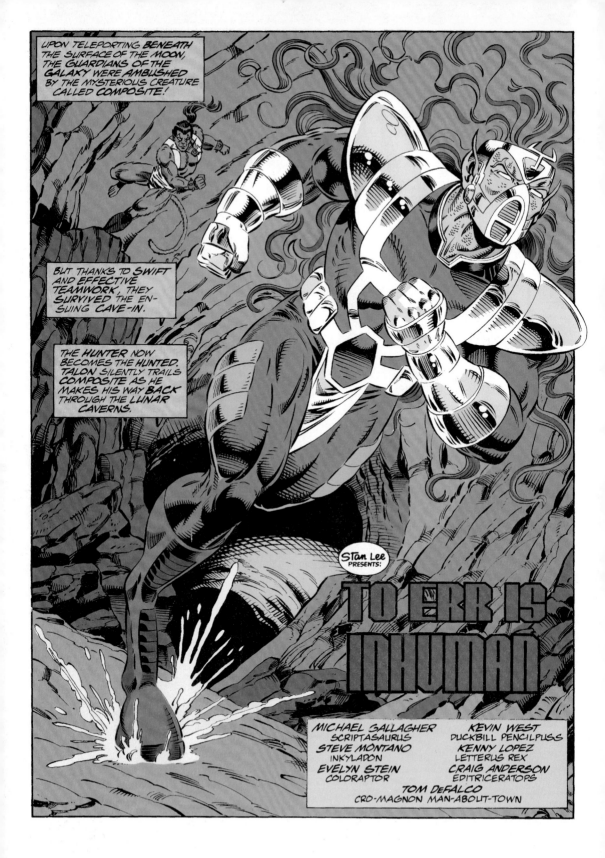

UPON TELEPORTING BENEATH THE SURFACE OF THE MOON, THE GUARDIANS OF THE GALAXY WERE AMBUSHED BY THE MYSTERIOUS CREATURE CALLED COMPOSITE!

BUT THANKS TO SWIFT AND EFFECTIVE TEAMWORK, THEY SURVIVED THE ENSUING CAVE-IN.

THE HUNTER NOW BECOMES THE HUNTED. TALON SILENTLY TRAILS COMPOSITE AS HE MAKES HIS WAY BACK THROUGH THE LUNAR CAVERNS.

STAN LEE PRESENTS:

TO ERR IS INHUMAN

MICHAEL GALLAGHER
SCRIPTASAURUS

STEVE MONTANO
INKYLADON

EVELYN STEIN
COLORAPTOR

KEVIN WEST
DUCKBILL PENCILPUSS

KENNY LOPEZ
LETTERUS REX

CRAIG ANDERSON
EDITRICERATORS

TOM DeFALCO
CRO-MAGNON MAN-ABOUT-TOWN

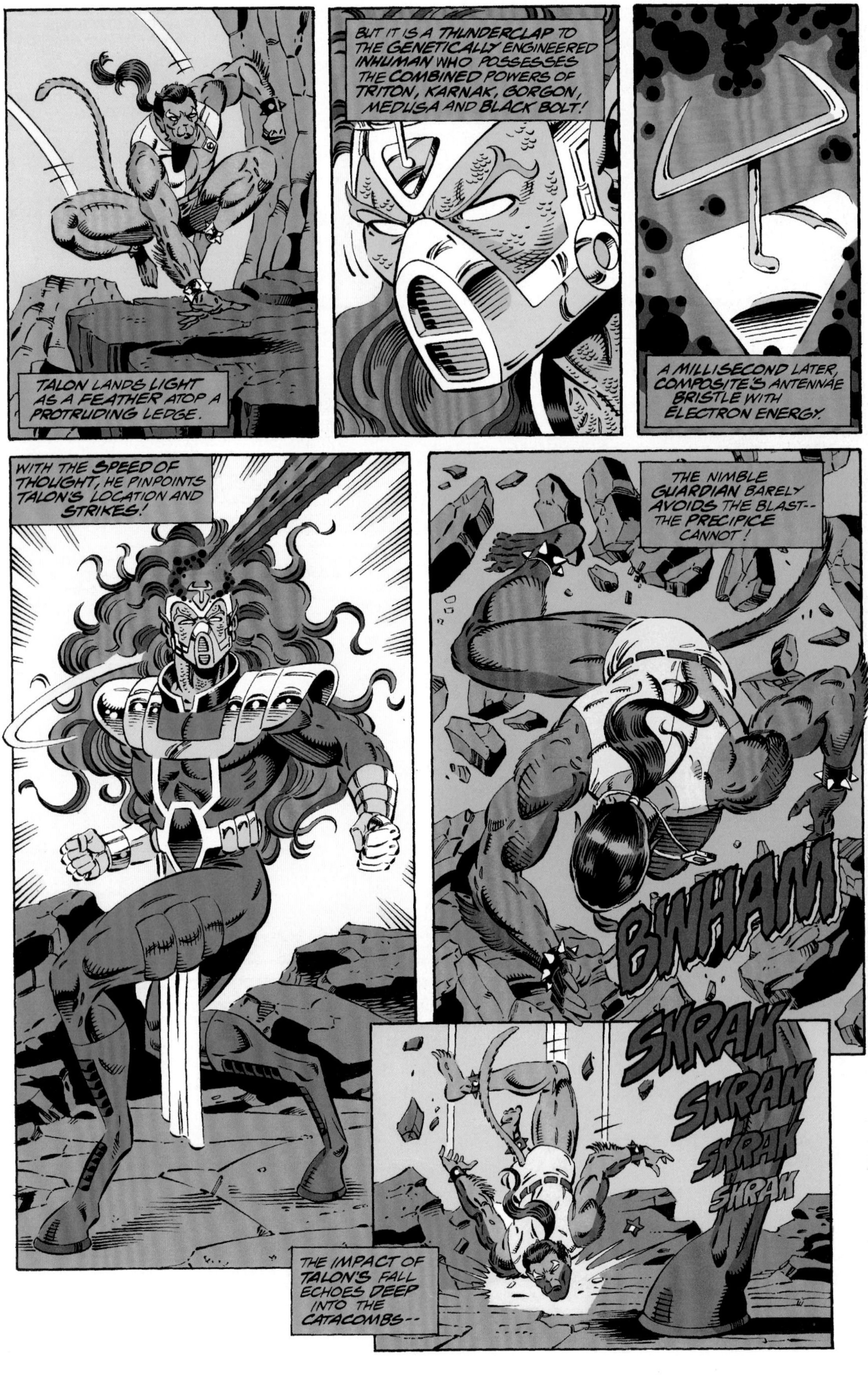
TALON LANDS LIGHT AS A FEATHER ATOP A PROTRUDING LEDGE.
BUT IT IS A THUNDERCLAP TO THE GENETICALLY ENGINEERED INHUMAN WHO POSSESSES THE COMBINED POWERS OF TRITON, KARNAK, GORGON, MEDUSA AND BLACK BOLT!
A MILLISECOND LATER, COMPOSITE'S ANTENNAE BRISTLE WITH ELECTRON ENERGY.
WITH THE SPEED OF THOUGHT, HE PINPOINTS TALON'S LOCATION AND STRIKES!
THE NIMBLE GUARDIAN BARELY AVOIDS THE BLAST-- THE PRECIPICE CANNOT!
BWHAM
SKRAK
SKRAK
SKRAK
SKRAK
THE IMPACT OF TALON'S FALL ECHOES DEEP INTO THE CATACOMBS--

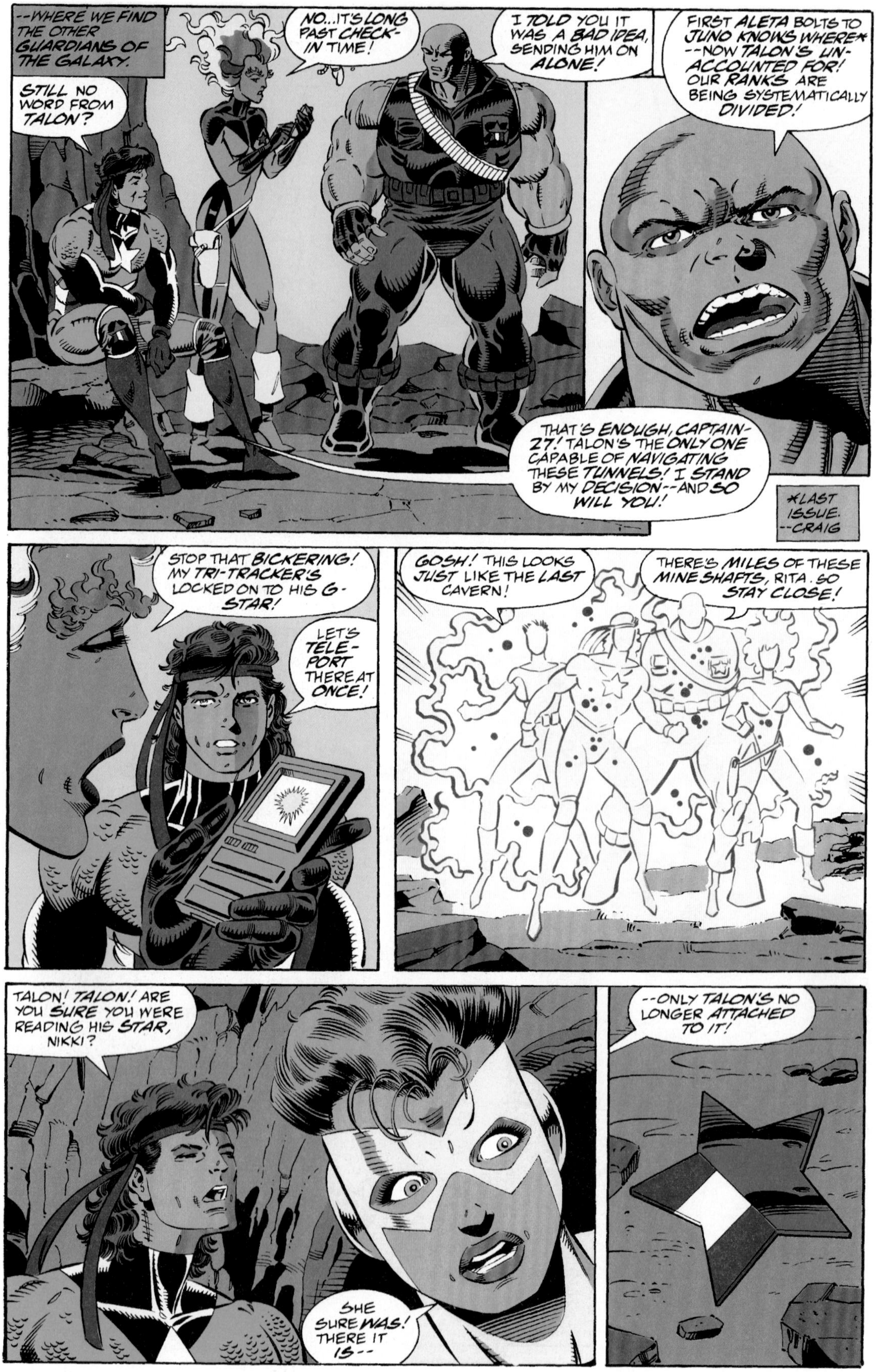
--WHERE WE FIND THE OTHER GUARDIANS OF THE GALAXY.
STILL NO WORD FROM TALON?
NO...IT'S LONG PAST CHECK-IN TIME!
I TOLD YOU IT WAS A BAD IDEA, SENDING HIM ON ALONE!
FIRST ALETA BOLTS TO JUNO KNOWS WHERE* --NOW TALON'S UN-ACCOUNTED FOR! OUR RANKS ARE BEING SYSTEMATICALLY DIVIDED!
THAT'S ENOUGH, CAPTAIN-27! TALON'S THE ONLY ONE CAPABLE OF NAVIGATING THESE TUNNELS! I STAND BY MY DECISION--AND SO WILL YOU!
*LAST ISSUE. --CRAIG
STOP THAT BICKERING! MY TRI-TRACKER'S LOCKED ON TO HIS G-STAR!
LET'S TELE-PORT THERE AT ONCE!
GOSH! THIS LOOKS JUST LIKE THE LAST CAVERN!
THERE'S MILES OF THESE MINE SHAFTS, RITA. SO STAY CLOSE!
TALON! TALON! ARE YOU SURE YOU WERE READING HIS STAR, NIKKI?
SHE SURE WAS! THERE IT IS--
--ONLY TALON'S NO LONGER ATTACHED TO IT!

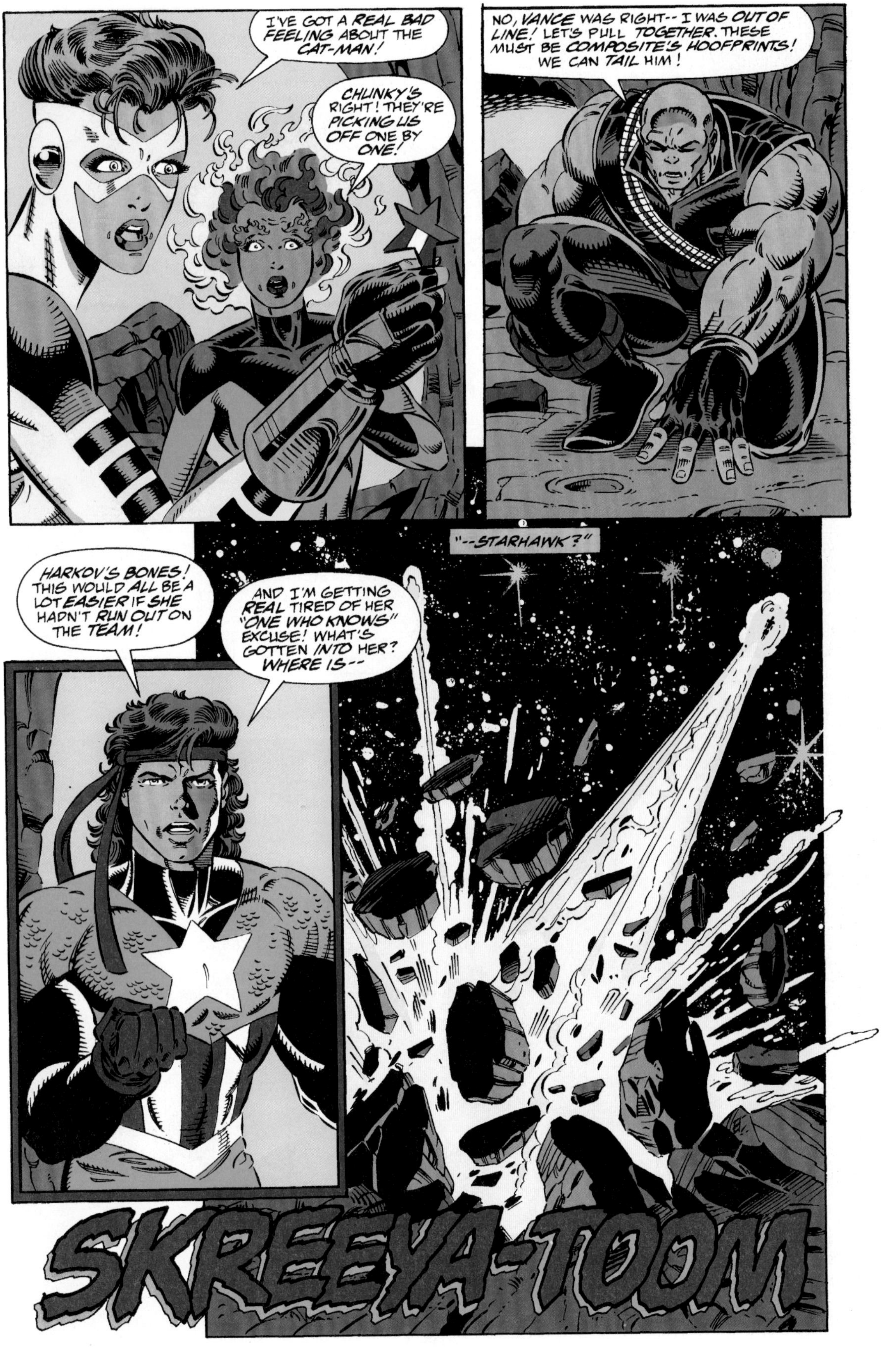
I'VE GOT A REAL BAD FEELING ABOUT THE CAT-MAN!
CHUNKY'S RIGHT! THEY'RE PICKING US OFF ONE BY ONE!
NO, VANCE WAS RIGHT-- I WAS OUT OF LINE! LET'S PULL TOGETHER. THESE MUST BE COMPOSITE'S HOOFPRINTS! WE CAN TAIL HIM!
HARKOV'S BONES! THIS WOULD ALL BE A LOT EASIER IF SHE HADN'T RUN OUT ON THE TEAM!
AND I'M GETTING REAL TIRED OF HER "ONE WHO KNOWS" EXCUSE! WHAT'S GOTTEN INTO HER? WHERE IS--
"--STARHAWK?"
SKREEYA-TOOM

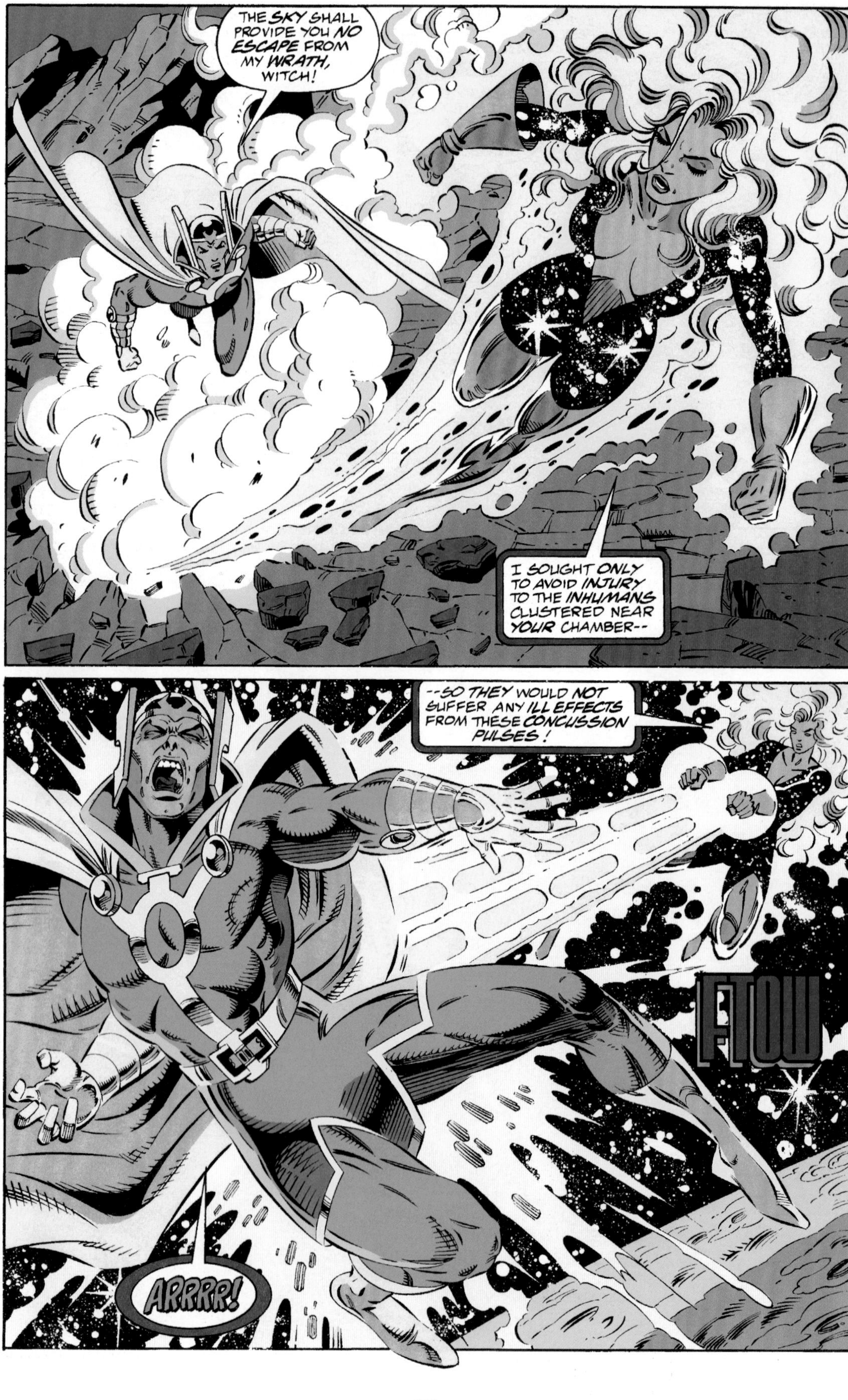
THE SKY SHALL PROVIDE YOU NO ESCAPE FROM MY WRATH, WITCH!
I SOUGHT ONLY TO AVOID INJURY TO THE INHUMANS CLUSTERED NEAR YOUR CHAMBER--
--SO THEY WOULD NOT SUFFER ANY ILL EFFECTS FROM THESE CONCUSSION PULSES!
FTOW
ARRRR!

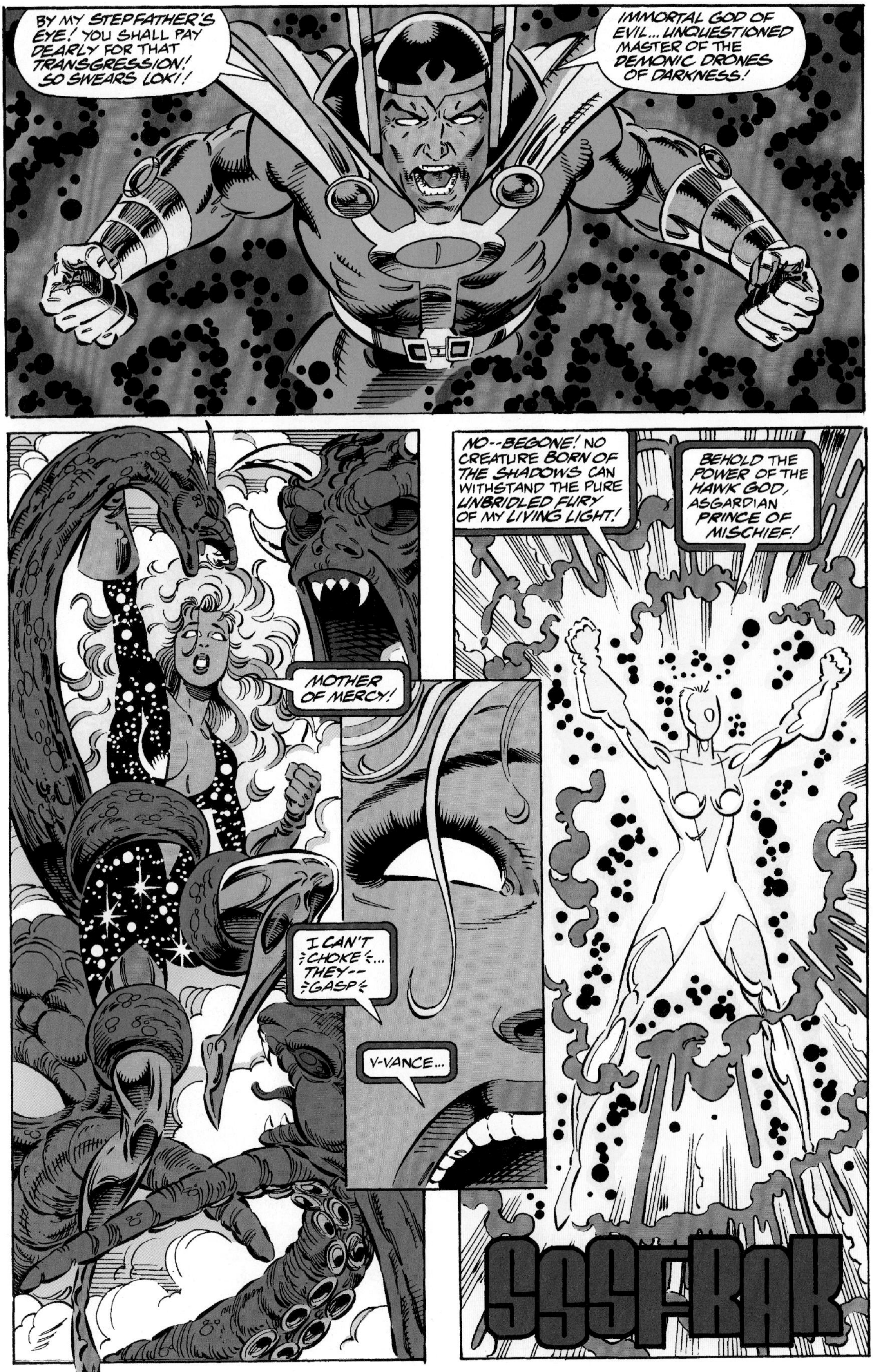
BY MY STEPFATHER'S EYE! YOU SHALL PAY DEARLY FOR THAT TRANSGRESSION! SO SWEARS LOKI!
IMMORTAL GOD OF EVIL... UNQUESTIONED MASTER OF THE DEMONIC DRONES OF DARKNESS!
MOTHER OF MERCY!
I CAN'T ...CHOKE... THEY-- ~GASP~
V-VANCE...
NO--BEGONE! NO CREATURE BORN OF THE SHADOWS CAN WITHSTAND THE PURE UNBRIDLED FURY OF MY LIVING LIGHT!
BEHOLD THE POWER OF THE HAWK GOD, ASGARDIAN PRINCE OF MISCHIEF!
SSSFRAK

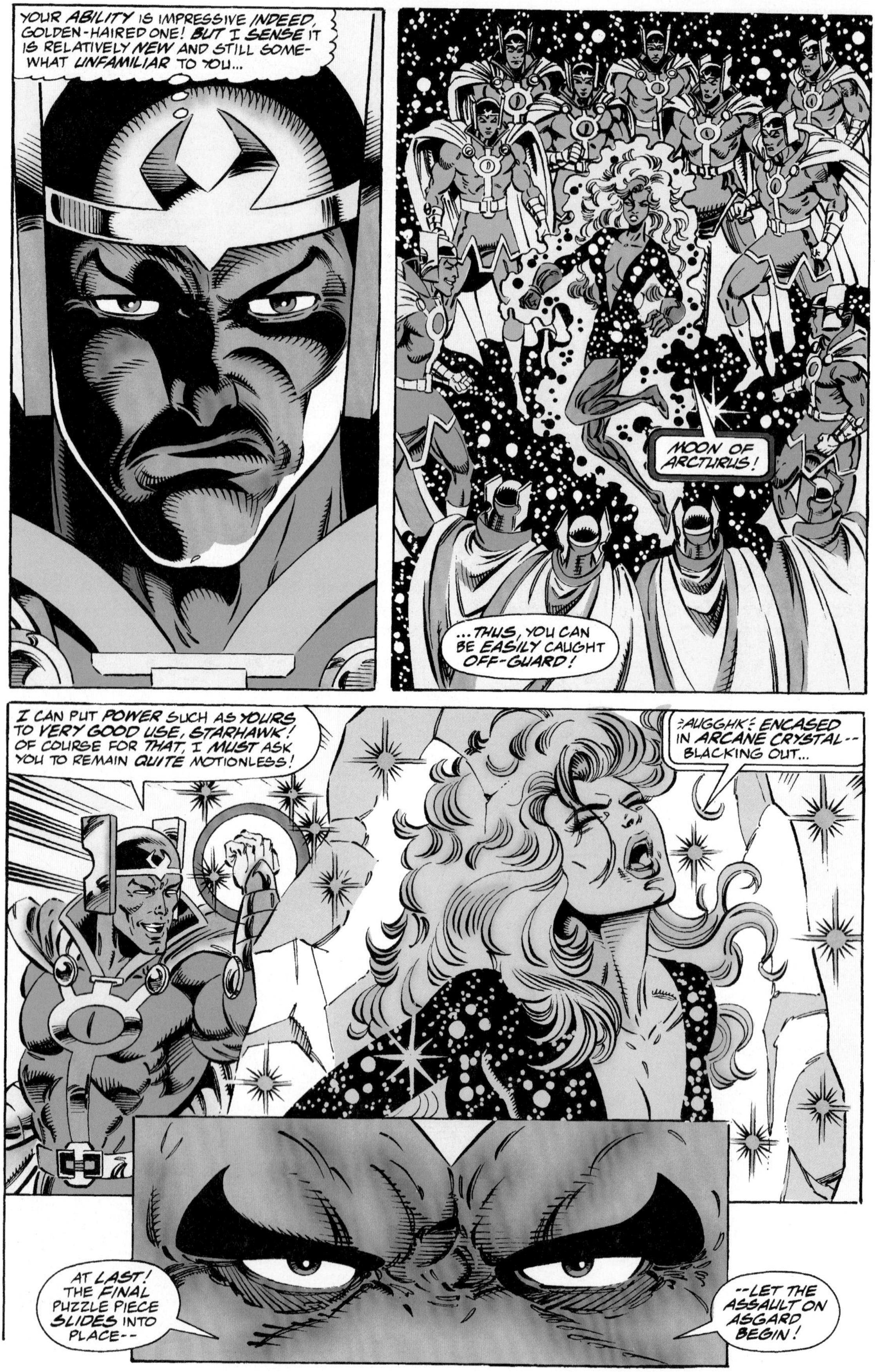

YOUR ABILITY IS IMPRESSIVE INDEED, GOLDEN-HAIRED ONE! BUT I SENSE IT IS RELATIVELY NEW AND STILL SOMEWHAT UNFAMILIAR TO YOU...
MOON OF ARCTURUS!
...THUS, YOU CAN BE EASILY CAUGHT OFF-GUARD!
I CAN PUT POWER SUCH AS YOURS TO VERY GOOD USE, STARHAWK! OF COURSE FOR THAT, I MUST ASK YOU TO REMAIN QUITE MOTIONLESS!
AUGGHK! ENCASED IN ARCANE CRYSTAL-- BLACKING OUT...
AT LAST! THE FINAL PUZZLE PIECE SLIDES INTO PLACE--
--LET THE ASSAULT ON ASGARD BEGIN!

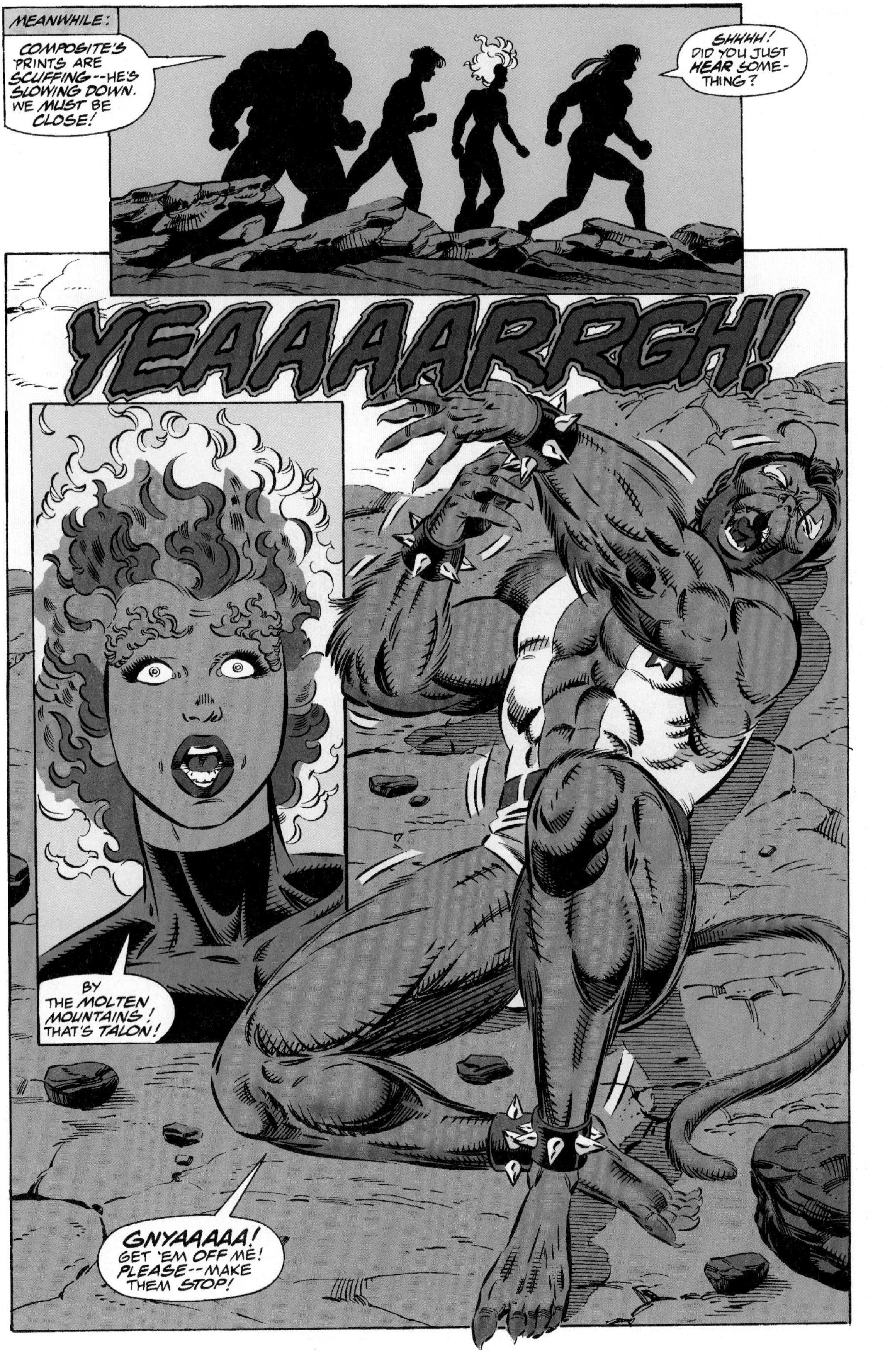
MEANWHILE:
COMPOSITE'S PRINTS ARE SCUFFING--HE'S SLOWING DOWN. WE MUST BE CLOSE!
SHHHH! DID YOU JUST HEAR SOME-THING?
YEAAAAARRGH!
BY THE MOLTEN MOUNTAINS! THAT'S TALON!
GNYAAAAA! GET 'EM OFF ME! PLEASE--MAKE THEM STOP!

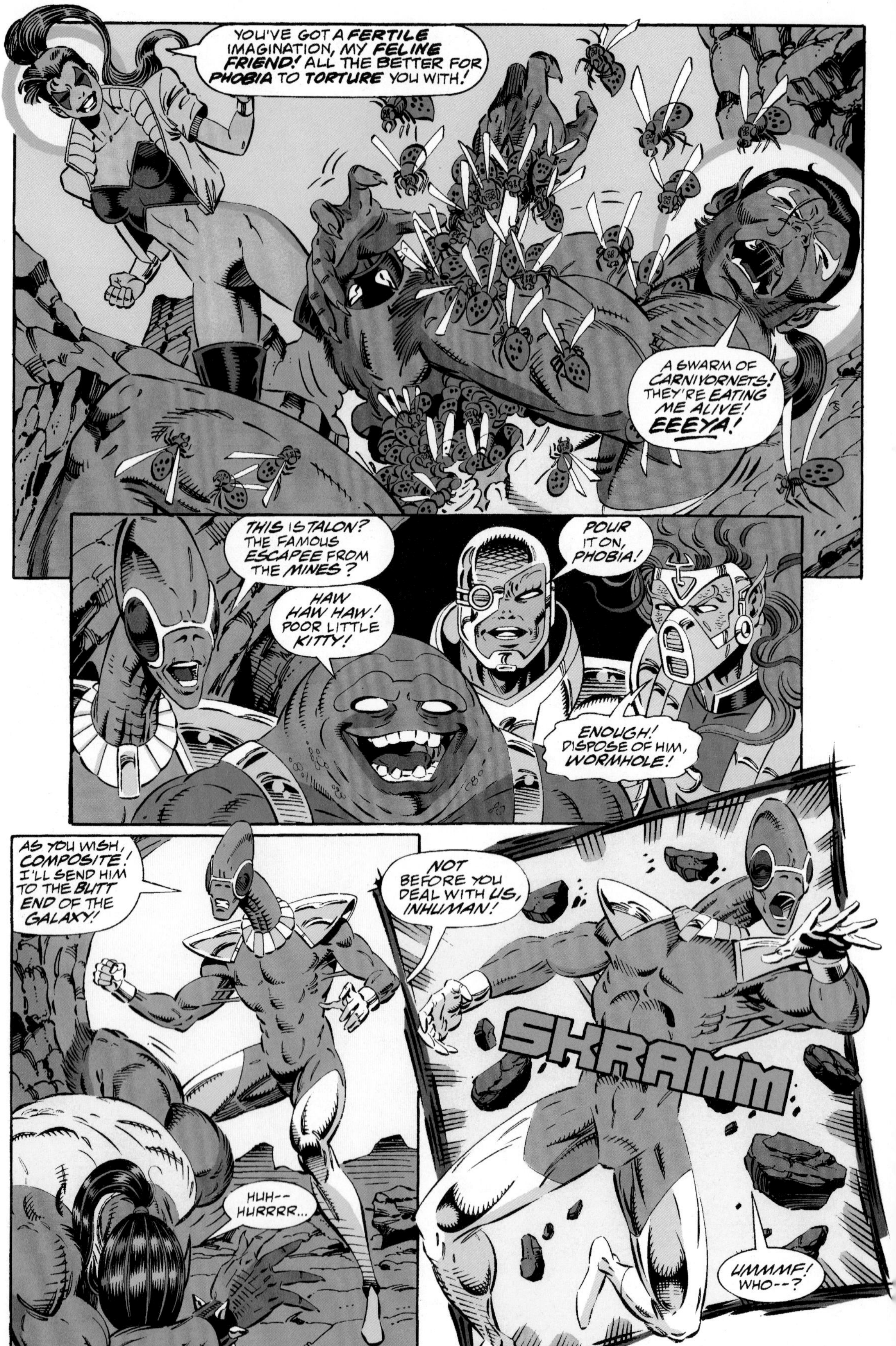
YOU'VE GOT A FERTILE IMAGINATION, MY FELINE FRIEND! ALL THE BETTER FOR PHOBIA TO TORTURE YOU WITH!
A SWARM OF CARNIVORNETS! THEY'RE EATING ME ALIVE! EEEYA!
THIS IS TALON? THE FAMOUS ESCAPEE FROM THE MINES?
HAW HAW HAW! POOR LITTLE KITTY!
POUR IT ON, PHOBIA!
ENOUGH! DISPOSE OF HIM, WORMHOLE!
AS YOU WISH, COMPOSITE! I'LL SEND HIM TO THE BUTT END OF THE GALAXY!
HUH-- HURRRR...
NOT BEFORE YOU DEAL WITH US, INHUMAN!
SKRAMM
UMMMF! WHO--?

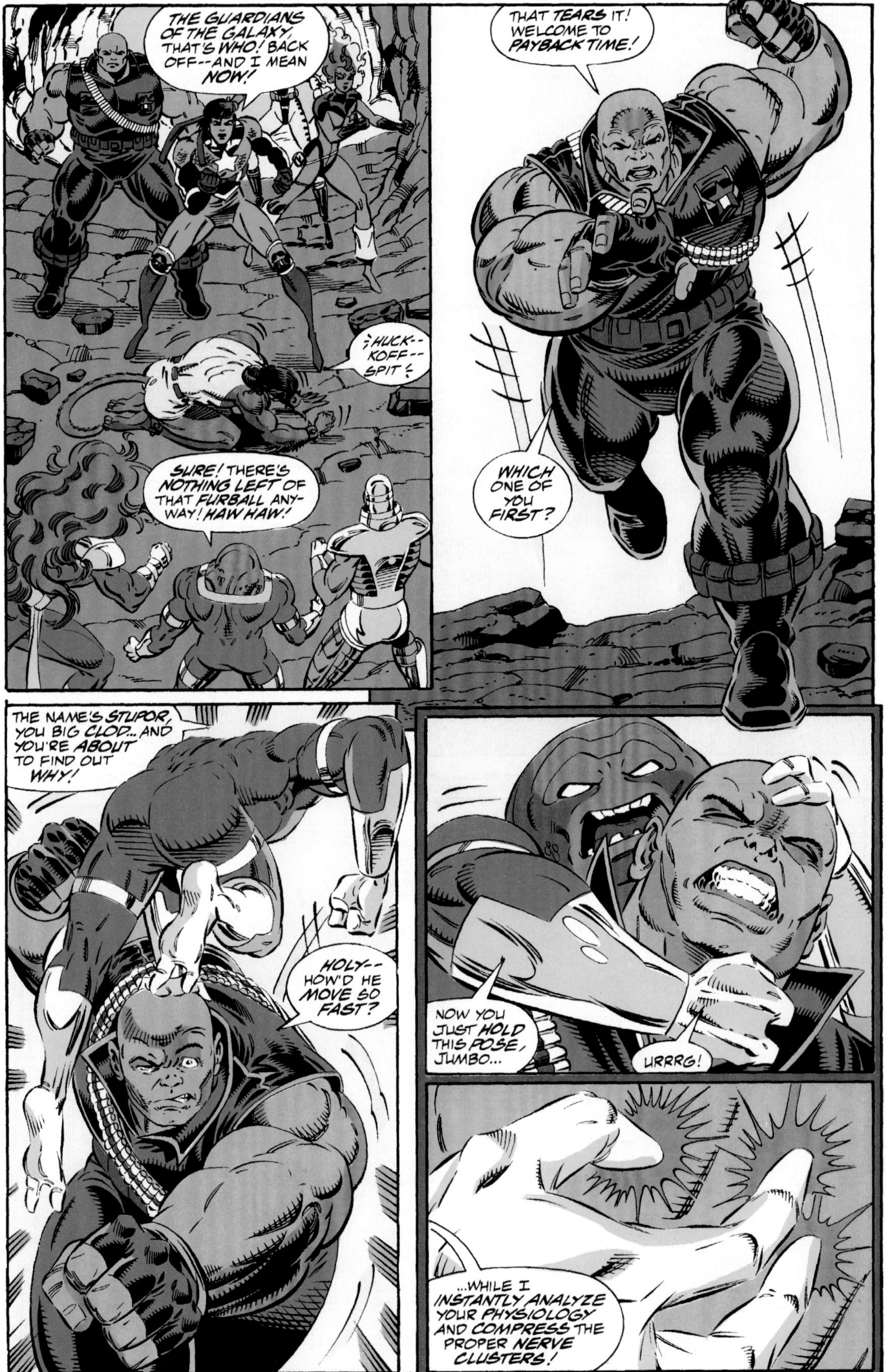
THE GUARDIANS OF THE GALAXY, THAT'S WHO! BACK OFF--AND I MEAN NOW!
;HUCK-KOFF--SPIT;
SURE! THERE'S NOTHING LEFT OF THAT FURBALL ANYWAY! HAW HAW!
THAT TEARS IT! WELCOME TO PAYBACK TIME!
WHICH ONE OF YOU FIRST?
THE NAME'S STUPOR, YOU BIG CLOD... AND YOU'RE ABOUT TO FIND OUT WHY!
HOLY-- HOW'D HE MOVE SO FAST?
NOW YOU JUST HOLD THIS POSE, JUMBO...
URRRG!
...WHILE I INSTANTLY ANALYZE YOUR PHYSIOLOGY AND COMPRESS THE PROPER NERVE CLUSTERS!

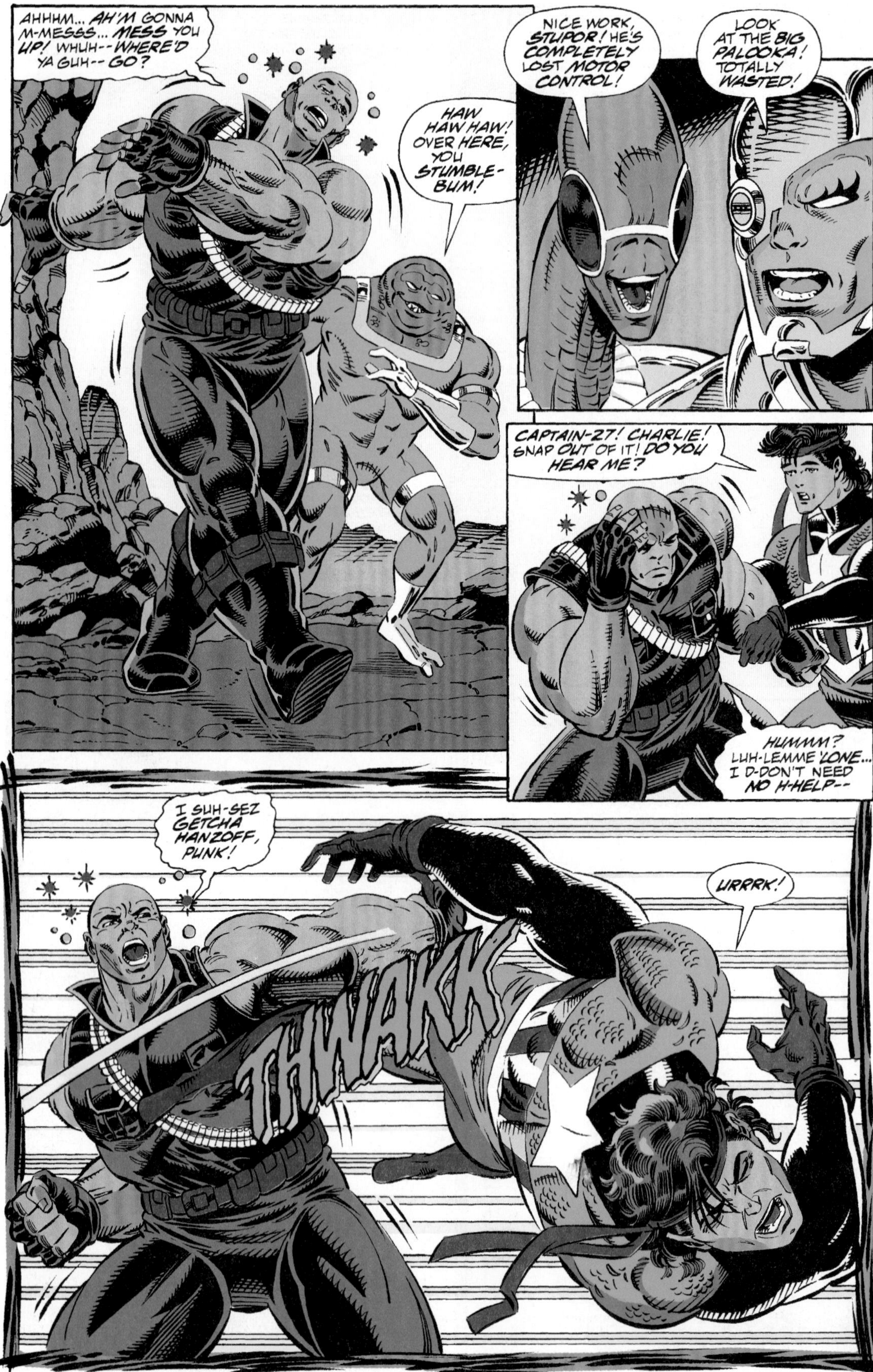
AHHHM... AH'M GONNA M-MESSS... MESS YOU UP! WHUH--WHERE'D YA GUH--GO?
HAW HAW HAW! OVER HERE, YOU STUMBLE-BUM!
NICE WORK, STUPOR! HE'S COMPLETELY LOST MOTOR CONTROL!
LOOK AT THE BIG PALOOKA! TOTALLY WASTED!
CAPTAIN-27! CHARLIE! SNAP OUT OF IT! DO YOU HEAR ME?
HUMMM? LUH-LEMME 'LONE... I D-DON'T NEED NO H-HELP--
I SUH-SEZ GETCHA HANZOFF, PUNK!
URRRK!
THWAKK

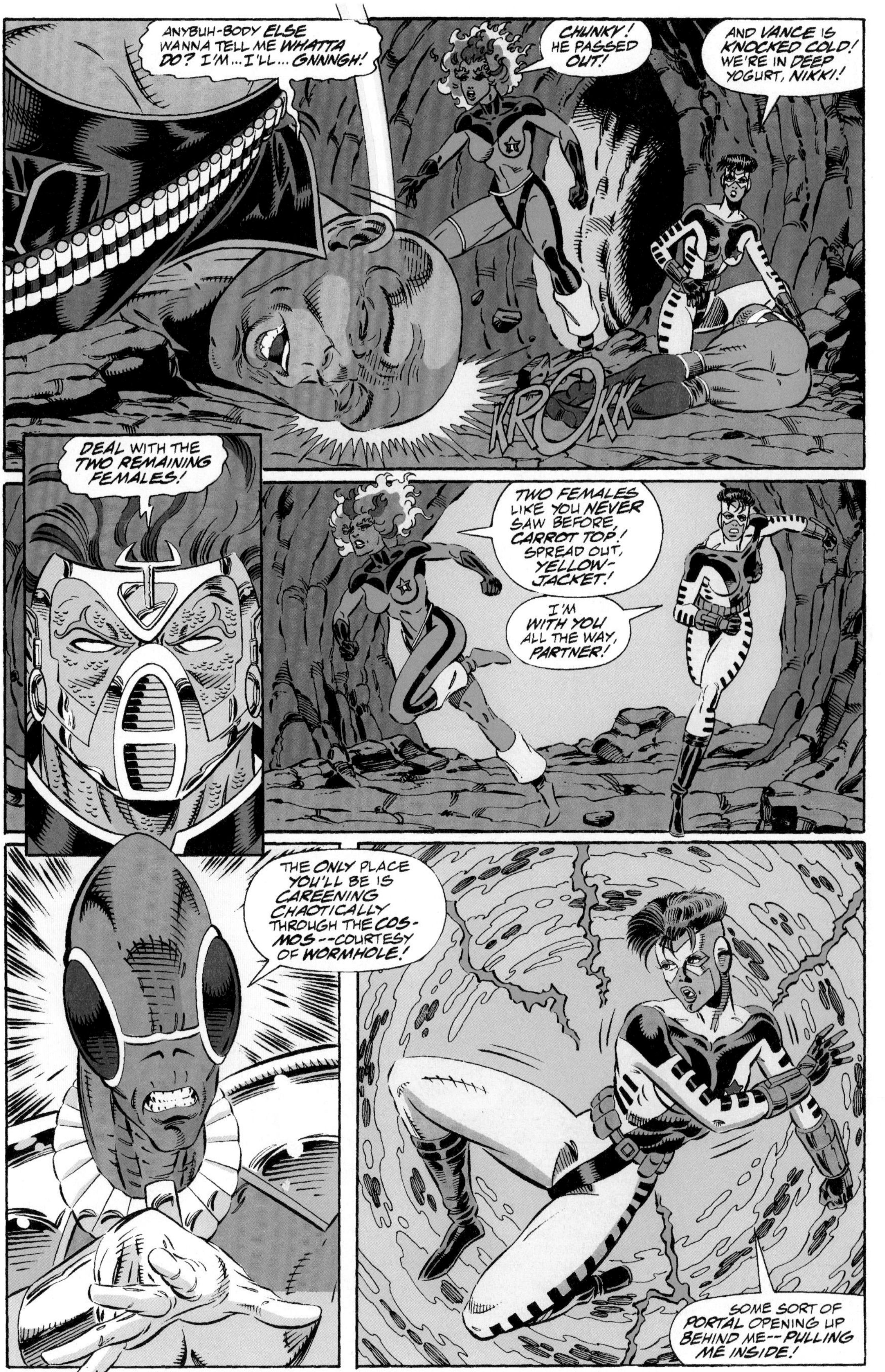
ANYBUH-BODY ELSE WANNA TELL ME WHATTA DO? I'M...I'LL... GNNNGH!
CHUNKY! HE PASSED OUT!
AND VANCE IS KNOCKED COLD! WE'RE IN DEEP YOGURT, NIKKI!
KROKK
DEAL WITH THE TWO REMAINING FEMALES!
TWO FEMALES LIKE YOU NEVER SAW BEFORE, CARROT TOP! SPREAD OUT, YELLOW-JACKET!
I'M WITH YOU ALL THE WAY, PARTNER!
THE ONLY PLACE YOU'LL BE IS CAREENING CHAOTICALLY THROUGH THE COS-MOS--COURTESY OF WORMHOLE!
SOME SORT OF PORTAL OPENING UP BEHIND ME-- PULLING ME INSIDE!

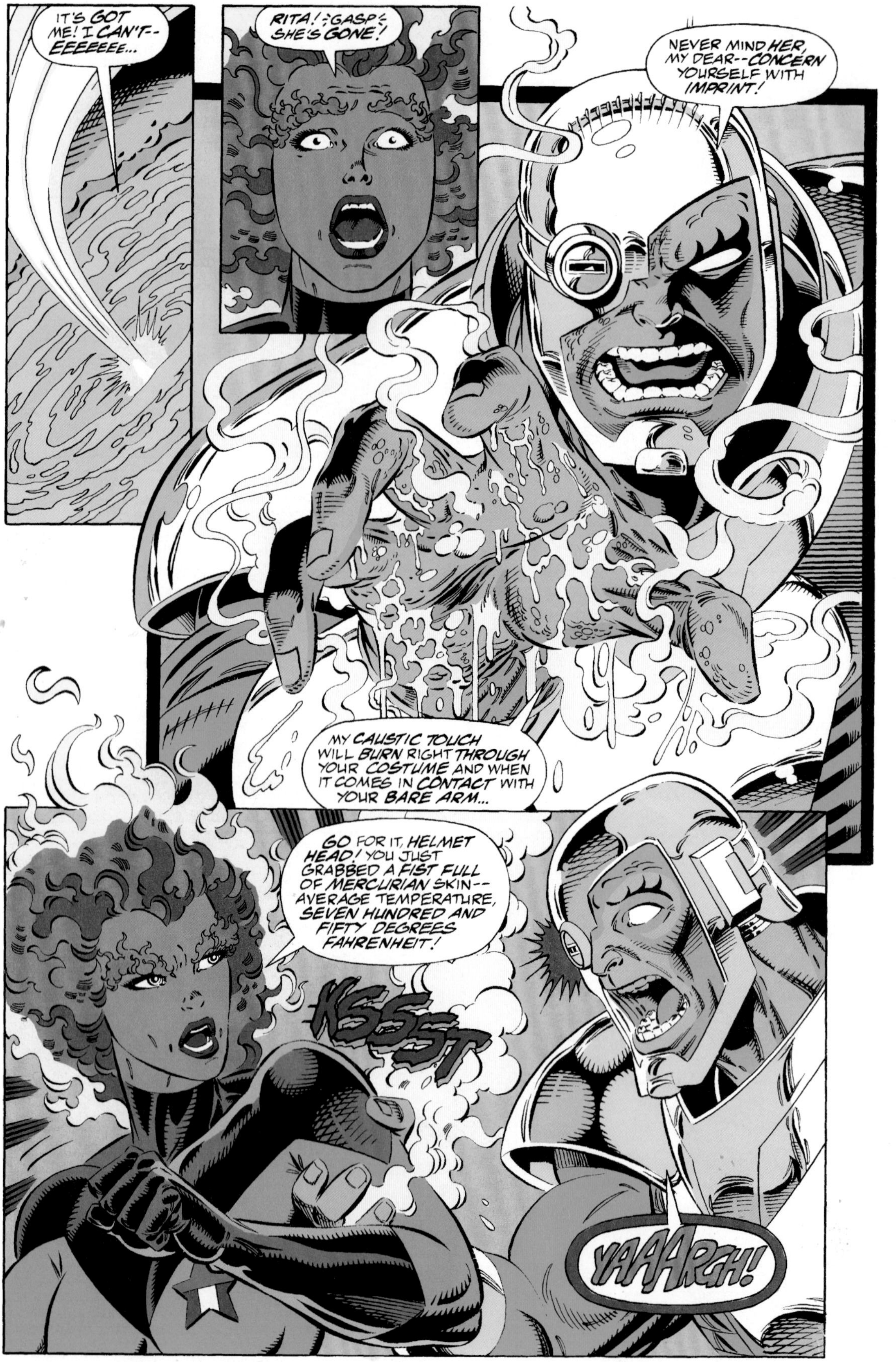
IT'S GOT ME! I CAN'T--EEEEEEE...
RITA! GASP SHE'S GONE!
NEVER MIND HER, MY DEAR--CONCERN YOURSELF WITH IMPRINT!
MY CAUSTIC TOUCH WILL BURN RIGHT THROUGH YOUR COSTUME AND WHEN IT COMES IN CONTACT WITH YOUR BARE ARM...
GO FOR IT, HELMET HEAD! YOU JUST GRABBED A FIST FULL OF MERCURIAN SKIN--AVERAGE TEMPERATURE, SEVEN HUNDRED AND FIFTY DEGREES FAHRENHEIT!
KSSST
YAAARGH!

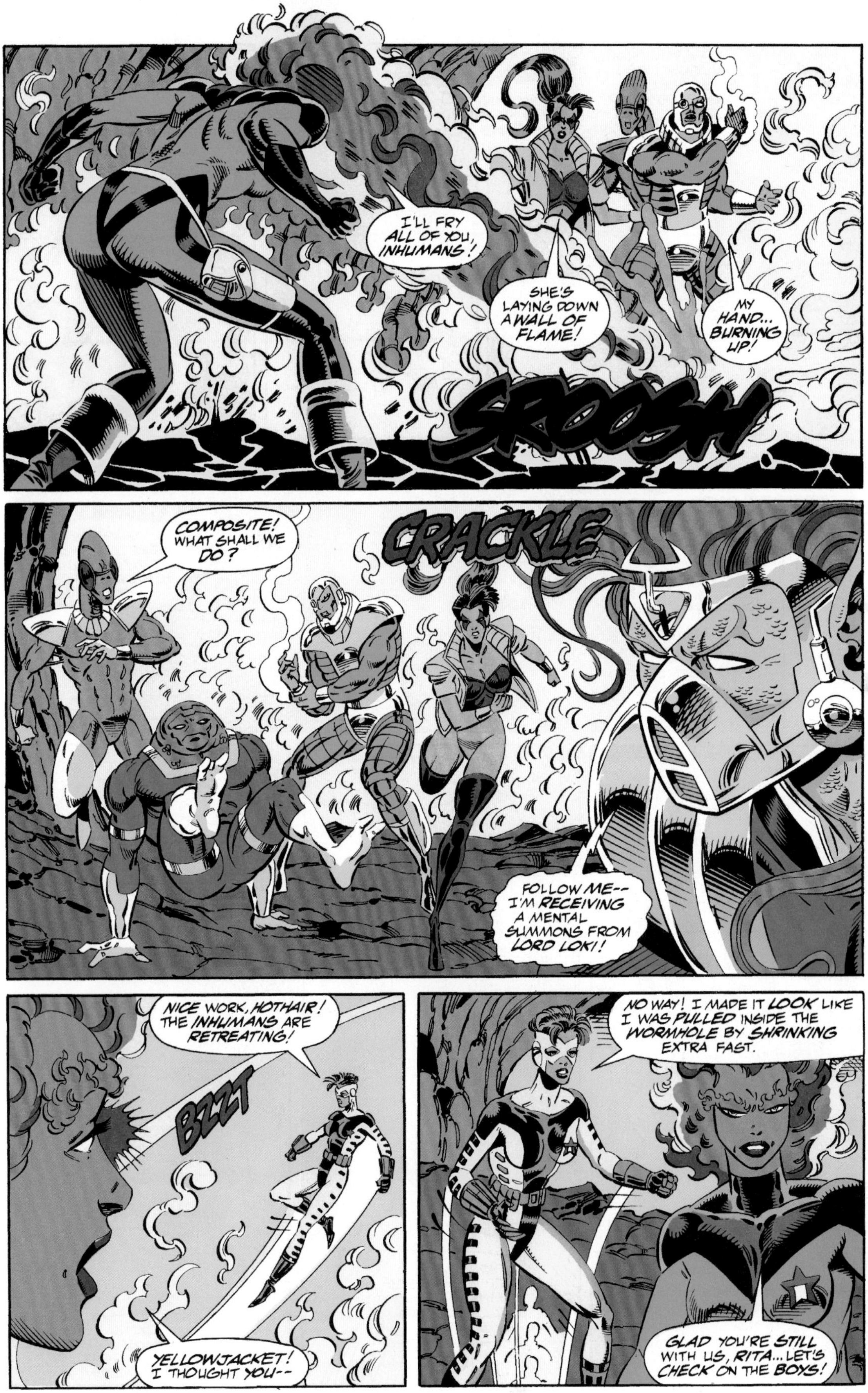
I'LL FRY ALL OF YOU, INHUMANS!
SHE'S LAYING DOWN A WALL OF FLAME!
MY HAND... BURNING UP!
SROOSH
COMPOSITE! WHAT SHALL WE DO?
CRACKLE
FOLLOW ME-- I'M RECEIVING A MENTAL SUMMONS FROM LORD LOKI!
NICE WORK, HOTHAIR! THE INHUMANS ARE RETREATING!
BZZT
YELLOWJACKET! I THOUGHT YOU--
NO WAY! I MADE IT LOOK LIKE I WAS PULLED INSIDE THE WORMHOLE BY SHRINKING EXTRA FAST.
GLAD YOU'RE STILL WITH US, RITA... LET'S CHECK ON THE BOYS!

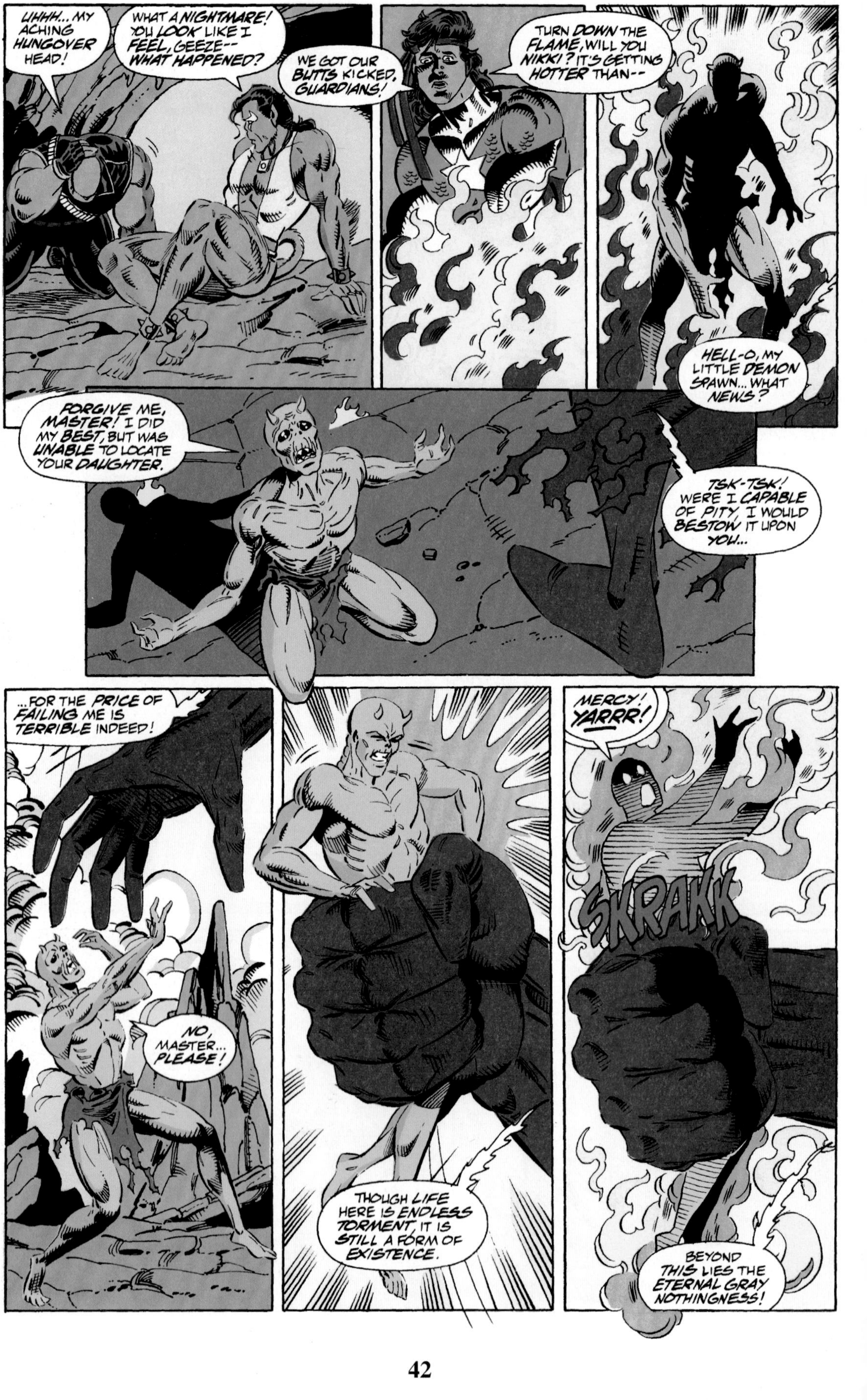
UHHH... MY ACHING HUNGOVER HEAD!
WHAT A NIGHTMARE! YOU LOOK LIKE I FEEL, GEEZE-- WHAT HAPPENED?
WE GOT OUR BUTTS KICKED, GUARDIANS!
TURN DOWN THE FLAME, WILL YOU NIKKI? IT'S GETTING HOTTER THAN--
HELL-O, MY LITTLE DEMON SPAWN... WHAT NEWS?
FORGIVE ME, MASTER! I DID MY BEST, BUT WAS UNABLE TO LOCATE YOUR DAUGHTER.
TSK-TSK! WERE I CAPABLE OF PITY, I WOULD BESTOW IT UPON YOU...
...FOR THE PRICE OF FAILING ME IS TERRIBLE INDEED!
NO, MASTER... PLEASE!
THOUGH LIFE HERE IS ENDLESS TORMENT, IT IS STILL A FORM OF EXISTENCE.
MERCY! YARRR!
SKRAKK
BEYOND THIS LIES THE ETERNAL GRAY NOTHINGNESS!

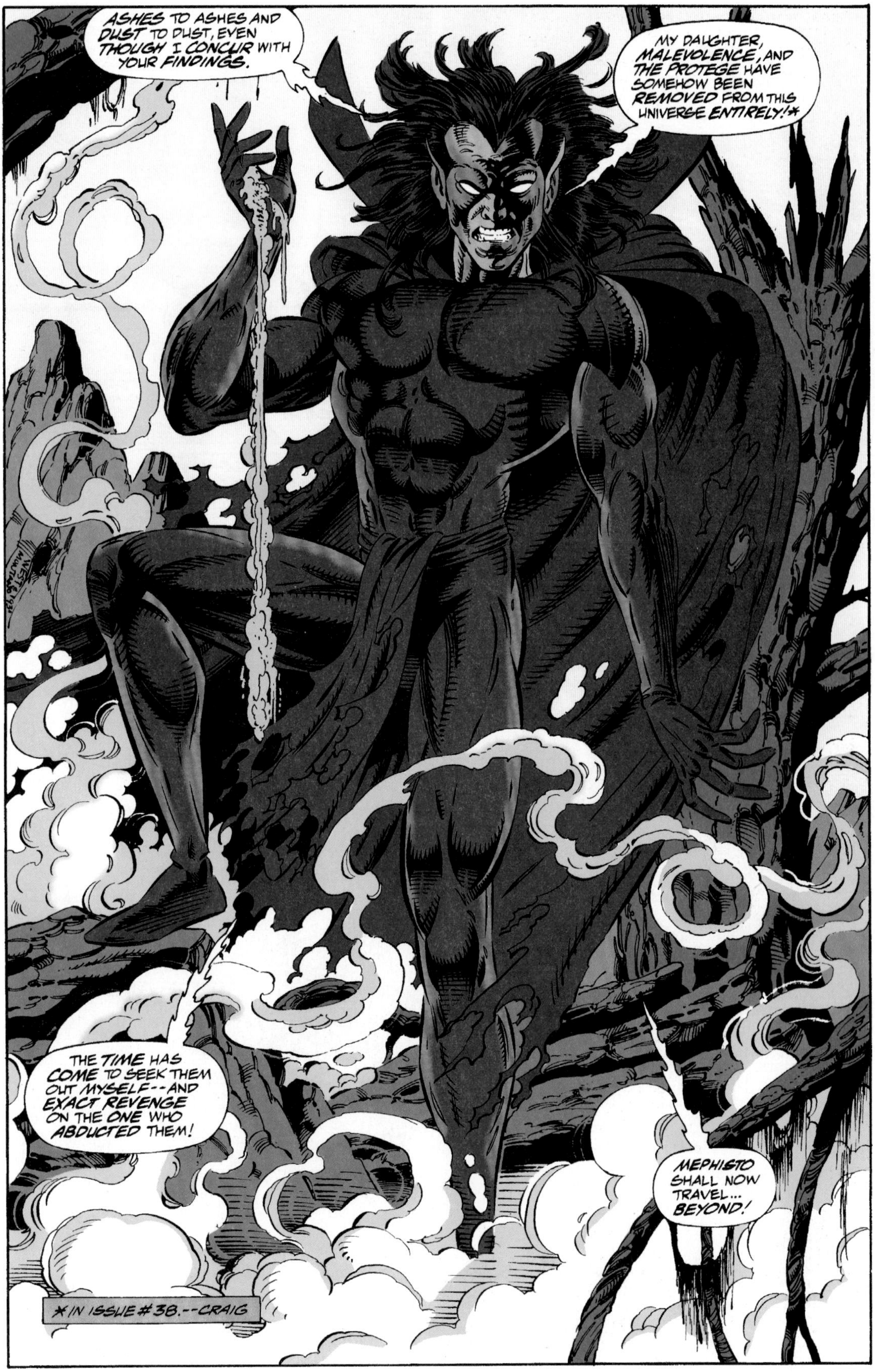
ASHES TO ASHES AND DUST TO DUST, EVEN THOUGH I CONCUR WITH YOUR FINDINGS.
MY DAUGHTER, MALEVOLENCE, AND THE PROTEGE HAVE SOMEHOW BEEN REMOVED FROM THIS UNIVERSE ENTIRELY!*
THE TIME HAS COME TO SEEK THEM OUT MYSELF--AND EXACT REVENGE ON THE ONE WHO ABDUCTED THEM!
MEPHISTO SHALL NOW TRAVEL... BEYOND!
*IN ISSUE #38.--CRAIG

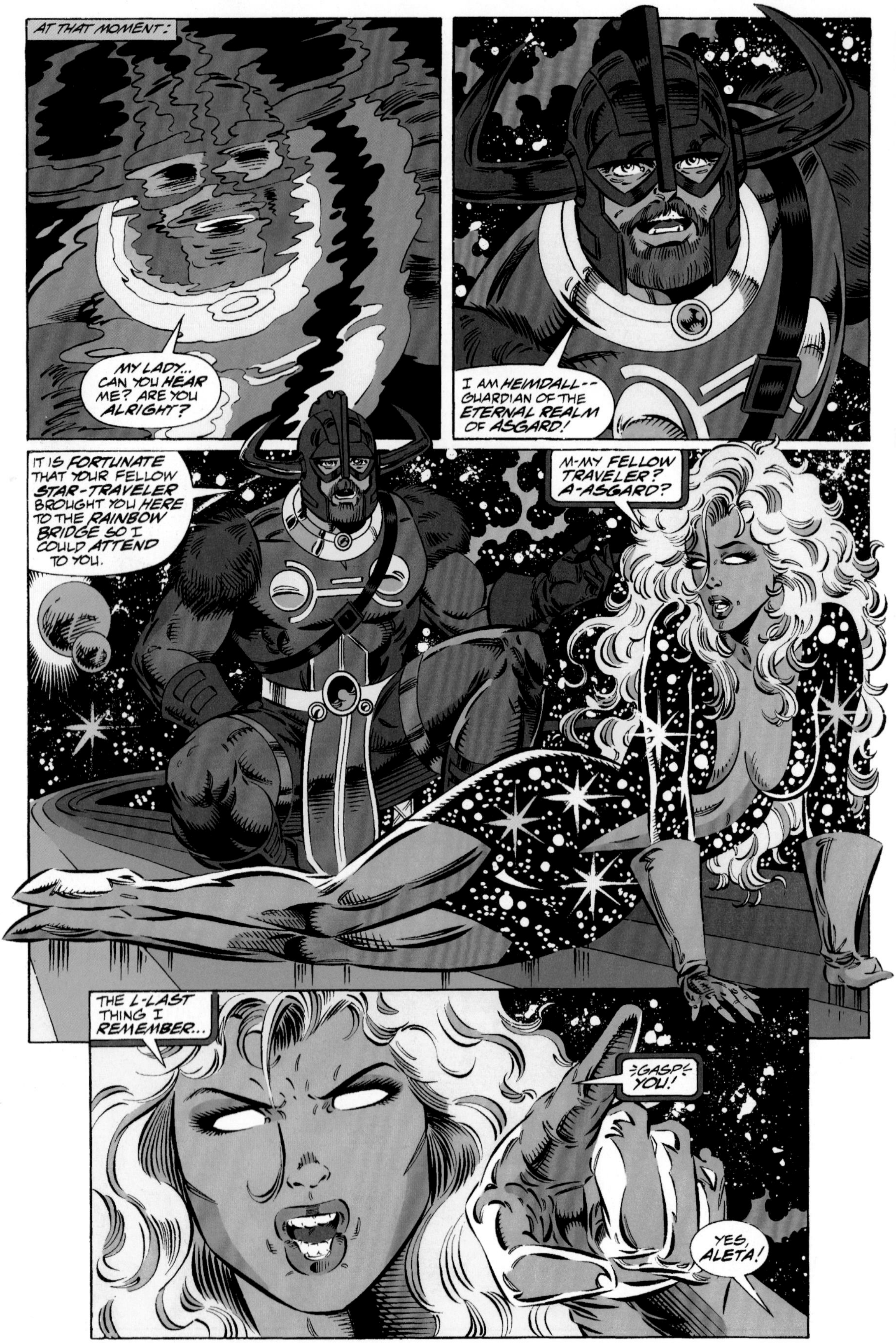
AT THAT MOMENT:
MY LADY... CAN YOU HEAR ME? ARE YOU ALRIGHT?
I AM HEIMDALL-- GUARDIAN OF THE ETERNAL REALM OF ASGARD!
IT IS FORTUNATE THAT YOUR FELLOW STAR-TRAVELER BROUGHT YOU HERE TO THE RAINBOW BRIDGE SO I COULD ATTEND TO YOU.
M-MY FELLOW TRAVELER? A-ASGARD?
THE L-LAST THING I REMEMBER...
GASP YOU!
YES, ALETA!

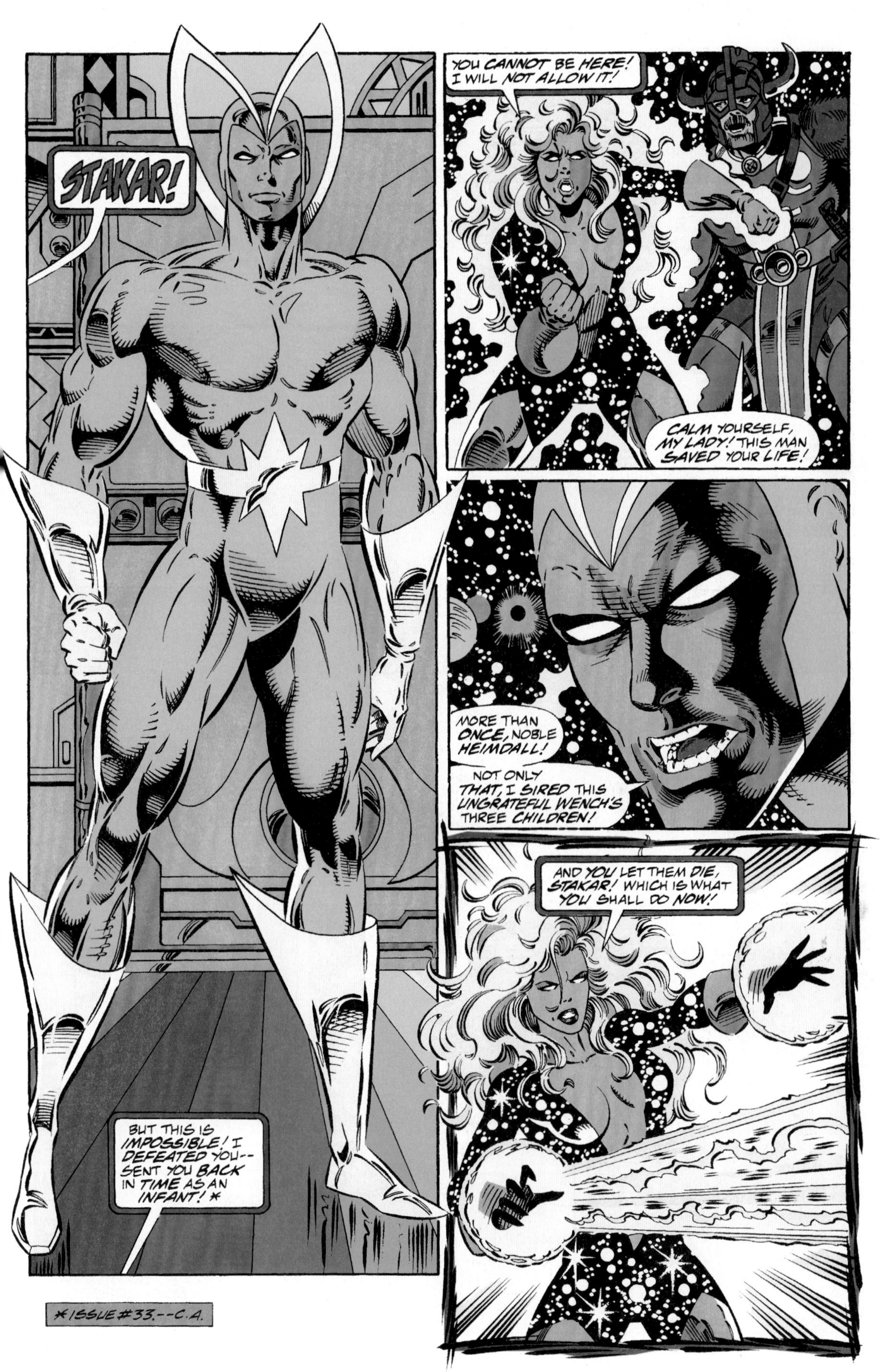
STAKAR!
BUT THIS IS IMPOSSIBLE! I DEFEATED YOU--SENT YOU BACK IN TIME AS AN INFANT! *
YOU CANNOT BE HERE! I WILL NOT ALLOW IT!
CALM YOURSELF, MY LADY! THIS MAN SAVED YOUR LIFE!
MORE THAN ONCE, NOBLE HEIMDALL!
NOT ONLY THAT, I SIRED THIS UNGRATEFUL WENCH'S THREE CHILDREN!
AND YOU LET THEM DIE, STAKAR! WHICH IS WHAT YOU SHALL DO NOW!

*ISSUE #33.--C.A.

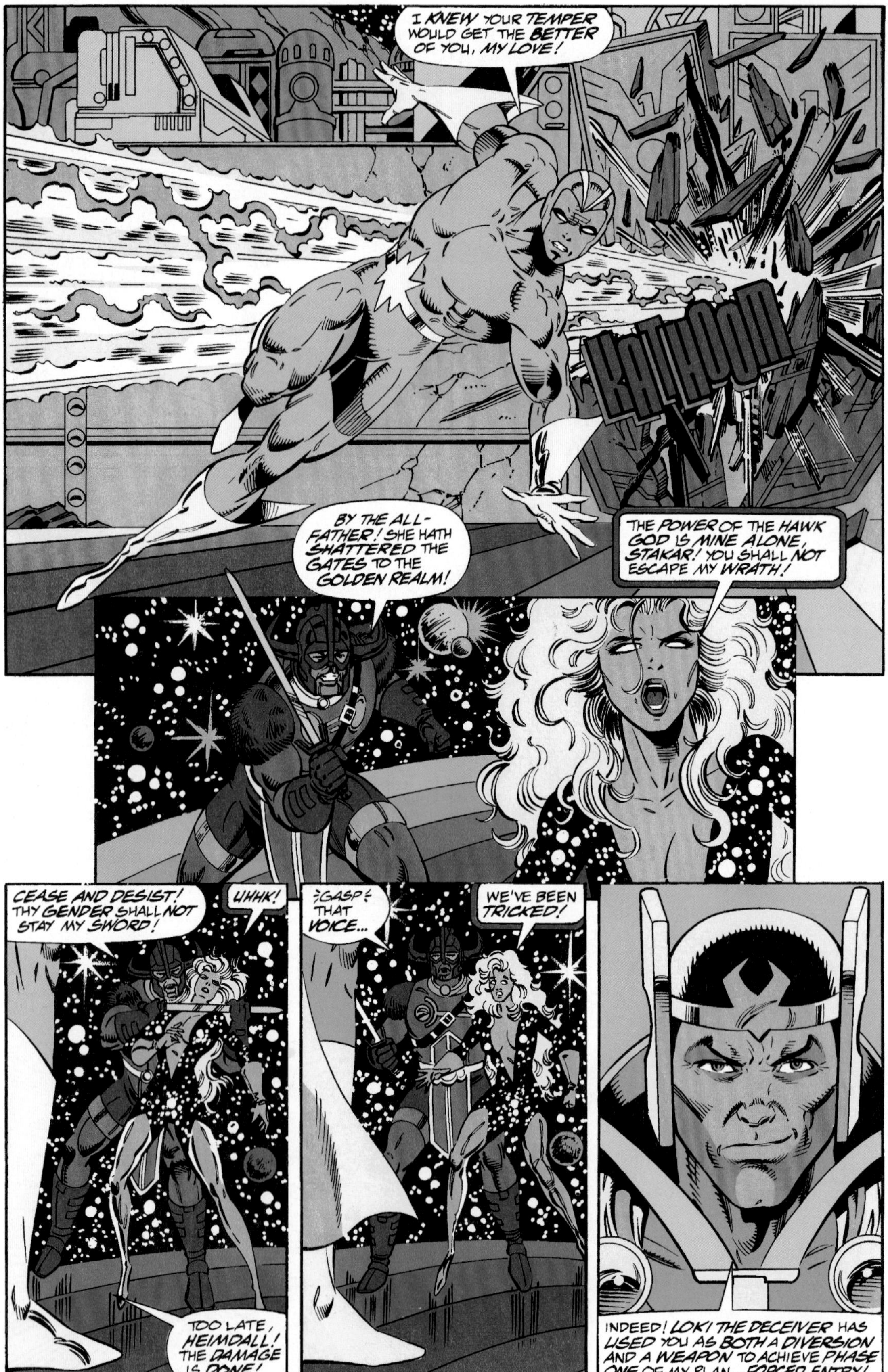
I KNEW YOUR TEMPER WOULD GET THE BETTER OF YOU, MY LOVE!
KATHOOM
BY THE ALL-FATHER! SHE HATH SHATTERED THE GATES TO THE GOLDEN REALM!
THE POWER OF THE HAWK GOD IS MINE ALONE, STAKAR! YOU SHALL NOT ESCAPE MY WRATH!
CEASE AND DESIST! THY GENDER SHALL NOT STAY MY SWORD!
UHHK!
TOO LATE, HEIMDALL! THE DAMAGE IS DONE!
GASP THAT VOICE...
WE'VE BEEN TRICKED!
INDEED! LOKI THE DECEIVER HAS USED YOU AS BOTH A DIVERSION AND A WEAPON TO ACHIEVE PHASE ONE OF MY PLAN... FORCED ENTRY!

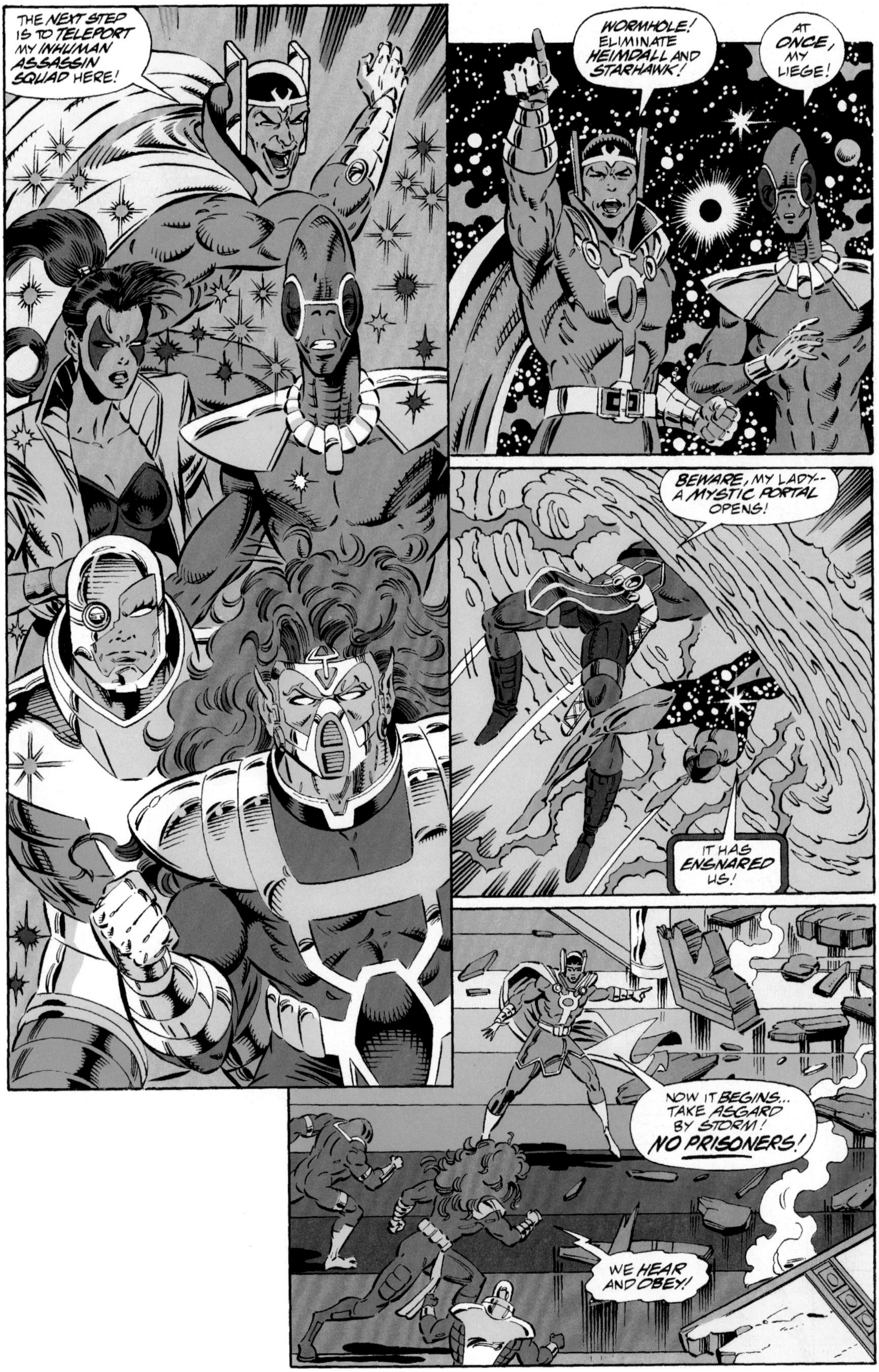
THE NEXT STEP IS TO TELEPORT MY INHUMAN ASSASSIN SQUAD HERE!
WORMHOLE! ELIMINATE HEIMDALL AND STARHAWK!
AT ONCE, MY LIEGE!
BEWARE, MY LADY-- A MYSTIC PORTAL OPENS!
IT HAS ENSNARED US!
NOW IT BEGINS... TAKE ASGARD BY STORM! NO PRISONERS!
WE HEAR AND OBEY!

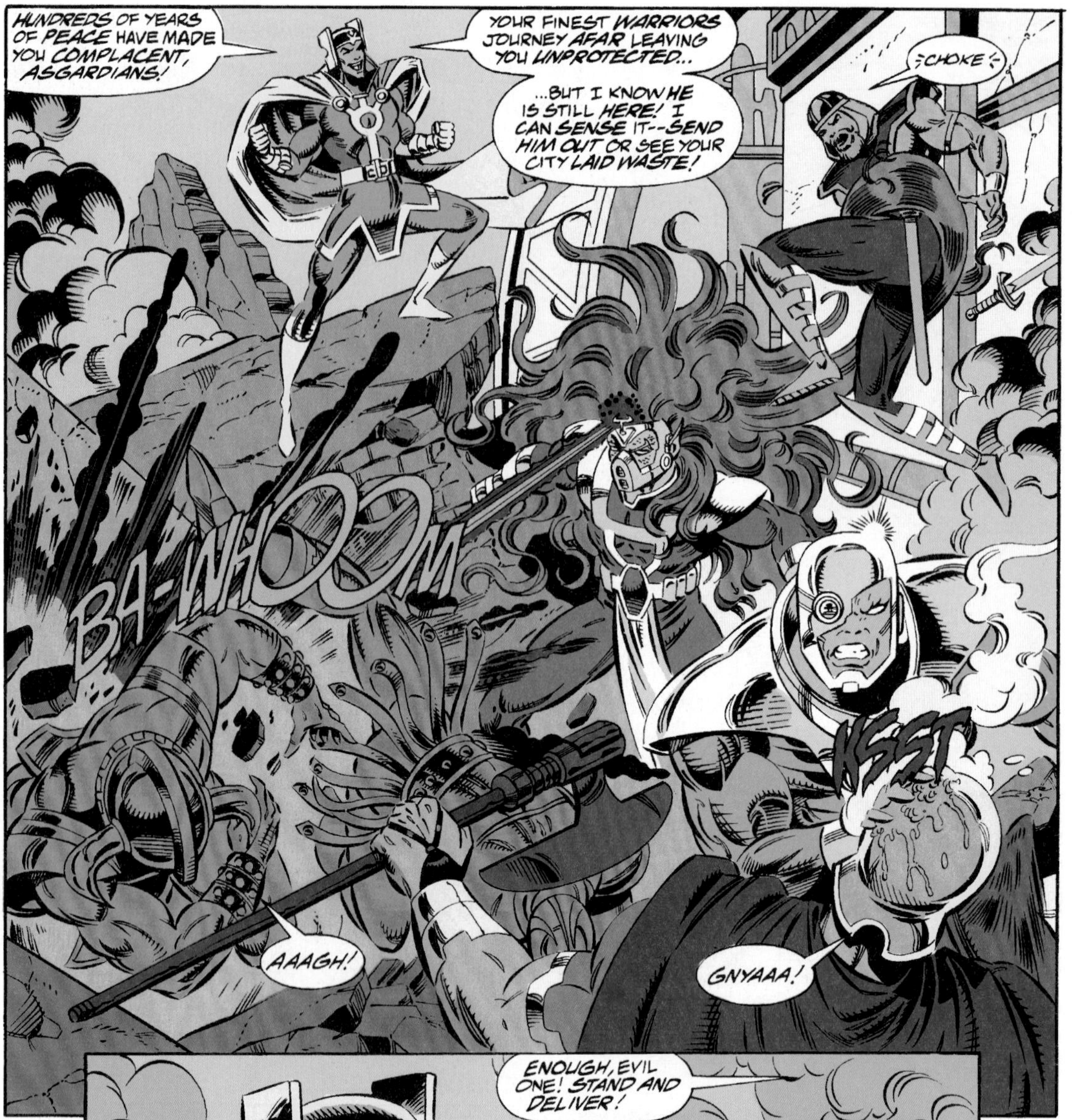
HUNDREDS OF YEARS OF PEACE HAVE MADE YOU COMPLACENT, ASGARDIANS!
YOUR FINEST WARRIORS JOURNEY AFAR LEAVING YOU UNPROTECTED...
...BUT I KNOW HE IS STILL HERE! I CAN SENSE IT--SEND HIM OUT OR SEE YOUR CITY LAID WASTE!
CHOKE
BA-WHOOM
ISST
AAAGH!
GNYAAA!

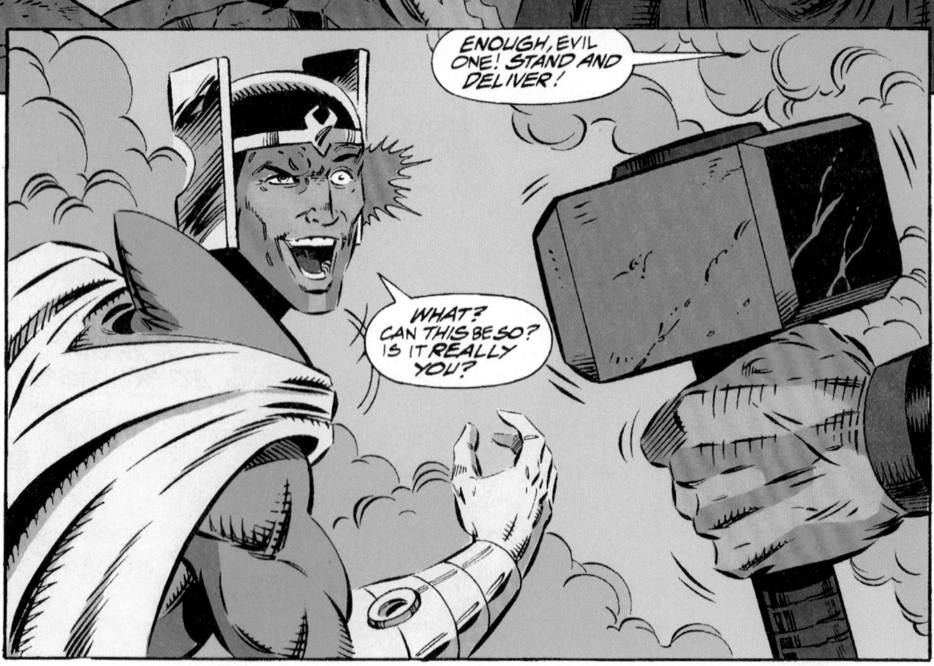
ENOUGH, EVIL ONE! STAND AND DELIVER!
WHAT? CAN THIS BE SO? IS IT REALLY YOU?

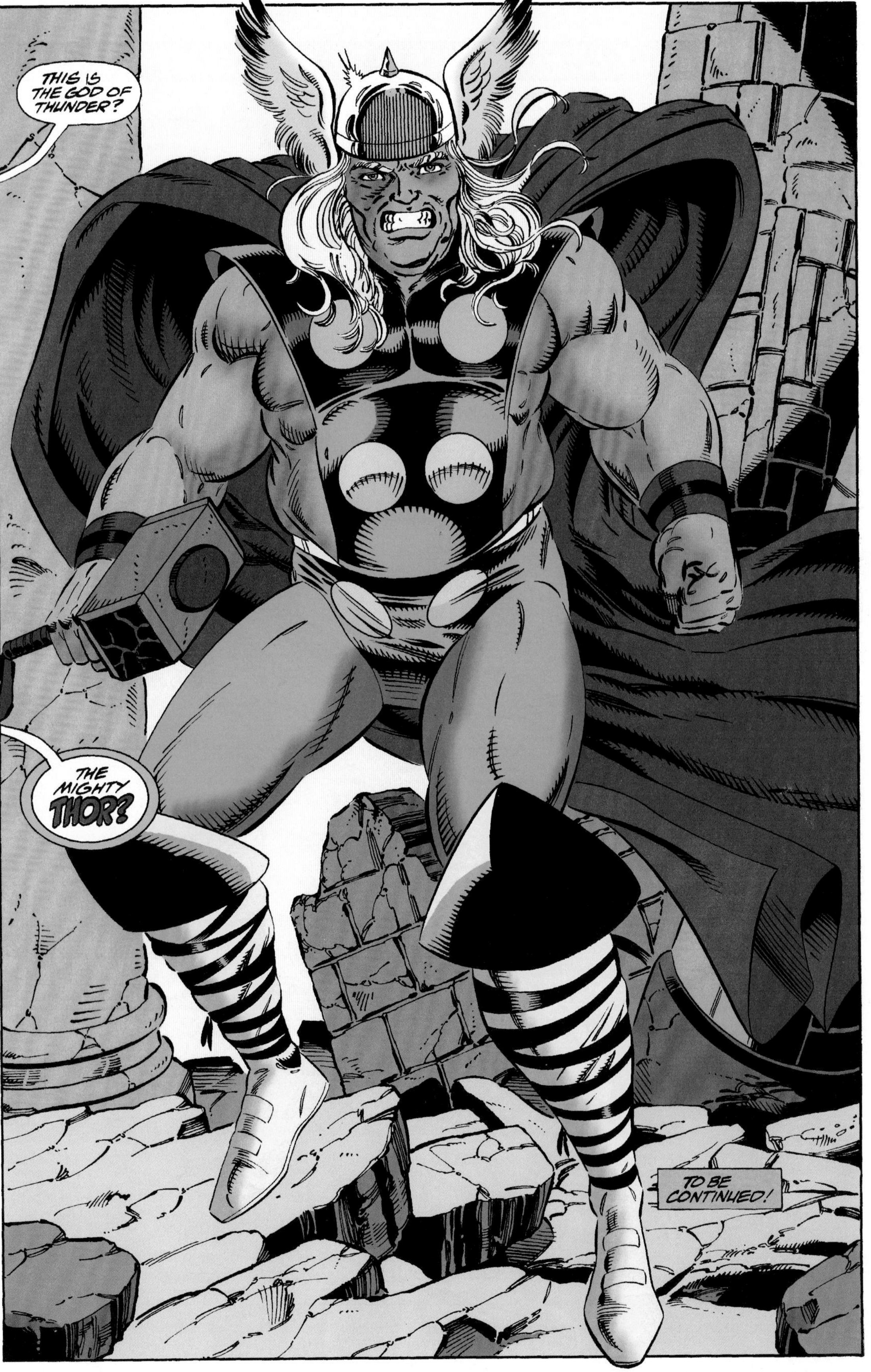

THIS IS THE GOD OF THUNDER?
THE MIGHTY THOR?
TO BE CONTINUED!

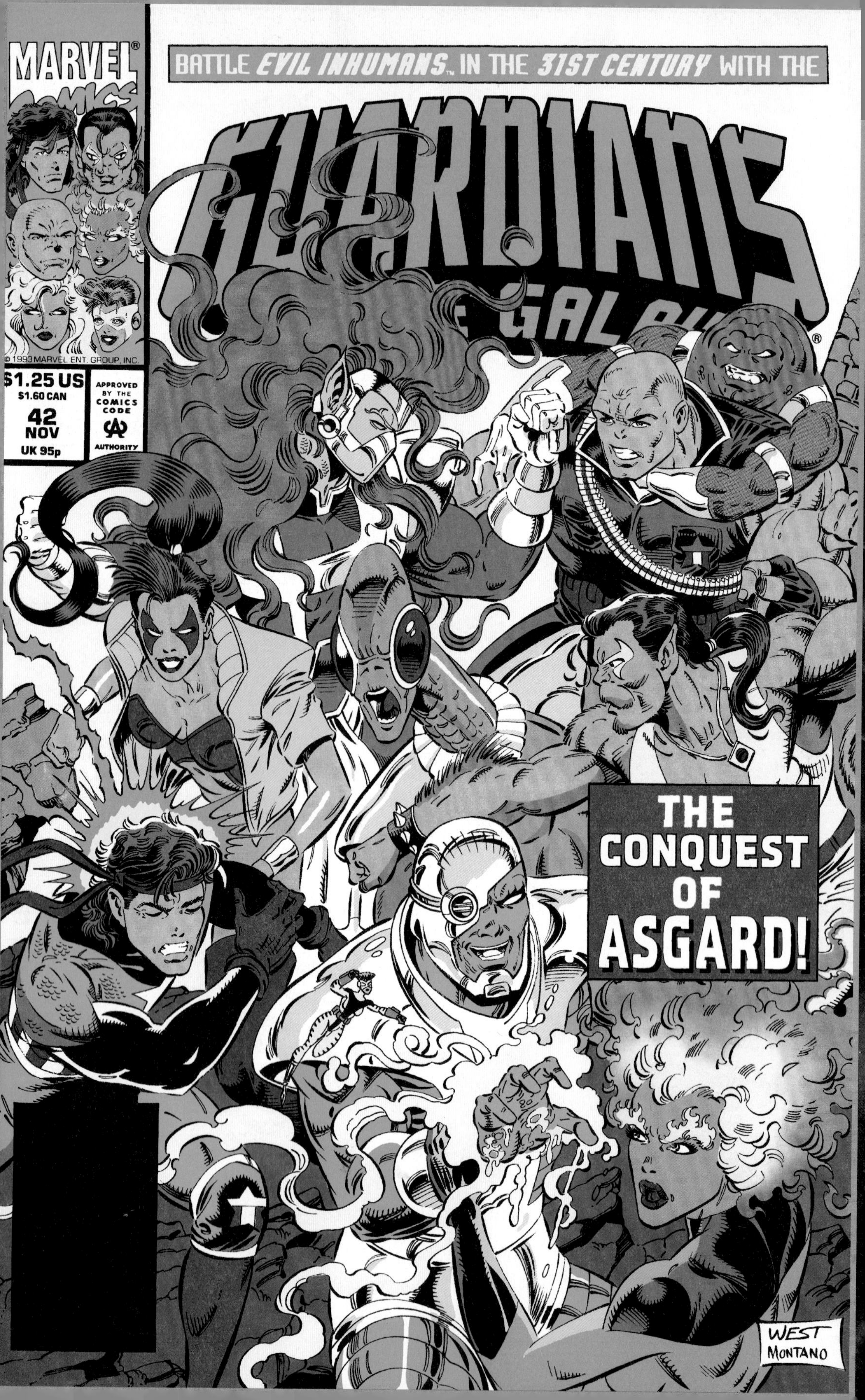
MARVEL COMICS
© 1993 MARVEL ENT. GROUP, INC.
$1.25 US
$1.60 CAN
42
NOV
UK 95p
APPROVED BY THE COMICS CODE AUTHORITY
BATTLE EVIL INHUMANS™ IN THE 31ST CENTURY WITH THE
GUARDIANS
THE CONQUEST OF ASGARD!
WEST
MONTANO

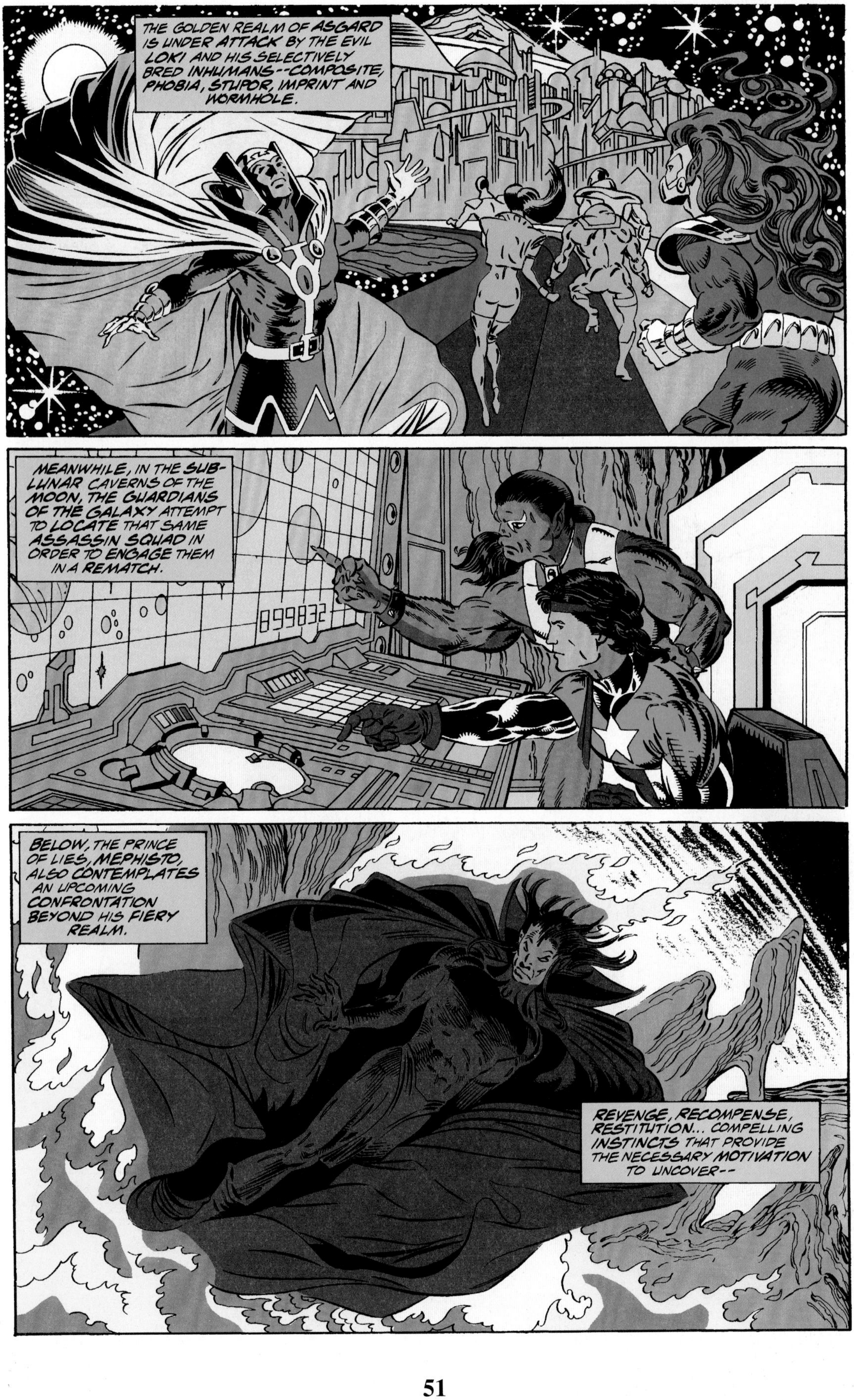
THE GOLDEN REALM OF ASGARD IS UNDER ATTACK BY THE EVIL LOKI AND HIS SELECTIVELY BRED INHUMANS--COMPOSITE, PHOBIA, STUPOR, IMPRINT AND WORMHOLE.
MEANWHILE, IN THE SUB-LUNAR CAVERNS OF THE MOON, THE GUARDIANS OF THE GALAXY ATTEMPT TO LOCATE THAT SAME ASSASSIN SQUAD IN ORDER TO ENGAGE THEM IN A REMATCH.
899832
BELOW, THE PRINCE OF LIES, MEPHISTO, ALSO CONTEMPLATES AN UPCOMING CONFRONTATION BEYOND HIS FIERY REALM.
REVENGE, RECOMPENSE, RESTITUTION... COMPELLING INSTINCTS THAT PROVIDE THE NECESSARY MOTIVATION TO UNCOVER--

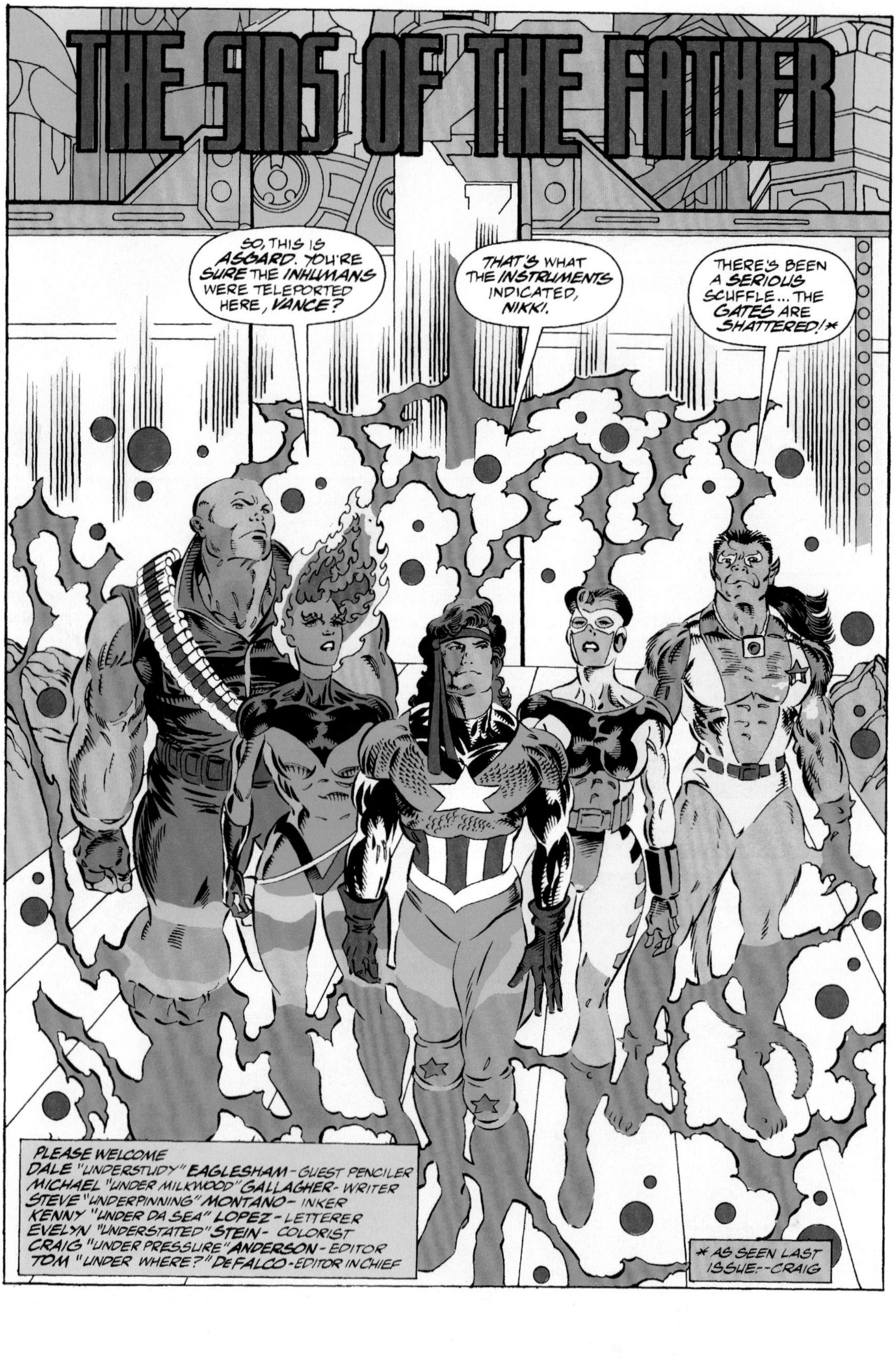
THE SINS OF THE FATHER
SO, THIS IS ASGARD. YOU'RE SURE THE INHUMANS WERE TELEPORTED HERE, VANCE?
THAT'S WHAT THE INSTRUMENTS INDICATED, NIKKI.
THERE'S BEEN A SERIOUS SCUFFLE... THE GATES ARE SHATTERED!*
PLEASE WELCOME
DALE "UNDERSTUDY" EAGLESHAM - GUEST PENCILER
MICHAEL "UNDER MILKWOOD" GALLAGHER - WRITER
STEVE "UNDERPINNING" MONTANO - INKER
KENNY "UNDER DA SEA" LOPEZ - LETTERER
EVELYN "UNDERSTATED" STEIN - COLORIST
CRAIG "UNDER PRESSURE" ANDERSON - EDITOR
TOM "UNDER WHERE?" DEFALCO - EDITOR IN CHIEF
* AS SEEN LAST ISSUE.--CRAIG

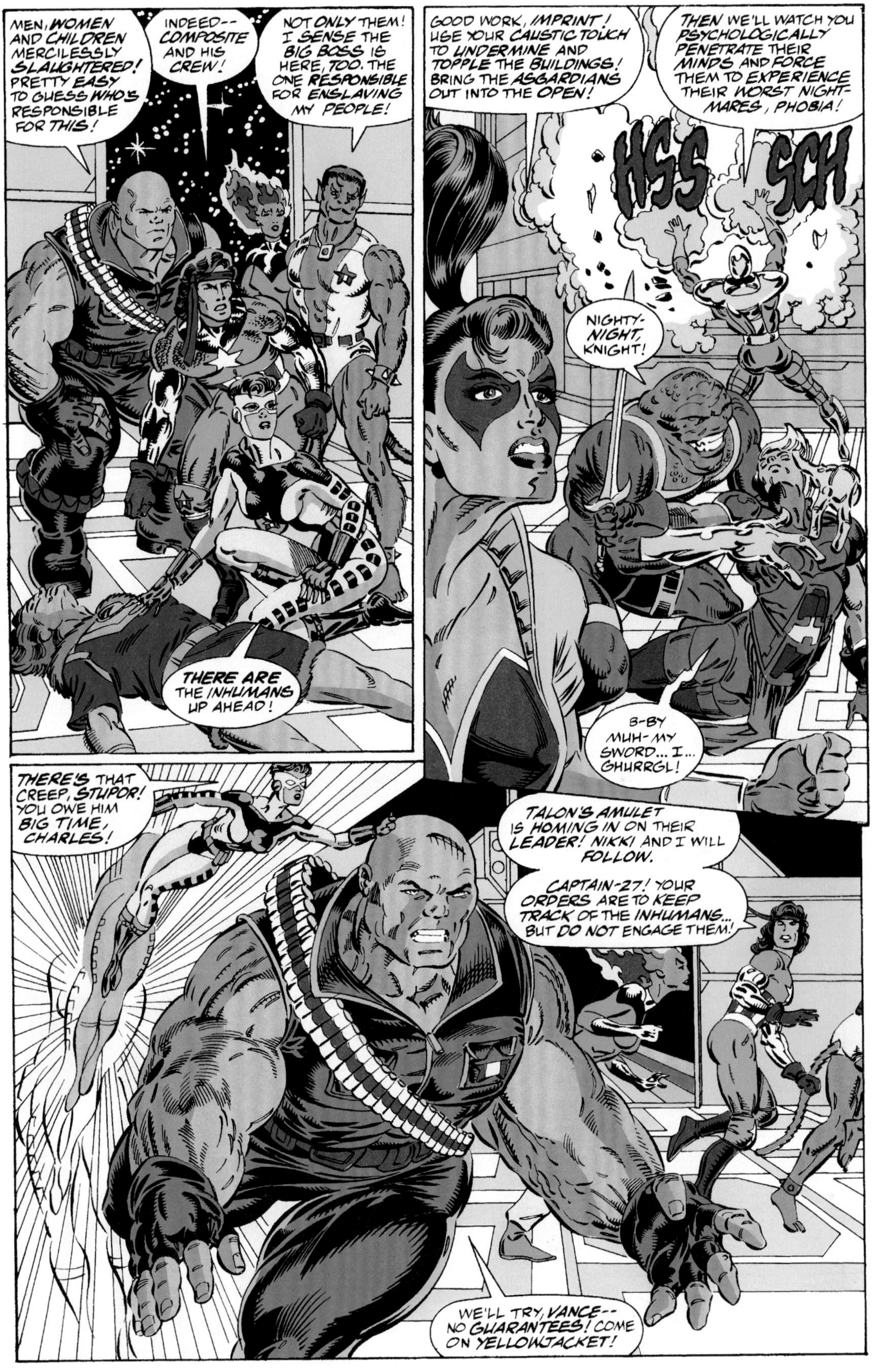

MEN, WOMEN AND CHILDREN MERCILESSLY SLAUGHTERED! PRETTY EASY TO GUESS WHO'S RESPONSIBLE FOR THIS!
INDEED-- COMPOSITE AND HIS CREW!
NOT ONLY THEM! I SENSE THE BIG BOSS IS HERE, TOO. THE ONE RESPONSIBLE FOR ENSLAVING MY PEOPLE!
THERE ARE THE INHUMANS UP AHEAD!
GOOD WORK, IMPRINT! USE YOUR CAUSTIC TOUCH TO UNDERMINE AND TOPPLE THE BUILDINGS! BRING THE ASGARDIANS OUT INTO THE OPEN!
THEN WE'LL WATCH YOU PSYCHOLOGICALLY PENETRATE THEIR MINDS AND FORCE THEM TO EXPERIENCE THEIR WORST NIGHT-MARES, PHOBIA!
HSS
SCH
NIGHTY-NIGHT, KNIGHT!
B-BY MUH-MY SWORD... I... GHURRGL!
THERE'S THAT CREEP, STUPOR! YOU OWE HIM BIG TIME, CHARLES!
TALON'S AMULET IS HOMING IN ON THEIR LEADER! NIKKI AND I WILL FOLLOW.
CAPTAIN-27! YOUR ORDERS ARE TO KEEP TRACK OF THE INHUMANS... BUT DO NOT ENGAGE THEM!
WE'LL TRY, VANCE-- NO GUARANTEES! COME ON YELLOWJACKET!

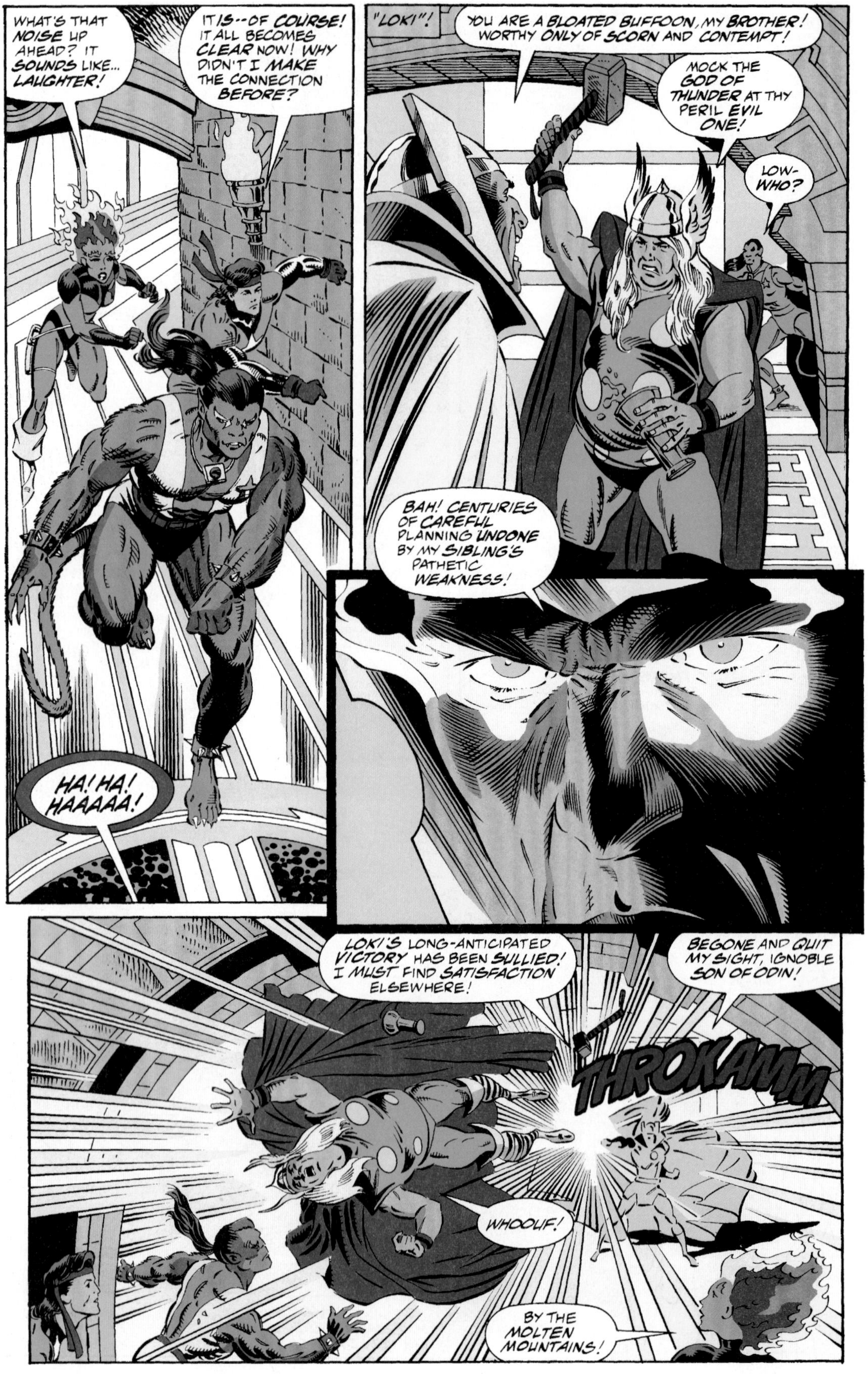
WHAT'S THAT NOISE UP AHEAD? IT SOUNDS LIKE... LAUGHTER!
IT IS--OF COURSE! IT ALL BECOMES CLEAR NOW! WHY DIDN'T I MAKE THE CONNECTION BEFORE?
HA! HA! HAAAAA!
"LOKI"!
YOU ARE A BLOATED BUFFOON, MY BROTHER! WORTHY ONLY OF SCORN AND CONTEMPT!
MOCK THE GOD OF THUNDER AT THY PERIL EVIL ONE!
LOW-WHO?
BAH! CENTURIES OF CAREFUL PLANNING UNDONE BY MY SIBLING'S PATHETIC WEAKNESS!
LOKI'S LONG-ANTICIPATED VICTORY HAS BEEN SULLIED! I MUST FIND SATISFACTION ELSEWHERE!
BEGONE AND QUIT MY SIGHT, IGNOBLE SON OF ODIN!
THROKAMM
WHOOUF!
BY THE MOLTEN MOUNTAINS!

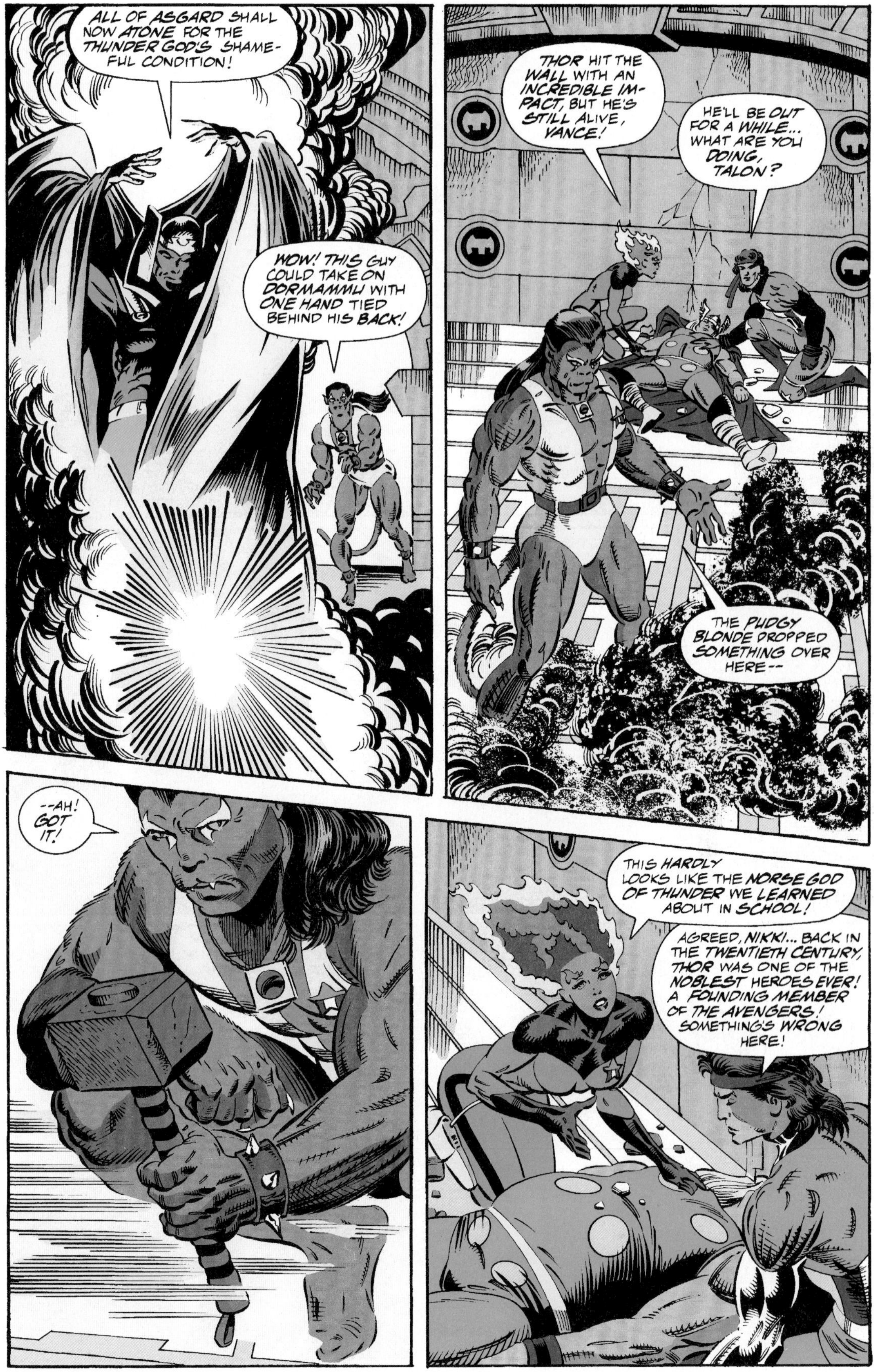
ALL OF ASGARD SHALL NOW ATONE FOR THE THUNDER GOD'S SHAME-FUL CONDITION!
WOW! THIS GUY COULD TAKE ON DORMAMMU WITH ONE HAND TIED BEHIND HIS BACK!
THOR HIT THE WALL WITH AN INCREDIBLE IM-PACT, BUT HE'S STILL ALIVE, VANCE!
HE'LL BE OUT FOR A WHILE... WHAT ARE YOU DOING, TALON?
THE PUDGY BLONDE DROPPED SOMETHING OVER HERE--
--AH! GOT IT!
THIS HARDLY LOOKS LIKE THE NORSE GOD OF THUNDER WE LEARNED ABOUT IN SCHOOL!
AGREED, NIKKI... BACK IN THE TWENTIETH CENTURY, THOR WAS ONE OF THE NOBLEST HEROES EVER! A FOUNDING MEMBER OF THE AVENGERS! SOMETHING'S WRONG HERE!

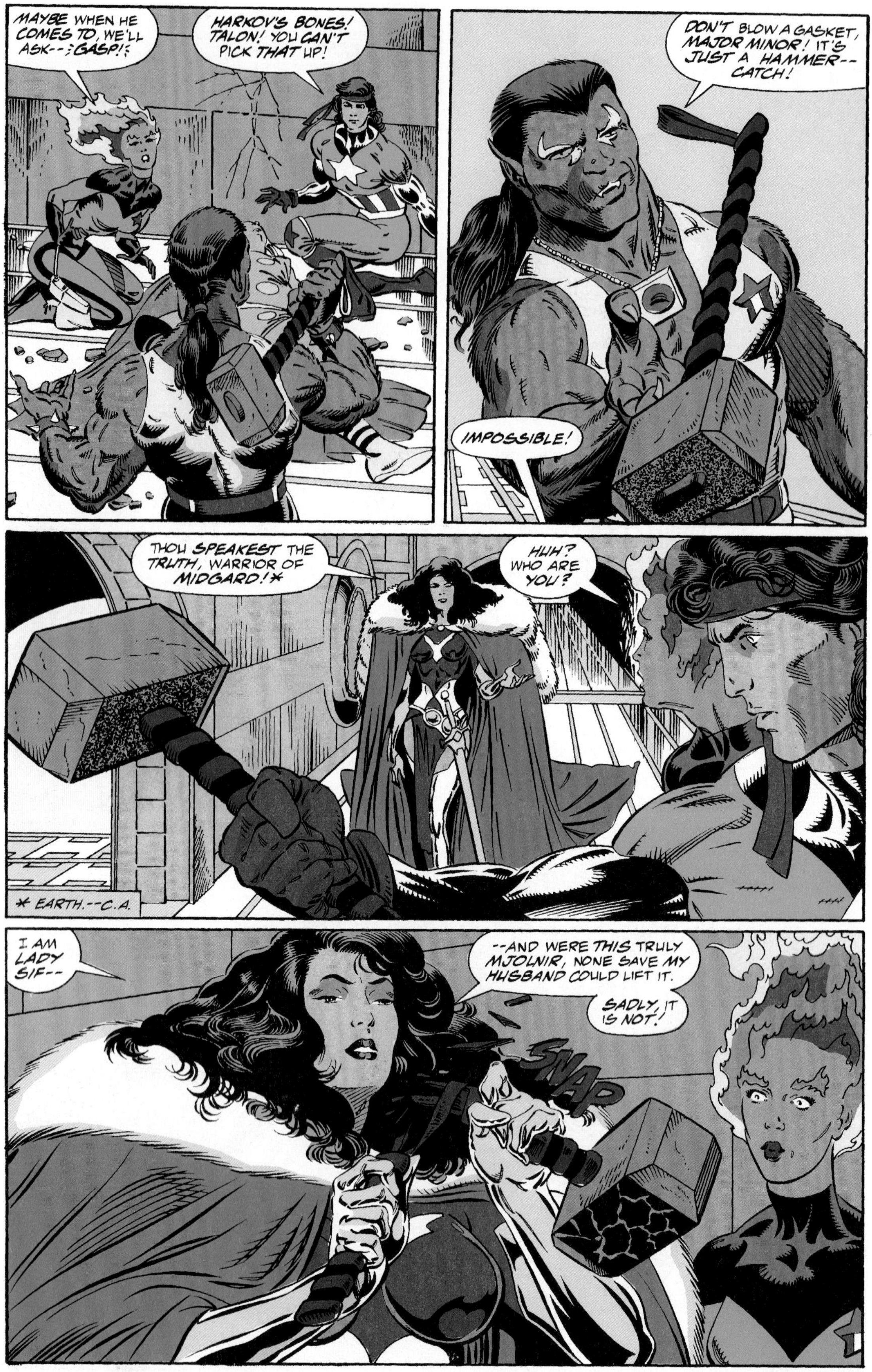
MAYBE WHEN HE COMES TO, WE'LL ASK-- ;GASP!;
HARKOV'S BONES! TALON! YOU CAN'T PICK THAT UP!
DON'T BLOW A GASKET, MAJOR MINOR! IT'S JUST A HAMMER-- CATCH!
IMPOSSIBLE!
THOU SPEAKEST THE TRUTH, WARRIOR OF MIDGARD!*
HUH? WHO ARE YOU?
* EARTH.--C.A.
I AM LADY SIF--
--AND WERE THIS TRULY MJOLNIR, NONE SAVE MY HUSBAND COULD LIFT IT.
SADLY, IT IS NOT!
SNAP

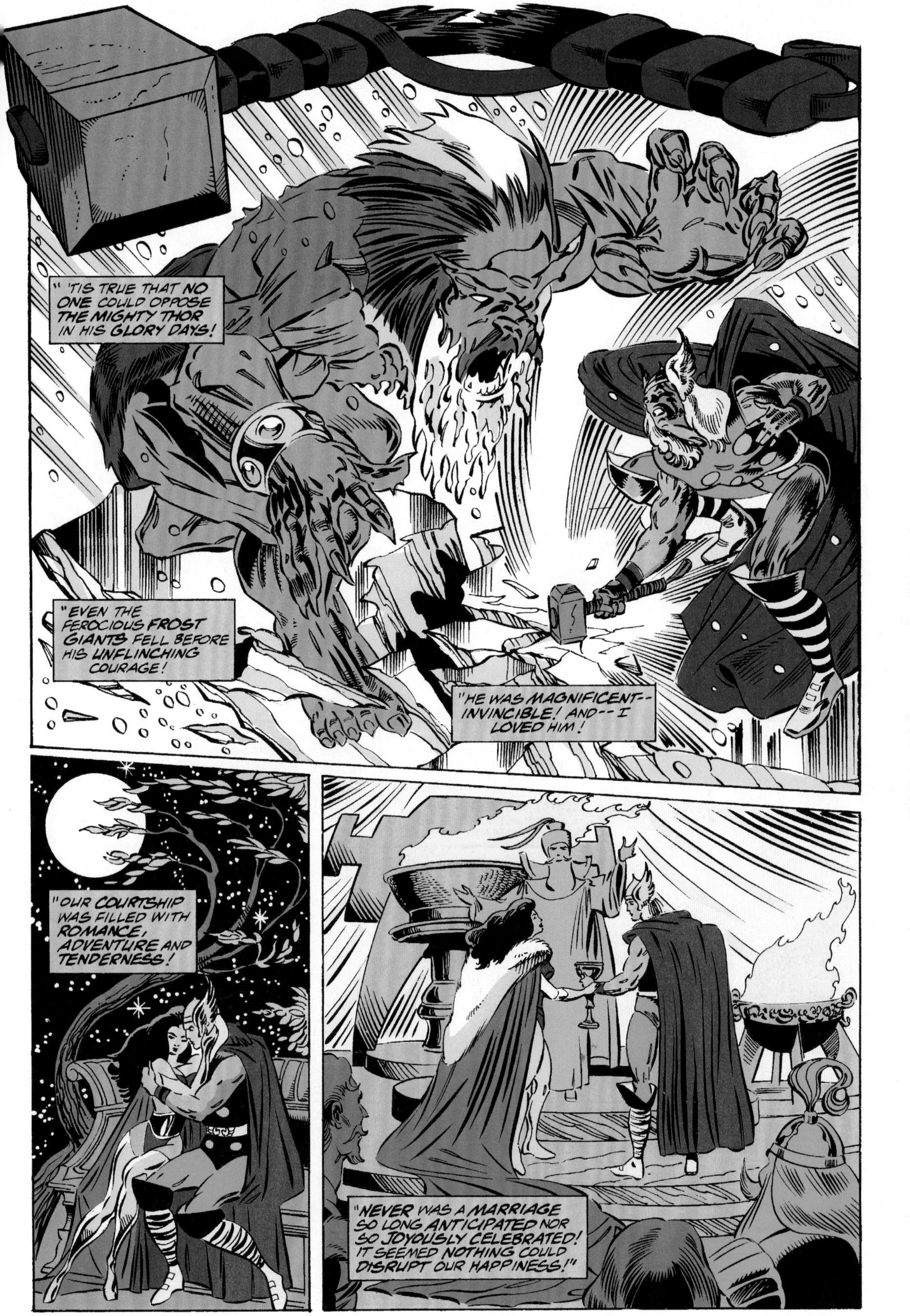
"'TIS TRUE THAT NO ONE COULD OPPOSE THE MIGHTY THOR IN HIS GLORY DAYS!
"EVEN THE FEROCIOUS FROST GIANTS FELL BEFORE HIS UNFLINCHING COURAGE!
"HE WAS MAGNIFICENT--INVINCIBLE! AND--I LOVED HIM!
"OUR COURTSHIP WAS FILLED WITH ROMANCE, ADVENTURE AND TENDERNESS!
"NEVER WAS A MARRIAGE SO LONG ANTICIPATED NOR SO JOYOUSLY CELEBRATED! IT SEEMED NOTHING COULD DISRUPT OUR HAPPINESS!"

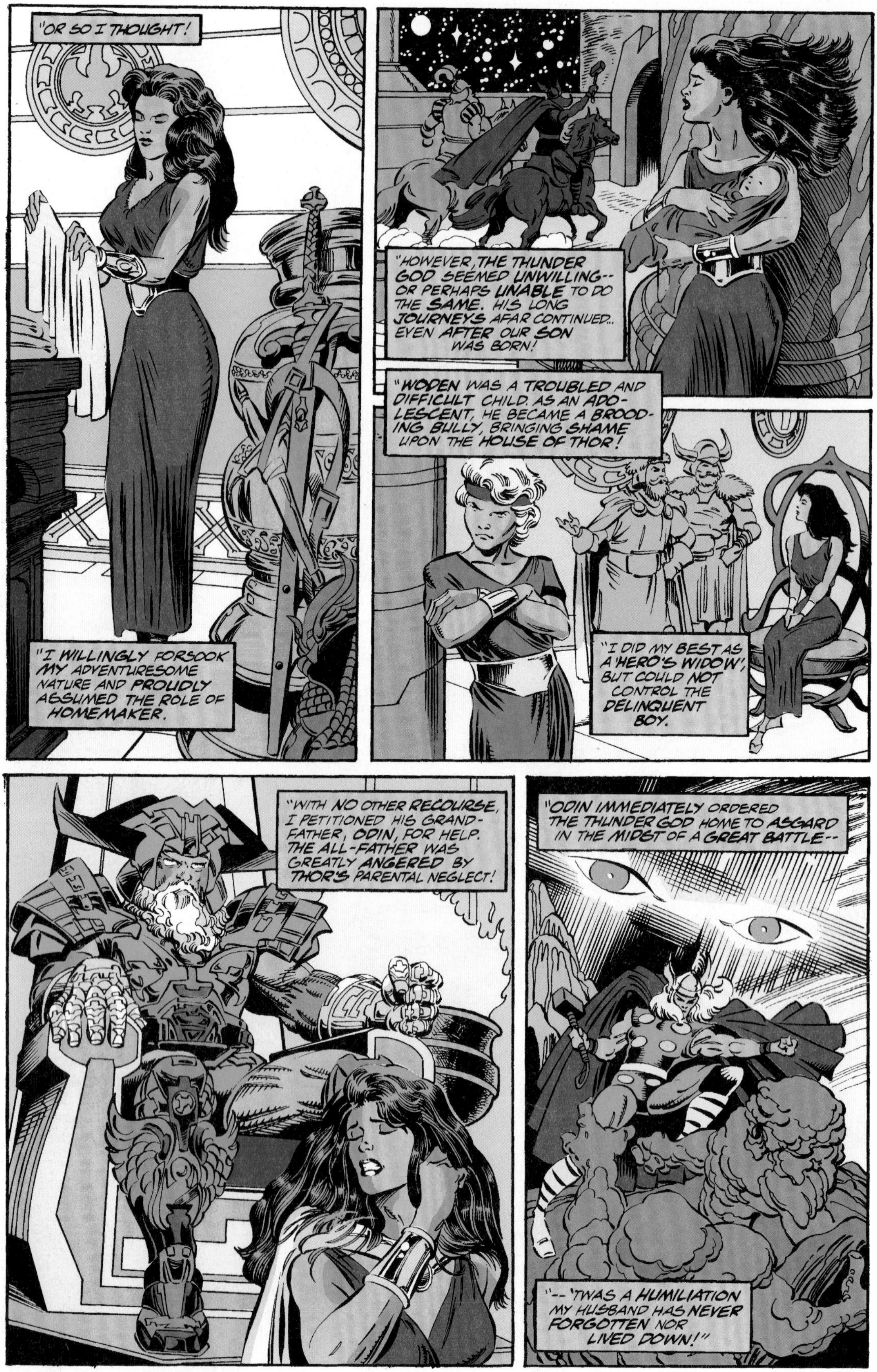
"OR SO I THOUGHT!
"I WILLINGLY FORSOOK MY ADVENTURESOME NATURE AND PROUDLY ASSUMED THE ROLE OF HOMEMAKER.
"HOWEVER, THE THUNDER GOD SEEMED UNWILLING-- OR PERHAPS UNABLE TO DO THE SAME. HIS LONG JOURNEYS AFAR CONTINUED... EVEN AFTER OUR SON WAS BORN!
"WODEN WAS A TROUBLED AND DIFFICULT CHILD. AS AN ADO-LESCENT, HE BECAME A BROOD-ING BULLY, BRINGING SHAME UPON THE HOUSE OF THOR!
"I DID MY BEST AS A 'HERO'S WIDOW', BUT COULD NOT CONTROL THE DELINQUENT BOY.
"WITH NO OTHER RECOURSE, I PETITIONED HIS GRAND-FATHER, ODIN, FOR HELP. THE ALL-FATHER WAS GREATLY ANGERED BY THOR'S PARENTAL NEGLECT!
"ODIN IMMEDIATELY ORDERED THE THUNDER GOD HOME TO ASGARD IN THE MIDST OF A GREAT BATTLE--
"--'TWAS A HUMILIATION MY HUSBAND HAS NEVER FORGOTTEN NOR LIVED DOWN!"

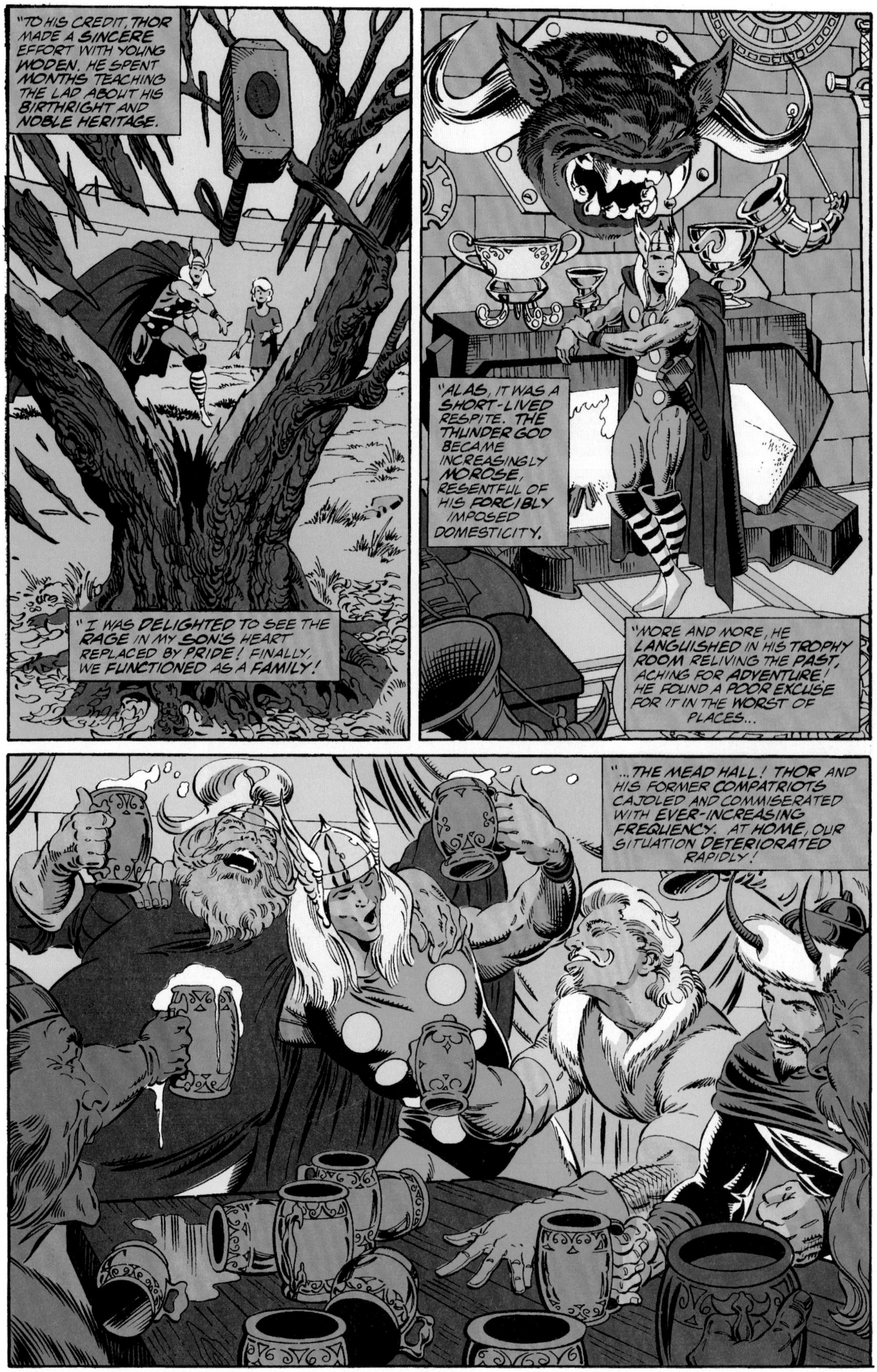
"TO HIS CREDIT, THOR MADE A SINCERE EFFORT WITH YOUNG WODEN. HE SPENT MONTHS TEACHING THE LAD ABOUT HIS BIRTHRIGHT AND NOBLE HERITAGE.
"I WAS DELIGHTED TO SEE THE RAGE IN MY SON'S HEART REPLACED BY PRIDE! FINALLY, WE FUNCTIONED AS A FAMILY!
"ALAS, IT WAS A SHORT-LIVED RESPITE. THE THUNDER GOD BECAME INCREASINGLY MOROSE, RESENTFUL OF HIS FORCIBLY IMPOSED DOMESTICITY.
"MORE AND MORE, HE LANGUISHED IN HIS TROPHY ROOM RELIVING THE PAST, ACHING FOR ADVENTURE! HE FOUND A POOR EXCUSE FOR IT IN THE WORST OF PLACES...
"...THE MEAD HALL! THOR AND HIS FORMER COMPATRIOTS CAJOLED AND COMMISERATED WITH EVER-INCREASING FREQUENCY. AT HOME, OUR SITUATION DETERIORATED RAPIDLY!

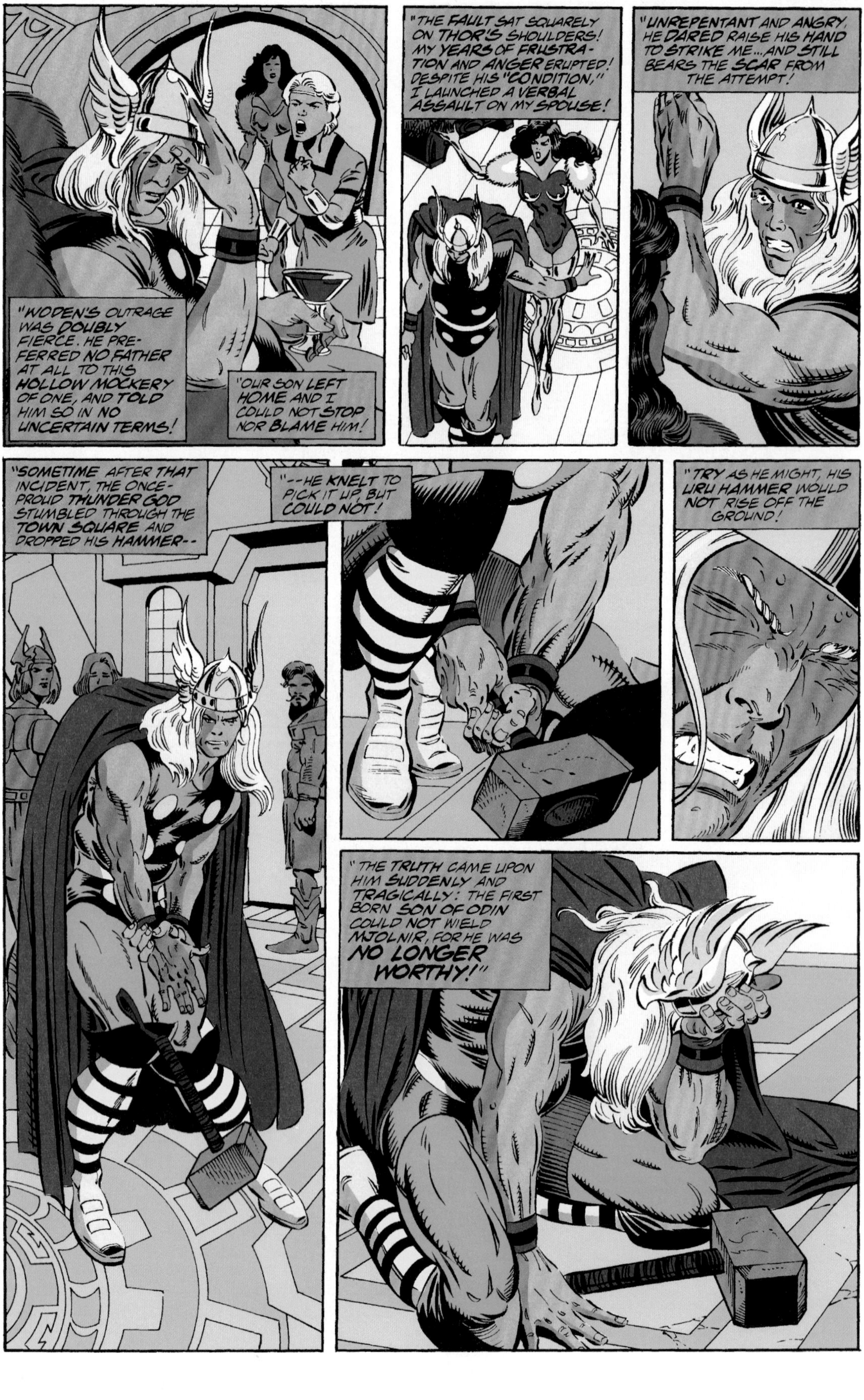
"WODEN'S OUTRAGE WAS DOUBLY FIERCE. HE PREFERRED NO FATHER AT ALL TO THIS HOLLOW MOCKERY OF ONE, AND TOLD HIM SO IN NO UNCERTAIN TERMS!
"OUR SON LEFT HOME AND I COULD NOT STOP NOR BLAME HIM!
"THE FAULT SAT SQUARELY ON THOR'S SHOULDERS! MY YEARS OF FRUSTRATION AND ANGER ERUPTED! DESPITE HIS "CONDITION," I LAUNCHED A VERBAL ASSAULT ON MY SPOUSE!
"UNREPENTANT AND ANGRY, HE DARED RAISE HIS HAND TO STRIKE ME... AND STILL BEARS THE SCAR FROM THE ATTEMPT!
"SOMETIME AFTER THAT INCIDENT, THE ONCE-PROUD THUNDER GOD STUMBLED THROUGH THE TOWN SQUARE AND DROPPED HIS HAMMER--
"--HE KNELT TO PICK IT UP BUT COULD NOT!
"TRY AS HE MIGHT, HIS URU HAMMER WOULD NOT RISE OFF THE GROUND!
"THE TRUTH CAME UPON HIM SUDDENLY AND TRAGICALLY: THE FIRST BORN SON OF ODIN COULD NOT WIELD MJOLNIR, FOR HE WAS NO LONGER WORTHY!"

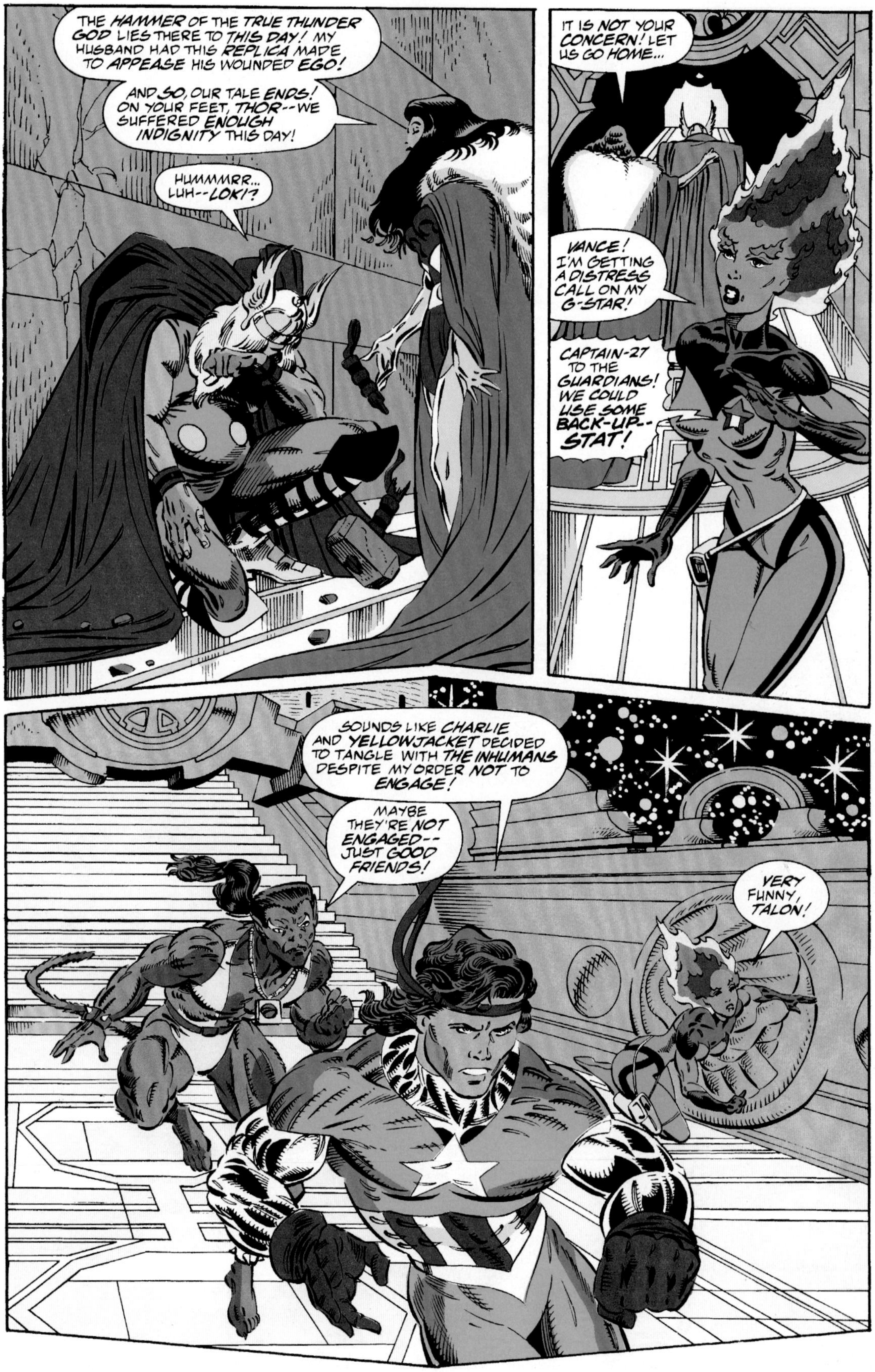

THE HAMMER OF THE TRUE THUNDER GOD LIES THERE TO THIS DAY! MY HUSBAND HAD THIS REPLICA MADE TO APPEASE HIS WOUNDED EGO!
AND SO, OUR TALE ENDS! ON YOUR FEET, THOR--WE SUFFERED ENOUGH INDIGNITY THIS DAY!
HUMMMRR... LUH--LOKI?
IT IS NOT YOUR CONCERN! LET US GO HOME...
VANCE! I'M GETTING A DISTRESS CALL ON MY G-STAR!
CAPTAIN-27 TO THE GUARDIANS! WE COULD USE SOME BACK-UP--STAT!
SOUNDS LIKE CHARLIE AND YELLOWJACKET DECIDED TO TANGLE WITH THE INHUMANS DESPITE MY ORDER NOT TO ENGAGE!
MAYBE THEY'RE NOT ENGAGED--JUST GOOD FRIENDS!
VERY FUNNY, TALON!

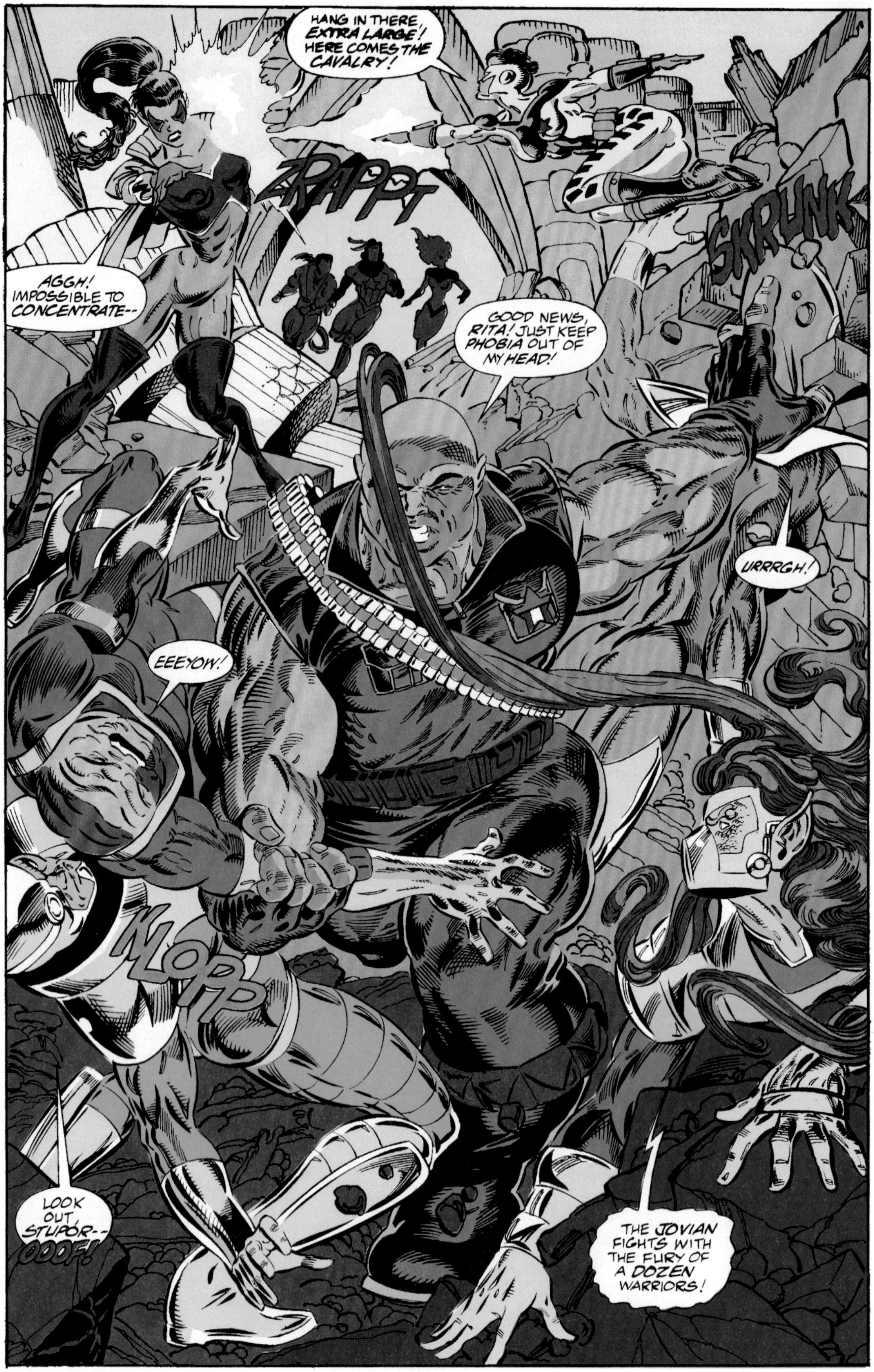
HANG IN THERE, EXTRA LARGE! HERE COMES THE CAVALRY!
ZRAPPT
SKRUNK
AGGH! IMPOSSIBLE TO CONCENTRATE--
GOOD NEWS, RITA! JUST KEEP PHOBIA OUT OF MY HEAD!
URRRGH!
EEEYOW!
WLORP
LOOK OUT, STUPOR-- OOOF!
THE JOVIAN FIGHTS WITH THE FURY OF A DOZEN WARRIORS!

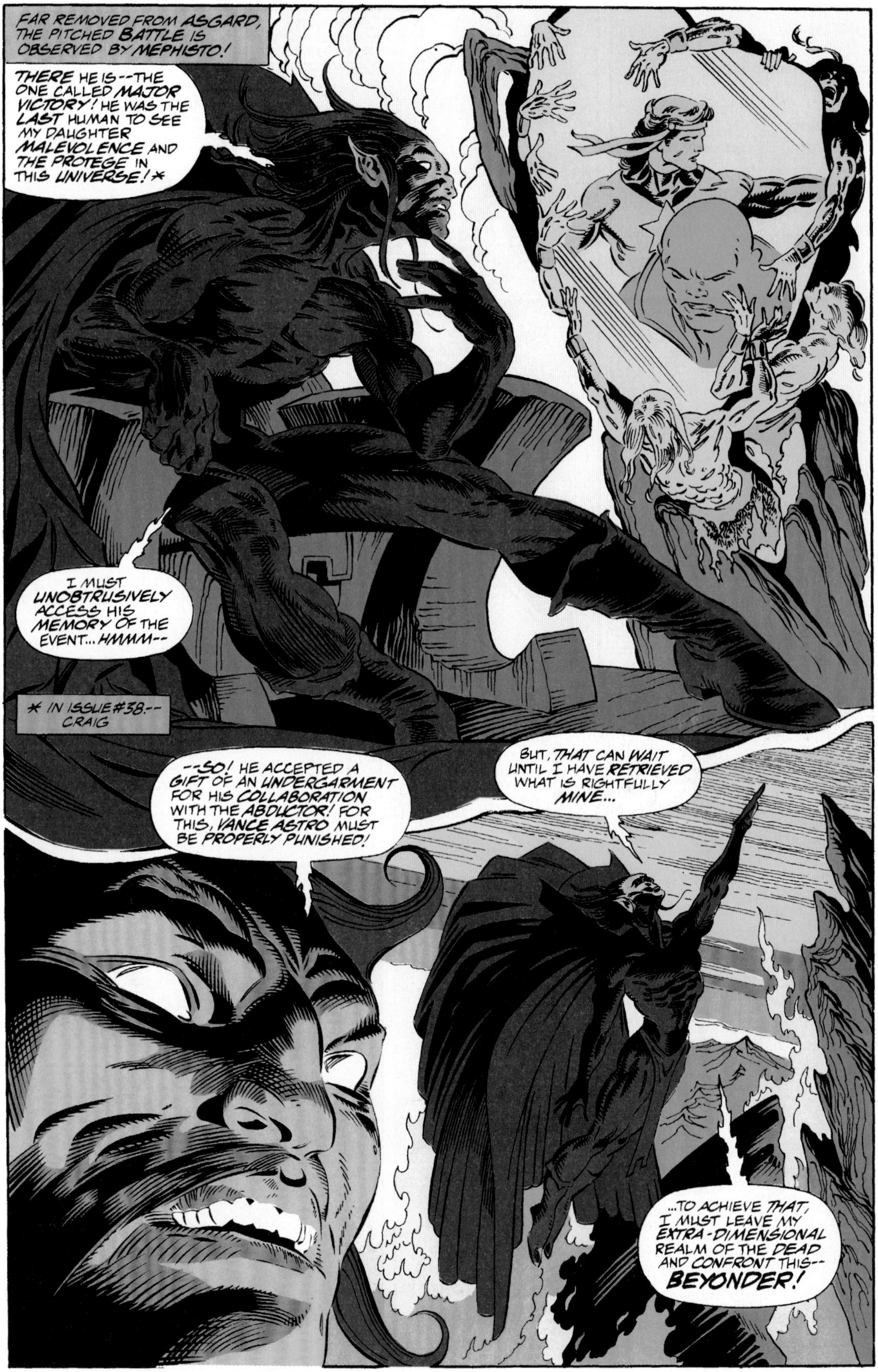
FAR REMOVED FROM ASGARD, THE PITCHED BATTLE IS OBSERVED BY MEPHISTO!
THERE HE IS--THE ONE CALLED MAJOR VICTORY! HE WAS THE LAST HUMAN TO SEE MY DAUGHTER MALEVOLENCE AND THE PROTEGE IN THIS UNIVERSE!*
I MUST UNOBTRUSIVELY ACCESS HIS MEMORY OF THE EVENT... HMMM--
* IN ISSUE #38.-- CRAIG
--SO! HE ACCEPTED A GIFT OF AN UNDERGARMENT FOR HIS COLLABORATION WITH THE ABDUCTOR! FOR THIS, VANCE ASTRO MUST BE PROPERLY PUNISHED!
BUT, THAT CAN WAIT UNTIL I HAVE RETRIEVED WHAT IS RIGHTFULLY MINE...
...TO ACHIEVE THAT, I MUST LEAVE MY EXTRA-DIMENSIONAL REALM OF THE DEAD AND CONFRONT THIS-- BEYONDER!

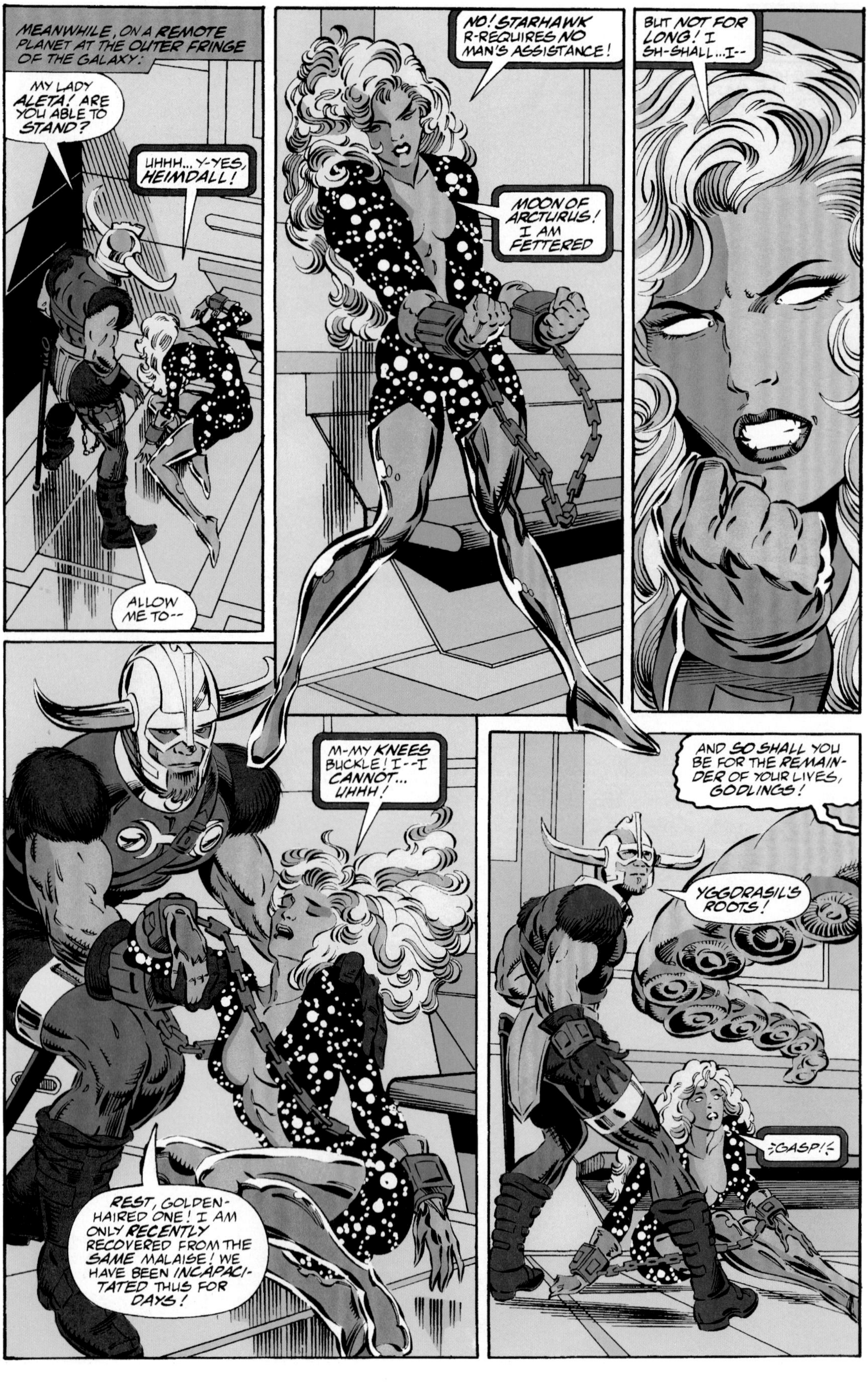
MEANWHILE, ON A REMOTE PLANET AT THE OUTER FRINGE OF THE GALAXY:
MY LADY ALETA! ARE YOU ABLE TO STAND?
UHHH... Y-YES, HEIMDALL!
ALLOW ME TO--
NO! STARHAWK R-REQUIRES NO MAN'S ASSISTANCE!
MOON OF ARCTURUS! I AM FETTERED
BUT NOT FOR LONG! I SH-SHALL...I--
M-MY KNEES BUCKLE! I--I CANNOT... UHHH!
REST, GOLDEN-HAIRED ONE! I AM ONLY RECENTLY RECOVERED FROM THE SAME MALAISE! WE HAVE BEEN INCAPACITATED THUS FOR DAYS!
AND SO SHALL YOU BE FOR THE REMAINDER OF YOUR LIVES, GODLINGS!
YGGDRASIL'S ROOTS!
GASP!

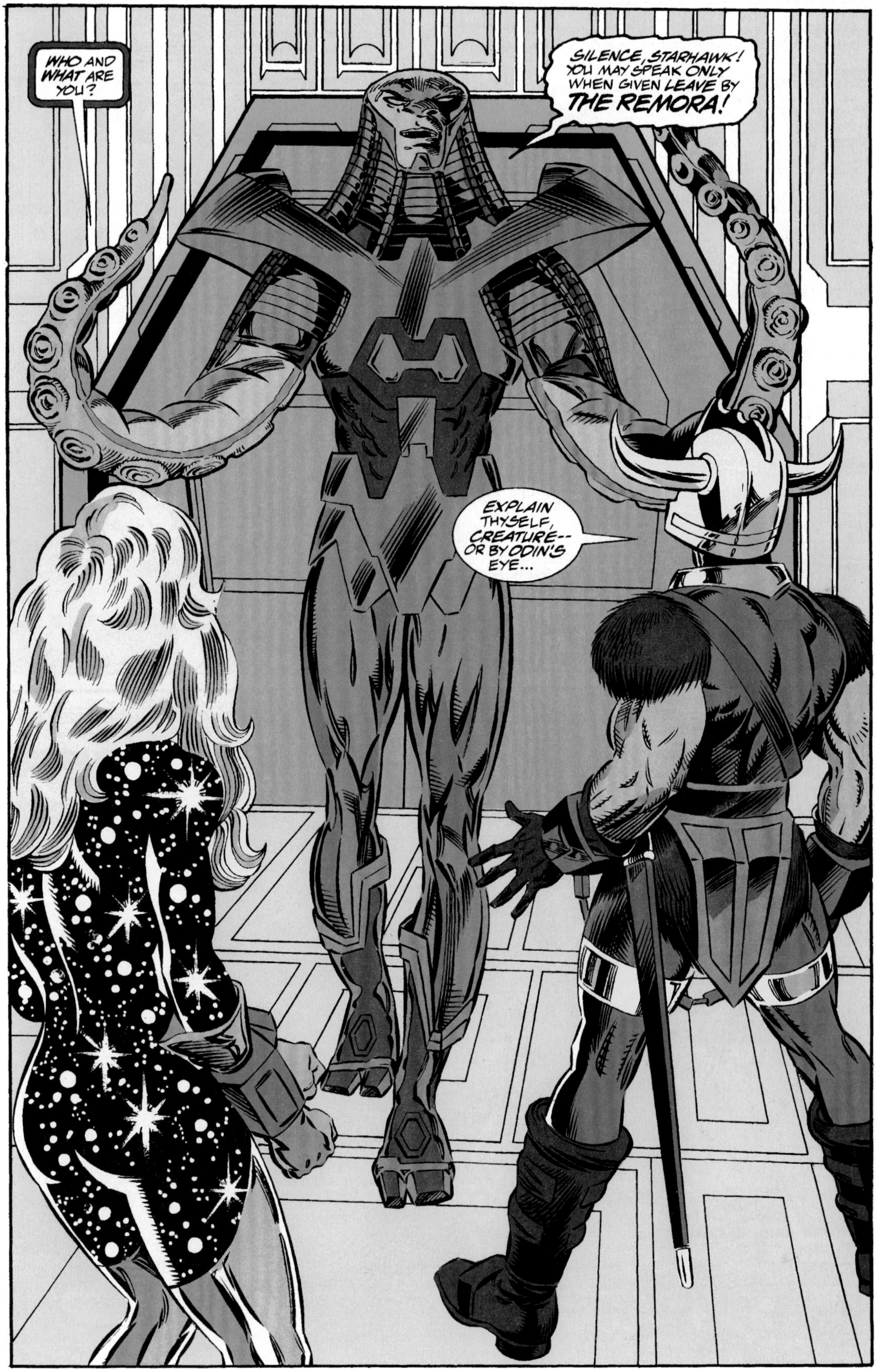
WHO AND WHAT ARE YOU?
SILENCE, STARHAWK! YOU MAY SPEAK ONLY WHEN GIVEN LEAVE BY THE REMORA!
EXPLAIN THYSELF, CREATURE-- OR BY ODIN'S EYE...

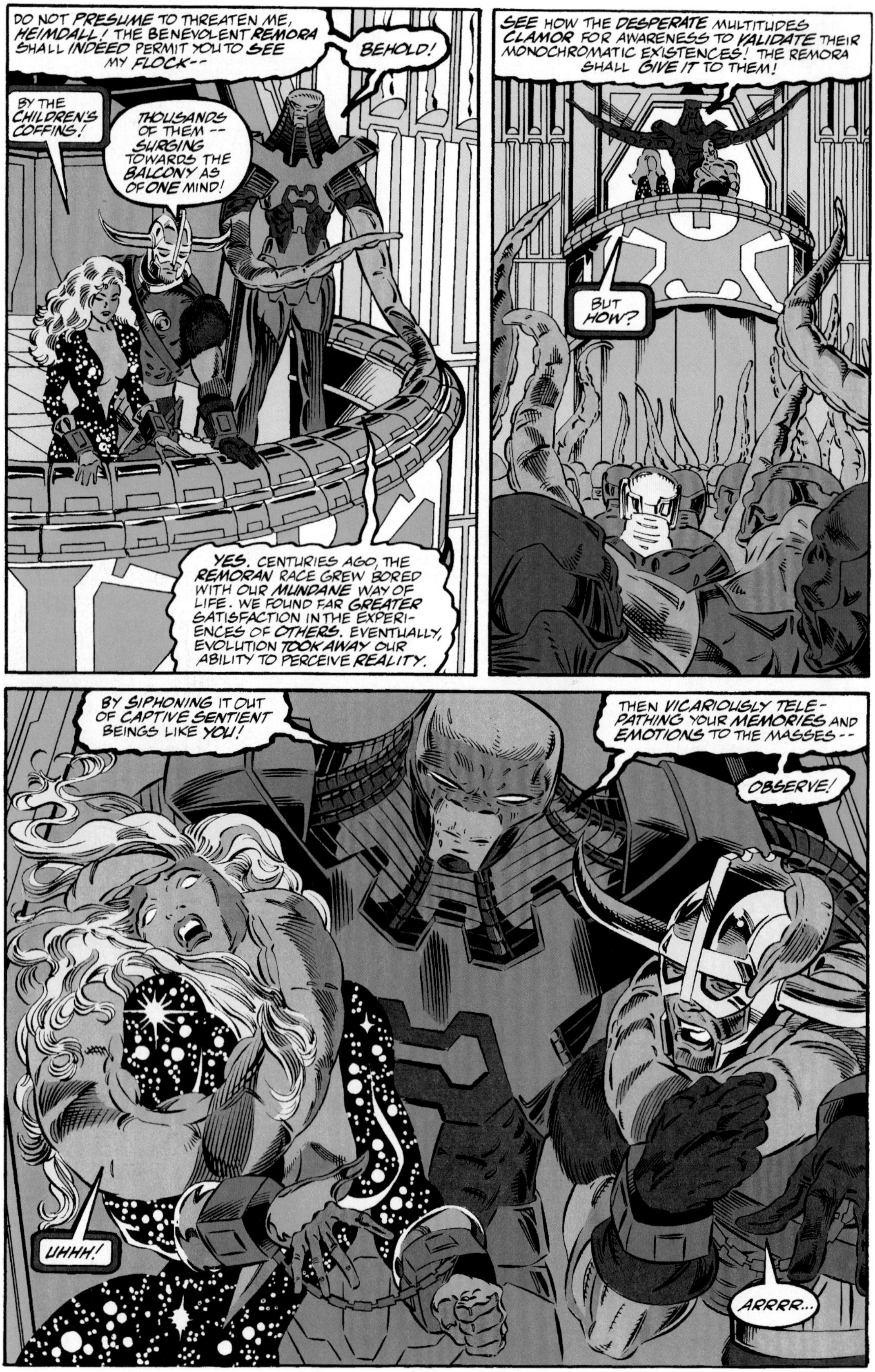

DO NOT PRESUME TO THREATEN ME, HEIMDALL! THE BENEVOLENT REMORA SHALL INDEED PERMIT YOU TO SEE MY FLOCK--
BEHOLD!
BY THE CHILDREN'S COFFINS!
THOUSANDS OF THEM -- SURGING TOWARDS THE BALCONY AS OF ONE MIND!
YES. CENTURIES AGO, THE REMORAN RACE GREW BORED WITH OUR MUNDANE WAY OF LIFE. WE FOUND FAR GREATER SATISFACTION IN THE EXPERIENCES OF OTHERS. EVENTUALLY, EVOLUTION TOOK AWAY OUR ABILITY TO PERCEIVE REALITY.
SEE HOW THE DESPERATE MULTITUDES CLAMOR FOR AWARENESS TO VALIDATE THEIR MONOCHROMATIC EXISTENCES! THE REMORA SHALL GIVE IT TO THEM!
BUT HOW?
BY SIPHONING IT OUT OF CAPTIVE SENTIENT BEINGS LIKE YOU!
THEN VICARIOUSLY TELEPATHING YOUR MEMORIES AND EMOTIONS TO THE MASSES--
OBSERVE!
UHHH!
ARRRR...

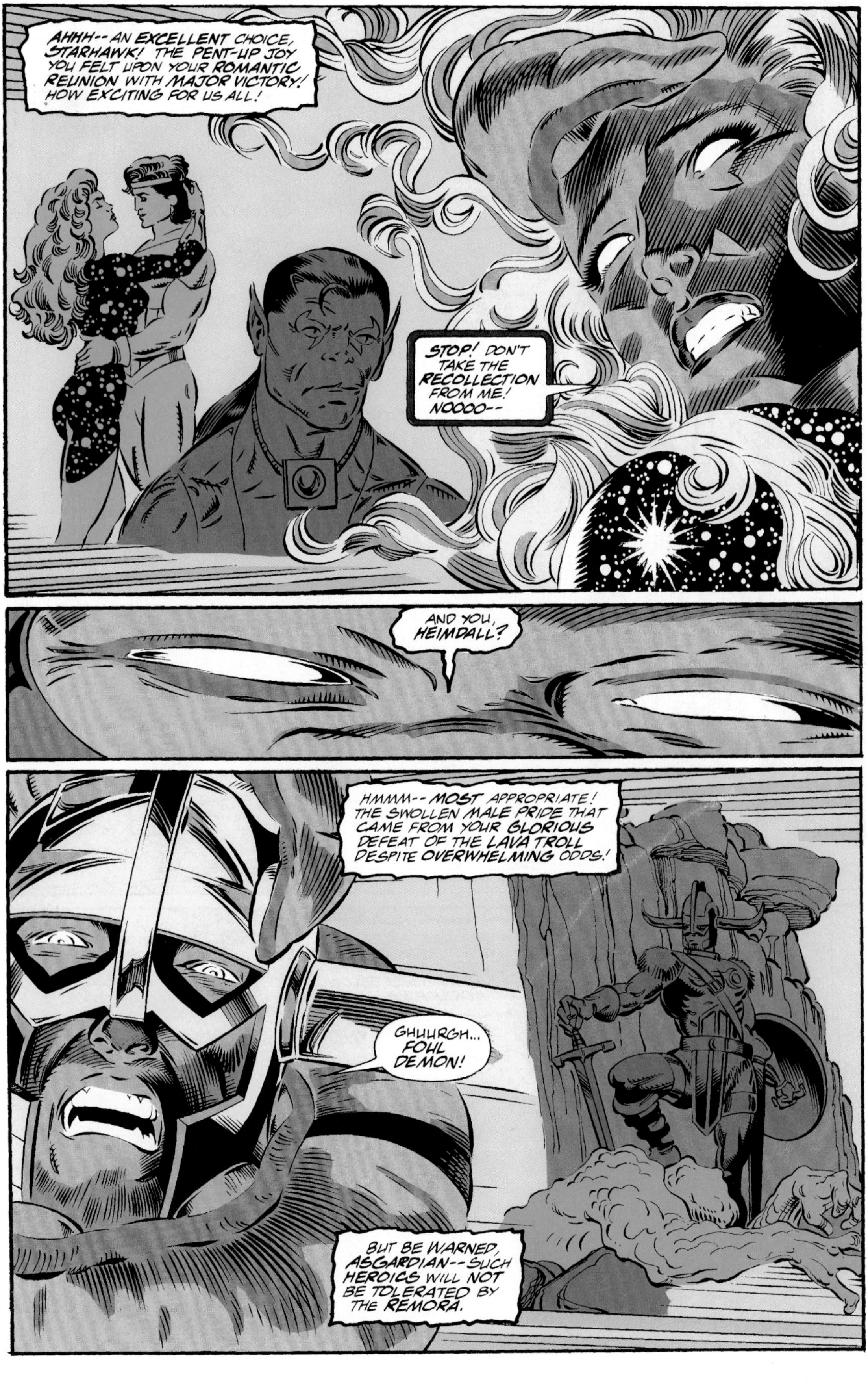
AHHH-- AN EXCELLENT CHOICE, STARHAWK! THE PENT-UP JOY YOU FELT UPON YOUR ROMANTIC REUNION WITH MAJOR VICTORY! HOW EXCITING FOR US ALL!
STOP! DON'T TAKE THE RECOLLECTION FROM ME! NOOOO--
AND YOU, HEIMDALL?
HMMM-- MOST APPROPRIATE! THE SWOLLEN MALE PRIDE THAT CAME FROM YOUR GLORIOUS DEFEAT OF THE LAVA TROLL DESPITE OVERWHELMING ODDS!
GHUURGH... FOUL DEMON!
BUT BE WARNED, ASGARDIAN-- SUCH HEROICS WILL NOT BE TOLERATED BY THE REMORA.

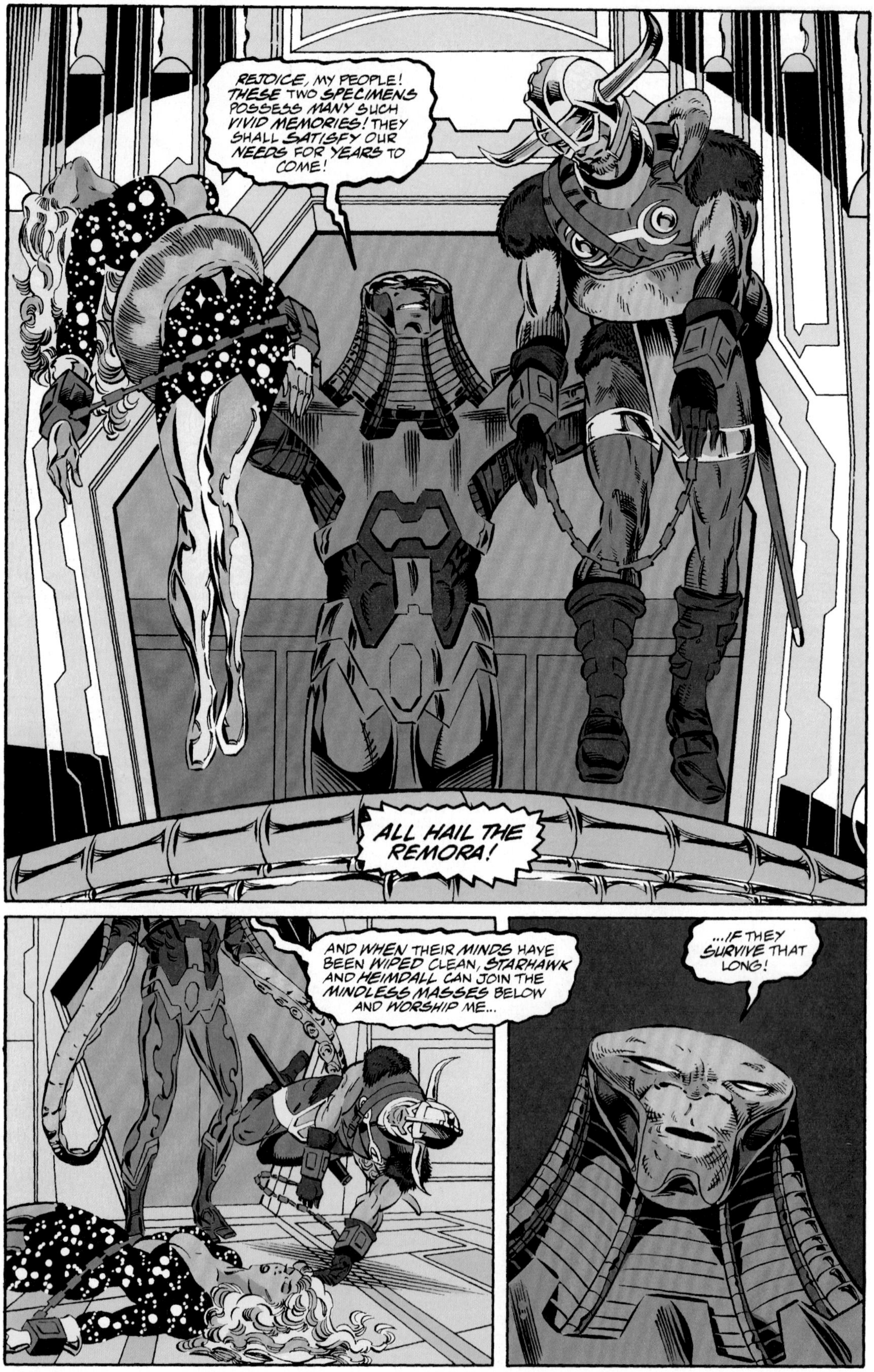
REJOICE, MY PEOPLE! THESE TWO SPECIMENS POSSESS MANY SUCH VIVID MEMORIES! THEY SHALL SATISFY OUR NEEDS FOR YEARS TO COME!
ALL HAIL THE REMORA!
AND WHEN THEIR MINDS HAVE BEEN WIPED CLEAN, STARHAWK AND HEIMDALL CAN JOIN THE MINDLESS MASSES BELOW AND WORSHIP ME...
...IF THEY SURVIVE THAT LONG!

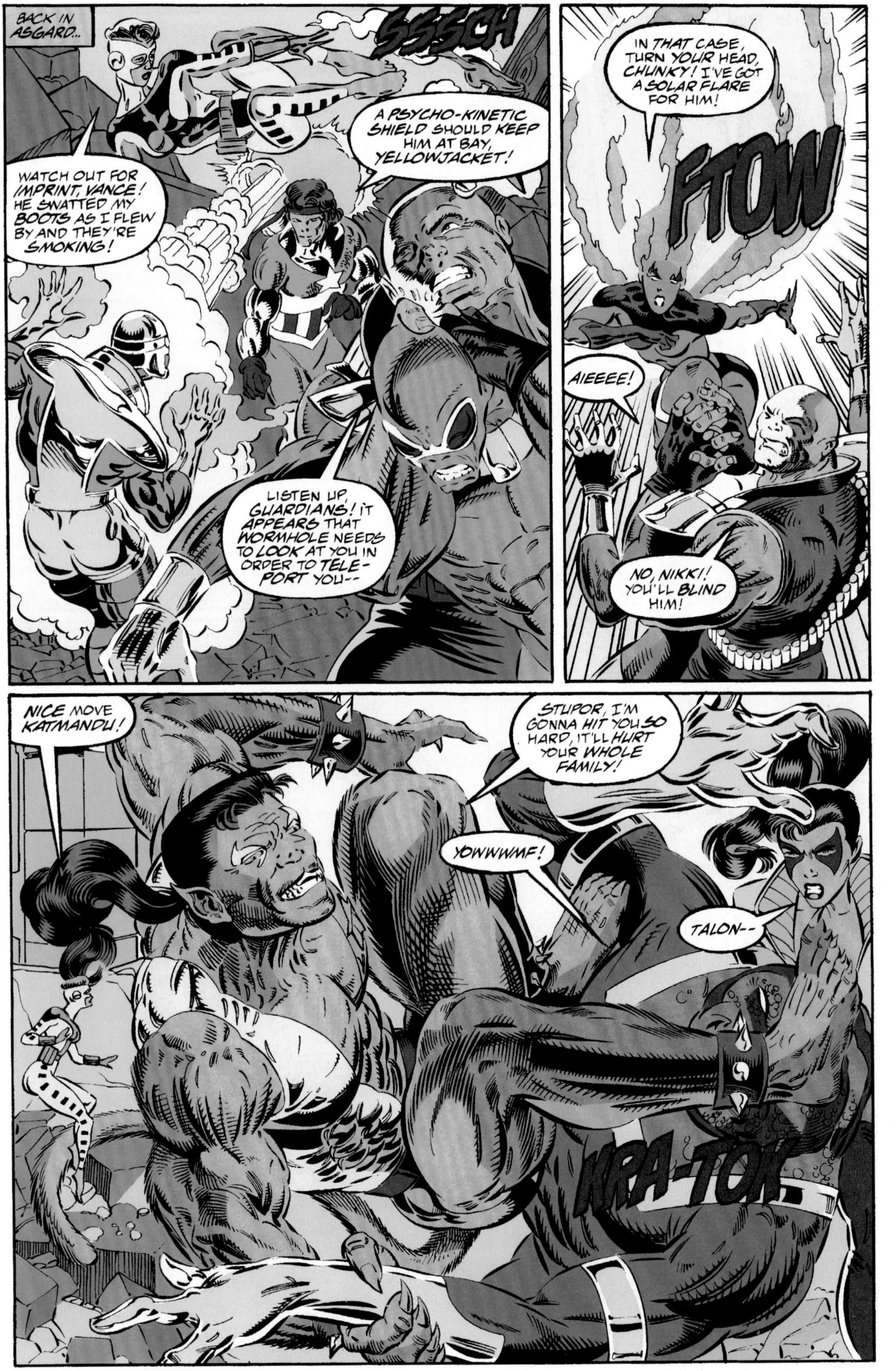
BACK IN ASGARD...
SSSCH
WATCH OUT FOR IMPRINT, VANCE! HE SWATTED MY BOOTS AS I FLEW BY AND THEY'RE SMOKING!
A PSYCHO-KINETIC SHIELD SHOULD KEEP HIM AT BAY, YELLOWJACKET!
LISTEN UP, GUARDIANS! IT APPEARS THAT WORMHOLE NEEDS TO LOOK AT YOU IN ORDER TO TELE-PORT YOU--
IN THAT CASE, TURN YOUR HEAD, CHUNKY! I'VE GOT A SOLAR FLARE FOR HIM!
FTOW
AIEEEE!
NO, NIKKI! YOU'LL BLIND HIM!
NICE MOVE KATMANDU!
STUPOR, I'M GONNA HIT YOU SO HARD, IT'LL HURT YOUR WHOLE FAMILY!
YOWWWMF!
TALON--
KRA-TOK

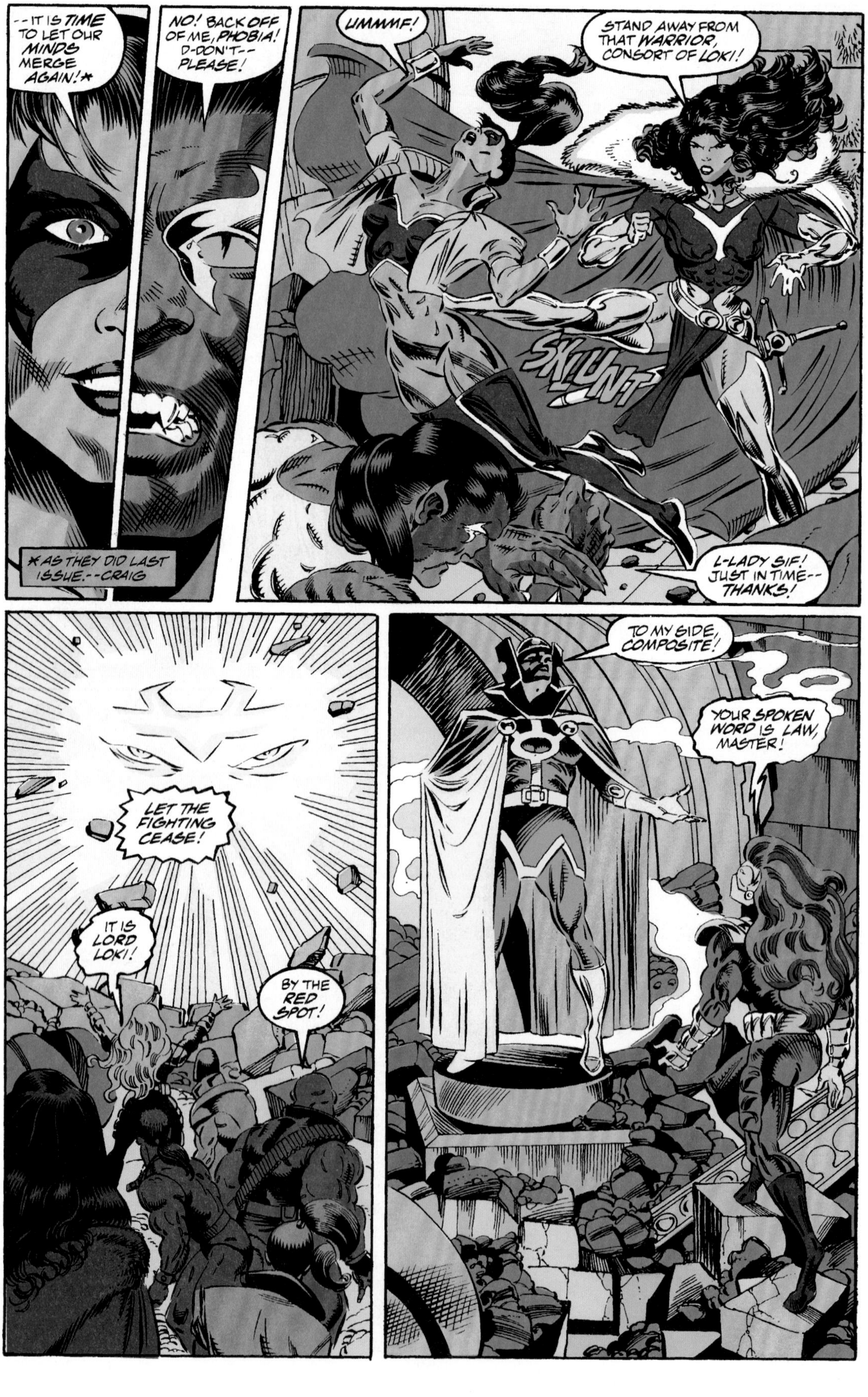
--IT IS TIME TO LET OUR MINDS MERGE AGAIN!*
*AS THEY DID LAST ISSUE.--CRAIG
NO! BACK OFF OF ME, PHOBIA! D-DON'T-- PLEASE!
UMMMF!
STAND AWAY FROM THAT WARRIOR, CONSORT OF LOKI!
SKLUNT
L-LADY SIF! JUST IN TIME-- THANKS!
LET THE FIGHTING CEASE!
IT IS LORD LOKI!
BY THE RED SPOT!
TO MY SIDE, COMPOSITE!
YOUR SPOKEN WORD IS LAW, MASTER!

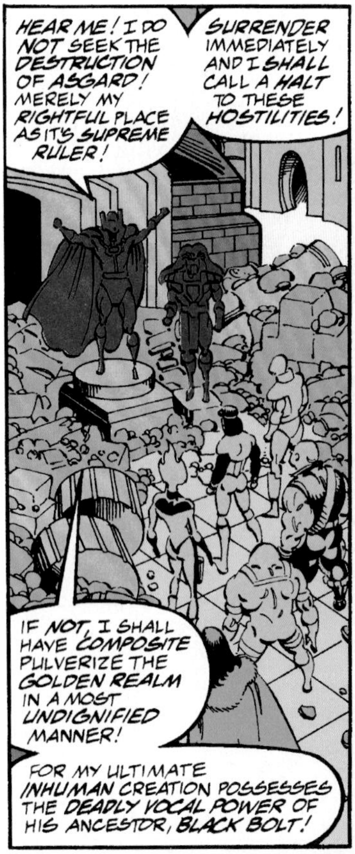
HEAR ME! I DO NOT SEEK THE DESTRUCTION OF ASGARD! MERELY MY RIGHTFUL PLACE AS IT'S SUPREME RULER!
SURRENDER IMMEDIATELY AND I SHALL CALL A HALT TO THESE HOSTILITIES!
IF NOT, I SHALL HAVE COMPOSITE PULVERIZE THE GOLDEN REALM IN A MOST UNDIGNIFIED MANNER!
FOR MY ULTIMATE INHUMAN CREATION POSSESSES THE DEADLY VOCAL POWER OF HIS ANCESTOR, BLACK BOLT!

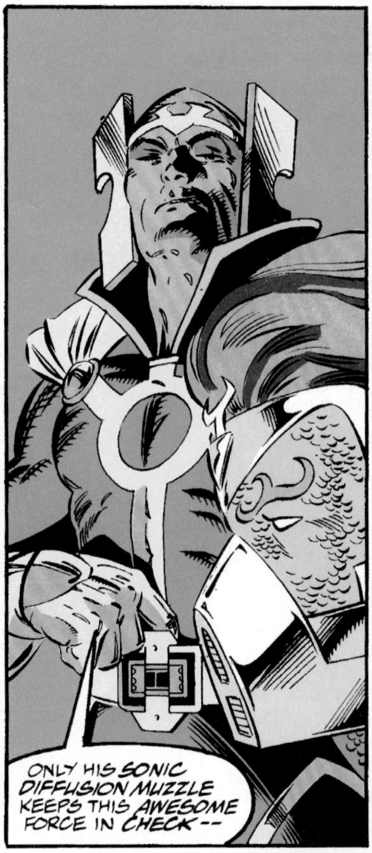
ONLY HIS SONIC DIFFUSION MUZZLE KEEPS THIS AWESOME FORCE IN CHECK--

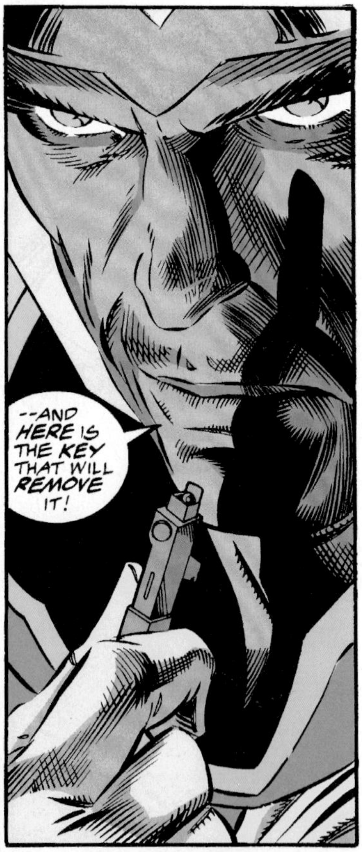
--AND HERE IS THE KEY THAT WILL REMOVE IT!

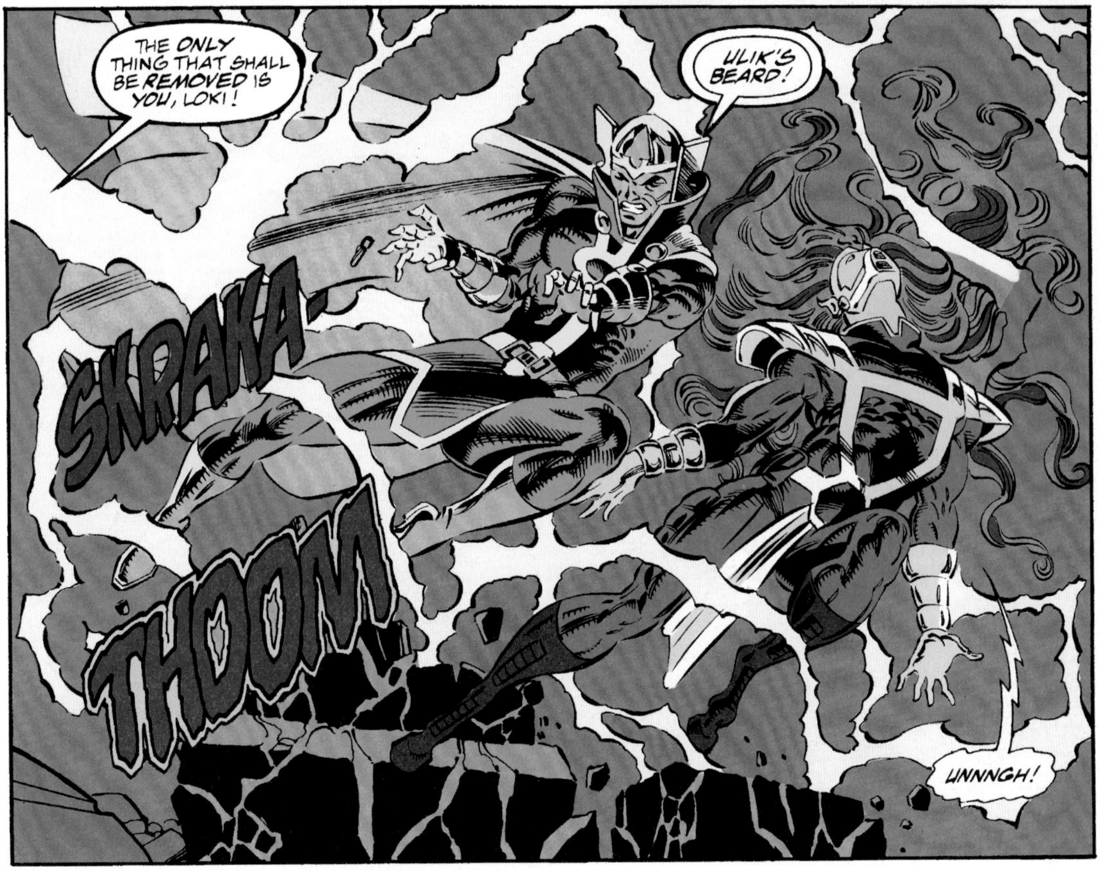
THE ONLY THING THAT SHALL BE REMOVED IS YOU, LOKI!
ULIK'S BEARD!
SKRAKA-
THOOM
UNNNGH!

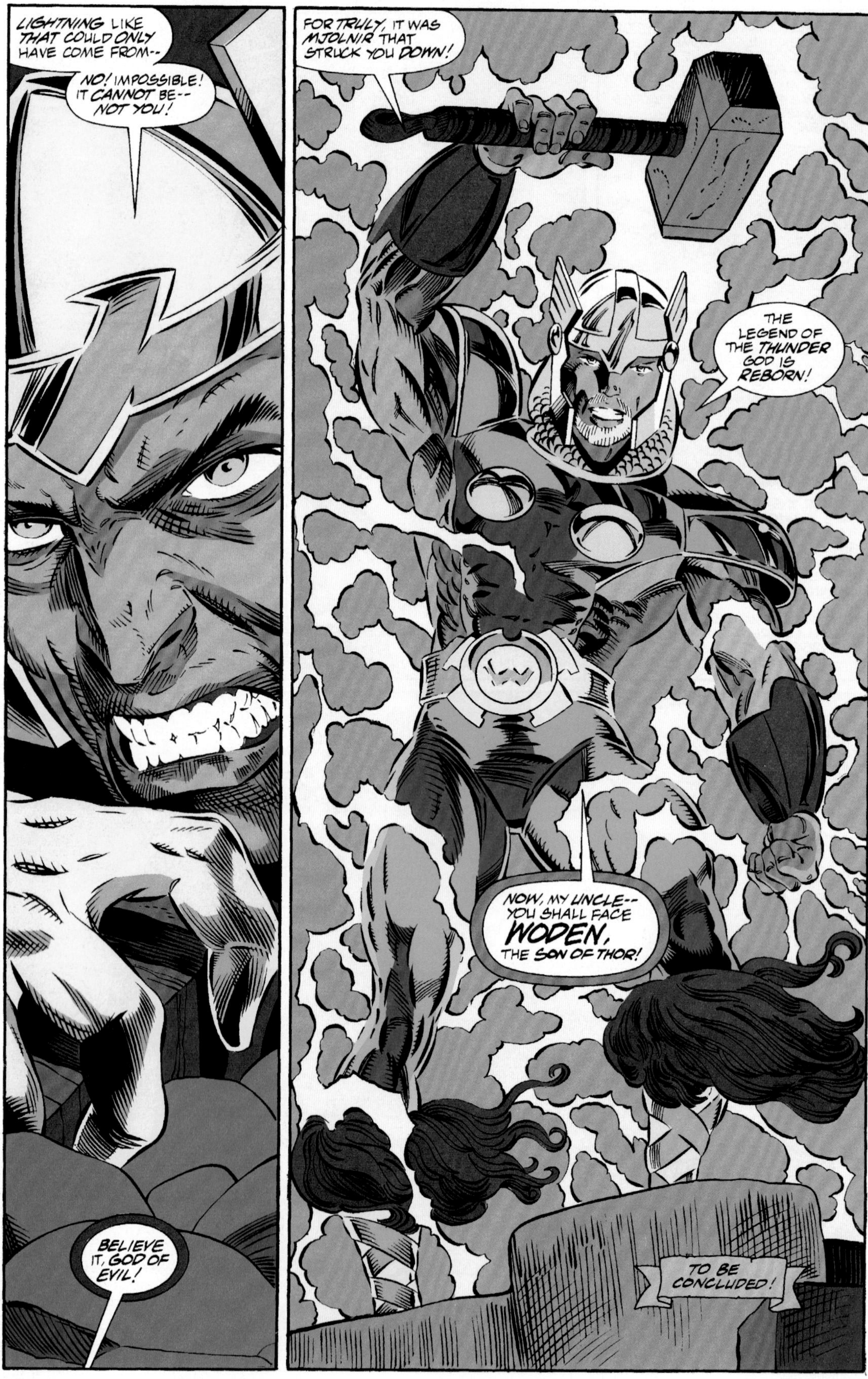
LIGHTNING LIKE THAT COULD ONLY HAVE COME FROM--
NO! IMPOSSIBLE! IT CANNOT BE-- NOT YOU!
BELIEVE IT, GOD OF EVIL!
FOR TRULY, IT WAS MJOLNIR THAT STRUCK YOU DOWN!
THE LEGEND OF THE THUNDER GOD IS REBORN!
NOW, MY UNCLE-- YOU SHALL FACE WODEN, THE SON OF THOR!
TO BE CONCLUDED!

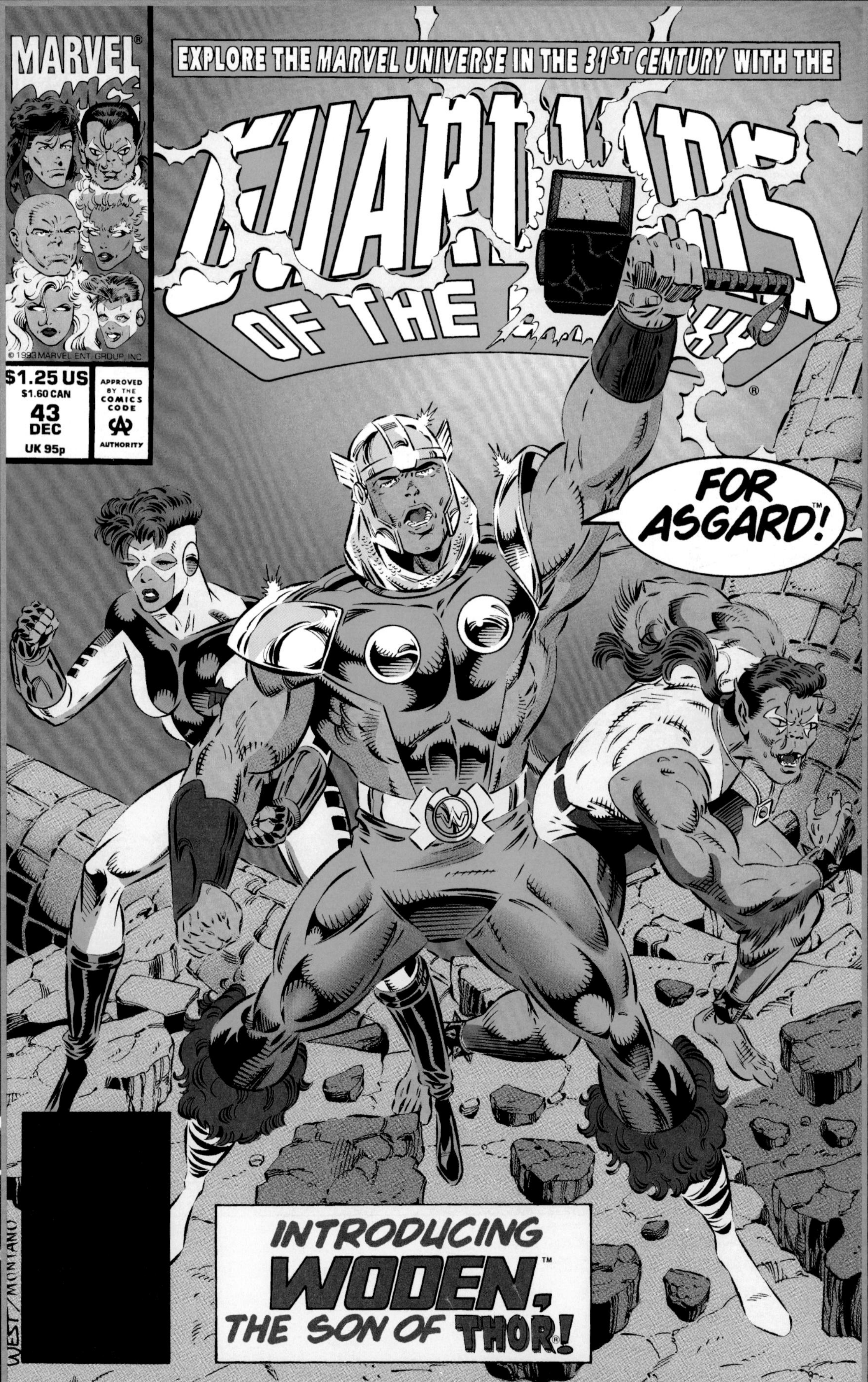
MARVEL® COMICS
EXPLORE THE MARVEL UNIVERSE IN THE 31ST CENTURY WITH THE
OF THE
©1993 MARVEL ENT. GROUP, INC
$1.25 US
$1.60 CAN
43
DEC
UK 95p
APPROVED BY THE COMICS CODE AUTHORITY
FOR ASGARD!™
INTRODUCING
WODEN,™
THE SON OF THOR®!
WEST/MONTANO

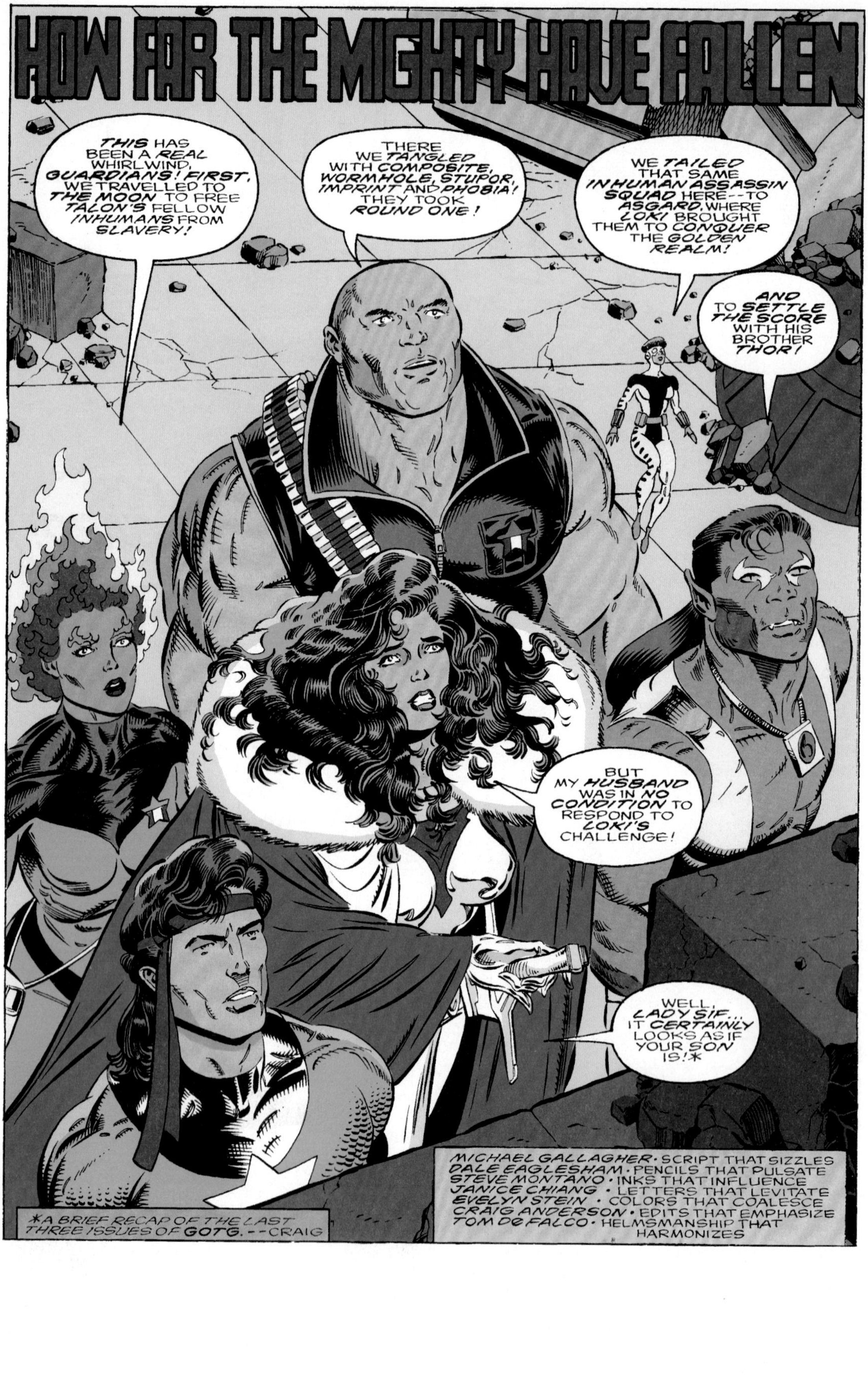

HOW FAR THE MIGHTY HAVE FALLEN
THIS HAS BEEN A REAL WHIRLWIND, GUARDIANS! FIRST, WE TRAVELLED TO THE MOON TO FREE TALON'S FELLOW INHUMANS FROM SLAVERY!
THERE WE TANGLED WITH COMPOSITE, WORMHOLE, STUPOR, IMPRINT AND PHOBIA! THEY TOOK ROUND ONE!
WE TAILED THAT SAME INHUMAN ASSASSIN SQUAD HERE--TO ASGARD, WHERE LOKI BROUGHT THEM TO CONQUER THE GOLDEN REALM!
AND TO SETTLE THE SCORE WITH HIS BROTHER THOR!
BUT MY HUSBAND WAS IN NO CONDITION TO RESPOND TO LOKI'S CHALLENGE!
WELL, LADY SIF... IT CERTAINLY LOOKS AS IF YOUR SON IS!*
MICHAEL GALLAGHER • SCRIPT THAT SIZZLES
DALE EAGLESHAM • PENCILS THAT PULSATE
STEVE MONTANO • INKS THAT INFLUENCE
JANICE CHIANG • LETTERS THAT LEVITATE
EVELYN STEIN • COLORS THAT COALESCE
CRAIG ANDERSON • EDITS THAT EMPHASIZE
TOM DE FALCO • HELMSMANSHIP THAT HARMONIZES
*A BRIEF RECAP OF THE LAST THREE ISSUES OF GOTG. --CRAIG

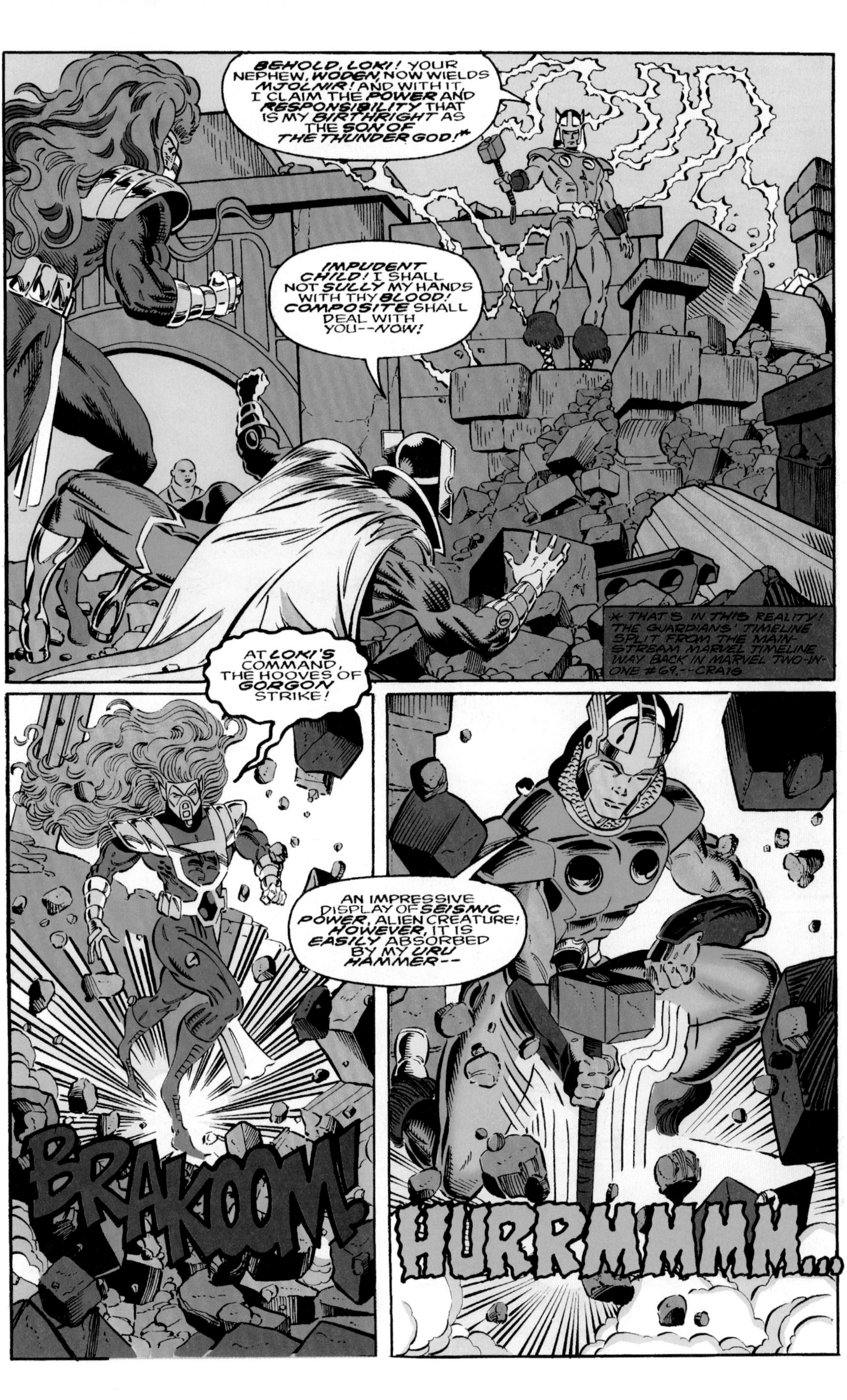

BEHOLD, LOKI! YOUR NEPHEW, WODEN, NOW WIELDS MJOLNIR! AND WITH IT, I CLAIM THE POWER AND RESPONSIBILITY THAT IS MY BIRTHRIGHT AS THE SON OF THE THUNDER GOD!*
IMPUDENT CHILD! I SHALL NOT SULLY MY HANDS WITH THY BLOOD! COMPOSITE SHALL DEAL WITH YOU--NOW!
*THAT'S IN THIS REALITY! THE GUARDIANS' TIMELINE SPLIT FROM THE MAIN-STREAM MARVEL TIMELINE WAY BACK IN MARVEL TWO-IN-ONE #69.--CRAIG
AT LOKI'S COMMAND, THE HOOVES OF GORGON STRIKE!
BRAKOOM!
AN IMPRESSIVE DISPLAY OF SEISMIC POWER, ALIEN CREATURE! HOWEVER, IT IS EASILY ABSORBED BY MY URU HAMMER--
HURRMMMM...

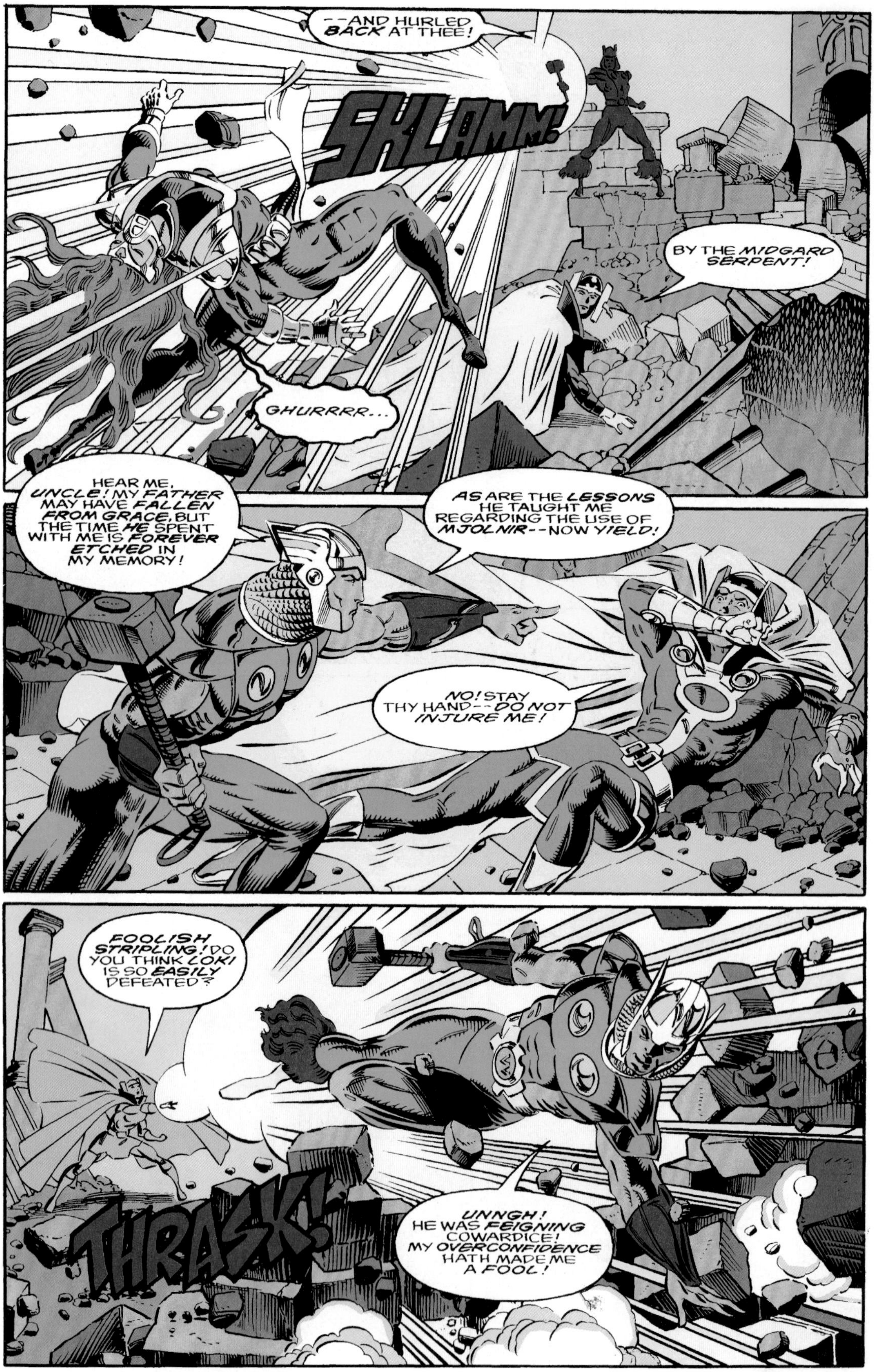
--AND HURLED BACK AT THEE!
SKLAMM!
BY THE MIDGARD SERPENT!
GHURRRR...
HEAR ME, UNCLE! MY FATHER MAY HAVE FALLEN FROM GRACE, BUT THE TIME HE SPENT WITH ME IS FOREVER ETCHED IN MY MEMORY!
AS ARE THE LESSONS HE TAUGHT ME REGARDING THE USE OF MJOLNIR--NOW YIELD!
NO! STAY THY HAND--DO NOT INJURE ME!
FOOLISH STRIPLING! DO YOU THINK LOKI IS SO EASILY DEFEATED?
THRASK!
UNNGH! HE WAS FEIGNING COWARDICE! MY OVERCONFIDENCE HATH MADE ME A FOOL!

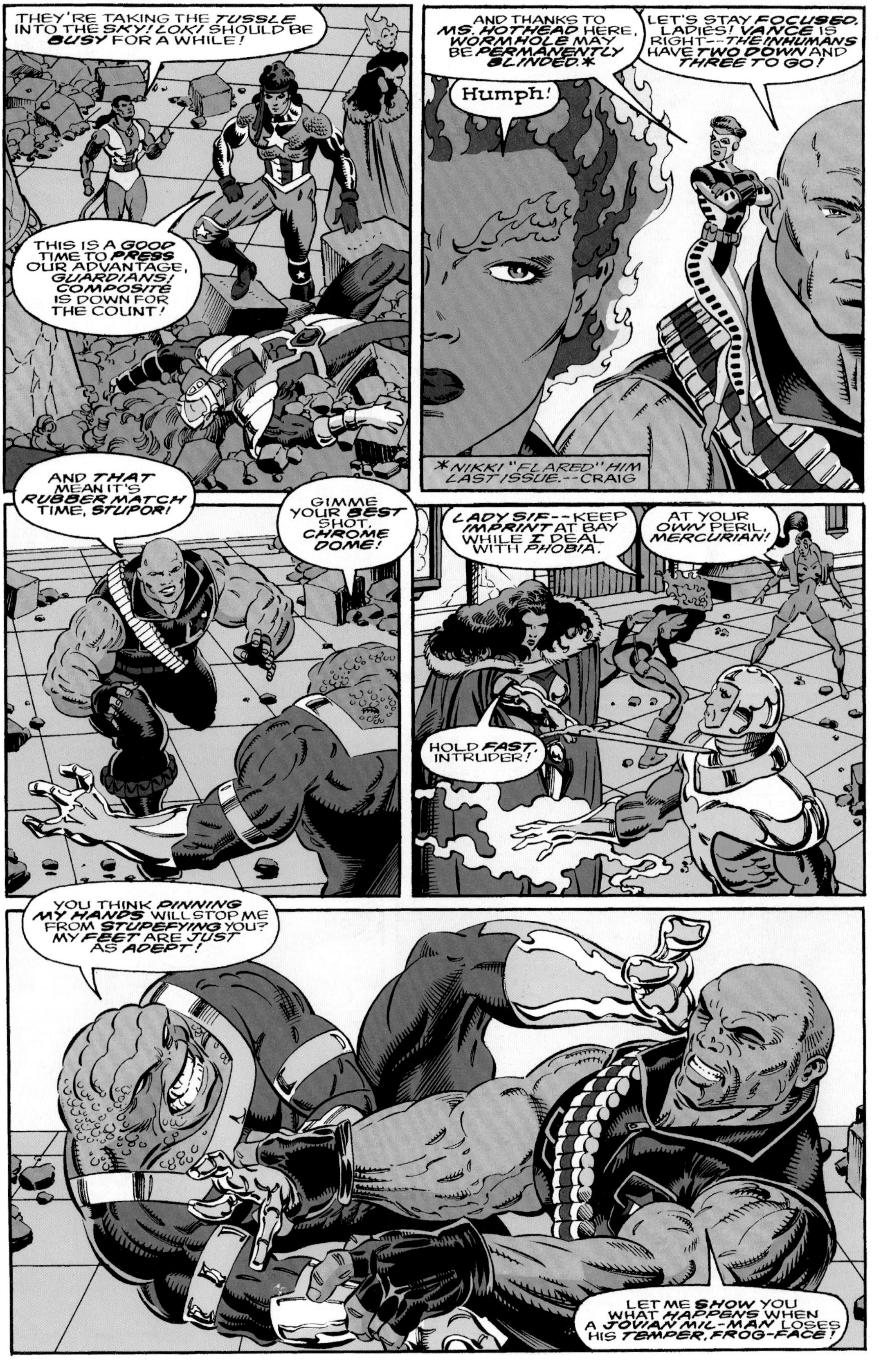
THEY'RE TAKING THE TUSSLE INTO THE SKY! LOKI SHOULD BE BUSY FOR A WHILE!
THIS IS A GOOD TIME TO PRESS OUR ADVANTAGE, GUARDIANS! COMPOSITE IS DOWN FOR THE COUNT!
AND THANKS TO MS. HOTHEAD HERE, WORMHOLE MAY BE PERMANENTLY BLINDED.*
Humph!
LET'S STAY FOCUSED, LADIES! VANCE IS RIGHT--THE INHUMANS HAVE TWO DOWN AND THREE TO GO!
*NIKKI "FLARED" HIM LAST ISSUE.--CRAIG
AND THAT MEAN IT'S RUBBER MATCH TIME, STUPOR!
GIMME YOUR BEST SHOT, CHROME DOME!
LADY SIF--KEEP IMPRINT AT BAY WHILE I DEAL WITH PHOBIA.
AT YOUR OWN PERIL, MERCURIAN!
HOLD FAST, INTRUDER!
YOU THINK PINNING MY HANDS WILL STOP ME FROM STUPEFYING YOU? MY FEET ARE JUST AS ADEPT!
LET ME SHOW YOU WHAT HAPPENS WHEN A JOVIAN MIL-MAN LOSES HIS TEMPER, FROG-FACE!

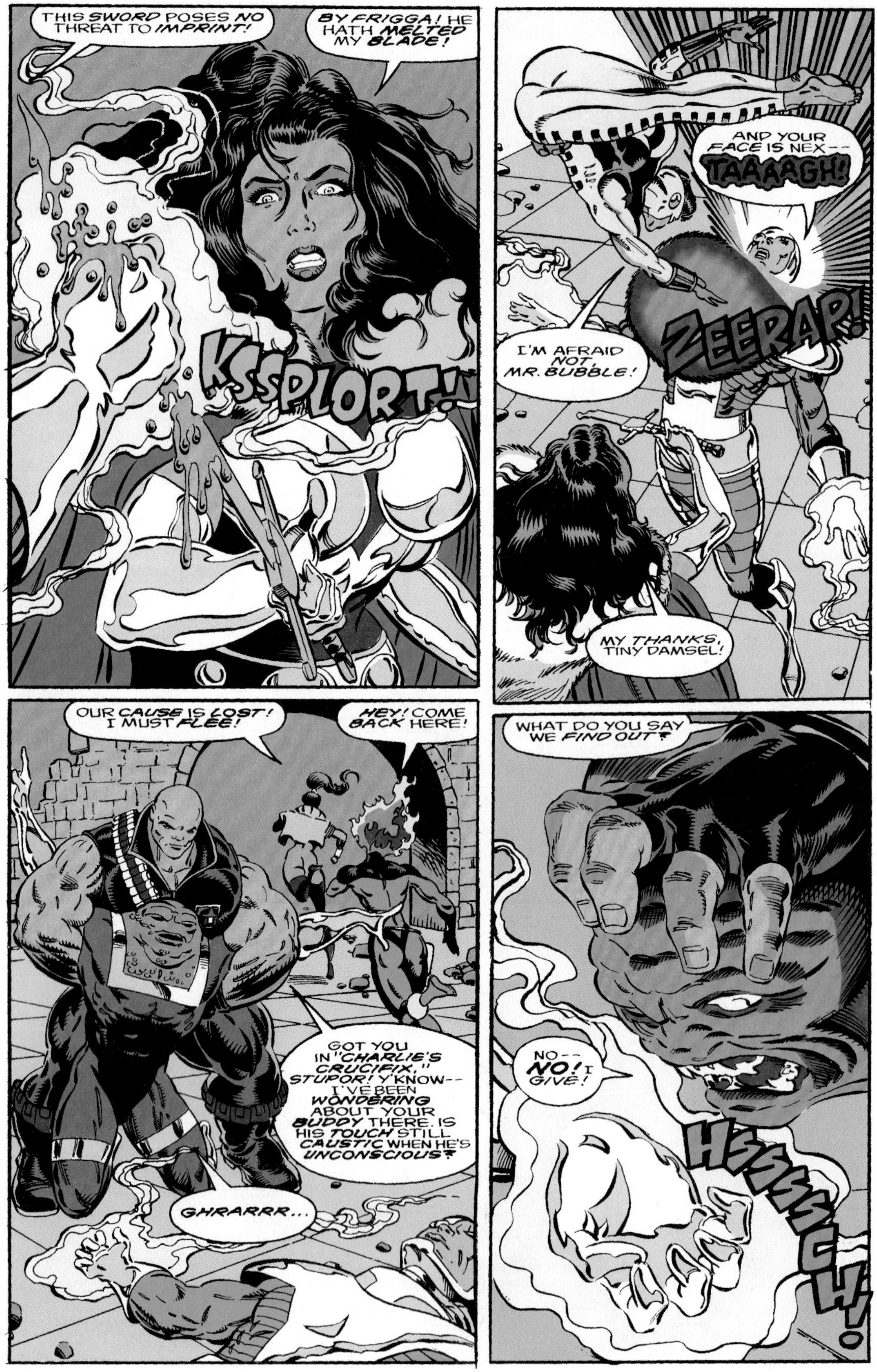

THIS SWORD POSES NO THREAT TO IMPRINT!
BY FRIGGA! HE HATH MELTED MY BLADE!
KSSPLORT!
AND YOUR FACE IS NEX-- TAAAAGH!
I'M AFRAID NOT, MR. BUBBLE!
ZEERAP!
MY THANKS, TINY DAMSEL!
OUR CAUSE IS LOST! I MUST FLEE!
HEY! COME BACK HERE!
GOT YOU IN "CHARLIE'S CRUCIFIX," STUPOR! Y'KNOW-- I'VE BEEN WONDERING ABOUT YOUR BUDDY THERE. IS HIS TOUCH STILL CAUSTIC WHEN HE'S UNCONSCIOUS?
GHRARRR...
WHAT DO YOU SAY WE FIND OUT?
NO-- NO! I GIVE!
HSSSSCH!

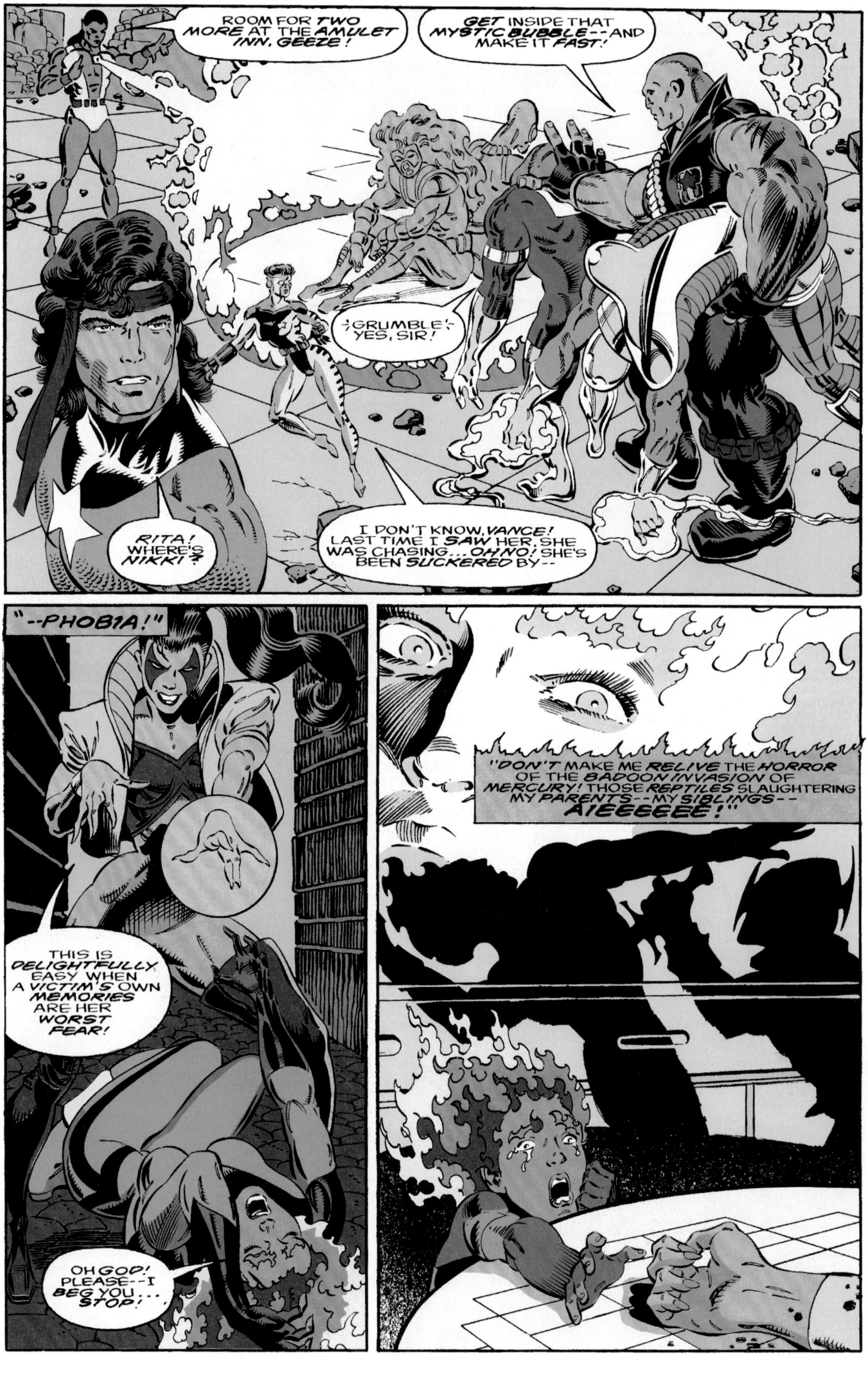
ROOM FOR TWO MORE AT THE AMULET INN, GEEZE!
GET INSIDE THAT MYSTIC BUBBLE--AND MAKE IT FAST!
-GRUMBLE- YES, SIR!
RITA! WHERE'S NIKKI?
I DON'T KNOW, VANCE! LAST TIME I SAW HER, SHE WAS CHASING... OH NO! SHE'S BEEN SUCKERED BY--
"--PHOBIA!"
THIS IS DELIGHTFULLY EASY WHEN A VICTIM'S OWN MEMORIES ARE HER WORST FEAR!
OH GOD! PLEASE--I BEG YOU... STOP!
"DON'T MAKE ME RELIVE THE HORROR OF THE BADOON INVASION OF MERCURY! THOSE REPTILES SLAUGHTERING MY PARENTS--MY SIBLINGS-- AIEEEEEE!"

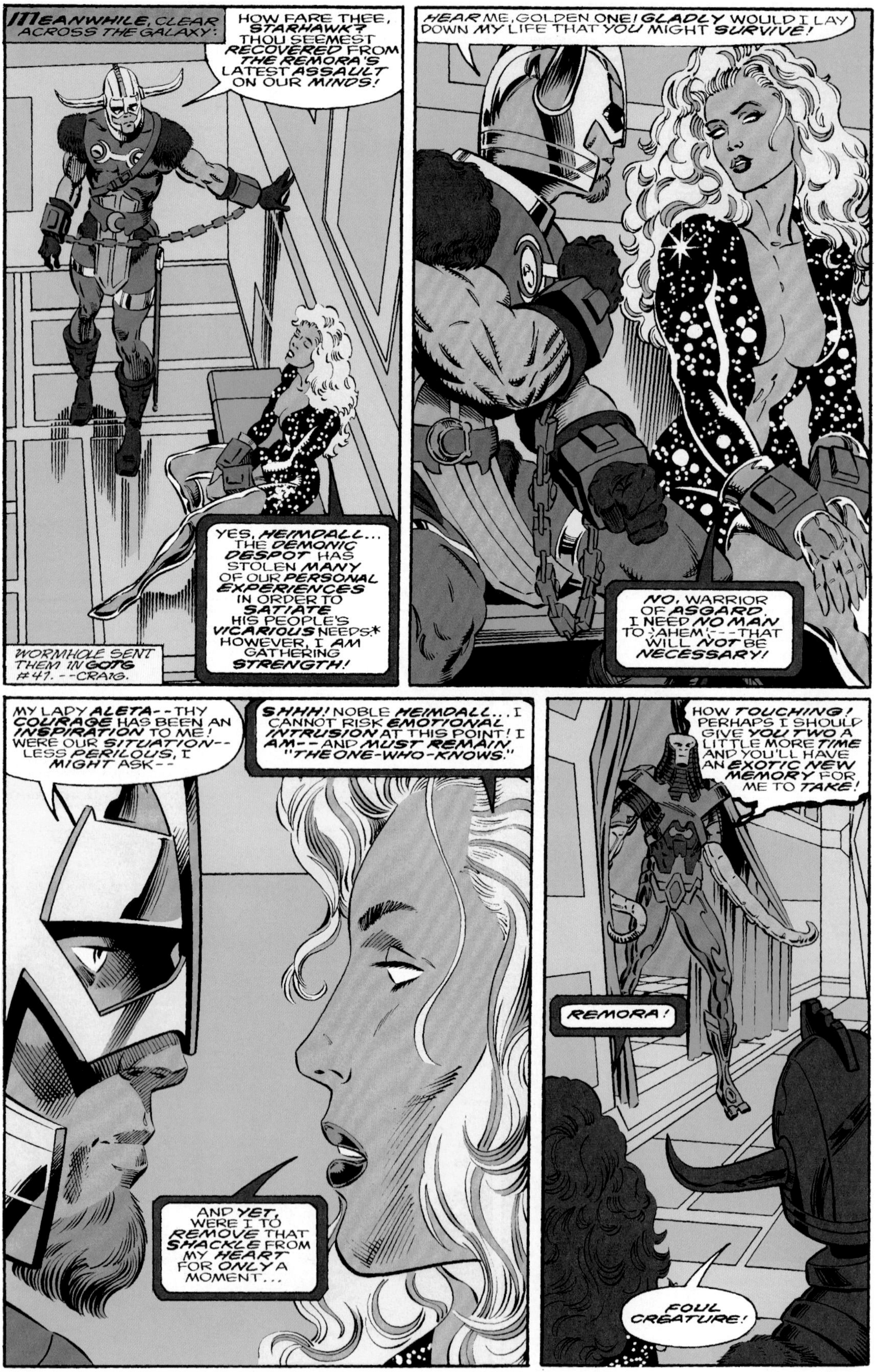
MEANWHILE, CLEAR ACROSS THE GALAXY:
HOW FARE THEE, STARHAWK? THOU SEEMEST RECOVERED FROM THE REMORA'S LATEST ASSAULT ON OUR MINDS!
YES, HEIMDALL... THE DEMONIC DESPOT HAS STOLEN MANY OF OUR PERSONAL EXPERIENCES IN ORDER TO SATIATE HIS PEOPLE'S VICARIOUS NEEDS.* HOWEVER, I AM GATHERING STRENGTH!
*WORMHOLE SENT THEM IN GOTG #41. --CRAIG.
HEAR ME, GOLDEN ONE! GLADLY WOULD I LAY DOWN MY LIFE THAT YOU MIGHT SURVIVE!
NO, WARRIOR OF ASGARD, I NEED NO MAN TO -AHEM- --THAT WILL NOT BE NECESSARY!
MY LADY ALETA--THY COURAGE HAS BEEN AN INSPIRATION TO ME! WERE OUR SITUATION--LESS PERILOUS, I MIGHT ASK--
SHHH! NOBLE HEIMDALL... I CANNOT RISK EMOTIONAL INTRUSION AT THIS POINT! I AM--AND MUST REMAIN "THE ONE-WHO-KNOWS."
AND YET, WERE I TO REMOVE THAT SHACKLE FROM MY HEART FOR ONLY A MOMENT...
HOW TOUCHING! PERHAPS I SHOULD GIVE YOU TWO A LITTLE MORE TIME AND YOU'LL HAVE AN EXOTIC NEW MEMORY FOR ME TO TAKE!
REMORA!
FOUL CREATURE!

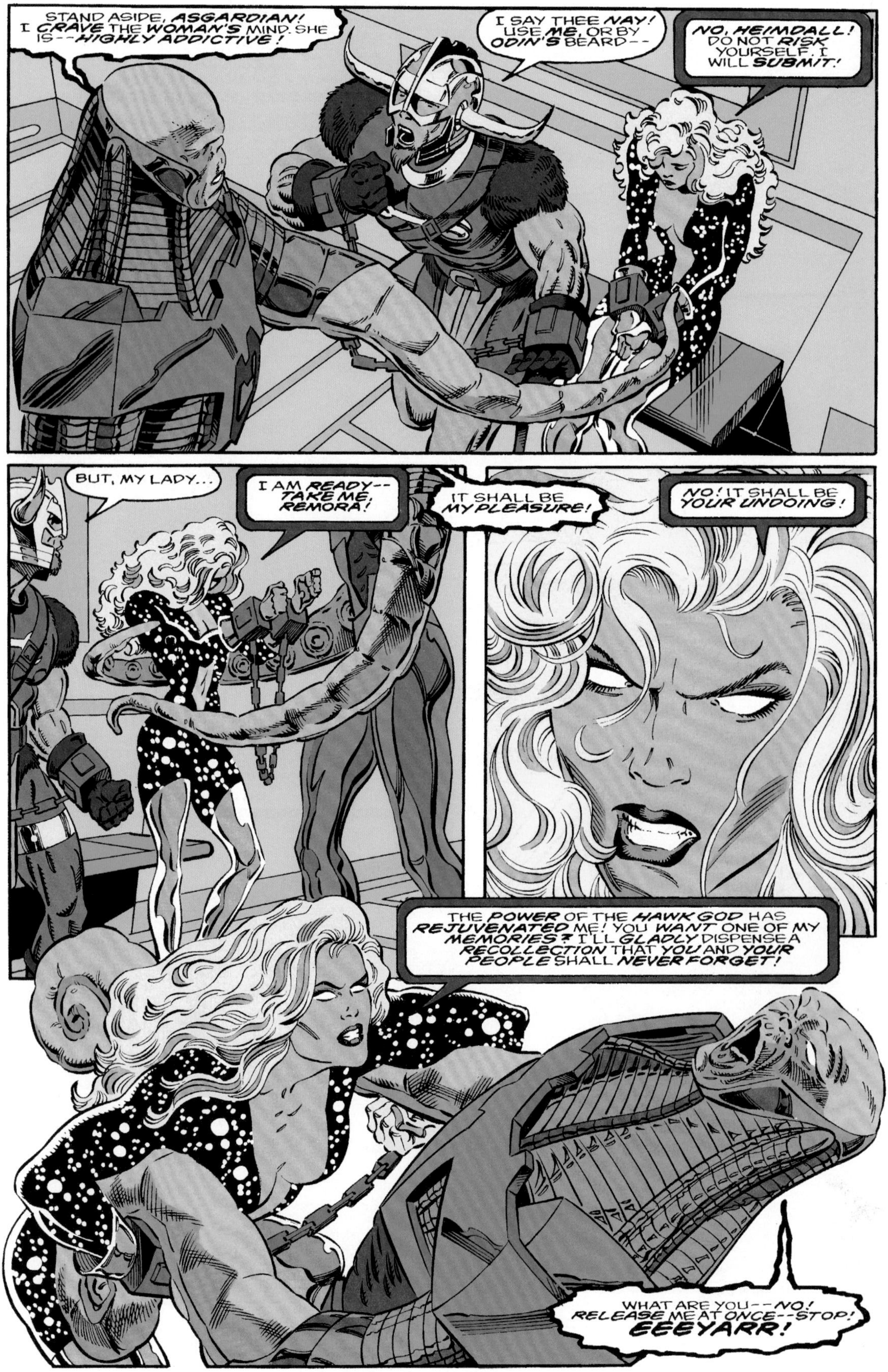
STAND ASIDE, ASGARDIAN! I CRAVE THE WOMAN'S MIND. SHE IS--HIGHLY ADDICTIVE!
I SAY THEE NAY! USE ME, OR BY ODIN'S BEARD--
NO, HEIMDALL! DO NOT RISK YOURSELF. I WILL SUBMIT!
BUT, MY LADY...
I AM READY--TAKE ME, REMORA!
IT SHALL BE MY PLEASURE!
NO! IT SHALL BE YOUR UNDOING!
THE POWER OF THE HAWK GOD HAS REJUVENATED ME! YOU WANT ONE OF MY MEMORIES? I'LL GLADLY DISPENSE A RECOLLECTION THAT YOU AND YOUR PEOPLE SHALL NEVER FORGET!
WHAT ARE YOU--NO! RELEASE ME AT ONCE--STOP! EEEYARR!

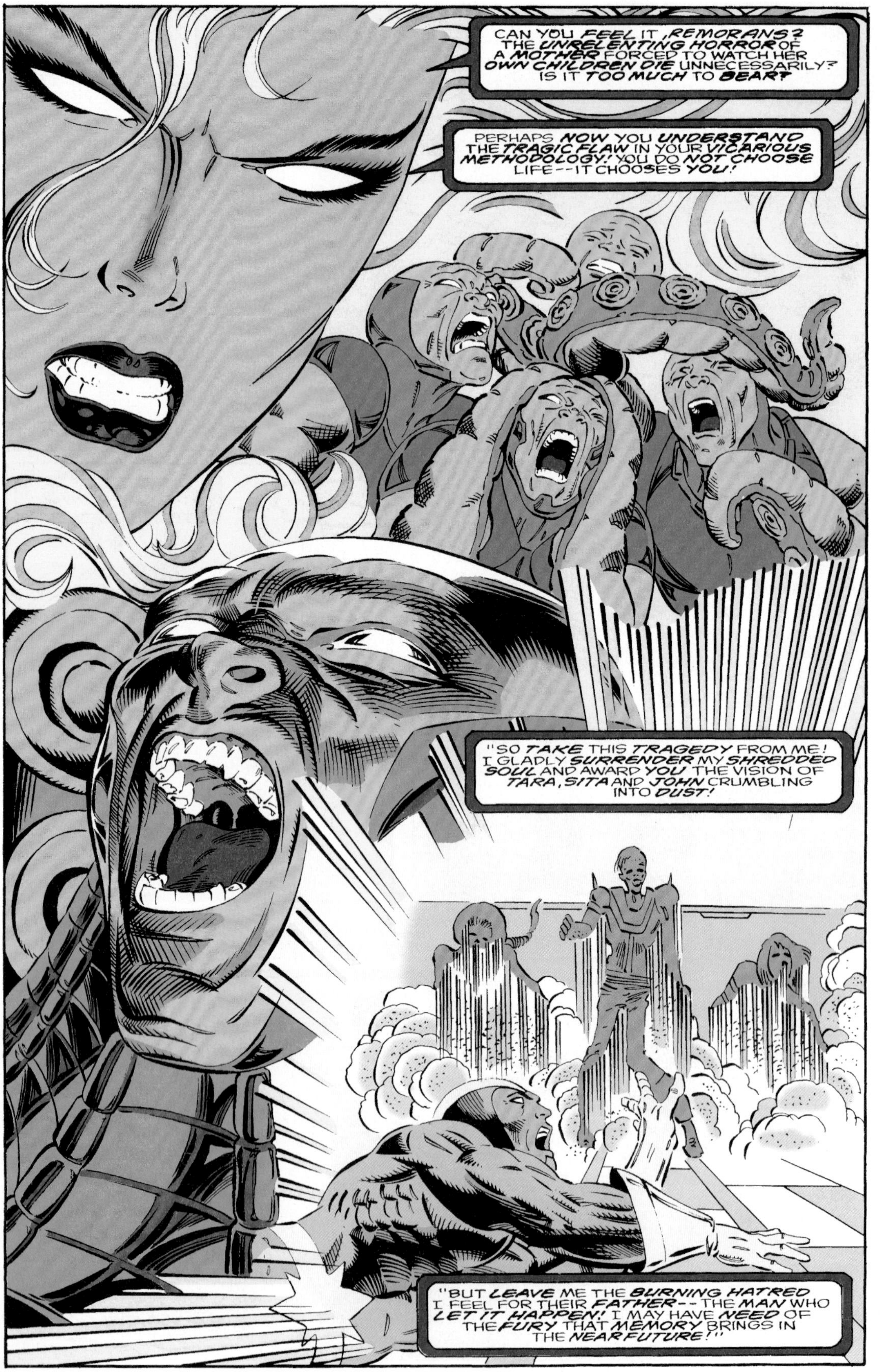
CAN YOU FEEL IT, REMORANS? THE UNRELENTING HORROR OF A MOTHER FORCED TO WATCH HER OWN CHILDREN DIE UNNECESSARILY? IS IT TOO MUCH TO BEAR?
PERHAPS NOW YOU UNDERSTAND THE TRAGIC FLAW IN YOUR VICARIOUS METHODOLOGY! YOU DO NOT CHOOSE LIFE--IT CHOOSES YOU!
"SO TAKE THIS TRAGEDY FROM ME! I GLADLY SURRENDER MY SHREDDED SOUL AND AWARD YOU THE VISION OF TARA, SITA AND JOHN CRUMBLING INTO DUST!
"BUT LEAVE ME THE BURNING HATRED I FEEL FOR THEIR FATHER--THE MAN WHO LET IT HAPPEN! I MAY HAVE NEED OF THE FURY THAT MEMORY BRINGS IN THE NEAR FUTURE!"

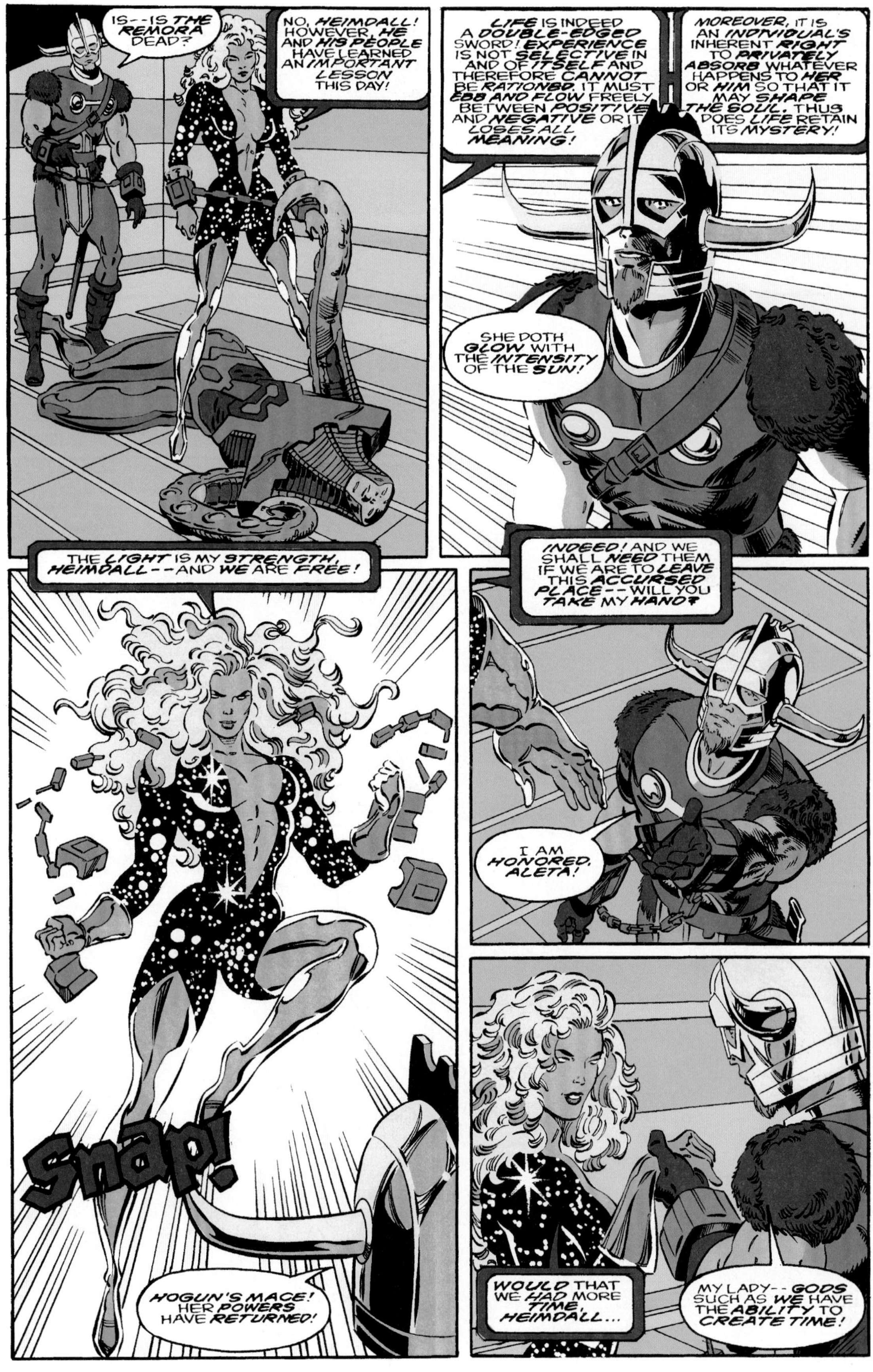

IS--IS THE REMORA DEAD?
NO, HEIMDALL! HOWEVER, HE AND HIS PEOPLE HAVE LEARNED AN IMPORTANT LESSON THIS DAY!
LIFE IS INDEED A DOUBLE-EDGED SWORD! EXPERIENCE IS NOT SELECTIVE IN AND OF ITSELF AND THEREFORE CANNOT BE RATIONED. IT MUST EBB AND FLOW FREELY BETWEEN POSITIVE AND NEGATIVE OR IT LOSES ALL MEANING!
MOREOVER, IT IS AN INDIVIDUAL'S INHERENT RIGHT TO PRIVATELY ABSORB WHATEVER HAPPENS TO HER OR HIM SO THAT IT MAY SHAPE THE SOUL. THUS DOES LIFE RETAIN ITS MYSTERY!
SHE DOTH GLOW WITH THE INTENSITY OF THE SUN!
THE LIGHT IS MY STRENGTH, HEIMDALL--AND WE ARE FREE!
SNAP!
HOGUN'S MACE! HER POWERS HAVE RETURNED!
INDEED! AND WE SHALL NEED THEM IF WE ARE TO LEAVE THIS ACCURSED PLACE--WILL YOU TAKE MY HAND?
I AM HONORED, ALETA!
WOULD THAT WE HAD MORE TIME, HEIMDALL...
MY LADY--GODS SUCH AS WE HAVE THE ABILITY TO CREATE TIME!

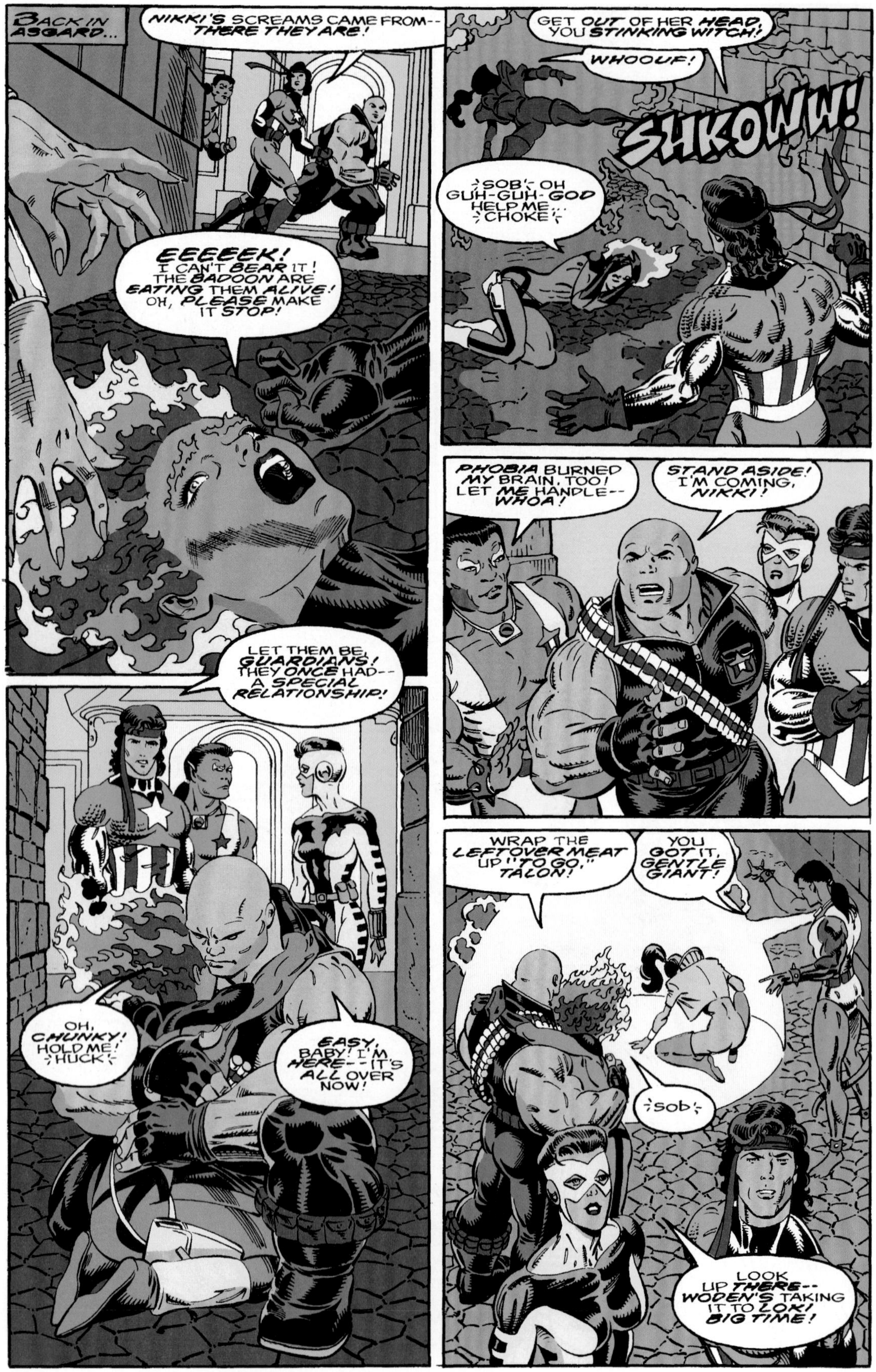

BACK IN ASGARD...
NIKKI'S SCREAMS CAME FROM-- THERE THEY ARE!
EEEEEK! I CAN'T BEAR IT! THE BADOON ARE EATING THEM ALIVE! OH, PLEASE MAKE IT STOP!
GET OUT OF HER HEAD, YOU STINKING WITCH!
WHOOUF!
SHKOWW!
SOB OH GUH-GUH-GOD HELP ME... CHOKE
LET THEM BE, GUARDIANS! THEY ONCE HAD-- A SPECIAL RELATIONSHIP!
OH, CHUNKY! HOLD ME! HUCK
EASY, BABY! I'M HERE--IT'S ALL OVER NOW!
PHOBIA BURNED MY BRAIN, TOO! LET ME HANDLE-- WHOA!
STAND ASIDE! I'M COMING, NIKKI!
WRAP THE LEFTOVER MEAT UP "TO GO," TALON!
YOU GOT IT, GENTLE GIANT!
SOB
LOOK UP THERE-- WODEN'S TAKING IT TO LOKI, BIG TIME!

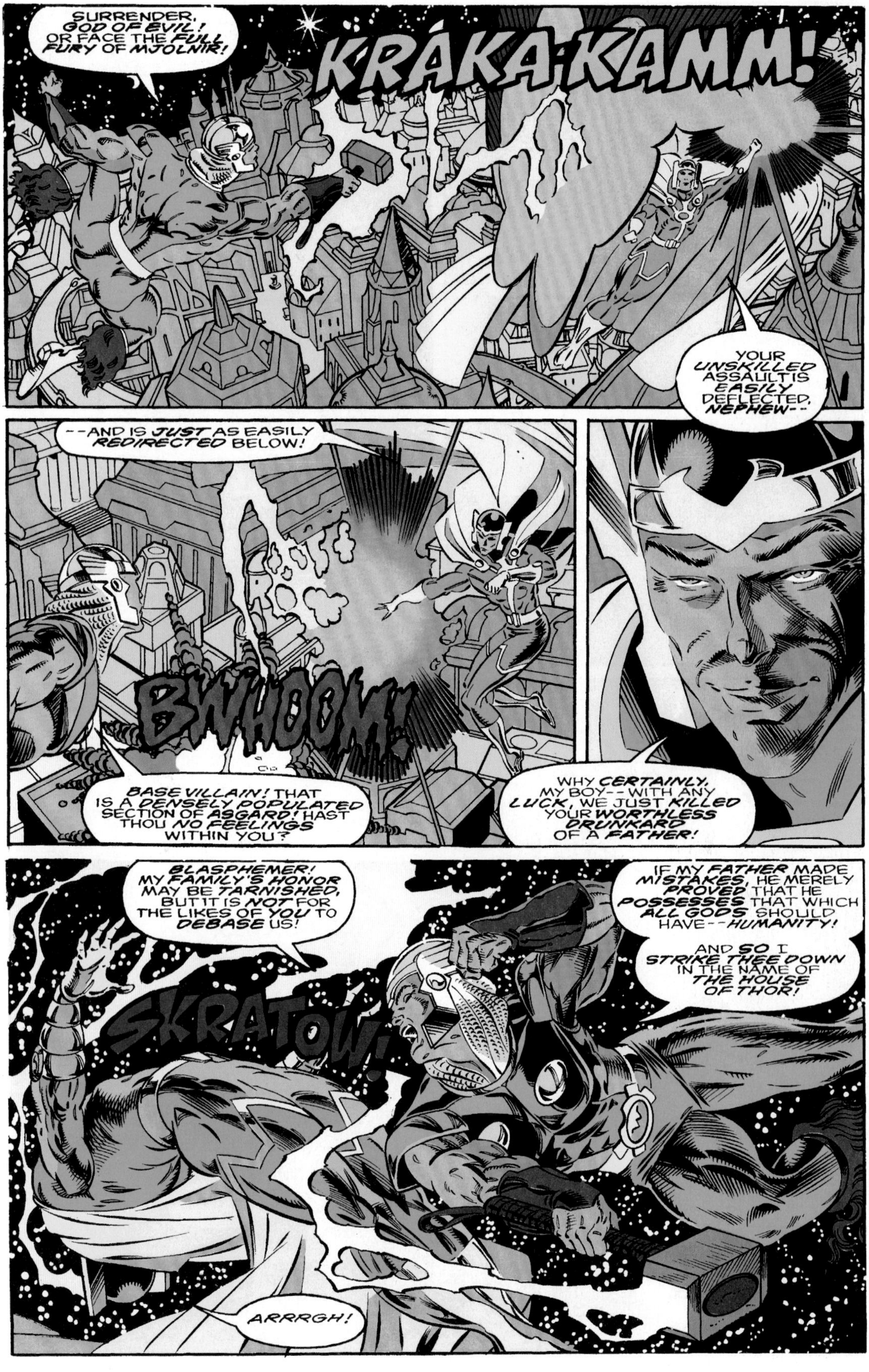
SURRENDER, GOD OF EVIL! OR FACE THE FULL FURY OF MJOLNIR!
KRAKA-KAMM!
YOUR UNSKILLED ASSAULT IS EASILY DEFLECTED, NEPHEW--
--AND IS JUST AS EASILY REDIRECTED BELOW!
BWHOOM!
BASE VILLAIN! THAT IS A DENSELY POPULATED SECTION OF ASGARD! HAST THOU NO FEELINGS WITHIN YOU?
WHY CERTAINLY, MY BOY-- WITH ANY LUCK, WE JUST KILLED YOUR WORTHLESS DRUNKARD OF A FATHER!
BLASPHEMER! MY FAMILY'S HONOR MAY BE TARNISHED, BUT IT IS NOT FOR THE LIKES OF YOU TO DEBASE US!
IF MY FATHER MADE MISTAKES, HE MERELY PROVED THAT HE POSSESSES THAT WHICH ALL GODS SHOULD HAVE--HUMANITY!
AND SO I STRIKE THEE DOWN IN THE NAME OF THE HOUSE OF THOR!
SKRATOW!
ARRRGH!

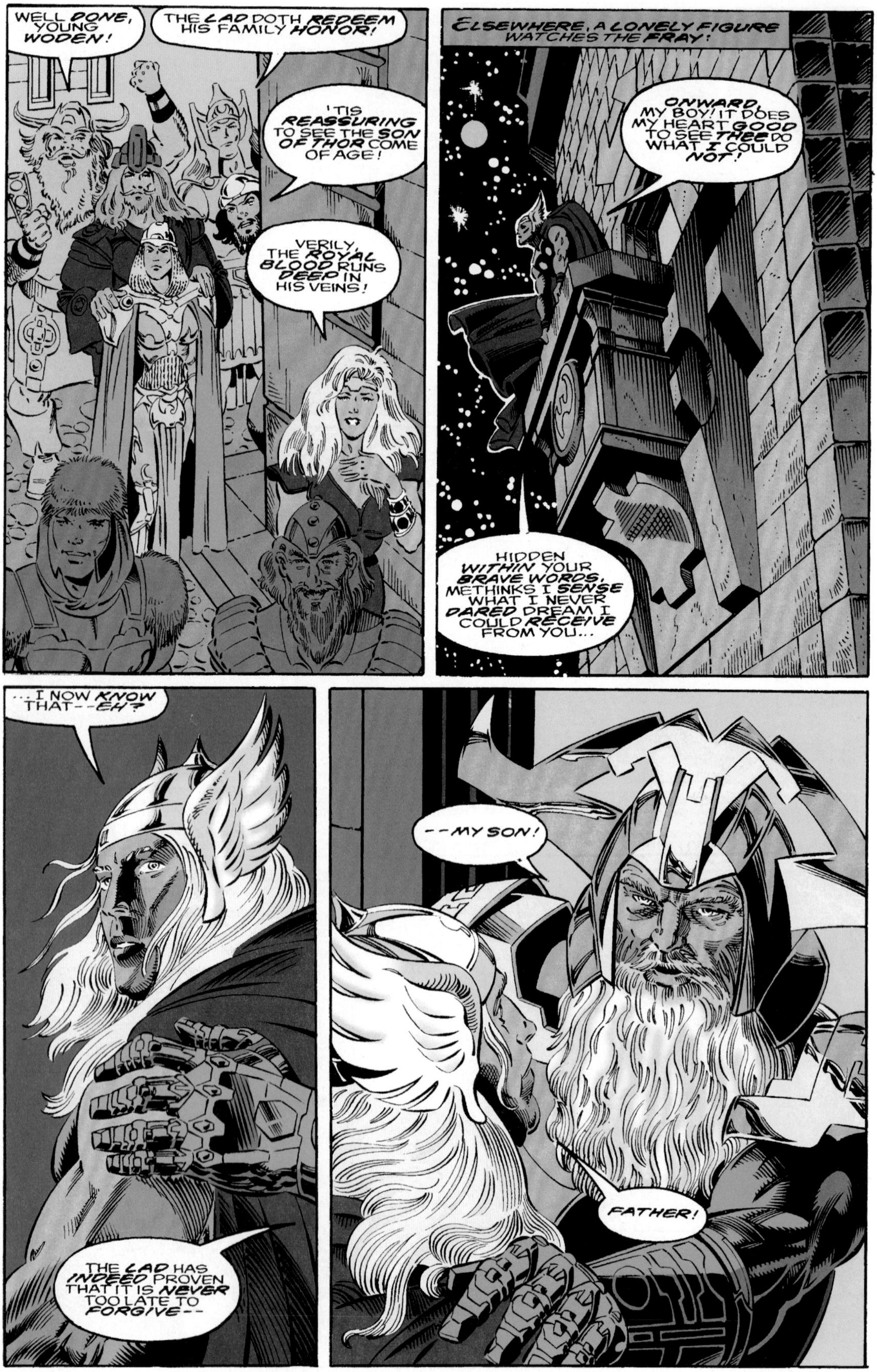
WELL DONE, YOUNG WODEN!
THE LAD DOTH REDEEM HIS FAMILY HONOR!
'TIS REASSURING TO SEE THE SON OF THOR COME OF AGE!
VERILY, THE ROYAL BLOOD RUNS DEEP IN HIS VEINS!
ELSEWHERE, A LONELY FIGURE WATCHES THE FRAY!
ONWARD, MY BOY! IT DOES MY HEART GOOD TO SEE THEE DO WHAT I COULD NOT!
HIDDEN WITHIN YOUR BRAVE WORDS, METHINKS I SENSE WHAT I NEVER DARED DREAM I COULD RECEIVE FROM YOU...
...I NOW KNOW THAT--EH?
THE LAD HAS INDEED PROVEN THAT IT IS NEVER TOO LATE TO FORGIVE--
--MY SON!
FATHER!

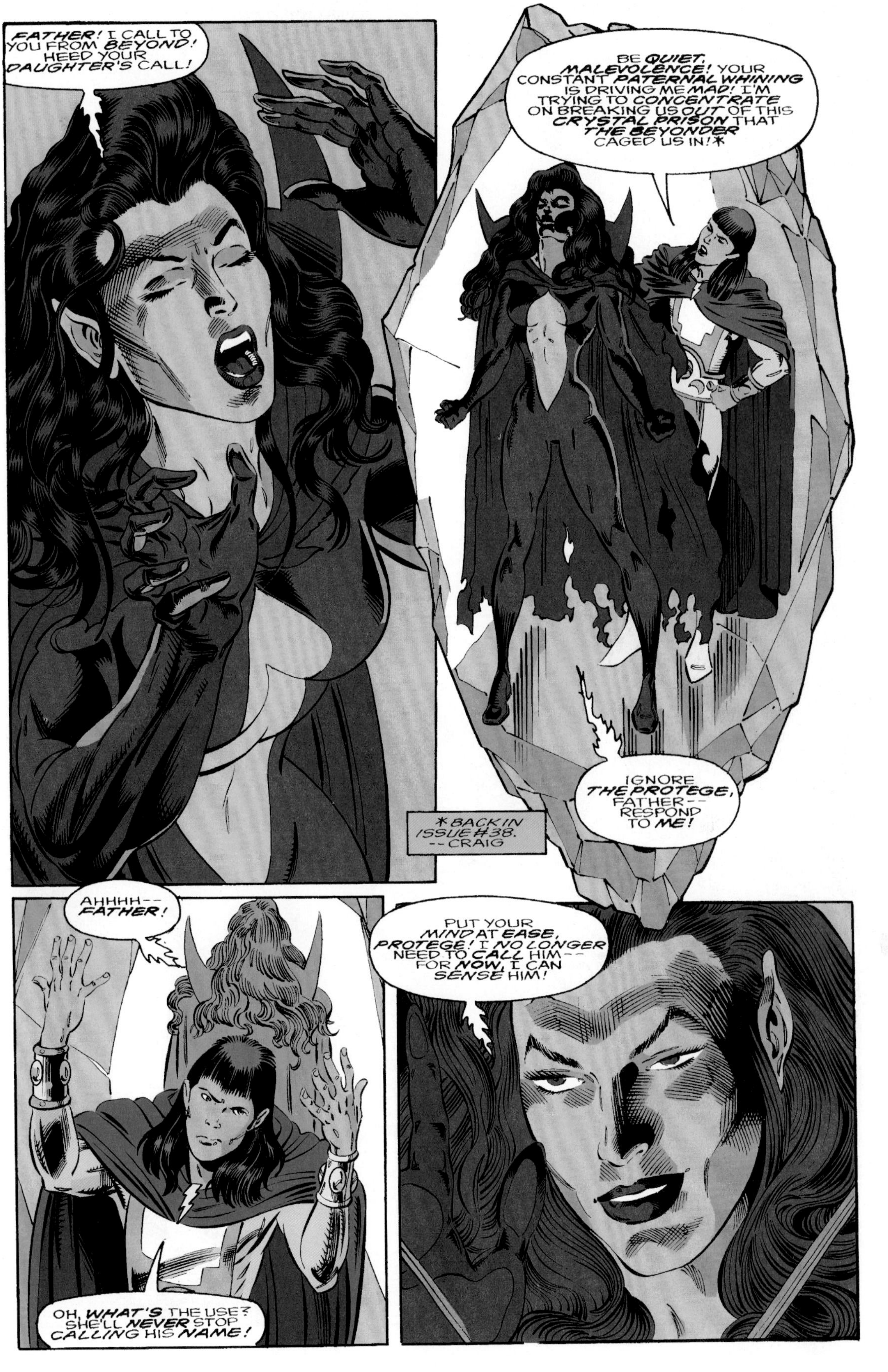
FATHER! I CALL TO YOU FROM BEYOND! HEED YOUR DAUGHTER'S CALL!
BE QUIET, MALEVOLENCE! YOUR CONSTANT PATERNAL WHINING IS DRIVING ME MAD! I'M TRYING TO CONCENTRATE ON BREAKING US OUT OF THIS CRYSTAL PRISON THAT THE BEYONDER CAGED US IN!*
IGNORE THE PROTEGE, FATHER-- RESPOND TO ME!
*BACK IN ISSUE #38. --CRAIG
AHHHH-- FATHER!
OH, WHAT'S THE USE? SHE'LL NEVER STOP CALLING HIS NAME!
PUT YOUR MIND AT EASE, PROTEGE! I NO LONGER NEED TO CALL HIM-- FOR NOW, I CAN SENSE HIM!

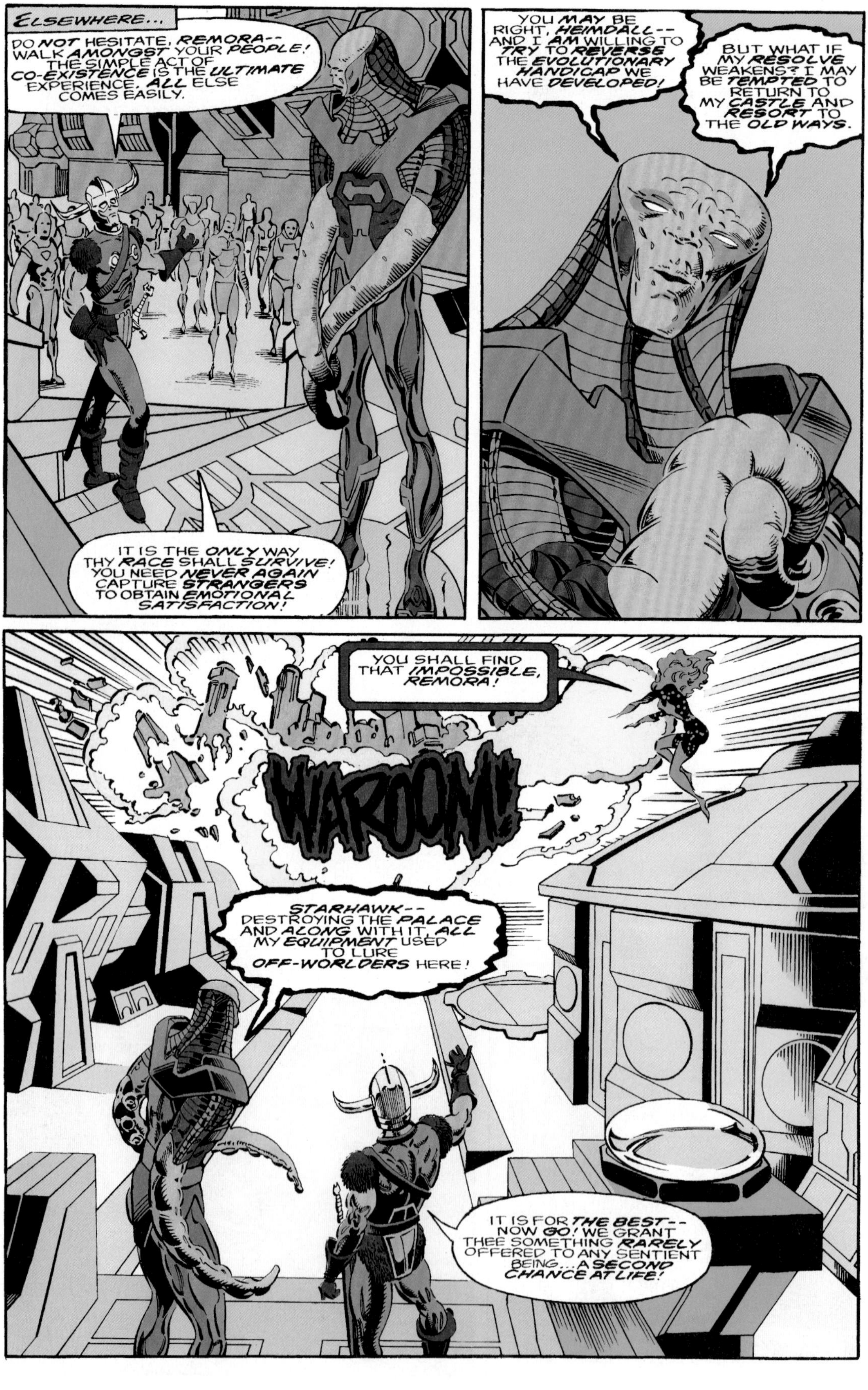
ELSEWHERE...
DO NOT HESITATE, REMORA-- WALK AMONGST YOUR PEOPLE! THE SIMPLE ACT OF CO-EXISTENCE IS THE ULTIMATE EXPERIENCE. ALL ELSE COMES EASILY.
IT IS THE ONLY WAY THY RACE SHALL SURVIVE! YOU NEED NEVER AGAIN CAPTURE STRANGERS TO OBTAIN EMOTIONAL SATISFACTION!
YOU MAY BE RIGHT, HEIMDALL-- AND I AM WILLING TO TRY TO REVERSE THE EVOLUTIONARY HANDICAP WE HAVE DEVELOPED!
BUT WHAT IF MY RESOLVE WEAKENS? I MAY BE TEMPTED TO RETURN TO MY CASTLE AND RESORT TO THE OLD WAYS.
YOU SHALL FIND THAT IMPOSSIBLE, REMORA!
WAROOM!
STARHAWK-- DESTROYING THE PALACE AND ALONG WITH IT, ALL MY EQUIPMENT USED TO LURE OFF-WORLDERS HERE!
IT IS FOR THE BEST-- NOW GO! WE GRANT THEE SOMETHING RARELY OFFERED TO ANY SENTIENT BEING... A SECOND CHANCE AT LIFE!

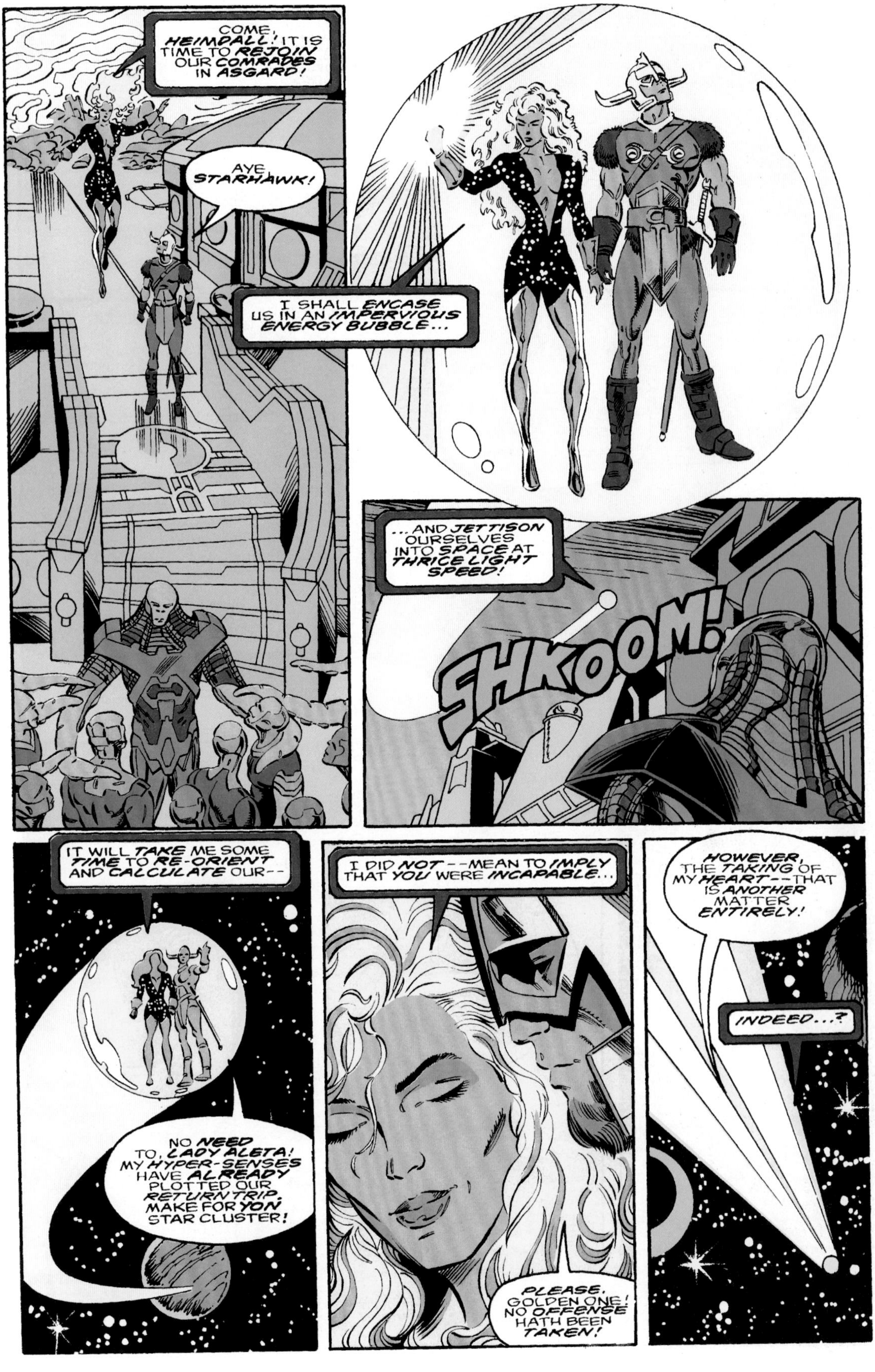
COME, HEIMDALL! IT IS TIME TO REJOIN OUR COMRADES IN ASGARD!
AYE STARHAWK!
I SHALL ENCASE US IN AN IMPERVIOUS ENERGY BUBBLE...
...AND JETTISON OURSELVES INTO SPACE AT THRICE LIGHT SPEED!
SHKOOM!
IT WILL TAKE ME SOME TIME TO RE-ORIENT AND CALCULATE OUR--
NO NEED TO, LADY ALETA! MY HYPER-SENSES HAVE ALREADY PLOTTED OUR RETURN TRIP. MAKE FOR YON STAR CLUSTER!
I DID NOT--MEAN TO IMPLY THAT YOU WERE INCAPABLE...
PLEASE, GOLDEN ONE! NO OFFENSE HATH BEEN TAKEN!
HOWEVER, THE TAKING OF MY HEART--THAT IS ANOTHER MATTER ENTIRELY!
INDEED...?

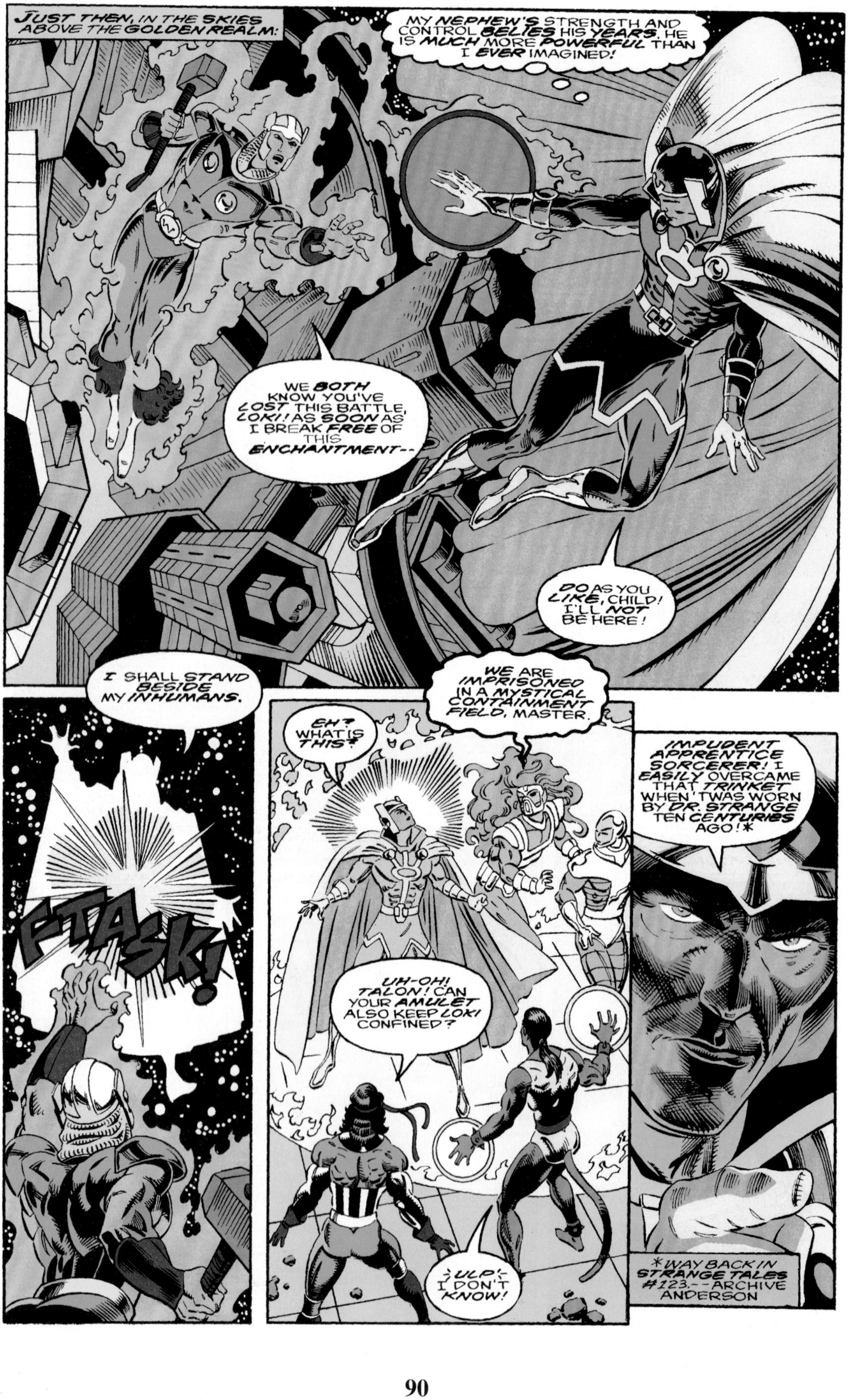

JUST THEN, IN THE SKIES ABOVE THE GOLDEN REALM:
MY NEPHEW'S STRENGTH AND CONTROL BELIES HIS YEARS. HE IS MUCH MORE POWERFUL THAN I EVER IMAGINED!
WE BOTH KNOW YOU'VE LOST THIS BATTLE, LOKI! AS SOON AS I BREAK FREE OF THIS ENCHANTMENT--
DO AS YOU LIKE, CHILD! I'LL NOT BE HERE!
I SHALL STAND BESIDE MY INHUMANS.
FTASK!
EH? WHAT IS THIS?
WE ARE IMPRISONED IN A MYSTICAL CONTAINMENT FIELD, MASTER.
UH-OH! TALON! CAN YOUR AMULET ALSO KEEP LOKI CONFINED?
ULP! I DON'T KNOW!
IMPUDENT APPRENTICE SORCERER! I EASILY OVERCAME THAT TRINKET WHEN 'TWAS WORN BY DR. STRANGE TEN CENTURIES AGO!*
*WAY BACK IN STRANGE TALES #123.--ARCHIVE ANDERSON

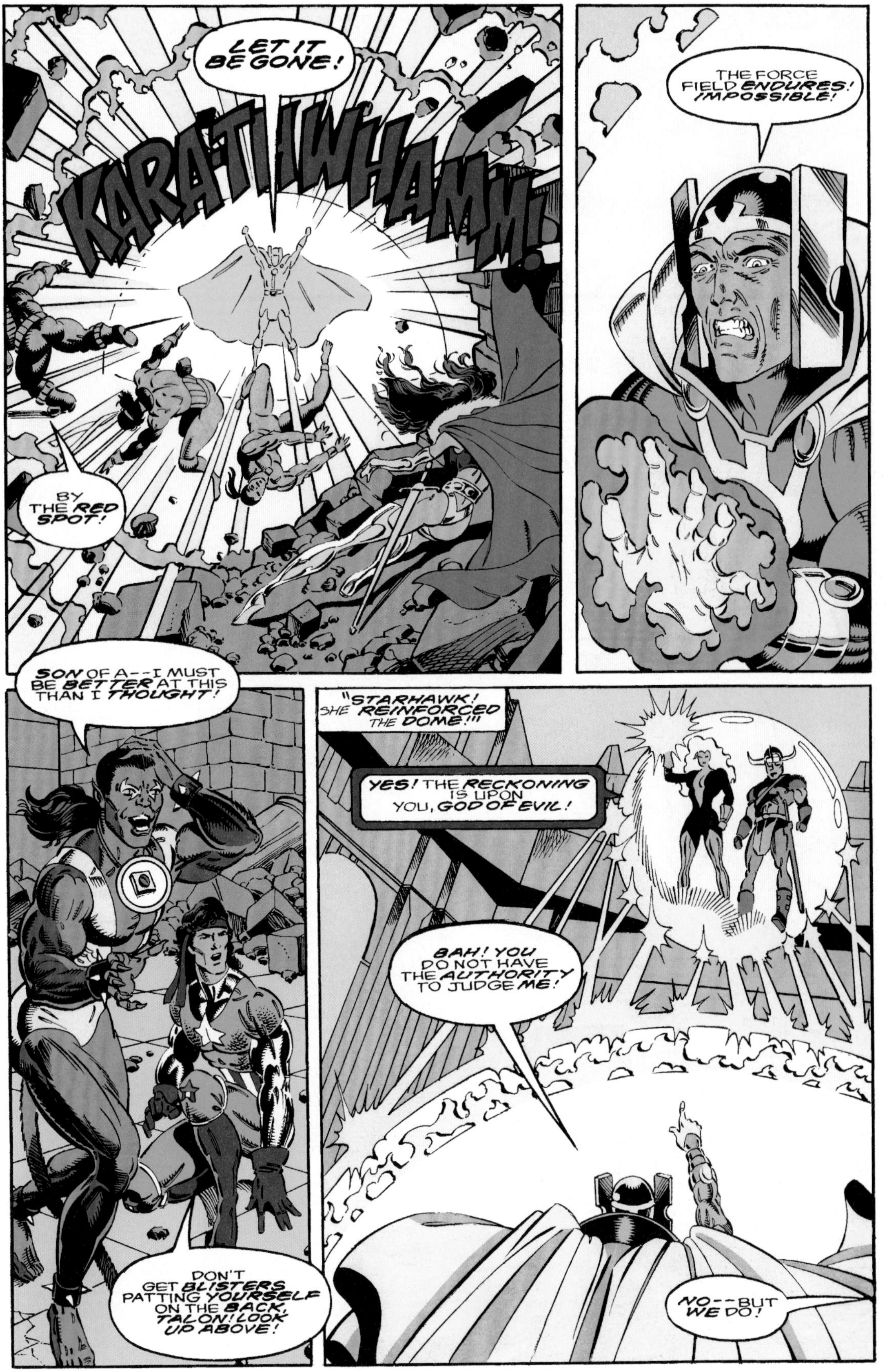
LET IT BE GONE!
KARATHWHAMM!
BY THE RED SPOT!
THE FORCE FIELD ENDURES! IMPOSSIBLE!
SON OF A--I MUST BE BETTER AT THIS THAN I THOUGHT!
DON'T GET BLISTERS PATTING YOURSELF ON THE BACK, TALON! LOOK UP ABOVE!
"STARHAWK! SHE REINFORCED THE DOME!"
YES! THE RECKONING IS UPON YOU, GOD OF EVIL!
BAH! YOU DO NOT HAVE THE AUTHORITY TO JUDGE ME!
NO--BUT WE DO!

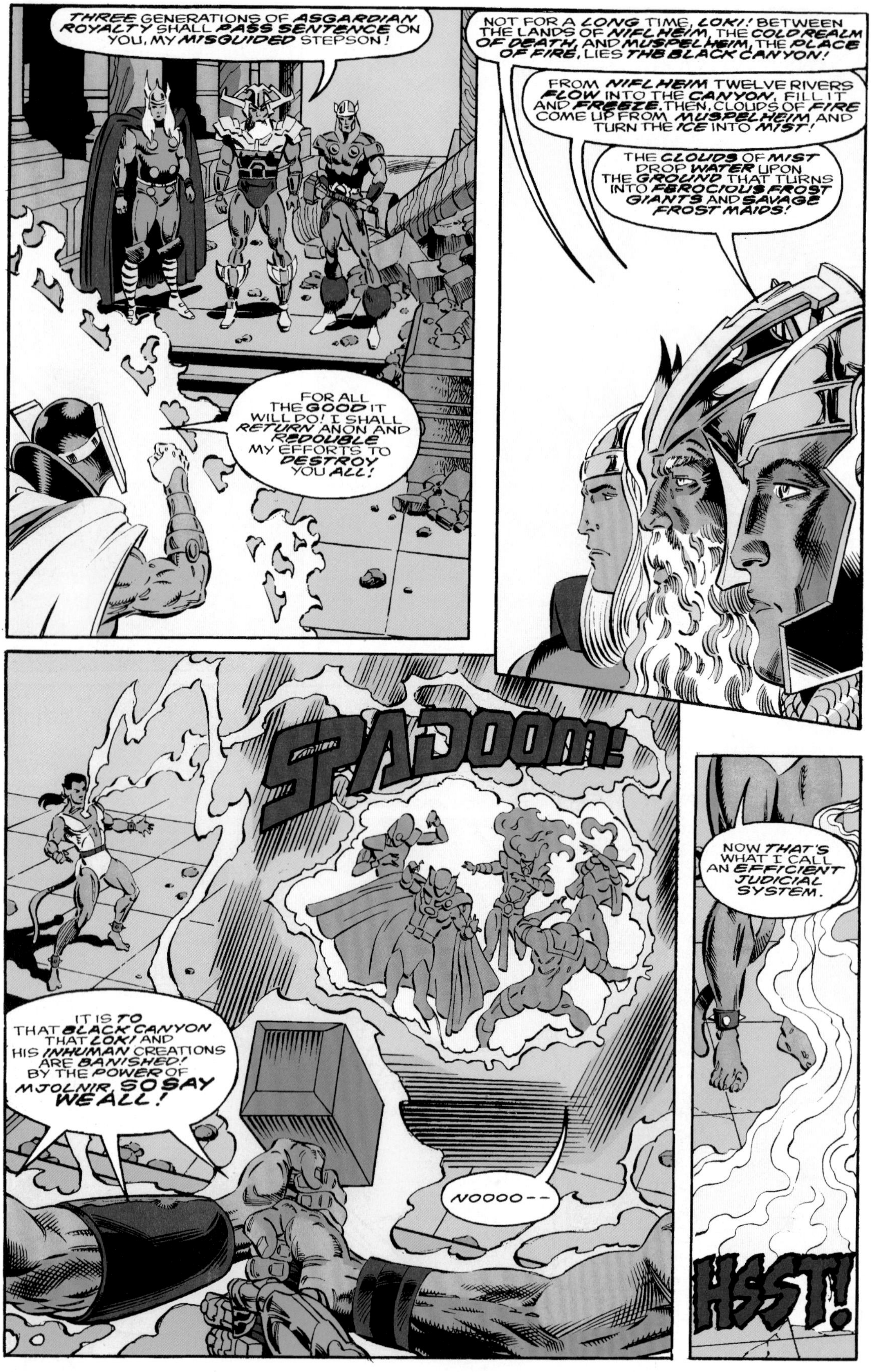
THREE GENERATIONS OF ASGARDIAN ROYALTY SHALL PASS SENTENCE ON YOU, MY MISGUIDED STEPSON!
FOR ALL THE GOOD IT WILL DO! I SHALL RETURN ANON AND REDOUBLE MY EFFORTS TO DESTROY YOU ALL!
NOT FOR A LONG TIME, LOKI! BETWEEN THE LANDS OF NIFLHEIM, THE COLD REALM OF DEATH, AND MUSPELHEIM, THE PLACE OF FIRE, LIES THE BLACK CANYON!
FROM NIFLHEIM TWELVE RIVERS FLOW INTO THE CANYON, FILL IT AND FREEZE. THEN, CLOUDS OF FIRE COME UP FROM MUSPELHEIM AND TURN THE ICE INTO MIST!
THE CLOUDS OF MIST DROP WATER UPON THE GROUND THAT TURNS INTO FEROCIOUS FROST GIANTS AND SAVAGE FROST MAIDS!
SPADOOM!
IT IS TO THAT BLACK CANYON THAT LOKI AND HIS INHUMAN CREATIONS ARE BANISHED! BY THE POWER OF MJOLNIR, SO SAY WE ALL!
NOOOO--
NOW THAT'S WHAT I CALL AN EFFICIENT JUDICIAL SYSTEM.
HSST!

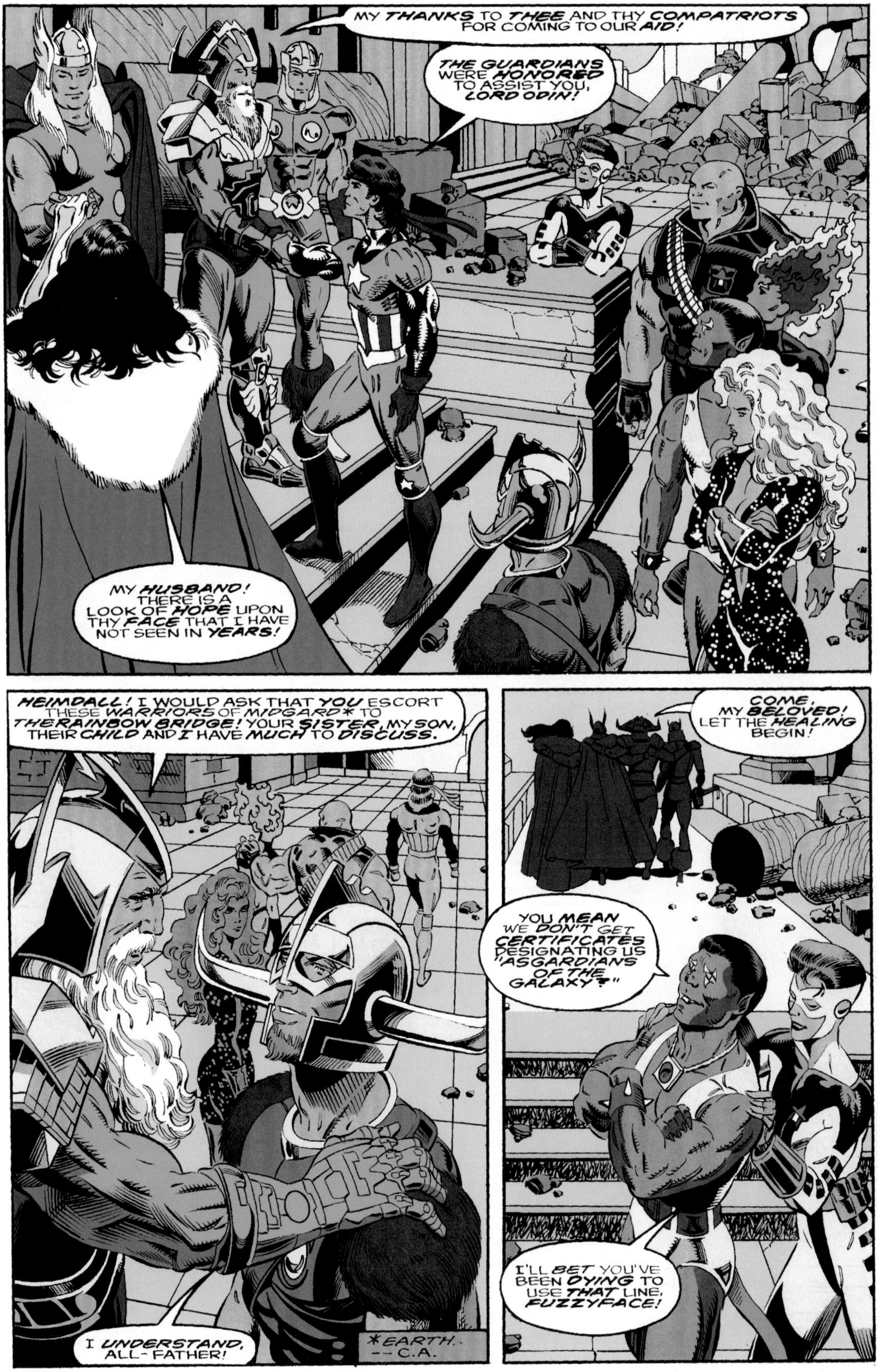
MY THANKS TO THEE AND THY COMPATRIOTS FOR COMING TO OUR AID!
THE GUARDIANS WERE HONORED TO ASSIST YOU, LORD ODIN!
MY HUSBAND! THERE IS A LOOK OF HOPE UPON THY FACE THAT I HAVE NOT SEEN IN YEARS!
HEIMDALL! I WOULD ASK THAT YOU ESCORT THESE WARRIORS OF MIDGARD* TO THE RAINBOW BRIDGE! YOUR SISTER, MY SON, THEIR CHILD AND I HAVE MUCH TO DISCUSS.
I UNDERSTAND, ALL-FATHER!
*EARTH. --C.A.
COME, MY BELOVED! LET THE HEALING BEGIN!
YOU MEAN WE DON'T GET CERTIFICATES DESIGNATING US "ASGARDIANS OF THE GALAXY?"
I'LL BET YOU'VE BEEN DYING TO USE THAT LINE, FUZZYFACE!

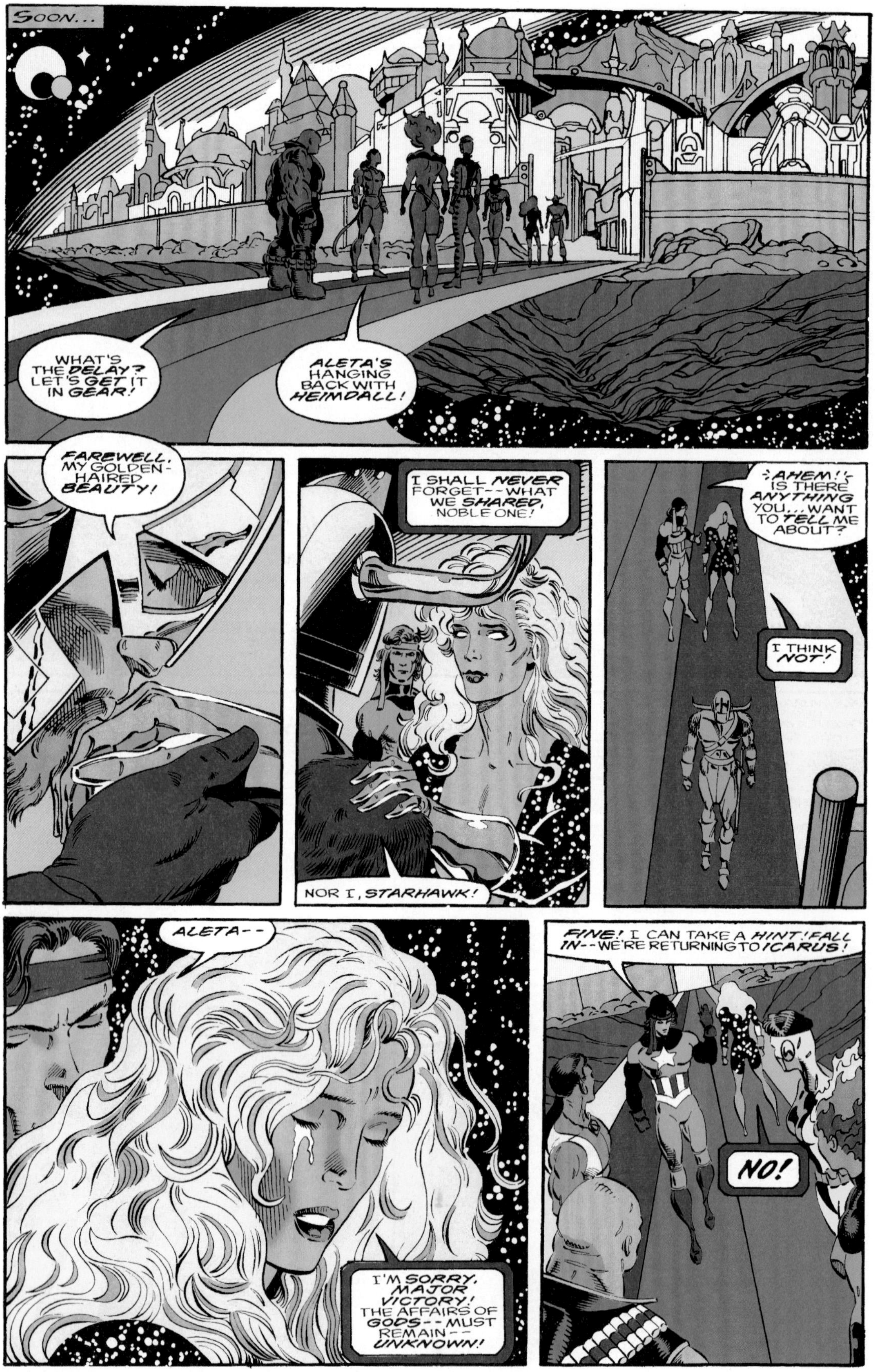
SOON...
WHAT'S THE DELAY? LET'S GET IT IN GEAR!
ALETA'S HANGING BACK WITH HEIMDALL!
FAREWELL, MY GOLDEN-HAIRED BEAUTY!
I SHALL NEVER FORGET-- WHAT WE SHARED, NOBLE ONE!
NOR I, STARHAWK!
AHEM! IS THERE ANYTHING YOU... WANT TO TELL ME ABOUT?
I THINK NOT!
ALETA--
I'M SORRY, MAJOR VICTORY! THE AFFAIRS OF GODS-- MUST REMAIN-- UNKNOWN!
FINE! I CAN TAKE A HINT! FALL IN-- WE'RE RETURNING TO ICARUS!
NO!

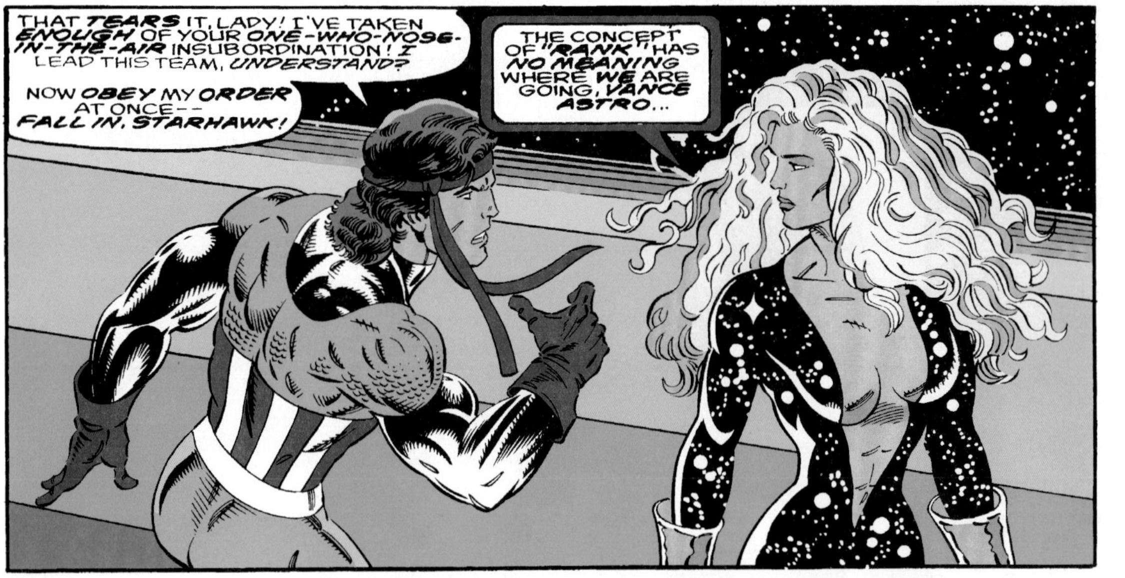
THAT TEARS IT, LADY! I'VE TAKEN ENOUGH OF YOUR ONE-WHO-NOSE-IN-THE-AIR INSUBORDINATION! I LEAD THIS TEAM, UNDERSTAND?
NOW OBEY MY ORDER AT ONCE-- FALL IN, STARHAWK!
THE CONCEPT OF "RANK" HAS NO MEANING WHERE WE ARE GOING, VANCE ASTRO...

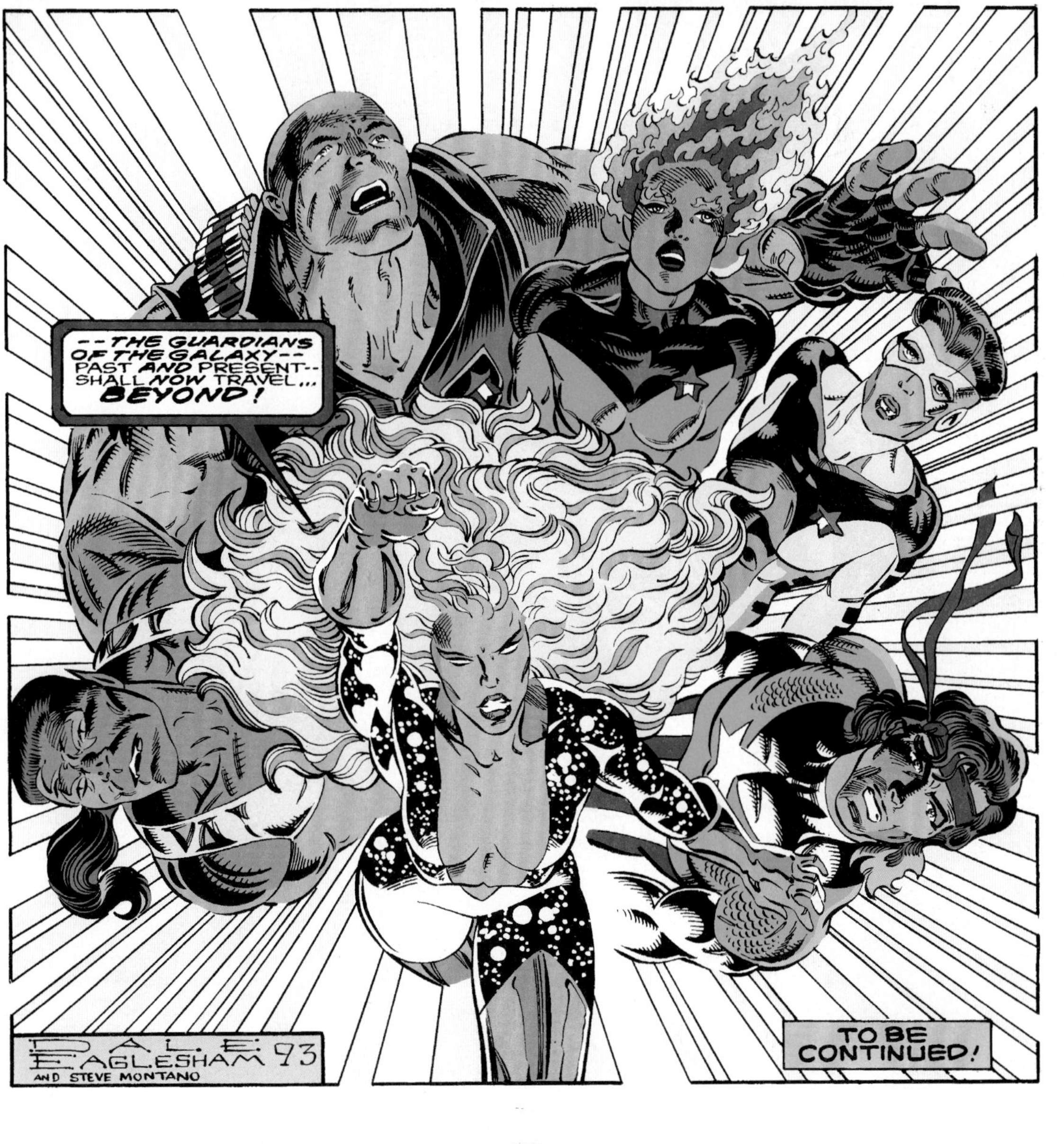
--THE GUARDIANS OF THE GALAXY-- PAST AND PRESENT-- SHALL NOW TRAVEL... BEYOND!
DALE EAGLESHAM 93
AND STEVE MONTANO
TO BE CONTINUED!

MARVEL® COMICS
EXPLORE THE MARVEL UNIVERSE IN THE 31ST CENTURY WITH THE
GUARDIANS
OF THE GA
© 1993 MARVEL ENT. GROUP, INC.
$1.25 US
$1.60 CAN
44
JAN
UK 95p
APPROVED BY THE COMICS CODE AUTHORITY
HE'S BACK...
...AND WE DON'T MEAN
YONDU
WEST & MONTIANO

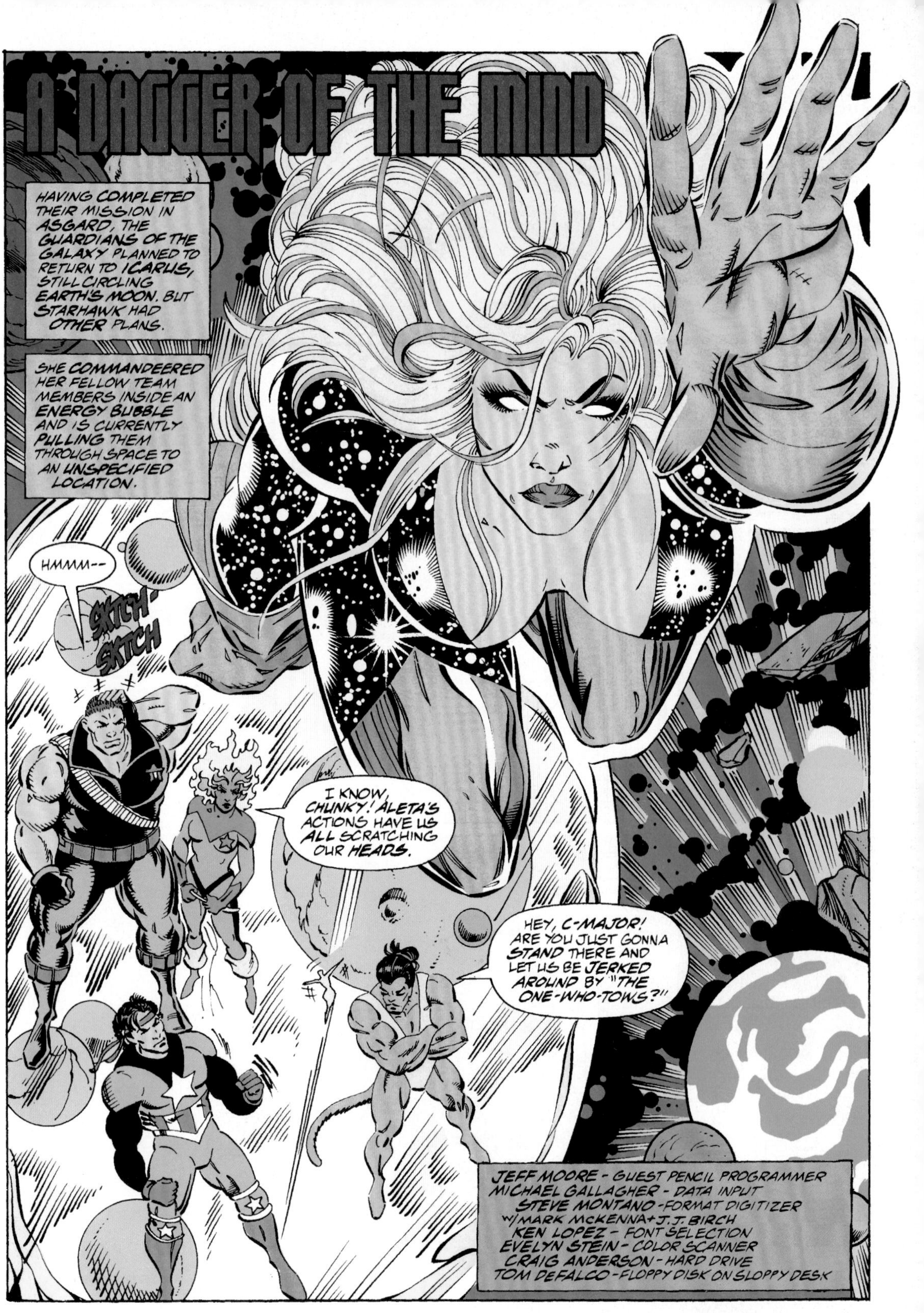
A DAGGER OF THE MIND
HAVING COMPLETED THEIR MISSION IN ASGARD, THE GUARDIANS OF THE GALAXY PLANNED TO RETURN TO ICARUS, STILL CIRCLING EARTH'S MOON. BUT STARHAWK HAD OTHER PLANS.
SHE COMMANDEERED HER FELLOW TEAM MEMBERS INSIDE AN ENERGY BUBBLE AND IS CURRENTLY PULLING THEM THROUGH SPACE TO AN UNSPECIFIED LOCATION.
HMMM--
SKTCH-SKTCH
I KNOW, CHUNKY! ALETA'S ACTIONS HAVE US ALL SCRATCHING OUR HEADS.
HEY, C-MAJOR! ARE YOU JUST GONNA STAND THERE AND LET US BE JERKED AROUND BY "THE ONE-WHO-TOWS?"
JEFF MOORE - GUEST PENCIL PROGRAMMER
MICHAEL GALLAGHER - DATA INPUT
STEVE MONTANO - FORMAT DIGITIZER w/MARK McKENNA + J.J. BIRCH
KEN LOPEZ - FONT SELECTION
EVELYN STEIN - COLOR SCANNER
CRAIG ANDERSON - HARD DRIVE
TOM DeFALCO - FLOPPY DISK ON SLOPPY DESK

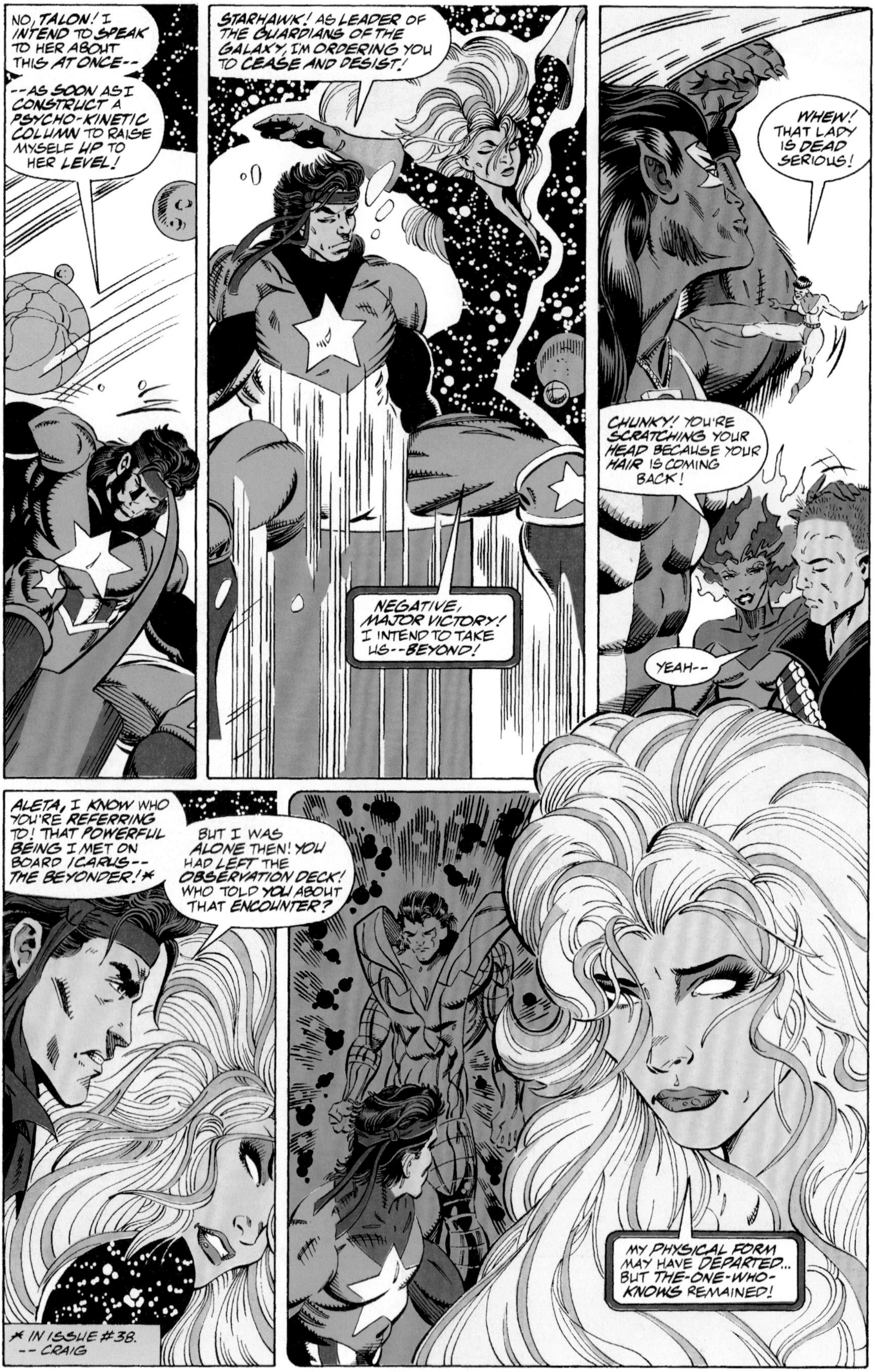
NO, TALON! I INTEND TO SPEAK TO HER ABOUT THIS AT ONCE--
--AS SOON AS I CONSTRUCT A PSYCHO-KINETIC COLUMN TO RAISE MYSELF UP TO HER LEVEL!
STARHAWK! AS LEADER OF THE GUARDIANS OF THE GALAXY, I'M ORDERING YOU TO CEASE AND DESIST!
NEGATIVE, MAJOR VICTORY! I INTEND TO TAKE US--BEYOND!
WHEW! THAT LADY IS DEAD SERIOUS!
CHUNKY! YOU'RE SCRATCHING YOUR HEAD BECAUSE YOUR HAIR IS COMING BACK!
YEAH--
ALETA, I KNOW WHO YOU'RE REFERRING TO! THAT POWERFUL BEING I MET ON BOARD ICARUS--THE BEYONDER!*
BUT I WAS ALONE THEN! YOU HAD LEFT THE OBSERVATION DECK! WHO TOLD YOU ABOUT THAT ENCOUNTER?
* IN ISSUE #38. --CRAIG
MY PHYSICAL FORM MAY HAVE DEPARTED... BUT THE-ONE-WHO-KNOWS REMAINED!

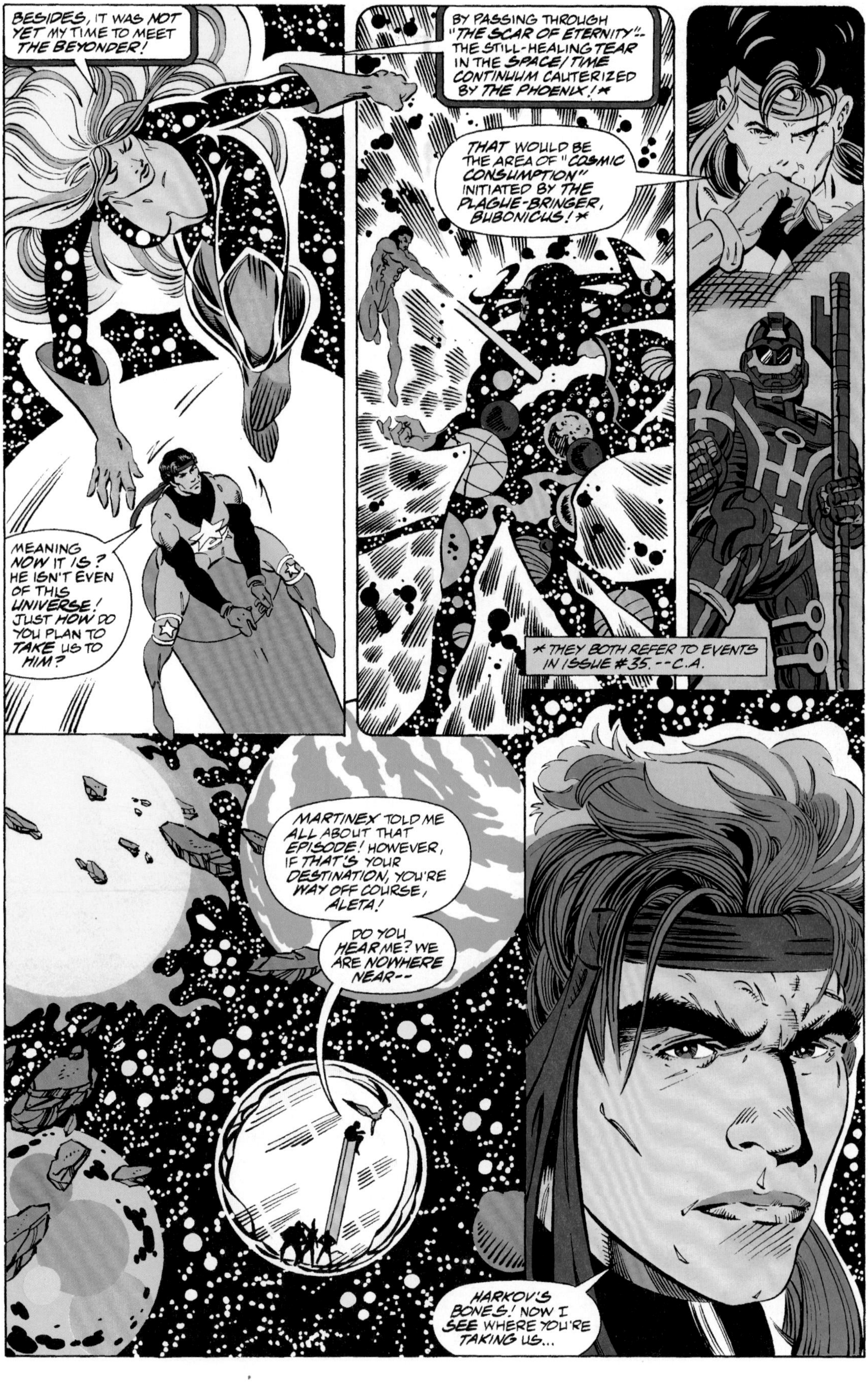
BESIDES, IT WAS NOT YET MY TIME TO MEET THE BEYONDER!
BY PASSING THROUGH "THE SCAR OF ETERNITY"-- THE STILL-HEALING TEAR IN THE SPACE/TIME CONTINUUM CAUTERIZED BY THE PHOENIX! *
THAT WOULD BE THE AREA OF "COSMIC CONSUMPTION" INITIATED BY THE PLAGUE-BRINGER, BUBONICUS! *
MEANING NOW IT IS? HE ISN'T EVEN OF THIS UNIVERSE! JUST HOW DO YOU PLAN TO TAKE US TO HIM?
* THEY BOTH REFER TO EVENTS IN ISSUE #35. --C.A.
MARTINEX TOLD ME ALL ABOUT THAT EPISODE! HOWEVER, IF THAT'S YOUR DESTINATION, YOU'RE WAY OFF COURSE, ALETA!
DO YOU HEAR ME? WE ARE NOWHERE NEAR--
HARKOV'S BONES! NOW I SEE WHERE YOU'RE TAKING US...

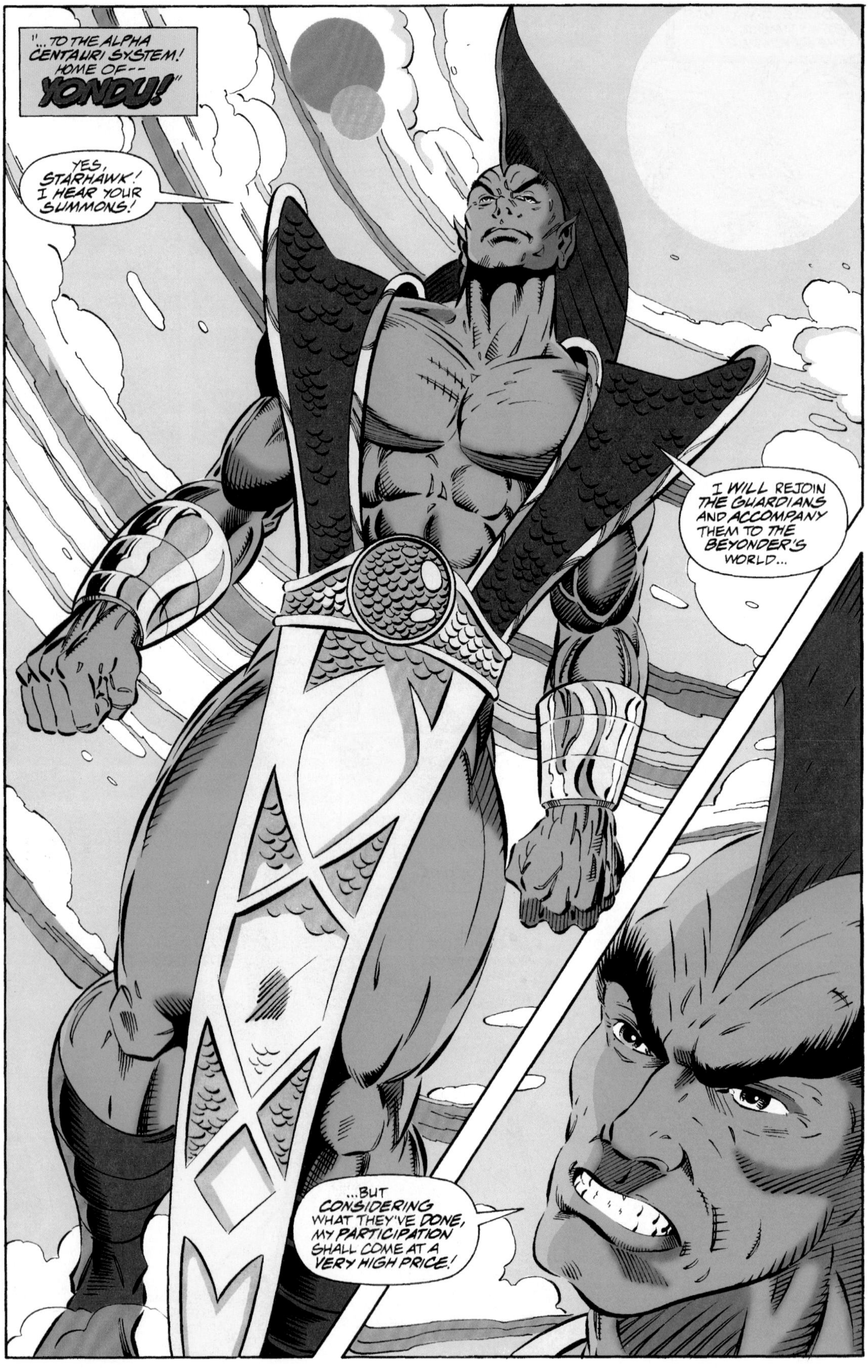
"...TO THE ALPHA CENTAURI SYSTEM! HOME OF-- YONDU!"
YES, STARHAWK! I HEAR YOUR SUMMONS!
I WILL REJOIN THE GUARDIANS AND ACCOMPANY THEM TO THE BEYONDER'S WORLD...
...BUT CONSIDERING WHAT THEY'VE DONE, MY PARTICIPATION SHALL COME AT A VERY HIGH PRICE!

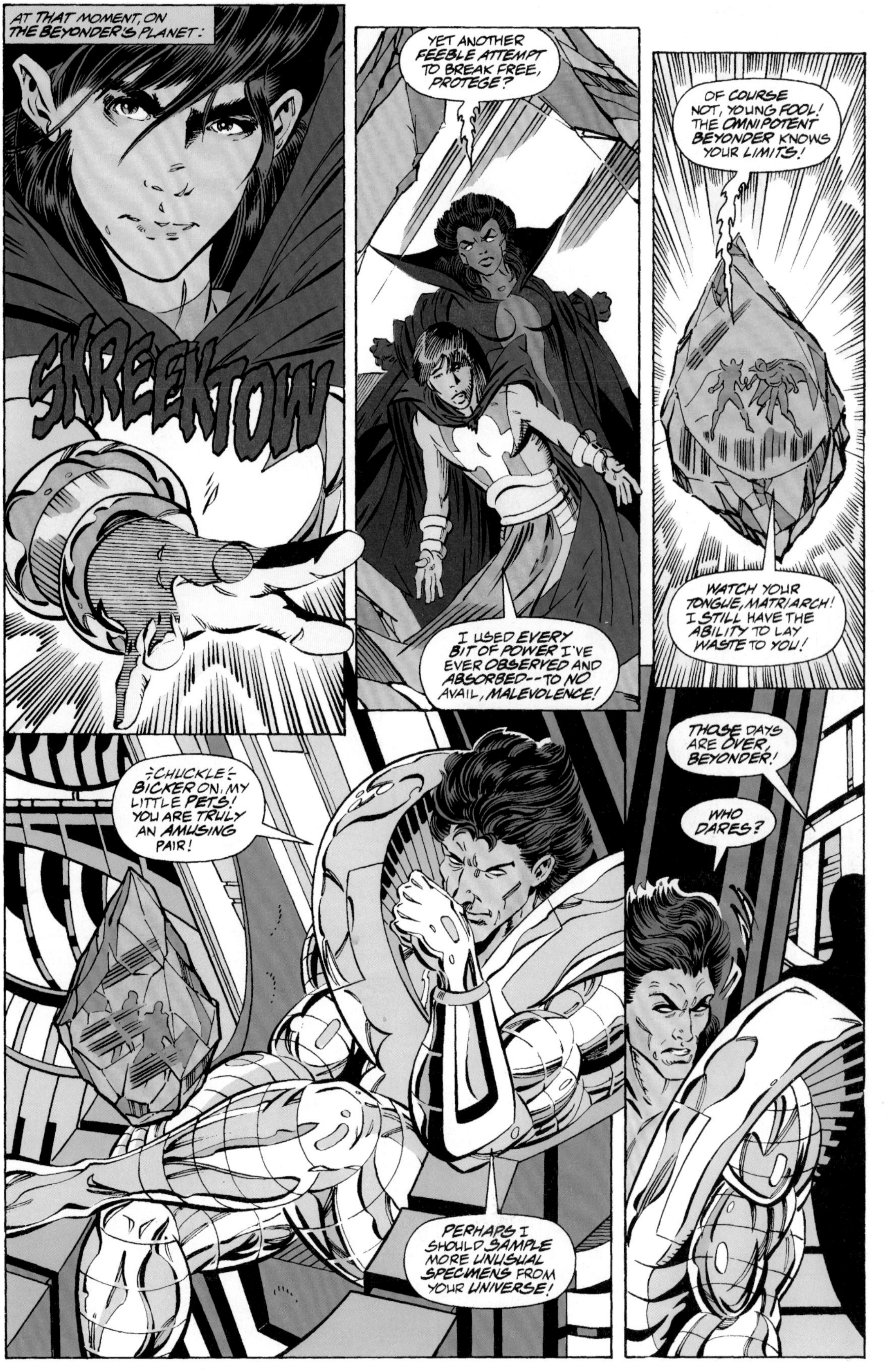
AT THAT MOMENT, ON THE BEYONDER'S PLANET:
SKREEKTOW
YET ANOTHER FEEBLE ATTEMPT TO BREAK FREE, PROTEGE?
I USED EVERY BIT OF POWER I'VE EVER OBSERVED AND ABSORBED--TO NO AVAIL, MALEVOLENCE!
OF COURSE NOT, YOUNG FOOL! THE OMNIPOTENT BEYONDER KNOWS YOUR LIMITS!
WATCH YOUR TONGUE, MATRIARCH! I STILL HAVE THE ABILITY TO LAY WASTE TO YOU!
=CHUCKLE= BICKER ON, MY LITTLE PETS! YOU ARE TRULY AN AMUSING PAIR!
PERHAPS I SHOULD SAMPLE MORE UNUSUAL SPECIMENS FROM YOUR UNIVERSE!
THOSE DAYS ARE OVER, BEYONDER!
WHO DARES?

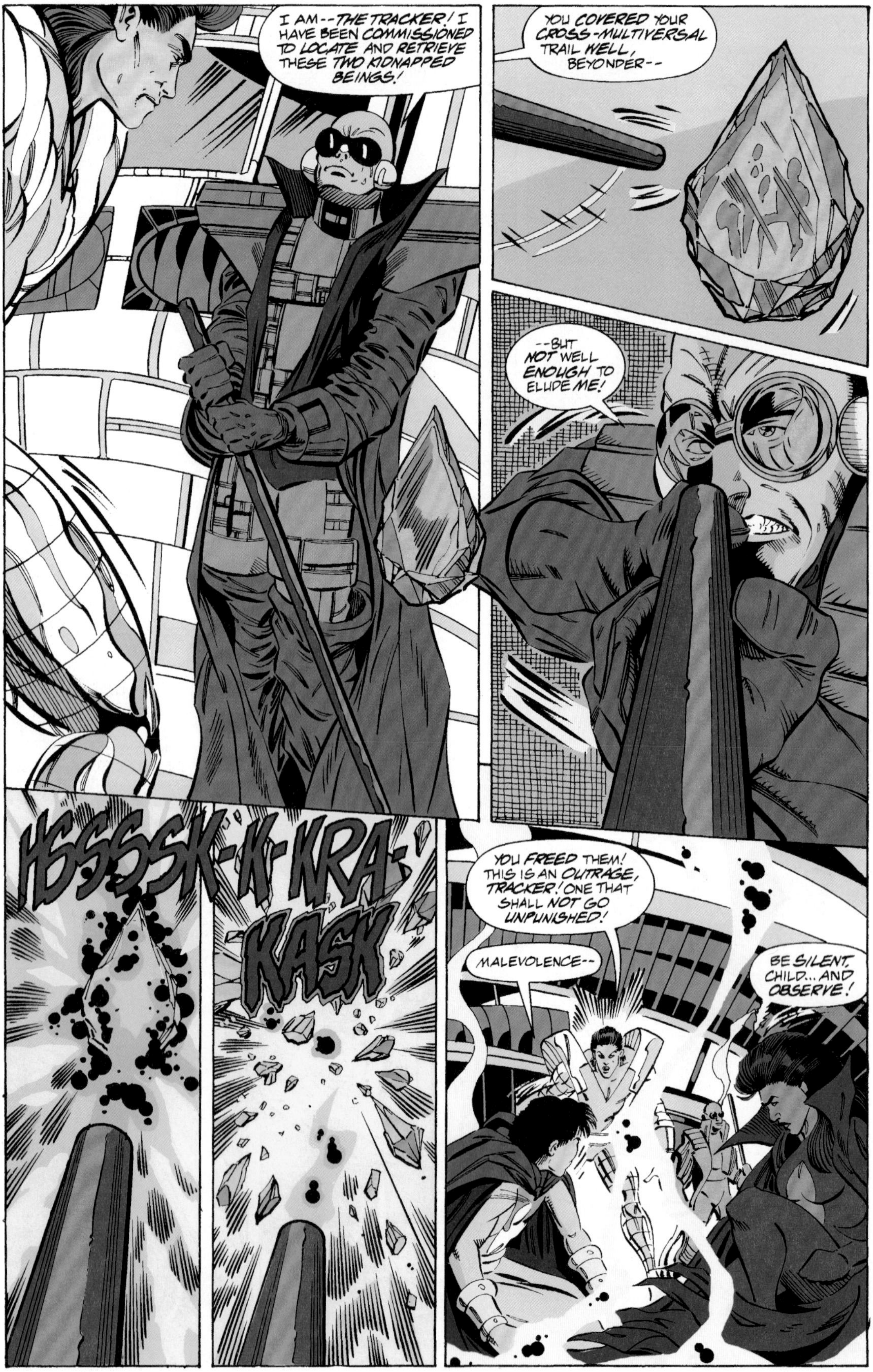
I AM--THE TRACKER! I HAVE BEEN COMMISSIONED TO LOCATE AND RETRIEVE THESE TWO KIDNAPPED BEINGS!
YOU COVERED YOUR CROSS-MULTIVERSAL TRAIL WELL, BEYONDER--
--BUT NOT WELL ENOUGH TO ELUDE ME!
HSSSSK-K-KRA-KASK
YOU FREED THEM! THIS IS AN OUTRAGE, TRACKER! ONE THAT SHALL NOT GO UNPUNISHED!
MALEVOLENCE--
BE SILENT, CHILD... AND OBSERVE!

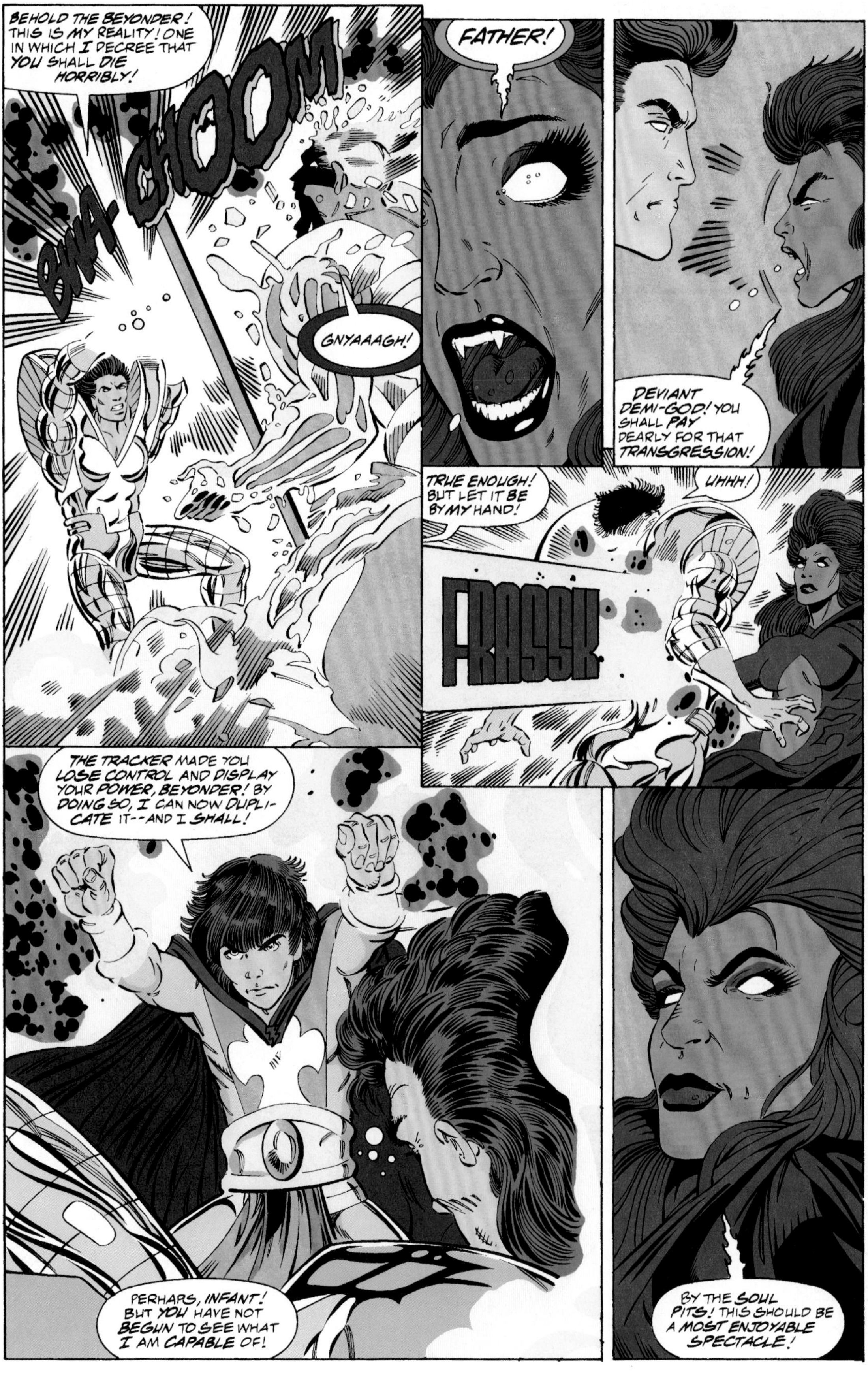

BEHOLD THE BEYONDER! THIS IS MY REALITY! ONE IN WHICH I DECREE THAT YOU SHALL DIE HORRIBLY!
BWA-CHOOM
GNYAAAGH!
FATHER!
DEVIANT DEMI-GOD! YOU SHALL PAY DEARLY FOR THAT TRANSGRESSION!
TRUE ENOUGH! BUT LET IT BE BY MY HAND!
UHHH!
FRASSK
THE TRACKER MADE YOU LOSE CONTROL AND DISPLAY YOUR POWER, BEYONDER! BY DOING SO, I CAN NOW DUPLICATE IT--AND I SHALL!
PERHAPS, INFANT! BUT YOU HAVE NOT BEGUN TO SEE WHAT I AM CAPABLE OF!
BY THE SOUL PITS! THIS SHOULD BE A MOST ENJOYABLE SPECTACLE!

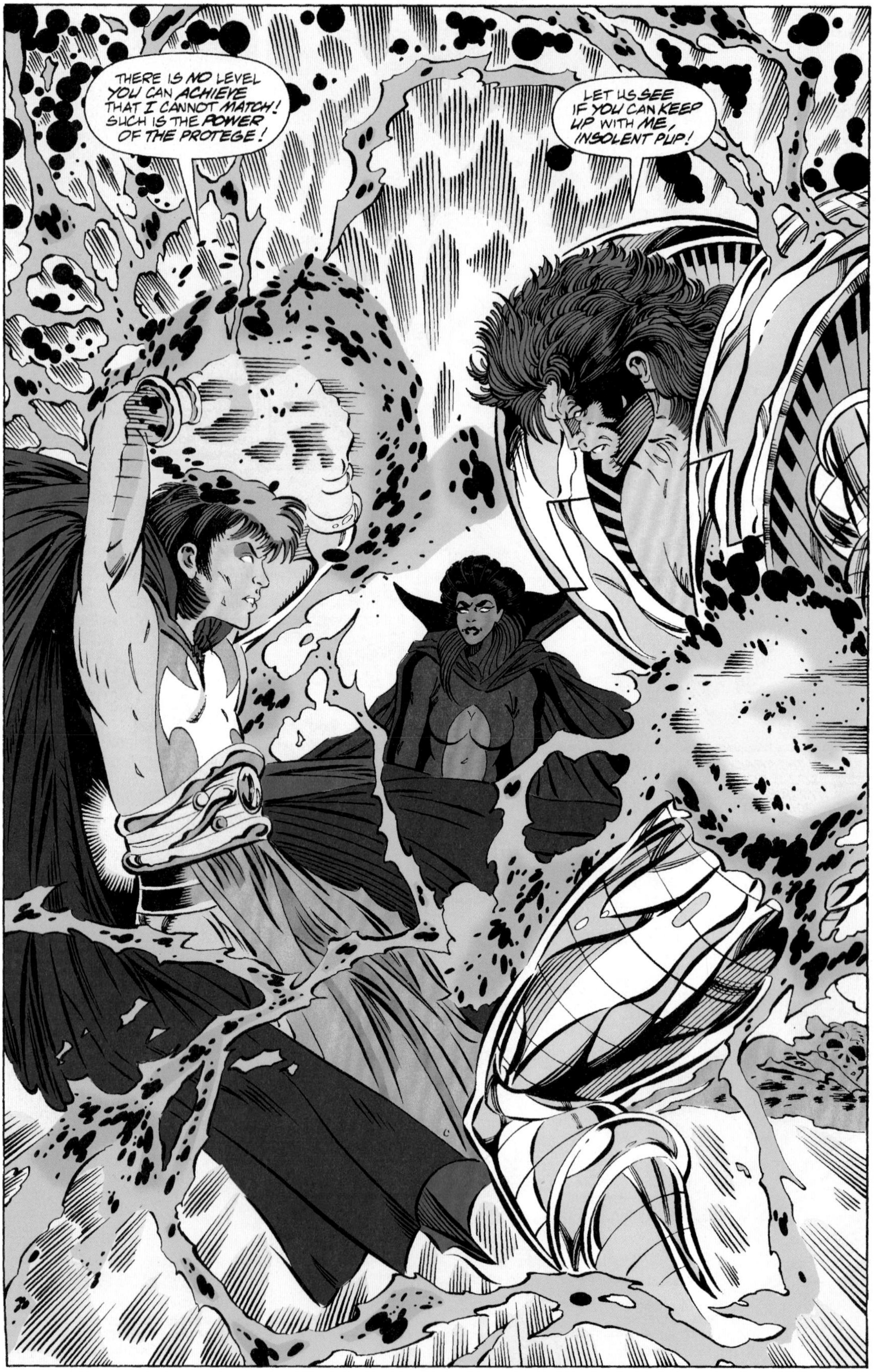
THERE IS NO LEVEL YOU CAN ACHIEVE THAT I CANNOT MATCH! SUCH IS THE POWER OF THE PROTEGE!
LET US SEE IF YOU CAN KEEP UP WITH ME, INSOLENT PUP!

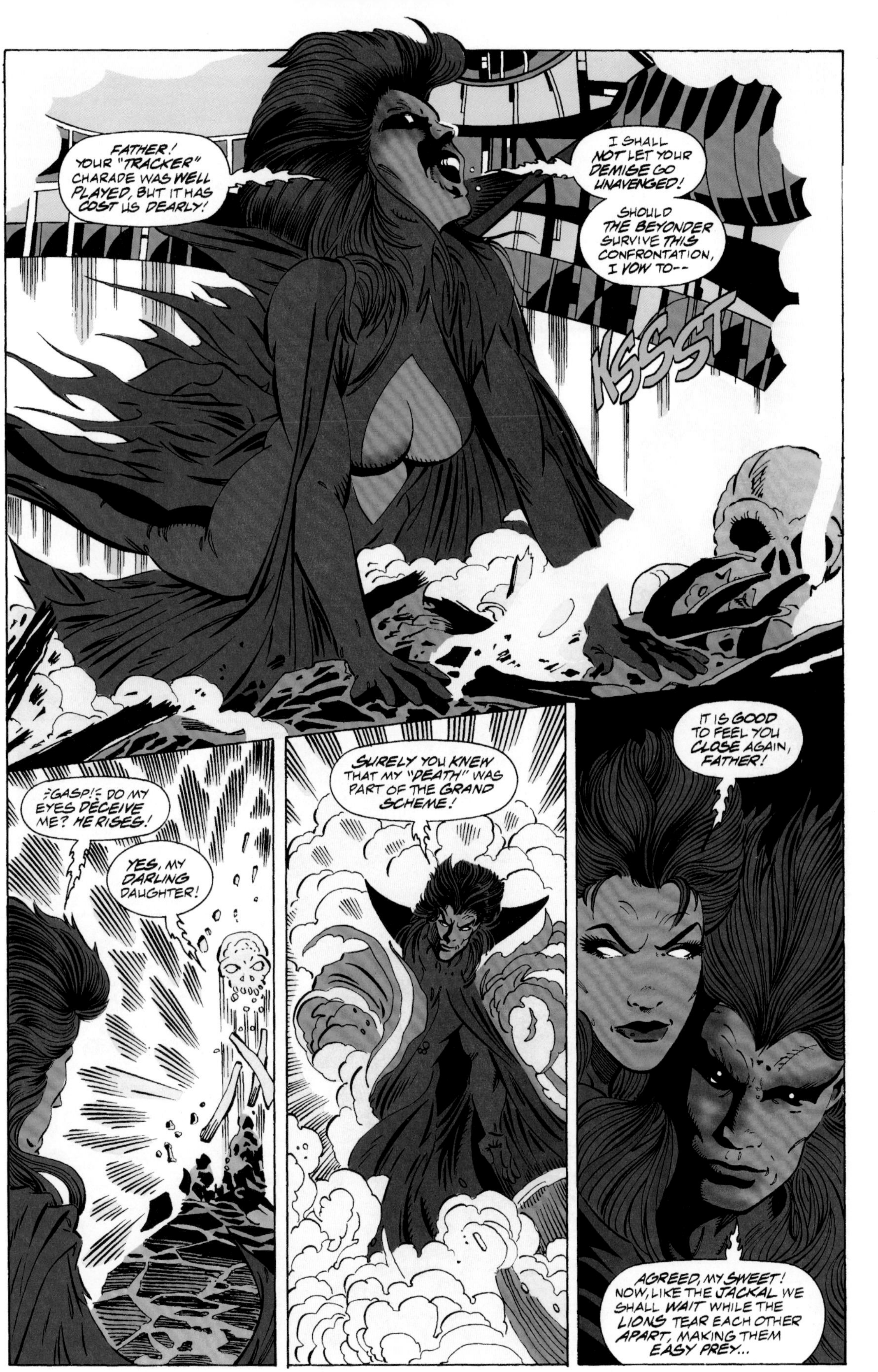
FATHER! YOUR "TRACKER" CHARADE WAS WELL PLAYED, BUT IT HAS COST US DEARLY!
I SHALL NOT LET YOUR DEMISE GO UNAVENGED!
SHOULD THE BEYONDER SURVIVE THIS CONFRONTATION, I VOW TO--
KSSST
GASP! DO MY EYES DECEIVE ME? HE RISES!
YES, MY DARLING DAUGHTER!
SURELY YOU KNEW THAT MY "DEATH" WAS PART OF THE GRAND SCHEME!
IT IS GOOD TO FEEL YOU CLOSE AGAIN, FATHER!
AGREED, MY SWEET! NOW, LIKE THE JACKAL WE SHALL WAIT WHILE THE LIONS TEAR EACH OTHER APART, MAKING THEM EASY PREY...

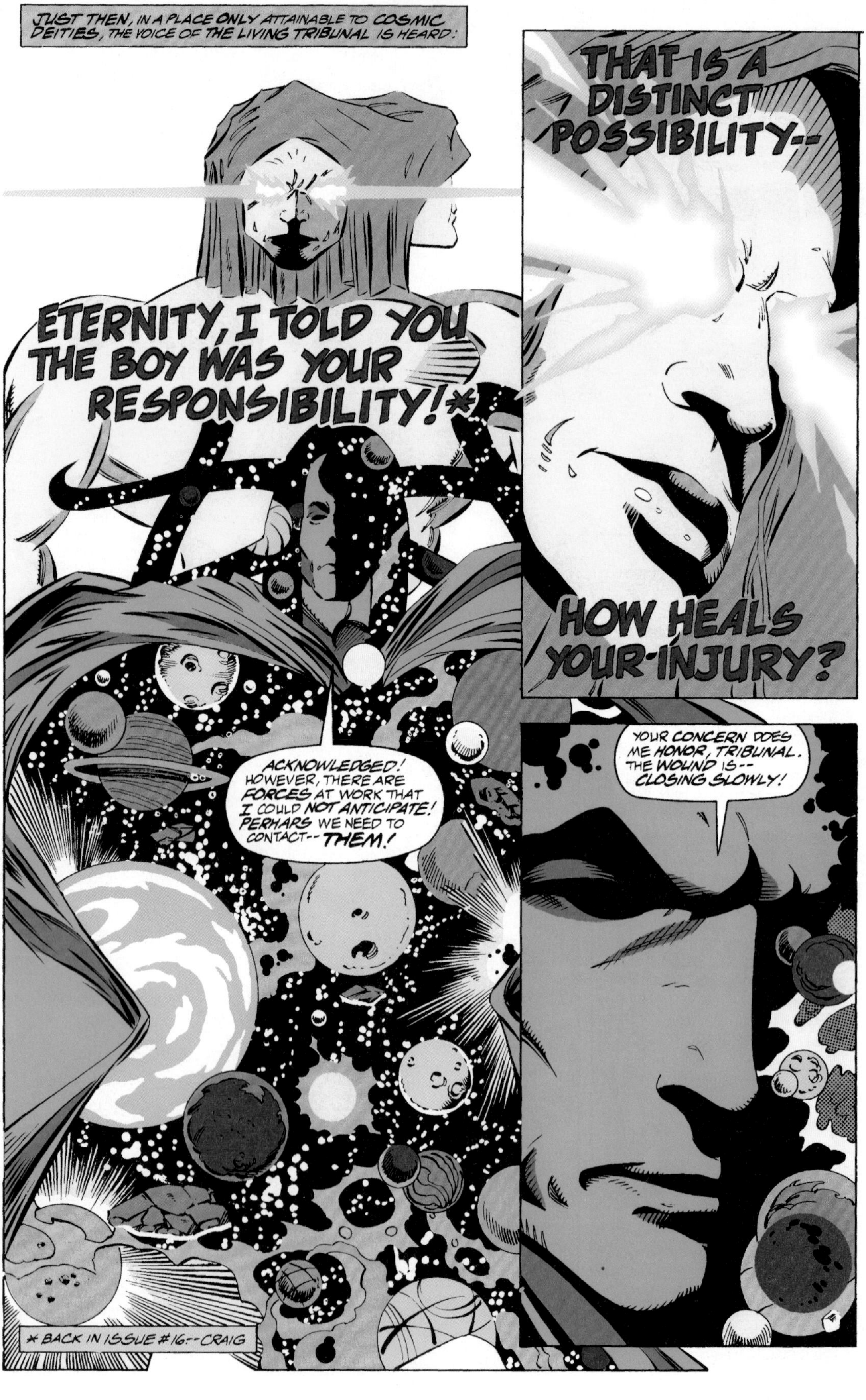
JUST THEN, IN A PLACE ONLY ATTAINABLE TO COSMIC DEITIES, THE VOICE OF THE LIVING TRIBUNAL IS HEARD:
ETERNITY, I TOLD YOU THE BOY WAS YOUR RESPONSIBILITY!*
ACKNOWLEDGED! HOWEVER, THERE ARE FORCES AT WORK THAT I COULD NOT ANTICIPATE! PERHAPS WE NEED TO CONTACT-- THEM!
* BACK IN ISSUE #16.--CRAIG
THAT IS A DISTINCT POSSIBILITY--
HOW HEALS YOUR INJURY?
YOUR CONCERN DOES ME HONOR, TRIBUNAL. THE WOUND IS-- CLOSING SLOWLY!

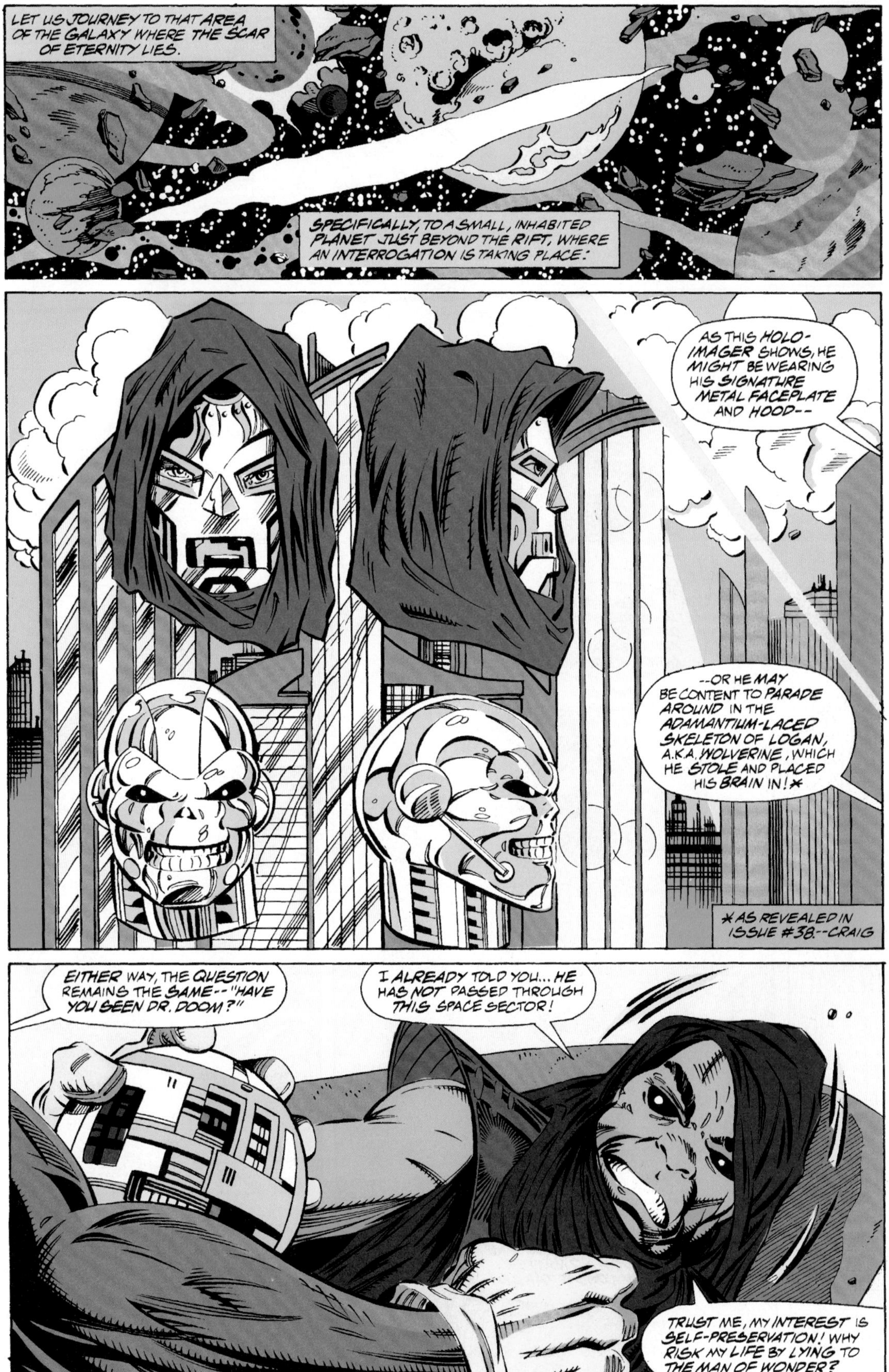
LET US JOURNEY TO THAT AREA OF THE GALAXY WHERE THE SCAR OF ETERNITY LIES.
SPECIFICALLY, TO A SMALL, INHABITED PLANET JUST BEYOND THE RIFT, WHERE AN INTERROGATION IS TAKING PLACE:
AS THIS HOLO-IMAGER SHOWS, HE MIGHT BE WEARING HIS SIGNATURE METAL FACEPLATE AND HOOD--
--OR HE MAY BE CONTENT TO PARADE AROUND IN THE ADAMANTIUM-LACED SKELETON OF LOGAN, A.K.A. WOLVERINE, WHICH HE STOLE AND PLACED HIS BRAIN IN! *
* AS REVEALED IN ISSUE #38.--CRAIG
EITHER WAY, THE QUESTION REMAINS THE SAME-- "HAVE YOU SEEN DR. DOOM?"
I ALREADY TOLD YOU... HE HAS NOT PASSED THROUGH THIS SPACE SECTOR!
TRUST ME, MY INTEREST IS SELF-PRESERVATION! WHY RISK MY LIFE BY LYING TO THE MAN OF WONDER?

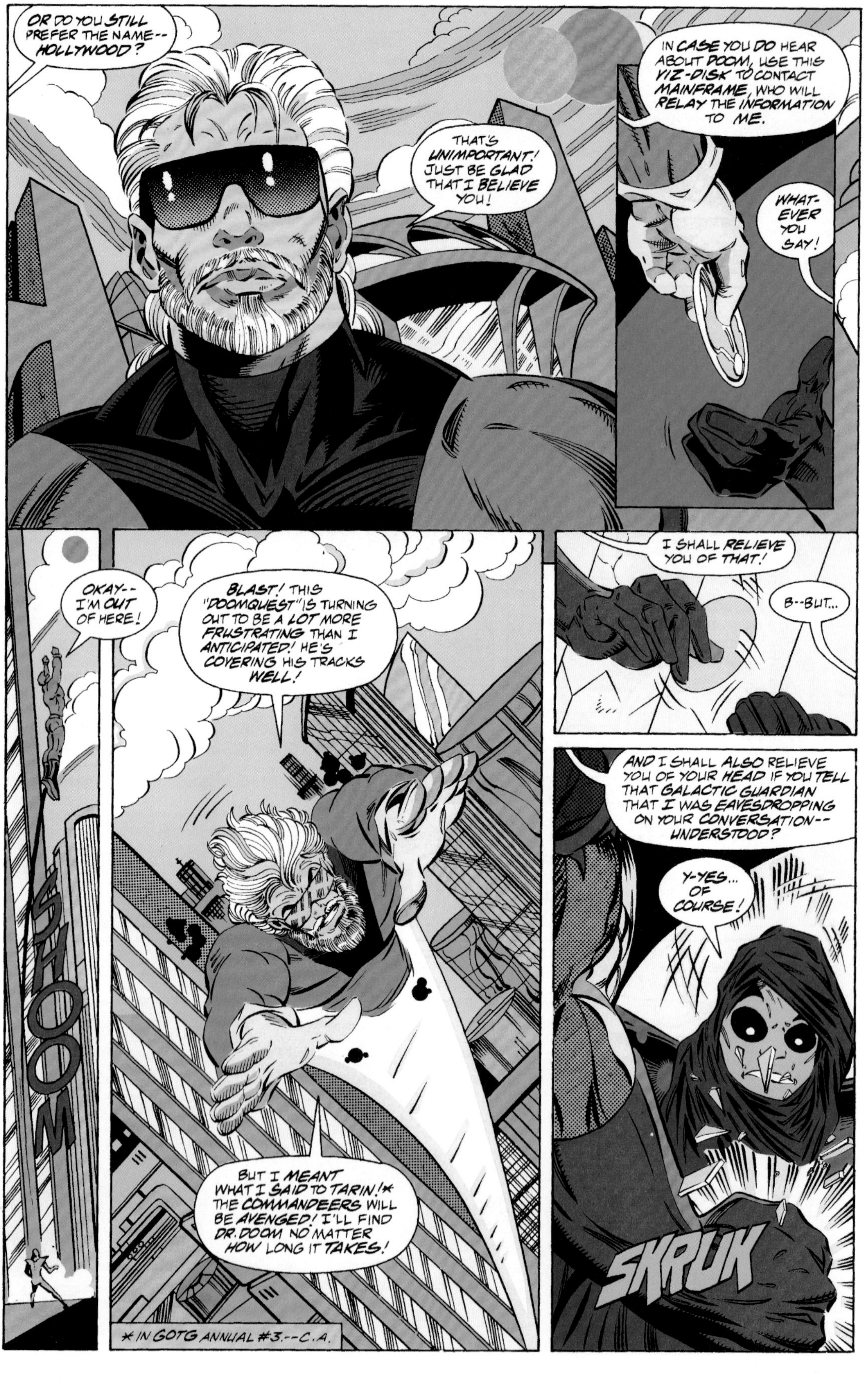
OR DO YOU STILL PREFER THE NAME-- HOLLYWOOD?
THAT'S UNIMPORTANT! JUST BE GLAD THAT I BELIEVE YOU!
IN CASE YOU DO HEAR ABOUT DOOM, USE THIS VIZ-DISK TO CONTACT MAINFRAME, WHO WILL RELAY THE INFORMATION TO ME.
WHAT-EVER YOU SAY!
OKAY-- I'M OUT OF HERE!
SHOOOM
BLAST! THIS "DOOMQUEST" IS TURNING OUT TO BE A LOT MORE FRUSTRATING THAN I ANTICIPATED! HE'S COVERING HIS TRACKS WELL!
BUT I MEANT WHAT I SAID TO TARIN!* THE COMMANDEERS WILL BE AVENGED! I'LL FIND DR. DOOM NO MATTER HOW LONG IT TAKES!
* IN GOTG ANNUAL #3.--C.A.
I SHALL RELIEVE YOU OF THAT!
B--BUT...
AND I SHALL ALSO RELIEVE YOU OF YOUR HEAD IF YOU TELL THAT GALACTIC GUARDIAN THAT I WAS EAVESDROPPING ON YOUR CONVERSATION-- UNDERSTOOD?
Y-YES... OF COURSE!
SKRUK

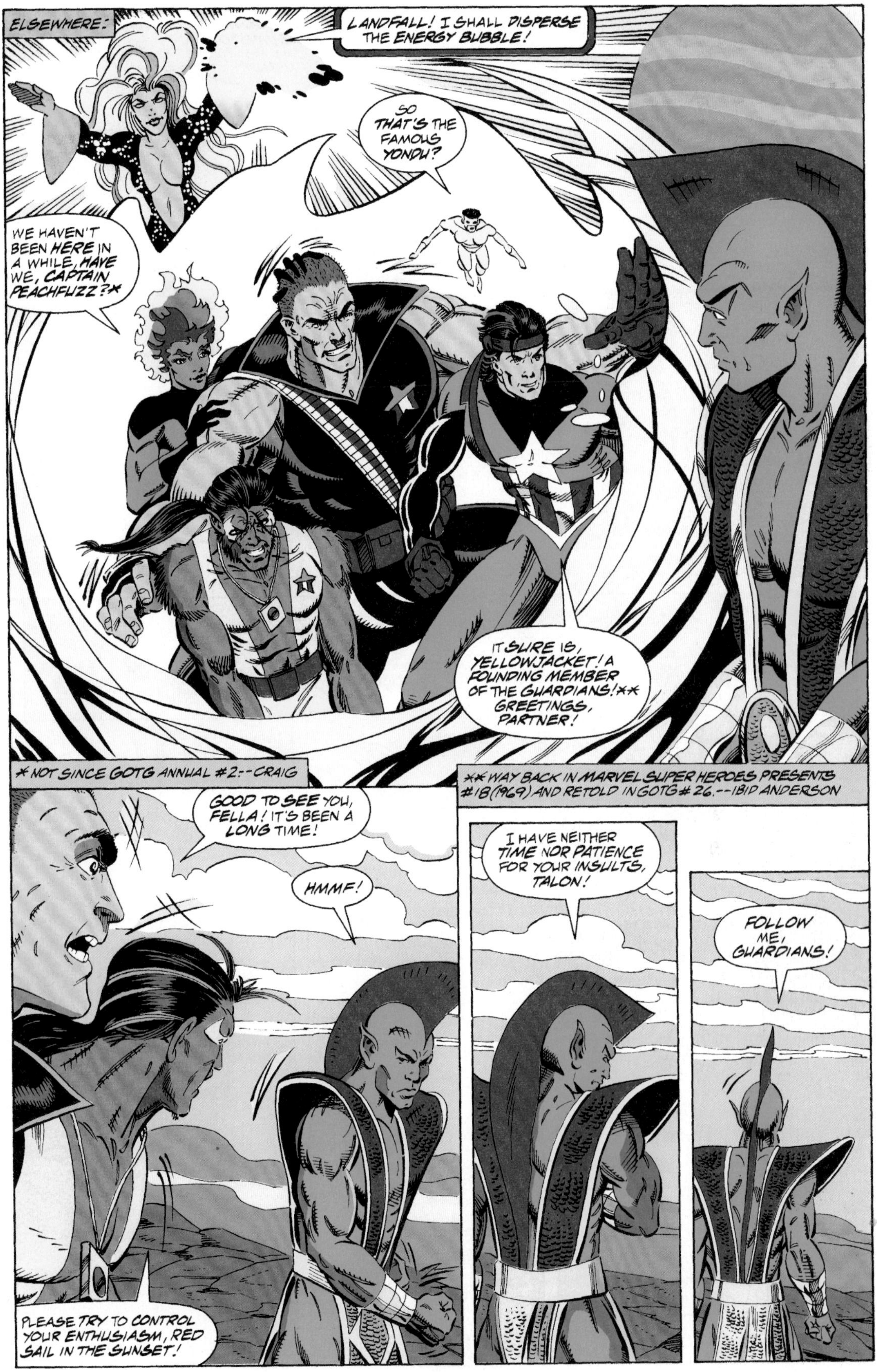
ELSEWHERE:
LANDFALL! I SHALL DISPERSE THE ENERGY BUBBLE!
SO THAT'S THE FAMOUS YONDU?
WE HAVEN'T BEEN HERE IN A WHILE, HAVE WE, CAPTAIN PEACHFUZZ?*
IT SURE IS, YELLOWJACKET! A FOUNDING MEMBER OF THE GUARDIANS!** GREETINGS, PARTNER!
* NOT SINCE GOTG ANNUAL #2.--CRAIG
** WAY BACK IN MARVEL SUPER HEROES PRESENTS #18 (1969) AND RETOLD IN GOTG #26.--IBID ANDERSON
GOOD TO SEE YOU, FELLA! IT'S BEEN A LONG TIME!
HMMF!
PLEASE TRY TO CONTROL YOUR ENTHUSIASM, RED SAIL IN THE SUNSET!
I HAVE NEITHER TIME NOR PATIENCE FOR YOUR INSULTS, TALON!
FOLLOW ME, GUARDIANS!

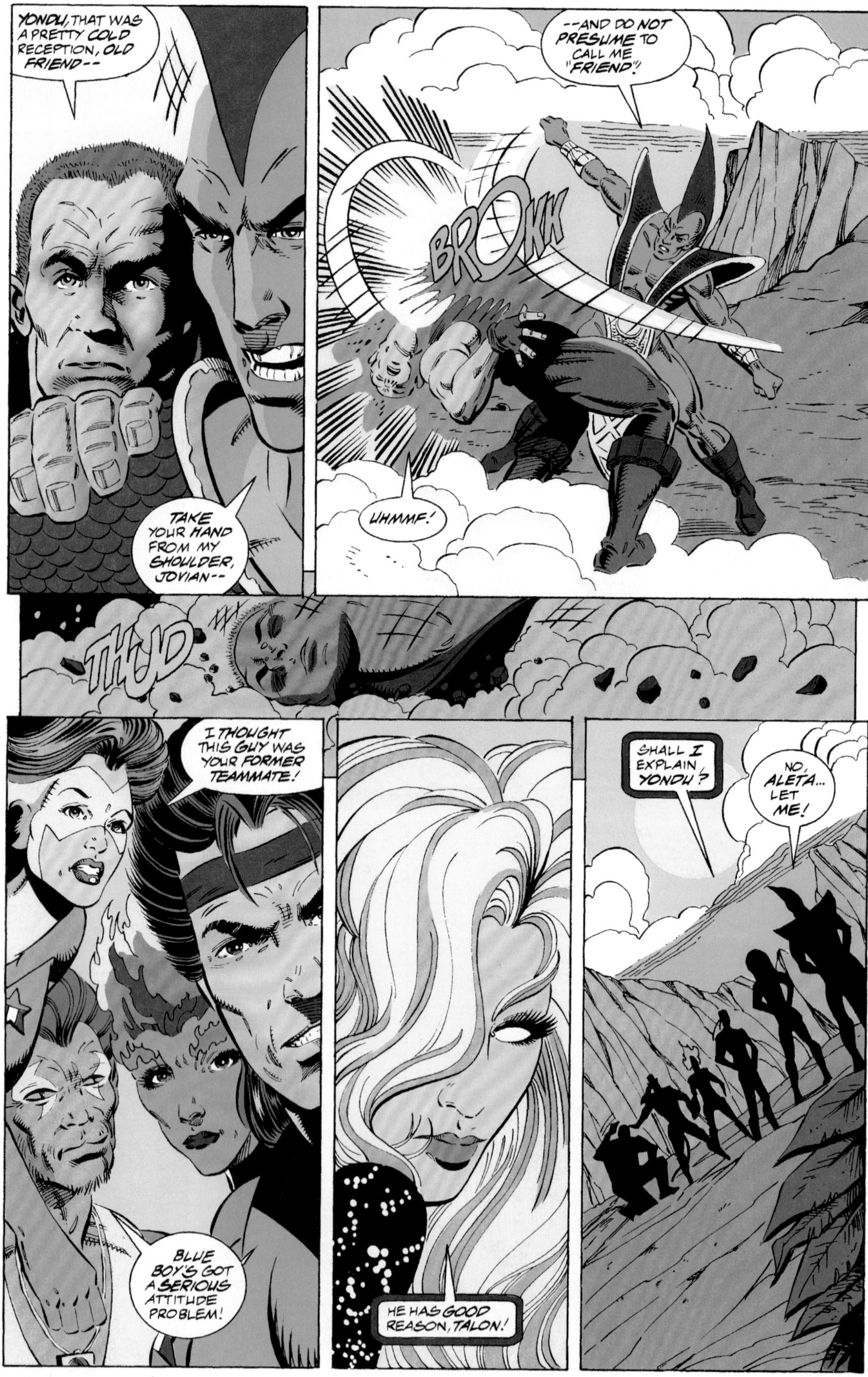
YONDU, THAT WAS A PRETTY COLD RECEPTION, OLD FRIEND--
TAKE YOUR HAND FROM MY SHOULDER, JOVIAN--
--AND DO NOT PRESUME TO CALL ME "FRIEND"!
BRONK
UHMMF!
THUD
I THOUGHT THIS GUY WAS YOUR FORMER TEAMMATE!
BLUE BOY'S GOT A SERIOUS ATTITUDE PROBLEM!
HE HAS GOOD REASON, TALON!
SHALL I EXPLAIN YONDU?
NO, ALETA... LET ME!

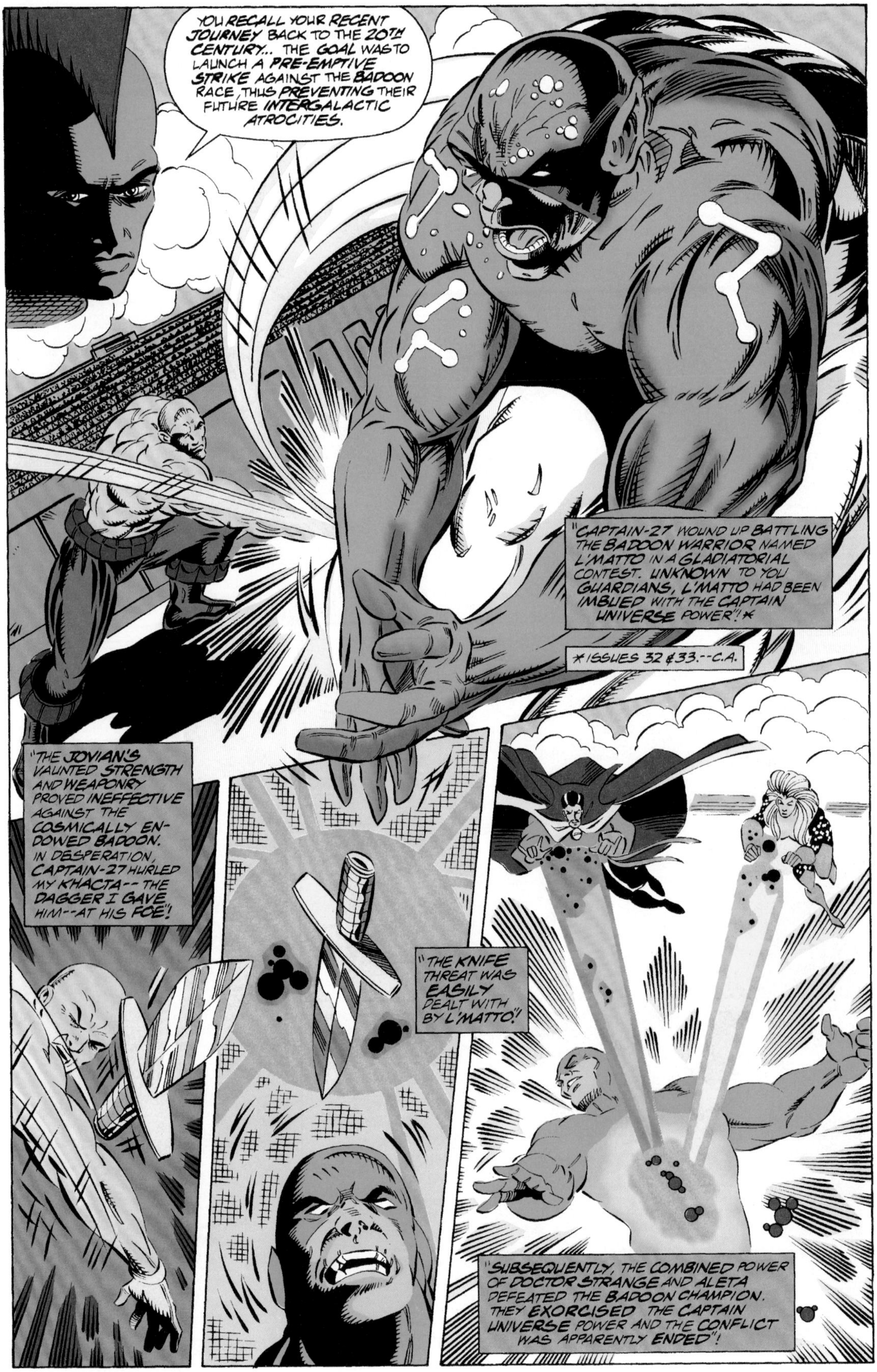
YOU RECALL YOUR RECENT JOURNEY BACK TO THE 20TH CENTURY... THE GOAL WAS TO LAUNCH A PRE-EMPTIVE STRIKE AGAINST THE BADOON RACE, THUS PREVENTING THEIR FUTURE INTERGALACTIC ATROCITIES.
"CAPTAIN-27 WOUND UP BATTLING THE BADOON WARRIOR NAMED L'MATTO IN A GLADIATORIAL CONTEST. UNKNOWN TO YOU GUARDIANS, L'MATTO HAD BEEN IMBUED WITH THE CAPTAIN UNIVERSE POWER"!*
*ISSUES 32 & 33.--C.A.
"THE JOVIAN'S VAUNTED STRENGTH AND WEAPONRY PROVED INEFFECTIVE AGAINST THE COSMICALLY ENDOWED BADOON. IN DESPERATION, CAPTAIN-27 HURLED MY KHACTA-- THE DAGGER I GAVE HIM--AT HIS FOE"!
"THE KNIFE THREAT WAS EASILY DEALT WITH BY L'MATTO"!
"SUBSEQUENTLY, THE COMBINED POWER OF DOCTOR STRANGE AND ALETA DEFEATED THE BADOON CHAMPION. THEY EXORCISED THE CAPTAIN UNIVERSE POWER AND THE CONFLICT WAS APPARENTLY ENDED"!

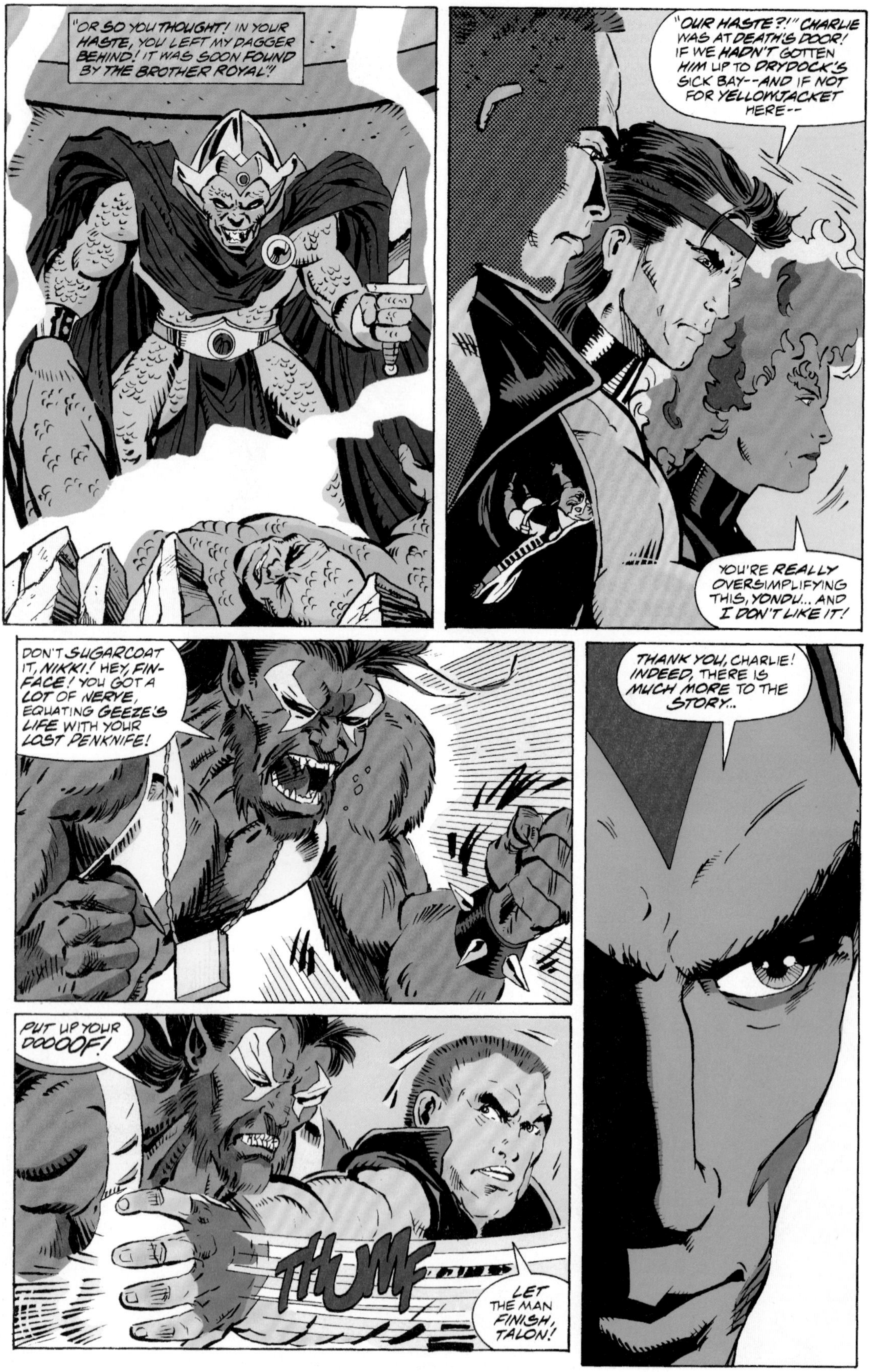
"OR SO YOU THOUGHT! IN YOUR HASTE, YOU LEFT MY DAGGER BEHIND! IT WAS SOON FOUND BY THE BROTHER ROYAL"!
"OUR HASTE?!" CHARLIE WAS AT DEATH'S DOOR! IF WE HADN'T GOTTEN HIM UP TO DRYDOCK'S SICK BAY--AND IF NOT FOR YELLOWJACKET HERE--
YOU'RE REALLY OVERSIMPLIFYING THIS, YONDU... AND I DON'T LIKE IT!
DON'T SUGARCOAT IT, NIKKI! HEY, FIN-FACE! YOU GOT A LOT OF NERVE, EQUATING GEEZE'S LIFE WITH YOUR LOST PENKNIFE!
PUT UP YOUR DOOOOF!
THUMF
LET THE MAN FINISH, TALON!
THANK YOU, CHARLIE! INDEED, THERE IS MUCH MORE TO THE STORY...

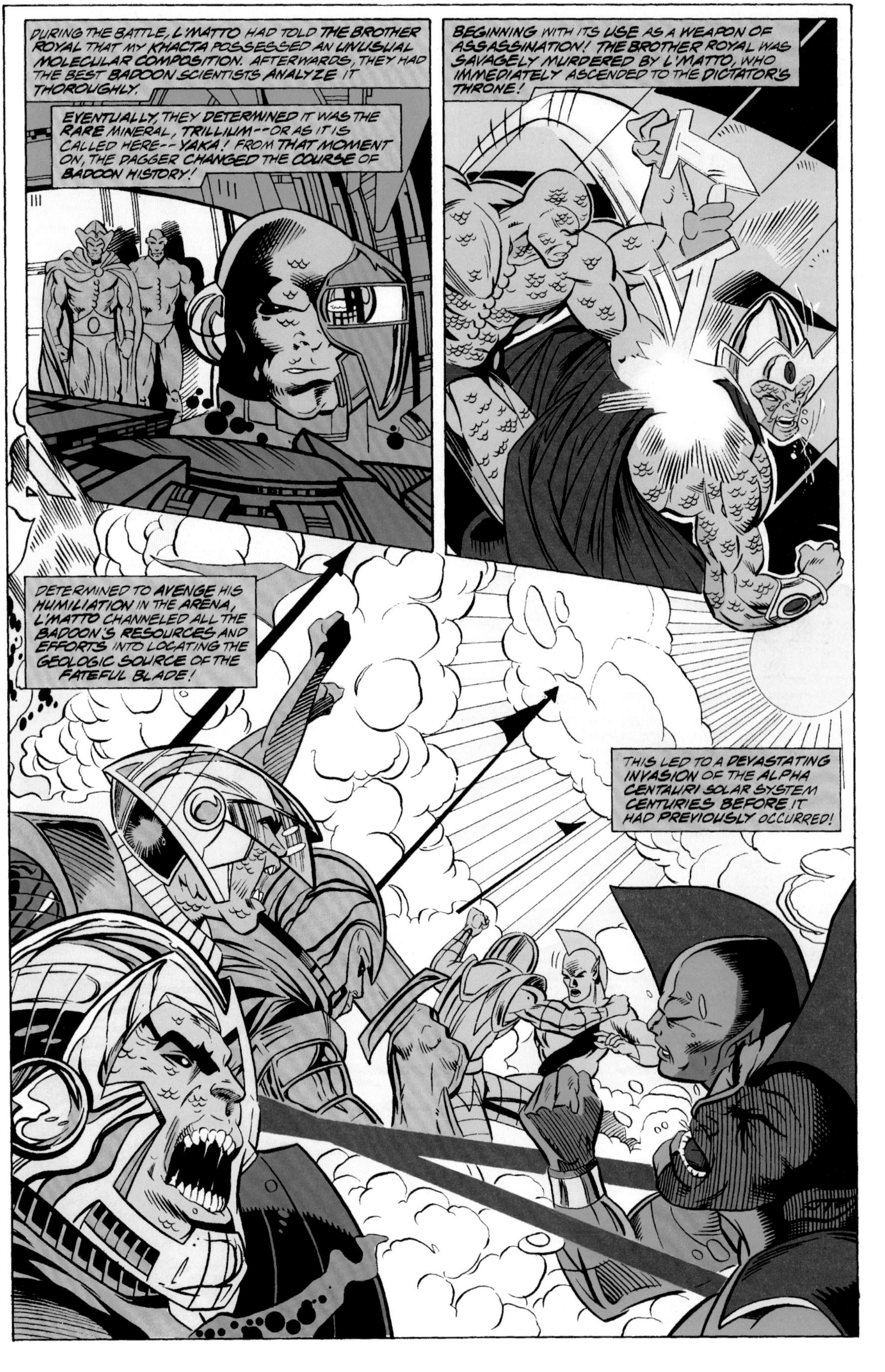
DURING THE BATTLE, L'MATTO HAD TOLD THE BROTHER ROYAL THAT MY KHACTA POSSESSED AN UNUSUAL MOLECULAR COMPOSITION. AFTERWARDS, THEY HAD THE BEST BADOON SCIENTISTS ANALYZE IT THOROUGHLY.
EVENTUALLY, THEY DETERMINED IT WAS THE RARE MINERAL, TRILLIUM--OR AS IT IS CALLED HERE--YAKA! FROM THAT MOMENT ON, THE DAGGER CHANGED THE COURSE OF BADOON HISTORY!
BEGINNING WITH ITS USE AS A WEAPON OF ASSASSINATION! THE BROTHER ROYAL WAS SAVAGELY MURDERED BY L'MATTO, WHO IMMEDIATELY ASCENDED TO THE DICTATOR'S THRONE!
DETERMINED TO AVENGE HIS HUMILIATION IN THE ARENA, L'MATTO CHANNELED ALL THE BADOON'S RESOURCES AND EFFORTS INTO LOCATING THE GEOLOGIC SOURCE OF THE FATEFUL BLADE!
THIS LED TO A DEVASTATING INVASION OF THE ALPHA CENTAURI SOLAR SYSTEM CENTURIES BEFORE IT HAD PREVIOUSLY OCCURRED!

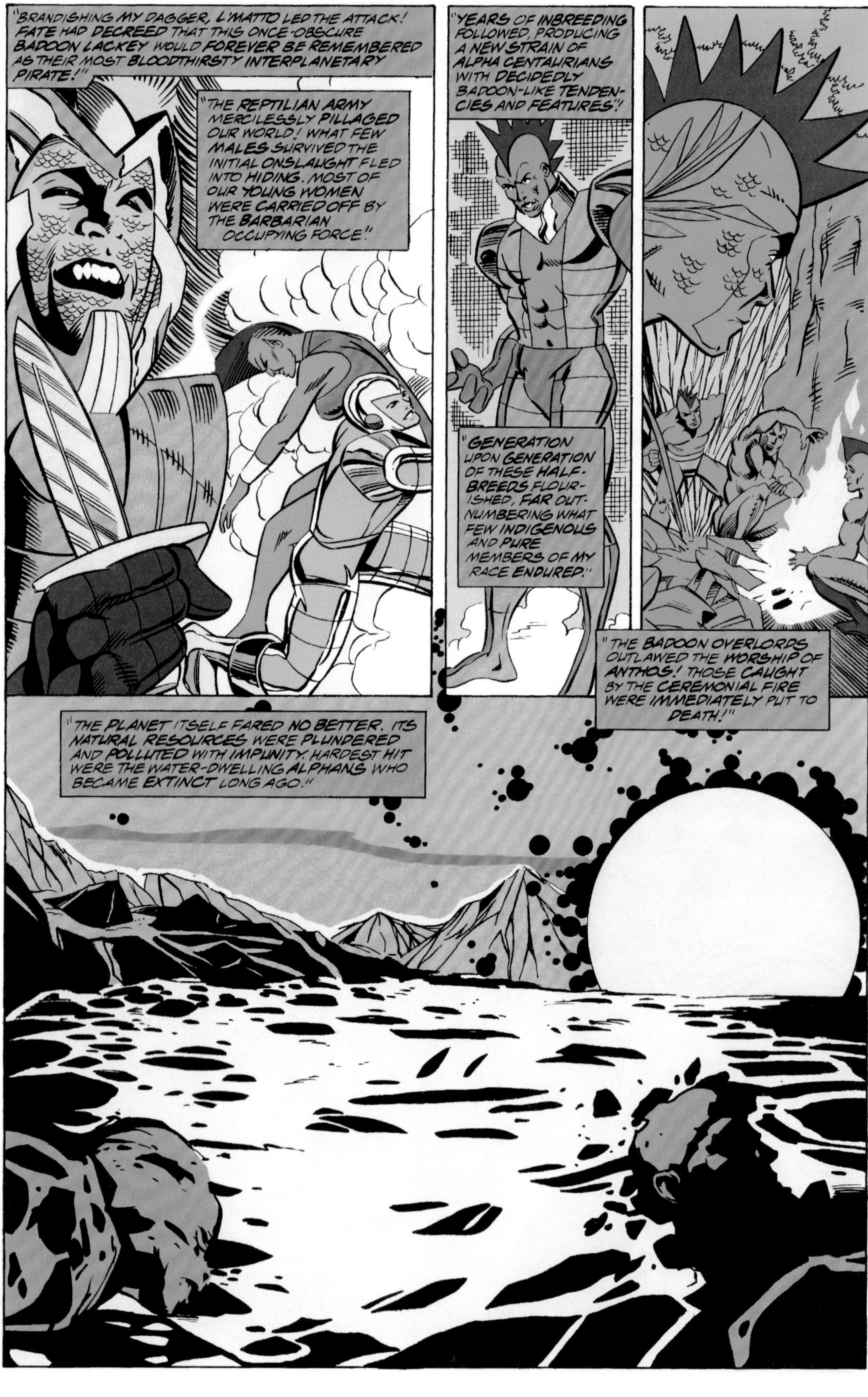
"BRANDISHING MY DAGGER, L'MATTO LED THE ATTACK! FATE HAD DECREED THAT THIS ONCE-OBSCURE BADOON LACKEY WOULD FOREVER BE REMEMBERED AS THEIR MOST BLOODTHIRSTY INTERPLANETARY PIRATE!"
"THE REPTILIAN ARMY MERCILESSLY PILLAGED OUR WORLD! WHAT FEW MALES SURVIVED THE INITIAL ONSLAUGHT FLED INTO HIDING. MOST OF OUR YOUNG WOMEN WERE CARRIED OFF BY THE BARBARIAN OCCUPYING FORCE!"
"YEARS OF INBREEDING FOLLOWED, PRODUCING A NEW STRAIN OF ALPHA CENTAURIANS WITH DECIDEDLY BADOON-LIKE TENDENCIES AND FEATURES!"
"GENERATION UPON GENERATION OF THESE HALF-BREEDS FLOURISHED, FAR OUTNUMBERING WHAT FEW INDIGENOUS AND PURE MEMBERS OF MY RACE ENDURED."
"THE BADOON OVERLORDS OUTLAWED THE WORSHIP OF ANTHOS! THOSE CAUGHT BY THE CEREMONIAL FIRE WERE IMMEDIATELY PUT TO DEATH!"
"THE PLANET ITSELF FARED NO BETTER. ITS NATURAL RESOURCES WERE PLUNDERED AND POLLUTED WITH IMPUNITY. HARDEST HIT WERE THE WATER-DWELLING ALPHANS WHO BECAME EXTINCT LONG AGO."

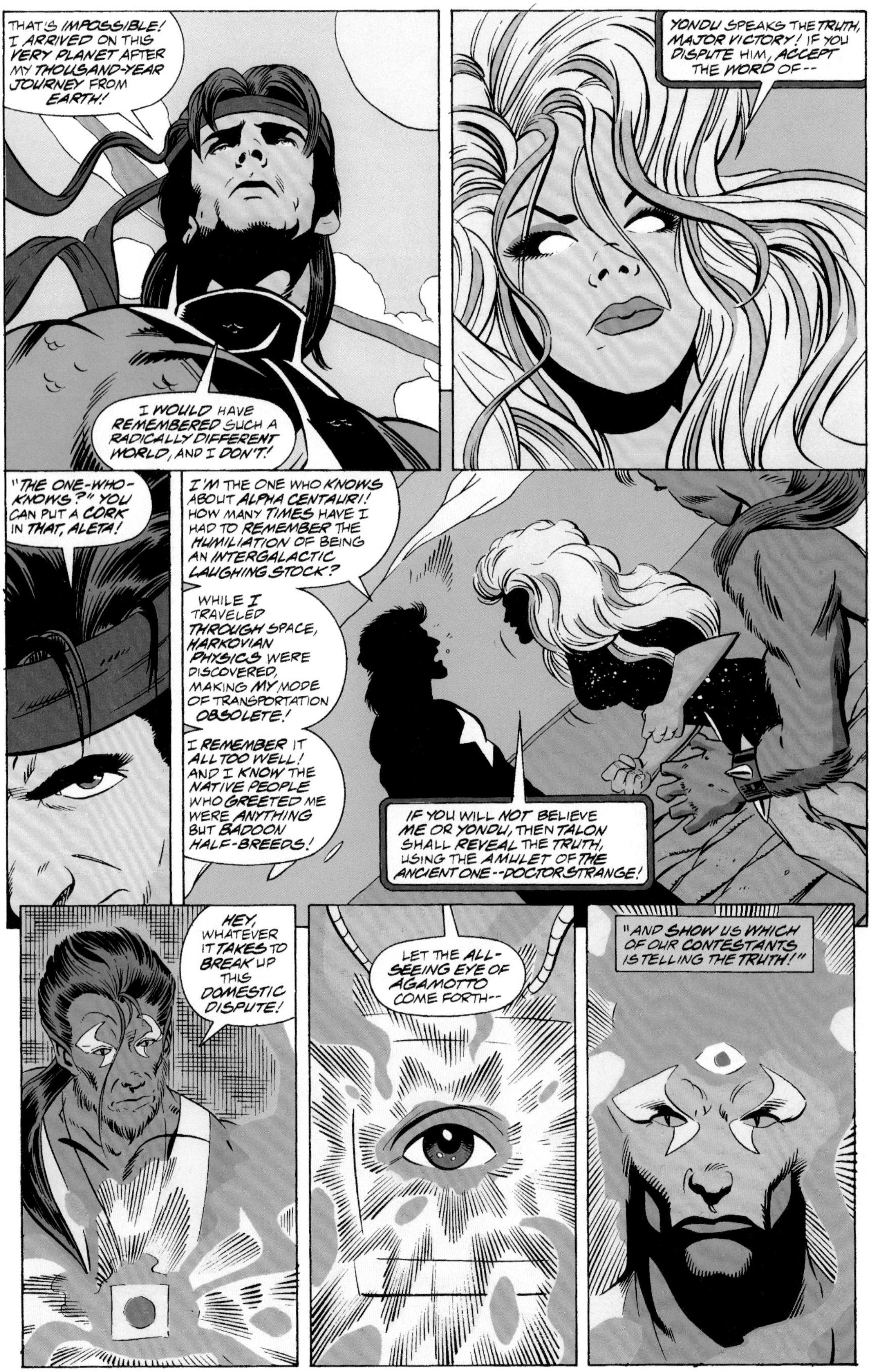
THAT'S IMPOSSIBLE! I ARRIVED ON THIS VERY PLANET AFTER MY THOUSAND-YEAR JOURNEY FROM EARTH!
I WOULD HAVE REMEMBERED SUCH A RADICALLY DIFFERENT WORLD, AND I DON'T!
YONDU SPEAKS THE TRUTH, MAJOR VICTORY! IF YOU DISPUTE HIM, ACCEPT THE WORD OF --
"THE ONE-WHO-KNOWS?" YOU CAN PUT A CORK IN THAT, ALETA!
I'M THE ONE WHO KNOWS ABOUT ALPHA CENTAURI! HOW MANY TIMES HAVE I HAD TO REMEMBER THE HUMILIATION OF BEING AN INTERGALACTIC LAUGHING STOCK?
WHILE I TRAVELED THROUGH SPACE, HARKOVIAN PHYSICS WERE DISCOVERED, MAKING MY MODE OF TRANSPORTATION OBSOLETE!
I REMEMBER IT ALL TOO WELL! AND I KNOW THE NATIVE PEOPLE WHO GREETED ME WERE ANYTHING BUT BADOON HALF-BREEDS!
IF YOU WILL NOT BELIEVE ME OR YONDU, THEN TALON SHALL REVEAL THE TRUTH, USING THE AMULET OF THE ANCIENT ONE -- DOCTOR STRANGE!
HEY, WHATEVER IT TAKES TO BREAK UP THIS DOMESTIC DISPUTE!
LET THE ALL-SEEING EYE OF AGAMOTTO COME FORTH --
"AND SHOW US WHICH OF OUR CONTESTANTS IS TELLING THE TRUTH!"

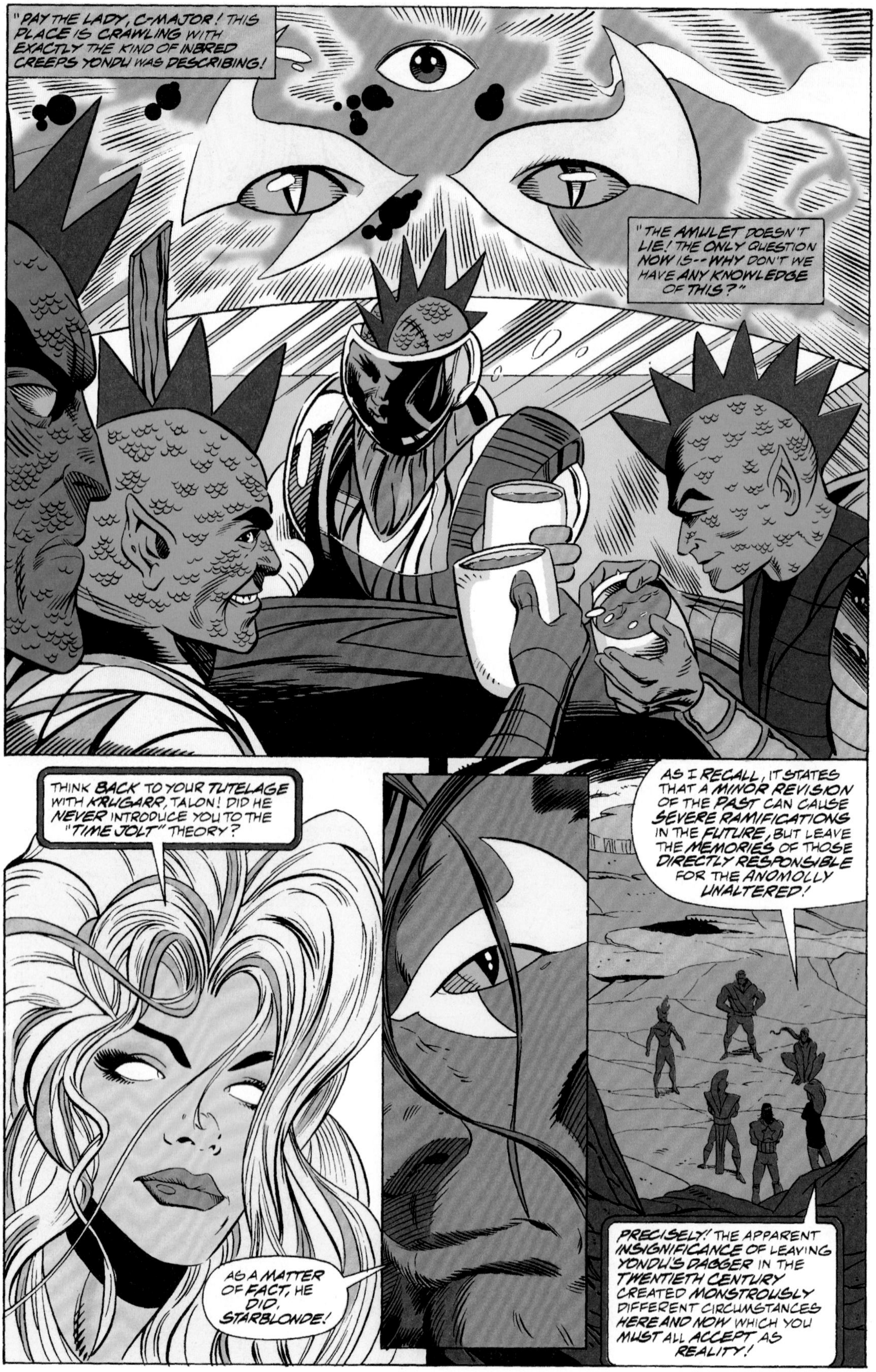
"PAY THE LADY, C-MAJOR! THIS PLACE IS CRAWLING WITH EXACTLY THE KIND OF INBRED CREEPS YONDU WAS DESCRIBING!
"THE AMULET DOESN'T LIE! THE ONLY QUESTION NOW IS-- WHY DON'T WE HAVE ANY KNOWLEDGE OF THIS?"
THINK BACK TO YOUR TUTELAGE WITH KRUGARR, TALON! DID HE NEVER INTRODUCE YOU TO THE "TIME JOLT" THEORY?
AS A MATTER OF FACT, HE DID, STARBLONDE!
AS I RECALL, IT STATES THAT A MINOR REVISION OF THE PAST CAN CAUSE SEVERE RAMIFICATIONS IN THE FUTURE, BUT LEAVE THE MEMORIES OF THOSE DIRECTLY RESPONSIBLE FOR THE ANOMOLLY UNALTERED!
PRECISELY! THE APPARENT INSIGNIFICANCE OF LEAVING YONDU'S DAGGER IN THE TWENTIETH CENTURY CREATED MONSTROUSLY DIFFERENT CIRCUMSTANCES HERE AND NOW WHICH YOU MUST ALL ACCEPT AS REALITY!

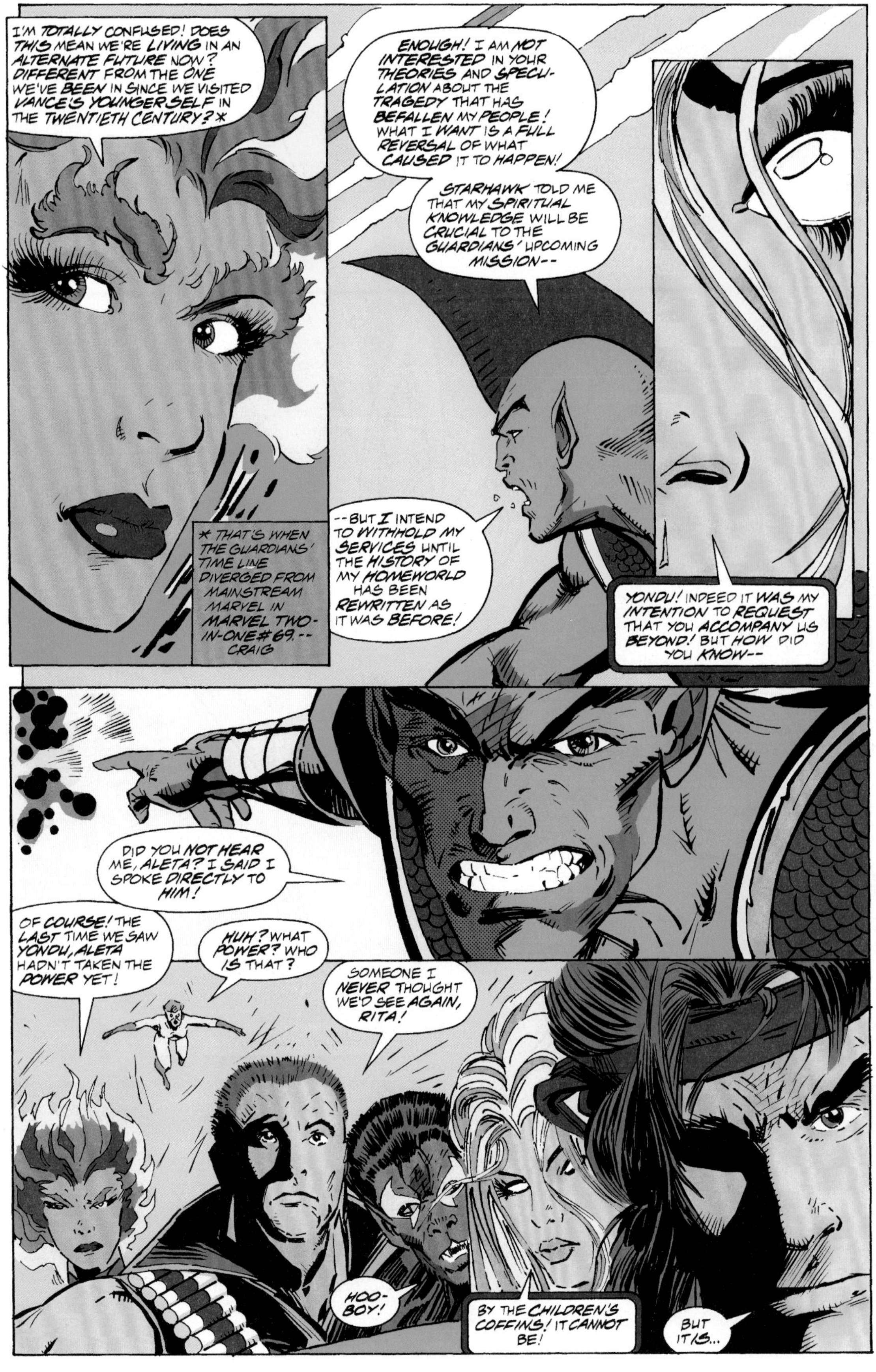
I'M TOTALLY CONFUSED! DOES THIS MEAN WE'RE LIVING IN AN ALTERNATE FUTURE NOW? DIFFERENT FROM THE ONE WE'VE BEEN IN SINCE WE VISITED VANCE'S YOUNGER SELF IN THE TWENTIETH CENTURY? *
* THAT'S WHEN THE GUARDIANS' TIME LINE DIVERGED FROM MAINSTREAM MARVEL IN MARVEL TWO-IN-ONE # 69. --CRAIG
ENOUGH! I AM NOT INTERESTED IN YOUR THEORIES AND SPECULATION ABOUT THE TRAGEDY THAT HAS BEFALLEN MY PEOPLE! WHAT I WANT IS A FULL REVERSAL OF WHAT CAUSED IT TO HAPPEN!
STARHAWK TOLD ME THAT MY SPIRITUAL KNOWLEDGE WILL BE CRUCIAL TO THE GUARDIANS' UPCOMING MISSION--
--BUT I INTEND TO WITHHOLD MY SERVICES UNTIL THE HISTORY OF MY HOMEWORLD HAS BEEN REWRITTEN AS IT WAS BEFORE!
YONDU! INDEED IT WAS MY INTENTION TO REQUEST THAT YOU ACCOMPANY US BEYOND! BUT HOW DID YOU KNOW--
DID YOU NOT HEAR ME, ALETA? I SAID I SPOKE DIRECTLY TO HIM!
OF COURSE! THE LAST TIME WE SAW YONDU, ALETA HADN'T TAKEN THE POWER YET!
HUH? WHAT POWER? WHO IS THAT?
SOMEONE I NEVER THOUGHT WE'D SEE AGAIN, RITA!
HOO-BOY!
BY THE CHILDREN'S COFFINS! IT CANNOT BE!
BUT IT IS...

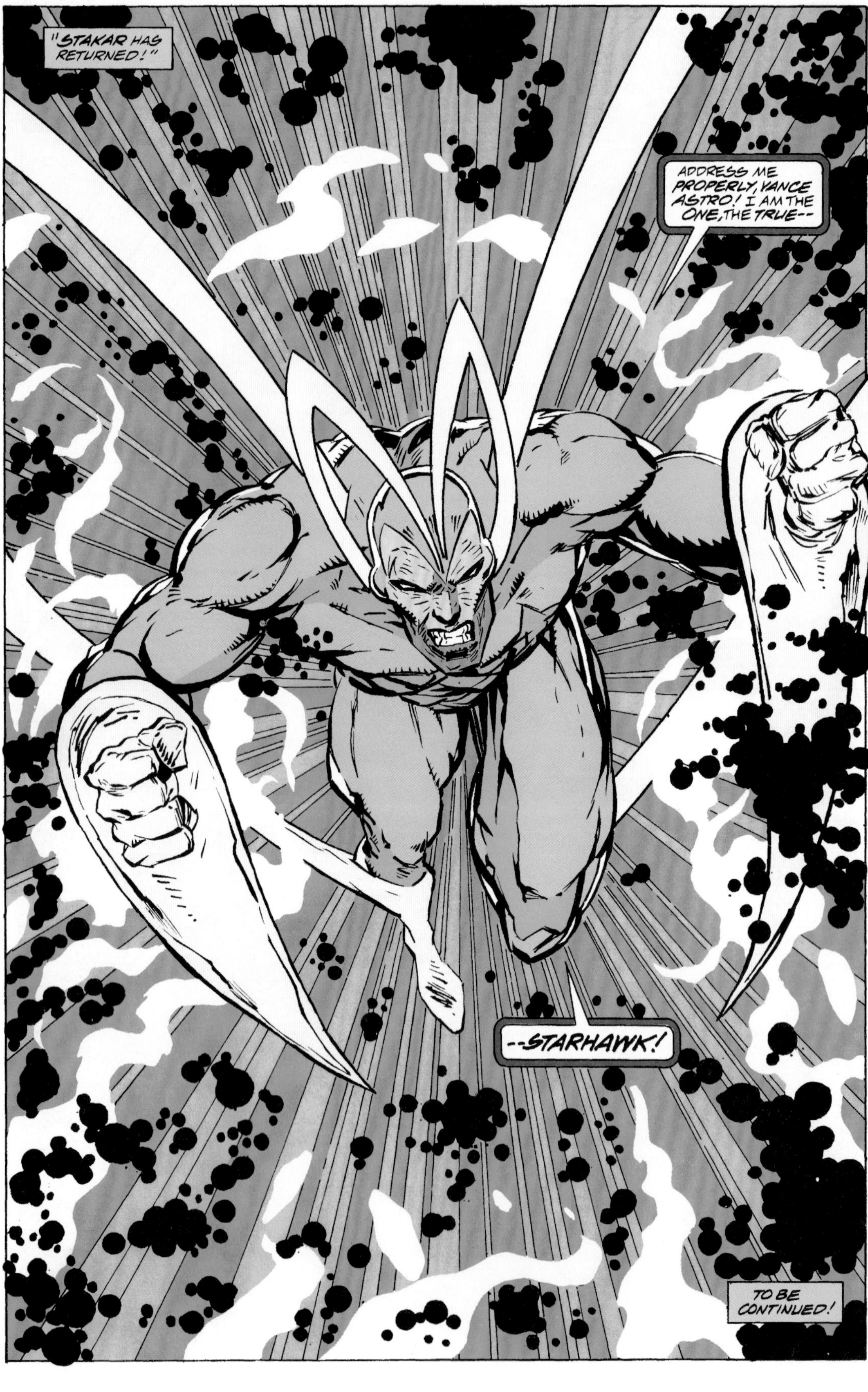
"STAKAR HAS RETURNED!"
ADDRESS ME PROPERLY, VANCE ASTRO! I AM THE ONE, THE TRUE--
--STARHAWK!
TO BE CONTINUED!

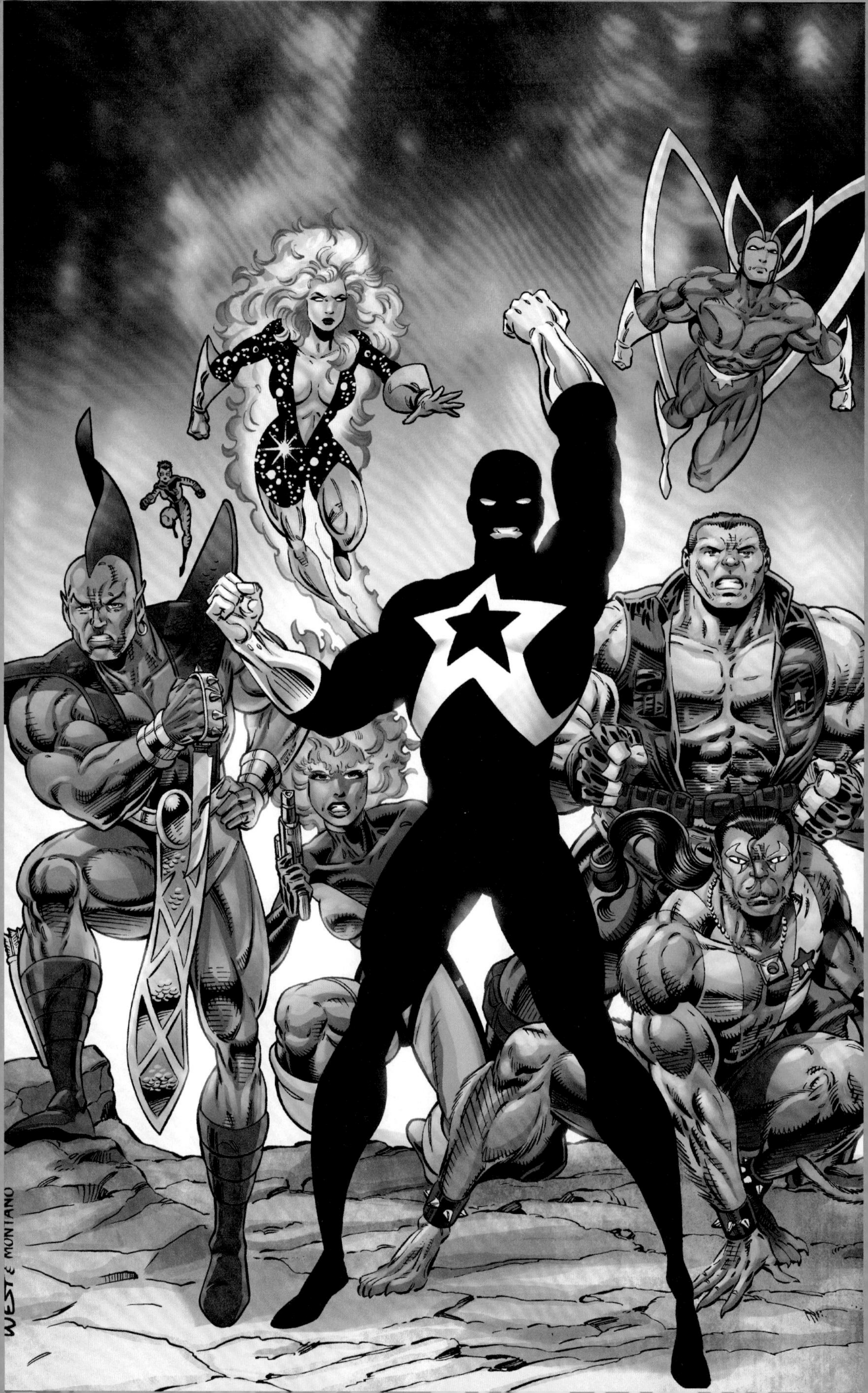
WEST & MONTANO

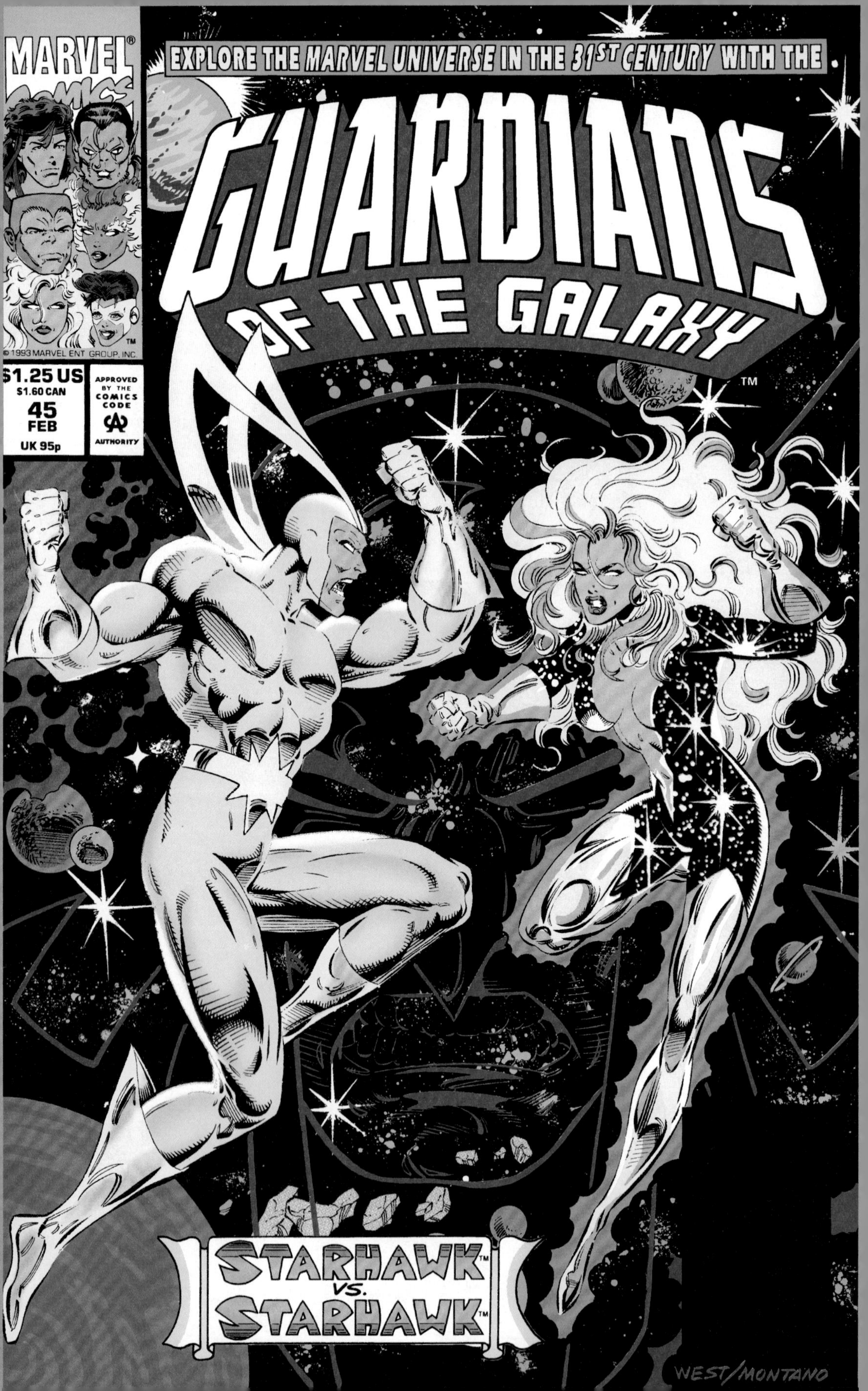
MARVEL® COMICS
EXPLORE THE MARVEL UNIVERSE IN THE 31ST CENTURY WITH THE
GUARDIANS OF THE GALAXY™
©1993 MARVEL ENT GROUP, INC.
$1.25 US
$1.60 CAN
45
FEB
UK 95p
APPROVED BY THE COMICS CODE AUTHORITY
STARHAWK™ VS. STARHAWK™
WEST/MONTANO

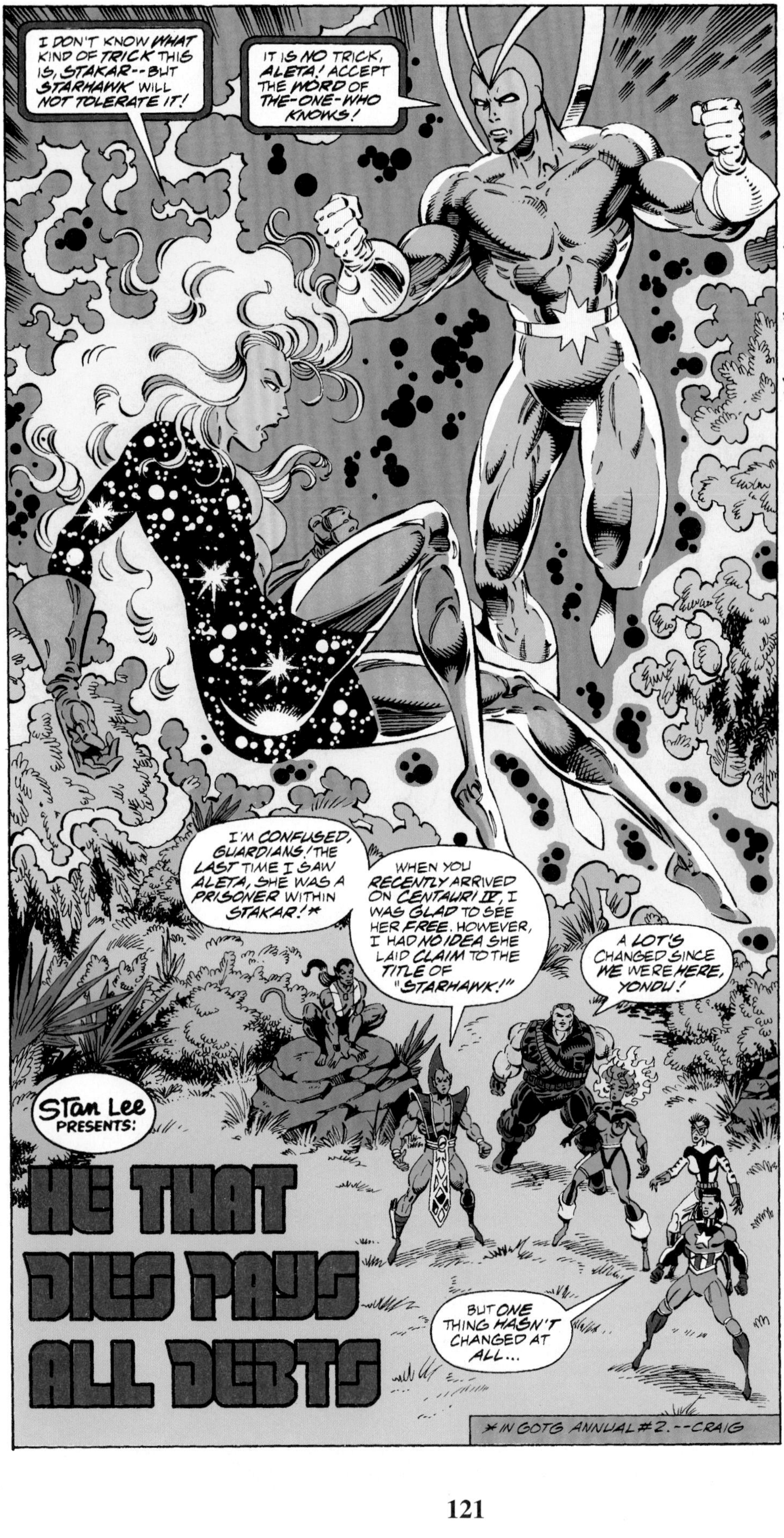
I DON'T KNOW WHAT KIND OF TRICK THIS IS, STAKAR--BUT STARHAWK WILL NOT TOLERATE IT!
IT IS NO TRICK, ALETA! ACCEPT THE WORD OF THE-ONE-WHO KNOWS!
I'M CONFUSED, GUARDIANS! THE LAST TIME I SAW ALETA, SHE WAS A PRISONER WITHIN STAKAR!*
WHEN YOU RECENTLY ARRIVED ON CENTAURI IV, I WAS GLAD TO SEE HER FREE. HOWEVER, I HAD NO IDEA SHE LAID CLAIM TO THE TITLE OF "STARHAWK!"
A LOT'S CHANGED SINCE WE WERE HERE, YONDU!
STAN LEE PRESENTS:
HE THAT DIES PAYS ALL DEBTS
BUT ONE THING HASN'T CHANGED AT ALL...
*IN GOTG ANNUAL #2.--CRAIG

PLEASE WELCOME BACK KEVIN "KEY" WEST - PENCILS
PLEASE ACKNOWLEDGE MICHAEL GALLAGHER - SCRIPT
PLEASE ENCOURAGE STEVE MONTANO - INKS
PLEASE PATRONIZE KENNY LOPEZ - LETTERS
PLEASE COMPLIMENT EVELYN STEIN - COLORS
PLEASE EMULATE CRAIG ANDERSON - EDITS
PLEASE DON'T FEED TOM DEFALCO - EDITOR IN CHIEF

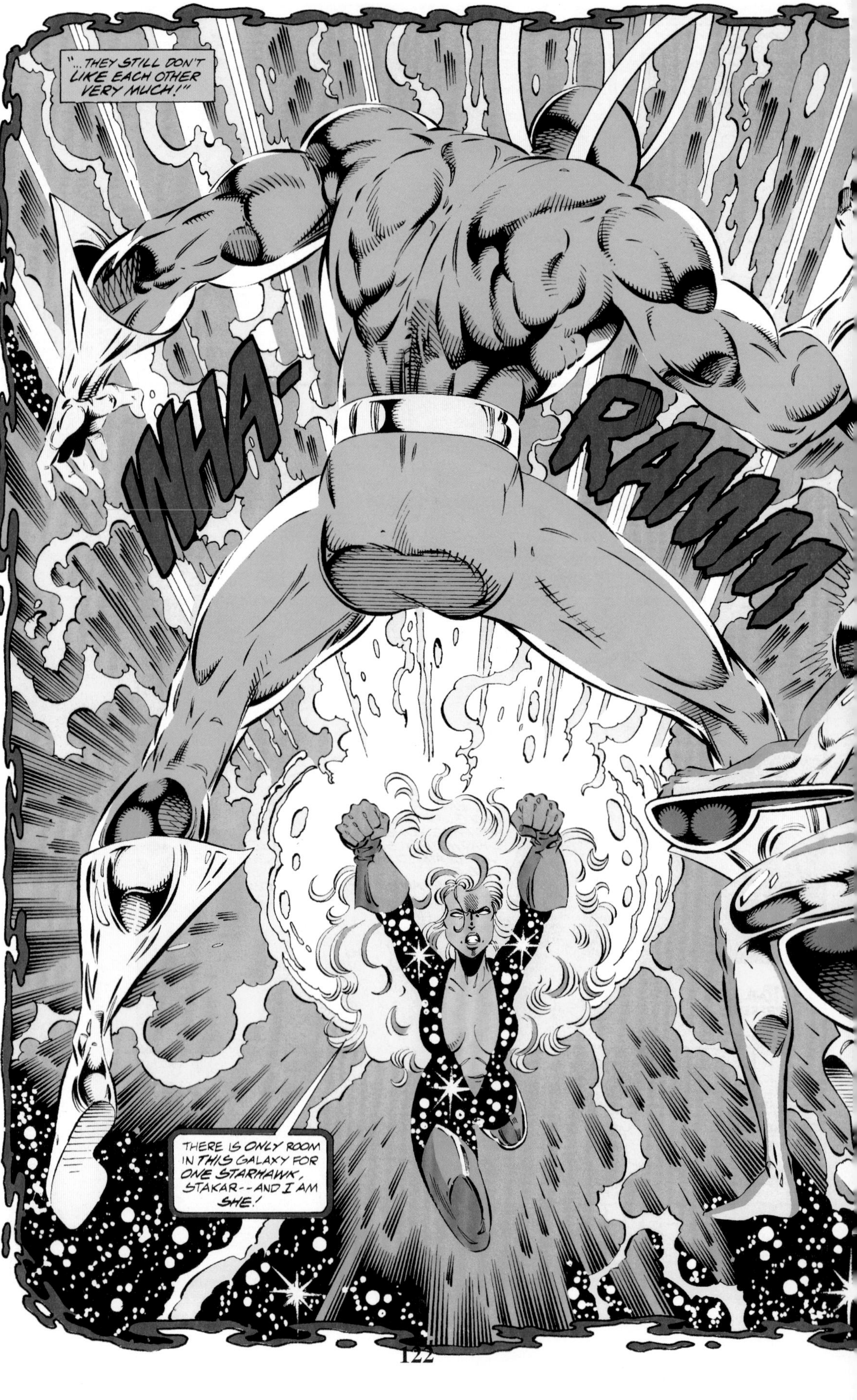

"...THEY STILL DON'T LIKE EACH OTHER VERY MUCH!"
WHA-
RAMM
THERE IS ONLY ROOM IN THIS GALAXY FOR ONE STARHAWK, STAKAR--AND I AM SHE!

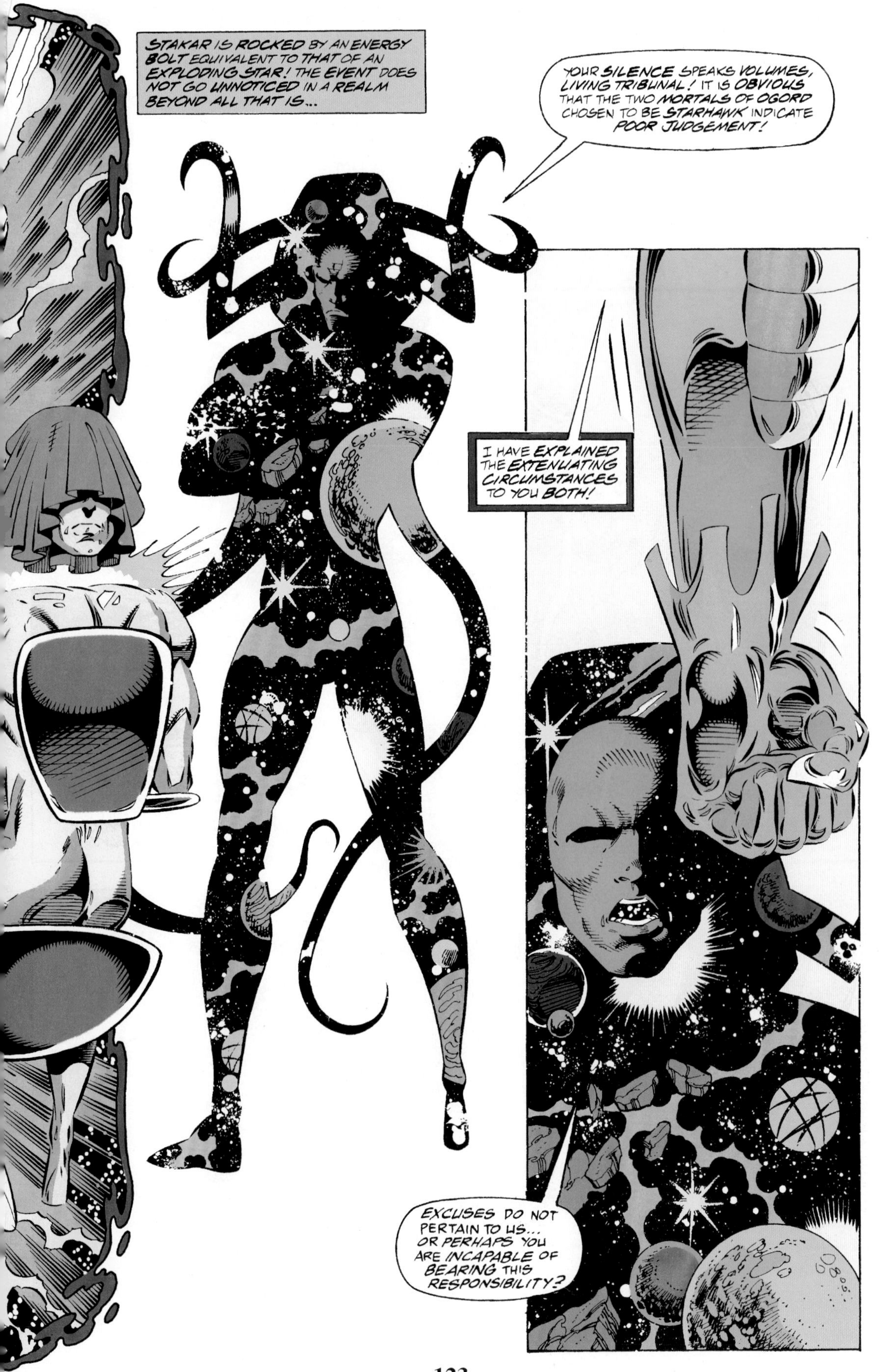
STAKAR IS ROCKED BY AN ENERGY BOLT EQUIVALENT TO THAT OF AN EXPLODING STAR! THE EVENT DOES NOT GO UNNOTICED IN A REALM BEYOND ALL THAT IS...
YOUR SILENCE SPEAKS VOLUMES, LIVING TRIBUNAL! IT IS OBVIOUS THAT THE TWO MORTALS OF OGORD CHOSEN TO BE STARHAWK INDICATE POOR JUDGEMENT!
I HAVE EXPLAINED THE EXTENUATING CIRCUMSTANCES TO YOU BOTH!
EXCUSES DO NOT PERTAIN TO US... OR PERHAPS YOU ARE INCAPABLE OF BEARING THIS RESPONSIBILITY?

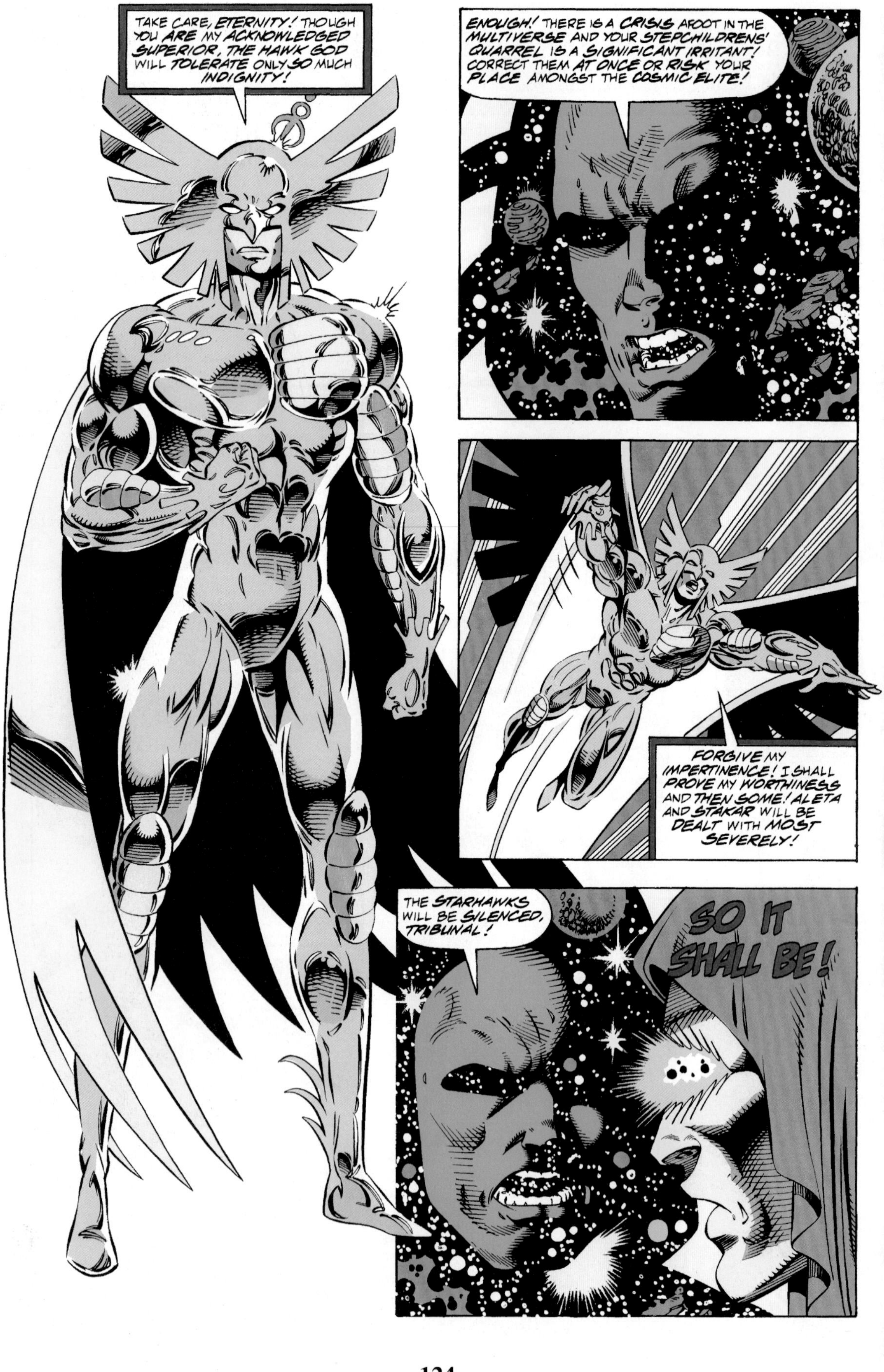

TAKE CARE, ETERNITY! THOUGH YOU ARE MY ACKNOWLEDGED SUPERIOR, THE HAWK GOD WILL TOLERATE ONLY SO MUCH INDIGNITY!
ENOUGH! THERE IS A CRISIS AFOOT IN THE MULTIVERSE AND YOUR STEPCHILDRENS' QUARREL IS A SIGNIFICANT IRRITANT! CORRECT THEM AT ONCE OR RISK YOUR PLACE AMONGST THE COSMIC ELITE!
FORGIVE MY IMPERTINENCE! I SHALL PROVE MY WORTHINESS AND THEN SOME! ALETA AND STAKAR WILL BE DEALT WITH MOST SEVERELY!
THE STARHAWKS WILL BE SILENCED, TRIBUNAL!
SO IT SHALL BE!

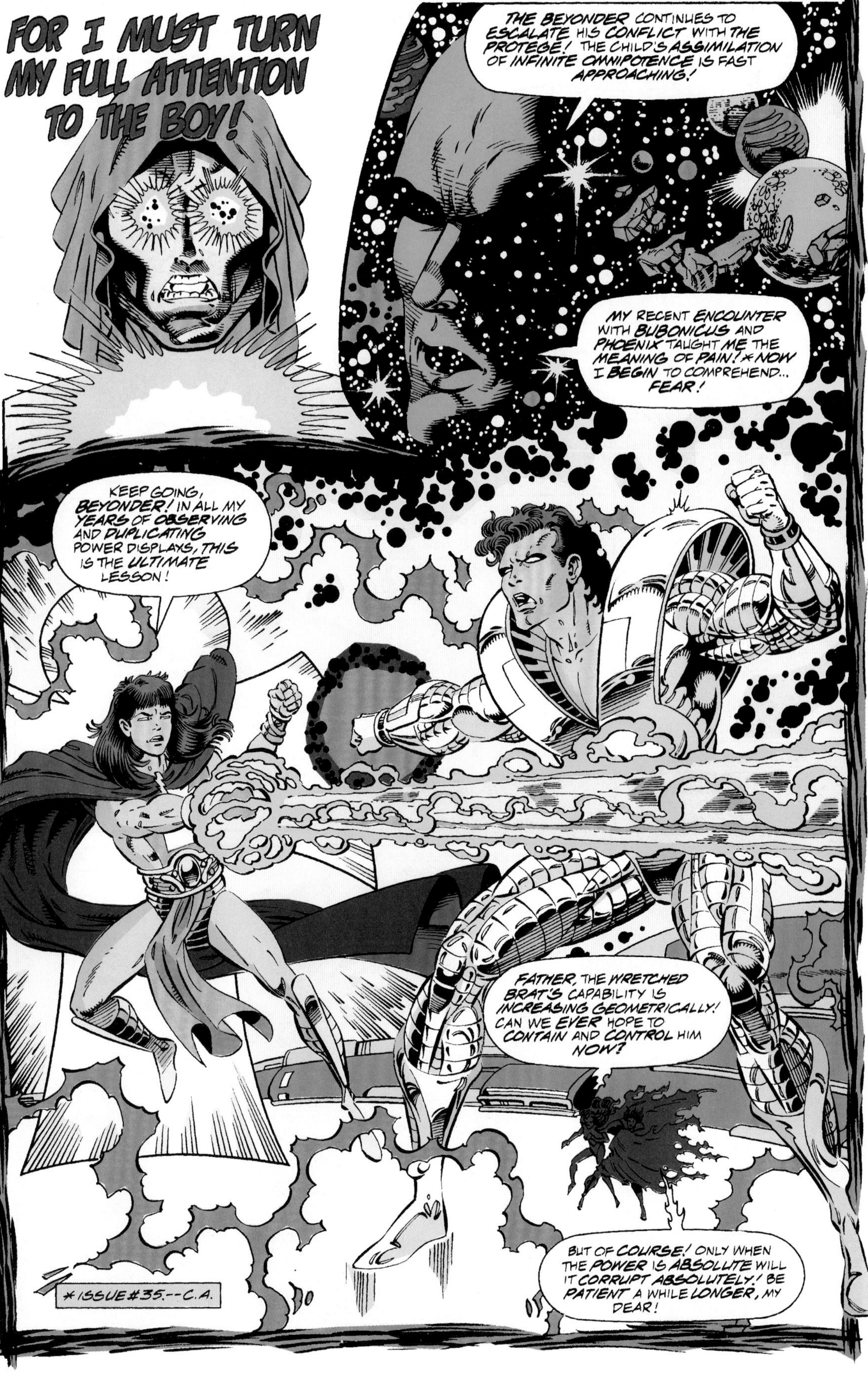
FOR I MUST TURN MY FULL ATTENTION TO THE BOY!
THE BEYONDER CONTINUES TO ESCALATE HIS CONFLICT WITH THE PROTEGE! THE CHILD'S ASSIMILATION OF INFINITE OMNIPOTENCE IS FAST APPROACHING!
MY RECENT ENCOUNTER WITH BUBONICUS AND PHOENIX TAUGHT ME THE MEANING OF PAIN! * NOW I BEGIN TO COMPREHEND... FEAR!
KEEP GOING, BEYONDER! IN ALL MY YEARS OF OBSERVING AND DUPLICATING POWER DISPLAYS, THIS IS THE ULTIMATE LESSON!
FATHER, THE WRETCHED BRAT'S CAPABILITY IS INCREASING GEOMETRICALLY! CAN WE EVER HOPE TO CONTAIN AND CONTROL HIM NOW?
* ISSUE #35.--C.A.
BUT OF COURSE! ONLY WHEN THE POWER IS ABSOLUTE WILL IT CORRUPT ABSOLUTELY! BE PATIENT A WHILE LONGER, MY DEAR!

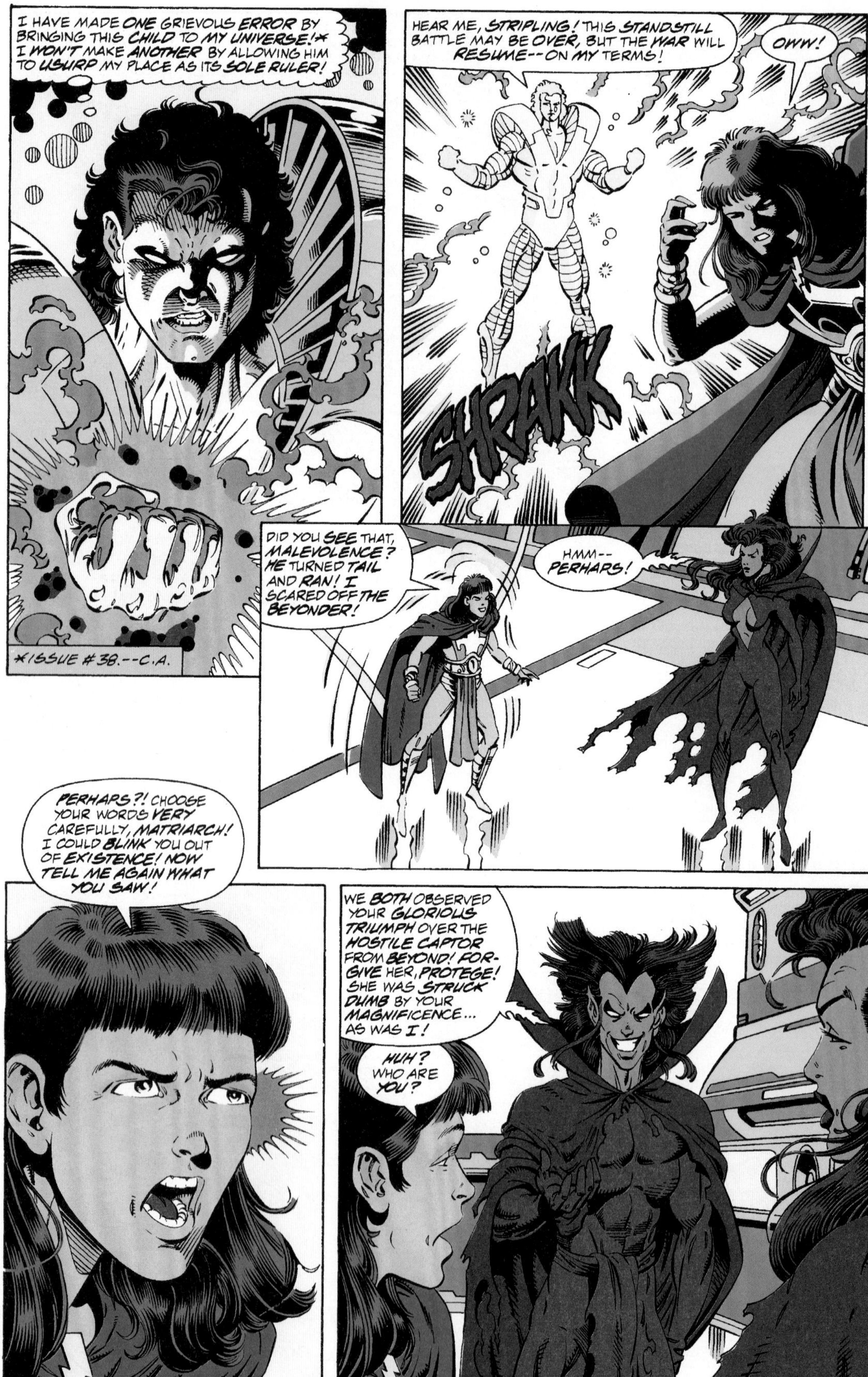

I HAVE MADE ONE GRIEVOUS ERROR BY BRINGING THIS CHILD TO MY UNIVERSE!* I WON'T MAKE ANOTHER BY ALLOWING HIM TO USURP MY PLACE AS ITS SOLE RULER!
*ISSUE #38.--C.A.
HEAR ME, STRIPLING! THIS STANDSTILL BATTLE MAY BE OVER, BUT THE WAR WILL RESUME--ON MY TERMS!
OWW!
SHRAKK
DID YOU SEE THAT, MALEVOLENCE? HE TURNED TAIL AND RAN! I SCARED OFF THE BEYONDER!
HMM-- PERHAPS!
PERHAPS?! CHOOSE YOUR WORDS VERY CAREFULLY, MATRIARCH! I COULD BLINK YOU OUT OF EXISTENCE! NOW TELL ME AGAIN WHAT YOU SAW!
WE BOTH OBSERVED YOUR GLORIOUS TRIUMPH OVER THE HOSTILE CAPTOR FROM BEYOND! FOR-GIVE HER, PROTEGE! SHE WAS STRUCK DUMB BY YOUR MAGNIFICENCE... AS WAS I!
HUH? WHO ARE YOU?

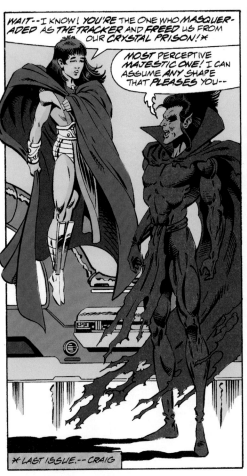

WAIT--I KNOW! YOU'RE THE ONE WHO MASQUERADED AS THE TRACKER AND FREED US FROM OUR CRYSTAL PRISON!*

MOST PERCEPTIVE MAJESTIC ONE! I CAN ASSUME ANY SHAPE THAT PLEASES YOU--

* LAST ISSUE.-- CRAIG

--FOR EXAMPLE, REPLICA, YOUR FORMER SKRULL PLAYMATE!

≥SNARL!≤

OH, EXCELLENT!

BUT I'M SURE THE ALL-POWERFUL PROTEGE HAS MORE IMPORTANT THINGS TO DO THAN OBSERVE MY PARLOR TRICKS!

NO, NO! I MISS MY FRIENDS! I WANT TO SEE MORE OF THEM! CAN YOU BECOME MY OLD ADVISOR, JILTRIN?

OF COURSE!

EXPLOITING THE BOY'S HOMESICKNESS AND SHORT ATTENTION SPAN! I APPLAUD YOUR STYLE, FATHER!

WOW! YOU'RE LOTS OF FUN! WHAT ELSE CAN WE DO TOGETHER?

OH, MANY THINGS, MY LORD! WE SHALL BECOME GREAT FRIENDS, YOU AND I...

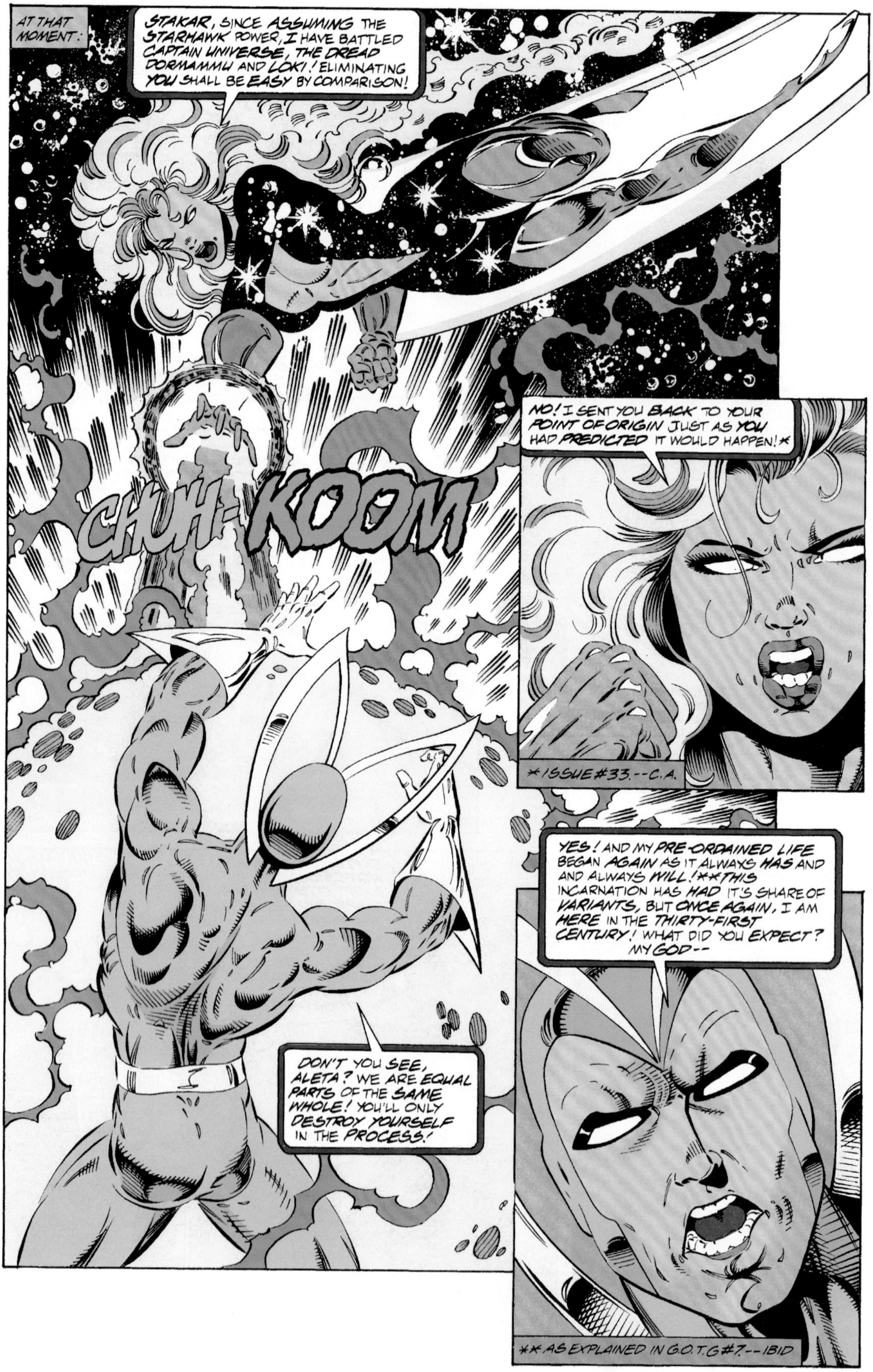
AT THAT MOMENT:
STAKAR, SINCE ASSUMING THE STARHAWK POWER, I HAVE BATTLED CAPTAIN UNIVERSE, THE DREAD DORMAMMU AND LOKI! ELIMINATING YOU SHALL BE EASY BY COMPARISON!
CHUH-KOOM
DON'T YOU SEE, ALETA? WE ARE EQUAL PARTS OF THE SAME WHOLE! YOU'LL ONLY DESTROY YOURSELF IN THE PROCESS!
NO! I SENT YOU BACK TO YOUR POINT OF ORIGIN JUST AS YOU HAD PREDICTED IT WOULD HAPPEN! *
* ISSUE #33. --C.A.
YES! AND MY PRE-ORDAINED LIFE BEGAN AGAIN AS IT ALWAYS HAS AND AND ALWAYS WILL! ** THIS INCARNATION HAS HAD IT'S SHARE OF VARIANTS, BUT ONCE AGAIN, I AM HERE IN THE THIRTY-FIRST CENTURY! WHAT DID YOU EXPECT? MY GOD--
** AS EXPLAINED IN G.O.T.G #7.--IBID

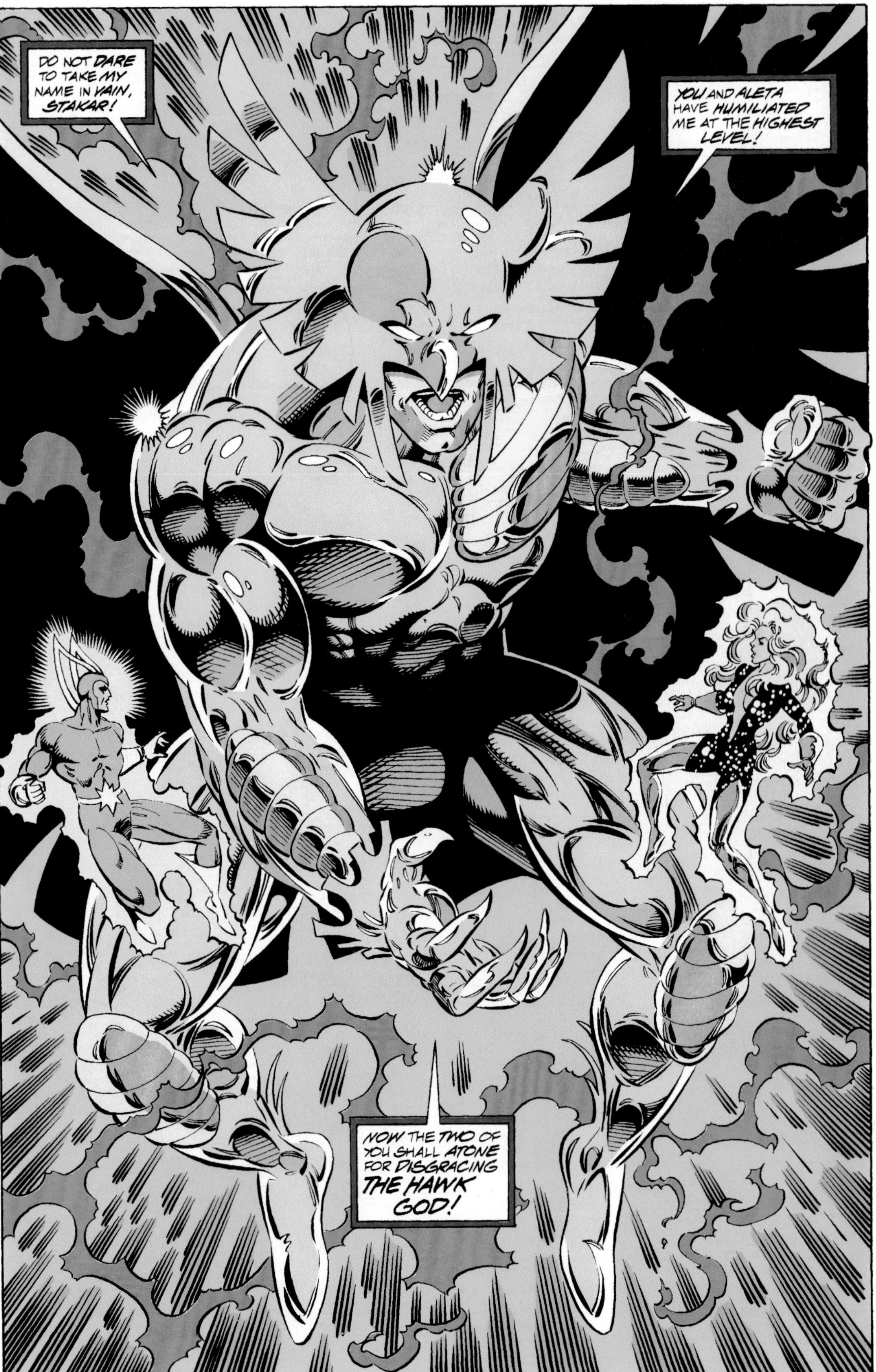
DO NOT DARE TO TAKE MY NAME IN VAIN, STAKAR!
YOU AND ALETA HAVE HUMILIATED ME AT THE HIGHEST LEVEL!
NOW THE TWO OF YOU SHALL ATONE FOR DISGRACING THE HAWK GOD!

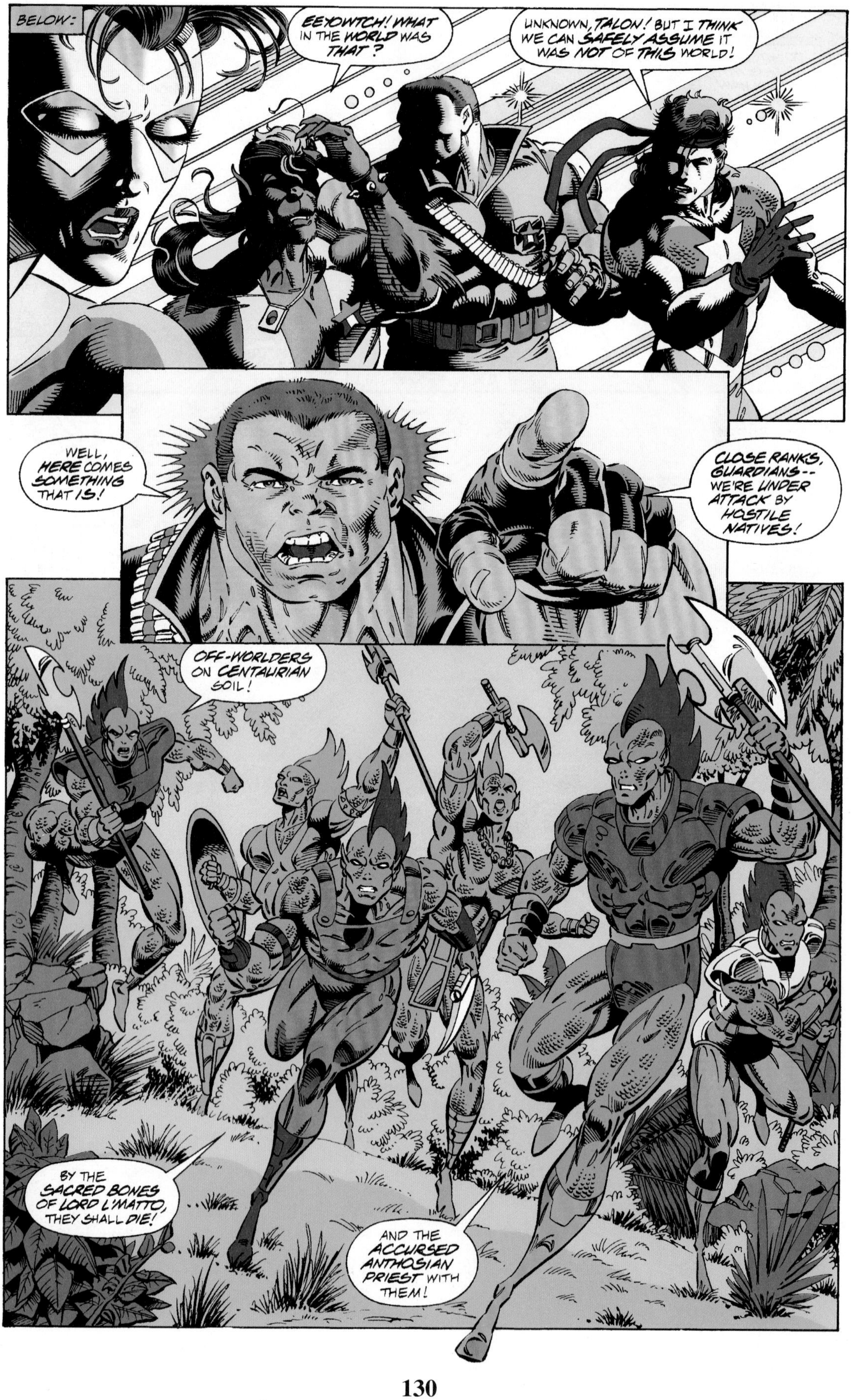
BELOW:
EEYOWTCH! WHAT IN THE WORLD WAS THAT?
UNKNOWN, TALON! BUT I THINK WE CAN SAFELY ASSUME IT WAS NOT OF THIS WORLD!
WELL, HERE COMES SOMETHING THAT IS!
CLOSE RANKS, GUARDIANS-- WE'RE UNDER ATTACK BY HOSTILE NATIVES!
OFF-WORLDERS ON CENTAURIAN SOIL!
BY THE SACRED BONES OF LORD L'MATTO, THEY SHALL DIE!
AND THE ACCURSED ANTHOSIAN PRIEST WITH THEM!

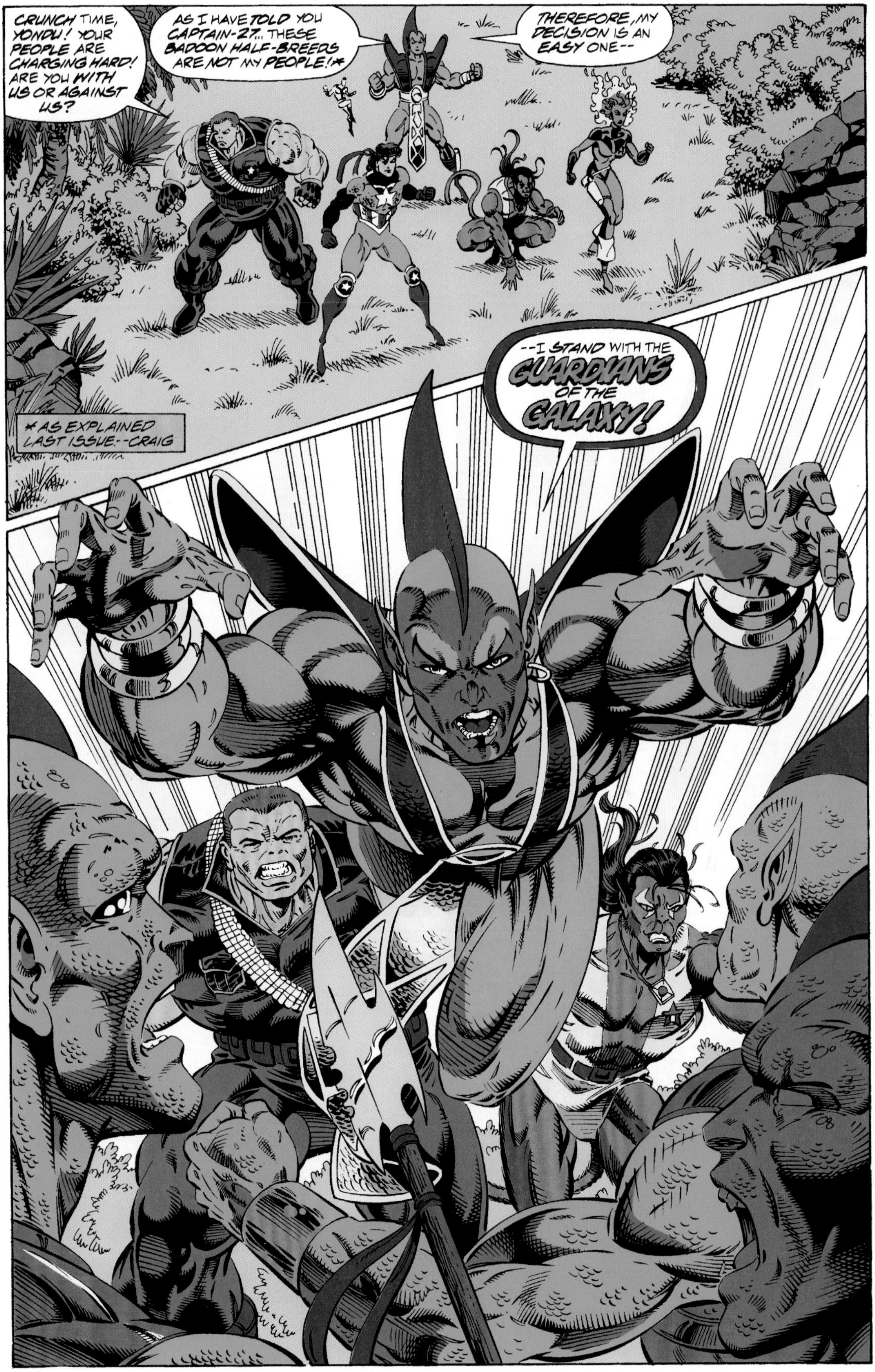
CRUNCH TIME, YONDU! YOUR PEOPLE ARE CHARGING HARD! ARE YOU WITH US OR AGAINST US?
AS I HAVE TOLD YOU CAPTAIN-27... THESE BADOON HALF-BREEDS ARE NOT MY PEOPLE!*
THEREFORE, MY DECISION IS AN EASY ONE--
*AS EXPLAINED LAST ISSUE--CRAIG
--I STAND WITH THE GUARDIANS OF THE GALAXY!

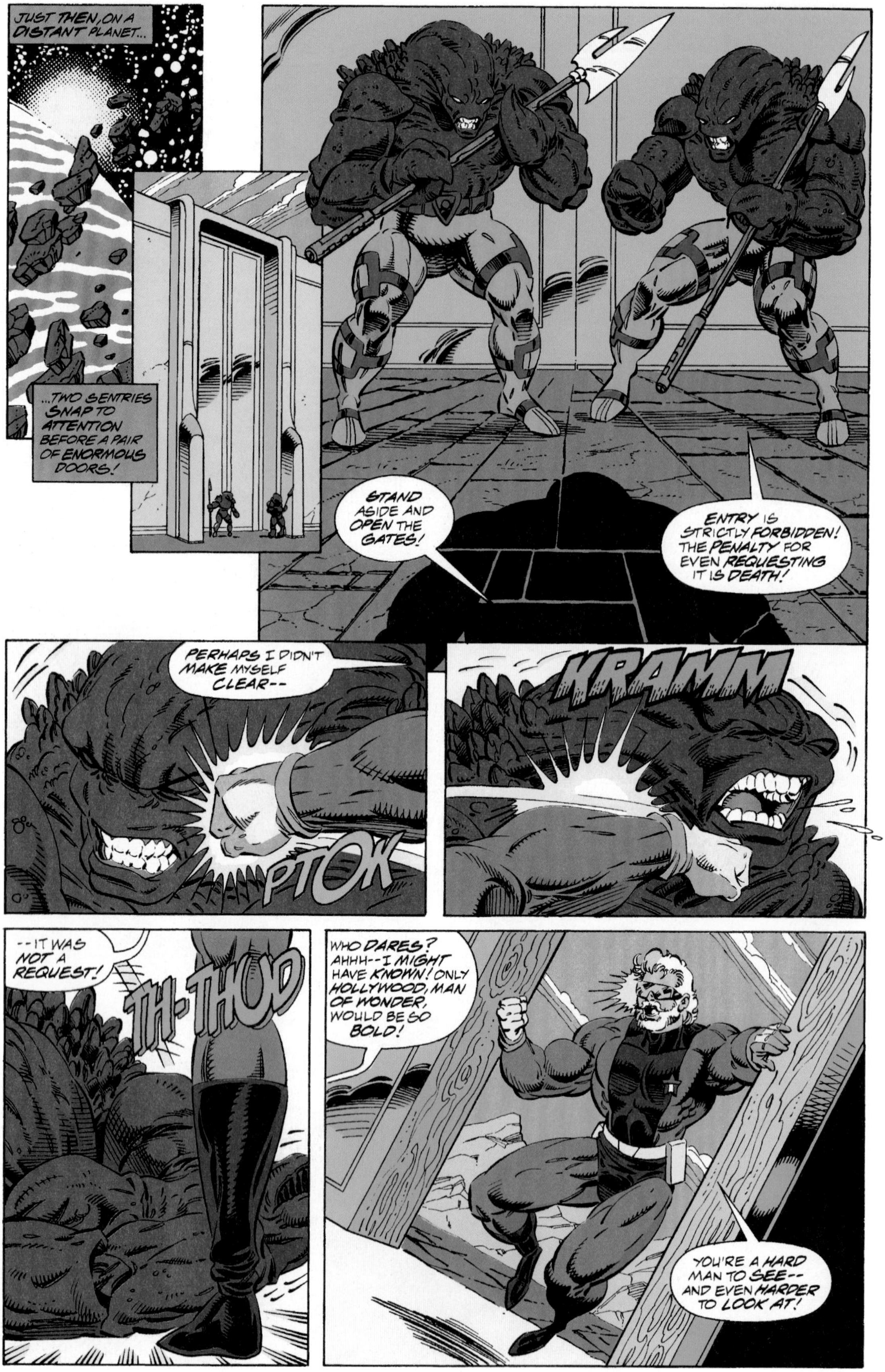
JUST THEN, ON A DISTANT PLANET...
...TWO SENTRIES SNAP TO ATTENTION BEFORE A PAIR OF ENORMOUS DOORS!
STAND ASIDE AND OPEN THE GATES!
ENTRY IS STRICTLY FORBIDDEN! THE PENALTY FOR EVEN REQUESTING IT IS DEATH!
PERHAPS I DIDN'T MAKE MYSELF CLEAR--
PTOK
KRAMM
--IT WAS NOT A REQUEST!
TH-THUD
WHO DARES? AHHH--I MIGHT HAVE KNOWN! ONLY HOLLYWOOD, MAN OF WONDER, WOULD BE SO BOLD!
YOU'RE A HARD MAN TO SEE--AND EVEN HARDER TO LOOK AT!

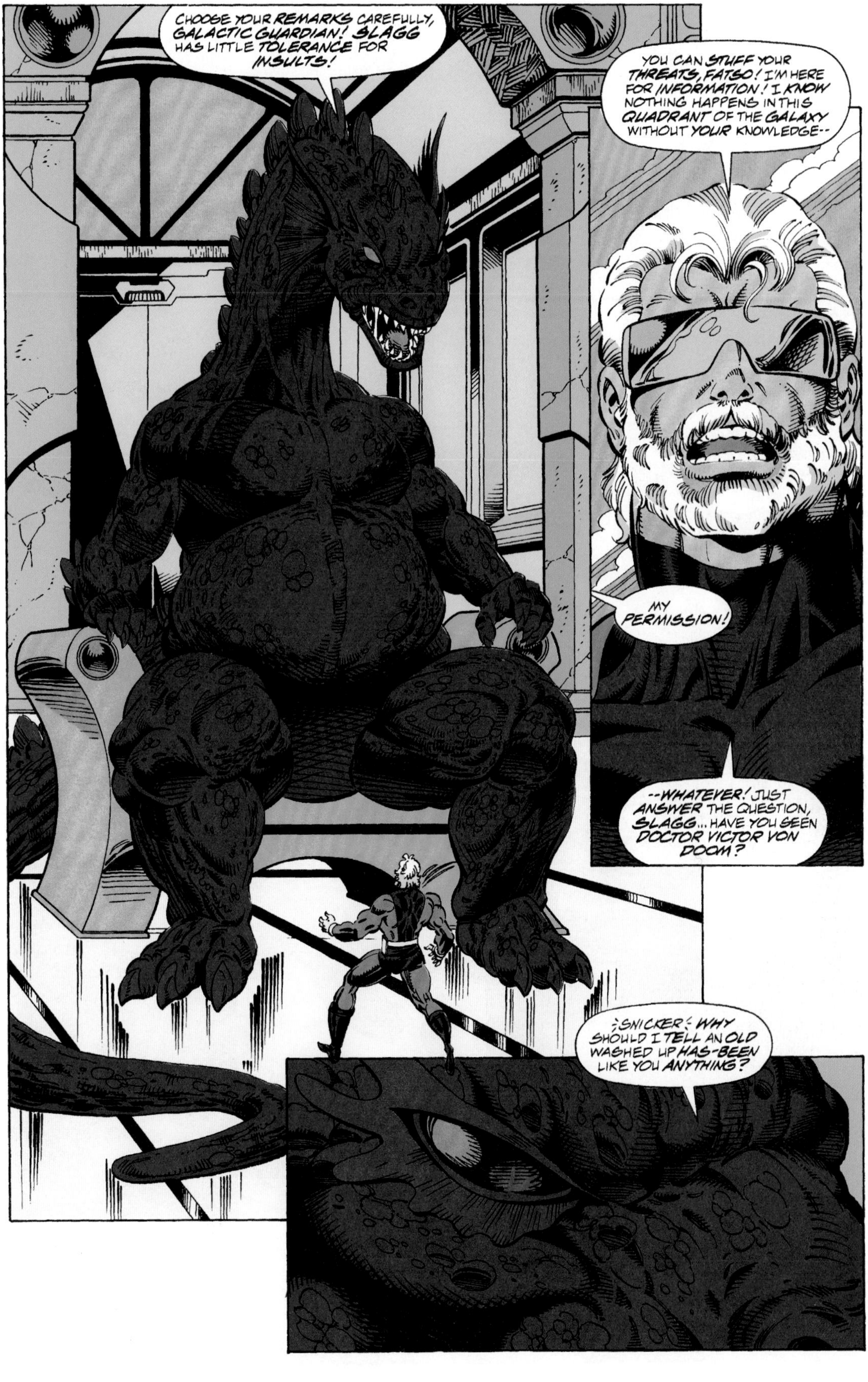
CHOOSE YOUR REMARKS CAREFULLY, GALACTIC GUARDIAN! SLAGG HAS LITTLE TOLERANCE FOR INSULTS!
YOU CAN STUFF YOUR THREATS, FATSO! I'M HERE FOR INFORMATION! I KNOW NOTHING HAPPENS IN THIS QUADRANT OF THE GALAXY WITHOUT YOUR KNOWLEDGE--
MY PERMISSION!
--WHATEVER! JUST ANSWER THE QUESTION, SLAGG... HAVE YOU SEEN DOCTOR VICTOR VON DOOM?
:SNICKER: WHY SHOULD I TELL AN OLD WASHED UP HAS-BEEN LIKE YOU ANYTHING?

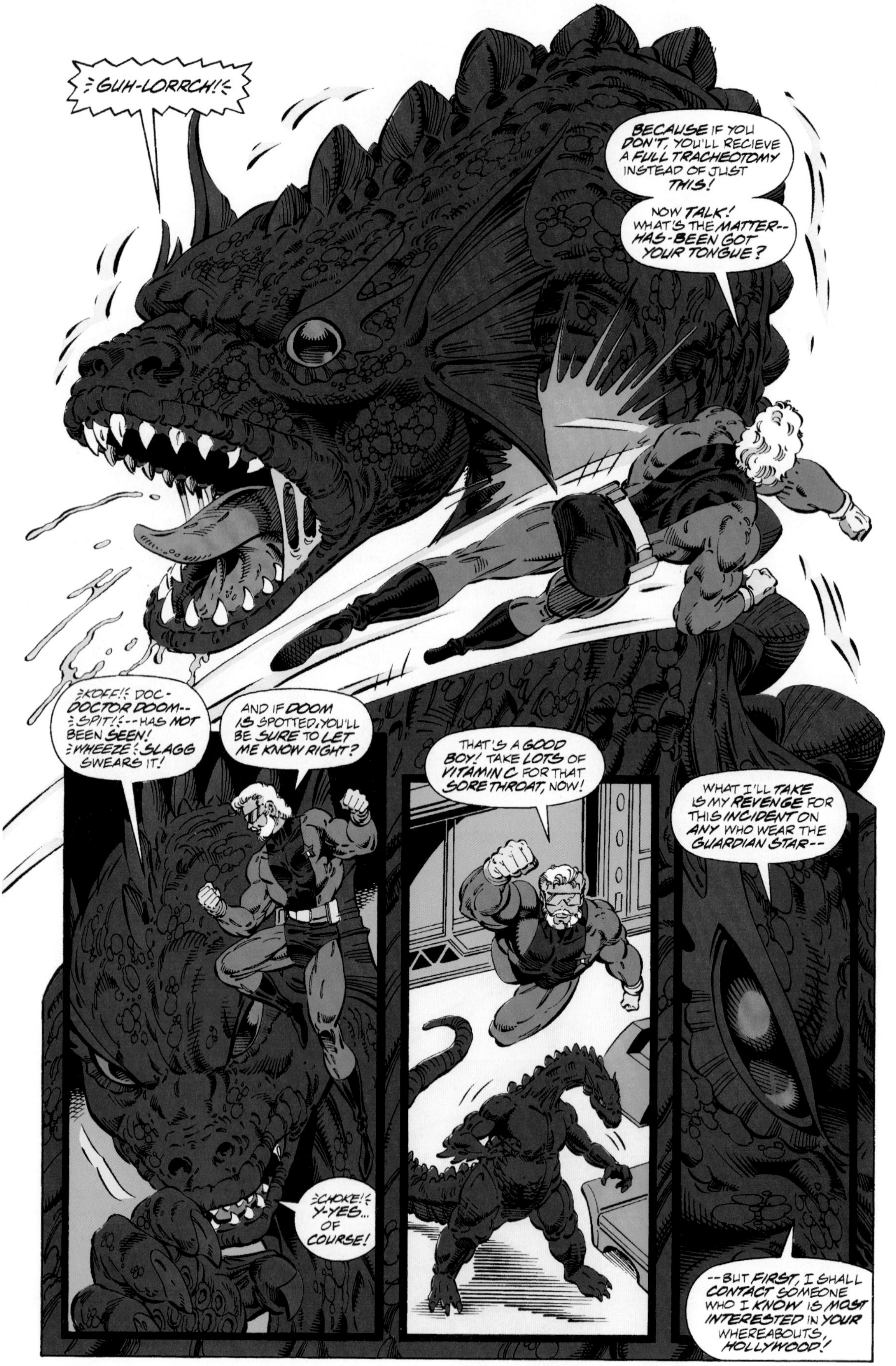
GUH-LORRCH!
BECAUSE IF YOU DON'T, YOU'LL RECIEVE A FULL TRACHEOTOMY INSTEAD OF JUST THIS!
NOW TALK! WHAT'S THE MATTER-- HAS-BEEN GOT YOUR TONGUE?
KOFF! DOC- DOCTOR DOOM-- SPIT! --HAS NOT BEEN SEEN! WHEEZE! SLAGG SWEARS IT!
AND IF DOOM IS SPOTTED, YOU'LL BE SURE TO LET ME KNOW RIGHT?
CHOKE! Y-YES... OF COURSE!
THAT'S A GOOD BOY! TAKE LOTS OF VITAMIN C FOR THAT SORE THROAT, NOW!
WHAT I'LL TAKE IS MY REVENGE FOR THIS INCIDENT ON ANY WHO WEAR THE GUARDIAN STAR--
--BUT FIRST, I SHALL CONTACT SOMEONE WHO I KNOW IS MOST INTERESTED IN YOUR WHEREABOUTS, HOLLYWOOD!

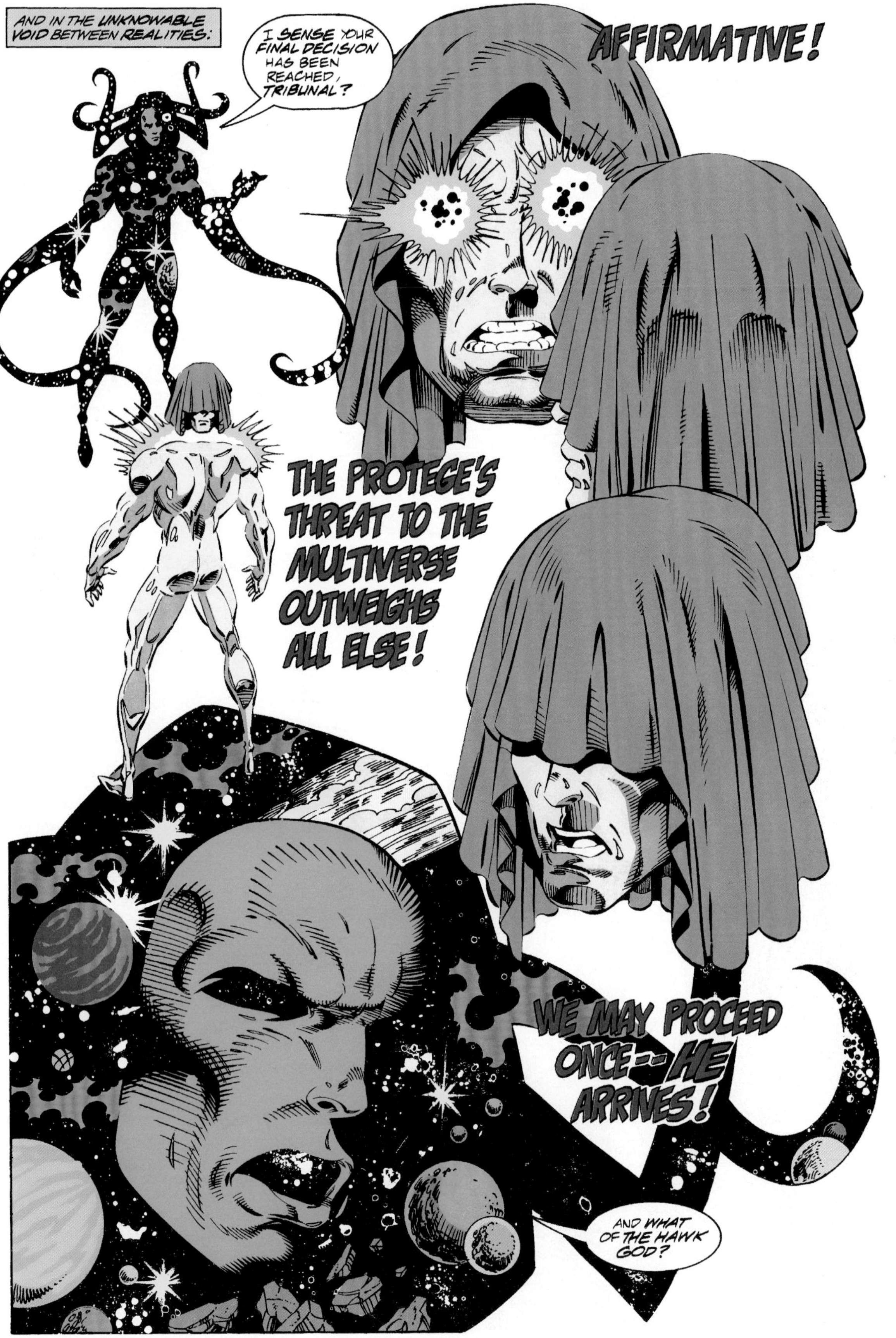
AND IN THE UNKNOWABLE VOID BETWEEN REALITIES:
I SENSE YOUR FINAL DECISION HAS BEEN REACHED, TRIBUNAL?
AFFIRMATIVE!
THE PROTEGE'S THREAT TO THE MULTIVERSE OUTWEIGHS ALL ELSE!
WE MAY PROCEED ONCE-- HE ARRIVES!
AND WHAT OF THE HAWK GOD?

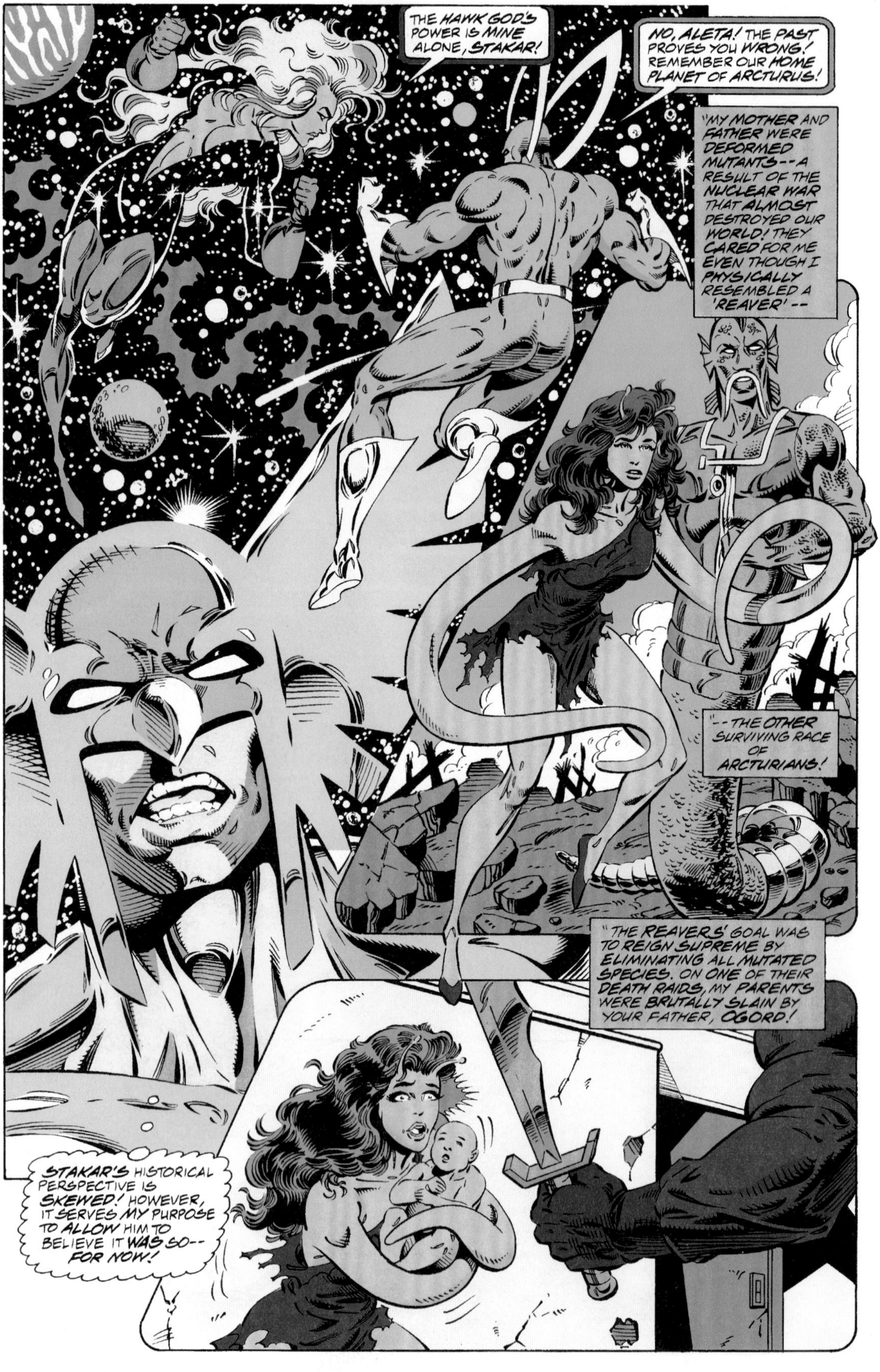

THE HAWK GOD'S POWER IS MINE ALONE, STAKAR!
NO, ALETA! THE PAST PROVES YOU WRONG! REMEMBER OUR HOME PLANET OF ARCTURUS!
"MY MOTHER AND FATHER WERE DEFORMED MUTANTS--A RESULT OF THE NUCLEAR WAR THAT ALMOST DESTROYED OUR WORLD! THEY CARED FOR ME EVEN THOUGH I PHYSICALLY RESEMBLED A 'REAVER'--
--THE OTHER SURVIVING RACE OF ARCTURIANS!
"THE REAVERS' GOAL WAS TO REIGN SUPREME BY ELIMINATING ALL MUTATED SPECIES. ON ONE OF THEIR DEATH RAIDS, MY PARENTS WERE BRUTALLY SLAIN BY YOUR FATHER, OGORD!
STAKAR'S HISTORICAL PERSPECTIVE IS SKEWED! HOWEVER, IT SERVES MY PURPOSE TO ALLOW HIM TO BELIEVE IT WAS SO--FOR NOW!

"MISTAKING ME FOR A HUMAN CHILD, HE AND YOUR MOTHER SALAAN ADOPTED ME, EVEN THOUGH SHE HAD RECENTLY GIVEN BIRTH TO A DAUGHTER.

"YOU, ALETA! AS WE GREW, OUR DIFFERENCES KEPT US DISTANT, BUT WE MANAGED TO DEVELOP A COMPATIBLE SIBLING RELATIONSHIP.

"MARRIAGE WAS INCONCEIVABLE TO US BOTH, LET ALONE OUR ULTIMATE DESTINY!

"UPON REACHING MATURITY, I FELT THE INCOMPREHENSIBLE NEED TO EXPLORE ARCTURUS' FORBIDDEN CITY! YOU FOLLOWED ME AND TOGETHER WE DISCOVERED-- HIM!

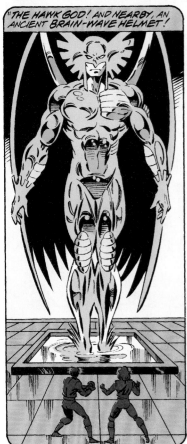

"THE HAWK GOD! AND NEARBY, AN ANCIENT BRAIN-WAVE HELMET!

"YOUR FAMOUS TEMPER ERUPTED AND YOU THREW THE HEADPIECE TO THE GROUND, ACTIVATING IT!

"THE HELMET INSTANTLY CONVERTED YOUR BODY INTO PURE ENERGY!

"I DONNED IT TO TRY AND SAVE YOU, BUT THE SAME FATE BEFELL ME! OUR CONSCIOUSNESSES MERGED AND WE WERE REFORMED INTO THE COMPOSITE BEING KNOWN AS:

STARHAWK!

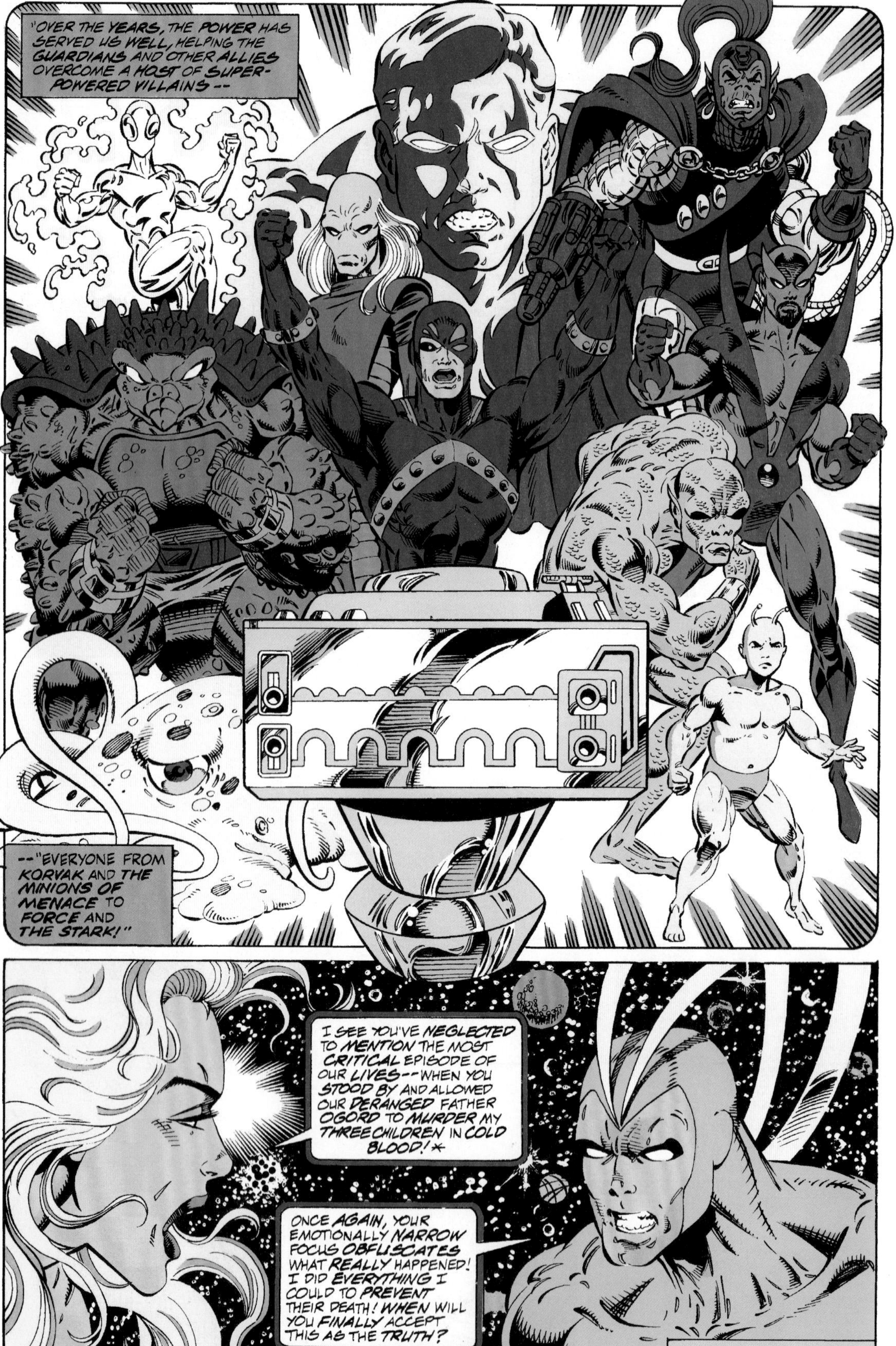
"OVER THE YEARS, THE POWER HAS SERVED US WELL, HELPING THE GUARDIANS AND OTHER ALLIES OVERCOME A HOST OF SUPER-POWERED VILLAINS --
--"EVERYONE FROM KORVAK AND THE MINIONS OF MENACE TO FORCE AND THE STARK!"
I SEE YOU'VE NEGLECTED TO MENTION THE MOST CRITICAL EPISODE OF OUR LIVES--WHEN YOU STOOD BY AND ALLOWED OUR DERANGED FATHER OGORD TO MURDER MY THREE CHILDREN IN COLD BLOOD! *
ONCE AGAIN, YOUR EMOTIONALLY NARROW FOCUS OBFUSCATES WHAT REALLY HAPPENED! I DID EVERYTHING I COULD TO PREVENT THEIR DEATH! WHEN WILL YOU FINALLY ACCEPT THIS AS THE TRUTH?
* MARVEL PRESENTS #11. -- CRAIG

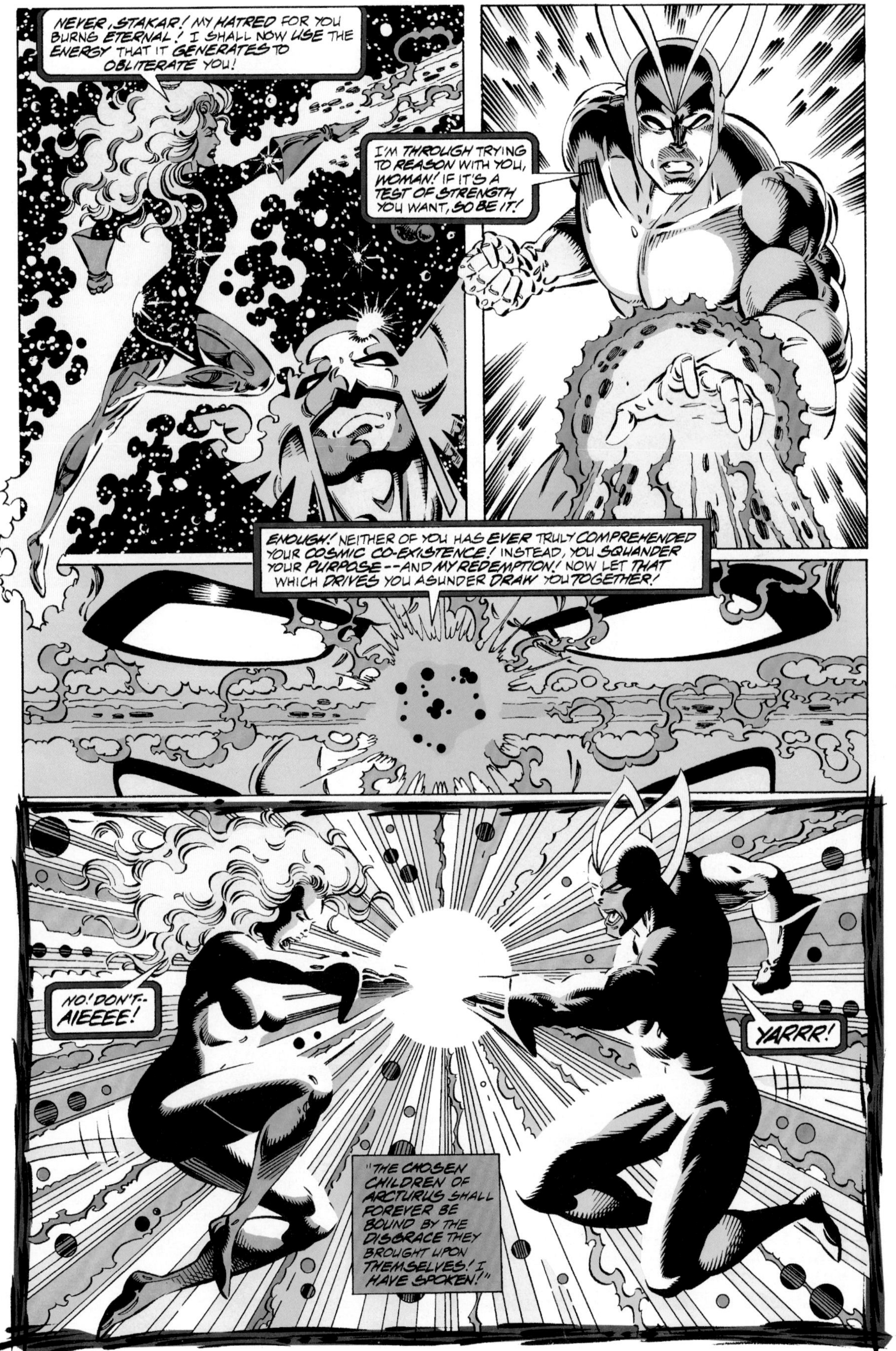
NEVER, STAKAR! MY HATRED FOR YOU BURNS ETERNAL! I SHALL NOW USE THE ENERGY THAT IT GENERATES TO OBLITERATE YOU!
I'M THROUGH TRYING TO REASON WITH YOU, WOMAN! IF IT'S A TEST OF STRENGTH YOU WANT, SO BE IT!
ENOUGH! NEITHER OF YOU HAS EVER TRULY COMPREHENDED YOUR COSMIC CO-EXISTENCE! INSTEAD, YOU SQUANDER YOUR PURPOSE--AND MY REDEMPTION! NOW LET THAT WHICH DRIVES YOU ASUNDER DRAW YOU TOGETHER!
NO! DON'T-- AIEEEE!
YARRR!
"THE CHOSEN CHILDREN OF ARCTURUS SHALL FOREVER BE BOUND BY THE DISGRACE THEY BROUGHT UPON THEMSELVES! I HAVE SPOKEN!"

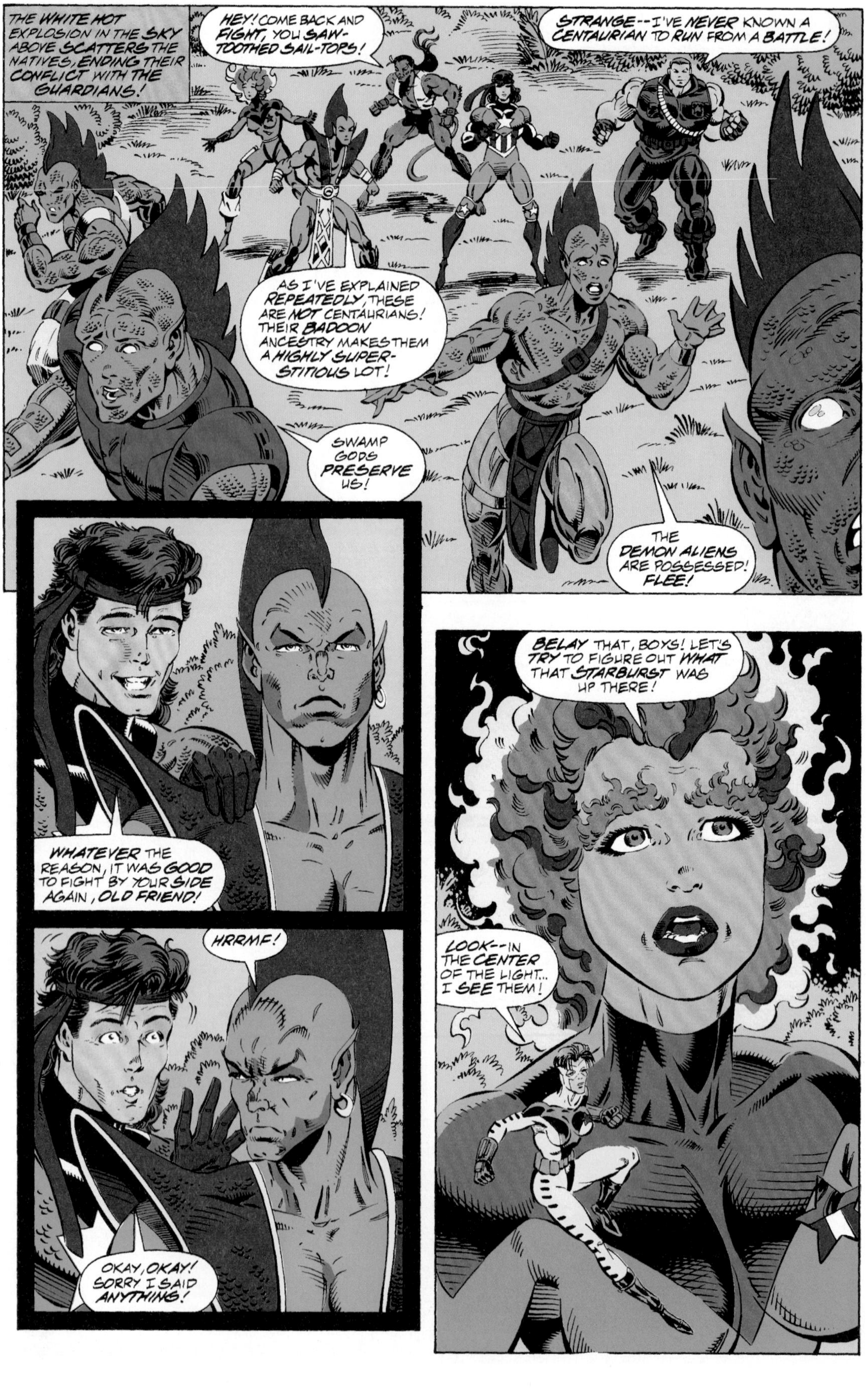
THE WHITE HOT EXPLOSION IN THE SKY ABOVE SCATTERS THE NATIVES, ENDING THEIR CONFLICT WITH THE GUARDIANS!
HEY! COME BACK AND FIGHT, YOU SAW-TOOTHED SAIL-TOPS!
STRANGE--I'VE NEVER KNOWN A CENTAURIAN TO RUN FROM A BATTLE!
AS I'VE EXPLAINED REPEATEDLY, THESE ARE NOT CENTAURIANS! THEIR BADOON ANCESTRY MAKES THEM A HIGHLY SUPER-STITIOUS LOT!
SWAMP GODS PRESERVE US!
THE DEMON ALIENS ARE POSSESSED! FLEE!
WHATEVER THE REASON, IT WAS GOOD TO FIGHT BY YOUR SIDE AGAIN, OLD FRIEND!
HRRMF!
OKAY, OKAY! SORRY I SAID ANYTHING!
BELAY THAT, BOYS! LET'S TRY TO FIGURE OUT WHAT THAT STARBURST WAS UP THERE!
LOOK--IN THE CENTER OF THE LIGHT... I SEE THEM!

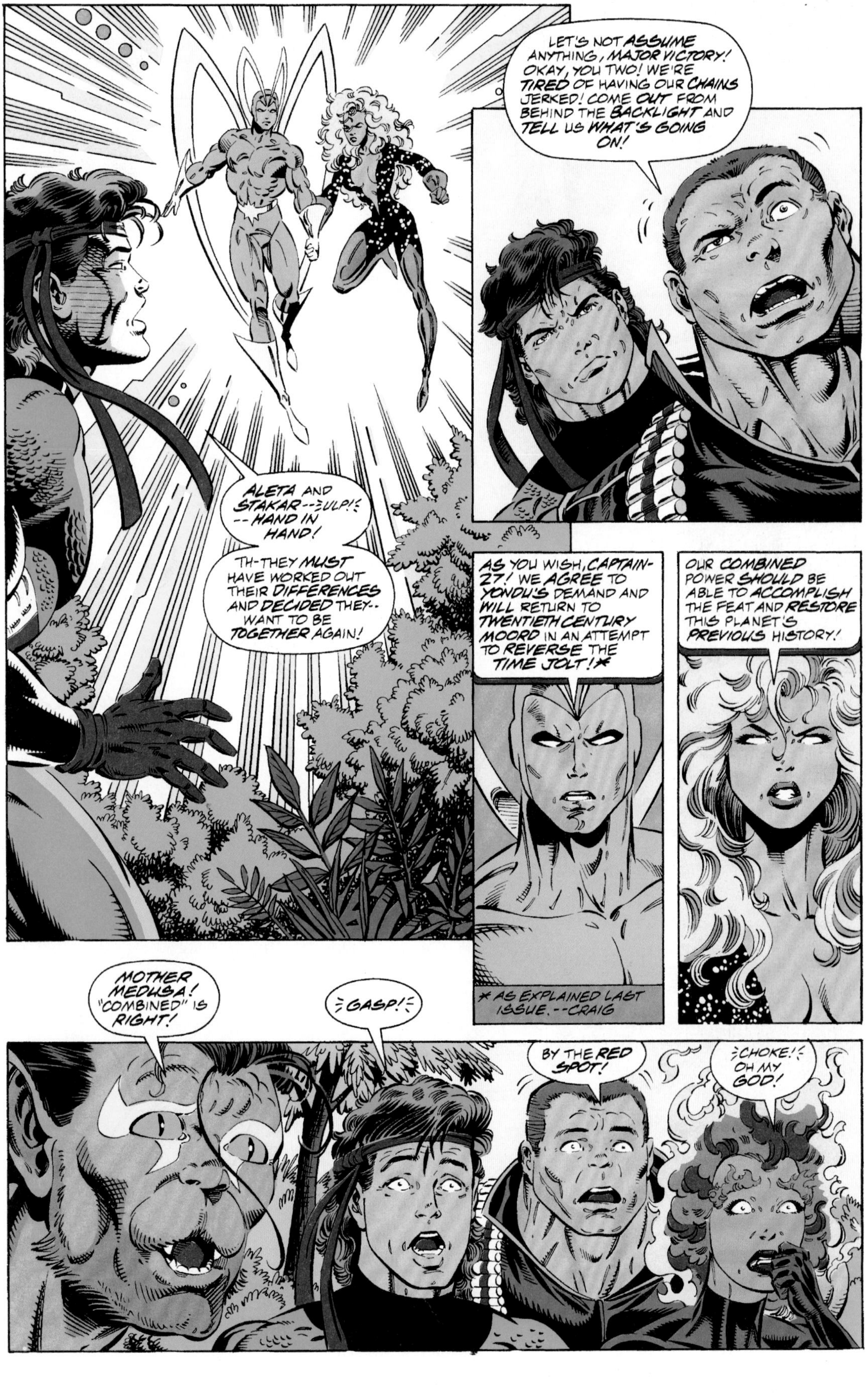
LET'S NOT ASSUME ANYTHING, MAJOR VICTORY! OKAY, YOU TWO! WE'RE TIRED OF HAVING OUR CHAINS JERKED! COME OUT FROM BEHIND THE BACKLIGHT AND TELL US WHAT'S GOING ON!
ALETA AND STAKAR--ULP!--HAND IN HAND!
TH-THEY MUST HAVE WORKED OUT THEIR DIFFERENCES AND DECIDED THEY--WANT TO BE TOGETHER AGAIN!
AS YOU WISH, CAPTAIN-27! WE AGREE TO YONDU'S DEMAND AND WILL RETURN TO TWENTIETH CENTURY MOORD IN AN ATTEMPT TO REVERSE THE TIME JOLT!*
* AS EXPLAINED LAST ISSUE. --CRAIG
OUR COMBINED POWER SHOULD BE ABLE TO ACCOMPLISH THE FEAT AND RESTORE THIS PLANET'S PREVIOUS HISTORY!
MOTHER MEDUSA! "COMBINED" IS RIGHT!
GASP!
BY THE RED SPOT!
CHOKE! OH MY GOD!

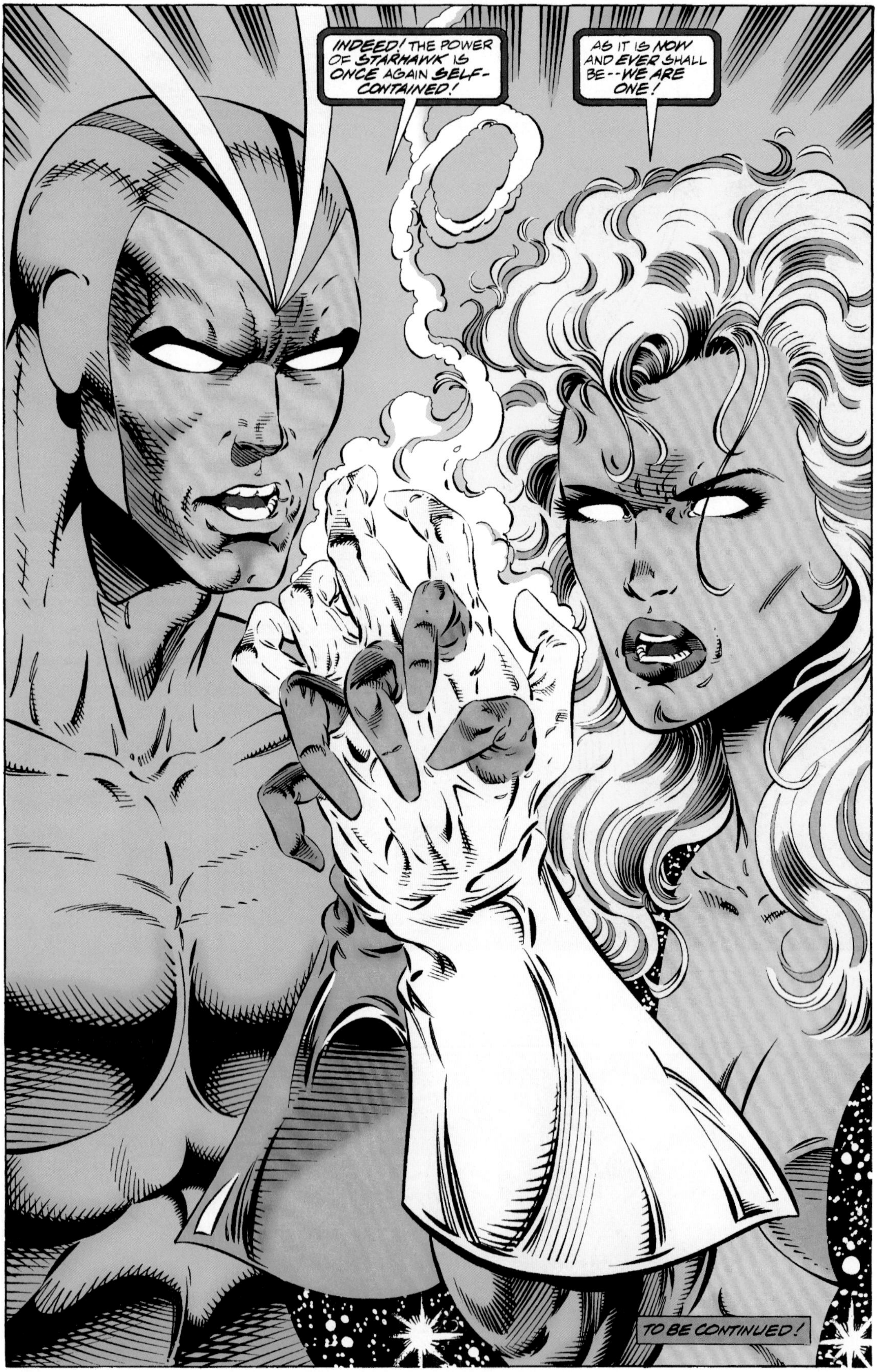
INDEED! THE POWER OF STARHAWK IS ONCE AGAIN SELF-CONTAINED!
AS IT IS NOW AND EVER SHALL BE--WE ARE ONE!
TO BE CONTINUED!

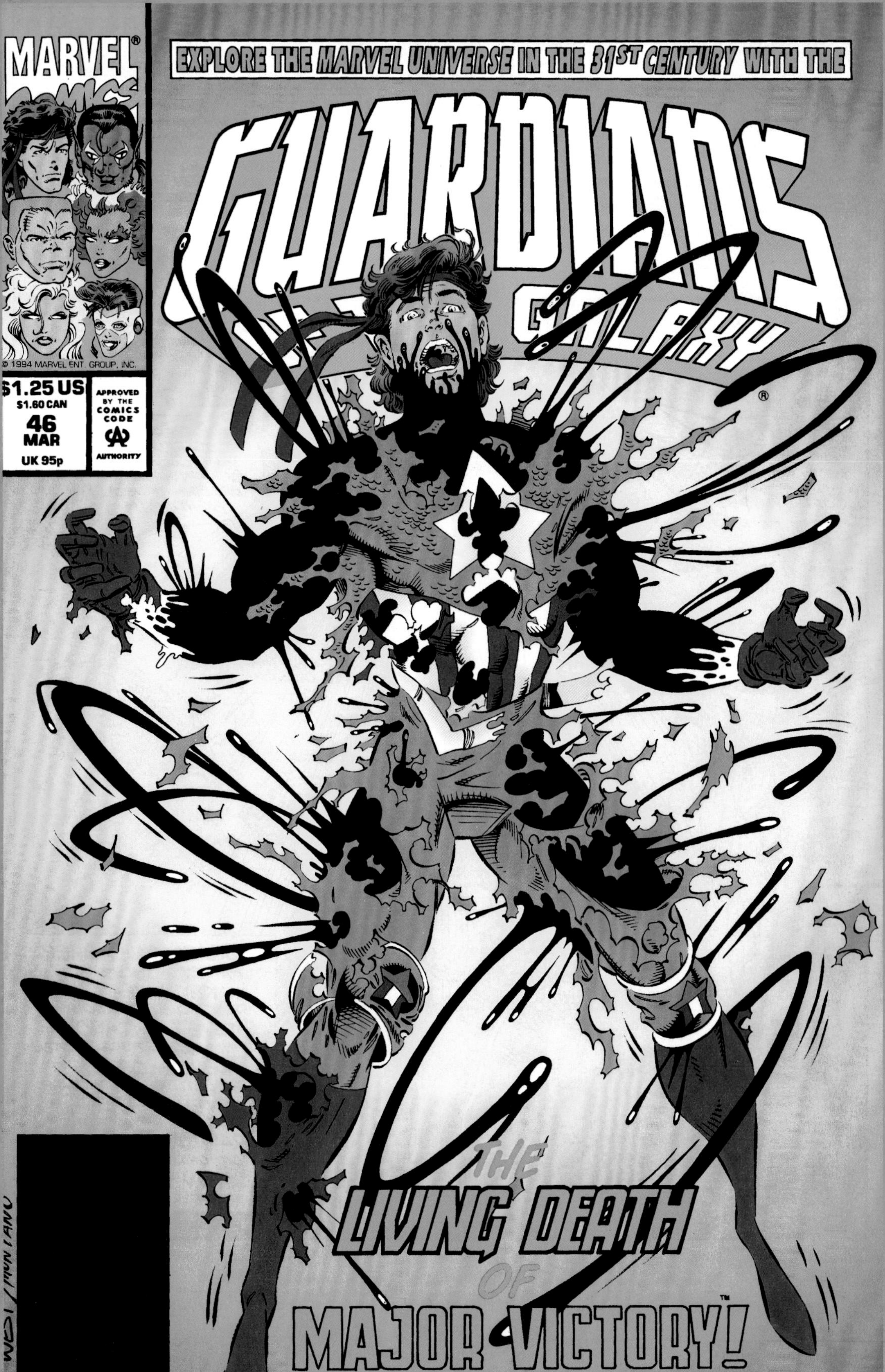
MARVEL
COMICS
© 1994 MARVEL ENT. GROUP, INC.
$1.25 US
$1.60 CAN
46
MAR
UK 95p
APPROVED BY THE COMICS CODE AUTHORITY
EXPLORE THE MARVEL UNIVERSE IN THE 31ST CENTURY WITH THE
GUARDIANS
GALAXY
THE LIVING DEATH OF MAJOR VICTORY!

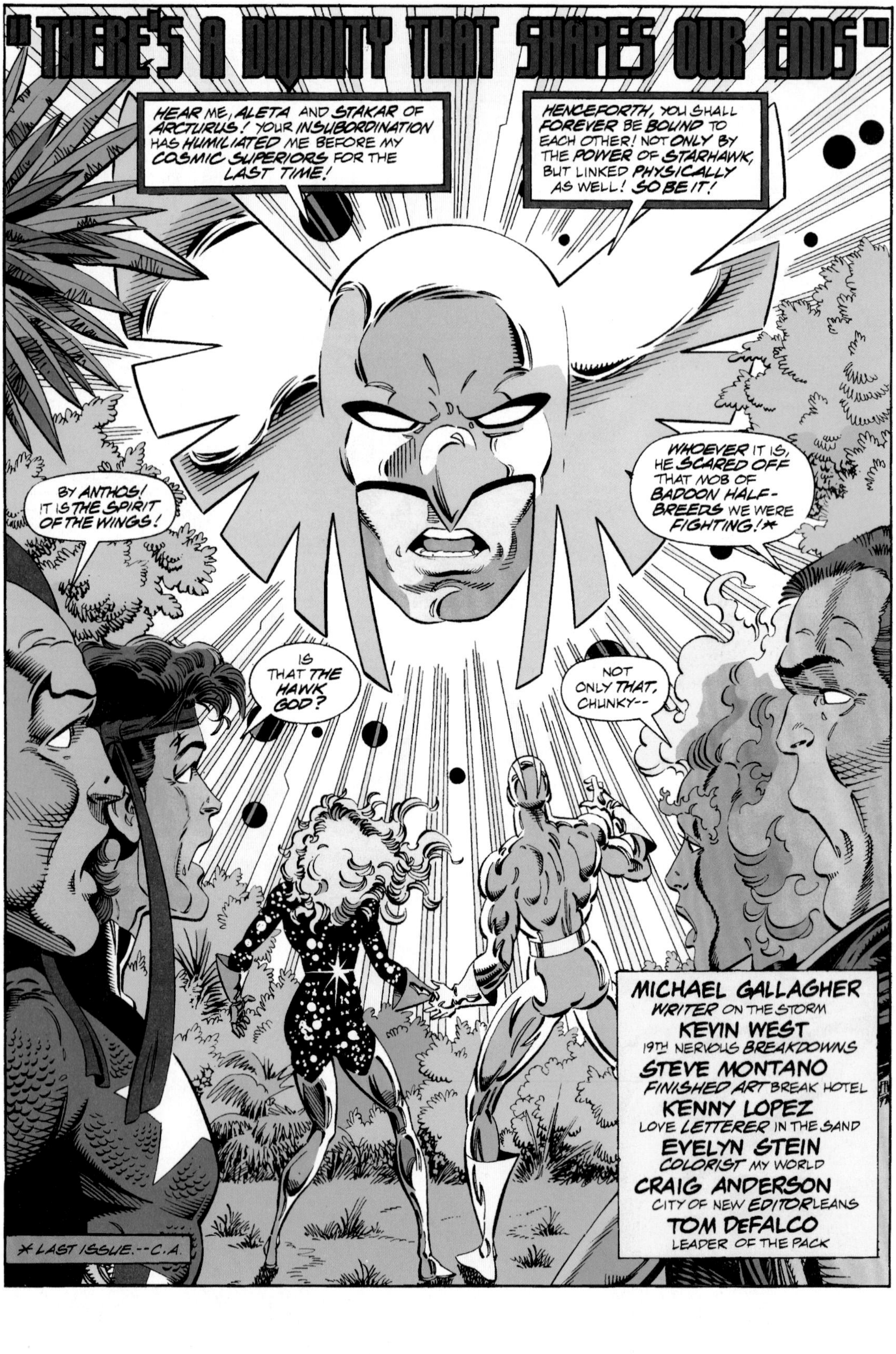
"THERE'S A DIVINITY THAT SHAPES OUR ENDS"
HEAR ME, ALETA AND STAKAR OF ARCTURUS! YOUR INSUBORDINATION HAS HUMILIATED ME BEFORE MY COSMIC SUPERIORS FOR THE LAST TIME!
HENCEFORTH, YOU SHALL FOREVER BE BOUND TO EACH OTHER! NOT ONLY BY THE POWER OF STARHAWK, BUT LINKED PHYSICALLY AS WELL! SO BE IT!
BY ANTHOS! IT IS THE SPIRIT OF THE WINGS!
WHOEVER IT IS, HE SCARED OFF THAT MOB OF BADOON HALF-BREEDS WE WERE FIGHTING!*
IS THAT THE HAWK GOD?
NOT ONLY THAT, CHUNKY--
*LAST ISSUE.--C.A.
MICHAEL GALLAGHER WRITER ON THE STORM
KEVIN WEST 19TH NERVOUS BREAKDOWNS
STEVE MONTANO FINISHED ART BREAK HOTEL
KENNY LOPEZ LOVE LETTERER IN THE SAND
EVELYN STEIN COLORIST MY WORLD
CRAIG ANDERSON CITY OF NEW EDITORLEANS
TOM DeFALCO LEADER OF THE PACK

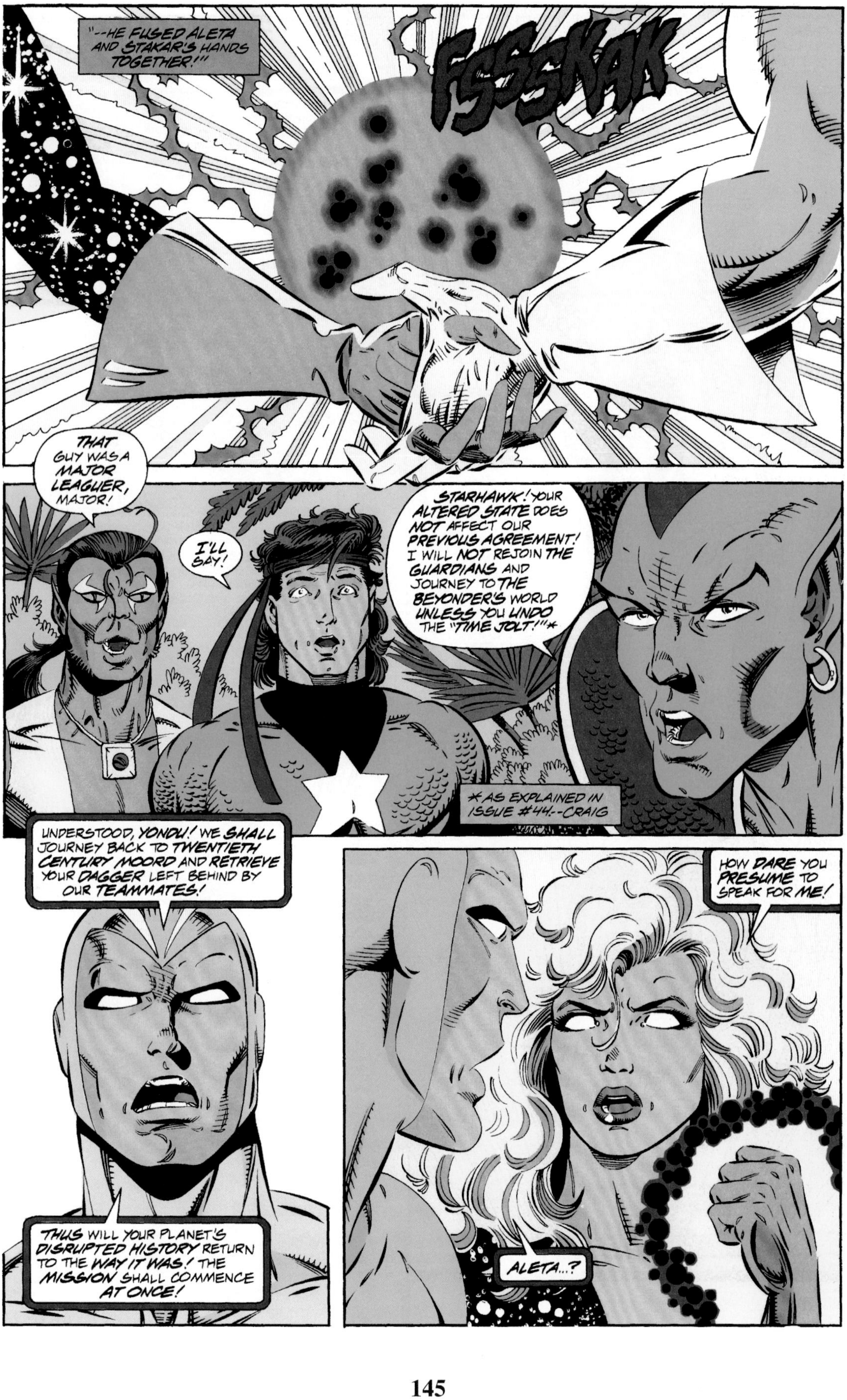

"--HE FUSED ALETA AND STAKAR'S HANDS TOGETHER!"
FSSSKAK
THAT GUY WAS A MAJOR LEAGUER, MAJOR!
I'LL SAY!
STARHAWK! YOUR ALTERED STATE DOES NOT AFFECT OUR PREVIOUS AGREEMENT! I WILL NOT REJOIN THE GUARDIANS AND JOURNEY TO THE BEYONDER'S WORLD UNLESS YOU UNDO THE "TIME JOLT"!*
* AS EXPLAINED IN ISSUE #44.--CRAIG
UNDERSTOOD, YONDU! WE SHALL JOURNEY BACK TO TWENTIETH CENTURY MOORD AND RETRIEVE YOUR DAGGER LEFT BEHIND BY OUR TEAMMATES!
THUS WILL YOUR PLANET'S DISRUPTED HISTORY RETURN TO THE WAY IT WAS! THE MISSION SHALL COMMENCE AT ONCE!
HOW DARE YOU PRESUME TO SPEAK FOR ME!
ALETA...?

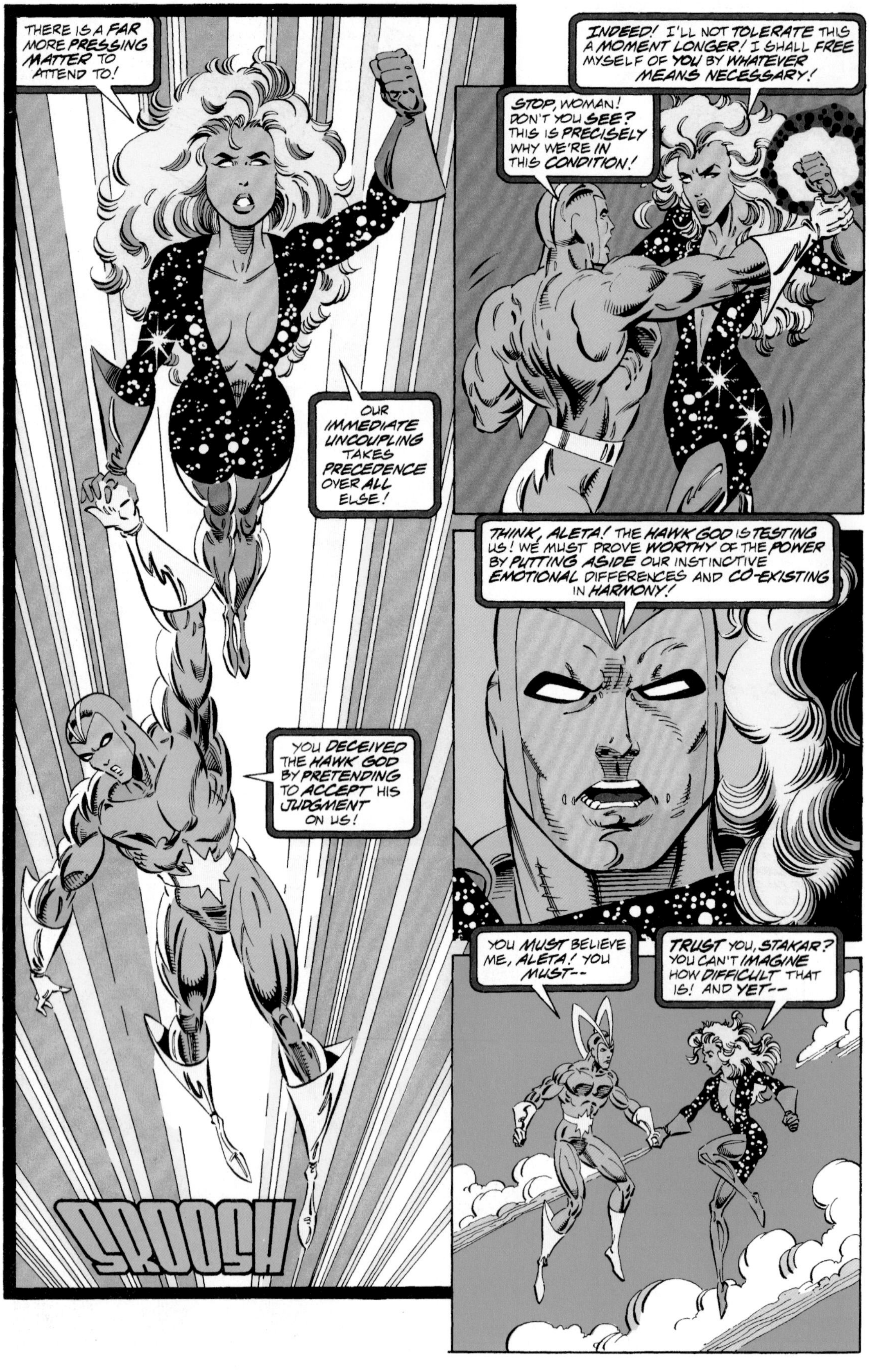
THERE IS A FAR MORE PRESSING MATTER TO ATTEND TO!
OUR IMMEDIATE UNCOUPLING TAKES PRECEDENCE OVER ALL ELSE!
YOU DECEIVED THE HAWK GOD BY PRETENDING TO ACCEPT HIS JUDGMENT ON US!
SROOSH
INDEED! I'LL NOT TOLERATE THIS A MOMENT LONGER! I SHALL FREE MYSELF OF YOU BY WHATEVER MEANS NECESSARY!
STOP, WOMAN! DON'T YOU SEE? THIS IS PRECISELY WHY WE'RE IN THIS CONDITION!
THINK, ALETA! THE HAWK GOD IS TESTING US! WE MUST PROVE WORTHY OF THE POWER BY PUTTING ASIDE OUR INSTINCTIVE EMOTIONAL DIFFERENCES AND CO-EXISTING IN HARMONY!
YOU MUST BELIEVE ME, ALETA! YOU MUST--
TRUST YOU, STAKAR? YOU CAN'T IMAGINE HOW DIFFICULT THAT IS! AND YET--

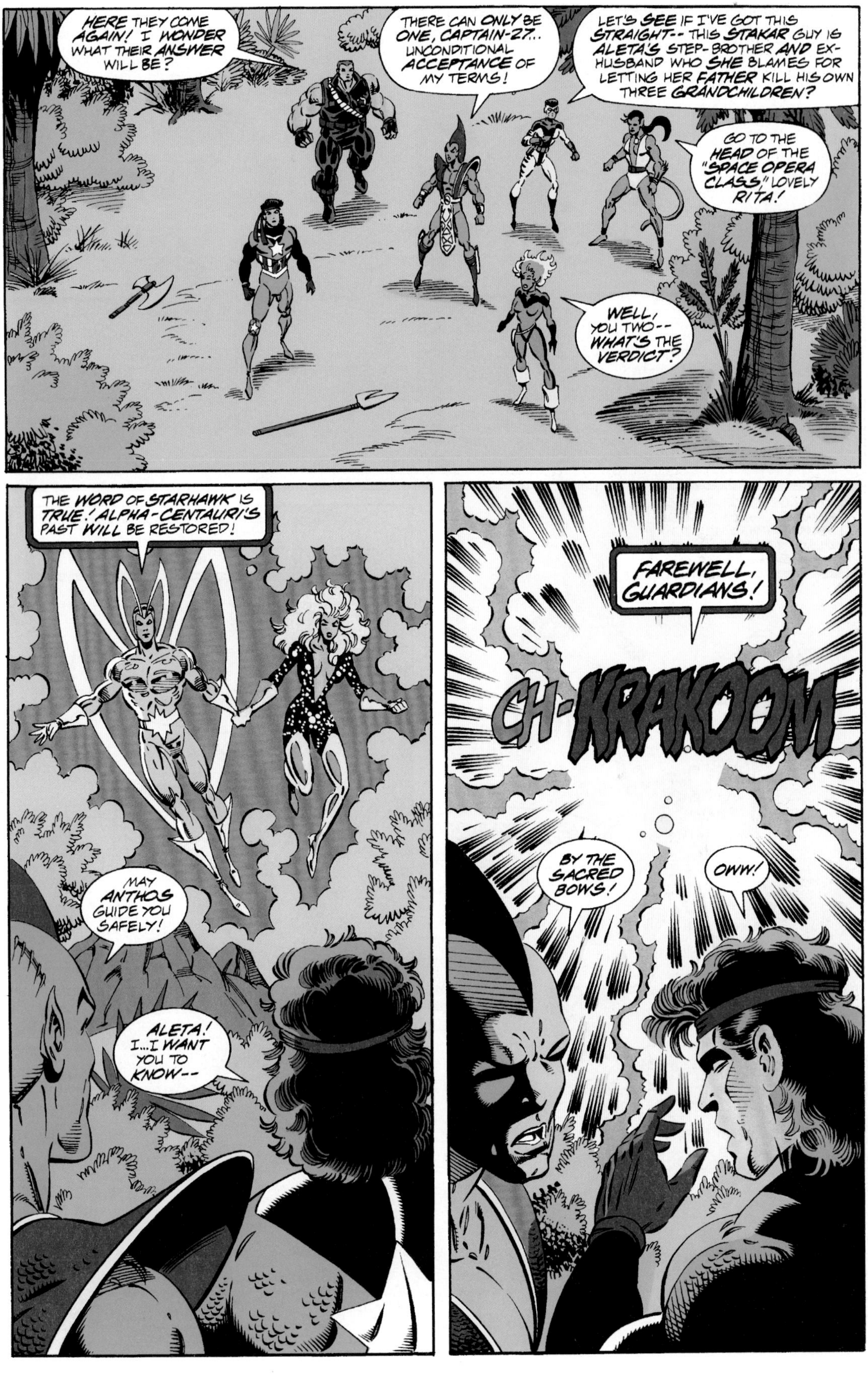

HERE THEY COME AGAIN! I WONDER WHAT THEIR ANSWER WILL BE?
THERE CAN ONLY BE ONE, CAPTAIN-27... UNCONDITIONAL ACCEPTANCE OF MY TERMS!
LET'S SEE IF I'VE GOT THIS STRAIGHT-- THIS STAKAR GUY IS ALETA'S STEP-BROTHER AND EX-HUSBAND WHO SHE BLAMES FOR LETTING HER FATHER KILL HIS OWN THREE GRANDCHILDREN?
GO TO THE HEAD OF THE "SPACE OPERA CLASS," LOVELY RITA!
WELL, YOU TWO-- WHAT'S THE VERDICT?
THE WORD OF STARHAWK IS TRUE! ALPHA-CENTAURI'S PAST WILL BE RESTORED!
MAY ANTHOS GUIDE YOU SAFELY!
ALETA! I...I WANT YOU TO KNOW--
FAREWELL, GUARDIANS!
CH-KRAKOOM
BY THE SACRED BOWS!
OWW!

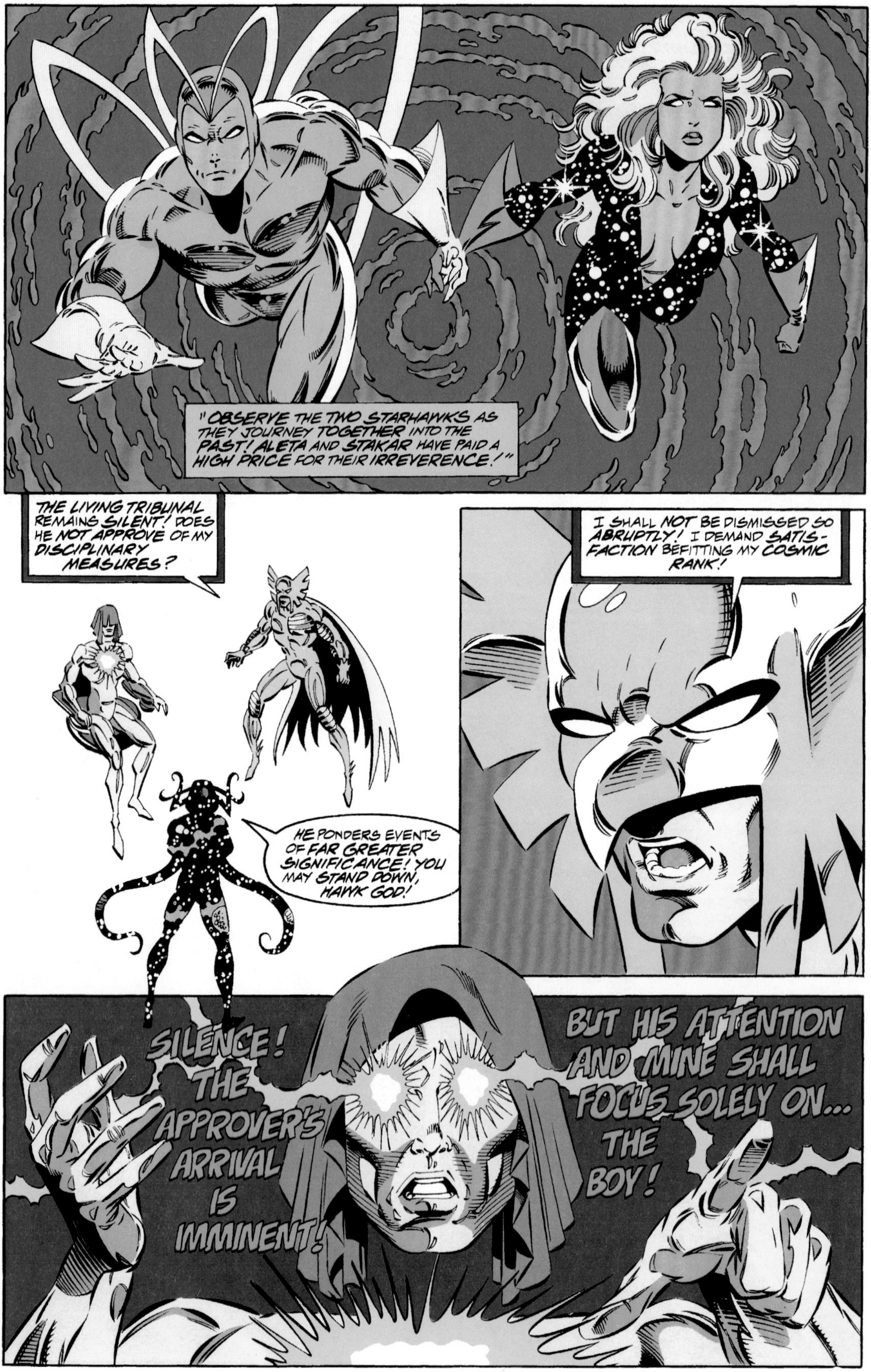
"OBSERVE THE TWO STARHAWKS AS THEY JOURNEY TOGETHER INTO THE PAST! ALETA AND STAKAR HAVE PAID A HIGH PRICE FOR THEIR IRREVERENCE!"
THE LIVING TRIBUNAL REMAINS SILENT! DOES HE NOT APPROVE OF MY DISCIPLINARY MEASURES?
HE PONDERS EVENTS OF FAR GREATER SIGNIFICANCE! YOU MAY STAND DOWN, HAWK GOD!
I SHALL NOT BE DISMISSED SO ABRUPTLY! I DEMAND SATISFACTION BEFITTING MY COSMIC RANK!
SILENCE! THE APPROVER'S ARRIVAL IS IMMINENT!
BUT HIS ATTENTION AND MINE SHALL FOCUS SOLELY ON... THE BOY!

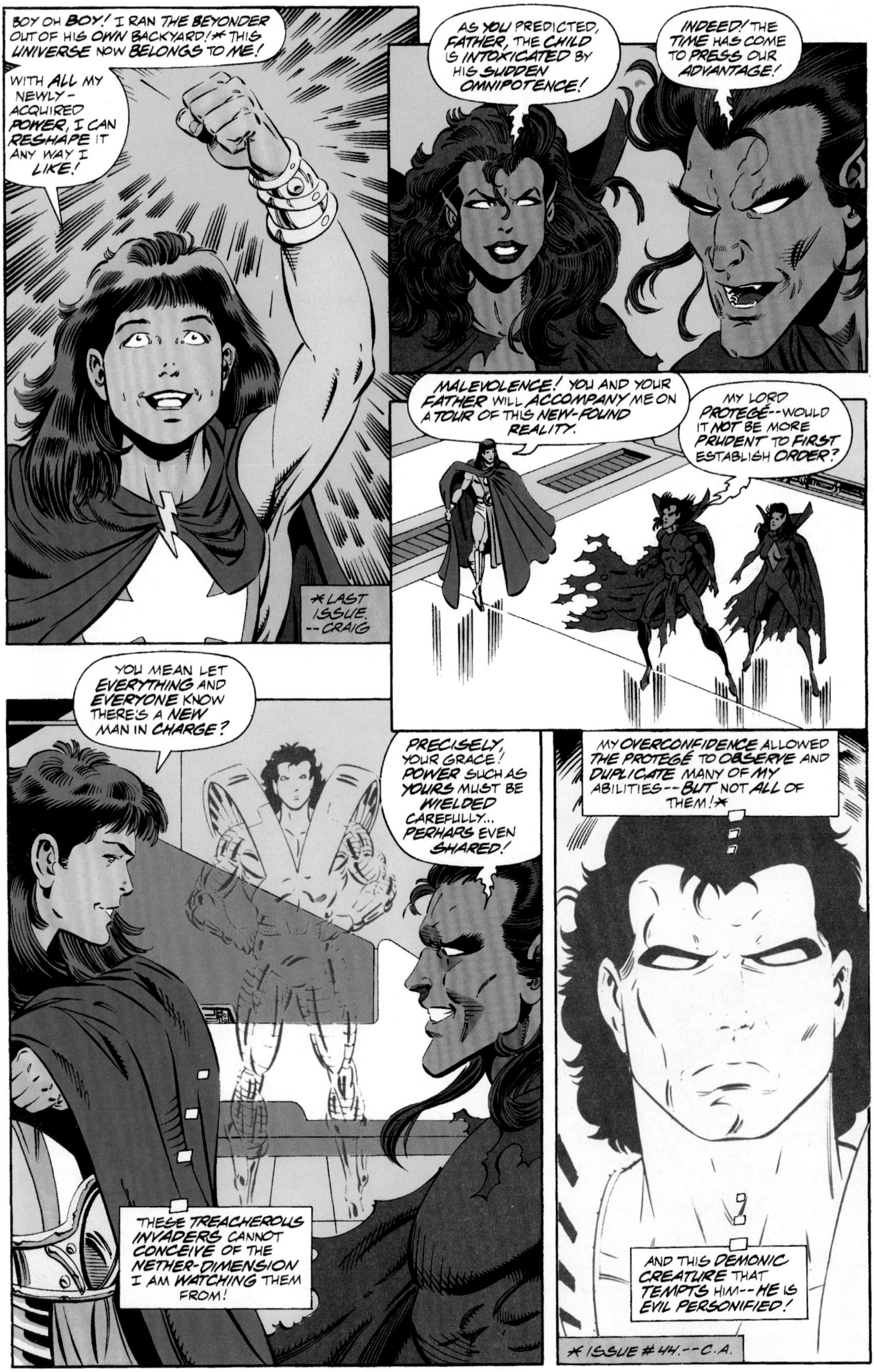

BOY OH BOY! I RAN THE BEYONDER OUT OF HIS OWN BACKYARD!* THIS UNIVERSE NOW BELONGS TO ME!
WITH ALL MY NEWLY-ACQUIRED POWER, I CAN RESHAPE IT ANY WAY I LIKE!
*LAST ISSUE --CRAIG
AS YOU PREDICTED, FATHER, THE CHILD IS INTOXICATED BY HIS SUDDEN OMNIPOTENCE!
INDEED! THE TIME HAS COME TO PRESS OUR ADVANTAGE!
MALEVOLENCE! YOU AND YOUR FATHER WILL ACCOMPANY ME ON A TOUR OF THIS NEW-FOUND REALITY.
MY LORD PROTEGÉ--WOULD IT NOT BE MORE PRUDENT TO FIRST ESTABLISH ORDER?
YOU MEAN LET EVERYTHING AND EVERYONE KNOW THERE'S A NEW MAN IN CHARGE?
PRECISELY, YOUR GRACE! POWER SUCH AS YOURS MUST BE WIELDED CAREFULLY... PERHAPS EVEN SHARED!
THESE TREACHEROUS INVADERS CANNOT CONCEIVE OF THE NETHER-DIMENSION I AM WATCHING THEM FROM!
MY OVERCONFIDENCE ALLOWED THE PROTEGÉ TO OBSERVE AND DUPLICATE MANY OF MY ABILITIES--BUT NOT ALL OF THEM!*
AND THIS DEMONIC CREATURE THAT TEMPTS HIM--HE IS EVIL PERSONIFIED!
*ISSUE #44.--C.A.

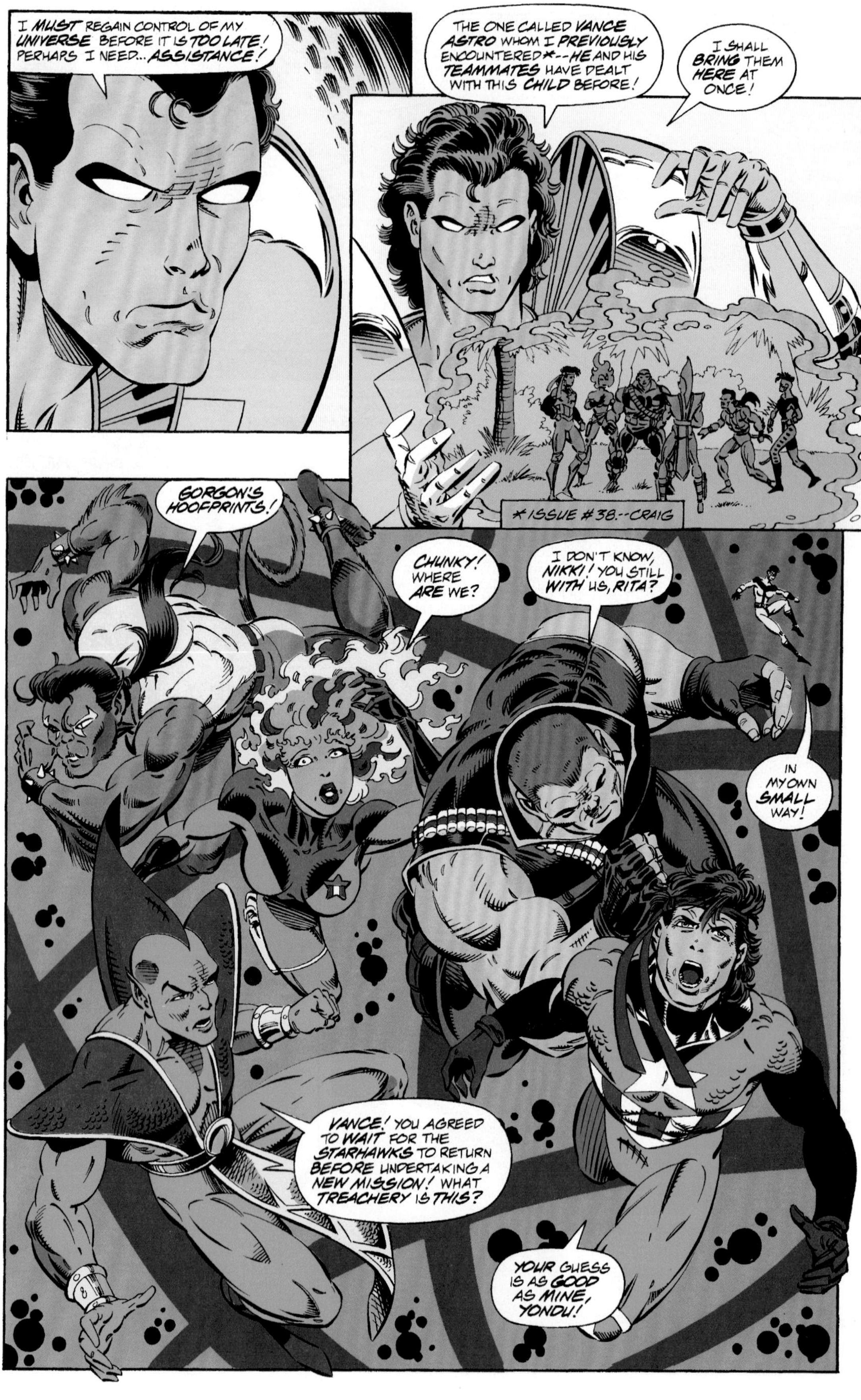
I MUST REGAIN CONTROL OF MY UNIVERSE BEFORE IT IS TOO LATE! PERHAPS I NEED... ASSISTANCE!
THE ONE CALLED VANCE ASTRO WHOM I PREVIOUSLY ENCOUNTERED*--HE AND HIS TEAMMATES HAVE DEALT WITH THIS CHILD BEFORE!
I SHALL BRING THEM HERE AT ONCE!
*ISSUE #38.--CRAIG
GORGON'S HOOFPRINTS!
CHUNKY! WHERE ARE WE?
I DON'T KNOW, NIKKI! YOU STILL WITH US, RITA?
IN MY OWN SMALL WAY!
VANCE! YOU AGREED TO WAIT FOR THE STARHAWKS TO RETURN BEFORE UNDERTAKING A NEW MISSION! WHAT TREACHERY IS THIS?
YOUR GUESS IS AS GOOD AS MINE, YONDU!

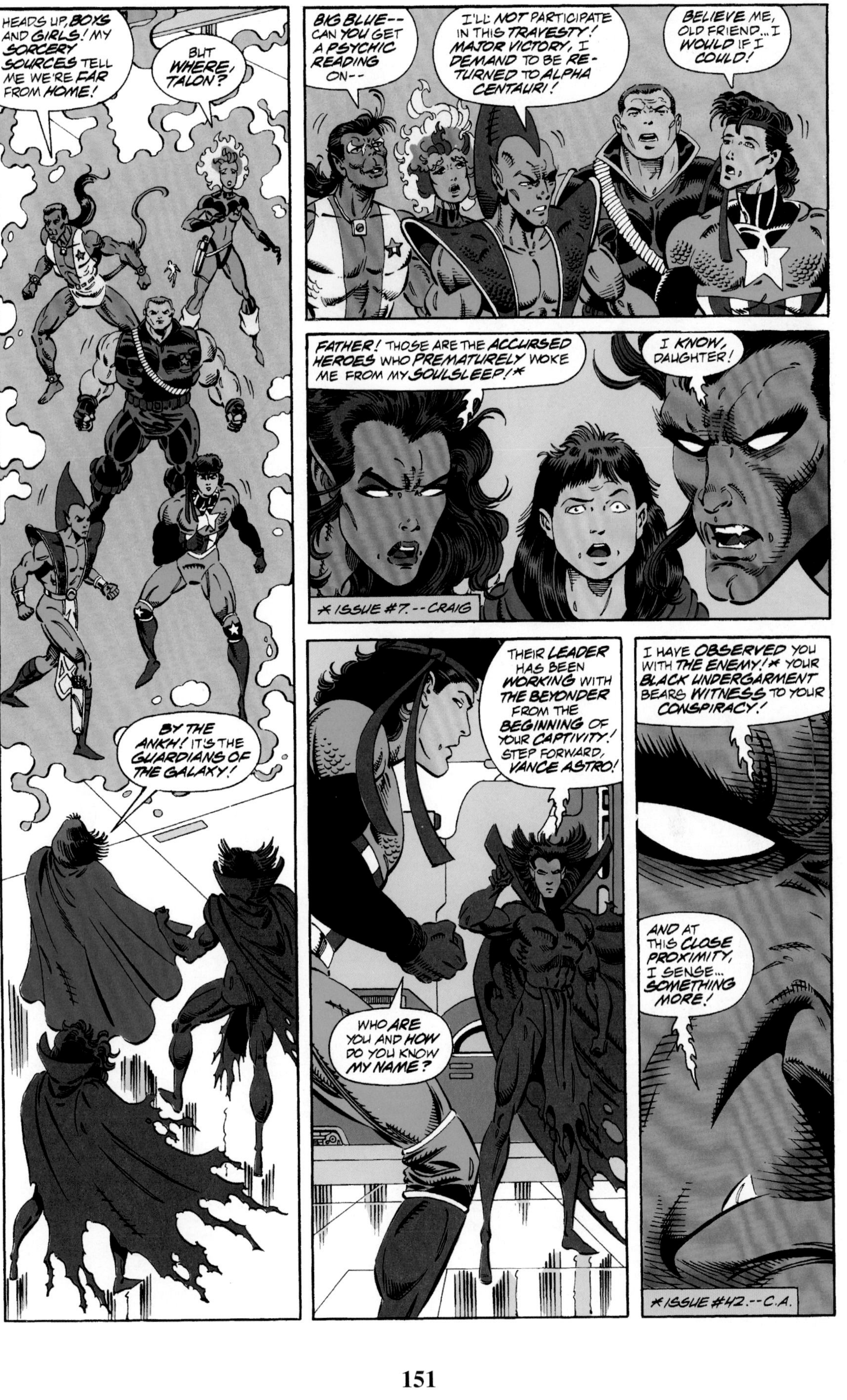
HEADS UP, BOYS AND GIRLS! MY SORCERY SOURCES TELL ME WE'RE FAR FROM HOME!
BUT WHERE, TALON?
BY THE ANKH! IT'S THE GUARDIANS OF THE GALAXY!
BIG BLUE-- CAN YOU GET A PSYCHIC READING ON--
I'LL NOT PARTICIPATE IN THIS TRAVESTY! MAJOR VICTORY, I DEMAND TO BE RE-TURNED TO ALPHA CENTAURI!
BELIEVE ME, OLD FRIEND... I WOULD IF I COULD!
FATHER! THOSE ARE THE ACCURSED HEROES WHO PREMATURELY WOKE ME FROM MY SOULSLEEP!*
I KNOW, DAUGHTER!
*ISSUE #7. --CRAIG
THEIR LEADER HAS BEEN WORKING WITH THE BEYONDER FROM THE BEGINNING OF YOUR CAPTIVITY! STEP FORWARD, VANCE ASTRO!
WHO ARE YOU AND HOW DO YOU KNOW MY NAME?
I HAVE OBSERVED YOU WITH THE ENEMY!* YOUR BLACK UNDERGARMENT BEARS WITNESS TO YOUR CONSPIRACY!
AND AT THIS CLOSE PROXIMITY, I SENSE... SOMETHING MORE!
*ISSUE #42. --C.A.

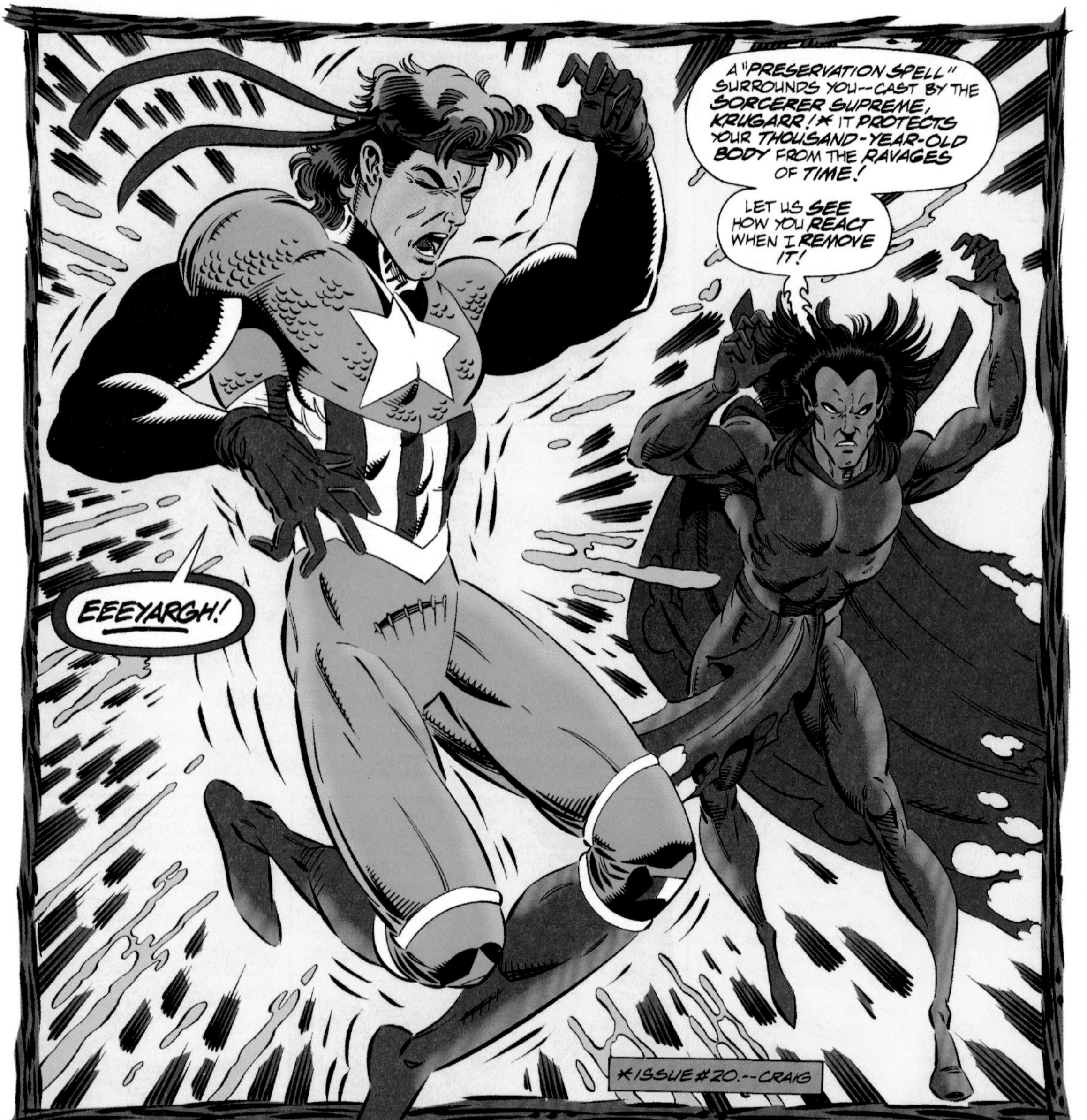
A "PRESERVATION SPELL" SURROUNDS YOU--CAST BY THE SORCERER SUPREME, KRUGARR! * IT PROTECTS YOUR THOUSAND-YEAR-OLD BODY FROM THE RAVAGES OF TIME!
LET US SEE HOW YOU REACT WHEN I REMOVE IT!
EEEYARGH!
* ISSUE #20.--CRAIG

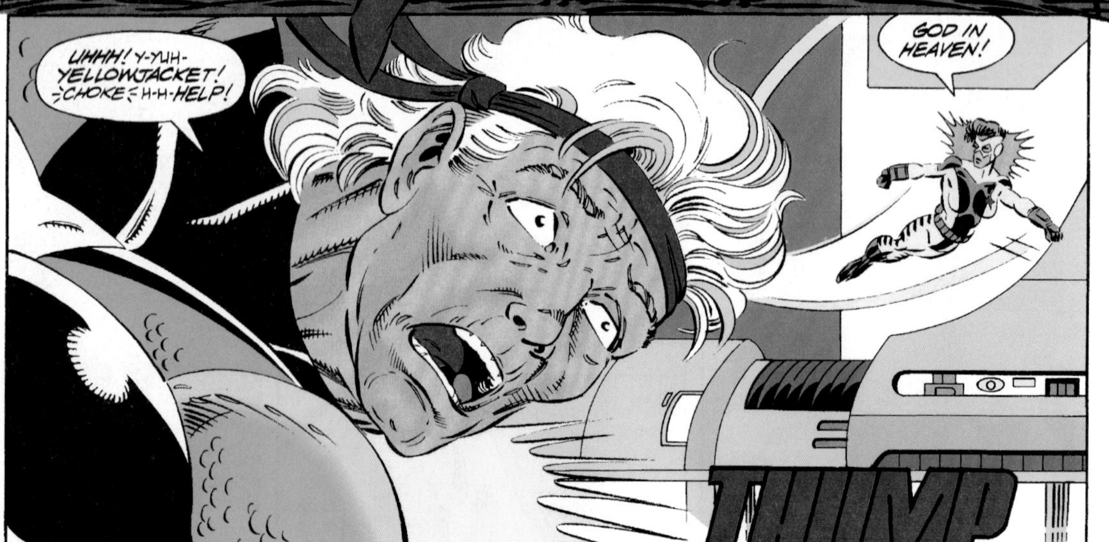
UHHH! Y-YUH-YELLOWJACKET! ~CHOKE~ H-H-HELP!
GOD IN HEAVEN!
THUMP

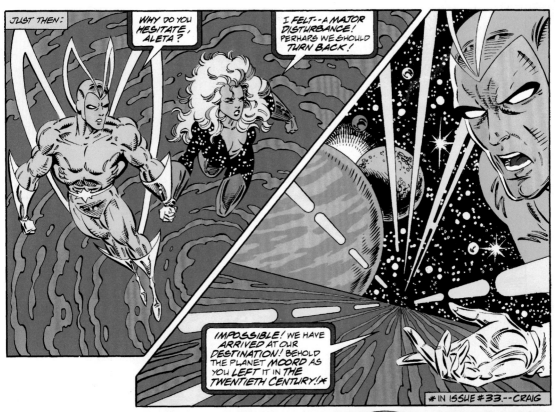

JUST THEN:

WHY DO YOU HESITATE, ALETA?

I FELT--A MAJOR DISTURBANCE! PERHAPS WE SHOULD TURN BACK!

IMPOSSIBLE! WE HAVE ARRIVED AT OUR DESTINATION! BEHOLD THE PLANET *MOORD* AS YOU *LEFT* IT IN *THE TWENTIETH CENTURY!**

*IN ISSUE #33.--CRAIG

AND *BELOW* US, THE *ARENA* WHERE CAPTAIN-27 BATTLED THE *BADOON* WARRIOR, L'MATTO!

OUR *JOVIAN* TEAMMATE NEVER *KNEW* HIS OPPONENT HAD BEEN IMBUED WITH THE CAPTAIN UNIVERSE POWER!

THERE HE LIES-- AFTER *DOCTOR STRANGE* EXORCISED THE *UNI-POWER* FROM HIM!

AND THERE *I* AM, WARNING *THE BROTHER ROYAL* NOT TO *INTERFERE* WITH *THE GUARD-IANS'* DEPARTURE!

153

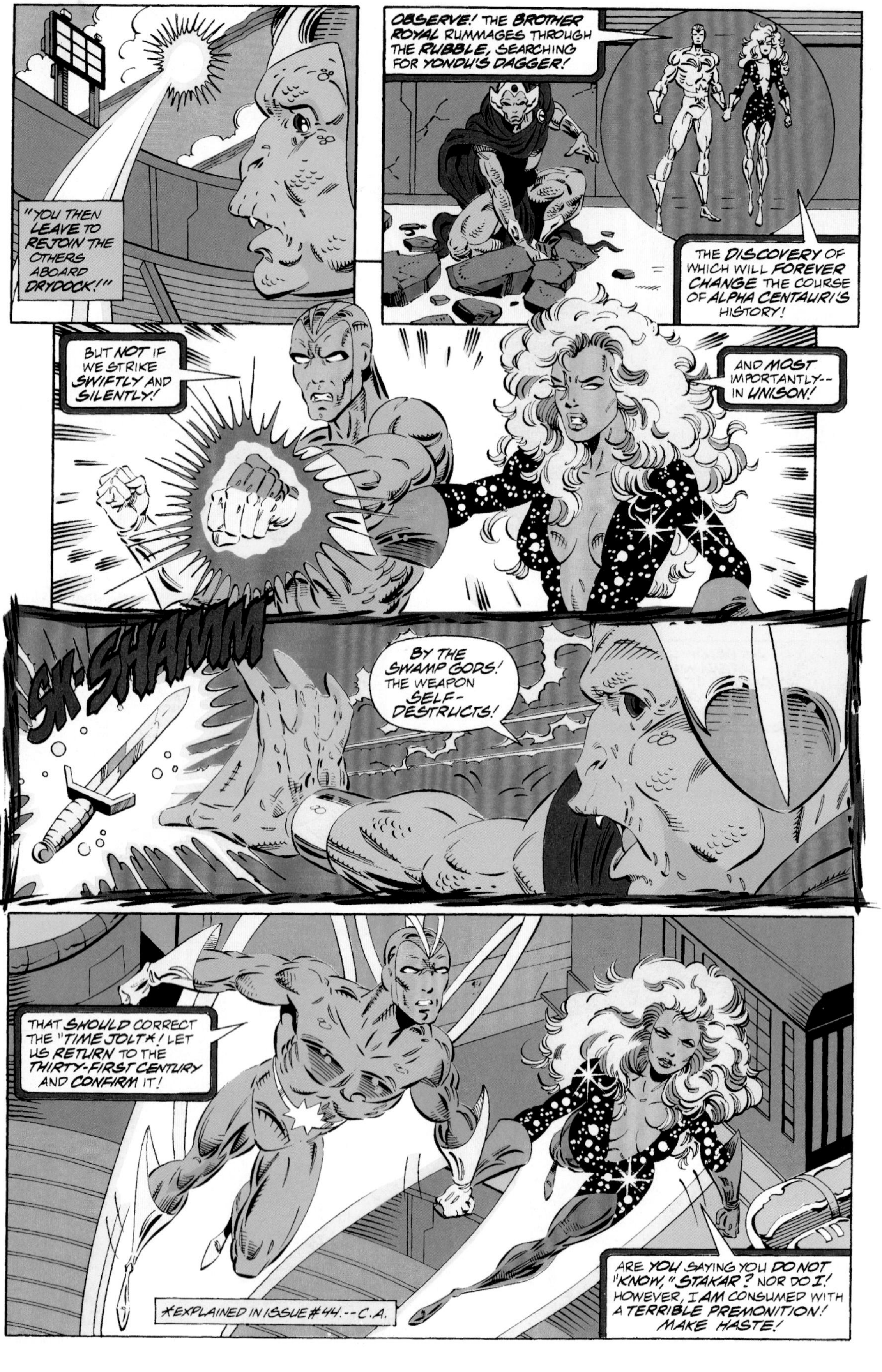
"YOU THEN LEAVE TO REJOIN THE OTHERS ABOARD DRYDOCK!"
OBSERVE! THE BROTHER ROYAL RUMMAGES THROUGH THE RUBBLE, SEARCHING FOR YONDU'S DAGGER!
THE DISCOVERY OF WHICH WILL FOREVER CHANGE THE COURSE OF ALPHA CENTAURI'S HISTORY!
BUT NOT IF WE STRIKE SWIFTLY AND SILENTLY!
AND MOST IMPORTANTLY-- IN UNISON!
SK-SHAMM
BY THE SWAMP GODS! THE WEAPON SELF-DESTRUCTS!
THAT SHOULD CORRECT THE "TIME JOLT*! LET US RETURN TO THE THIRTY-FIRST CENTURY AND CONFIRM IT!
ARE YOU SAYING YOU DO NOT "KNOW," STAKAR? NOR DO I! HOWEVER, I AM CONSUMED WITH A TERRIBLE PREMONITION! MAKE HASTE!
*EXPLAINED IN ISSUE #44.--C.A.

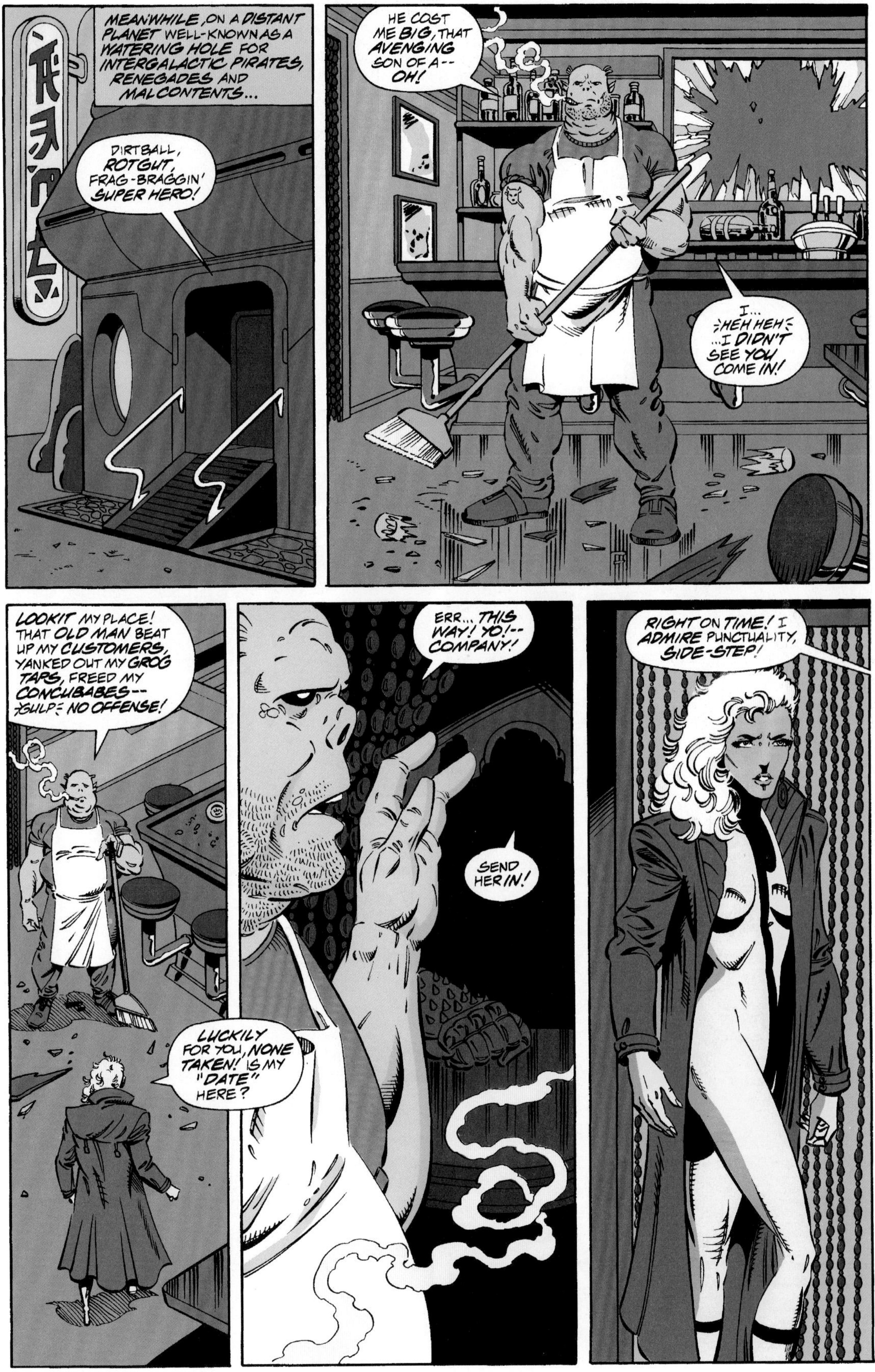
MEANWHILE, ON A DISTANT PLANET WELL-KNOWN AS A WATERING HOLE FOR INTERGALACTIC PIRATES, RENEGADES AND MALCONTENTS...
DIRTBALL, ROTGUT, FRAG-BRAGGIN' SUPER HERO!
HE COST ME BIG, THAT AVENGING SON OF A-- OH!
I... HEH HEH ...I DIDN'T SEE YOU COME IN!
LOOKIT MY PLACE! THAT OLD MAN BEAT UP MY CUSTOMERS, YANKED OUT MY GROG TAPS, FREED MY CONCUBABES-- GULP NO OFFENSE!
LUCKILY FOR YOU, NONE TAKEN! IS MY "DATE" HERE?
ERR... THIS WAY! YO!-- COMPANY!
SEND HER IN!
RIGHT ON TIME! I ADMIRE PUNCTUALITY, SIDE-STEP!

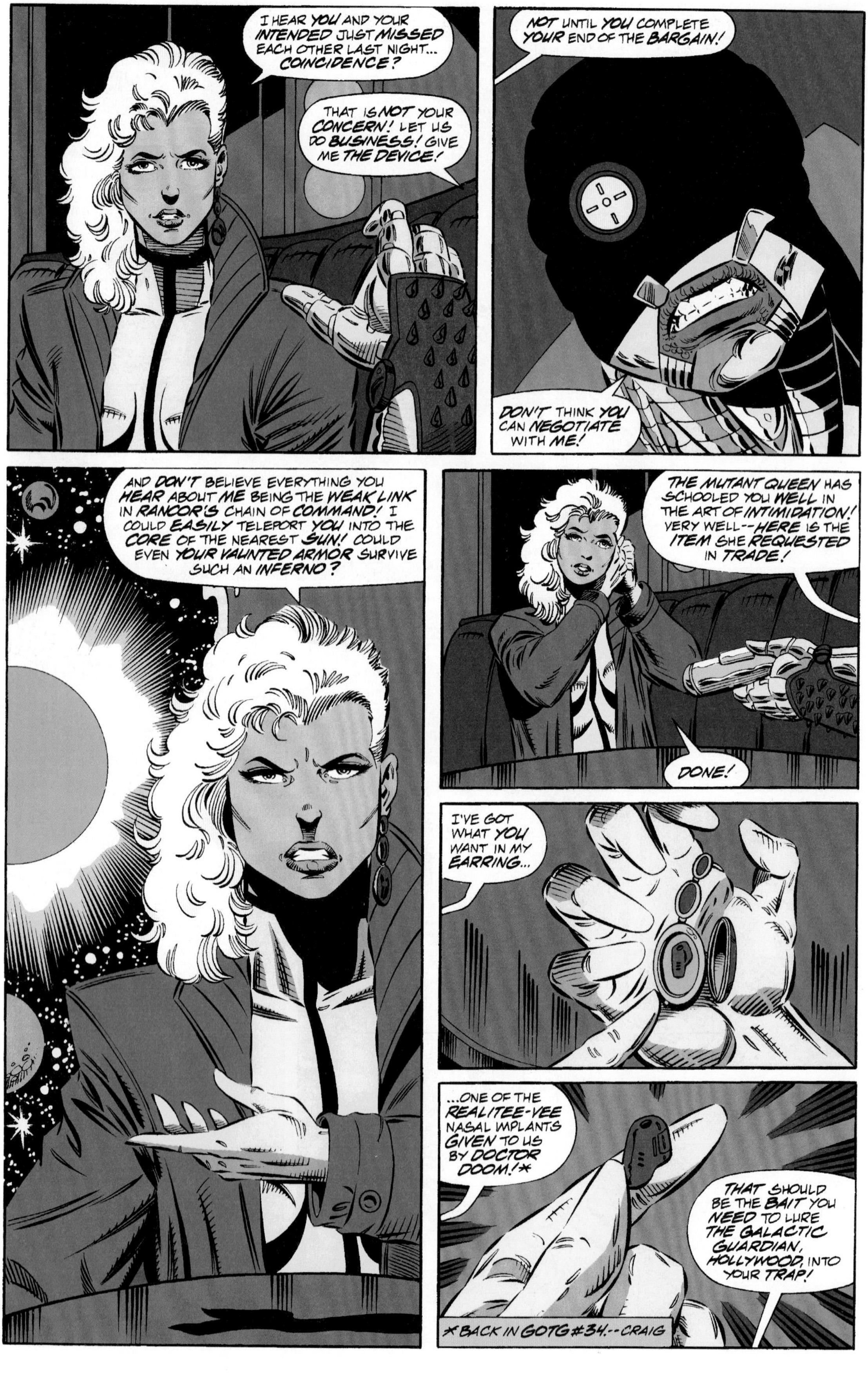
I HEAR YOU AND YOUR INTENDED JUST MISSED EACH OTHER LAST NIGHT... COINCIDENCE?
THAT IS NOT YOUR CONCERN! LET US DO BUSINESS! GIVE ME THE DEVICE!
NOT UNTIL YOU COMPLETE YOUR END OF THE BARGAIN!
DON'T THINK YOU CAN NEGOTIATE WITH ME!
AND DON'T BELIEVE EVERYTHING YOU HEAR ABOUT ME BEING THE WEAK LINK IN RANCOR'S CHAIN OF COMMAND! I COULD EASILY TELEPORT YOU INTO THE CORE OF THE NEAREST SUN! COULD EVEN YOUR VAUNTED ARMOR SURVIVE SUCH AN INFERNO?
THE MUTANT QUEEN HAS SCHOOLED YOU WELL IN THE ART OF INTIMIDATION! VERY WELL--HERE IS THE ITEM SHE REQUESTED IN TRADE!
DONE!
I'VE GOT WHAT YOU WANT IN MY EARRING...
...ONE OF THE REALITEE-VEE NASAL IMPLANTS GIVEN TO US BY DOCTOR DOOM!*
THAT SHOULD BE THE BAIT YOU NEED TO LURE THE GALACTIC GUARDIAN, HOLLYWOOD, INTO YOUR TRAP!
*BACK IN GOTG #34.--CRAIG

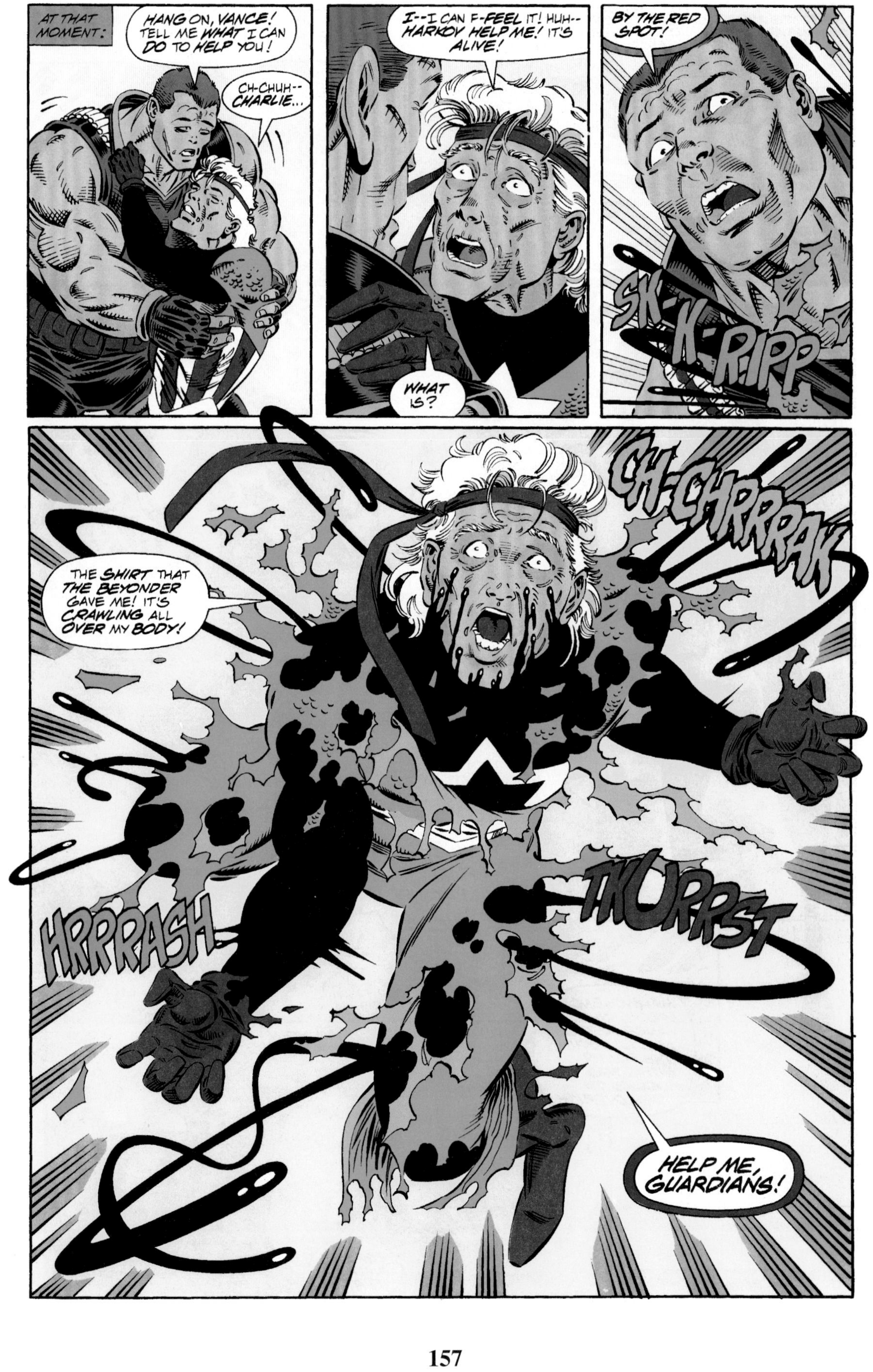
AT THAT MOMENT:
HANG ON, VANCE! TELL ME WHAT I CAN DO TO HELP YOU!
CH-CHUH-- CHARLIE...
I--I CAN F-FEEL IT! HUH-- HARKOV HELP ME! IT'S ALIVE!
WHAT IS?
BY THE RED SPOT!
SK-K-RIPP
CH-CHRRRAK
THE SHIRT THAT THE BEYONDER GAVE ME! IT'S CRAWLING ALL OVER MY BODY!
HRRRASH
TKURRST
HELP ME, GUARDIANS!

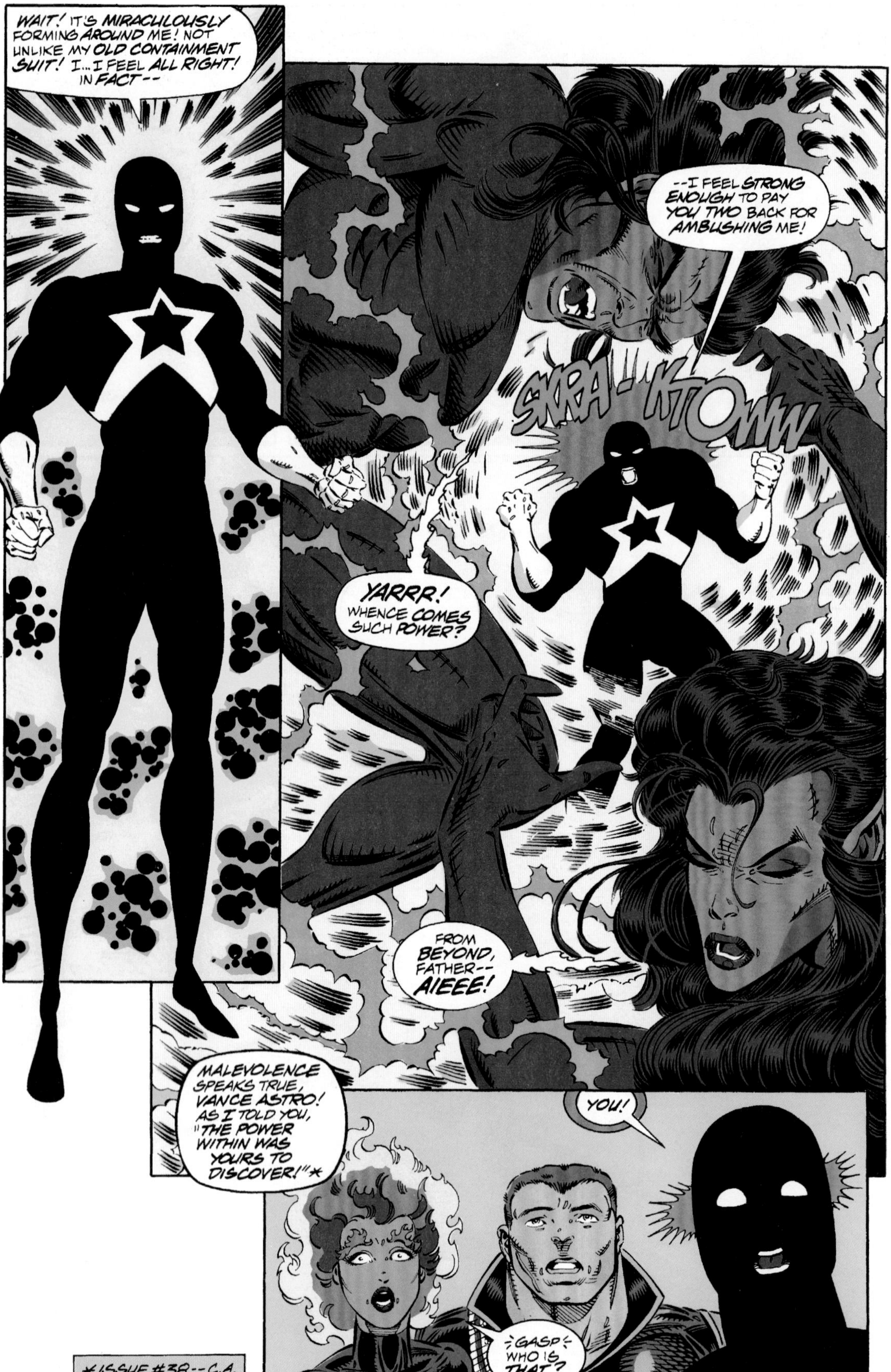
WAIT! IT'S MIRACULOUSLY FORMING AROUND ME! NOT UNLIKE MY OLD CONTAINMENT SUIT! I...I FEEL ALL RIGHT! IN FACT--
--I FEEL STRONG ENOUGH TO PAY YOU TWO BACK FOR AMBUSHING ME!
SKRA-KTOWW
YARRR! WHENCE COMES SUCH POWER?
FROM BEYOND, FATHER-- AIEEE!
MALEVOLENCE SPEAKS TRUE, VANCE ASTRO! AS I TOLD YOU, "THE POWER WITHIN WAS YOURS TO DISCOVER!"*
YOU!
GASP WHO IS THAT?
*ISSUE #38.--C.A.

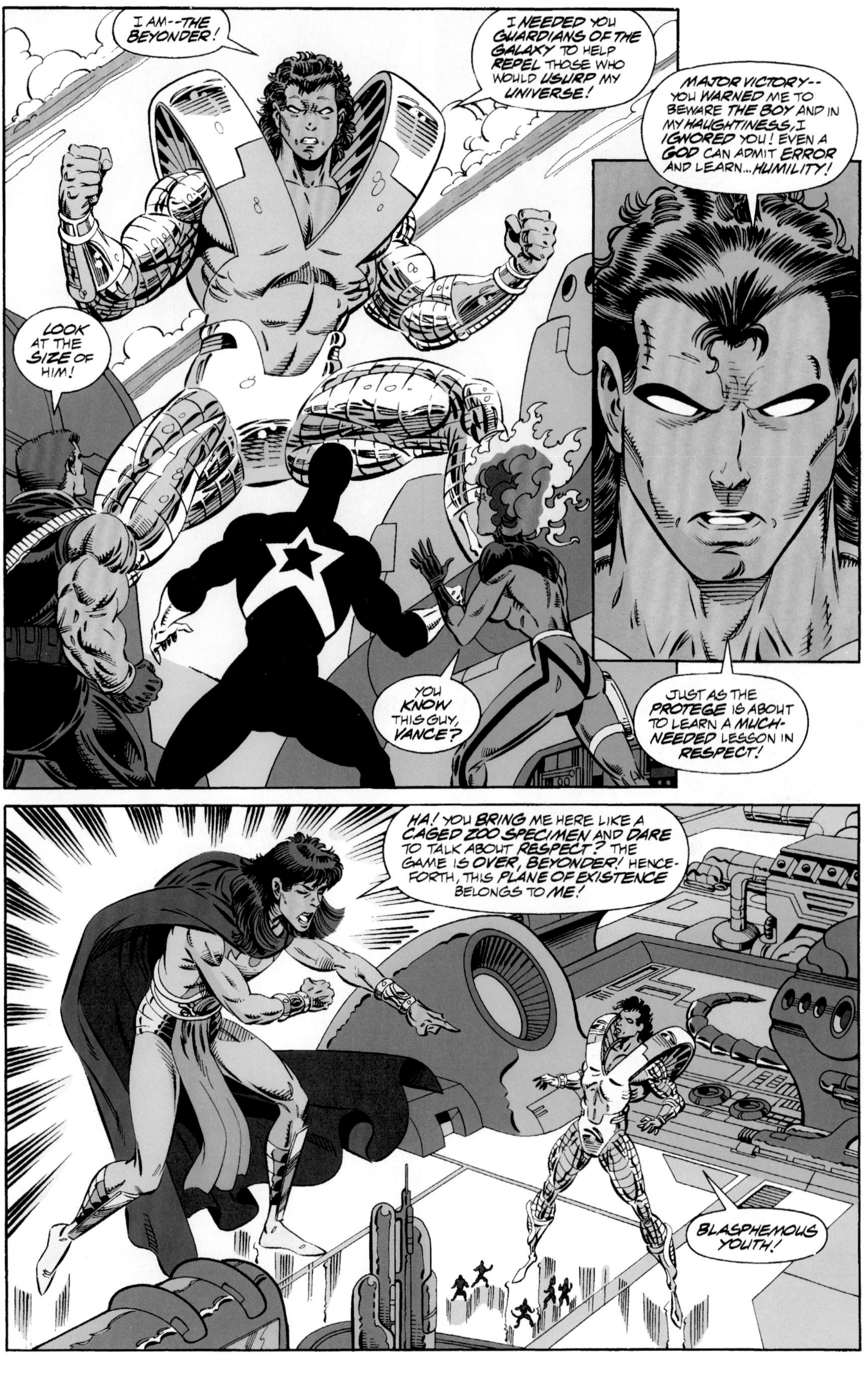
I AM--THE BEYONDER!
I NEEDED YOU GUARDIANS OF THE GALAXY TO HELP REPEL THOSE WHO WOULD USURP MY UNIVERSE!
MAJOR VICTORY--YOU WARNED ME TO BEWARE THE BOY AND IN MY HAUGHTINESS, I IGNORED YOU! EVEN A GOD CAN ADMIT ERROR AND LEARN... HUMILITY!
LOOK AT THE SIZE OF HIM!
YOU KNOW THIS GUY, VANCE?
JUST AS THE PROTEGE IS ABOUT TO LEARN A MUCH-NEEDED LESSON IN RESPECT!
HA! YOU BRING ME HERE LIKE A CAGED ZOO SPECIMEN AND DARE TO TALK ABOUT RESPECT? THE GAME IS OVER, BEYONDER! HENCE-FORTH, THIS PLANE OF EXISTENCE BELONGS TO ME!
BLASPHEMOUS YOUTH!

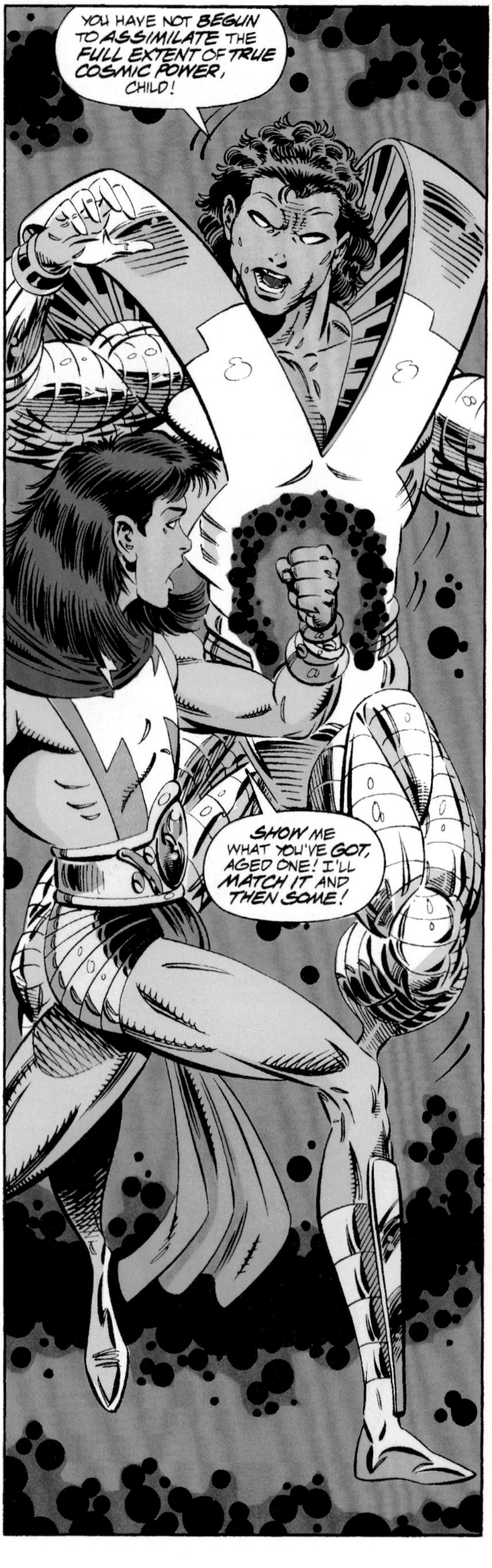
YOU HAVE NOT BEGUN TO ASSIMILATE THE FULL EXTENT OF TRUE COSMIC POWER, CHILD!
SHOW ME WHAT YOU'VE GOT, AGED ONE! I'LL MATCH IT AND THEN SOME!

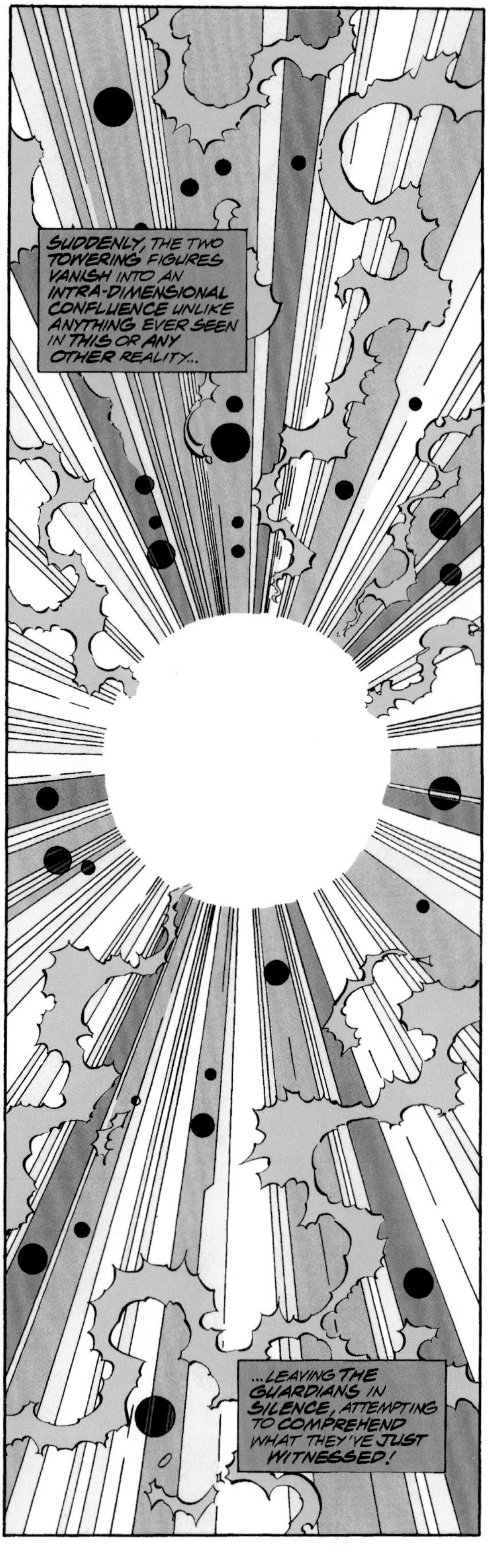
SUDDENLY, THE TWO TOWERING FIGURES VANISH INTO AN INTRA-DIMENSIONAL CONFLUENCE UNLIKE ANYTHING EVER SEEN IN THIS OR ANY OTHER REALITY...
...LEAVING THE GUARDIANS IN SILENCE, ATTEMPTING TO COMPREHEND WHAT THEY'VE JUST WITNESSED!

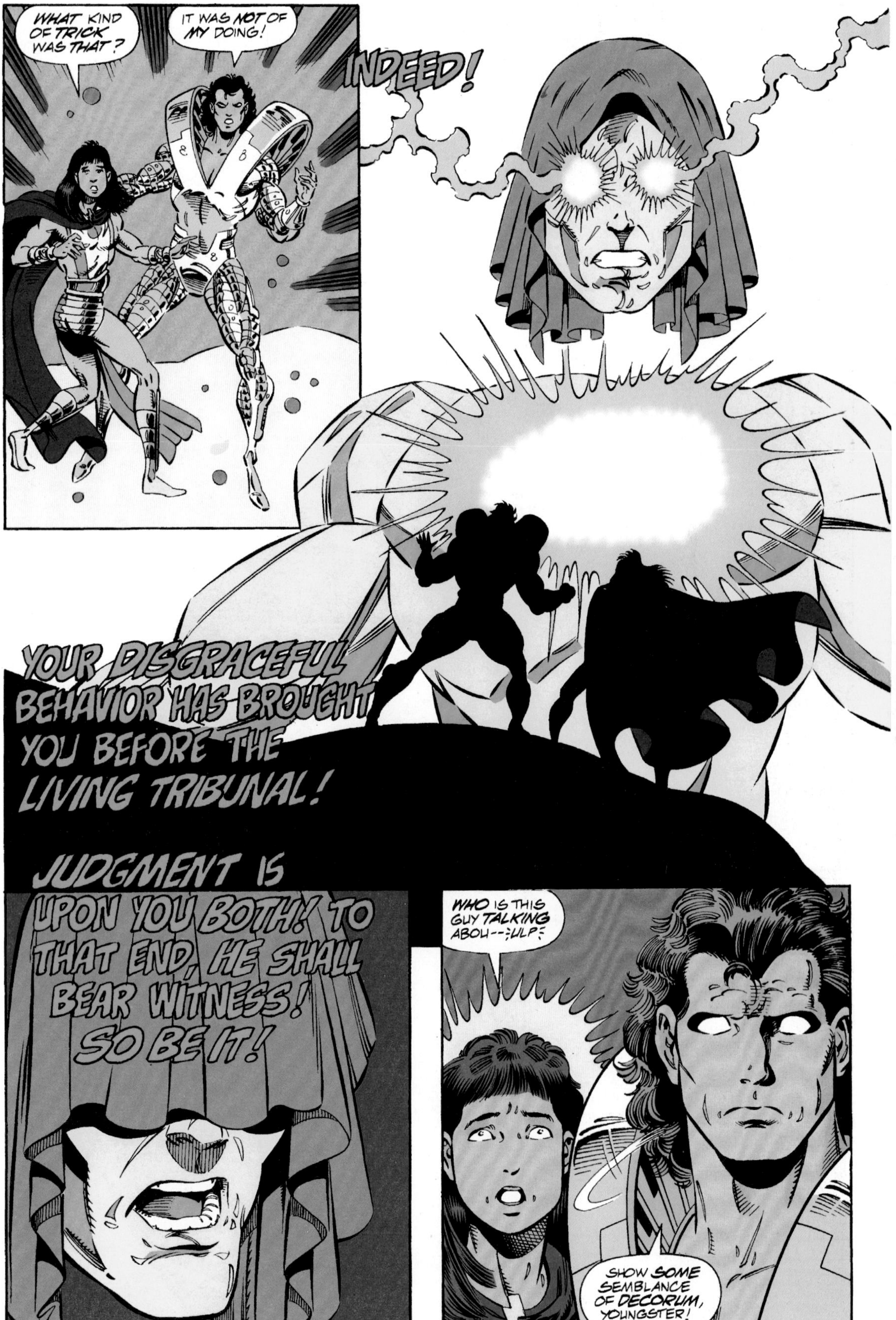
WHAT KIND OF TRICK WAS THAT?
IT WAS NOT OF MY DOING!
INDEED!
YOUR DISGRACEFUL BEHAVIOR HAS BROUGHT YOU BEFORE THE LIVING TRIBUNAL!
JUDGMENT IS UPON YOU BOTH! TO THAT END, HE SHALL BEAR WITNESS! SO BE IT!
WHO IS THIS GUY TALKING ABOU--ULP!
SHOW SOME SEMBLANCE OF DECORUM, YOUNGSTER!

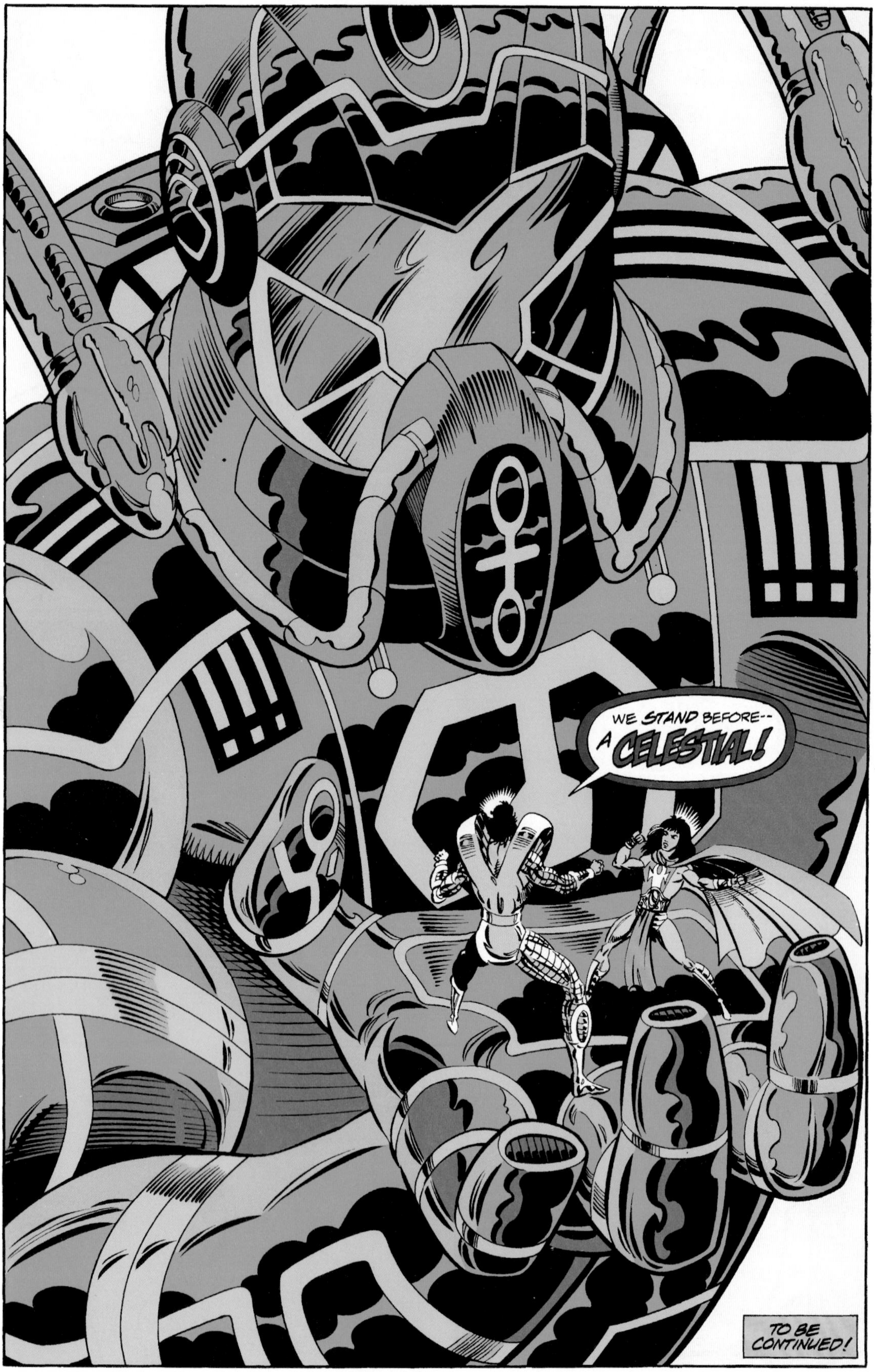
WE STAND BEFORE-- A CELESTIAL!
TO BE CONTINUED!

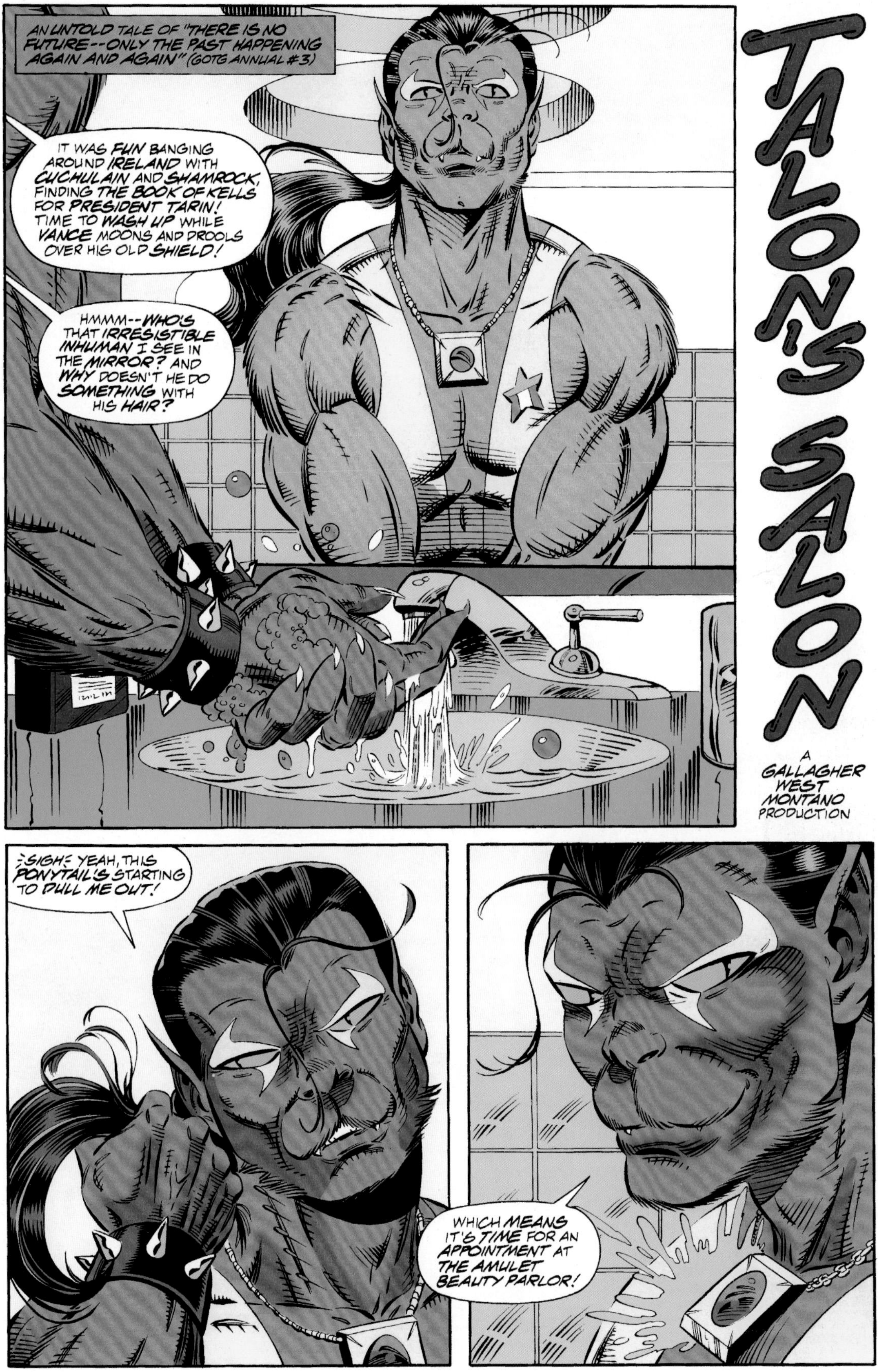
AN UNTOLD TALE OF "THERE IS NO FUTURE--ONLY THE PAST HAPPENING AGAIN AND AGAIN" (GOTG ANNUAL #3)
TALON'S SALON
A GALLAGHER WEST MONTANO PRODUCTION
IT WAS FUN BANGING AROUND IRELAND WITH CUCHULAIN AND SHAMROCK, FINDING THE BOOK OF KELLS FOR PRESIDENT TARIN! TIME TO WASH UP WHILE VANCE MOONS AND DROOLS OVER HIS OLD SHIELD!
HMMM--WHO'S THAT IRRESISTIBLE INHUMAN I SEE IN THE MIRROR? AND WHY DOESN'T HE DO SOMETHING WITH HIS HAIR?
=SIGH= YEAH, THIS PONYTAIL'S STARTING TO DULL ME OUT!
WHICH MEANS IT'S TIME FOR AN APPOINTMENT AT THE AMULET BEAUTY PARLOR!

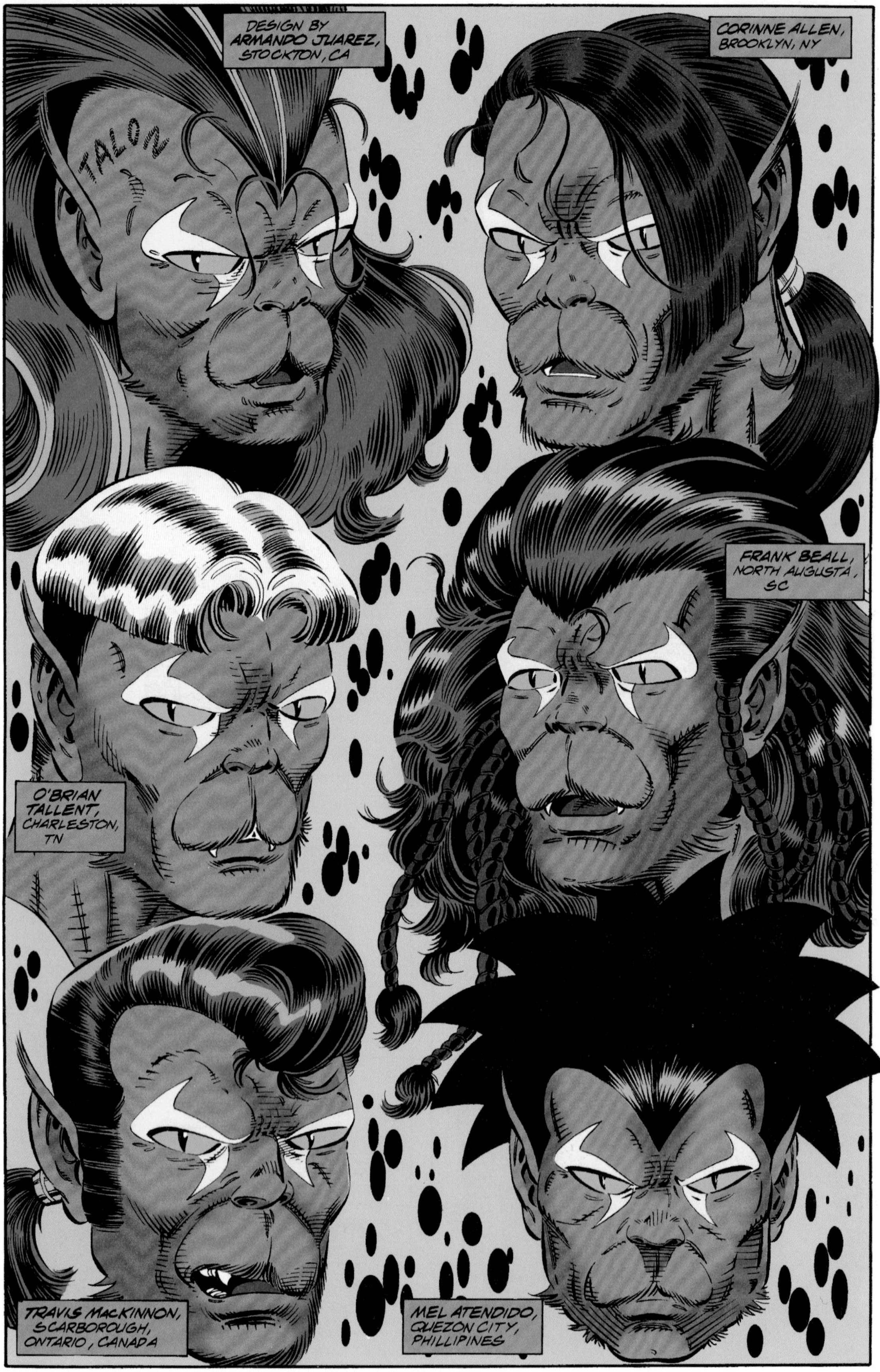
DESIGN BY ARMANDO JUAREZ, STOCKTON, CA
TALON
CORINNE ALLEN, BROOKLYN, NY
FRANK BEALL, NORTH AUGUSTA, SC
O'BRIAN TALLENT, CHARLESTON, TN
TRAVIS MACKINNON, SCARBOROUGH, ONTARIO, CANADA
MEL ATENDIDO, QUEZON CITY, PHILLIPINES

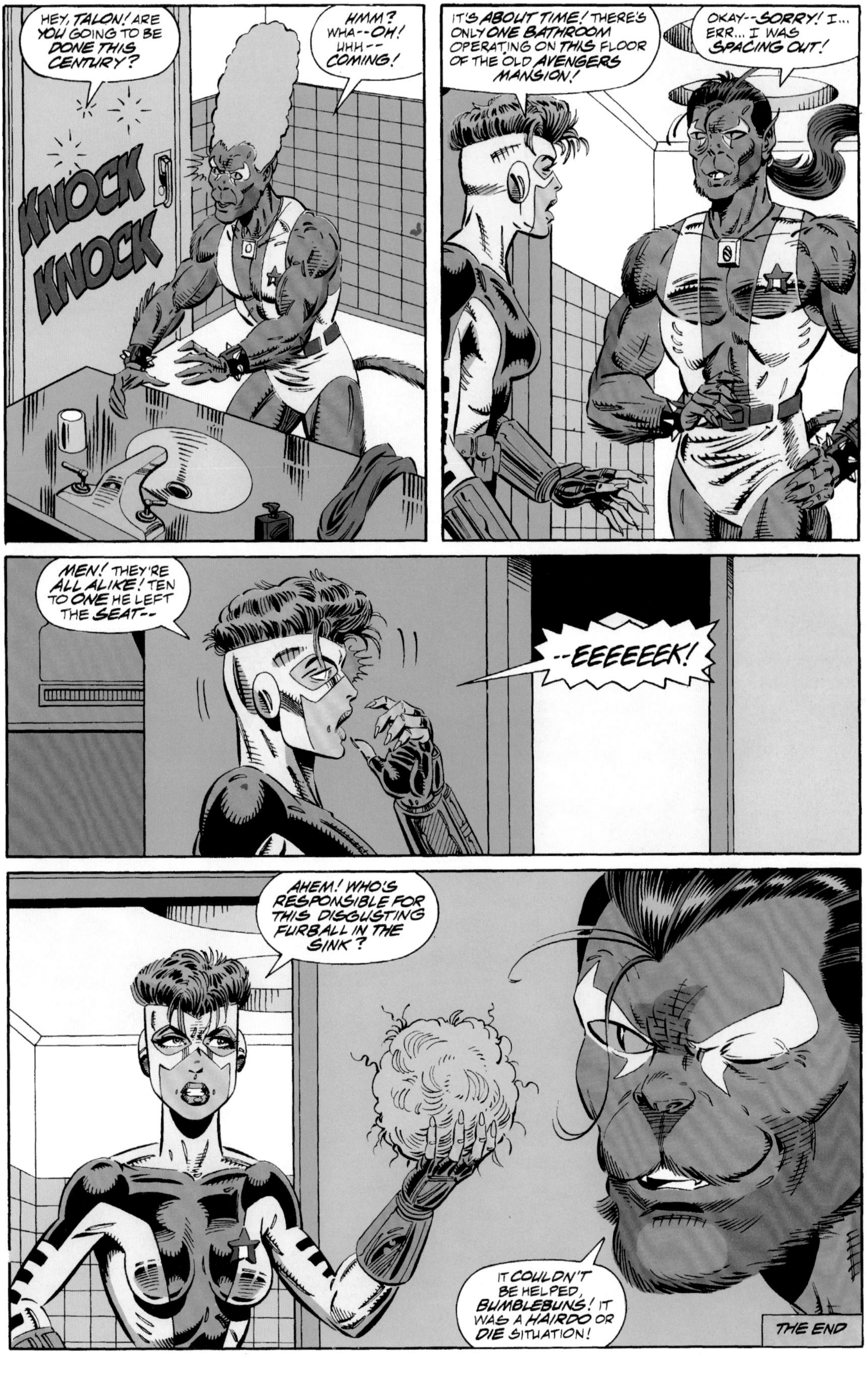
HEY, TALON! ARE YOU GOING TO BE DONE THIS CENTURY?
KNOCK KNOCK
HMM? WHA--OH! UHH-- COMING!
IT'S ABOUT TIME! THERE'S ONLY ONE BATHROOM OPERATING ON THIS FLOOR OF THE OLD AVENGERS MANSION!
OKAY--SORRY! I... ERR... I WAS SPACING OUT!
MEN! THEY'RE ALL ALIKE! TEN TO ONE HE LEFT THE SEAT--
--EEEEEEK!
AHEM! WHO'S RESPONSIBLE FOR THIS DISGUSTING FURBALL IN THE SINK?
IT COULDN'T BE HELPED, BUMBLEBUNS! IT WAS A HAIRDO OR DIE SITUATION!
THE END

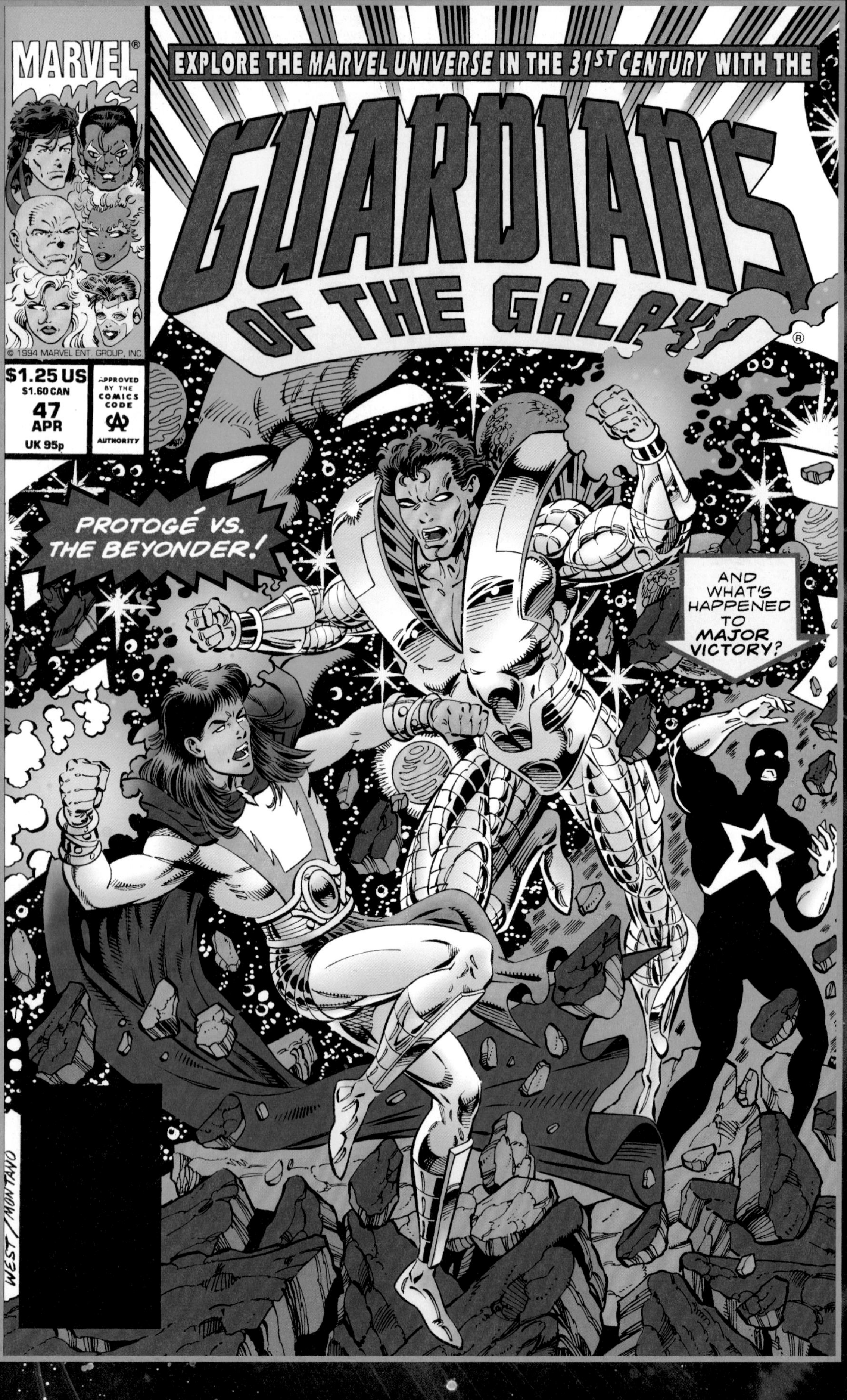
MARVEL COMICS
EXPLORE THE MARVEL UNIVERSE IN THE 31ST CENTURY WITH THE
GUARDIANS OF THE GALAXY
© 1994 MARVEL ENT. GROUP, INC.
$1.25 US
$1.60 CAN
47
APR
UK 95p
APPROVED BY THE COMICS CODE AUTHORITY
PROTOGÉ VS. THE BEYONDER!
AND WHAT'S HAPPENED TO MAJOR VICTORY?
WEST/MONTANO

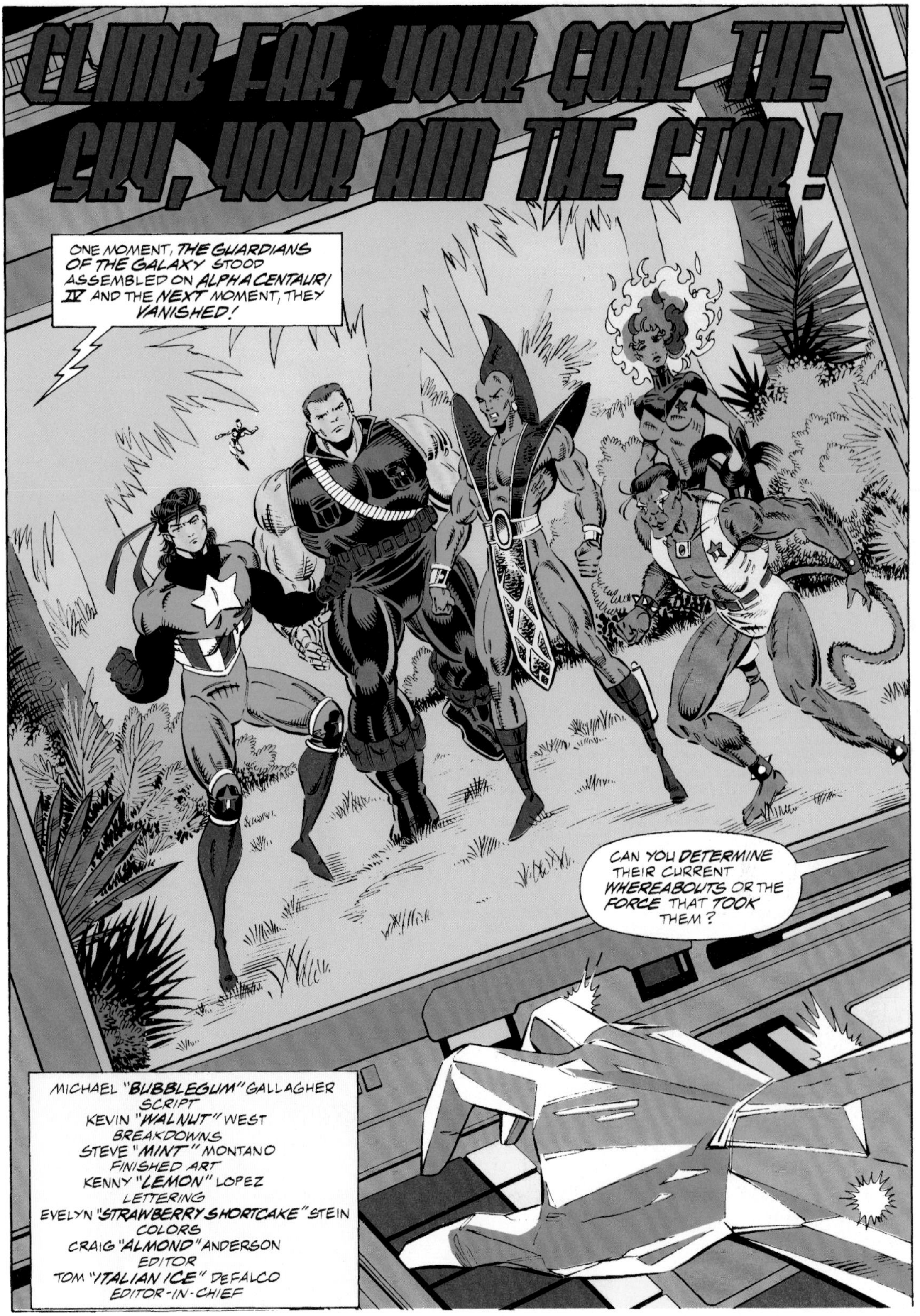
CLIMB FAR, YOUR GOAL THE SKY, YOUR AIM THE STAR!
ONE MOMENT, THE GUARDIANS OF THE GALAXY STOOD ASSEMBLED ON ALPHA CENTAURI IV AND THE NEXT MOMENT, THEY VANISHED!
CAN YOU DETERMINE THEIR CURRENT WHEREABOUTS OR THE FORCE THAT TOOK THEM?
MICHAEL "BUBBLEGUM" GALLAGHER SCRIPT
KEVIN "WALNUT" WEST BREAKDOWNS
STEVE "MINT" MONTANO FINISHED ART
KENNY "LEMON" LOPEZ LETTERING
EVELYN "STRAWBERRY SHORTCAKE" STEIN COLORS
CRAIG "ALMOND" ANDERSON EDITOR
TOM "ITALIAN ICE" DEFALCO EDITOR-IN-CHIEF

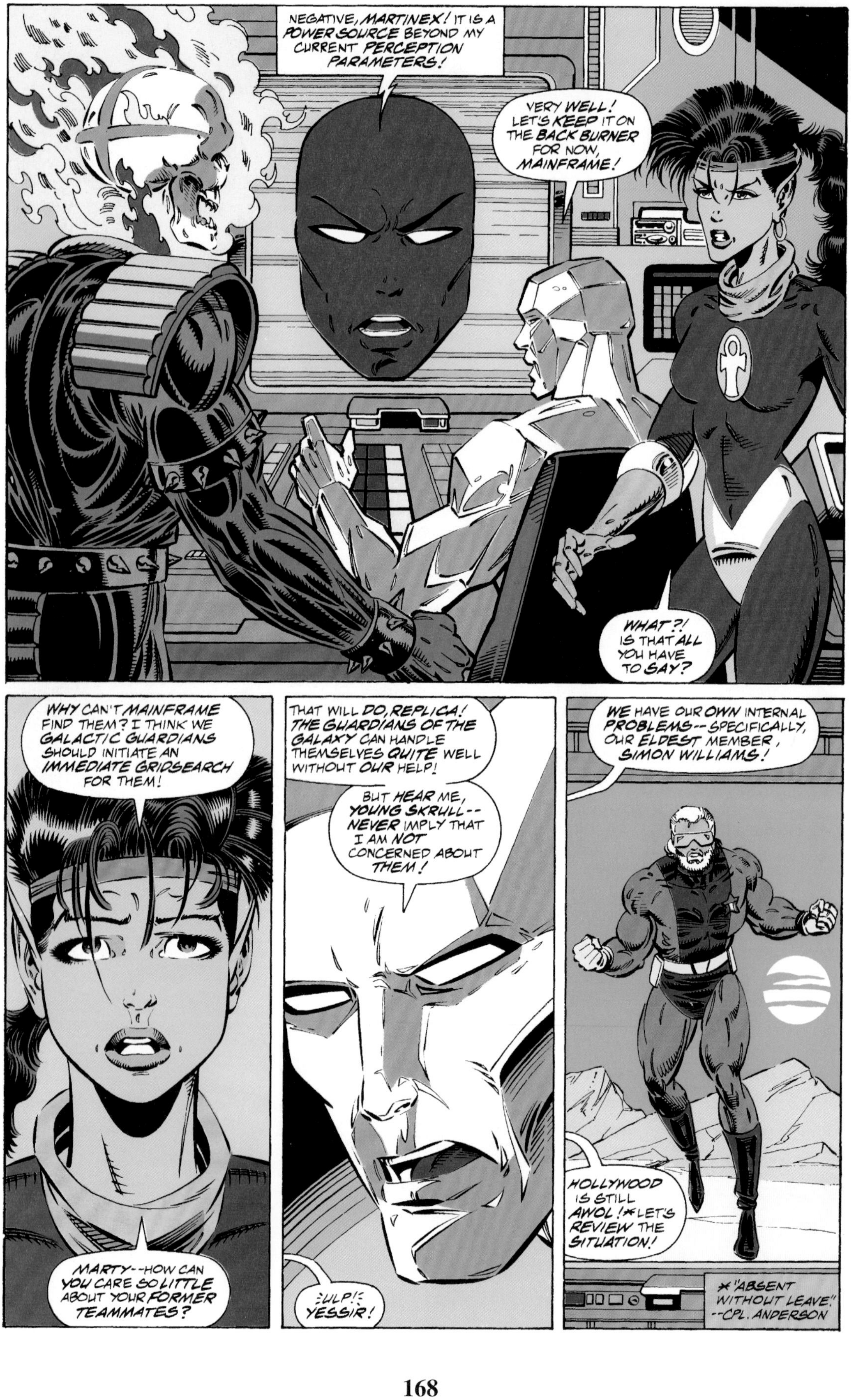
NEGATIVE, MARTINEX! IT IS A POWER SOURCE BEYOND MY CURRENT PERCEPTION PARAMETERS!
VERY WELL! LET'S KEEP IT ON THE BACK BURNER FOR NOW, MAINFRAME!
WHAT?! IS THAT ALL YOU HAVE TO SAY?
WHY CAN'T MAINFRAME FIND THEM? I THINK WE GALACTIC GUARDIANS SHOULD INITIATE AN IMMEDIATE GRIDSEARCH FOR THEM!
MARTY--HOW CAN YOU CARE SO LITTLE ABOUT YOUR FORMER TEAMMATES?
THAT WILL DO, REPLICA! THE GUARDIANS OF THE GALAXY CAN HANDLE THEMSELVES QUITE WELL WITHOUT OUR HELP!
BUT HEAR ME, YOUNG SKRULL--NEVER IMPLY THAT I AM NOT CONCERNED ABOUT THEM!
!ULP!! YESSIR!
WE HAVE OUR OWN INTERNAL PROBLEMS--SPECIFICALLY, OUR ELDEST MEMBER, SIMON WILLIAMS!
HOLLYWOOD IS STILL AWOL!* LET'S REVIEW THE SITUATION!
*"ABSENT WITHOUT LEAVE." --CPL. ANDERSON

AFFIRMATIVE! PREVIOUS TO JOINING *THE GALACTIC GUARDIANS*, *SIMON WILLIAMS*, *A.K.A. HOLLYWOOD AND/OR WONDER MAN*, WORKED IN CONJUNCTION WITH THE *COMMANDEERS*!

LED BY *TARIN*, CURRENT *PRESIDENT OF EARTH'S NORTHEAST CORRIDOR*, THE *COMMANDEERS* TRIED TO MAINTAIN *ORDER* IN THE *POST-WAR ZONE OF MANHATTAN*!

"OPPOSING THEM WERE THE *PUNISHERS*--A SAVAGE *CULT* THAT LOOSELY BASED ITS *CHARTER* ON THE *LEGEND* OF *FRANK CASTLE* FROM THE *TWENTIETH CENTURY*!*

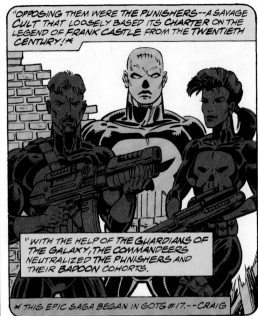

"WITH THE HELP OF *THE GUARDIANS OF THE GALAXY*, THE *COMMANDEERS* NEUTRALIZED THE *PUNISHERS* AND THEIR *BADOON* COHORTS.

* THIS EPIC SAGA BEGAN IN *GOTG #17.*--CRAIG

"HOWEVER, THEY WERE SOON *SUPPLANTED* BY A DERANGED MOB OF 'REALITEE-VEE' ADDICTS CALLED *RETOX*!

"DRIVEN *MAD* BY THE NEED FOR *RTV*, *RETOX* AMBUSHED THE *COMMANDEERS*, LEAVING ONLY *TARIN* AND *OLD REDD* ALIVE!

"*SUBSEQUENT* EVENTS INVOLVING *RANCOR*, FORMER *MUTANT QUEEN OF HAVEN*, REVEALED THE TRUE *MASTERMIND* THAT ENGINEERED IT ALL--*VICTOR VON DOOM*!**

** THE SHADOW OF DR. DOOM BEGAN FALLING IN ISSUE #30. --CRAIG

"SOON AFTER THE *GALACTIC GUARDIANS* FORMED TO DEFEAT *KORVAC*, *HOLLYWOOD* LEARNED ABOUT THE *COMMANDEERS'* FATE VIA A *CONVERSATION* WITH PRESIDENT TARIN. HE IMMEDIATELY JOURNEYED TO *EARTH* FOR ALL THE DETAILS. ***

"UPON HEARING THEM, SIMON UNDERTOOK A *PERSONAL QUEST* TO SEEK OUT *DOCTOR DOOM* AND BRING HIM *JUSTICE*

--BY WHATEVER *MEANS NECESSARY* AND TO THE *EXCLUSION OF ALL ELSE*!

*** ANNUAL #3.--C.A.

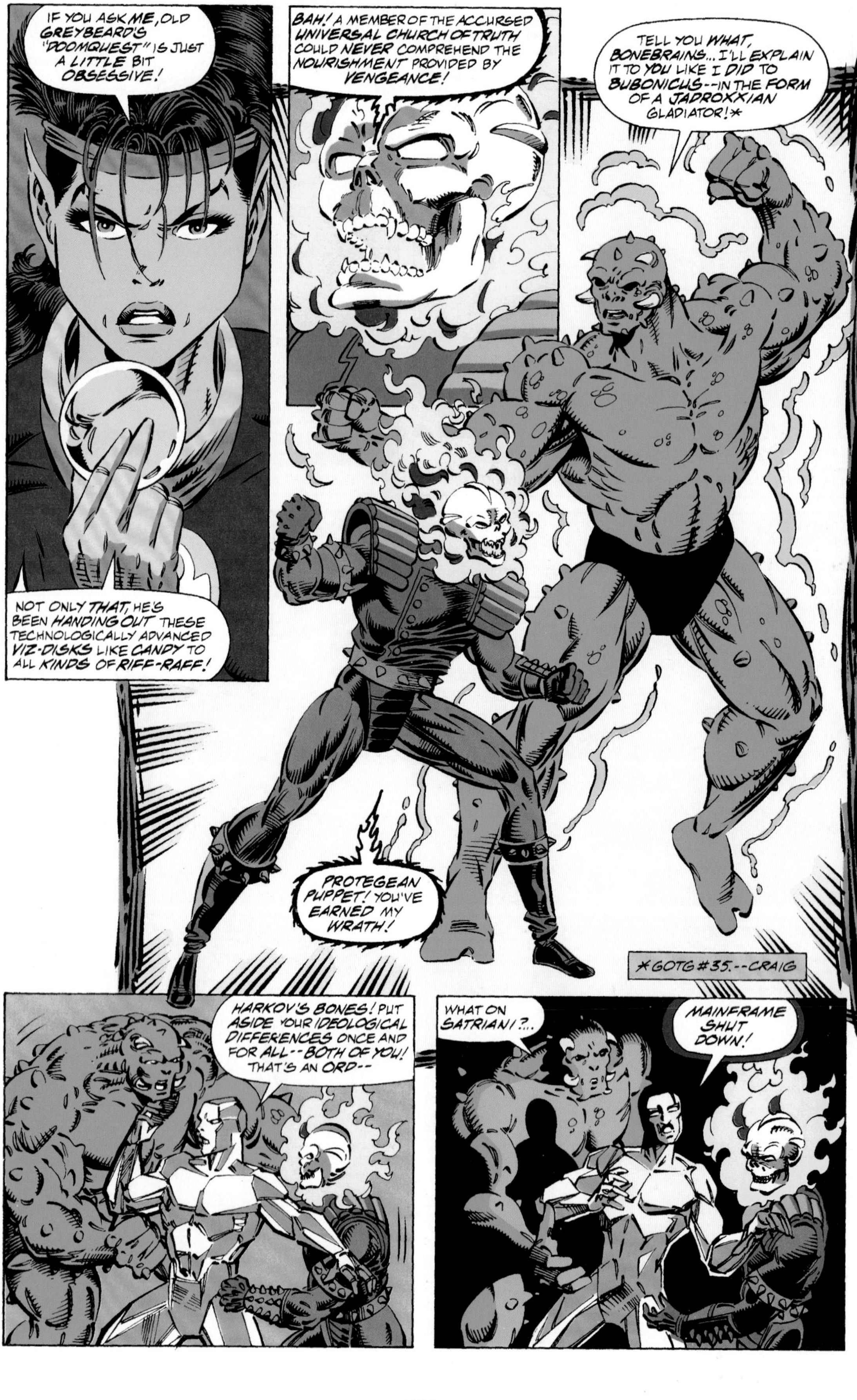

IF YOU ASK ME, OLD GREYBEARD'S "DOOMQUEST" IS JUST A LITTLE BIT OBSESSIVE!
NOT ONLY THAT, HE'S BEEN HANDING OUT THESE TECHNOLOGICALLY ADVANCED VIZ-DISKS LIKE CANDY TO ALL KINDS OF RIFF-RAFF!
BAH! A MEMBER OF THE ACCURSED UNIVERSAL CHURCH OF TRUTH COULD NEVER COMPREHEND THE NOURISHMENT PROVIDED BY VENGEANCE!
TELL YOU WHAT, BONEBRAINS... I'LL EXPLAIN IT TO YOU LIKE I DID TO BUBONICUS--IN THE FORM OF A JADROXXIAN GLADIATOR!*
PROTEGEAN PUPPET! YOU'VE EARNED MY WRATH!
*GOTG #35.--CRAIG
HARKOV'S BONES! PUT ASIDE YOUR IDEOLOGICAL DIFFERENCES ONCE AND FOR ALL--BOTH OF YOU! THAT'S AN ORD--
WHAT ON SATRIANI!?...
MAINFRAME SHUT DOWN!

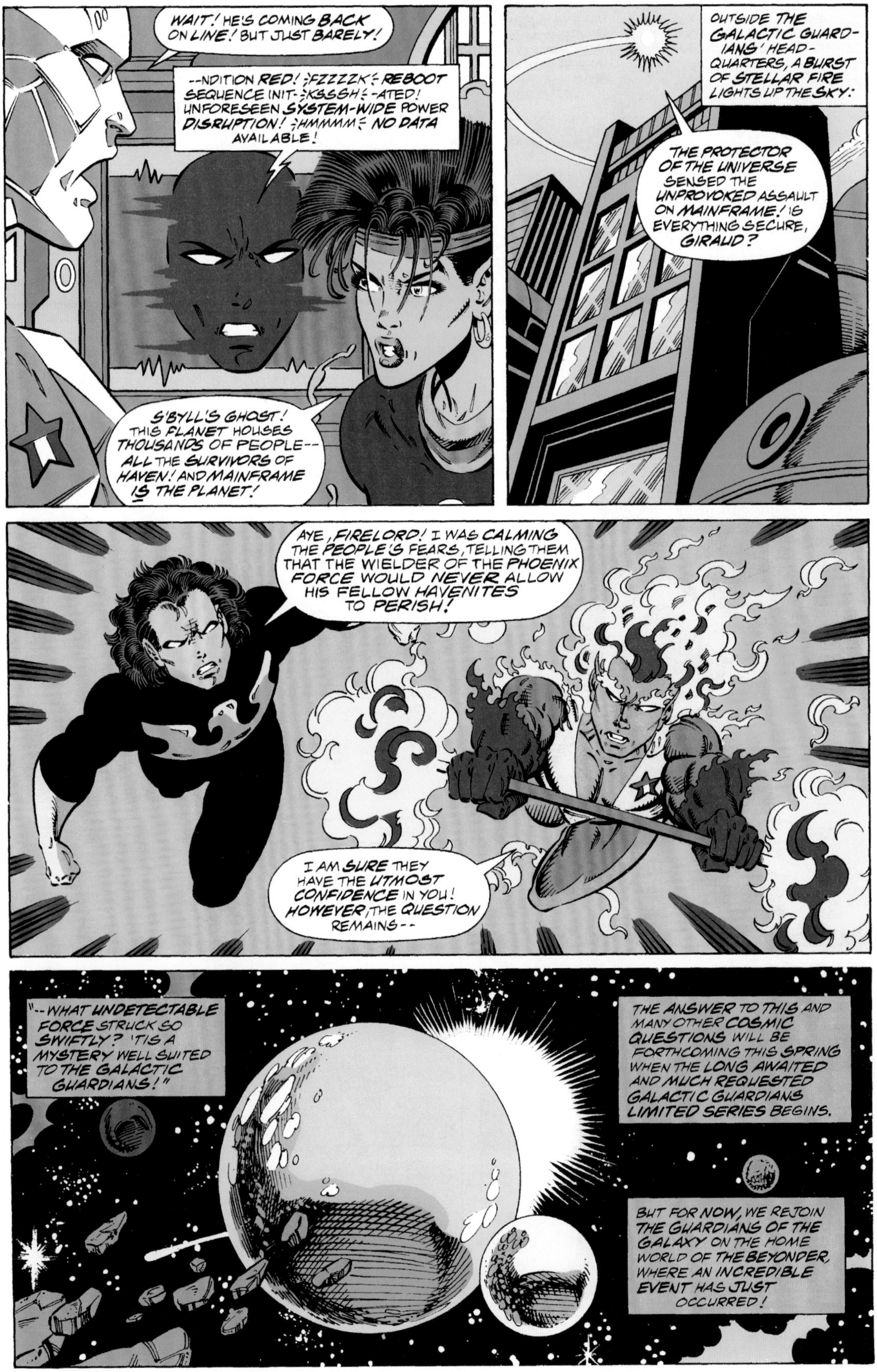
WAIT! HE'S COMING BACK ON LINE! BUT JUST BARELY!
--NDITION RED! -FZZZZK- REBOOT SEQUENCE INIT- -KSSGH- -ATED! UNFORESEEN SYSTEM-WIDE POWER DISRUPTION! -HMMMM- NO DATA AVAILABLE!
S'BYLL'S GHOST! THIS PLANET HOUSES THOUSANDS OF PEOPLE-- ALL THE SURVIVORS OF HAVEN! AND MAINFRAME IS THE PLANET!
OUTSIDE THE GALACTIC GUARDIANS' HEAD-QUARTERS, A BURST OF STELLAR FIRE LIGHTS UP THE SKY:
THE PROTECTOR OF THE UNIVERSE SENSED THE UNPROVOKED ASSAULT ON MAINFRAME! IS EVERYTHING SECURE, GIRAUD?
AYE, FIRELORD! I WAS CALMING THE PEOPLE'S FEARS, TELLING THEM THAT THE WIELDER OF THE PHOENIX FORCE WOULD NEVER ALLOW HIS FELLOW HAVENITES TO PERISH!
I AM SURE THEY HAVE THE UTMOST CONFIDENCE IN YOU! HOWEVER, THE QUESTION REMAINS--
"--WHAT UNDETECTABLE FORCE STRUCK SO SWIFTLY? 'TIS A MYSTERY WELL SUITED TO THE GALACTIC GUARDIANS!"
THE ANSWER TO THIS AND MANY OTHER COSMIC QUESTIONS WILL BE FORTHCOMING THIS SPRING WHEN THE LONG AWAITED AND MUCH REQUESTED GALACTIC GUARDIANS LIMITED SERIES BEGINS.
BUT FOR NOW, WE REJOIN THE GUARDIANS OF THE GALAXY ON THE HOME WORLD OF THE BEYONDER, WHERE AN INCREDIBLE EVENT HAS JUST OCCURRED!

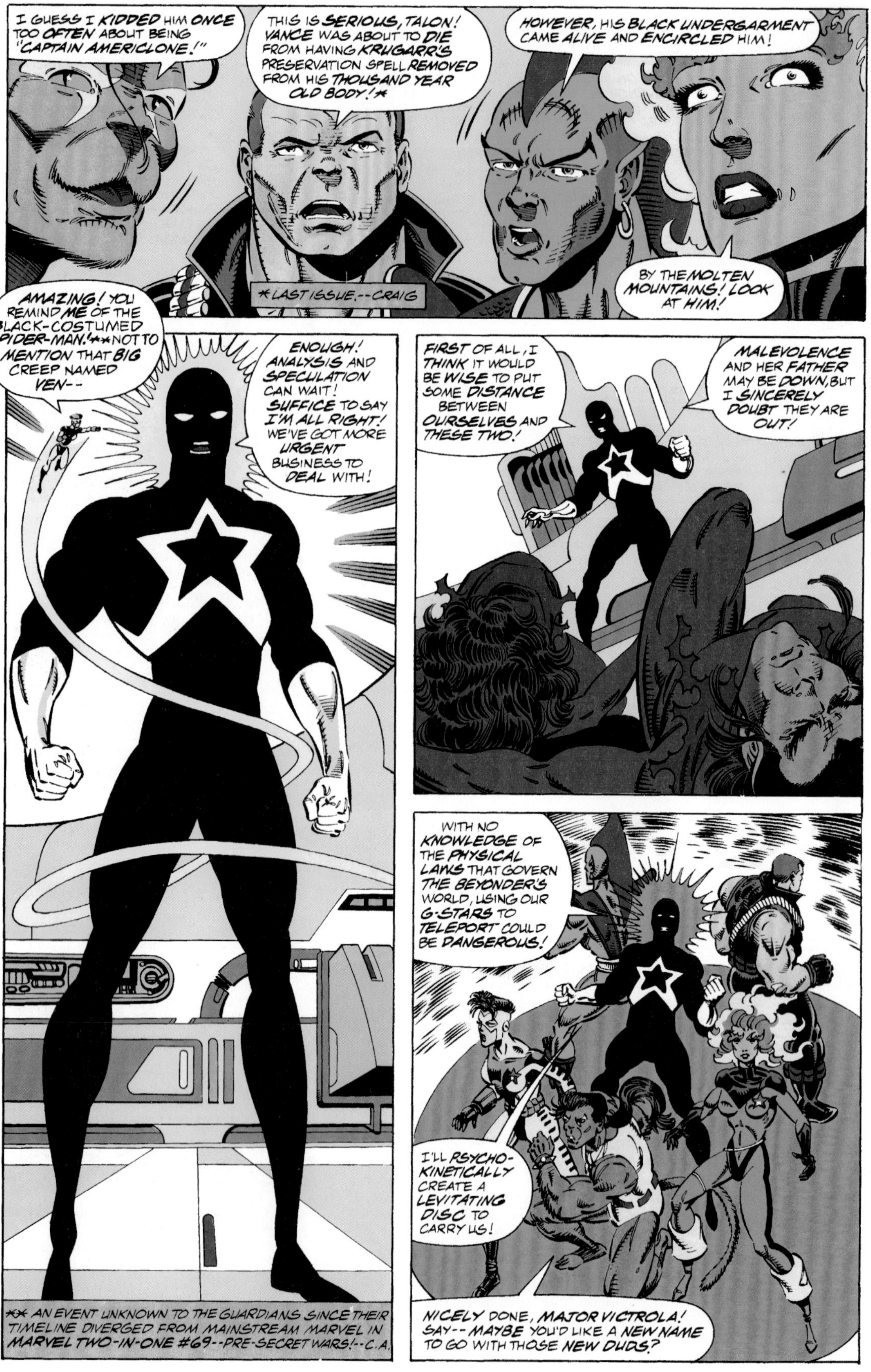
I GUESS I KIDDED HIM ONCE TOO OFTEN ABOUT BEING "CAPTAIN AMERICLONE!"
THIS IS SERIOUS, TALON! VANCE WAS ABOUT TO DIE FROM HAVING KRUGARR'S PRESERVATION SPELL REMOVED FROM HIS THOUSAND YEAR OLD BODY!*
HOWEVER, HIS BLACK UNDERGARMENT CAME ALIVE AND ENCIRCLED HIM!
BY THE MOLTEN MOUNTAINS! LOOK AT HIM!
*LAST ISSUE.--CRAIG
AMAZING! YOU REMIND ME OF THE BLACK-COSTUMED SPIDER-MAN!** NOT TO MENTION THAT BIG CREEP NAMED VEN--
ENOUGH! ANALYSIS AND SPECULATION CAN WAIT! SUFFICE TO SAY I'M ALL RIGHT! WE'VE GOT MORE URGENT BUSINESS TO DEAL WITH!
**AN EVENT UNKNOWN TO THE GUARDIANS SINCE THEIR TIMELINE DIVERGED FROM MAINSTREAM MARVEL IN MARVEL TWO-IN-ONE #69--PRE-SECRET WARS!--C.A.
FIRST OF ALL, I THINK IT WOULD BE WISE TO PUT SOME DISTANCE BETWEEN OURSELVES AND THESE TWO!
MALEVOLENCE AND HER FATHER MAY BE DOWN, BUT I SINCERELY DOUBT THEY ARE OUT!
WITH NO KNOWLEDGE OF THE PHYSICAL LAWS THAT GOVERN THE BEYONDER'S WORLD, USING OUR G-STARS TO TELEPORT COULD BE DANGEROUS!
I'LL PSYCHO-KINETICALLY CREATE A LEVITATING DISC TO CARRY US!
NICELY DONE, MAJOR VICTROLA! SAY-- MAYBE YOU'D LIKE A NEW NAME TO GO WITH THOSE NEW DUDS?

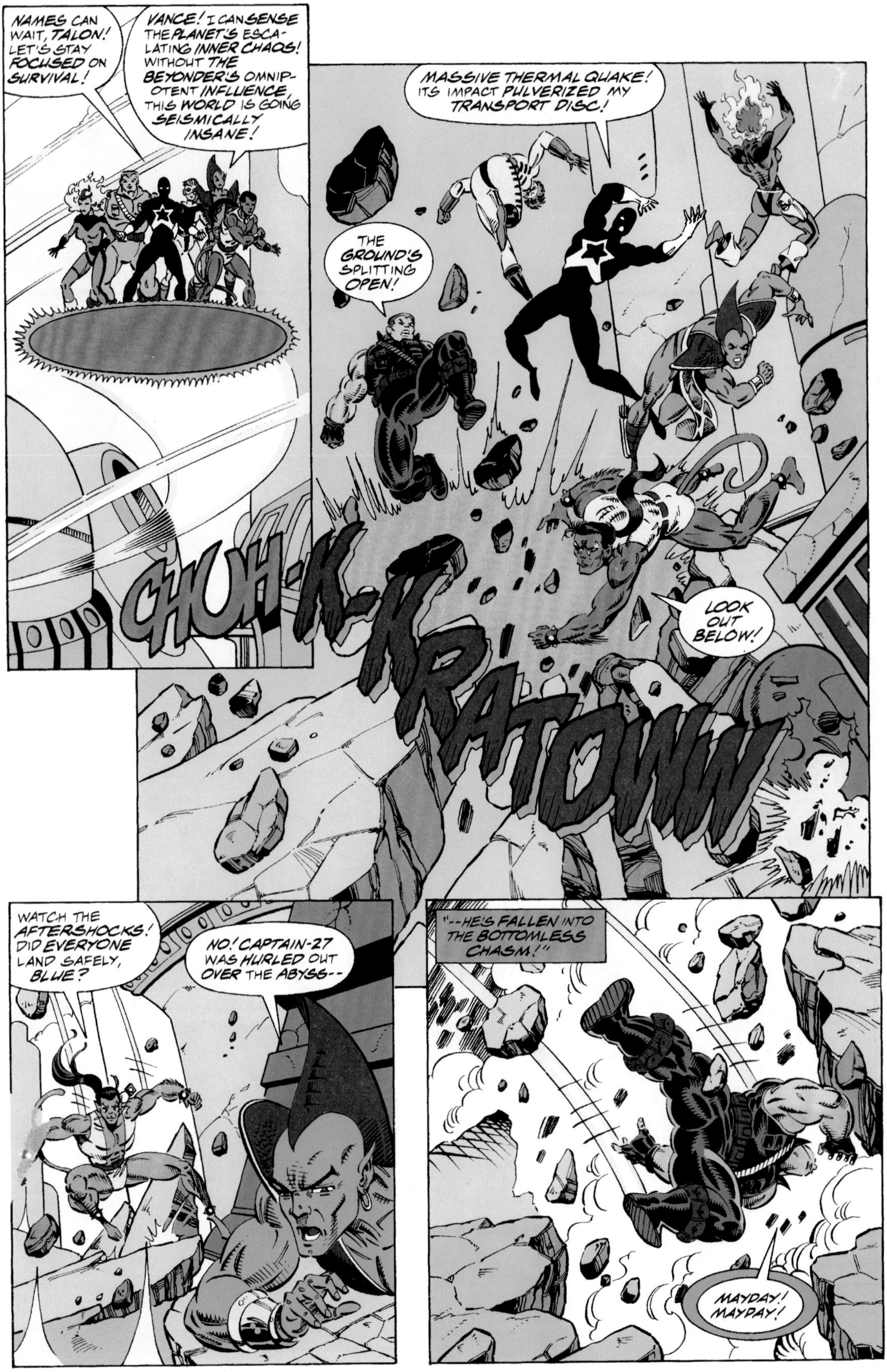
NAMES CAN WAIT, TALON! LET'S STAY FOCUSED ON SURVIVAL!
VANCE! I CAN SENSE THE PLANET'S ESCALATING INNER CHAOS! WITHOUT THE BEYONDER'S OMNIPOTENT INFLUENCE, THIS WORLD IS GOING SEISMICALLY INSANE!
MASSIVE THERMAL QUAKE! ITS IMPACT PULVERIZED MY TRANSPORT DISC!
THE GROUND'S SPLITTING OPEN!
CHUH-K-KRATOWW
LOOK OUT BELOW!
WATCH THE AFTERSHOCKS! DID EVERYONE LAND SAFELY, BLUE?
NO! CAPTAIN-27 WAS HURLED OUT OVER THE ABYSS--
"--HE'S FALLEN INTO THE BOTTOMLESS CHASM!"
MAYDAY! MAYDAY!

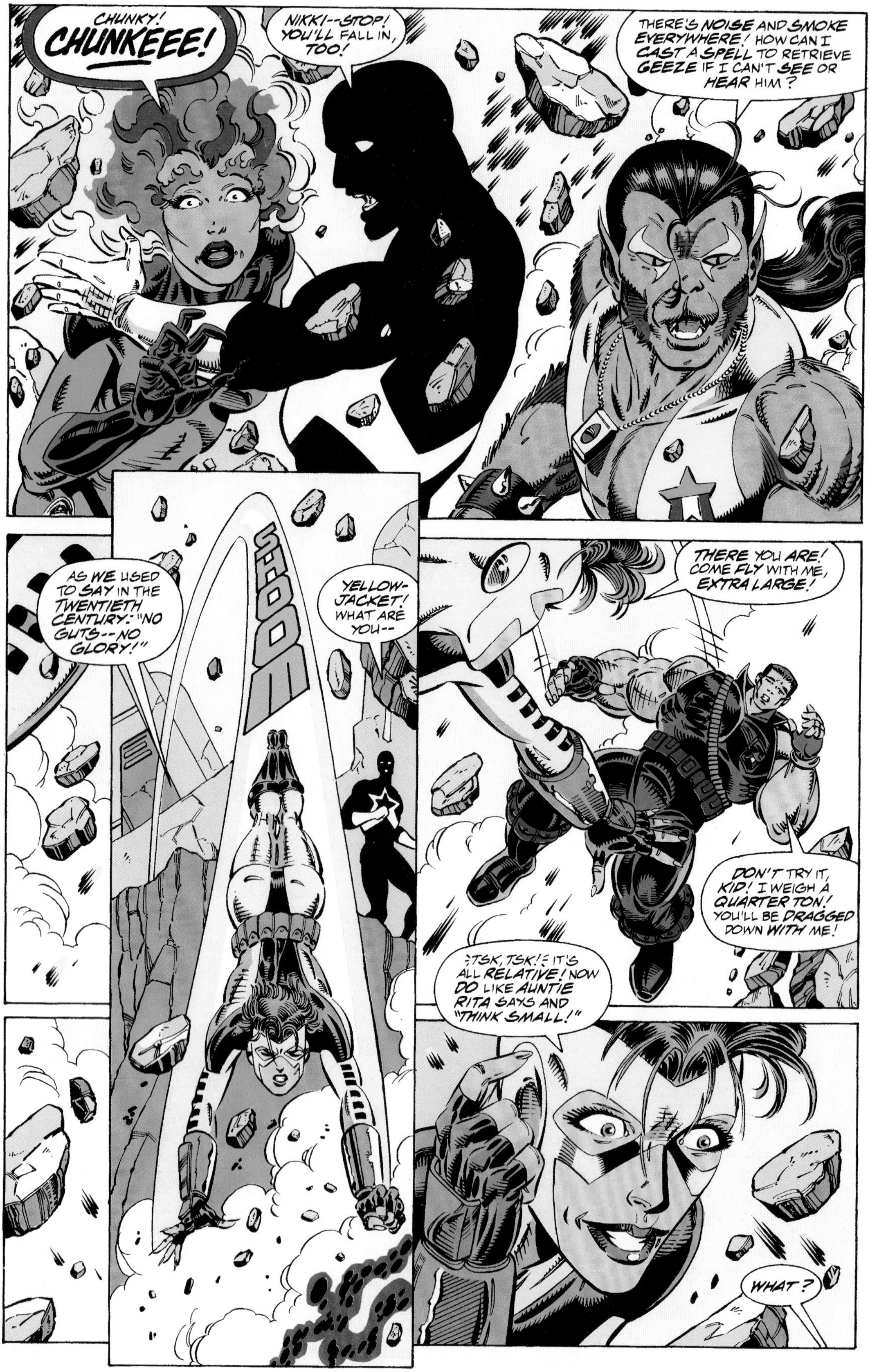
CHUNKY! CHUNKEEE!
NIKKI--STOP! YOU'LL FALL IN, TOO!
THERE'S NOISE AND SMOKE EVERYWHERE! HOW CAN I CAST A SPELL TO RETRIEVE GEEZE IF I CAN'T SEE OR HEAR HIM?
AS WE USED TO SAY IN THE TWENTIETH CENTURY: "NO GUTS--NO GLORY!"
SHOOOM
YELLOW-JACKET! WHAT ARE YOU--
THERE YOU ARE! COME FLY WITH ME, EXTRA LARGE!
DON'T TRY IT, KID! I WEIGH A QUARTER TON! YOU'LL BE DRAGGED DOWN WITH ME!
TSK, TSK! IT'S ALL RELATIVE! NOW DO LIKE AUNTIE RITA SAYS AND "THINK SMALL!"
WHAT?

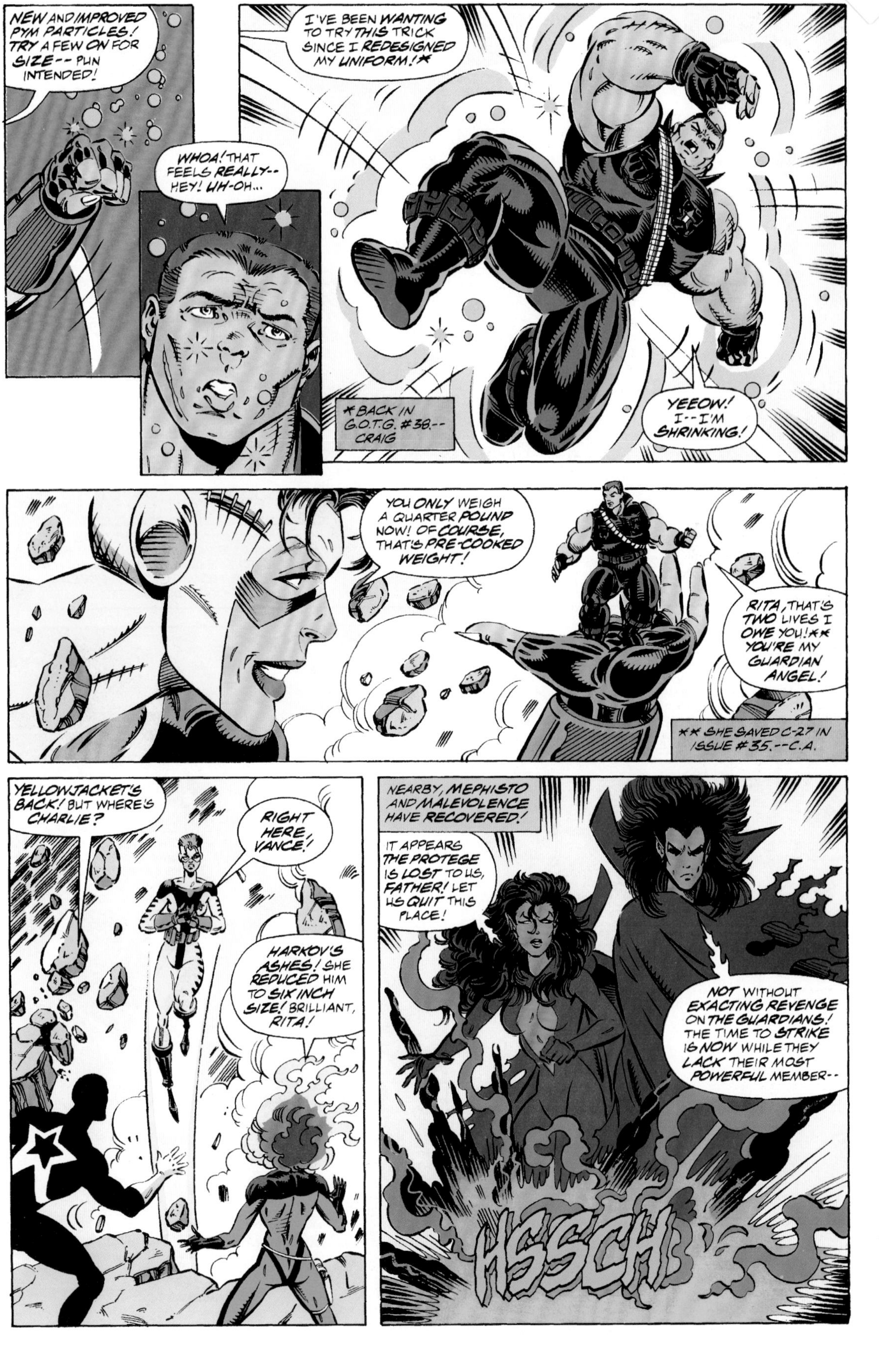

NEW AND IMPROVED PYM PARTICLES! TRY A FEW ON FOR SIZE-- PUN INTENDED!
WHOA! THAT FEELS REALLY-- HEY! UH-OH...
I'VE BEEN WANTING TO TRY THIS TRICK SINCE I REDESIGNED MY UNIFORM!*
*BACK IN G.O.T.G. #38.-- CRAIG
YEEOW! I--I'M SHRINKING!
YOU ONLY WEIGH A QUARTER POUND NOW! OF COURSE, THAT'S PRE-COOKED WEIGHT!
RITA, THAT'S TWO LIVES I OWE YOU!** YOU'RE MY GUARDIAN ANGEL!
**SHE SAVED C-27 IN ISSUE #35.--C.A.
YELLOWJACKET'S BACK! BUT WHERE'S CHARLIE?
RIGHT HERE, VANCE!
HARKOV'S ASHES! SHE REDUCED HIM TO SIX INCH SIZE! BRILLIANT, RITA!
NEARBY, MEPHISTO AND MALEVOLENCE HAVE RECOVERED!
IT APPEARS THE PROTEGE IS LOST TO US, FATHER! LET US QUIT THIS PLACE!
NOT WITHOUT EXACTING REVENGE ON THE GUARDIANS! THE TIME TO STRIKE IS NOW WHILE THEY LACK THEIR MOST POWERFUL MEMBER--
HSSCH!

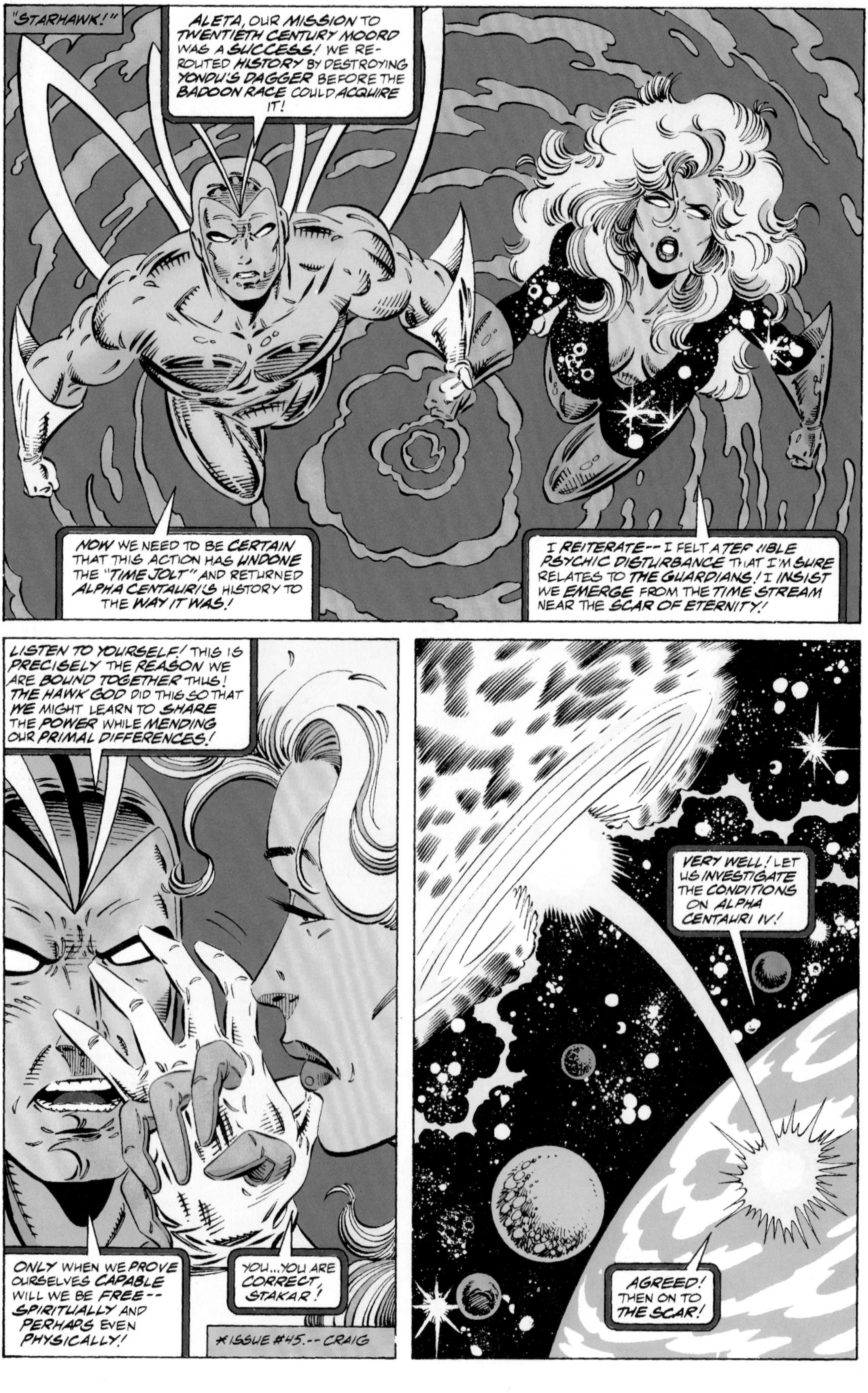
"STARHAWK!"
ALETA, OUR MISSION TO TWENTIETH CENTURY MOORD WAS A SUCCESS! WE RE-ROUTED HISTORY BY DESTROYING YONDU'S DAGGER BEFORE THE BADOON RACE COULD ACQUIRE IT!
NOW WE NEED TO BE CERTAIN THAT THIS ACTION HAS UNDONE THE "TIME JOLT" AND RETURNED ALPHA CENTAURI'S HISTORY TO THE WAY IT WAS!
I REITERATE-- I FELT A TERRIBLE PSYCHIC DISTURBANCE THAT I'M SURE RELATES TO THE GUARDIANS! I INSIST WE EMERGE FROM THE TIME STREAM NEAR THE SCAR OF ETERNITY!
LISTEN TO YOURSELF! THIS IS PRECISELY THE REASON WE ARE BOUND TOGETHER THUS! THE HAWK GOD DID THIS SO THAT WE MIGHT LEARN TO SHARE THE POWER WHILE MENDING OUR PRIMAL DIFFERENCES!
ONLY WHEN WE PROVE OURSELVES CAPABLE WILL WE BE FREE-- SPIRITUALLY AND PERHAPS EVEN PHYSICALLY!
YOU...YOU ARE CORRECT, STAKAR!
*ISSUE #45.--CRAIG
VERY WELL! LET US INVESTIGATE THE CONDITIONS ON ALPHA CENTAURI IV!
AGREED! THEN ON TO THE SCAR!

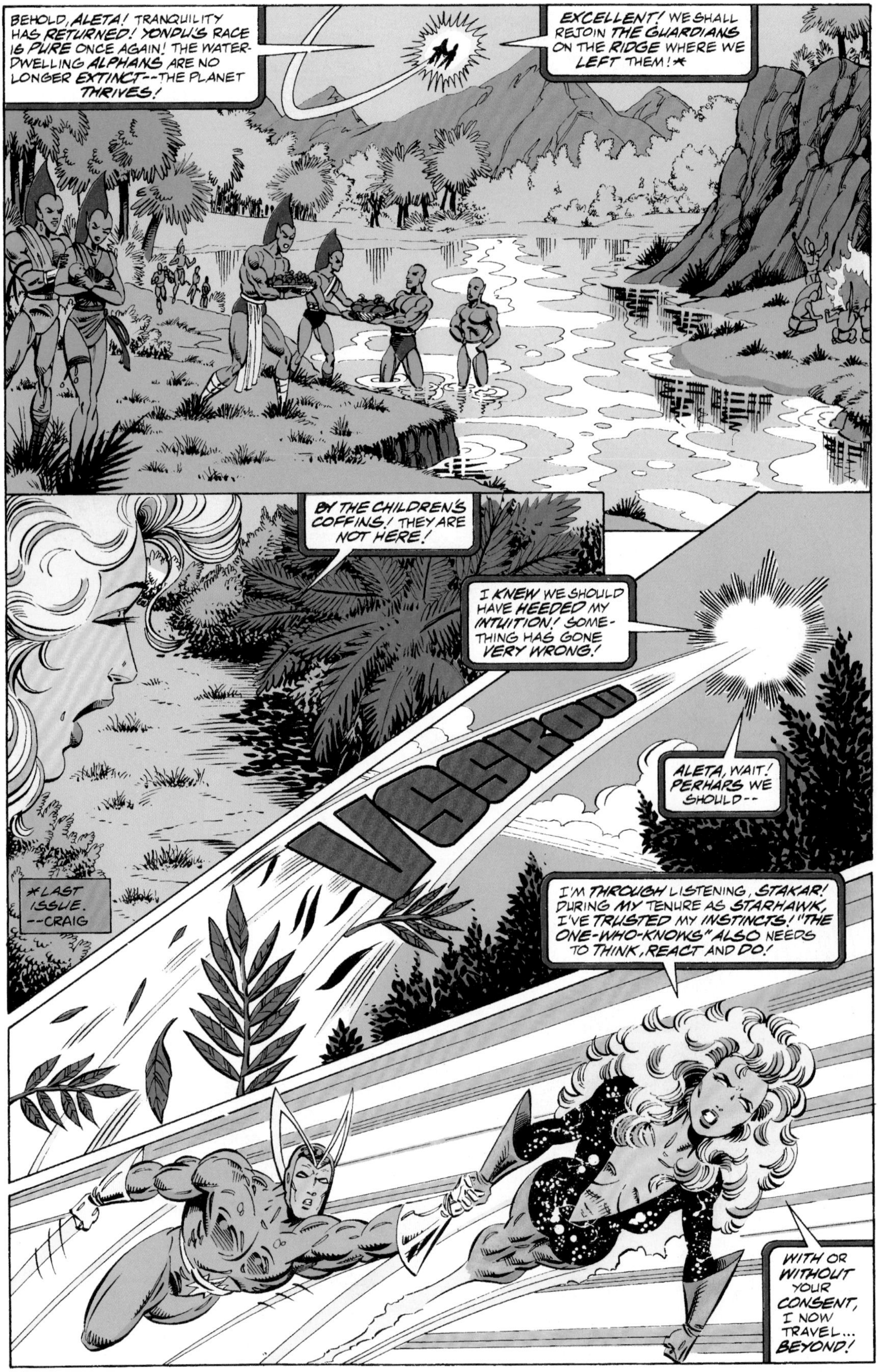

BEHOLD, ALETA! TRANQUILITY HAS RETURNED! YONDU'S RACE IS PURE ONCE AGAIN! THE WATER-DWELLING ALPHANS ARE NO LONGER EXTINCT--THE PLANET THRIVES!
EXCELLENT! WE SHALL REJOIN THE GUARDIANS ON THE RIDGE WHERE WE LEFT THEM! *
BY THE CHILDREN'S COFFINS! THEY ARE NOT HERE!
I KNEW WE SHOULD HAVE HEEDED MY INTUITION! SOMETHING HAS GONE VERY WRONG!
VSSKOW
ALETA, WAIT! PERHAPS WE SHOULD--
* LAST ISSUE. --CRAIG
I'M THROUGH LISTENING, STAKAR! DURING MY TENURE AS STARHAWK, I'VE TRUSTED MY INSTINCTS! "THE ONE-WHO-KNOWS" ALSO NEEDS TO THINK, REACT AND DO!
WITH OR WITHOUT YOUR CONSENT, I NOW TRAVEL... BEYOND!

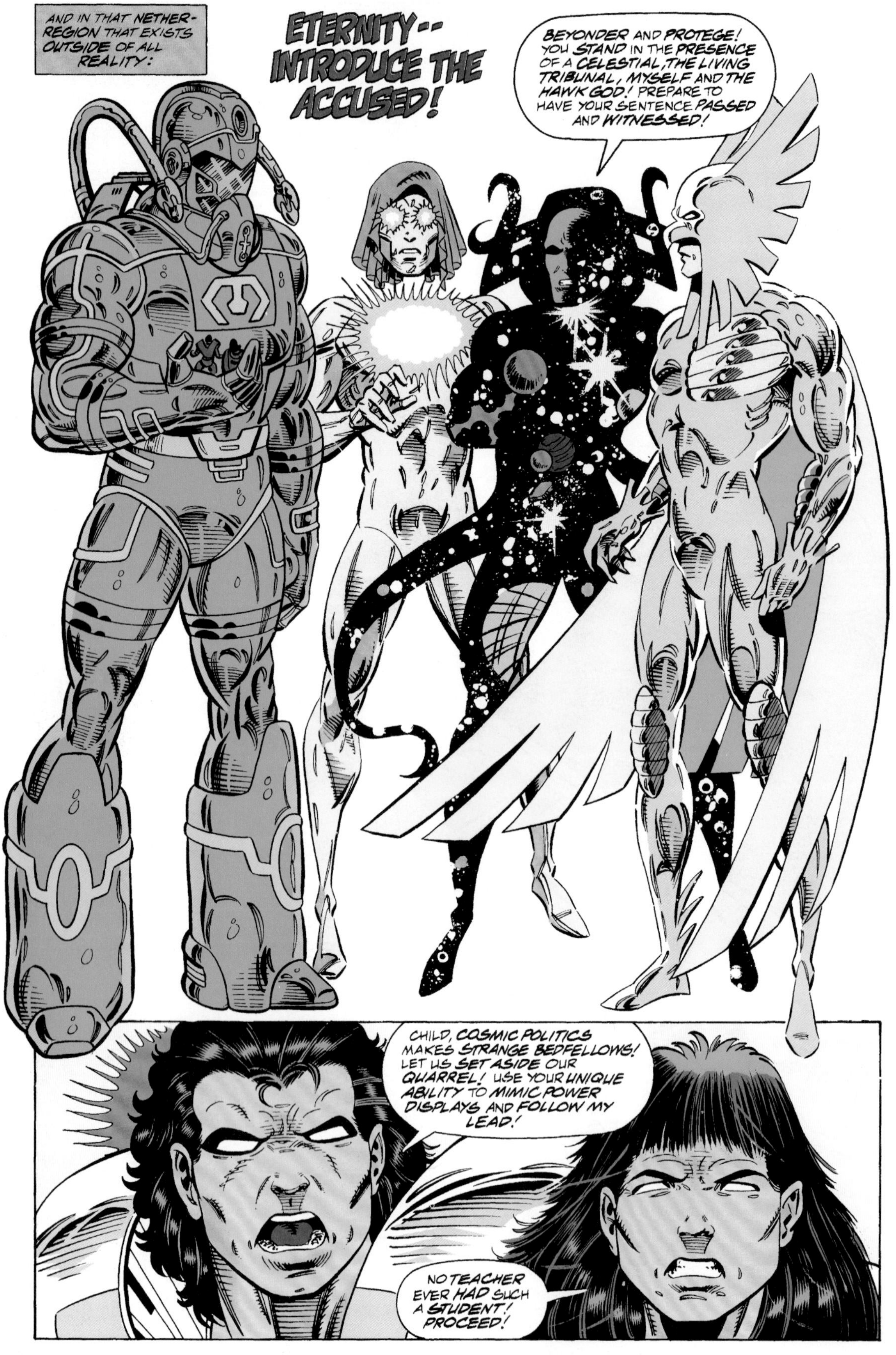
AND IN THAT NETHER-REGION THAT EXISTS OUTSIDE OF ALL REALITY:
ETERNITY-- INTRODUCE THE ACCUSED!
BEYONDER AND PROTEGE! YOU STAND IN THE PRESENCE OF A CELESTIAL, THE LIVING TRIBUNAL, MYSELF AND THE HAWK GOD! PREPARE TO HAVE YOUR SENTENCE PASSED AND WITNESSED!
CHILD, COSMIC POLITICS MAKES STRANGE BEDFELLOWS! LET US SET ASIDE OUR QUARREL! USE YOUR UNIQUE ABILITY TO MIMIC POWER DISPLAYS AND FOLLOW MY LEAD!
NO TEACHER EVER HAD SUCH A STUDENT! PROCEED!

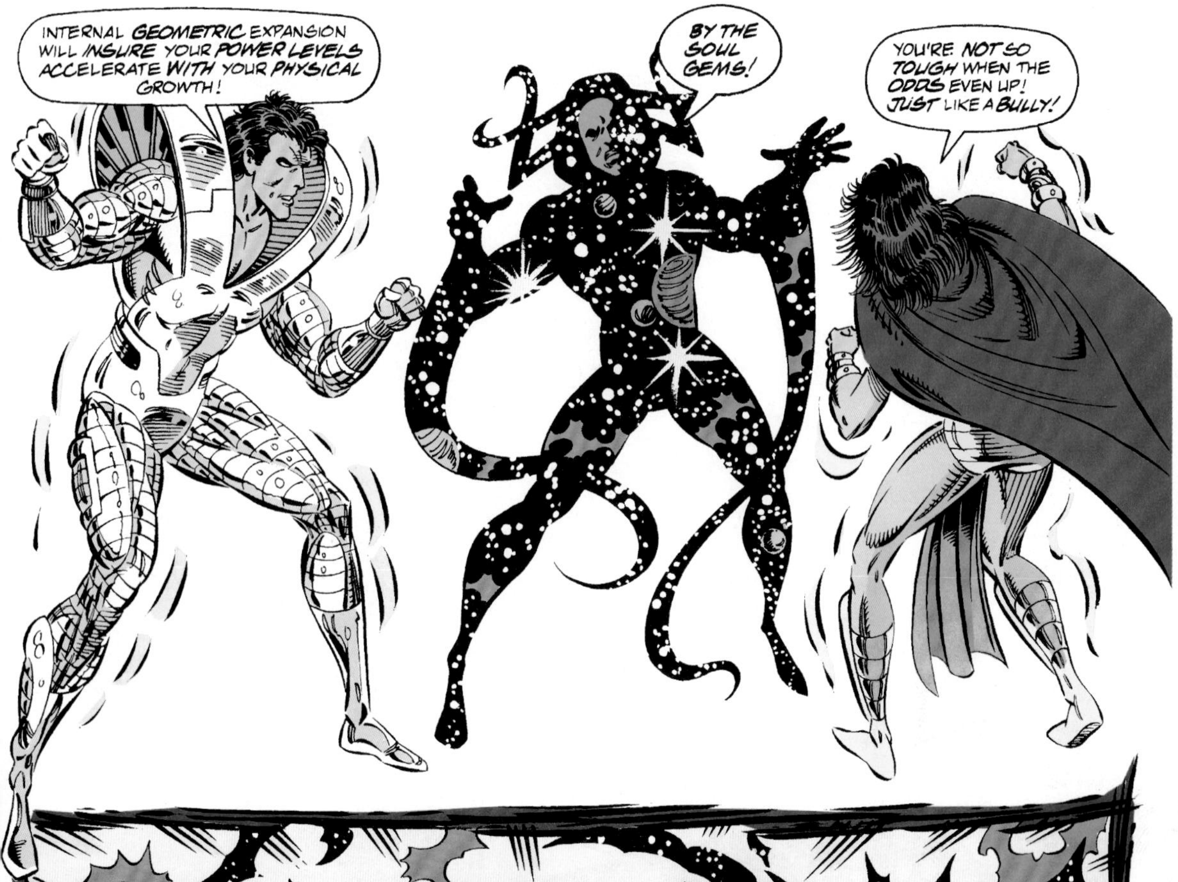
INTERNAL GEOMETRIC EXPANSION WILL INSURE YOUR POWER LEVELS ACCELERATE WITH YOUR PHYSICAL GROWTH!
BY THE SOUL GEMS!
YOU'RE NOT SO TOUGH WHEN THE ODDS EVEN UP! JUST LIKE A BULLY!

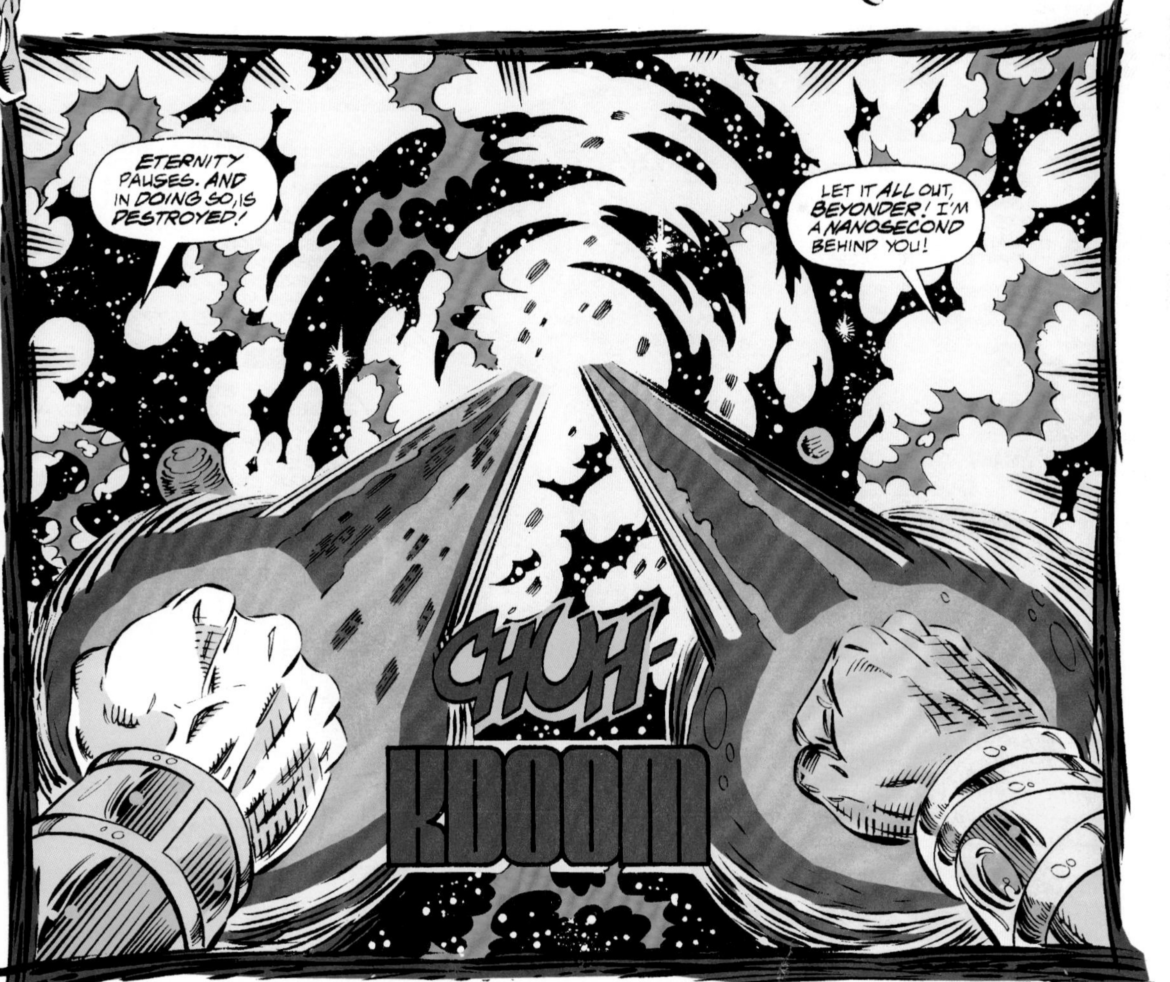
ETERNITY PAUSES. AND IN DOING SO, IS DESTROYED!
LET IT ALL OUT, BEYONDER! I'M A NANOSECOND BEHIND YOU!
CHUH-
KDOOM

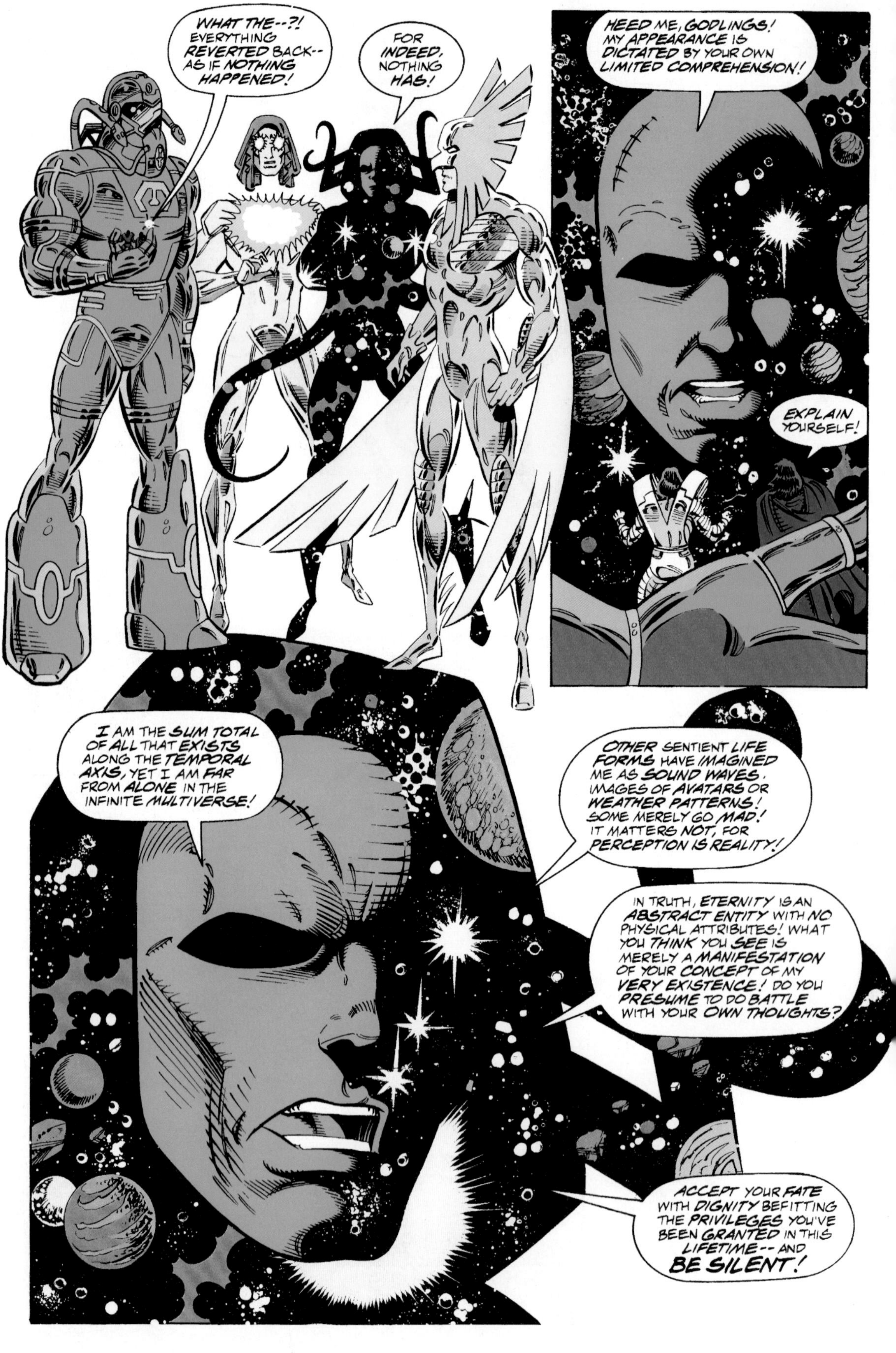
WHAT THE--?! EVERYTHING REVERTED BACK-- AS IF NOTHING HAPPENED!
FOR INDEED, NOTHING HAS!
HEED ME, GODLINGS! MY APPEARANCE IS DICTATED BY YOUR OWN LIMITED COMPREHENSION!
EXPLAIN YOURSELF!
I AM THE SUM TOTAL OF ALL THAT EXISTS ALONG THE TEMPORAL AXIS, YET I AM FAR FROM ALONE IN THE INFINITE MULTIVERSE!
OTHER SENTIENT LIFE FORMS HAVE IMAGINED ME AS SOUND WAVES, IMAGES OF AVATARS OR WEATHER PATTERNS! SOME MERELY GO MAD! IT MATTERS NOT, FOR PERCEPTION IS REALITY!
IN TRUTH, ETERNITY IS AN ABSTRACT ENTITY WITH NO PHYSICAL ATTRIBUTES! WHAT YOU THINK YOU SEE IS MERELY A MANIFESTATION OF YOUR CONCEPT OF MY VERY EXISTENCE! DO YOU PRESUME TO DO BATTLE WITH YOUR OWN THOUGHTS?
ACCEPT YOUR FATE WITH DIGNITY BEFITTING THE PRIVILEGES YOU'VE BEEN GRANTED IN THIS LIFETIME-- AND BE SILENT!

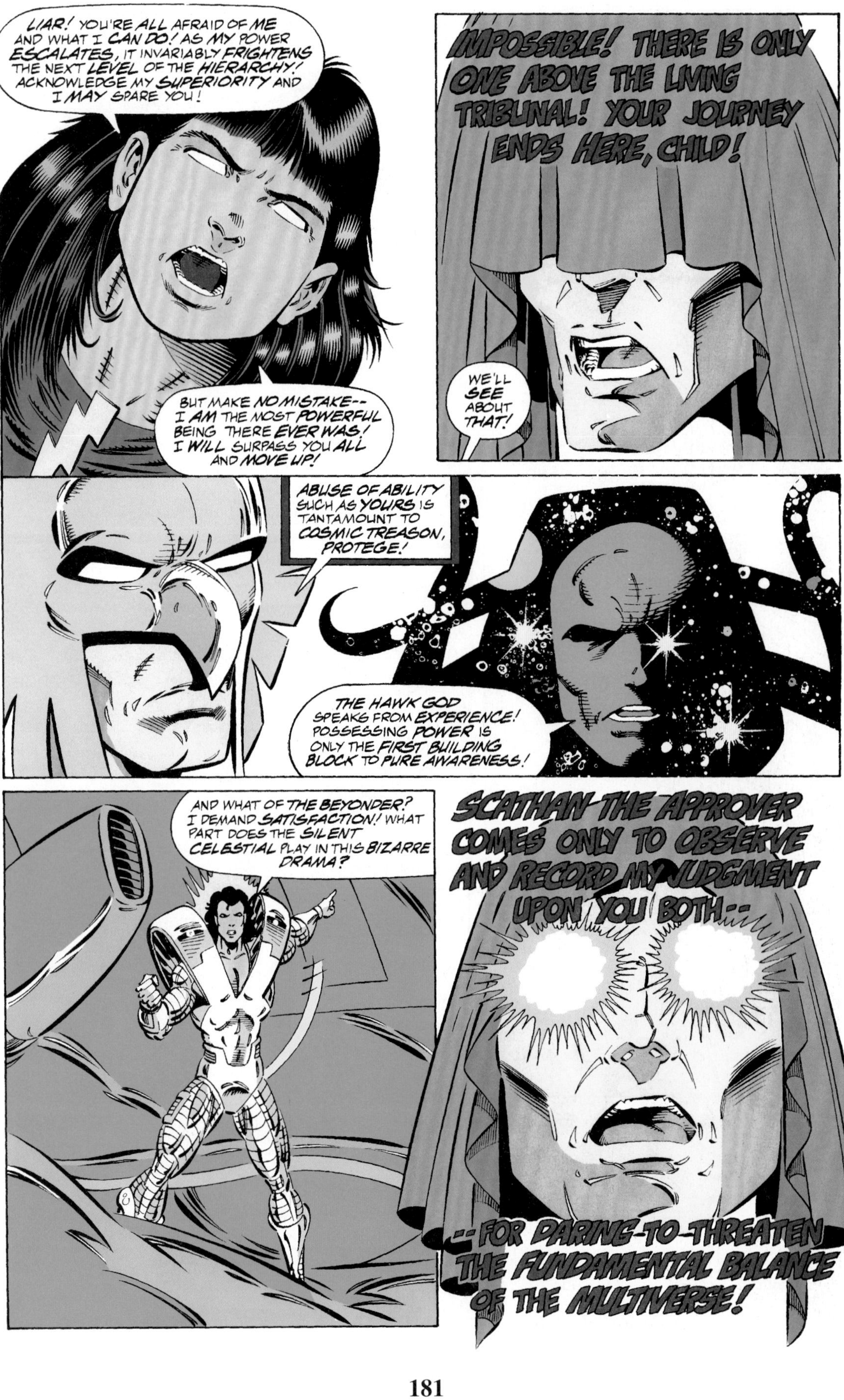
LIAR! YOU'RE ALL AFRAID OF ME AND WHAT I CAN DO! AS MY POWER ESCALATES, IT INVARIABLY FRIGHTENS THE NEXT LEVEL OF THE HIERARCHY! ACKNOWLEDGE MY SUPERIORITY AND I MAY SPARE YOU!
BUT MAKE NO MISTAKE-- I AM THE MOST POWERFUL BEING THERE EVER WAS! I WILL SURPASS YOU ALL AND MOVE UP!
IMPOSSIBLE! THERE IS ONLY ONE ABOVE THE LIVING TRIBUNAL! YOUR JOURNEY ENDS HERE, CHILD!
WE'LL SEE ABOUT THAT!
ABUSE OF ABILITY SUCH AS YOURS IS TANTAMOUNT TO COSMIC TREASON, PROTEGE!
THE HAWK GOD SPEAKS FROM EXPERIENCE! POSSESSING POWER IS ONLY THE FIRST BUILDING BLOCK TO PURE AWARENESS!
AND WHAT OF THE BEYONDER? I DEMAND SATISFACTION! WHAT PART DOES THE SILENT CELESTIAL PLAY IN THIS BIZARRE DRAMA?
SCATHAN THE APPROVER COMES ONLY TO OBSERVE AND RECORD MY JUDGMENT UPON YOU BOTH--
--FOR DARING TO THREATEN THE FUNDAMENTAL BALANCE OF THE MULTIVERSE!

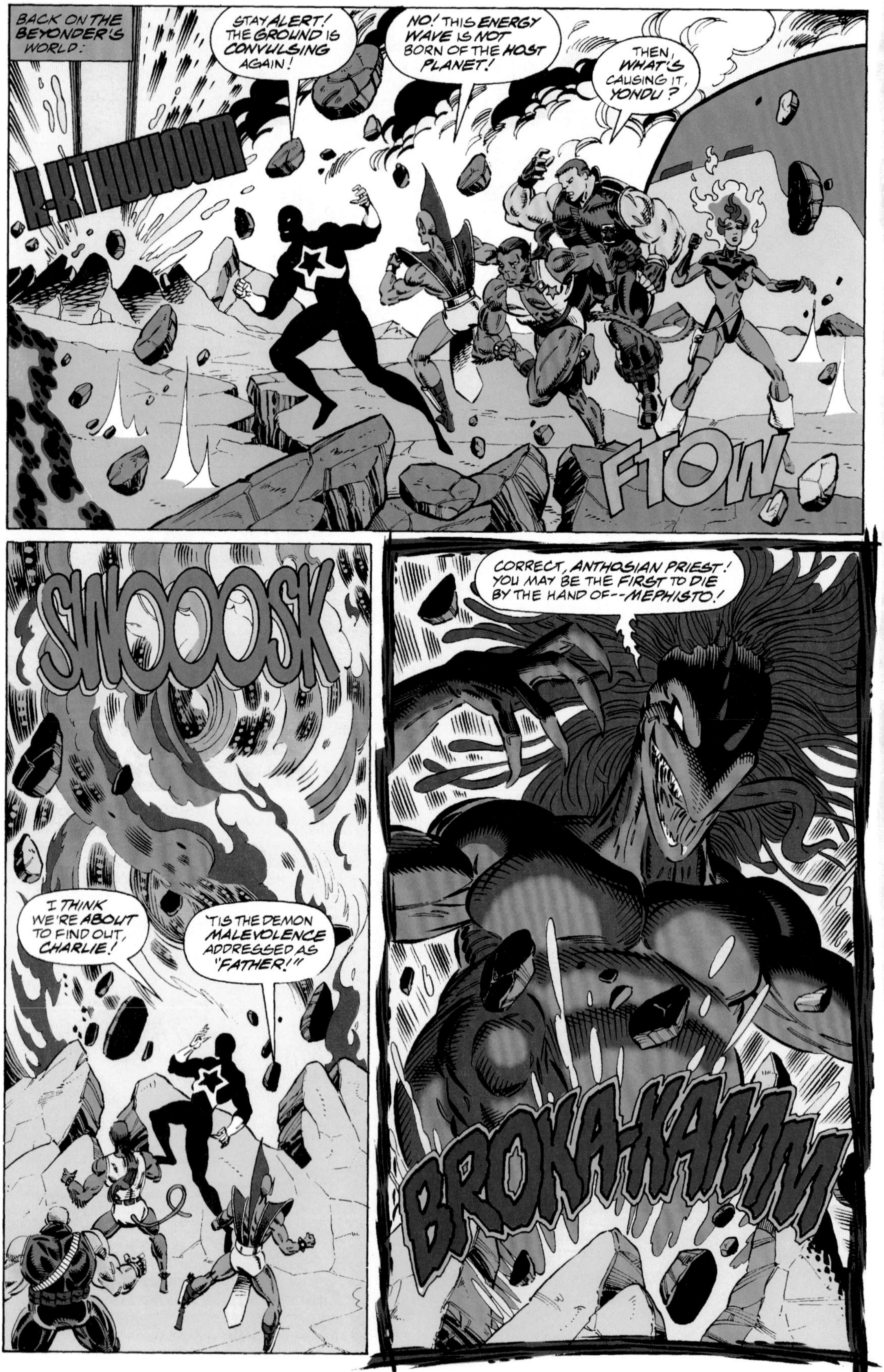
BACK ON THE BEYONDER'S WORLD:
STAY ALERT! THE GROUND IS CONVULSING AGAIN!
NO! THIS ENERGY WAVE IS NOT BORN OF THE HOST PLANET!
THEN, WHAT'S CAUSING IT, YONDU?
K-KTHWHOOM
FTOW
SWOOOSK
I THINK WE'RE ABOUT TO FIND OUT, CHARLIE!
'TIS THE DEMON MALEVOLENCE ADDRESSED AS "FATHER!"
CORRECT, ANTHOSIAN PRIEST! YOU MAY BE THE FIRST TO DIE BY THE HAND OF--MEPHISTO!
BROKA-KAMM

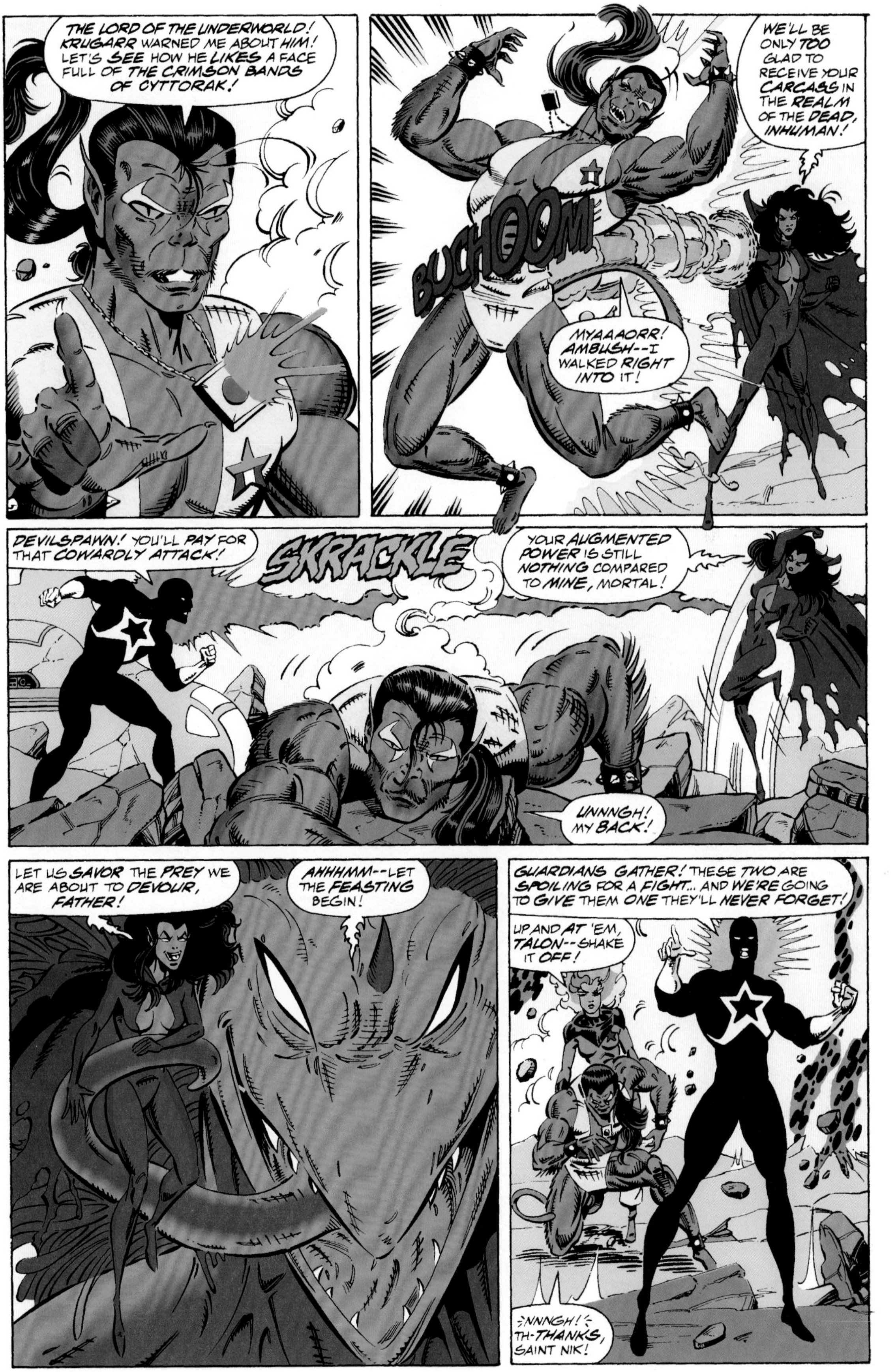
THE LORD OF THE UNDERWORLD! KRUGARR WARNED ME ABOUT HIM! LET'S SEE HOW HE LIKES A FACE FULL OF THE CRIMSON BANDS OF CYTTORAK!
WE'LL BE ONLY TOO GLAD TO RECEIVE YOUR CARCASS IN THE REALM OF THE DEAD, INHUMAN!
BUCHOOM
MYAAAORR! AMBUSH--I WALKED RIGHT INTO IT!
DEVILSPAWN! YOU'LL PAY FOR THAT COWARDLY ATTACK!
SKRACKLE
YOUR AUGMENTED POWER IS STILL NOTHING COMPARED TO MINE, MORTAL!
UNNNGH! MY BACK!
LET US SAVOR THE PREY WE ARE ABOUT TO DEVOUR, FATHER!
AHHHMMM--LET THE FEASTING BEGIN!
GUARDIANS GATHER! THESE TWO ARE SPOILING FOR A FIGHT... AND WE'RE GOING TO GIVE THEM ONE THEY'LL NEVER FORGET!
UP AND AT 'EM, TALON--SHAKE IT OFF!
NNNGH! TH-THANKS, SAINT NIK!

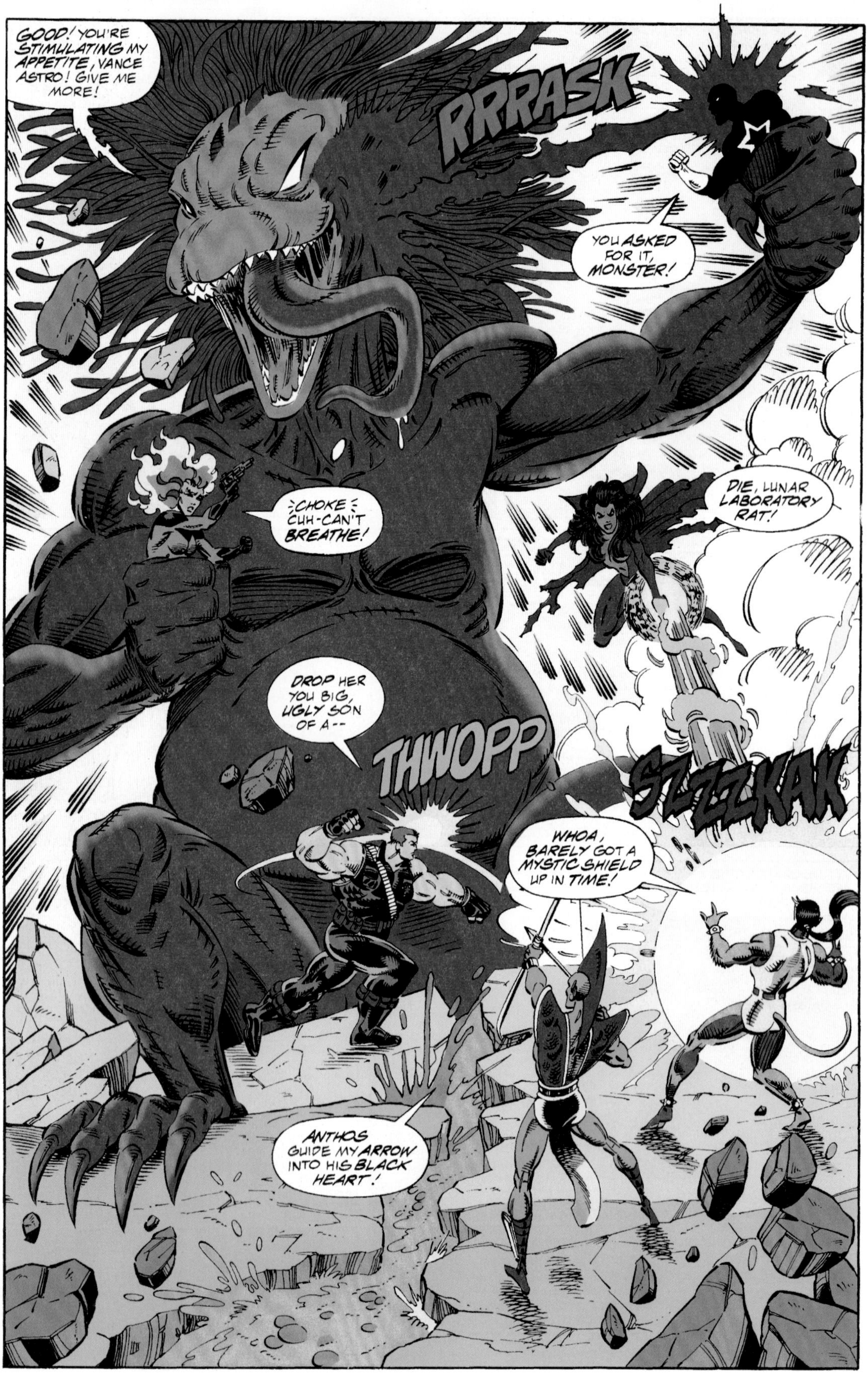
GOOD! YOU'RE STIMULATING MY APPETITE, VANCE ASTRO! GIVE ME MORE!
RRRASK
YOU ASKED FOR IT, MONSTER!
CHOKE CUH-CAN'T BREATHE!
DIE, LUNAR LABORATORY RAT!
DROP HER YOU BIG, UGLY SON OF A--
THWOPP
SZZZKAK
WHOA, BARELY GOT A MYSTIC SHIELD UP IN TIME!
ANTHOS GUIDE MY ARROW INTO HIS BLACK HEART!

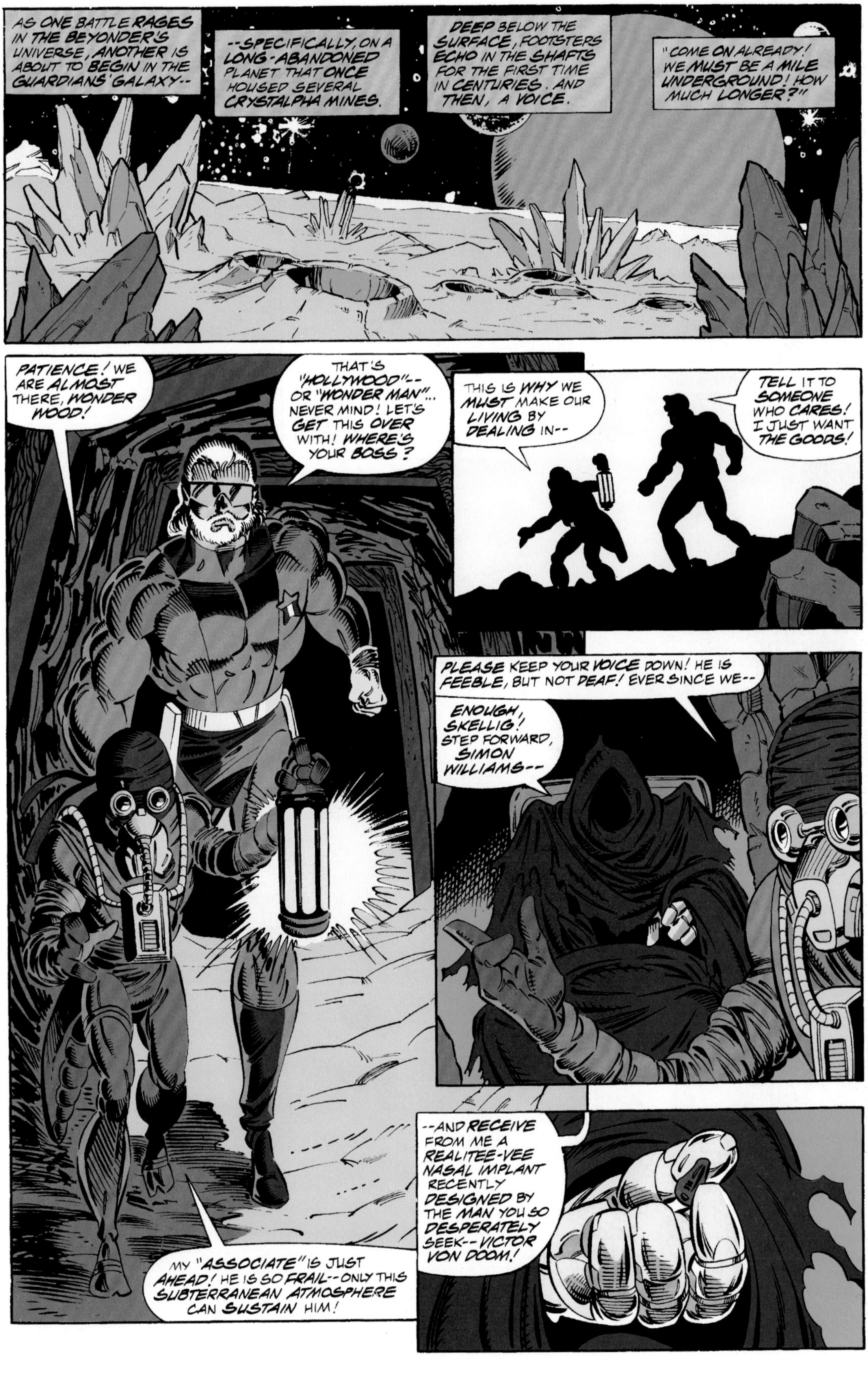

AS ONE BATTLE RAGES IN THE BEYONDER'S UNIVERSE, ANOTHER IS ABOUT TO BEGIN IN THE GUARDIANS' GALAXY--
--SPECIFICALLY, ON A LONG-ABANDONED PLANET THAT ONCE HOUSED SEVERAL CRYSTALPHA MINES.
DEEP BELOW THE SURFACE, FOOTSTEPS ECHO IN THE SHAFTS FOR THE FIRST TIME IN CENTURIES. AND THEN, A VOICE.
"COME ON ALREADY! WE MUST BE A MILE UNDERGROUND! HOW MUCH LONGER?"
PATIENCE! WE ARE ALMOST THERE, WONDER WOOD!
THAT'S "HOLLYWOOD"-- OR "WONDER MAN"... NEVER MIND! LET'S GET THIS OVER WITH! WHERE'S YOUR BOSS?
MY "ASSOCIATE" IS JUST AHEAD! HE IS SO FRAIL--ONLY THIS SUBTERRANEAN ATMOSPHERE CAN SUSTAIN HIM!
THIS IS WHY WE MUST MAKE OUR LIVING BY DEALING IN--
TELL IT TO SOMEONE WHO CARES! I JUST WANT THE GOODS!
PLEASE KEEP YOUR VOICE DOWN! HE IS FEEBLE, BUT NOT DEAF! EVER SINCE WE--
ENOUGH, SKELLIG! STEP FORWARD, SIMON WILLIAMS--
--AND RECEIVE FROM ME A REALITEE-VEE NASAL IMPLANT RECENTLY DESIGNED BY THE MAN YOU SO DESPERATELY SEEK--VICTOR VON DOOM!

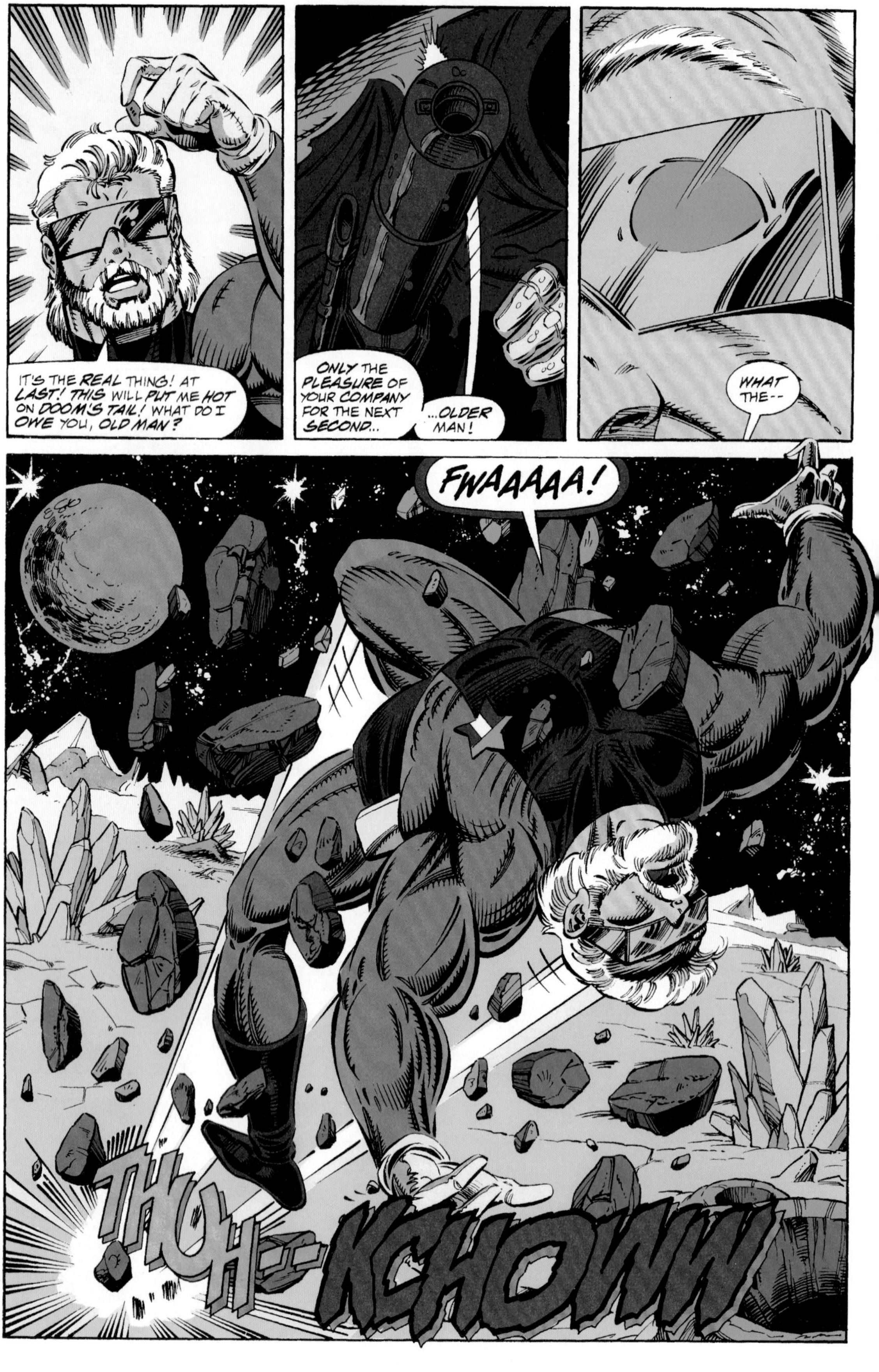
IT'S THE REAL THING! AT LAST! THIS WILL PUT ME HOT ON DOOM'S TAIL! WHAT DO I OWE YOU, OLD MAN?
ONLY THE PLEASURE OF YOUR COMPANY FOR THE NEXT SECOND...
...OLDER MAN!
WHAT THE--
FWAAAAA!
THCH--KCHOWW

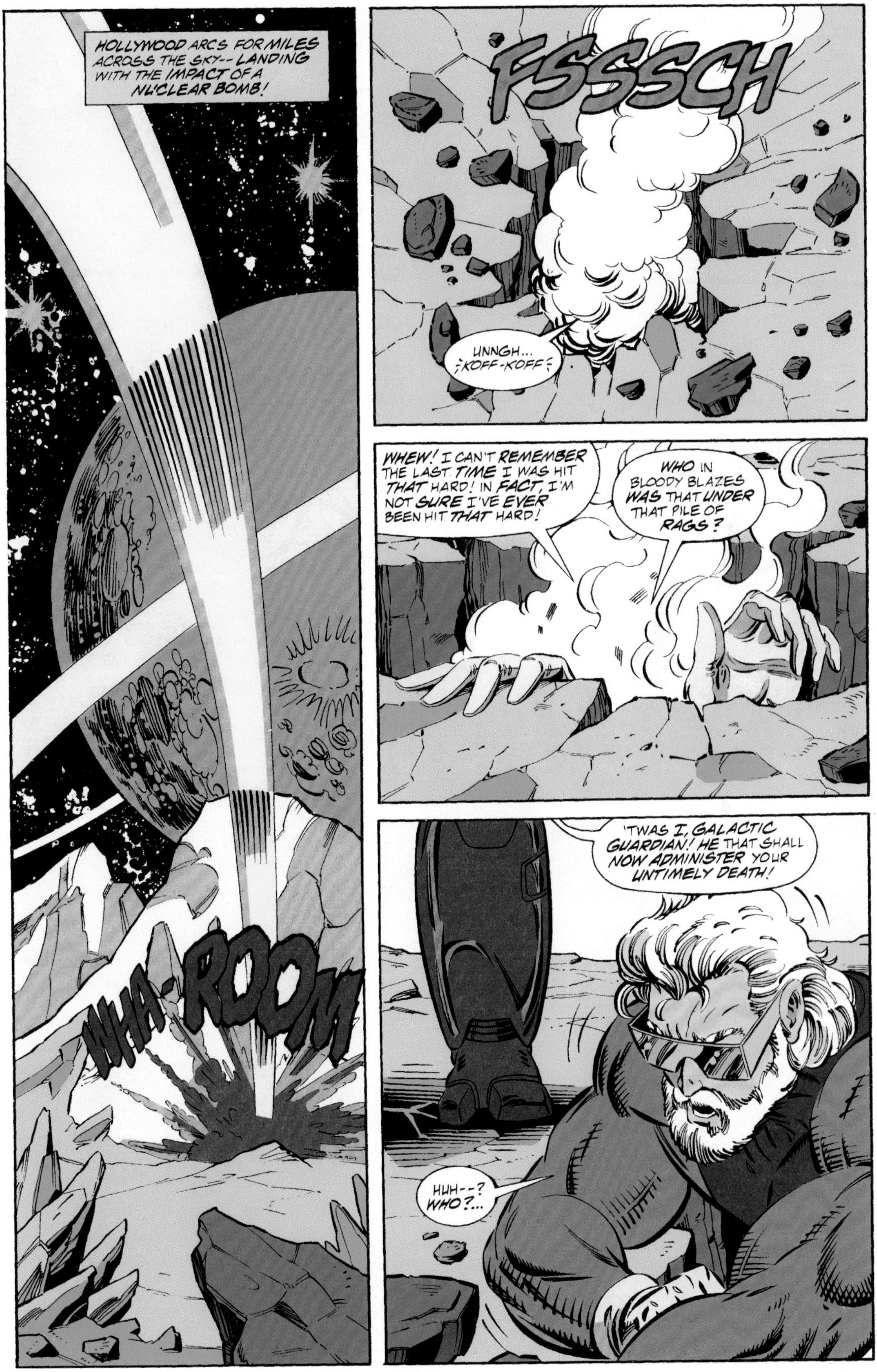
HOLLYWOOD ARCS FOR MILES ACROSS THE SKY-- LANDING WITH THE IMPACT OF A NUCLEAR BOMB!
WHA-ROOM
FSSSCH
UNNGH... KOFF-KOFF
WHEW! I CAN'T REMEMBER THE LAST TIME I WAS HIT THAT HARD! IN FACT, I'M NOT SURE I'VE EVER BEEN HIT THAT HARD!
WHO IN BLOODY BLAZES WAS THAT UNDER THAT PILE OF RAGS?
'TWAS I, GALACTIC GUARDIAN! HE THAT SHALL NOW ADMINISTER YOUR UNTIMELY DEATH!
HUH--? WHO?...

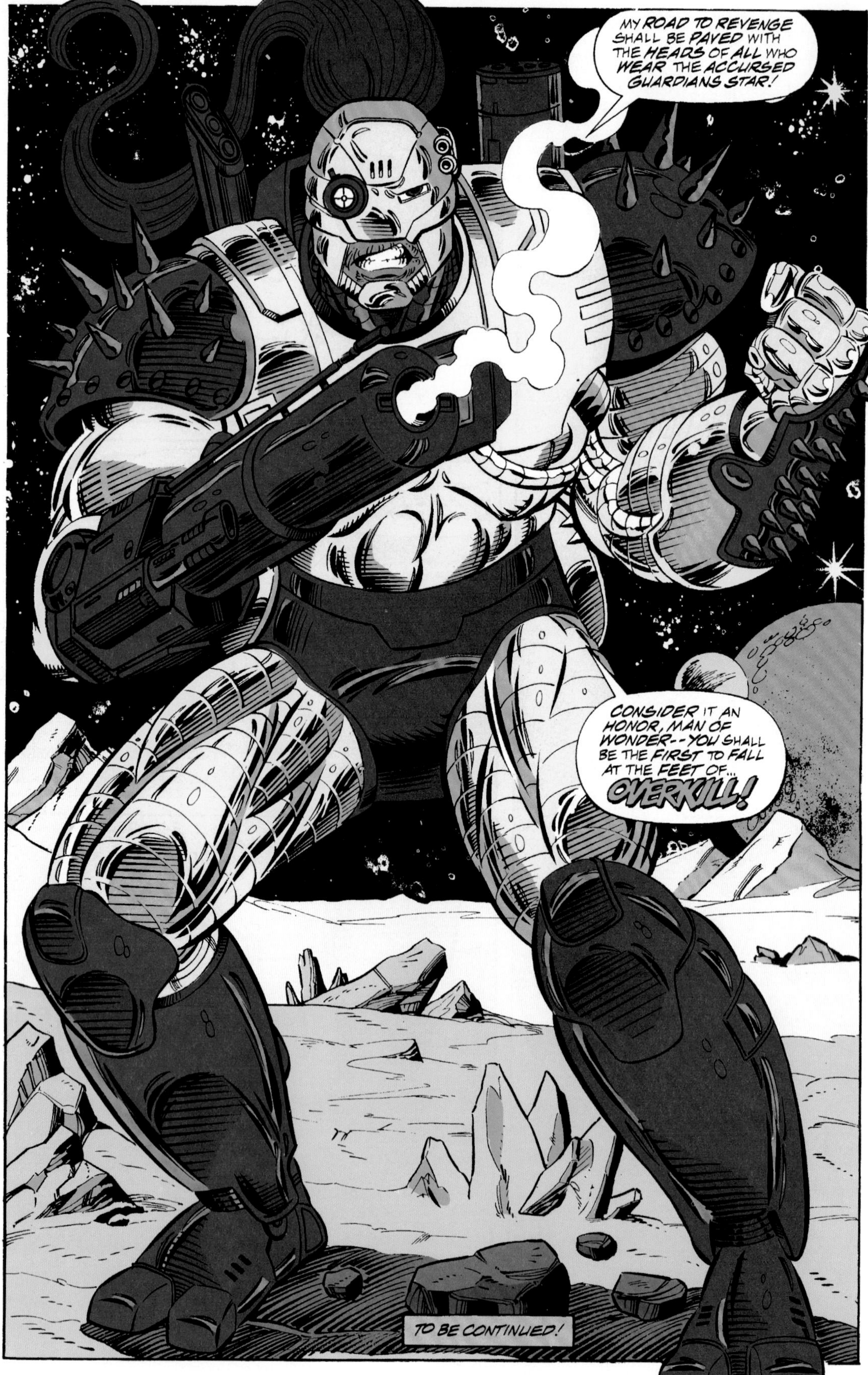
MY ROAD TO REVENGE SHALL BE PAVED WITH THE HEADS OF ALL WHO WEAR THE ACCURSED GUARDIANS STAR!
CONSIDER IT AN HONOR, MAN OF WONDER--YOU SHALL BE THE FIRST TO FALL AT THE FEET OF... OVERKILL!
TO BE CONTINUED!

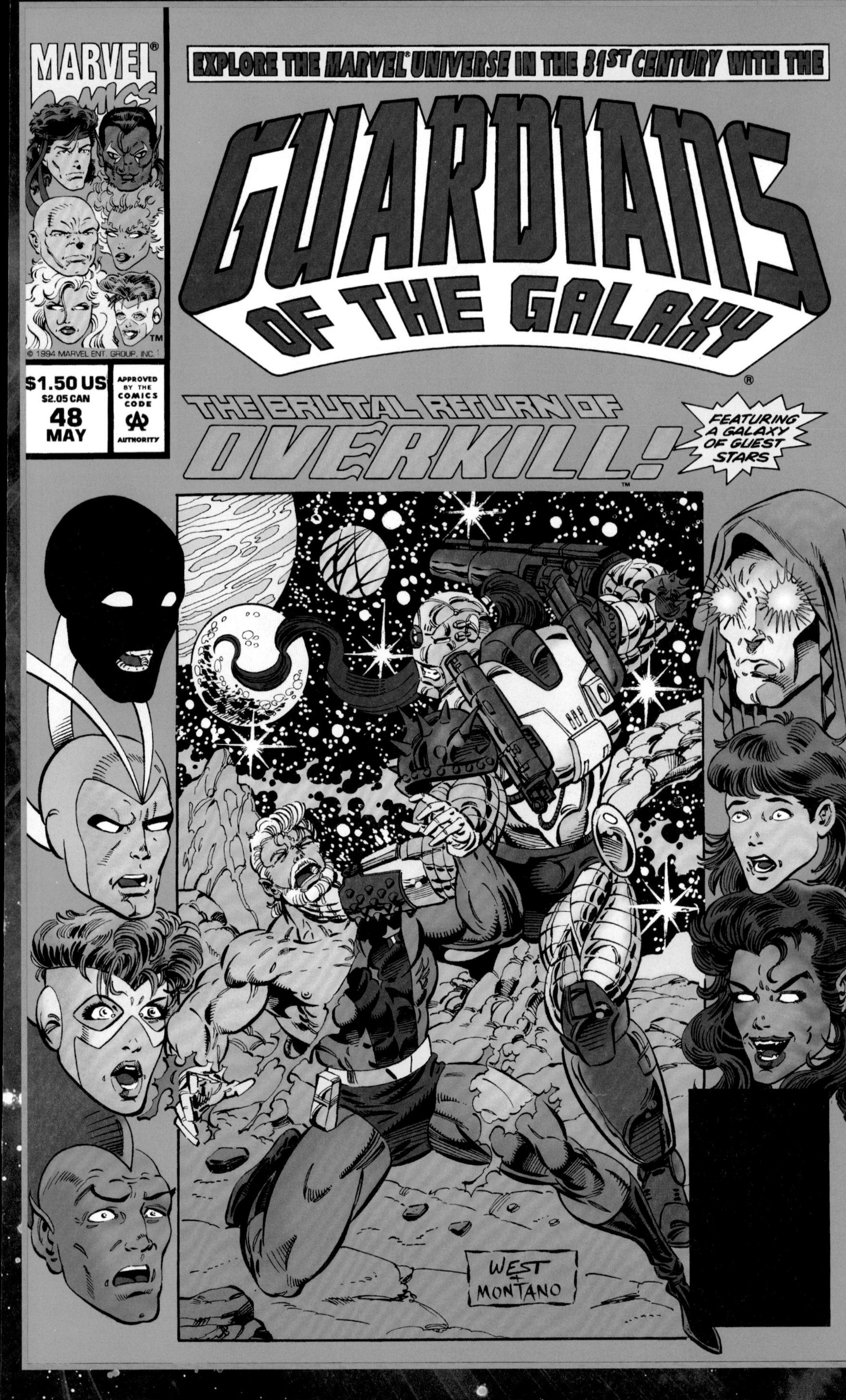
MARVEL® COMICS
™
© 1994 MARVEL ENT. GROUP, INC.
$1.50 US
$2.05 CAN
48
MAY
APPROVED BY THE COMICS CODE AUTHORITY
EXPLORE THE MARVEL® UNIVERSE IN THE 31ST CENTURY WITH THE
GUARDIANS OF THE GALAXY®
THE BRUTAL RETURN OF
OVERKILL!™
FEATURING A GALAXY OF GUEST STARS
WEST + MONTANO

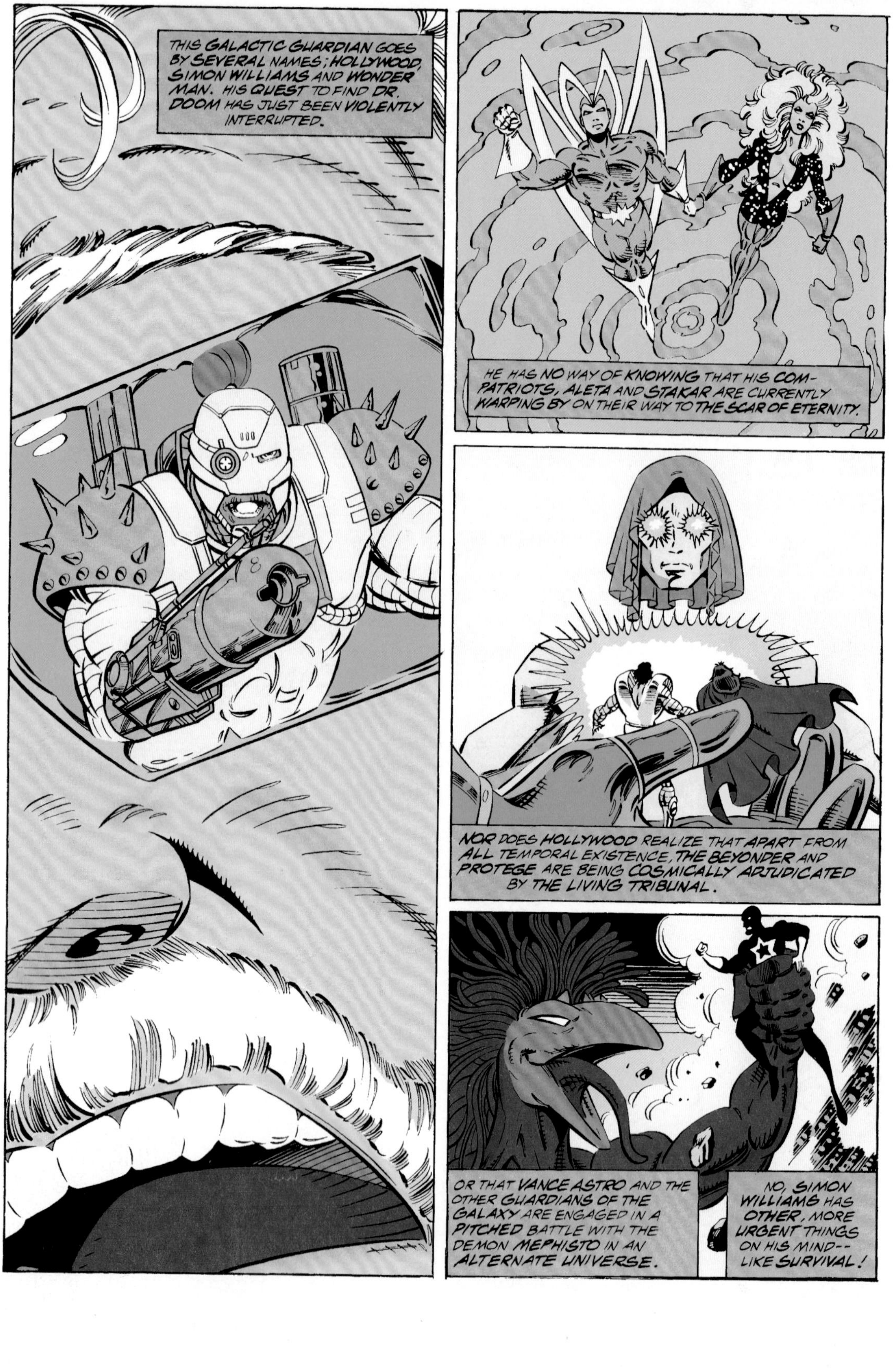
THIS GALACTIC GUARDIAN GOES BY SEVERAL NAMES; HOLLYWOOD, SIMON WILLIAMS AND WONDER MAN. HIS QUEST TO FIND DR. DOOM HAS JUST BEEN VIOLENTLY INTERRUPTED.
HE HAS NO WAY OF KNOWING THAT HIS COMPATRIOTS, ALETA AND STAKAR ARE CURRENTLY WARPING BY ON THEIR WAY TO THE SCAR OF ETERNITY.
NOR DOES HOLLYWOOD REALIZE THAT APART FROM ALL TEMPORAL EXISTENCE, THE BEYONDER AND PROTEGE ARE BEING COSMICALLY ADJUDICATED BY THE LIVING TRIBUNAL.
OR THAT VANCE ASTRO AND THE OTHER GUARDIANS OF THE GALAXY ARE ENGAGED IN A PITCHED BATTLE WITH THE DEMON MEPHISTO IN AN ALTERNATE UNIVERSE.
NO, SIMON WILLIAMS HAS OTHER, MORE URGENT THINGS ON HIS MIND-- LIKE SURVIVAL!

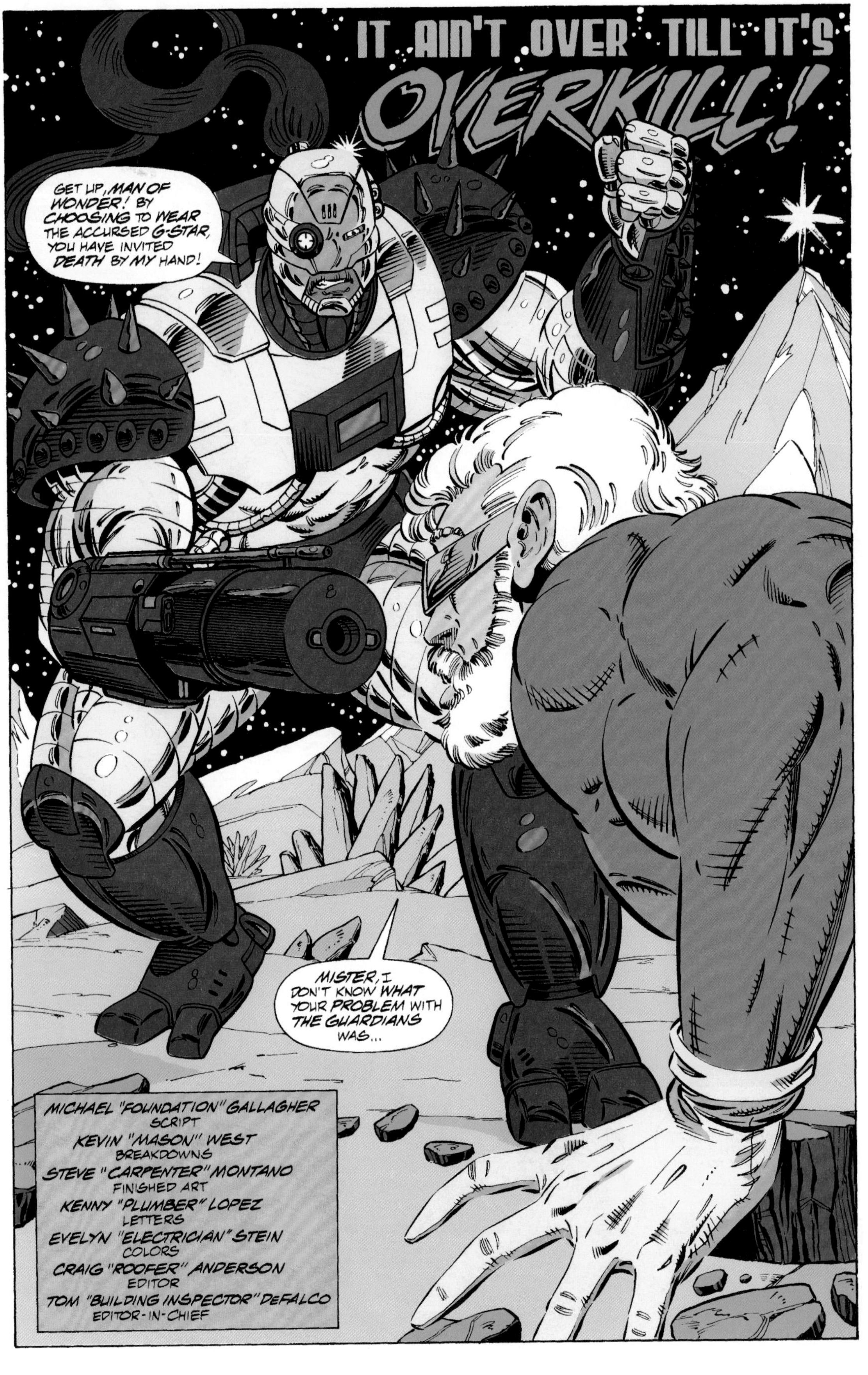
IT AIN'T OVER TILL IT'S
OVERKILL!
GET UP, MAN OF WONDER! BY CHOOSING TO WEAR THE ACCURSED G-STAR, YOU HAVE INVITED DEATH BY MY HAND!
MISTER, I DON'T KNOW WHAT YOUR PROBLEM WITH THE GUARDIANS WAS...
MICHAEL "FOUNDATION" GALLAGHER SCRIPT
KEVIN "MASON" WEST BREAKDOWNS
STEVE "CARPENTER" MONTANO FINISHED ART
KENNY "PLUMBER" LOPEZ LETTERS
EVELYN "ELECTRICIAN" STEIN COLORS
CRAIG "ROOFER" ANDERSON EDITOR
TOM "BUILDING INSPECTOR" DeFALCO EDITOR-IN-CHIEF

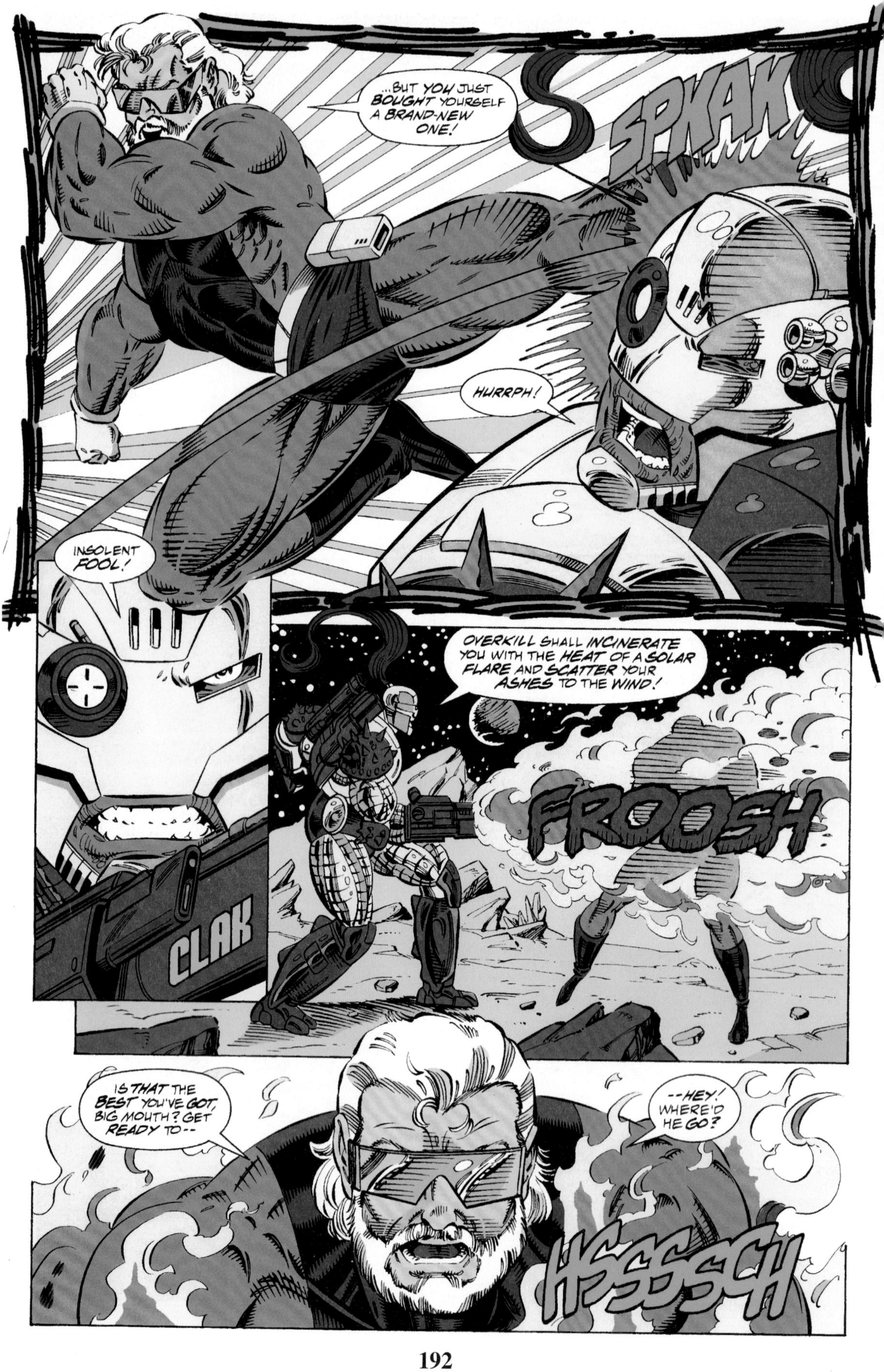
...BUT YOU JUST BOUGHT YOURSELF A BRAND-NEW ONE!
SPKAK
HURRPH!
INSOLENT FOOL!
CLAK
OVERKILL SHALL INCINERATE YOU WITH THE HEAT OF A SOLAR FLARE AND SCATTER YOUR ASHES TO THE WIND!
FROOSH
IS THAT THE BEST YOU'VE GOT, BIG MOUTH? GET READY TO--
--HEY! WHERE'D HE GO?
HSSSSCH

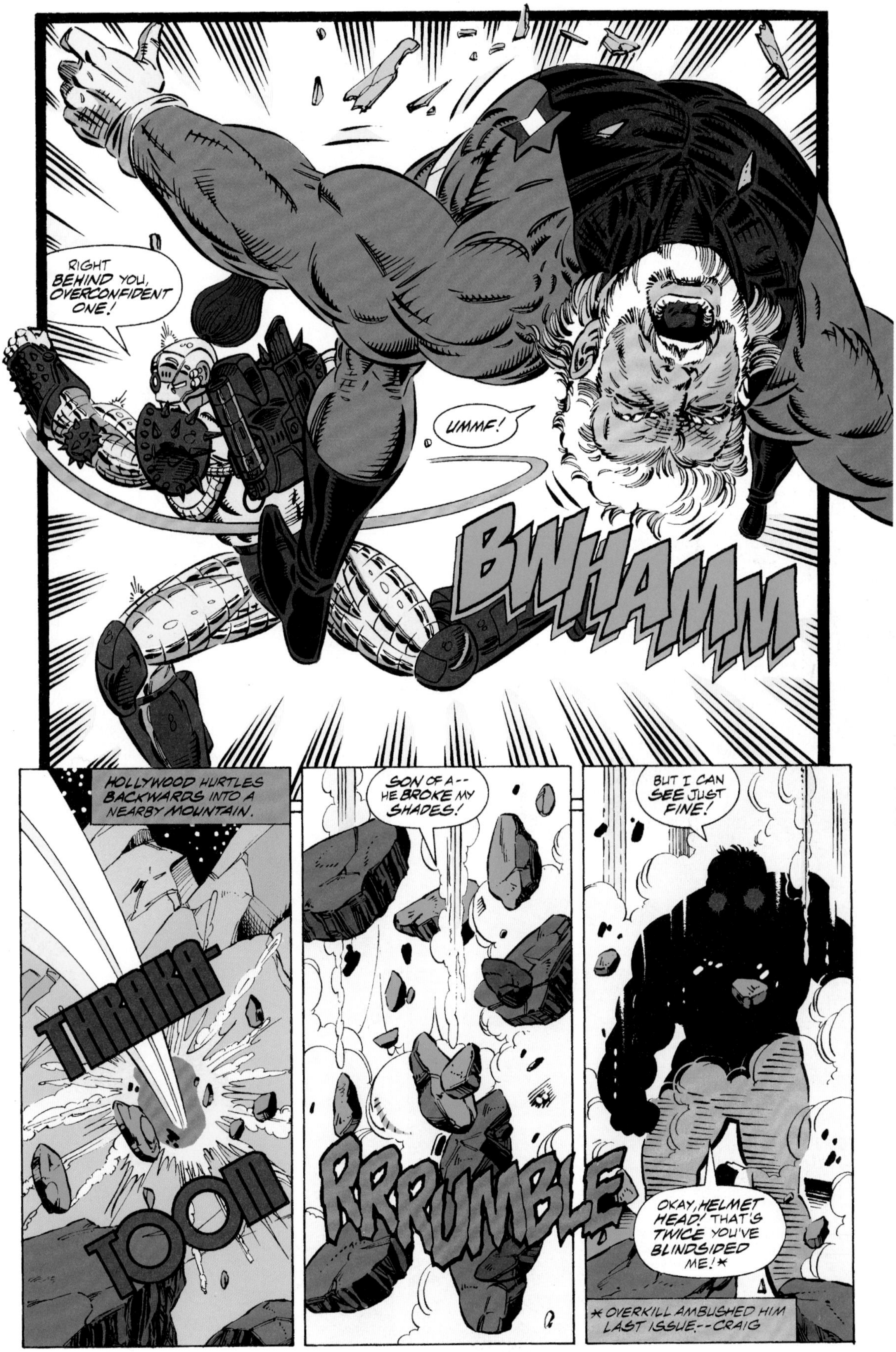
RIGHT BEHIND YOU, OVERCONFIDENT ONE!
UMMF!
BWHAMM
HOLLYWOOD HURTLES BACKWARDS INTO A NEARBY MOUNTAIN.
THRAKA-TOOM
SON OF A-- HE BROKE MY SHADES!
RRRUMBLE
BUT I CAN SEE JUST FINE!
OKAY, HELMET HEAD! THAT'S TWICE YOU'VE BLINDSIDED ME!*
*OVERKILL AMBUSHED HIM LAST ISSUE.--CRAIG

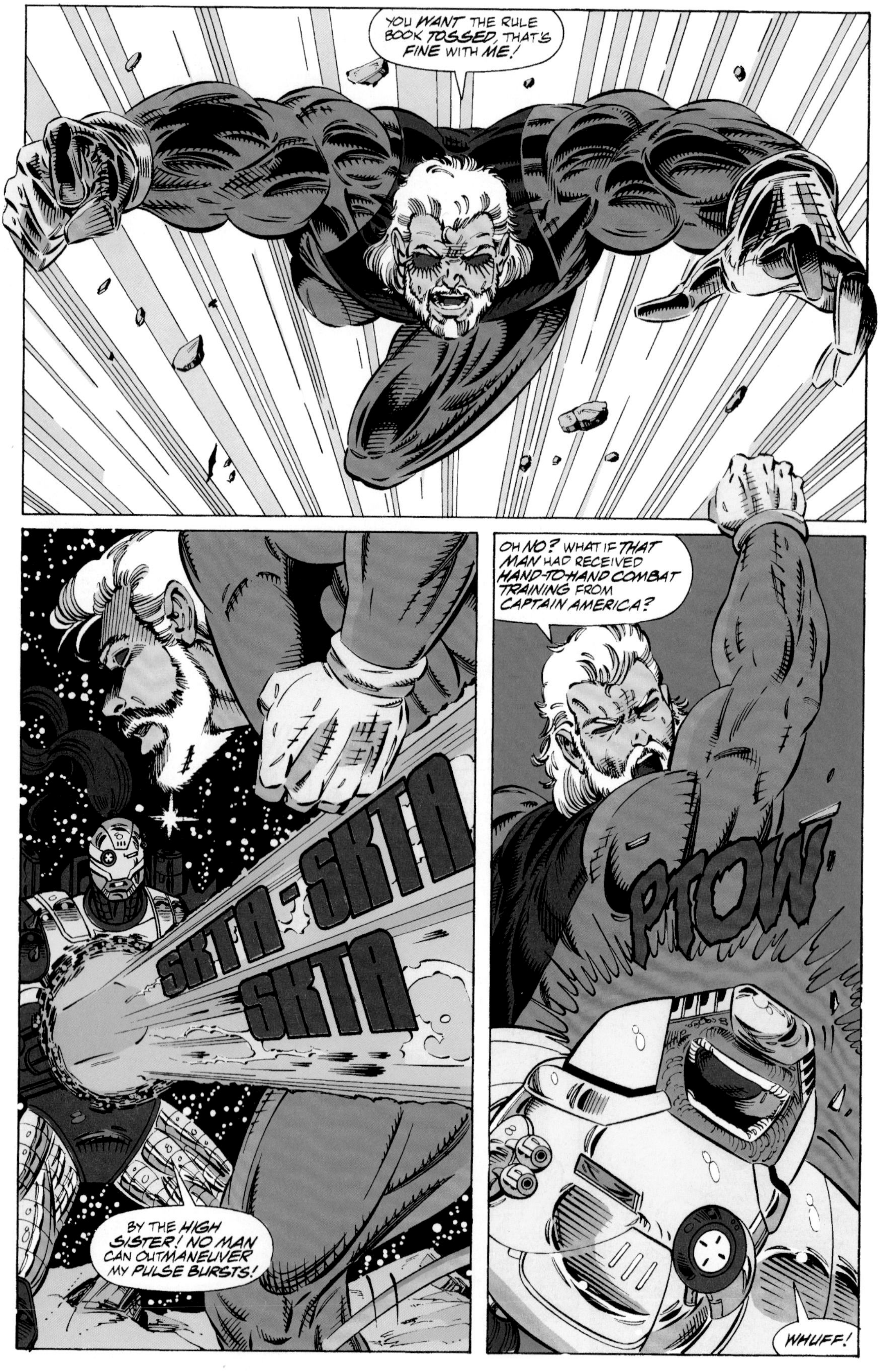
YOU WANT THE RULE BOOK TOSSED, THAT'S FINE WITH ME!
SKTA-SKTA SKTA
BY THE HIGH SISTER! NO MAN CAN OUTMANEUVER MY PULSE BURSTS!
OH NO? WHAT IF THAT MAN HAD RECEIVED HAND-TO-HAND COMBAT TRAINING FROM CAPTAIN AMERICA?
PTOW
WHUFF!

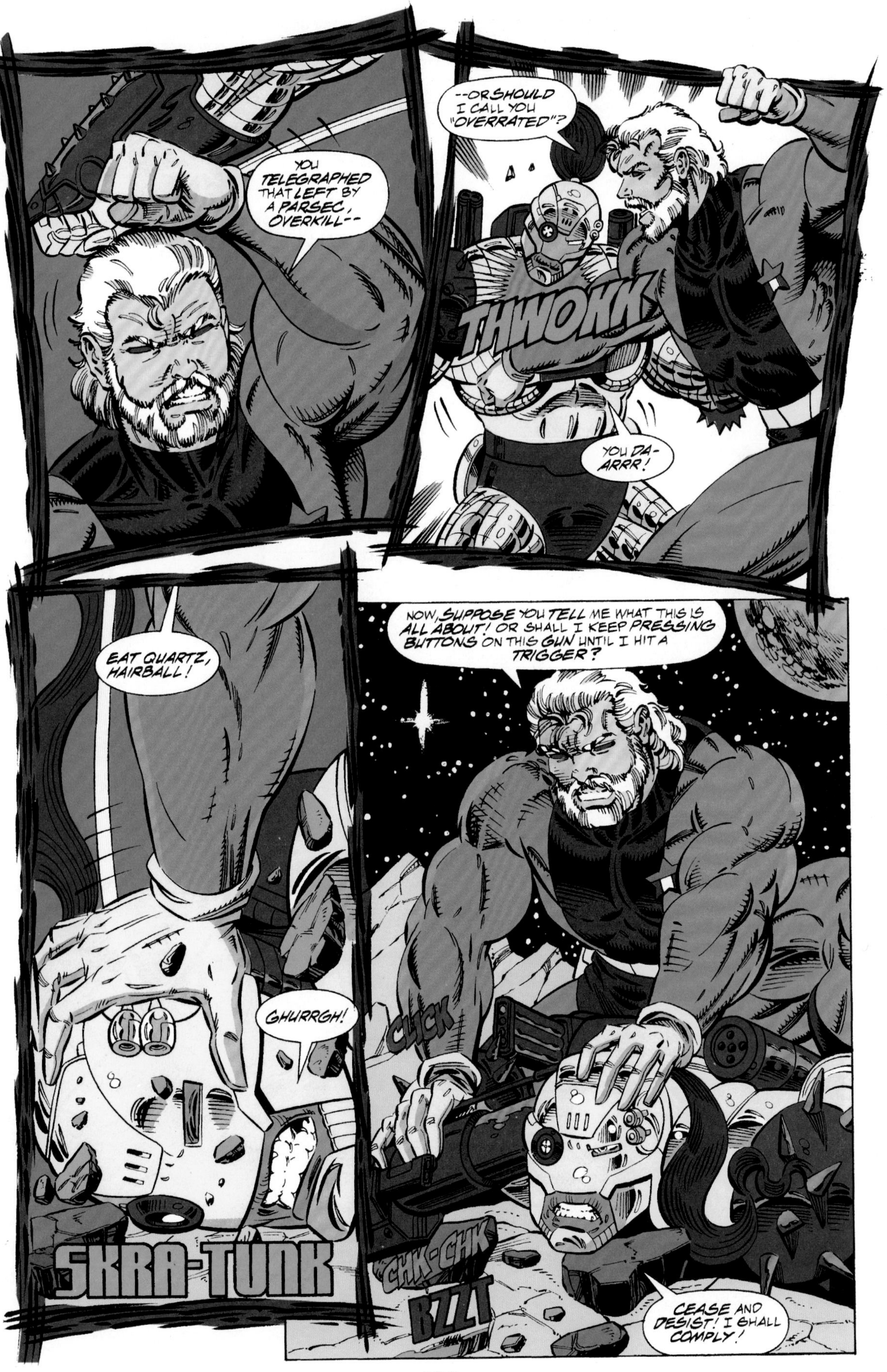
YOU TELEGRAPHED THAT LEFT BY A PARSEC, OVERKILL--
--OR SHOULD I CALL YOU "OVERRATED"?
THWOKK
YOU DA-ARRR!
EAT QUARTZ, HAIRBALL!
GHURRGH!
SKRA-TUNK
NOW, SUPPOSE YOU TELL ME WHAT THIS IS ALL ABOUT! OR SHALL I KEEP PRESSING BUTTONS ON THIS GUN UNTIL I HIT A TRIGGER?
CLICK
CHK-CHK
BZZT
CEASE AND DESIST! I SHALL COMPLY!

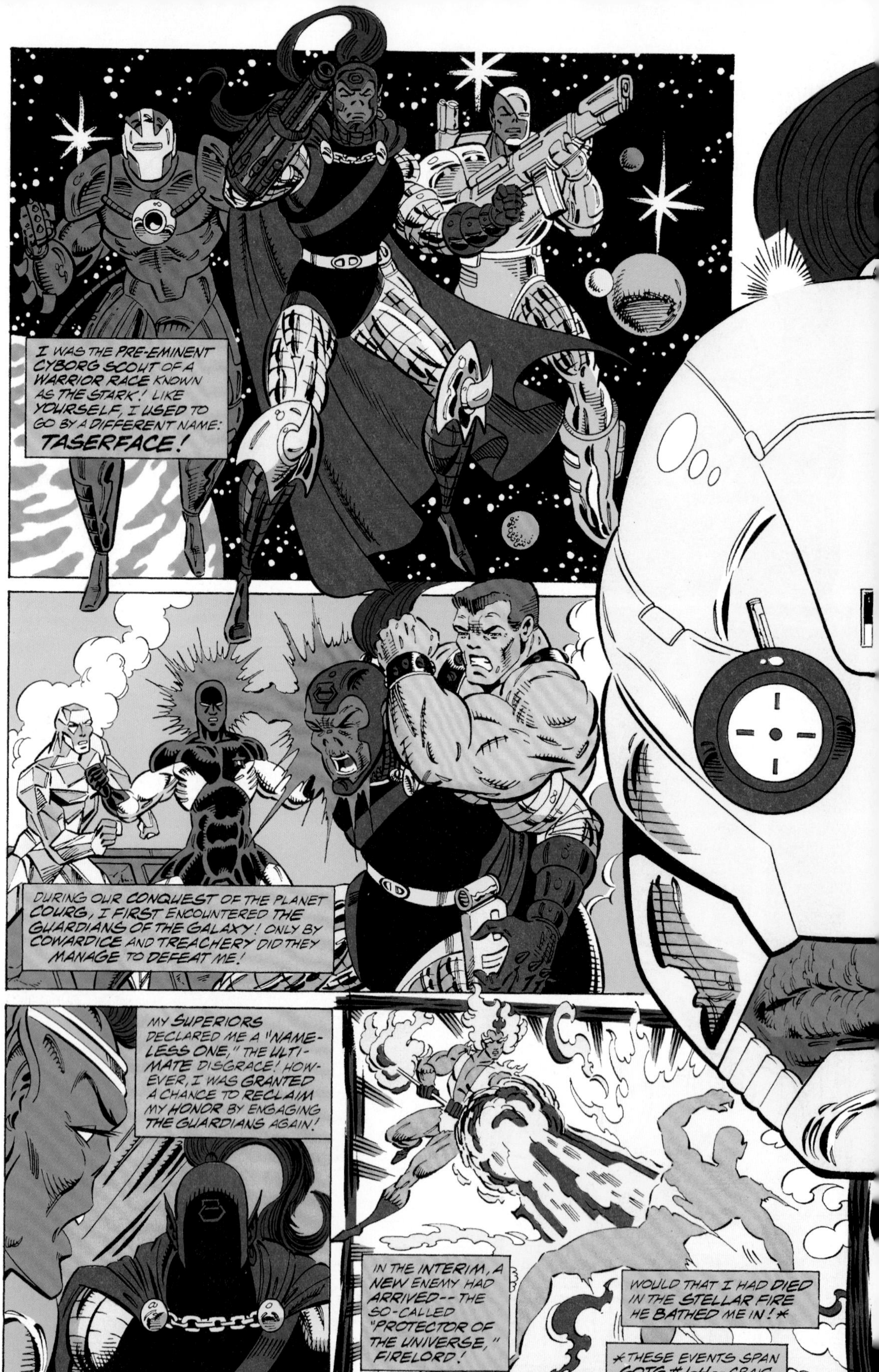
I WAS THE PRE-EMINENT CYBORG SCOUT OF A WARRIOR RACE KNOWN AS THE STARK! LIKE YOURSELF, I USED TO GO BY A DIFFERENT NAME: TASERFACE!
DURING OUR CONQUEST OF THE PLANET COURG, I FIRST ENCOUNTERED THE GUARDIANS OF THE GALAXY! ONLY BY COWARDICE AND TREACHERY DID THEY MANAGE TO DEFEAT ME!
MY SUPERIORS DECLARED ME A "NAME-LESS ONE," THE ULTI-MATE DISGRACE! HOW-EVER, I WAS GRANTED A CHANCE TO RECLAIM MY HONOR BY ENGAGING THE GUARDIANS AGAIN!
IN THE INTERIM, A NEW ENEMY HAD ARRIVED-- THE SO-CALLED "PROTECTOR OF THE UNIVERSE," FIRELORD!
WOULD THAT I HAD DIED IN THE STELLAR FIRE HE BATHED ME IN! *
*THESE EVENTS SPAN GOTG #1-4.--CRAIG

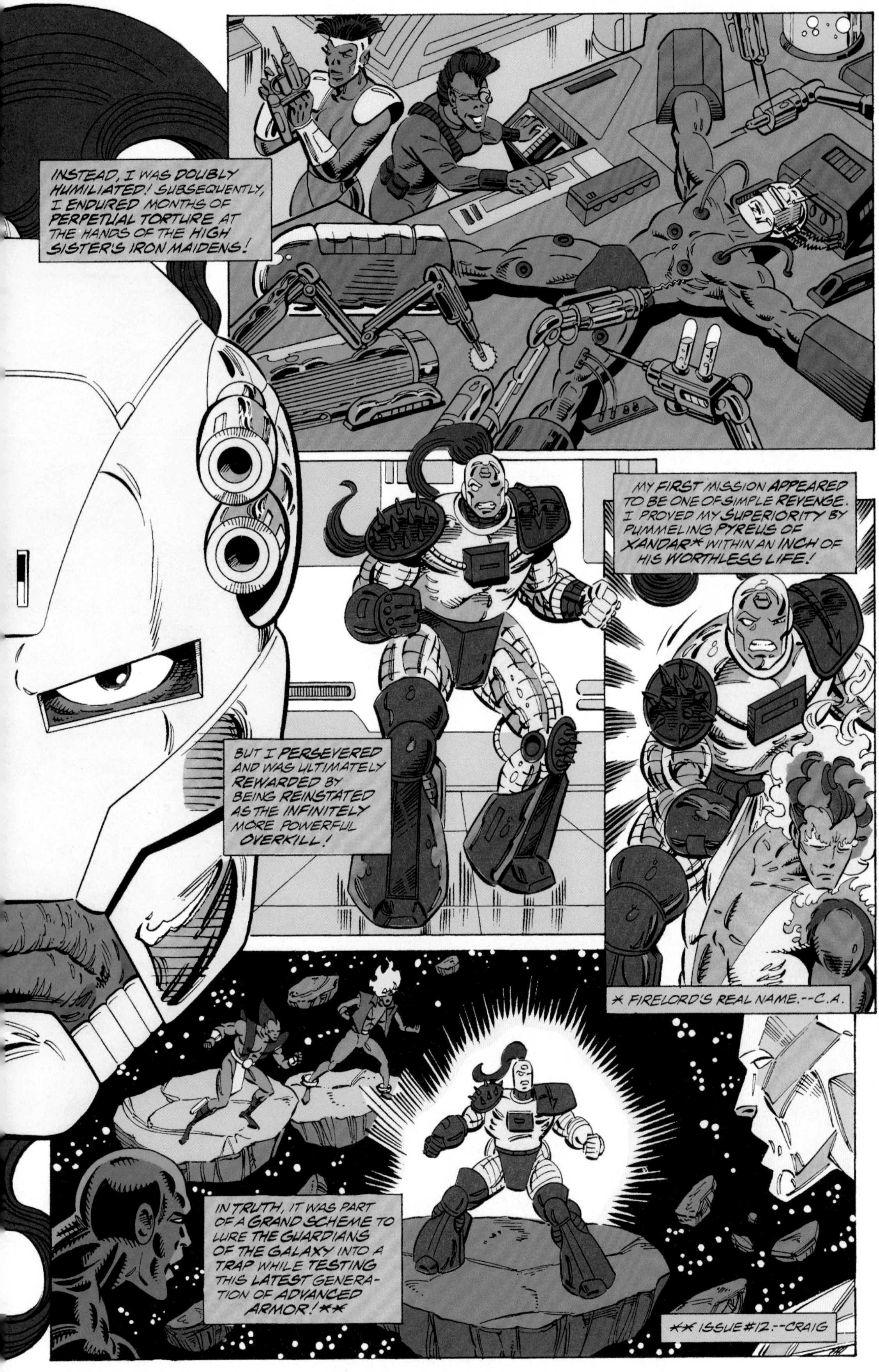
INSTEAD, I WAS DOUBLY HUMILIATED! SUBSEQUENTLY, I ENDURED MONTHS OF PERPETUAL TORTURE AT THE HANDS OF THE HIGH SISTER'S IRON MAIDENS!
BUT I PERSEVERED AND WAS ULTIMATELY REWARDED BY BEING REINSTATED AS THE INFINITELY MORE POWERFUL OVERKILL!
MY FIRST MISSION APPEARED TO BE ONE OF SIMPLE REVENGE. I PROVED MY SUPERIORITY BY PUMMELING PYREUS OF XANDAR* WITHIN AN INCH OF HIS WORTHLESS LIFE!
* FIRELORD'S REAL NAME.--C.A.
IN TRUTH, IT WAS PART OF A GRAND SCHEME TO LURE THE GUARDIANS OF THE GALAXY INTO A TRAP WHILE TESTING THIS LATEST GENERATION OF ADVANCED ARMOR!**
** ISSUE #12.--CRAIG

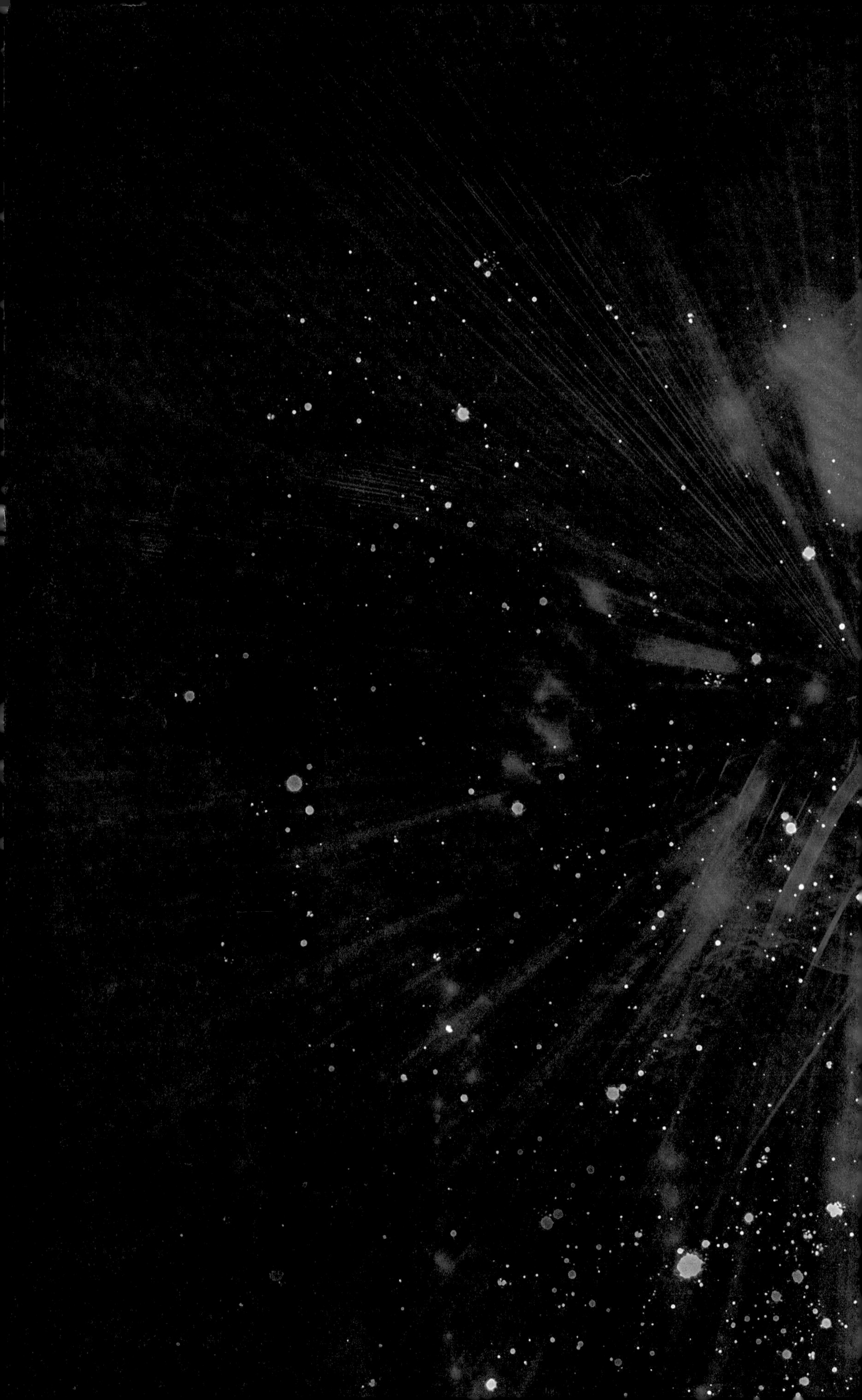

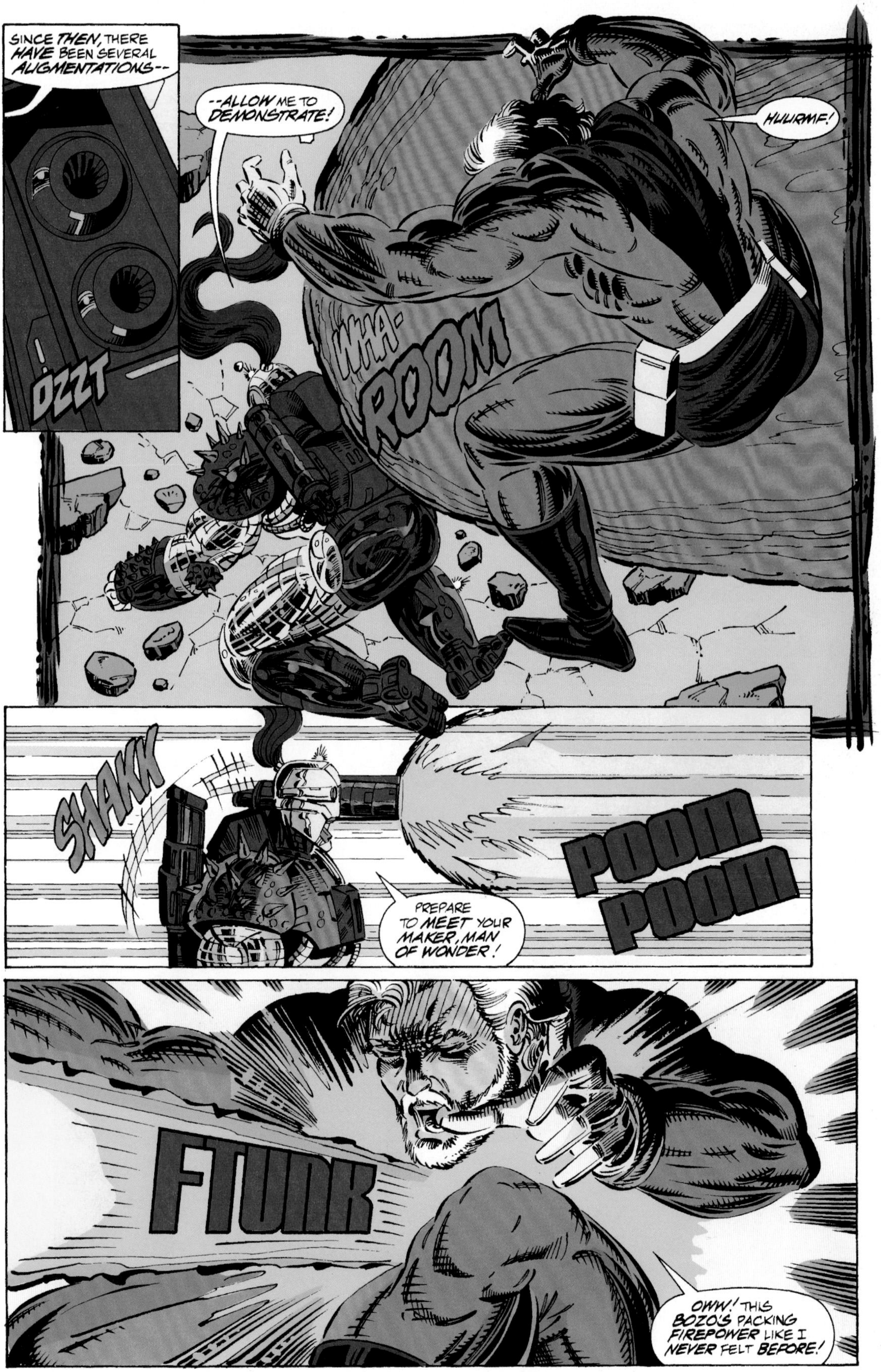
SINCE THEN, THERE HAVE BEEN SEVERAL AUGMENTATIONS--
DZZT
--ALLOW ME TO DEMONSTRATE!
HUURMF!
WHA-ROOM
SHAKK
POOM POOM
PREPARE TO MEET YOUR MAKER, MAN OF WONDER!
FTUNK
OWW! THIS BOZO'S PACKING FIREPOWER LIKE I NEVER FELT BEFORE!

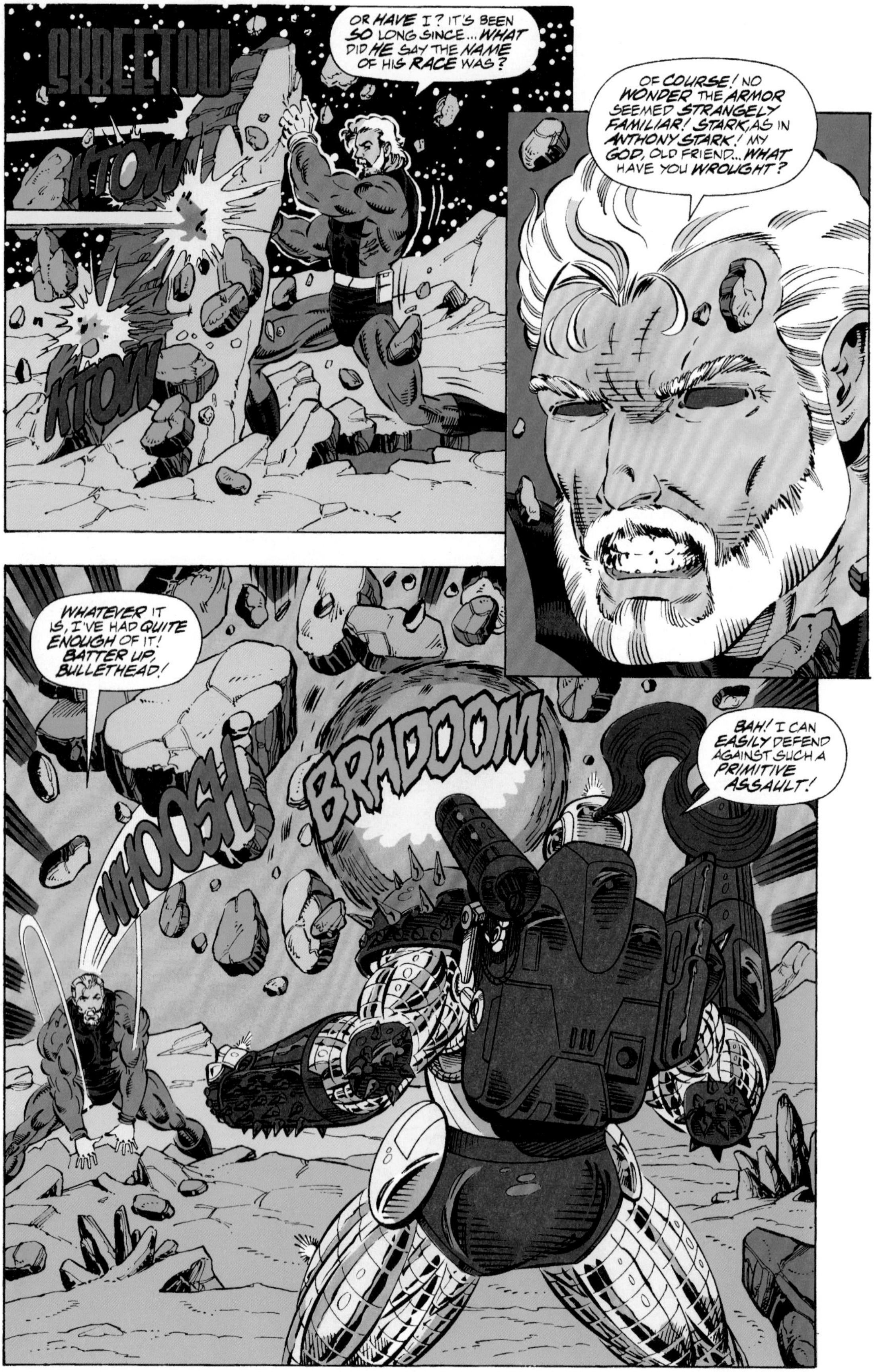
SKREETOU
OR HAVE I? IT'S BEEN SO LONG SINCE... WHAT DID HE SAY THE NAME OF HIS RACE WAS?
KTOW
KTOW
OF COURSE! NO WONDER THE ARMOR SEEMED STRANGELY FAMILIAR! STARK, AS IN ANTHONY STARK! MY GOD, OLD FRIEND... WHAT HAVE YOU WROUGHT?
WHATEVER IT IS, I'VE HAD QUITE ENOUGH OF IT! BATTER UP, BULLETHEAD!
WHOOSH
BRADOOM
BAH! I CAN EASILY DEFEND AGAINST SUCH A PRIMITIVE ASSAULT!

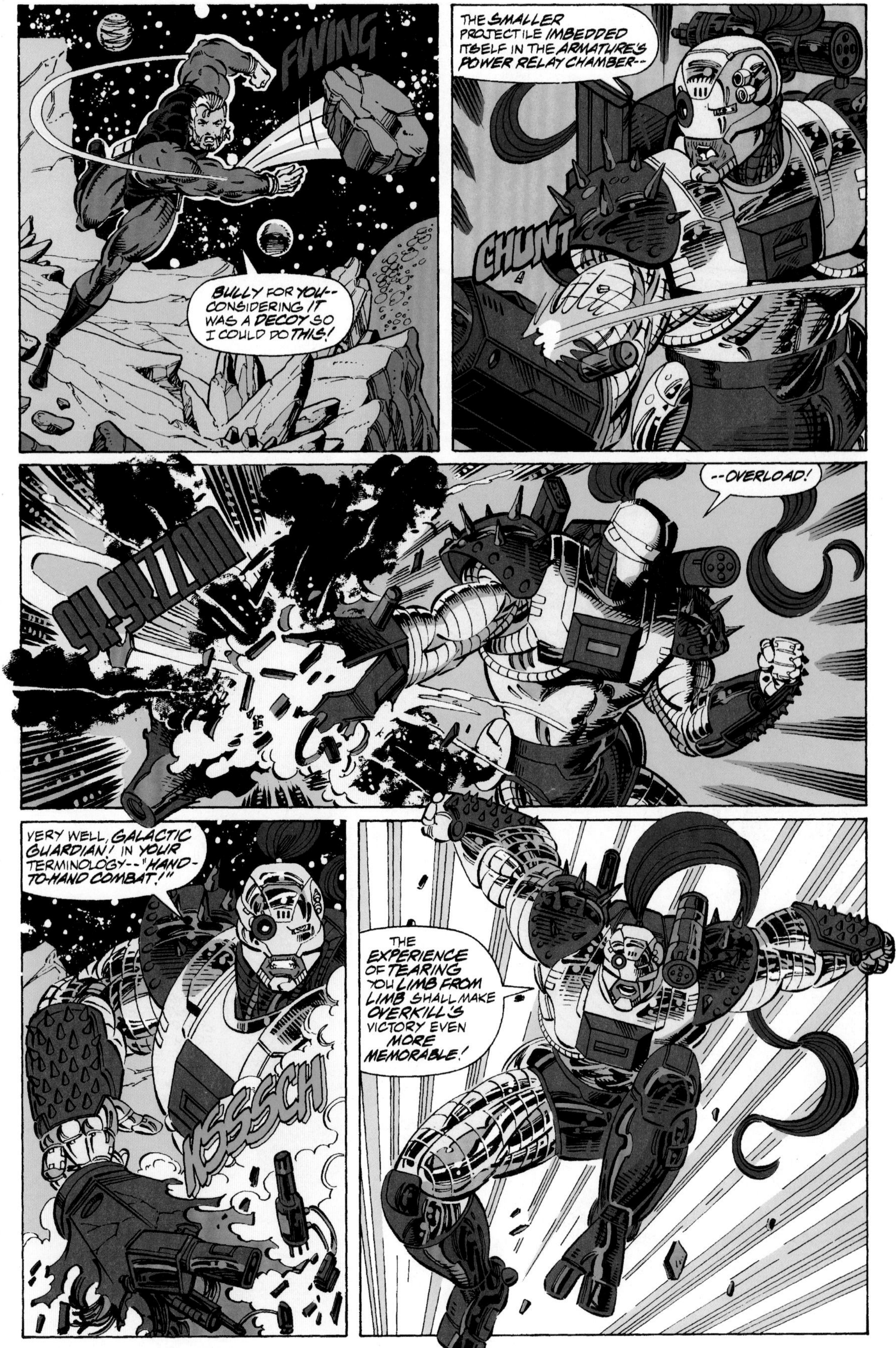
FWING
BULLY FOR YOU-- CONSIDERING IT WAS A DECOY SO I COULD DO THIS!
THE SMALLER PROJECTILE IMBEDDED ITSELF IN THE ARMATURE'S POWER RELAY CHAMBER--
CHUNT
SK-SKZZAM
--OVERLOAD!
VERY WELL, GALACTIC GUARDIAN! IN YOUR TERMINOLOGY--"HAND-TO-HAND COMBAT!"
KSSSCH
THE EXPERIENCE OF TEARING YOU LIMB FROM LIMB SHALL MAKE OVERKILL'S VICTORY EVEN MORE MEMORABLE!

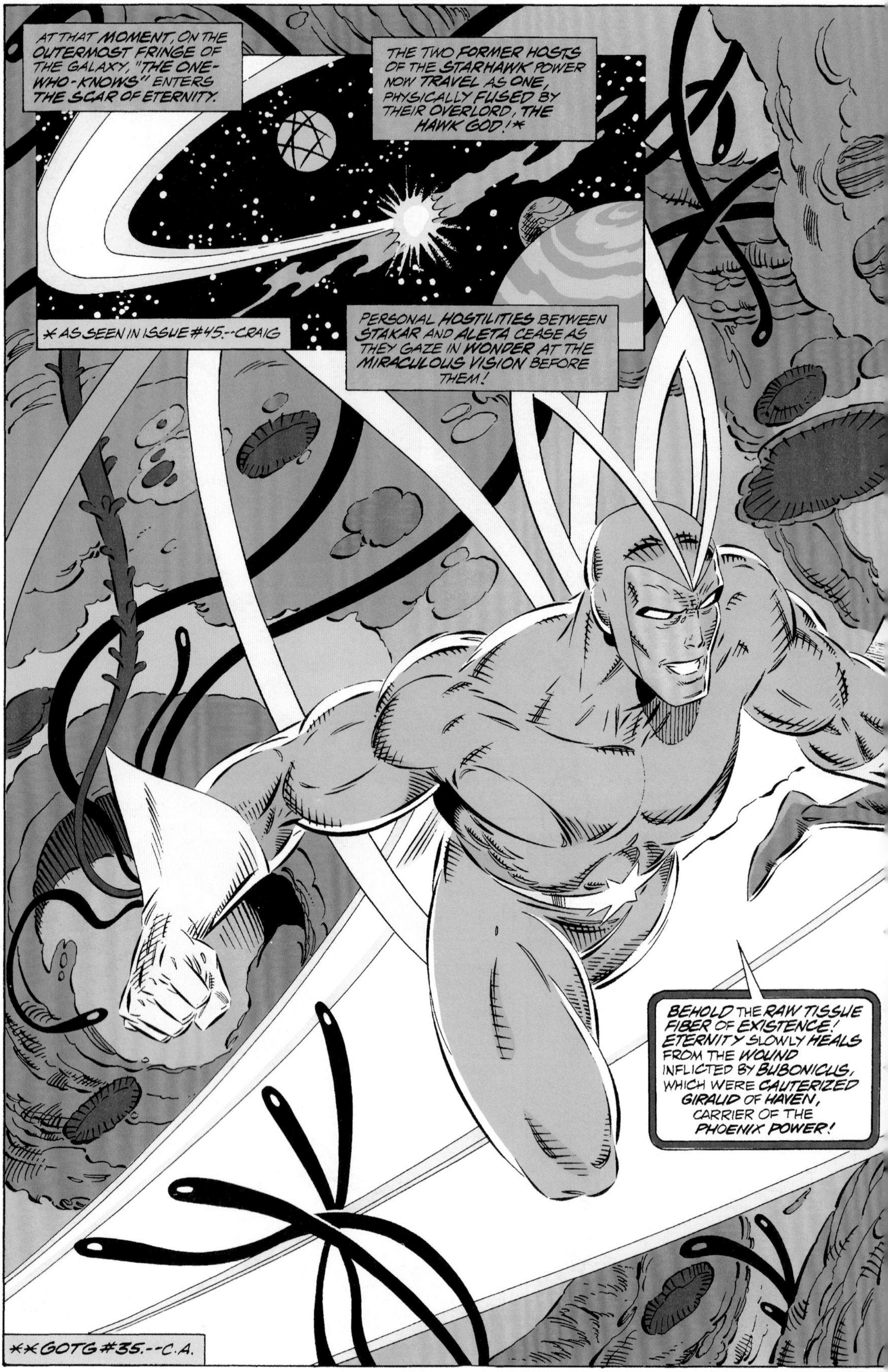
AT THAT MOMENT, ON THE OUTERMOST FRINGE OF THE GALAXY, "THE ONE-WHO-KNOWS" ENTERS THE SCAR OF ETERNITY.
THE TWO FORMER HOSTS OF THE STARHAWK POWER NOW TRAVEL AS ONE, PHYSICALLY FUSED BY THEIR OVERLORD, THE HAWK GOD!*
*AS SEEN IN ISSUE #45.--CRAIG
PERSONAL HOSTILITIES BETWEEN STAKAR AND ALETA CEASE AS THEY GAZE IN WONDER AT THE MIRACULOUS VISION BEFORE THEM!
BEHOLD THE RAW TISSUE FIBER OF EXISTENCE! ETERNITY SLOWLY HEALS FROM THE WOUND INFLICTED BY BUBONICUS, WHICH WERE CAUTERIZED GIRALID OF HAVEN, CARRIER OF THE PHOENIX POWER!
**GOTG #35.--C.A.

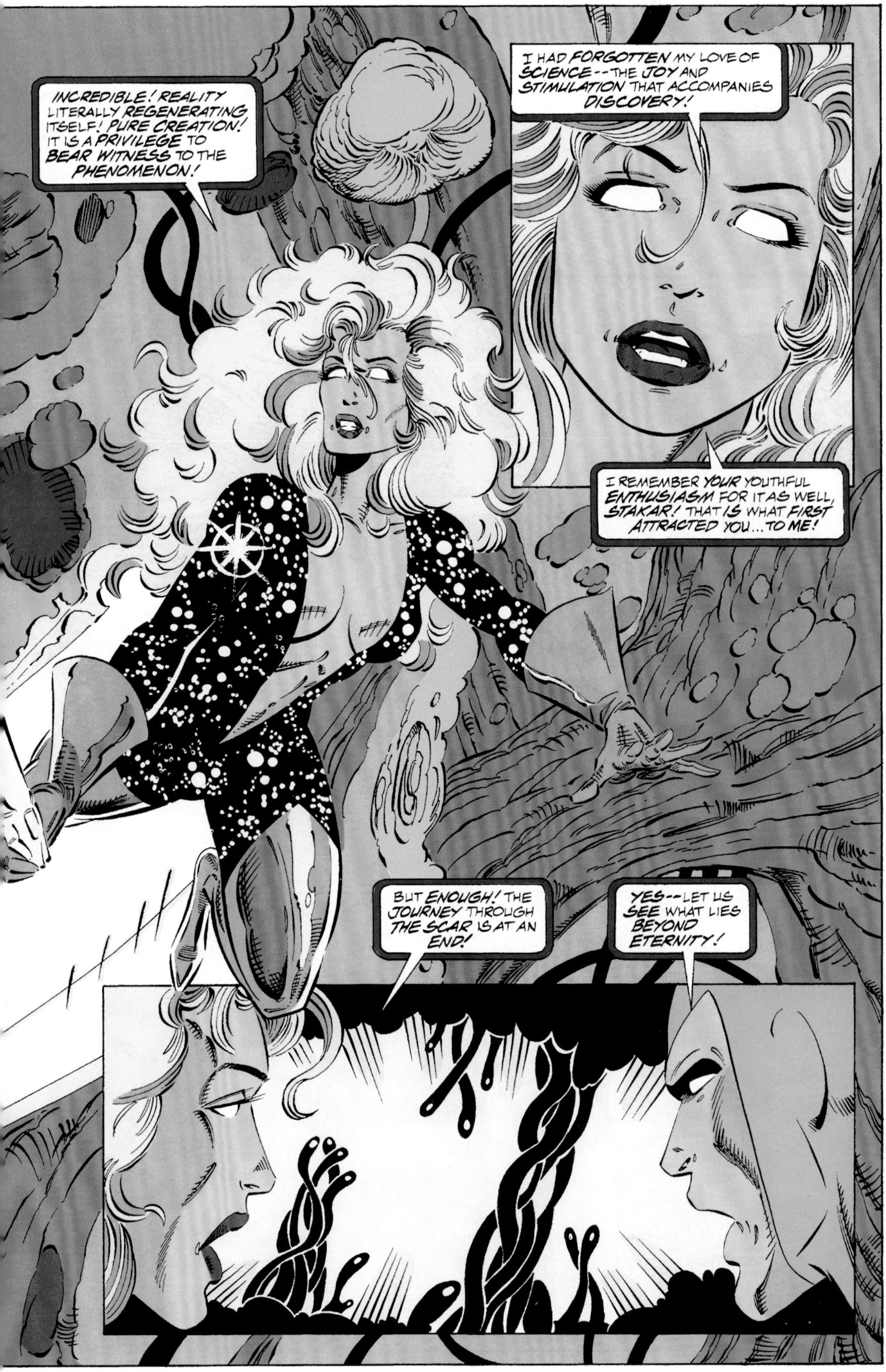
INCREDIBLE! REALITY LITERALLY REGENERATING ITSELF! PURE CREATION! IT IS A PRIVILEGE TO BEAR WITNESS TO THE PHENOMENON!
I HAD FORGOTTEN MY LOVE OF SCIENCE--THE JOY AND STIMULATION THAT ACCOMPANIES DISCOVERY!
I REMEMBER YOUR YOUTHFUL ENTHUSIASM FOR IT AS WELL, STAKAR! THAT IS WHAT FIRST ATTRACTED YOU...TO ME!
BUT ENOUGH! THE JOURNEY THROUGH THE SCAR IS AT AN END!
YES--LET US SEE WHAT LIES BEYOND ETERNITY!

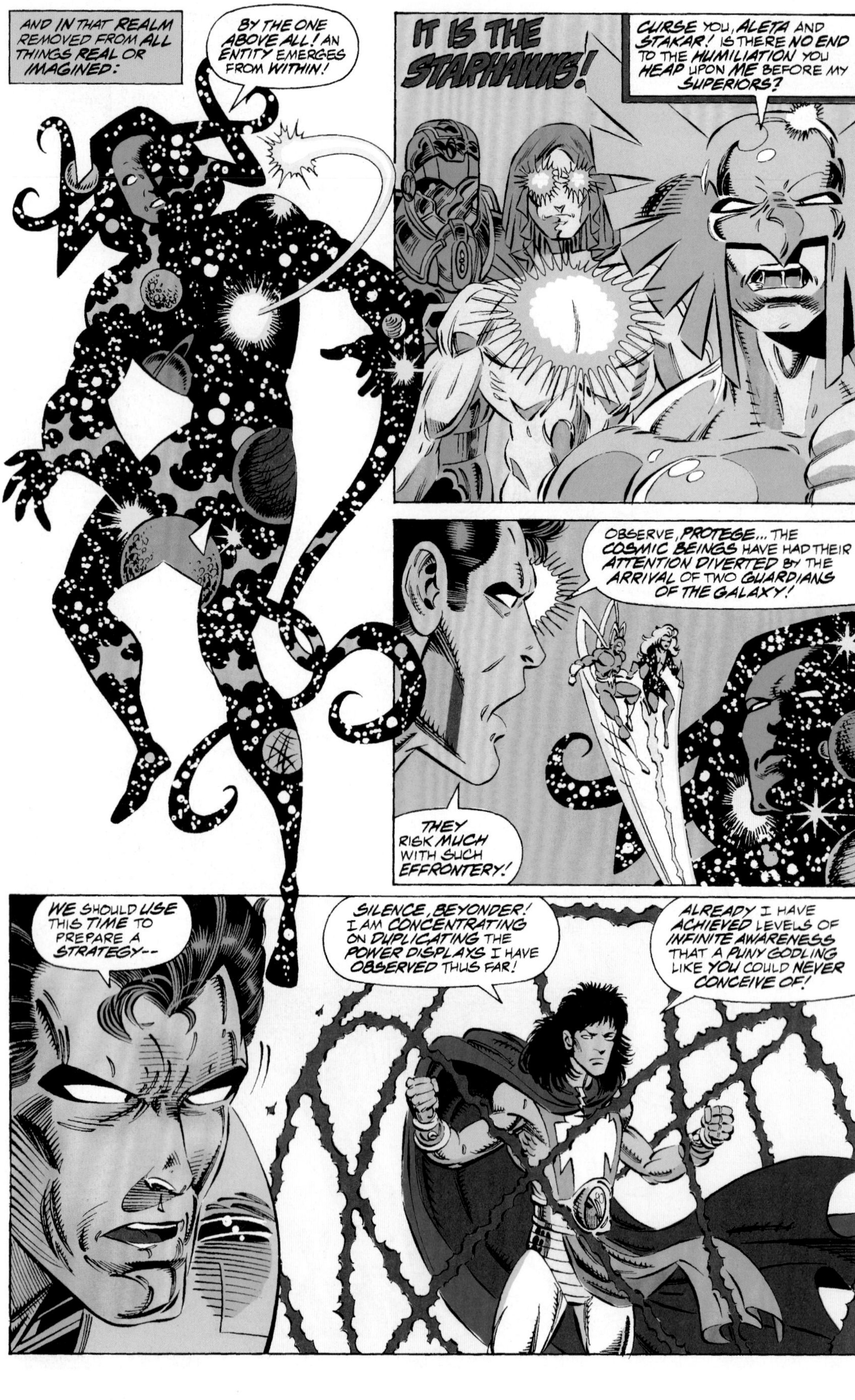
AND IN THAT REALM REMOVED FROM ALL THINGS REAL OR IMAGINED:
BY THE ONE ABOVE ALL! AN ENTITY EMERGES FROM WITHIN!
IT IS THE STARHAWKS!
CURSE YOU, ALETA AND STAKAR! IS THERE NO END TO THE HUMILIATION YOU HEAP UPON ME BEFORE MY SUPERIORS?
OBSERVE, PROTEGE... THE COSMIC BEINGS HAVE HAD THEIR ATTENTION DIVERTED BY THE ARRIVAL OF TWO GUARDIANS OF THE GALAXY!
THEY RISK MUCH WITH SUCH EFFRONTERY!
WE SHOULD USE THIS TIME TO PREPARE A STRATEGY--
SILENCE, BEYONDER! I AM CONCENTRATING ON DUPLICATING THE POWER DISPLAYS I HAVE OBSERVED THUS FAR!
ALREADY I HAVE ACHIEVED LEVELS OF INFINITE AWARENESS THAT A PUNY GODLING LIKE YOU COULD NEVER CONCEIVE OF!

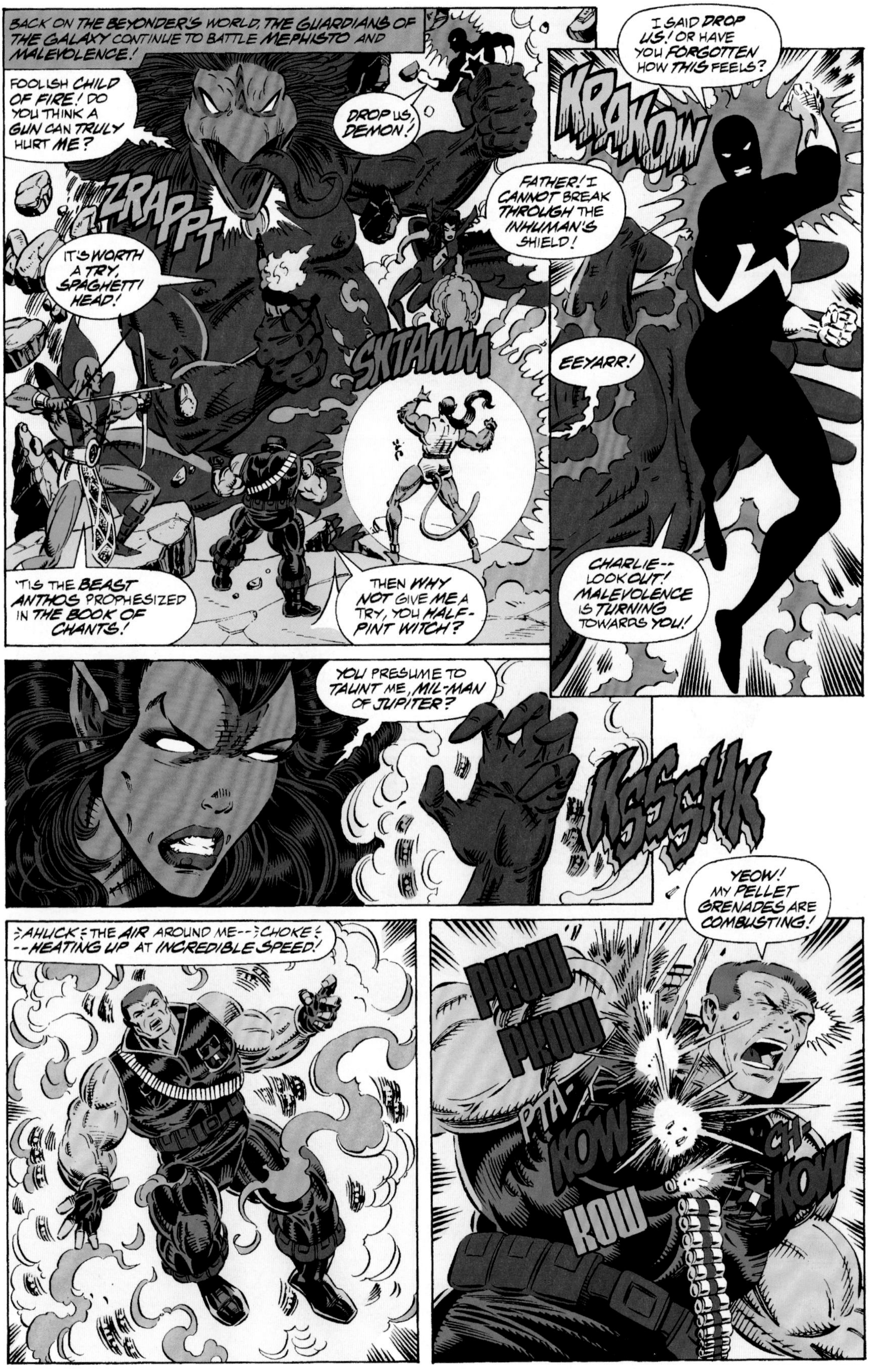
BACK ON THE BEYONDER'S WORLD, THE GUARDIANS OF THE GALAXY CONTINUE TO BATTLE MEPHISTO AND MALEVOLENCE!
FOOLISH CHILD OF FIRE! DO YOU THINK A GUN CAN TRULY HURT ME?
DROP US, DEMON!
ZRAPPT
IT'S WORTH A TRY, SPAGHETTI HEAD!
I SAID DROP US! OR HAVE YOU FORGOTTEN HOW THIS FEELS?
KRAKOW
FATHER! I CANNOT BREAK THROUGH THE INHUMAN'S SHIELD!
SKTAMM
EEYARR!
'TIS THE BEAST ANTHOS PROPHESIZED IN THE BOOK OF CHANTS!
THEN WHY NOT GIVE ME A TRY, YOU HALF-PINT WITCH?
CHARLIE-- LOOK OUT! MALEVOLENCE IS TURNING TOWARDS YOU!
YOU PRESUME TO TAUNT ME, MIL-MAN OF JUPITER?
KSSSHK
AHUCK THE AIR AROUND ME-- *CHOKE* --HEATING UP AT INCREDIBLE SPEED!
YEOW! MY PELLET GRENADES ARE COMBUSTING!
PHOW
PHOW
PTA-KOW
CH-KOW
KOW

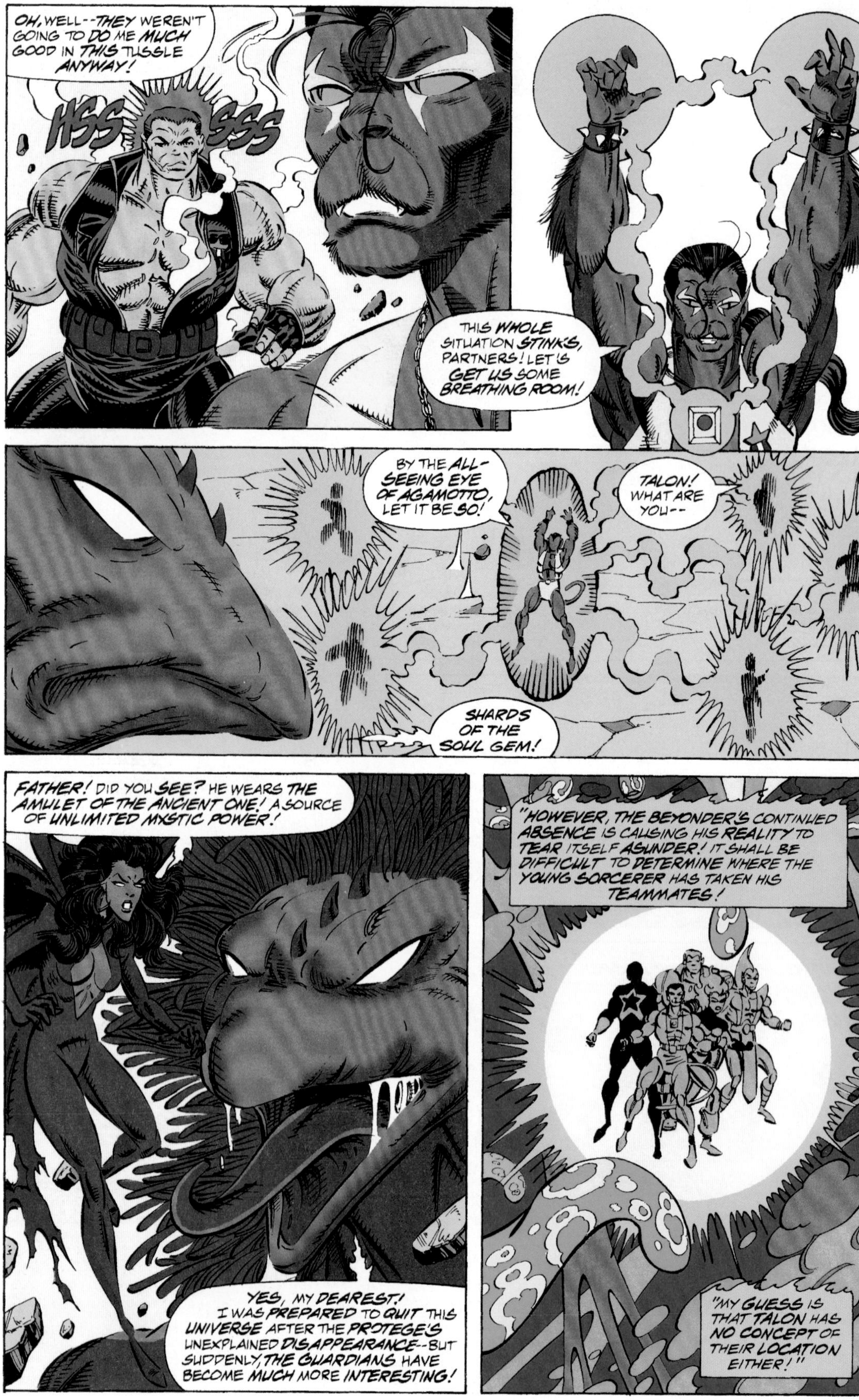
OH, WELL--THEY WEREN'T GOING TO DO ME MUCH GOOD IN THIS TUSSLE ANYWAY!
HSSSSS
THIS WHOLE SITUATION STINKS, PARTNERS! LET'S GET US SOME BREATHING ROOM!
BY THE ALL-SEEING EYE OF AGAMOTTO, LET IT BE SO!
TALON! WHAT ARE YOU--
SHARDS OF THE SOUL GEM!
FATHER! DID YOU SEE? HE WEARS THE AMULET OF THE ANCIENT ONE! A SOURCE OF UNLIMITED MYSTIC POWER!
YES, MY DEAREST! I WAS PREPARED TO QUIT THIS UNIVERSE AFTER THE PROTEGE'S UNEXPLAINED DISAPPEARANCE--BUT SUDDENLY, THE GUARDIANS HAVE BECOME MUCH MORE INTERESTING!
"HOWEVER, THE BEYONDER'S CONTINUED ABSENCE IS CAUSING HIS REALITY TO TEAR ITSELF ASUNDER! IT SHALL BE DIFFICULT TO DETERMINE WHERE THE YOUNG SORCERER HAS TAKEN HIS TEAMMATES!
"MY GUESS IS THAT TALON HAS NO CONCEPT OF THEIR LOCATION EITHER!"

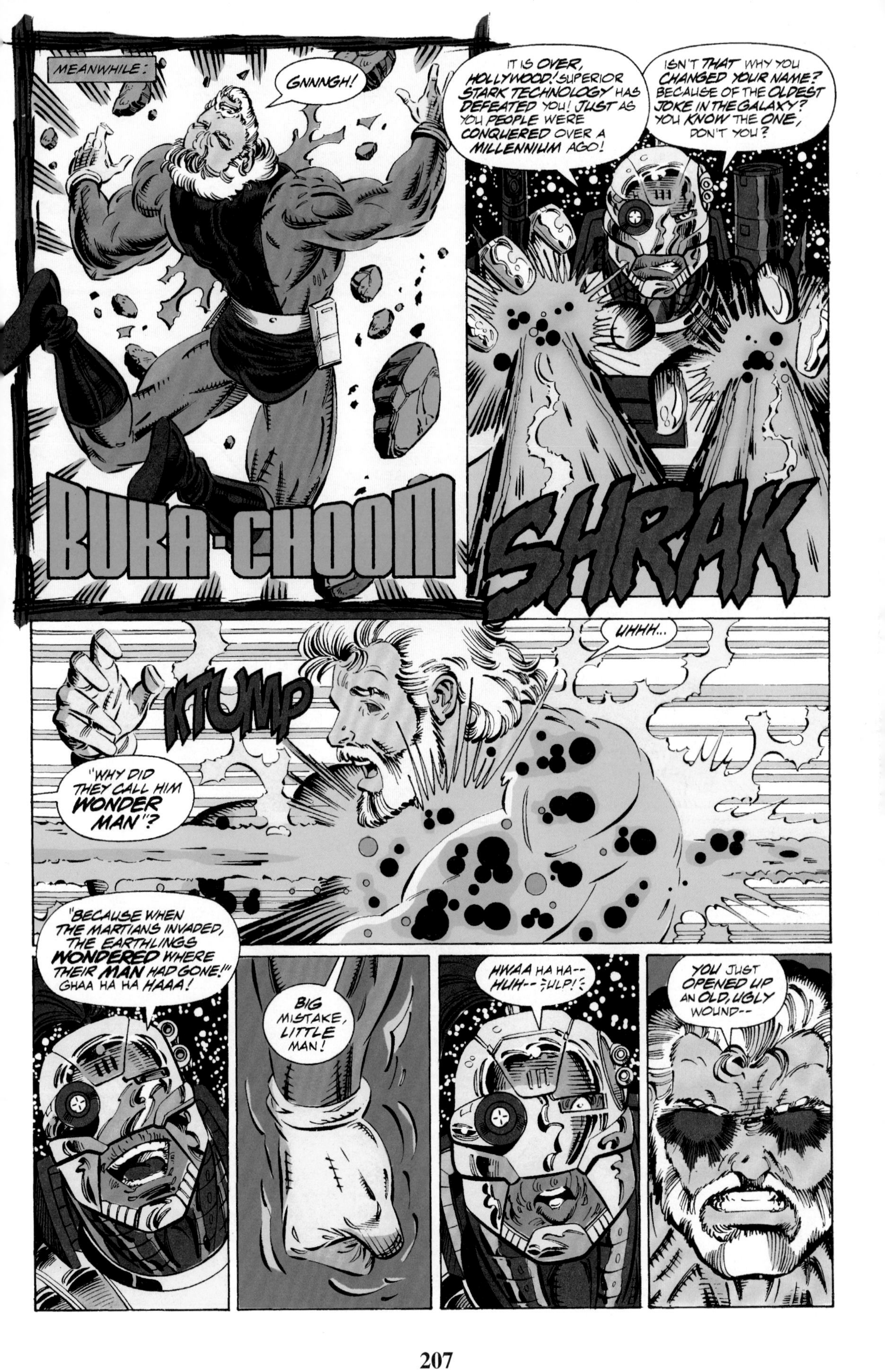
MEANWHILE:
GNNNGH!
BUKA-CHOOM
IT IS OVER, HOLLYWOOD! SUPERIOR STARK TECHNOLOGY HAS DEFEATED YOU! JUST AS YOU PEOPLE WERE CONQUERED OVER A MILLENNIUM AGO!
ISN'T THAT WHY YOU CHANGED YOUR NAME? BECAUSE OF THE OLDEST JOKE IN THE GALAXY? YOU KNOW THE ONE, DON'T YOU?
SHRAK
KTUMP
UHHH...
"WHY DID THEY CALL HIM WONDER MAN"?
"BECAUSE WHEN THE MARTIANS INVADED, THE EARTHLINGS WONDERED WHERE THEIR MAN HAD GONE!" GHAA HA HA HAAA!
BIG MISTAKE, LITTLE MAN!
HWAA HA HA-- HUH-- ¿ULP!?
YOU JUST OPENED UP AN OLD, UGLY WOUND--

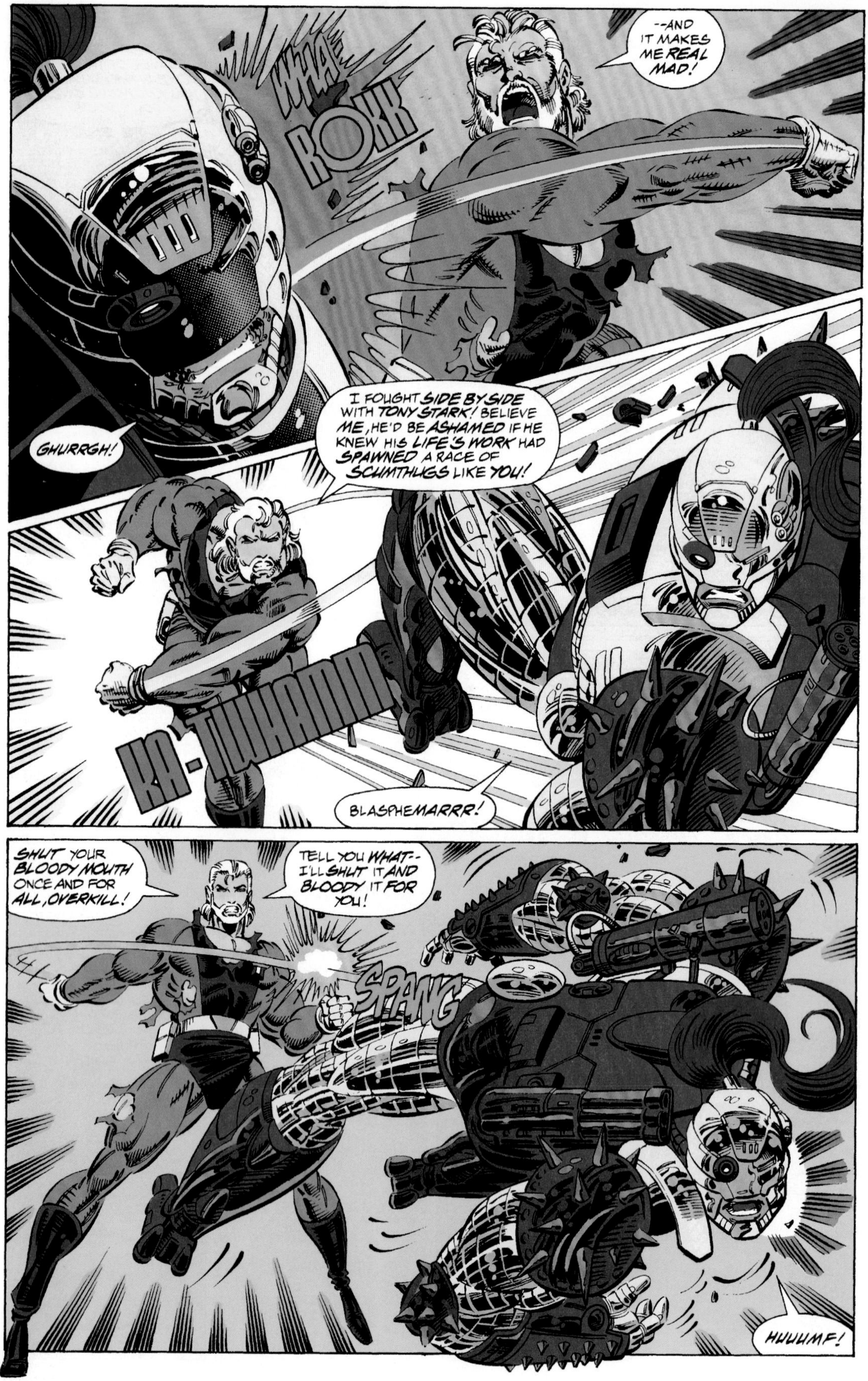
--AND IT MAKES ME REAL MAD!
WHA
ROKK
GHURRGH!
I FOUGHT SIDE BY SIDE WITH TONY STARK! BELIEVE ME, HE'D BE ASHAMED IF HE KNEW HIS LIFE'S WORK HAD SPAWNED A RACE OF SCUMTHUGS LIKE YOU!
KA-THWAMM
BLASPHEMARRR!
SHUT YOUR BLOODY MOUTH ONCE AND FOR ALL, OVERKILL!
TELL YOU WHAT-- I'LL SHUT IT AND BLOODY IT FOR YOU!
SPANG
HUUUMF!

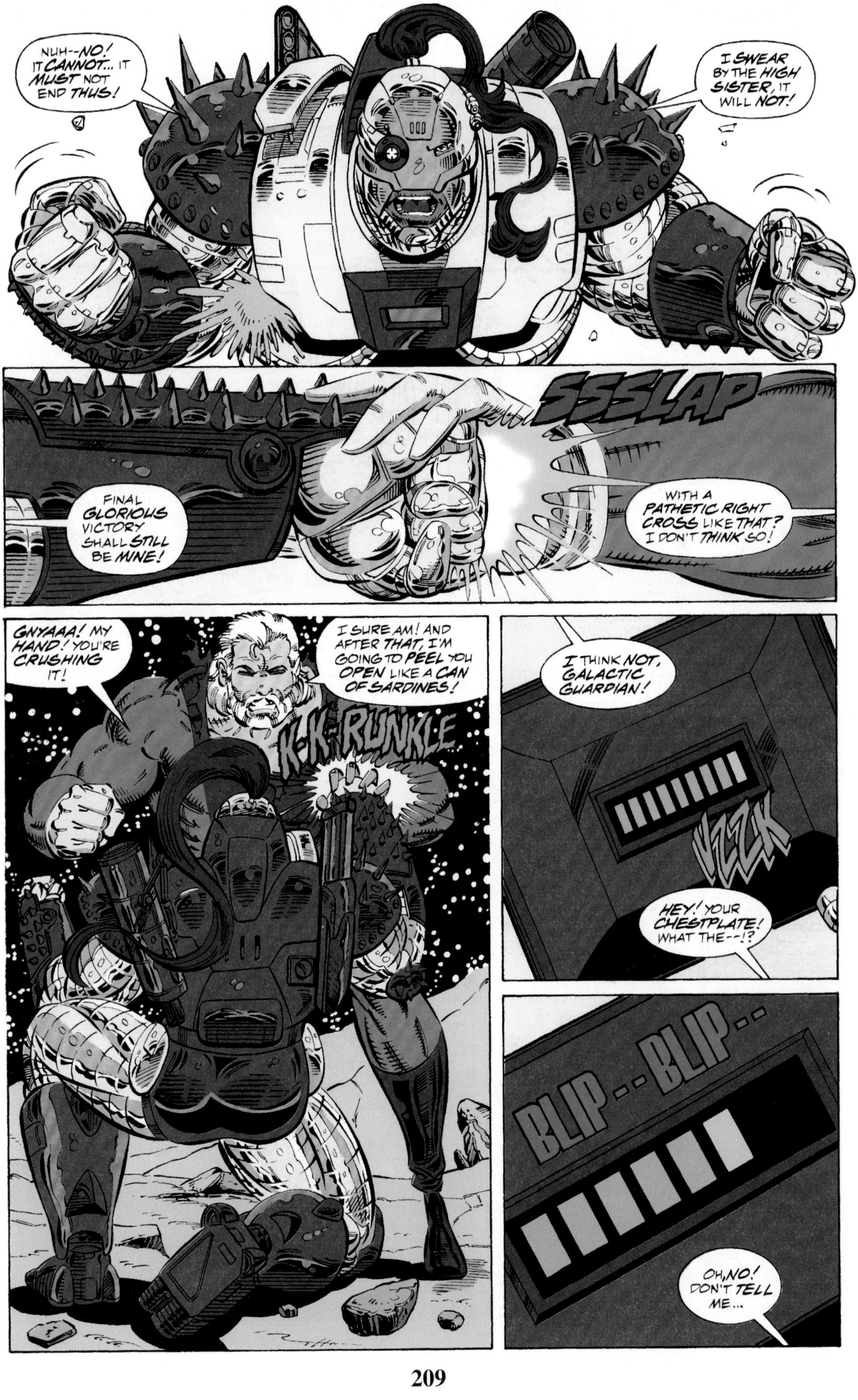
NUH--NO! IT CANNOT... IT MUST NOT END THUS!
I SWEAR BY THE HIGH SISTER, IT WILL NOT!
SSSLAP
FINAL GLORIOUS VICTORY SHALL STILL BE MINE!
WITH A PATHETIC RIGHT CROSS LIKE THAT? I DON'T THINK SO!
GNYAAA! MY HAND! YOU'RE CRUSHING IT!
I SURE AM! AND AFTER THAT, I'M GOING TO PEEL YOU OPEN LIKE A CAN OF SARDINES!
K-K-RUNKLE
I THINK NOT, GALACTIC GUARDIAN!
VZZK
HEY! YOUR CHESTPLATE! WHAT THE--!?
BLIP--BLIP--
OH, NO! DON'T TELL ME...

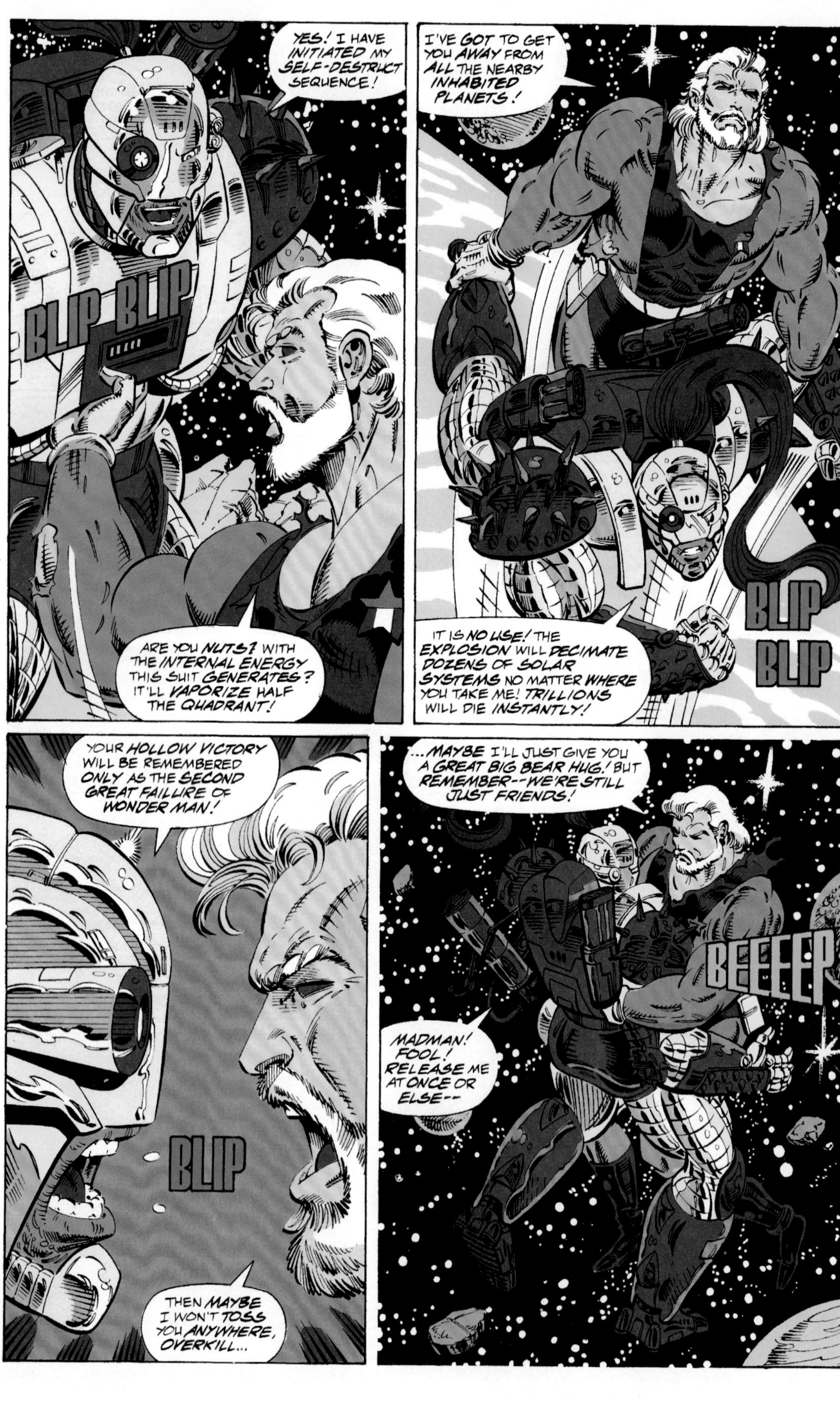
YES! I HAVE INITIATED MY SELF-DESTRUCT SEQUENCE!
BLIP BLIP
ARE YOU NUTS? WITH THE INTERNAL ENERGY THIS SUIT GENERATES? IT'LL VAPORIZE HALF THE QUADRANT!
I'VE GOT TO GET YOU AWAY FROM ALL THE NEARBY INHABITED PLANETS!
IT IS NO USE! THE EXPLOSION WILL DECIMATE DOZENS OF SOLAR SYSTEMS NO MATTER WHERE YOU TAKE ME! TRILLIONS WILL DIE INSTANTLY!
BLIP BLIP
YOUR HOLLOW VICTORY WILL BE REMEMBERED ONLY AS THE SECOND GREAT FAILURE OF WONDER MAN!
BLIP
THEN MAYBE I WON'T TOSS YOU ANYWHERE, OVERKILL...
...MAYBE I'LL JUST GIVE YOU A GREAT BIG BEAR HUG! BUT REMEMBER--WE'RE STILL JUST FRIENDS!
BEEEEP
MADMAN! FOOL! RELEASE ME AT ONCE OR ELSE--

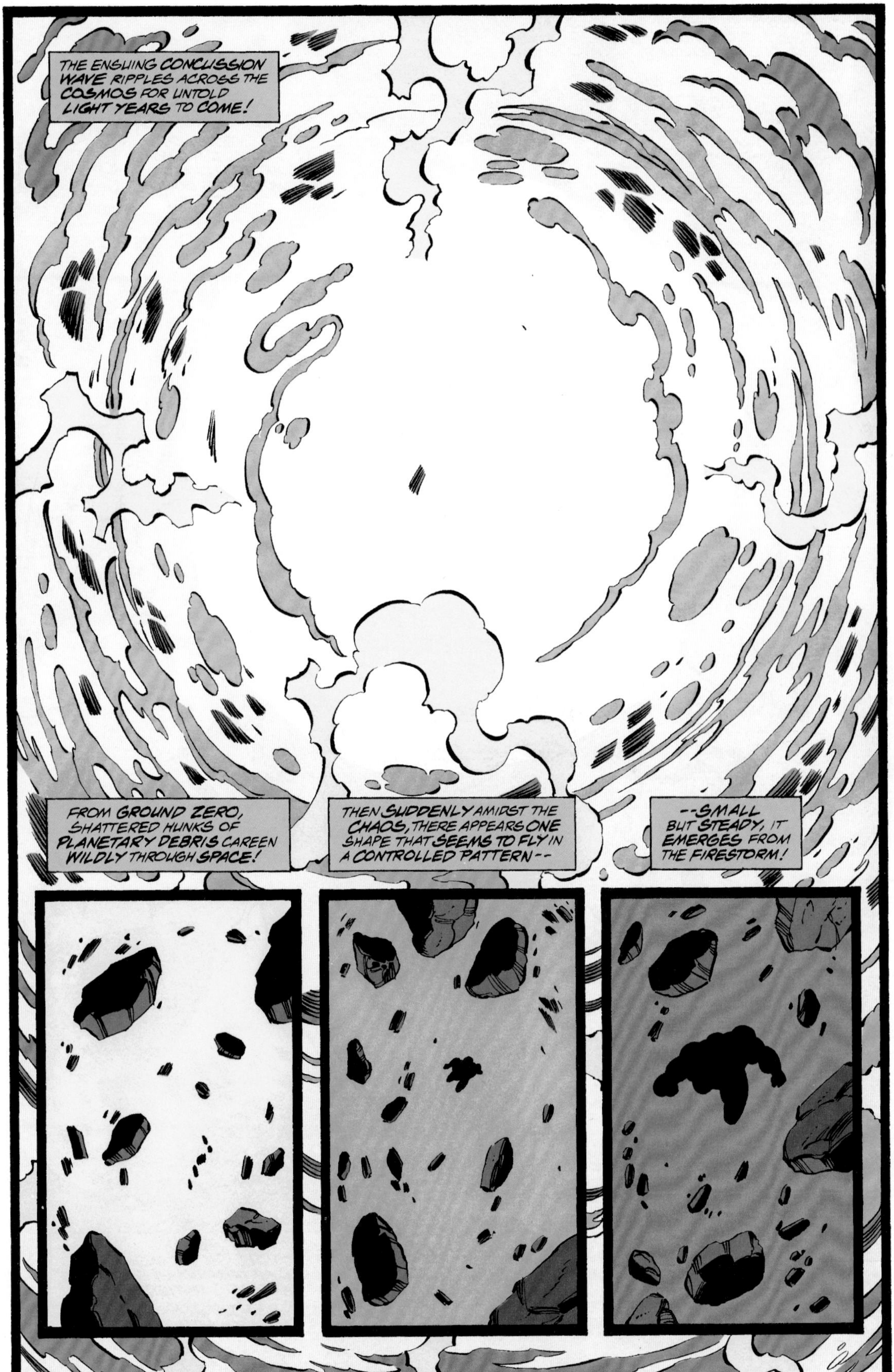
THE ENSUING CONCUSSION WAVE RIPPLES ACROSS THE COSMOS FOR UNTOLD LIGHT YEARS TO COME!
FROM GROUND ZERO, SHATTERED HUNKS OF PLANETARY DEBRIS CAREEN WILDLY THROUGH SPACE!
THEN SUDDENLY AMIDST THE CHAOS, THERE APPEARS ONE SHAPE THAT SEEMS TO FLY IN A CONTROLLED PATTERN--
--SMALL BUT STEADY, IT EMERGES FROM THE FIRESTORM!

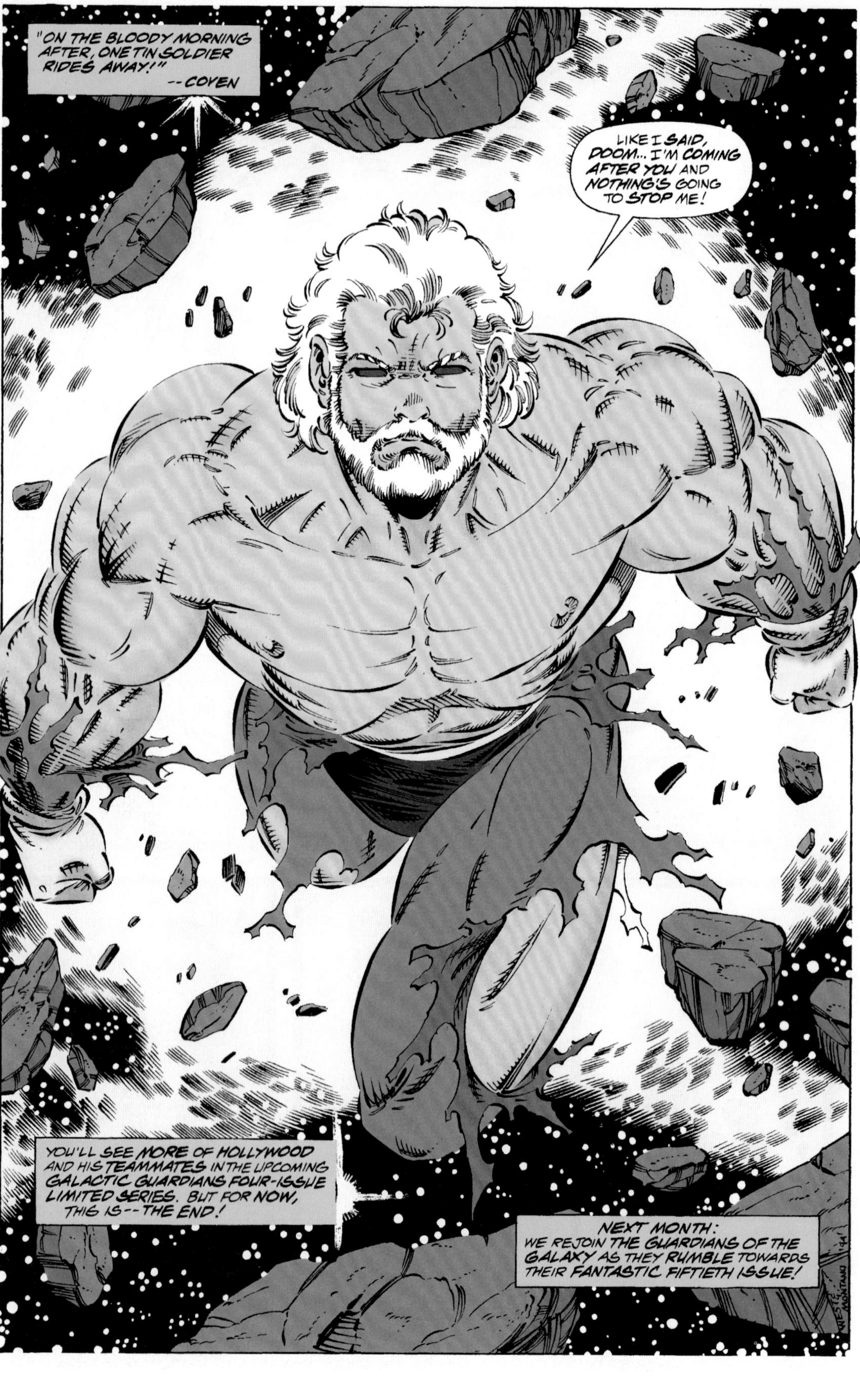

"ON THE BLOODY MORNING AFTER, ONE TIN SOLDIER RIDES AWAY!" --COYEN
LIKE I SAID, DOOM... I'M COMING AFTER YOU AND NOTHING'S GOING TO STOP ME!
YOU'LL SEE MORE OF HOLLYWOOD AND HIS TEAMMATES IN THE UPCOMING GALACTIC GUARDIANS FOUR-ISSUE LIMITED SERIES. BUT FOR NOW, THIS IS--THE END!
NEXT MONTH: WE REJOIN THE GUARDIANS OF THE GALAXY AS THEY RUMBLE TOWARDS THEIR FANTASTIC FIFTIETH ISSUE!

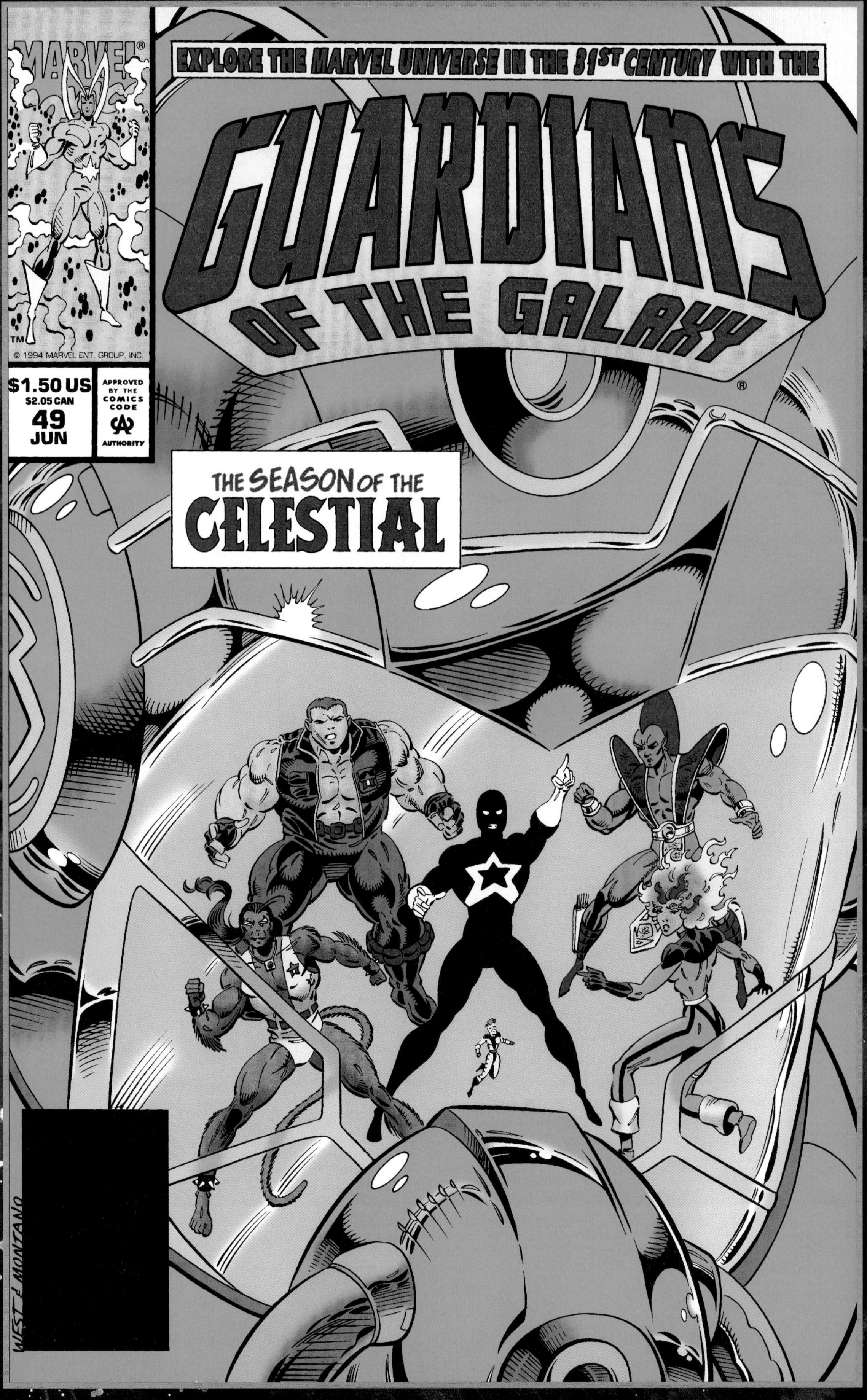
MARVEL®
EXPLORE THE MARVEL UNIVERSE IN THE 31ST CENTURY WITH THE
GUARDIANS OF THE GALAXY®
TM
© 1994 MARVEL ENT. GROUP, INC.
$1.50 US
$2.05 CAN
49
JUN
APPROVED BY THE COMICS CODE AUTHORITY
THE SEASON OF THE CELESTIAL
WEST & MONTANO

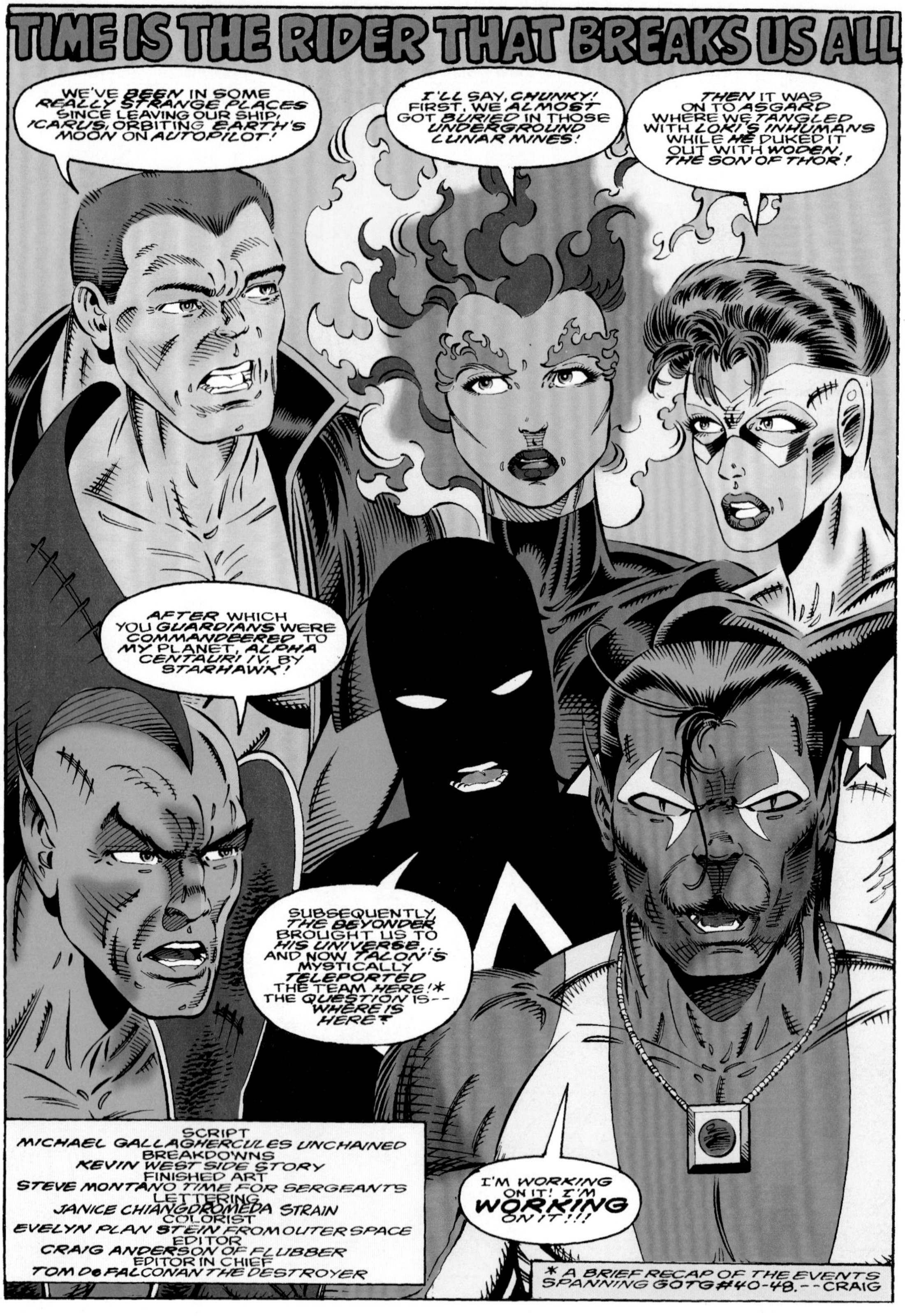
TIME IS THE RIDER THAT BREAKS US ALL
WE'VE BEEN IN SOME REALLY STRANGE PLACES SINCE LEAVING OUR SHIP, ICARUS, ORBITING EARTH'S MOON ON AUTOPILOT!
I'LL SAY, CHUNKY! FIRST, WE ALMOST GOT BURIED IN THOSE UNDERGROUND LUNAR MINES!
THEN IT WAS ON TO ASGARD WHERE WE TANGLED WITH LOKI'S INHUMANS WHILE HE DUKED IT OUT WITH WODEN, THE SON OF THOR!
AFTER WHICH YOU GUARDIANS WERE COMMANDEERED TO MY PLANET, ALPHA CENTAURI IV, BY STARHAWK!
SUBSEQUENTLY, THE BEYONDER BROUGHT US TO HIS UNIVERSE... AND NOW TALON'S MYSTICALLY TELEPORTED THE TEAM HERE!* THE QUESTION IS-- WHERE IS HERE?
I'M WORKING ON IT! I'M WORKING ON IT!!!
SCRIPT
MICHAEL GALLAGHERCULES UNCHAINED
BREAKDOWNS
KEVIN WEST SIDE STORY
FINISHED ART
STEVE MONTANO TIME FOR SERGEANTS
LETTERING
JANICE CHIANGDROMEDA STRAIN
COLORIST
EVELYN PLAN STEIN FROM OUTER SPACE
EDITOR
CRAIG ANDERSON OF FLUBBER
EDITOR IN CHIEF
TOM DeFALCONAN THE DESTROYER
* A BRIEF RECAP OF THE EVENTS SPANNING GOTG #40-48. --CRAIG

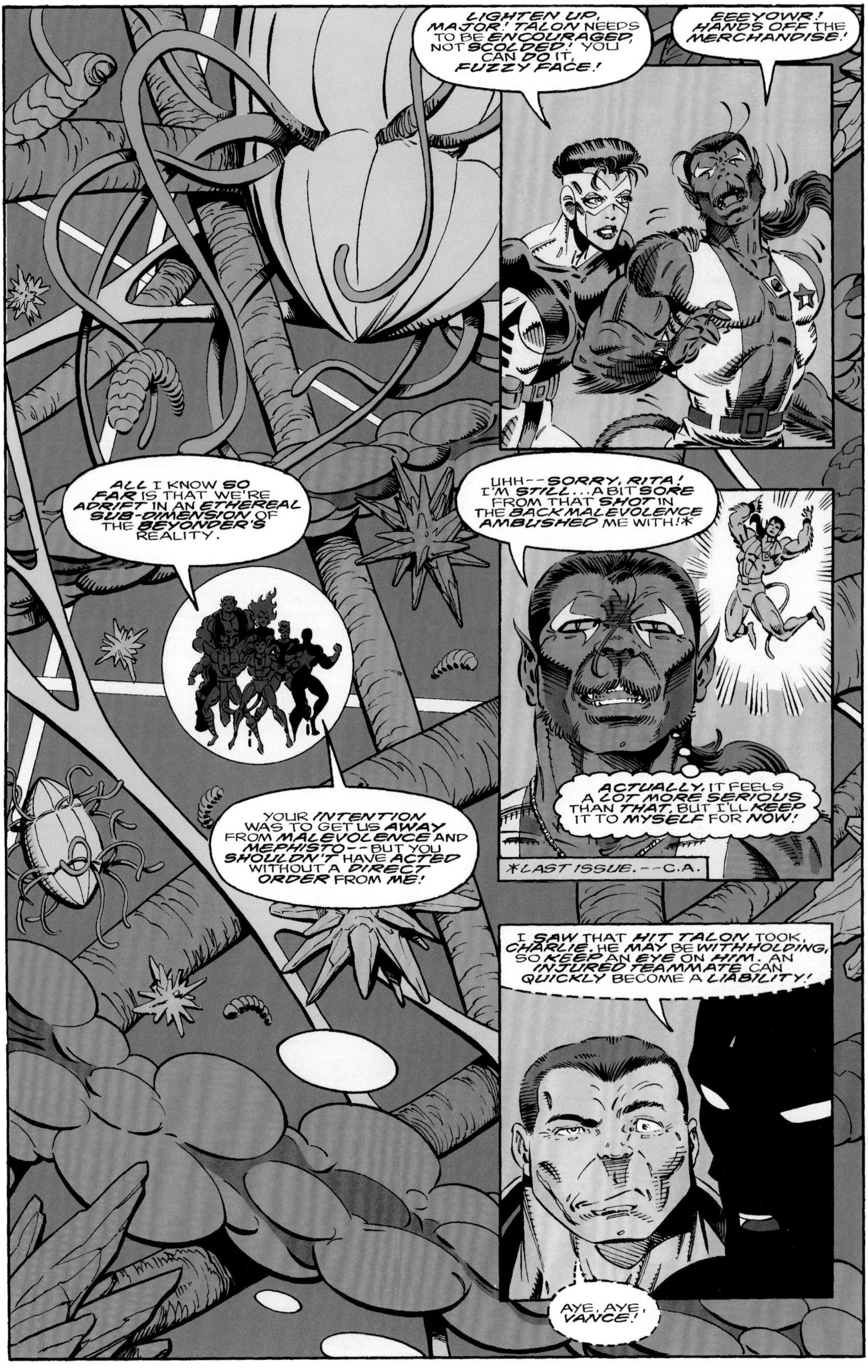
LIGHTEN UP, MAJOR! TALON NEEDS TO BE ENCOURAGED, NOT SCOLDED! YOU CAN DO IT, FUZZY FACE!
EEEYOWR! HANDS OFF THE MERCHANDISE!
ALL I KNOW SO FAR IS THAT WE'RE ADRIFT IN AN ETHEREAL SUB-DIMENSION OF THE BEYONDER'S REALITY.
UHH--SORRY, RITA! I'M STILL...A BIT SORE FROM THAT SHOT IN THE BACK MALEVOLENCE AMBUSHED ME WITH!*
ACTUALLY, IT FEELS A LOT MORE SERIOUS THAN THAT, BUT I'LL KEEP IT TO MYSELF FOR NOW!
*LAST ISSUE. --C.A.
YOUR INTENTION WAS TO GET US AWAY FROM MALEVOLENCE AND MEPHISTO--BUT YOU SHOULDN'T HAVE ACTED WITHOUT A DIRECT ORDER FROM ME!
I SAW THAT HIT TALON TOOK, CHARLIE. HE MAY BE WITHHOLDING, SO KEEP AN EYE ON HIM. AN INJURED TEAMMATE CAN QUICKLY BECOME A LIABILITY!
AYE, AYE, VANCE!

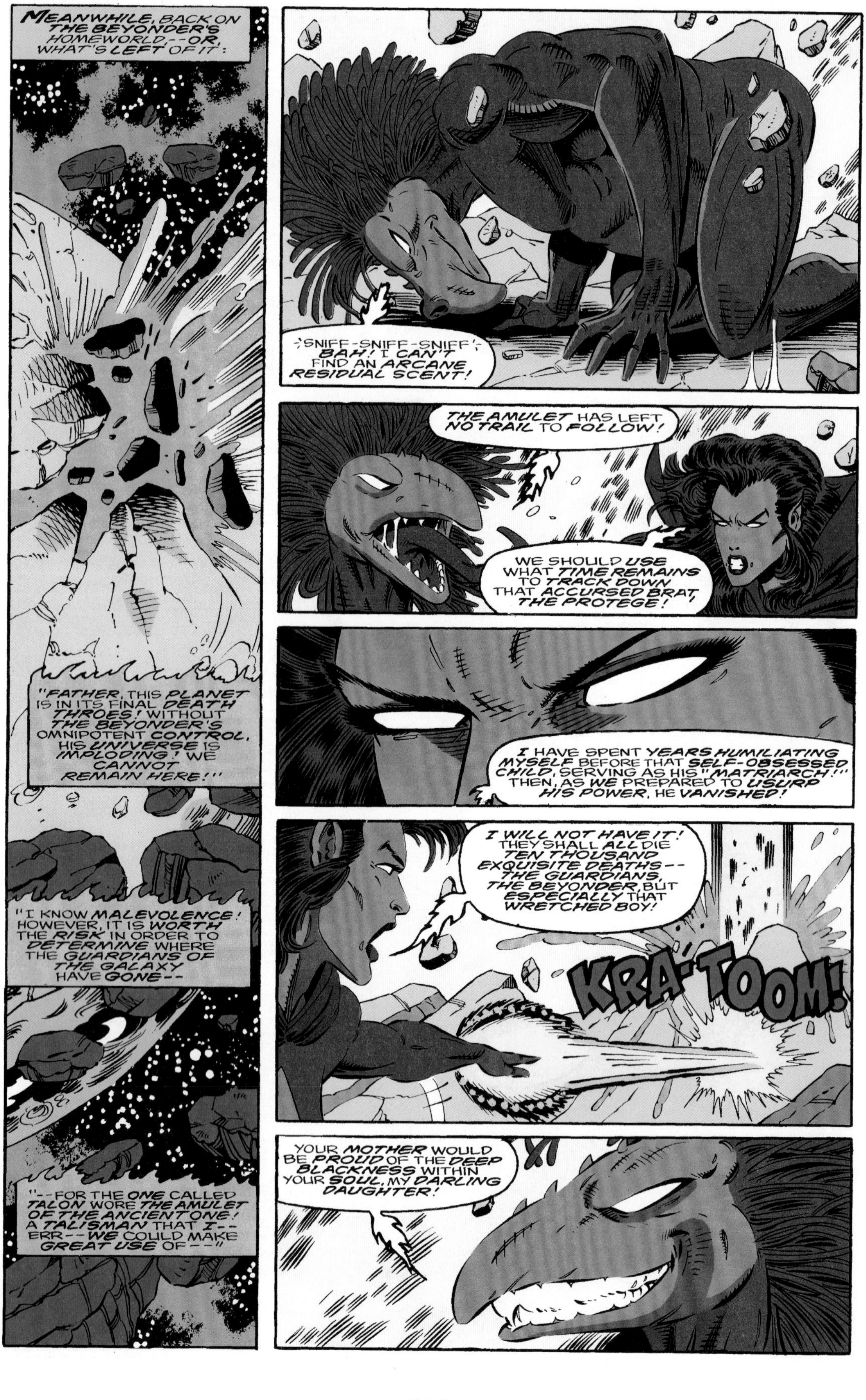

MEANWHILE, BACK ON THE BEYONDER'S HOMEWORLD--OR, WHAT'S LEFT OF IT:
"FATHER, THIS PLANET IS IN ITS FINAL DEATH THROES! WITHOUT THE BEYONDER'S OMNIPOTENT CONTROL, HIS UNIVERSE IS IMPLODING! WE CANNOT REMAIN HERE!"
"I KNOW MALEVOLENCE! HOWEVER, IT IS WORTH THE RISK IN ORDER TO DETERMINE WHERE THE GUARDIANS OF THE GALAXY HAVE GONE--
"--FOR THE ONE CALLED TALON WORE THE AMULET OF THE ANCIENT ONE! A TALISMAN THAT I-- ERR--WE COULD MAKE GREAT USE OF--"
SNIFF-SNIFF-SNIFF BAH! I CAN'T FIND AN ARCANE RESIDUAL SCENT!
THE AMULET HAS LEFT NO TRAIL TO FOLLOW!
WE SHOULD USE WHAT TIME REMAINS TO TRACK DOWN THAT ACCURSED BRAT, THE PROTEGE!
I HAVE SPENT YEARS HUMILIATING MYSELF BEFORE THAT SELF-OBSESSED CHILD, SERVING AS HIS "MATRIARCH!" THEN, AS WE PREPARED TO USURP HIS POWER, HE VANISHED!
I WILL NOT HAVE IT! THEY SHALL ALL DIE TEN THOUSAND EXQUISITE DEATHS--THE GUARDIANS, THE BEYONDER, BUT ESPECIALLY THAT WRETCHED BOY!
KRA-TOOM!
YOUR MOTHER WOULD BE PROUD OF THE DEEP BLACKNESS WITHIN YOUR SOUL, MY DARLING DAUGHTER!

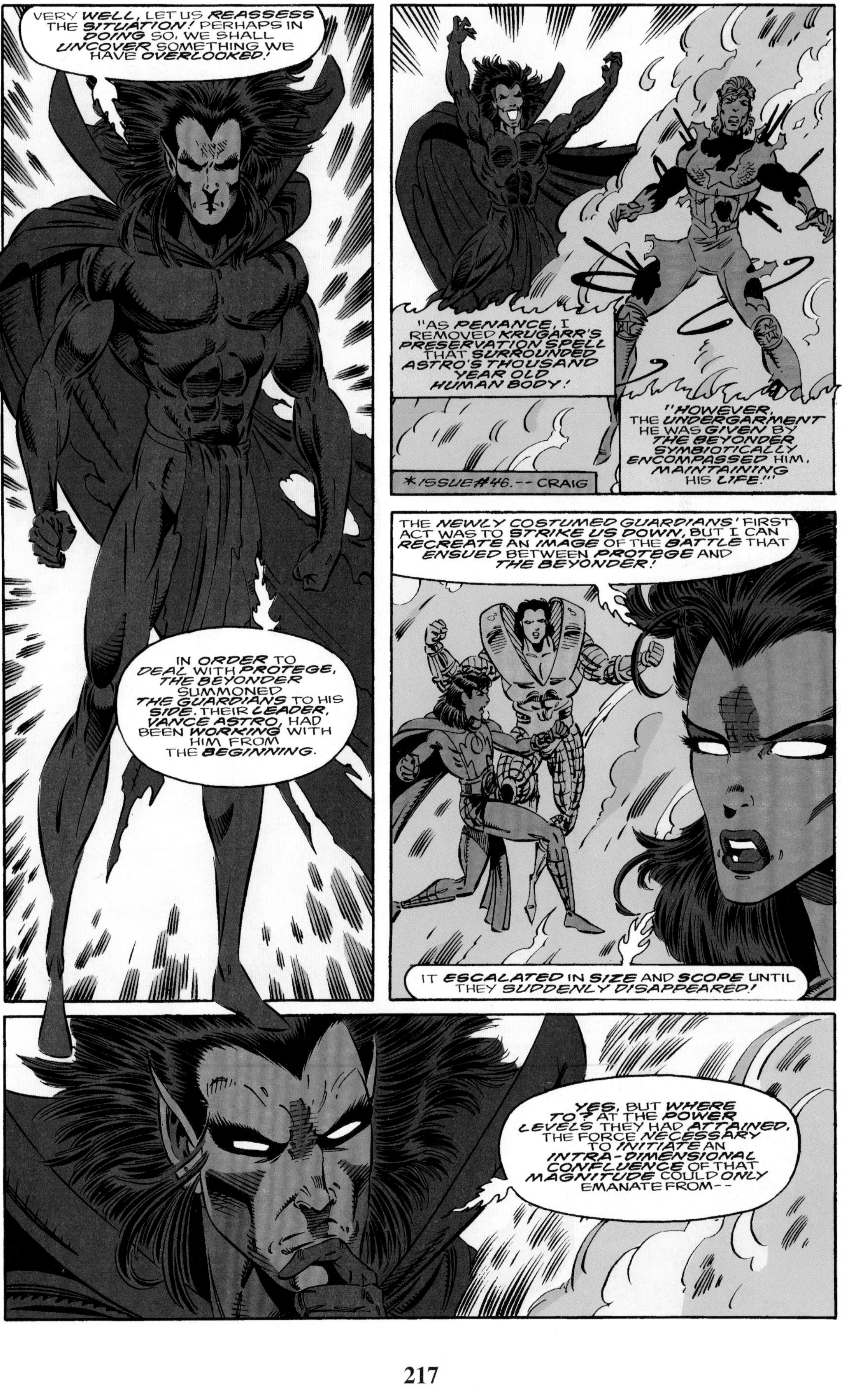
VERY WELL, LET US REASSESS THE SITUATION! PERHAPS IN DOING SO, WE SHALL UNCOVER SOMETHING WE HAVE OVERLOOKED!
IN ORDER TO DEAL WITH PROTEGE, THE BEYONDER SUMMONED THE GUARDIANS TO HIS SIDE. THEIR LEADER, VANCE ASTRO, HAD BEEN WORKING WITH HIM FROM THE BEGINNING.
"AS PENANCE, I REMOVED KRUGARR'S PRESERVATION SPELL THAT SURROUNDED ASTRO'S THOUSAND YEAR OLD HUMAN BODY!
*ISSUE #46. -- CRAIG
"HOWEVER, THE UNDERGARMENT HE WAS GIVEN BY THE BEYONDER SYMBIOTICALLY ENCOMPASSED HIM, MAINTAINING HIS LIFE."
THE NEWLY COSTUMED GUARDIANS' FIRST ACT WAS TO STRIKE US DOWN, BUT I CAN RECREATE AN IMAGE OF THE BATTLE THAT ENSUED BETWEEN PROTEGE AND THE BEYONDER!
IT ESCALATED IN SIZE AND SCOPE UNTIL THEY SUDDENLY DISAPPEARED!
YES, BUT WHERE TO? AT THE POWER LEVELS THEY HAD ATTAINED, THE FORCE NECESSARY TO INITIATE AN INTRA-DIMENSIONAL CONFLUENCE OF THAT MAGNITUDE COULD ONLY EMANATE FROM--

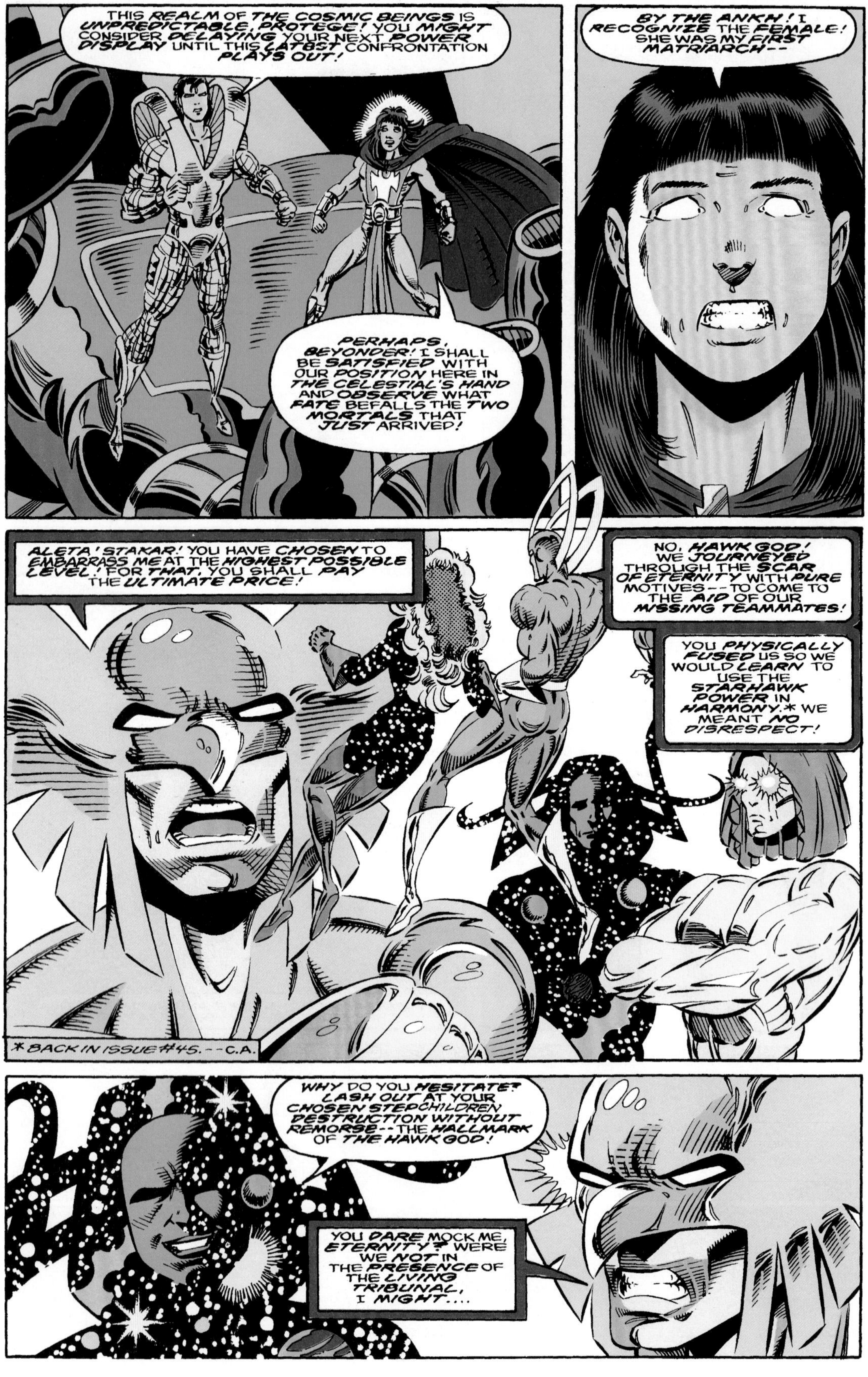

THIS REALM OF THE COSMIC BEINGS IS UNPREDICTABLE, PROTEGE! YOU MIGHT CONSIDER DELAYING YOUR NEXT POWER DISPLAY UNTIL THIS LATEST CONFRONTATION PLAYS OUT!
PERHAPS, BEYONDER! I SHALL BE SATISFIED WITH OUR POSITION HERE IN THE CELESTIAL'S HAND AND OBSERVE WHAT FATE BEFALLS THE TWO MORTALS THAT JUST ARRIVED!
BY THE ANKH! I RECOGNIZE THE FEMALE! SHE WAS MY FIRST MATRIARCH--
ALETA! STAKAR! YOU HAVE CHOSEN TO EMBARRASS ME AT THE HIGHEST POSSIBLE LEVEL! FOR THAT, YOU SHALL PAY THE ULTIMATE PRICE!
NO, HAWK GOD! WE JOURNEYED THROUGH THE SCAR OF ETERNITY WITH PURE MOTIVES--TO COME TO THE AID OF OUR MISSING TEAMMATES!
YOU PHYSICALLY FUSED US SO WE WOULD LEARN TO USE THE STARHAWK POWER IN HARMONY.* WE MEANT NO DISRESPECT!
* BACK IN ISSUE #45. --C.A.
WHY DO YOU HESITATE? LASH OUT AT YOUR CHOSEN STEPCHILDREN DESTRUCTION WITHOUT REMORSE--THE HALLMARK OF THE HAWK GOD!
YOU DARE MOCK ME, ETERNITY? WERE WE NOT IN THE PRESENCE OF THE LIVING TRIBUNAL, I MIGHT....

BUT SUCH *COSMIC CONFRONTATIONS* ARE *NOT* FOR THE *EYES* OF *MORTALS!*

THEREFORE, I SHALL *DEVOLVE* THE *ARCTURIAN ORPHANS* INTO *ELEMENTAL CARBON-PLASM ENERGY PODS!*

INTERESTING! YOU HAVE LET THEM *LIVE* --

"-- *STRIPPED* OF ALL *POWER* AND *CONTAINED* WITHIN A *TERRIFYING FORMAT!* YET, BY *YOUR* STANDARDS, ONE COULD CONSIDER THIS... *MERCIFUL!*"

ARE *WE* TO *ASSUME* YOUR *METHODOLOGY* IS *MODIFYING?* AFTER *UNTOLD MILLENNIA,* IS YOUR *MULTIVERSAL MATURITY* FINALLY AT *HAND?*

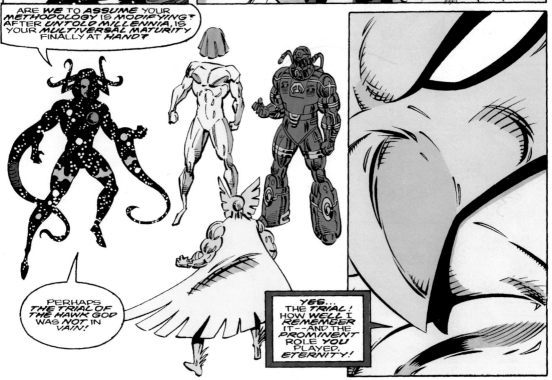

PERHAPS *THE TRIAL OF THE HAWK GOD* WAS *NOT* IN *VAIN!*

YES... THE *TRIAL!* HOW *WELL* I *REMEMBER* IT -- AND THE *PROMINENT ROLE YOU* PLAYED, *ETERNITY!*

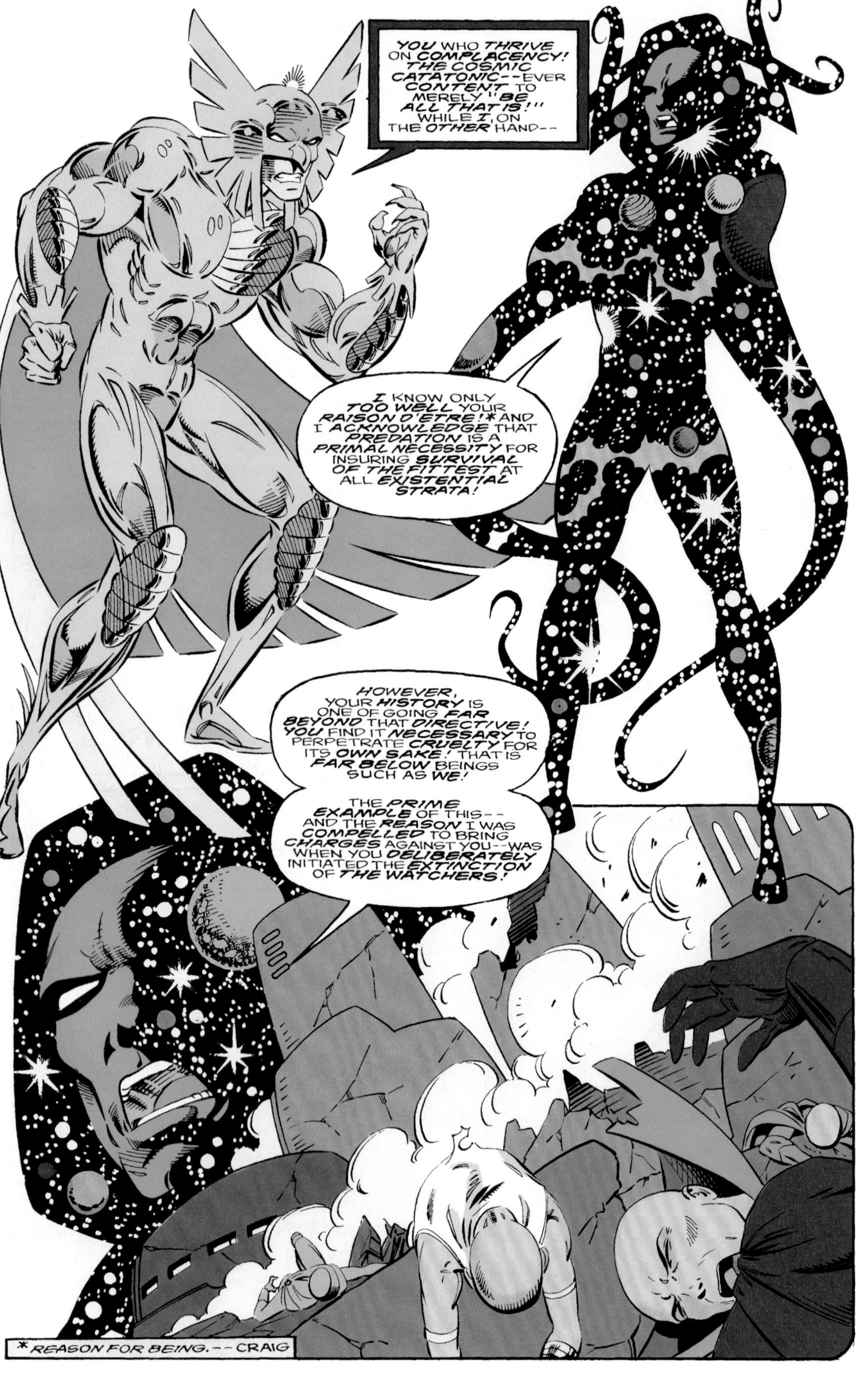
YOU WHO THRIVE ON COMPLACENCY! THE COSMIC CATATONIC--EVER CONTENT TO MERELY "BE ALL THAT IS!" WHILE I, ON THE OTHER HAND--
I KNOW ONLY TOO WELL YOUR RAISON D'ETRE!* AND I ACKNOWLEDGE THAT PREDATION IS A PRIMAL NECESSITY FOR INSURING SURVIVAL OF THE FITTEST AT ALL EXISTENTIAL STRATA!
HOWEVER, YOUR HISTORY IS ONE OF GOING FAR BEYOND THAT DIRECTIVE! YOU FIND IT NECESSARY TO PERPETRATE CRUELTY FOR ITS OWN SAKE! THAT IS FAR BELOW BEINGS SUCH AS WE!
THE PRIME EXAMPLE OF THIS--AND THE REASON I WAS COMPELLED TO BRING CHARGES AGAINST YOU--WAS WHEN YOU DELIBERATELY INITIATED THE EXTINCTION OF THE WATCHERS!
*REASON FOR BEING. --CRAIG

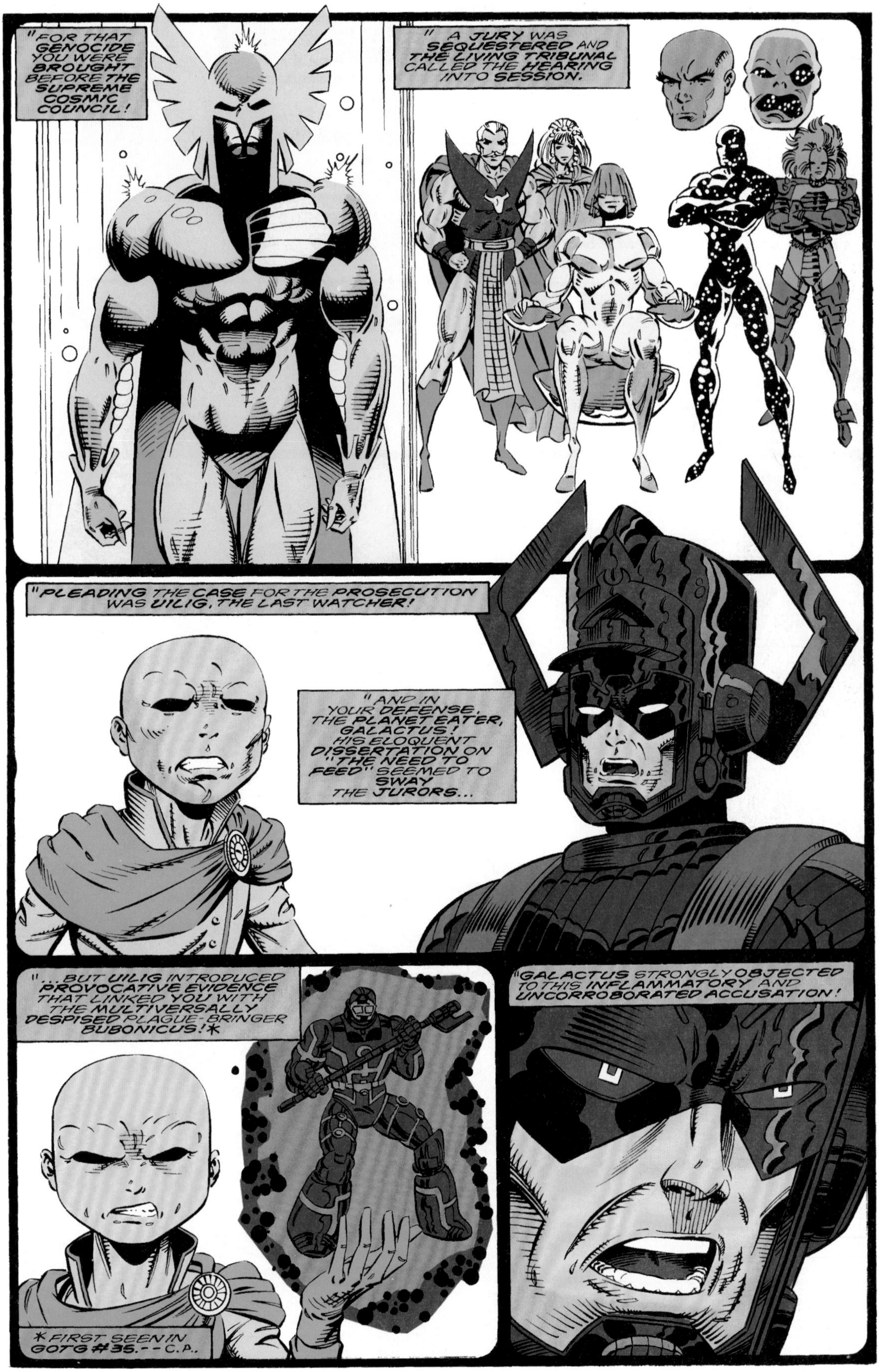
"FOR THAT GENOCIDE YOU WERE BROUGHT BEFORE THE SUPREME COSMIC COUNCIL!
" A JURY WAS SEQUESTERED AND THE LIVING TRIBUNAL CALLED THE HEARING INTO SESSION.
"PLEADING THE CASE FOR THE PROSECUTION WAS UILIG, THE LAST WATCHER!
" AND IN YOUR DEFENSE, THE PLANET EATER, GALACTUS! HIS ELOQUENT DISSERTATION ON "THE NEED TO FEED" SEEMED TO SWAY THE JURORS...
"...BUT UILIG INTRODUCED PROVOCATIVE EVIDENCE THAT LINKED YOU WITH THE MULTIVERSALLY DESPISED PLAGUE-BRINGER BUBONICUS!*
*FIRST SEEN IN GOTG #35.--C.P.
"GALACTUS STRONGLY OBJECTED TO THIS INFLAMMATORY AND UNCORROBORATED ACCUSATION!

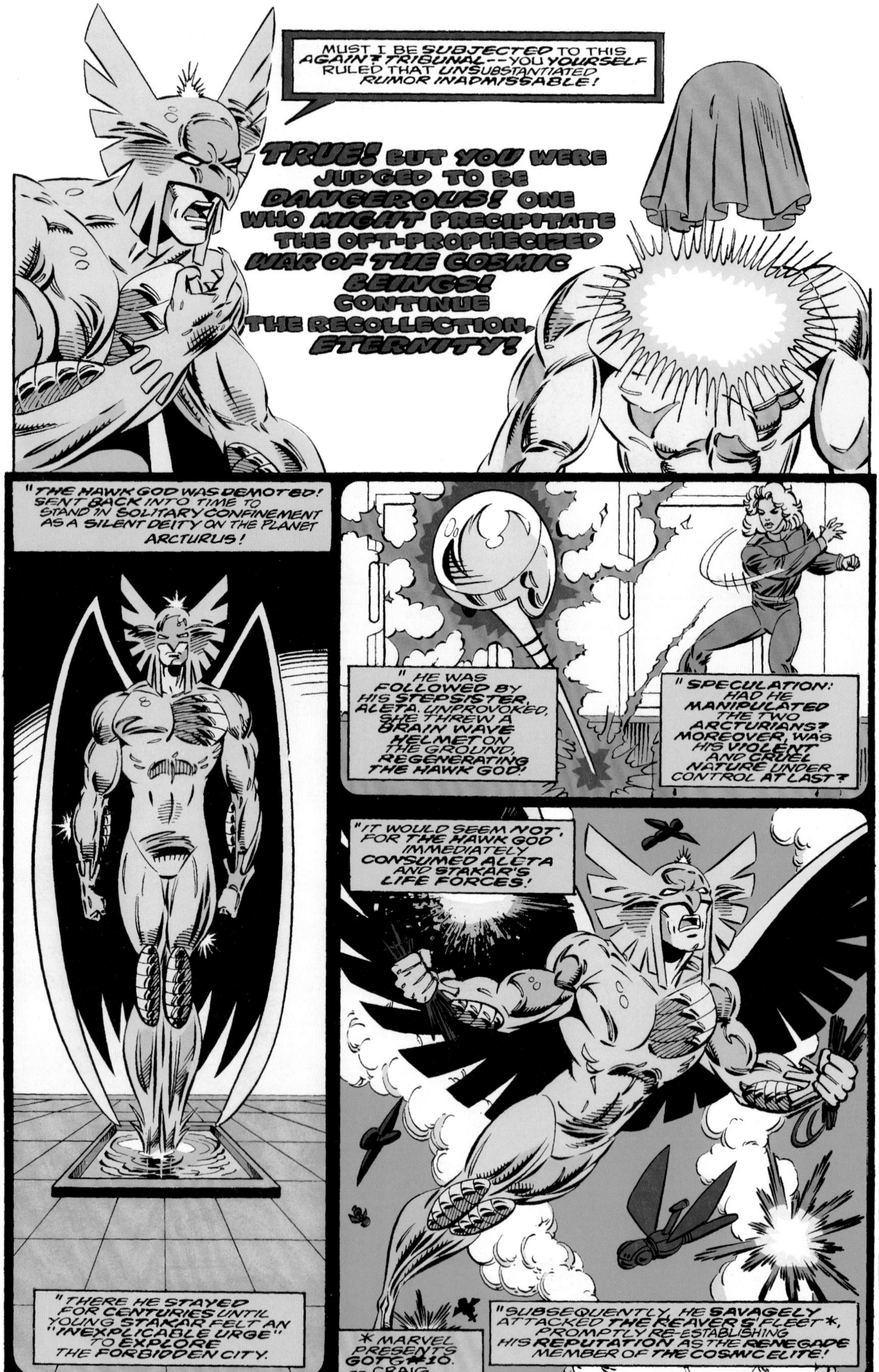

MUST I BE SUBJECTED TO THIS AGAIN? TRIBUNAL--YOU YOURSELF RULED THAT UNSUBSTANTIATED RUMOR INADMISSABLE!
TRUE! BUT YOU WERE JUDGED TO BE DANGEROUS! ONE WHO MIGHT PRECIPITATE THE OFT-PROPHECIZED WAR OF THE COSMIC BEINGS! CONTINUE THE RECOLLECTION, ETERNITY!
"THE HAWK GOD WAS DEMOTED! SENT BACK INTO TIME TO STAND IN SOLITARY CONFINEMENT AS A SILENT DEITY ON THE PLANET ARCTURUS!
"THERE HE STAYED FOR CENTURIES UNTIL YOUNG STAKAR FELT AN "INEXPLICABLE URGE" TO EXPLORE THE FORBIDDEN CITY.
"HE WAS FOLLOWED BY HIS STEPSISTER, ALETA. UNPROVOKED, SHE THREW A BRAIN WAVE HELMET ON THE GROUND, REGENERATING THE HAWK GOD!
"SPECULATION: HAD HE MANIPULATED THE TWO ARCTURIANS? MOREOVER, WAS HIS VIOLENT AND CRUEL NATURE UNDER CONTROL AT LAST?
"IT WOULD SEEM NOT, FOR THE HAWK GOD IMMEDIATELY CONSUMED ALETA AND STAKAR'S LIFE FORCES!
"SUBSEQUENTLY, HE SAVAGELY ATTACKED THE REAVER'S FLEET*, PROMPTLY RE-ESTABLISHING HIS REPUTATION AS THE RENEGADE MEMBER OF THE COSMIC ELITE!
*MARVEL PRESENTS GOTG #10. --CRAIG

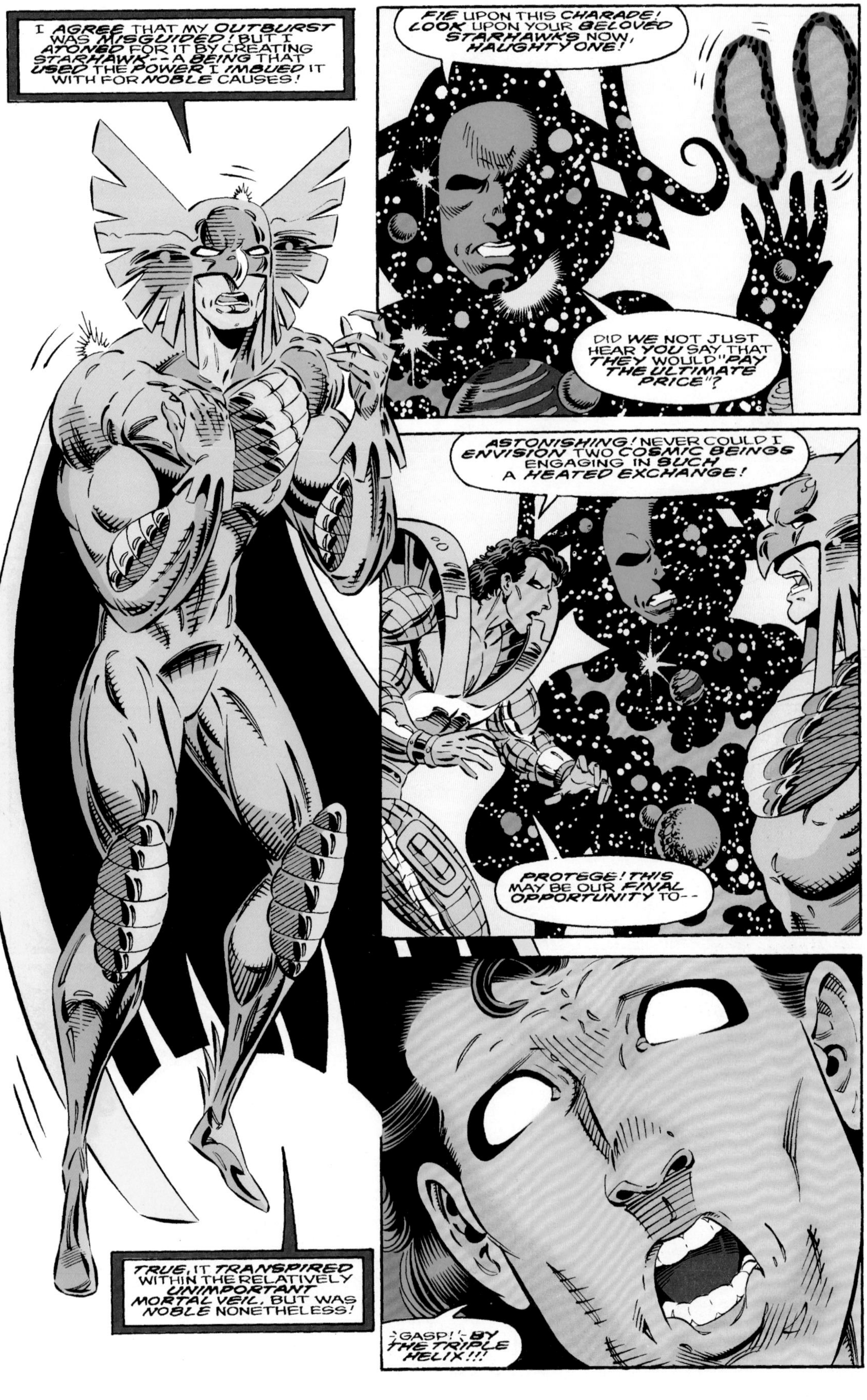
I AGREE THAT MY OUTBURST WAS MISGUIDED! BUT I ATONED FOR IT BY CREATING STARHAWK--A BEING THAT USED THE POWER I IMBUED IT WITH FOR NOBLE CAUSES!
TRUE, IT TRANSPIRED WITHIN THE RELATIVELY UNIMPORTANT MORTAL VEIL, BUT WAS NOBLE NONETHELESS!
FIE UPON THIS CHARADE! LOOK UPON YOUR BELOVED STARHAWKS NOW, HAUGHTY ONE!
DID WE NOT JUST HEAR YOU SAY THAT THEY WOULD "PAY THE ULTIMATE PRICE"?
ASTONISHING! NEVER COULD I ENVISION TWO COSMIC BEINGS ENGAGING IN SUCH A HEATED EXCHANGE!
PROTEGE! THIS MAY BE OUR FINAL OPPORTUNITY TO--
-GASP!- BY THE TRIPLE HELIX!!!

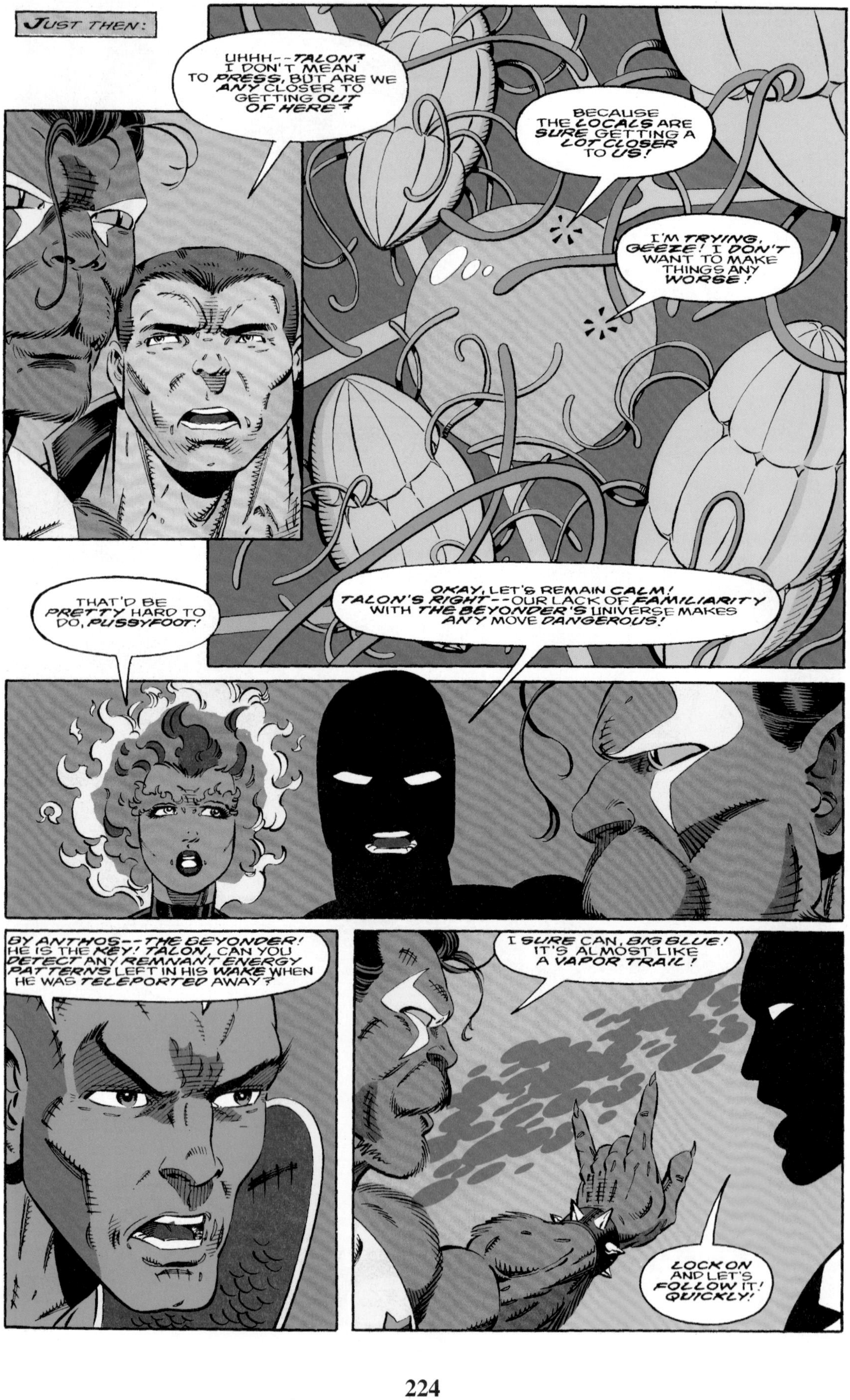
JUST THEN:
UHHH--TALON? I DON'T MEAN TO PRESS, BUT ARE WE ANY CLOSER TO GETTING OUT OF HERE?
BECAUSE THE LOCALS ARE SURE GETTING A LOT CLOSER TO US!
I'M TRYING, GEEZE! I DON'T WANT TO MAKE THINGS ANY WORSE!
THAT'D BE PRETTY HARD TO DO, PUSSYFOOT!
OKAY, LET'S REMAIN CALM! TALON'S RIGHT--OUR LACK OF FAMILIARITY WITH THE BEYONDER'S UNIVERSE MAKES ANY MOVE DANGEROUS!
BY ANTHOS--THE BEYONDER! HE IS THE KEY! TALON, CAN YOU DETECT ANY REMNANT ENERGY PATTERNS LEFT IN HIS WAKE WHEN HE WAS TELEPORTED AWAY?
I SURE CAN, BIG BLUE! IT'S ALMOST LIKE A VAPOR TRAIL!
LOCK ON AND LET'S FOLLOW IT! QUICKLY!

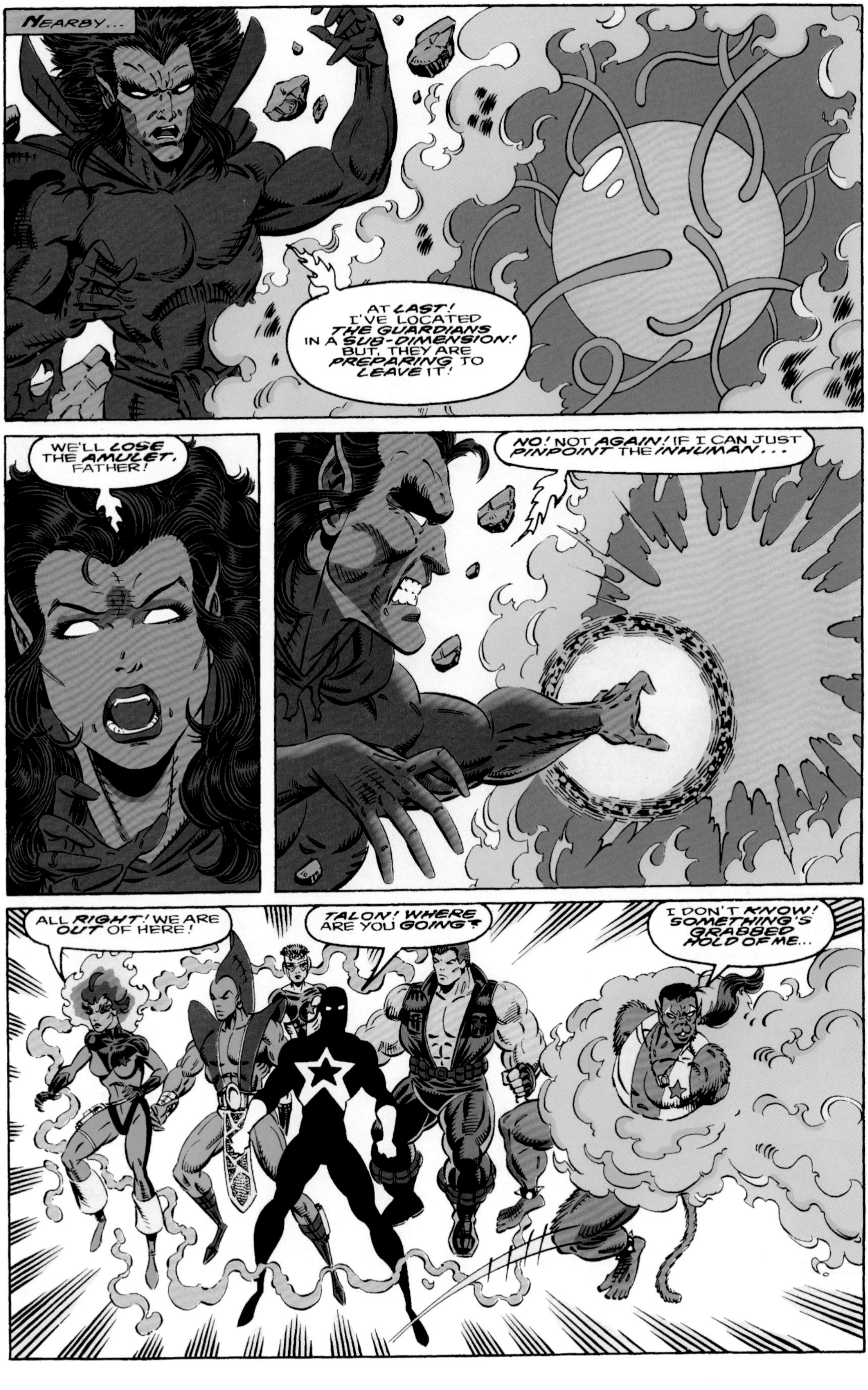
NEARBY...
AT LAST! I'VE LOCATED THE GUARDIANS IN A SUB-DIMENSION! BUT, THEY ARE PREPARING TO LEAVE IT!
WE'LL LOSE THE AMULET, FATHER!
NO! NOT AGAIN! IF I CAN JUST PINPOINT THE INHUMAN...
ALL RIGHT! WE ARE OUT OF HERE!
TALON! WHERE ARE YOU GOING?
I DON'T KNOW! SOMETHING'S GRABBED HOLD OF ME...

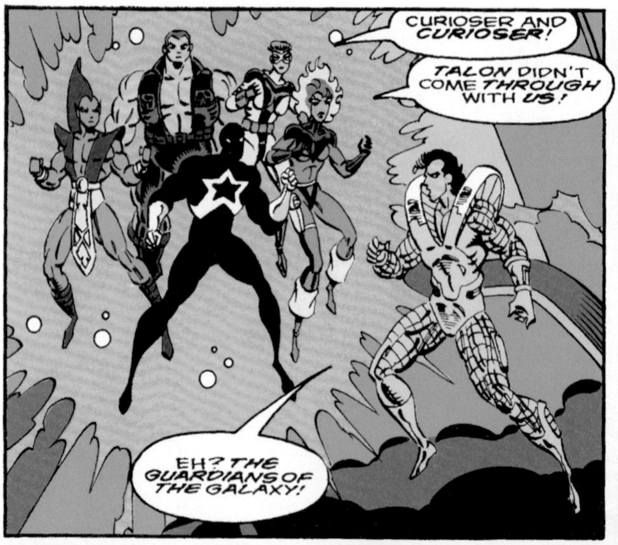
CURIOSER AND CURIOSER!
TALON DIDN'T COME THROUGH WITH US!
EH? THE GUARDIANS OF THE GALAXY!

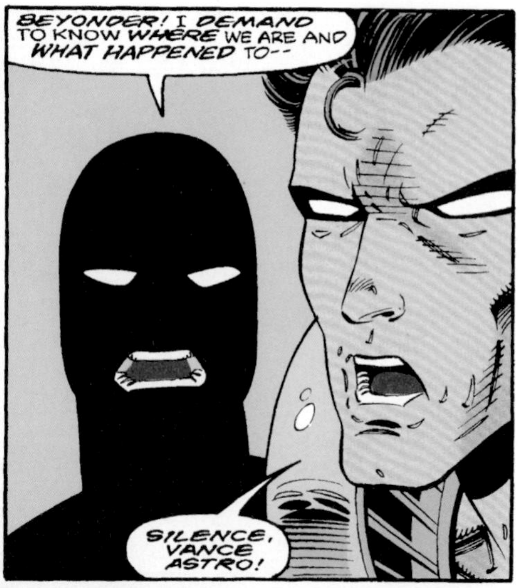
BEYONDER! I DEMAND TO KNOW WHERE WE ARE AND WHAT HAPPENED TO--
SILENCE, VANCE ASTRO!

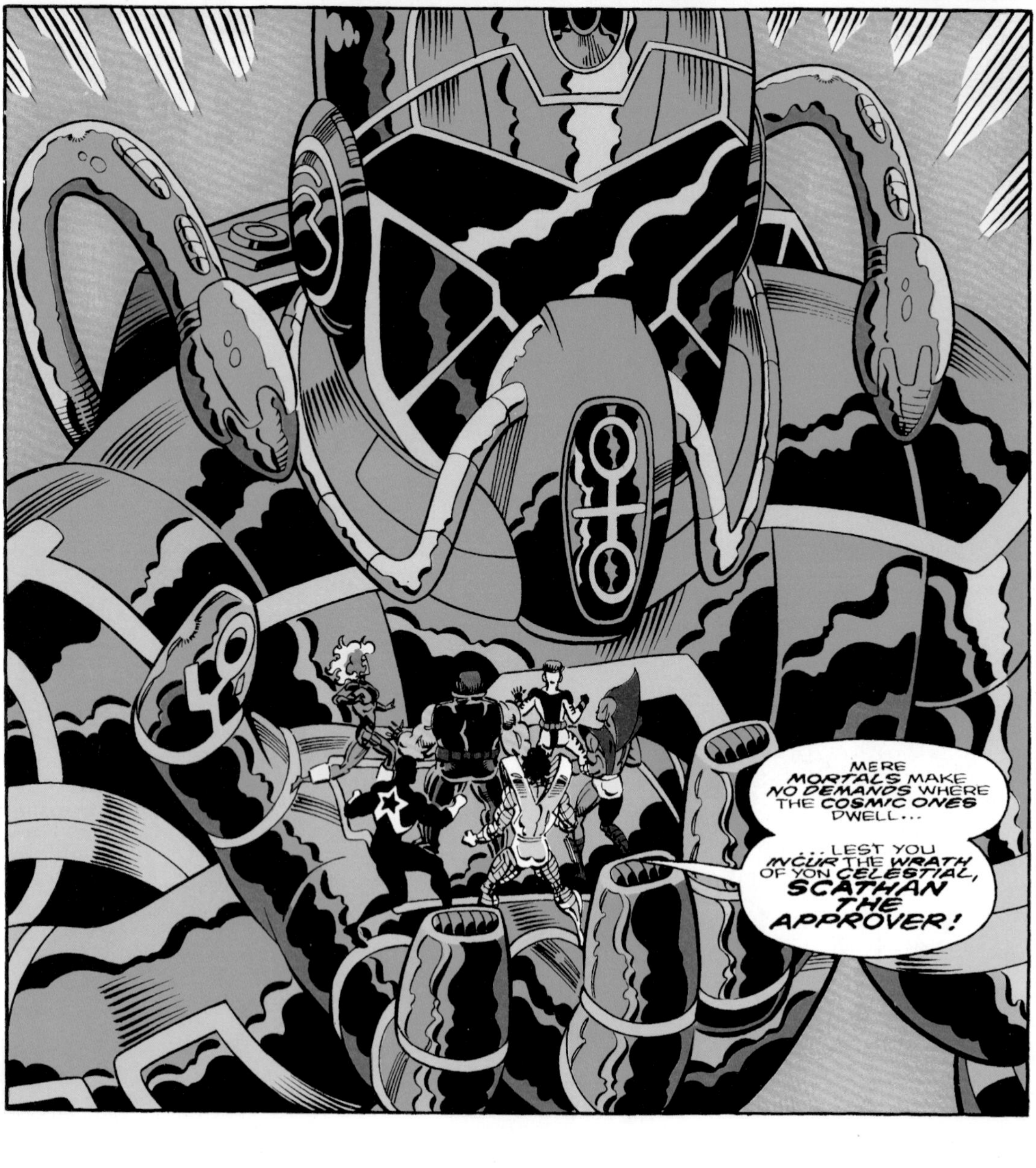
MERE MORTALS MAKE NO DEMANDS WHERE THE COSMIC ONES DWELL...
...LEST YOU INCUR THE WRATH OF YON CELESTIAL, SCATHAN THE APPROVER!

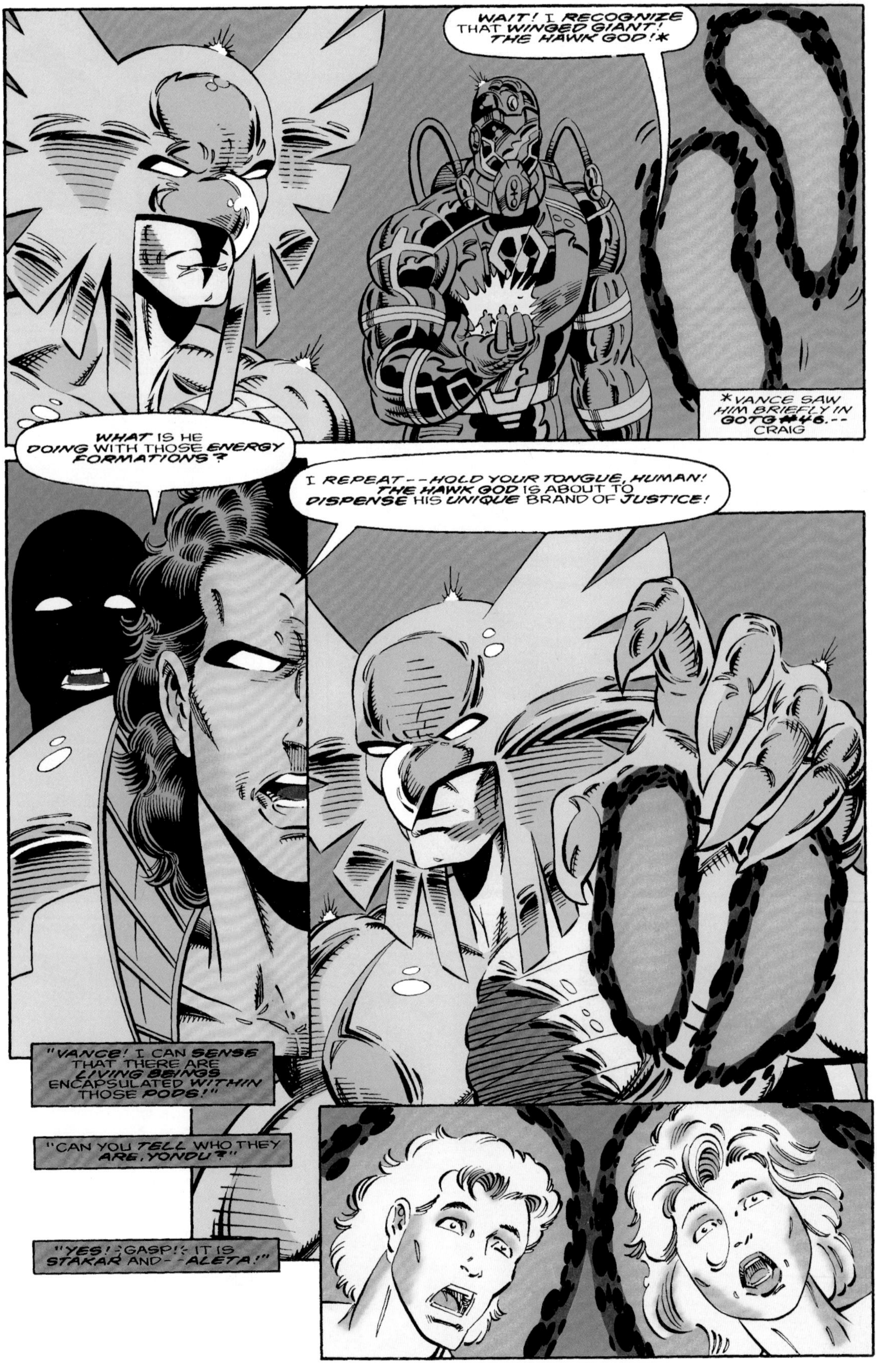
WAIT! I RECOGNIZE THAT WINGED GIANT! THE HAWK GOD!*
*VANCE SAW HIM BRIEFLY IN GOTG #46.--CRAIG
WHAT IS HE DOING WITH THOSE ENERGY FORMATIONS?
I REPEAT--HOLD YOUR TONGUE, HUMAN! THE HAWK GOD IS ABOUT TO DISPENSE HIS UNIQUE BRAND OF JUSTICE!
"VANCE! I CAN SENSE THAT THERE ARE LIVING BEINGS ENCAPSULATED WITHIN THOSE PODS!"
"CAN YOU TELL WHO THEY ARE, YONDU?"
"YES! -GASP!- IT IS STAKAR AND--ALETA!"

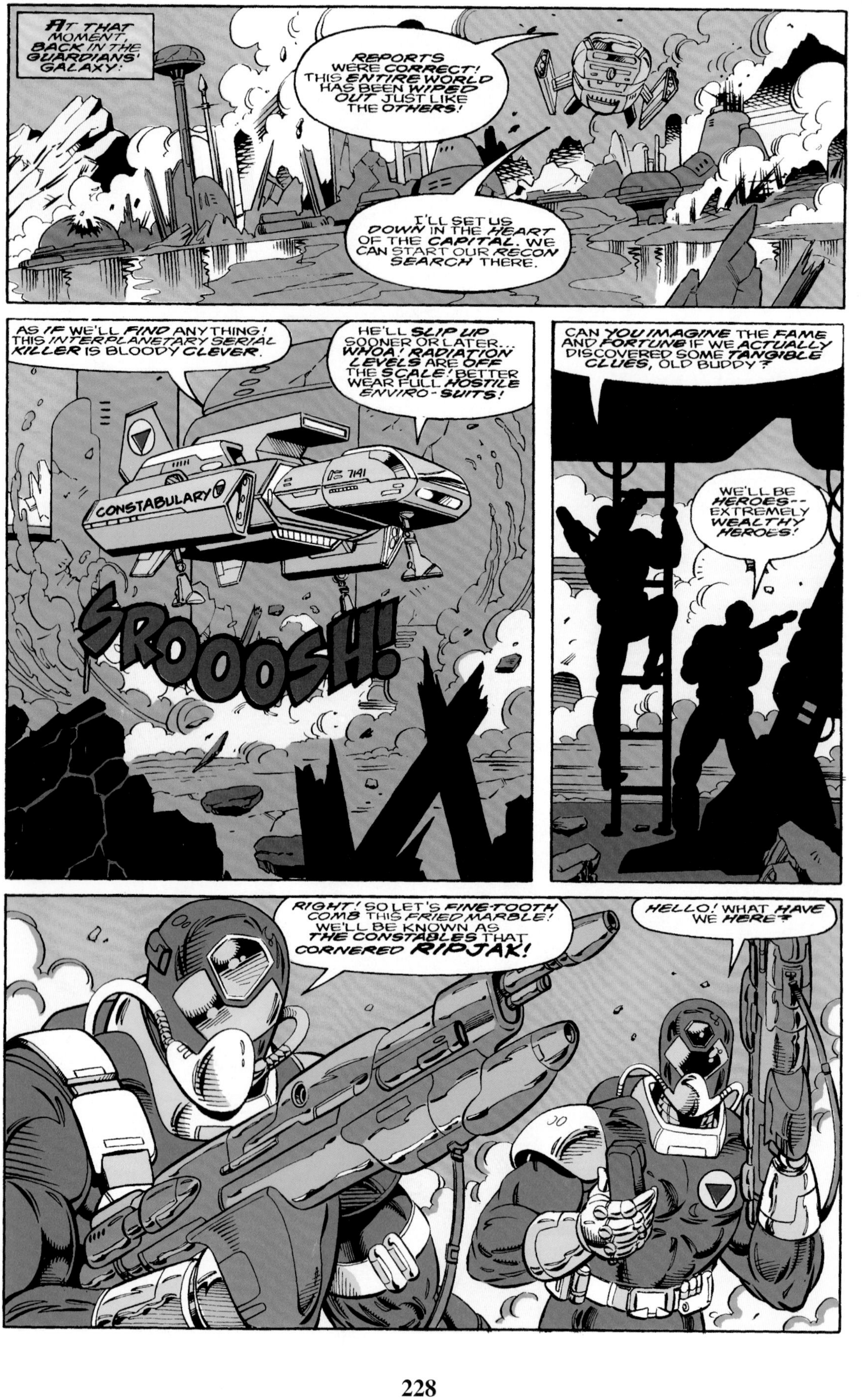
AT THAT MOMENT, BACK IN THE GUARDIANS' GALAXY:
REPORTS WERE CORRECT! THIS ENTIRE WORLD HAS BEEN WIPED OUT JUST LIKE THE OTHERS!
I'LL SET US DOWN IN THE HEART OF THE CAPITAL. WE CAN START OUR RECON SEARCH THERE.
AS IF WE'LL FIND ANYTHING! THIS INTERPLANETARY SERIAL KILLER IS BLOODY CLEVER.
HE'LL SLIP UP SOONER OR LATER... WHOA! RADIATION LEVELS ARE OFF THE SCALE! BETTER WEAR FULL HOSTILE ENVIRO-SUITS!
CONSTABULARY
7141
SROOOSH!
CAN YOU IMAGINE THE FAME AND FORTUNE IF WE ACTUALLY DISCOVERED SOME TANGIBLE CLUES, OLD BUDDY?
WE'LL BE HEROES-- EXTREMELY WEALTHY HEROES!
RIGHT! SO LET'S FINE-TOOTH COMB THIS FRIED MARBLE! WE'LL BE KNOWN AS THE CONSTABLES THAT CORNERED RIPJAK!
HELLO! WHAT HAVE WE HERE?

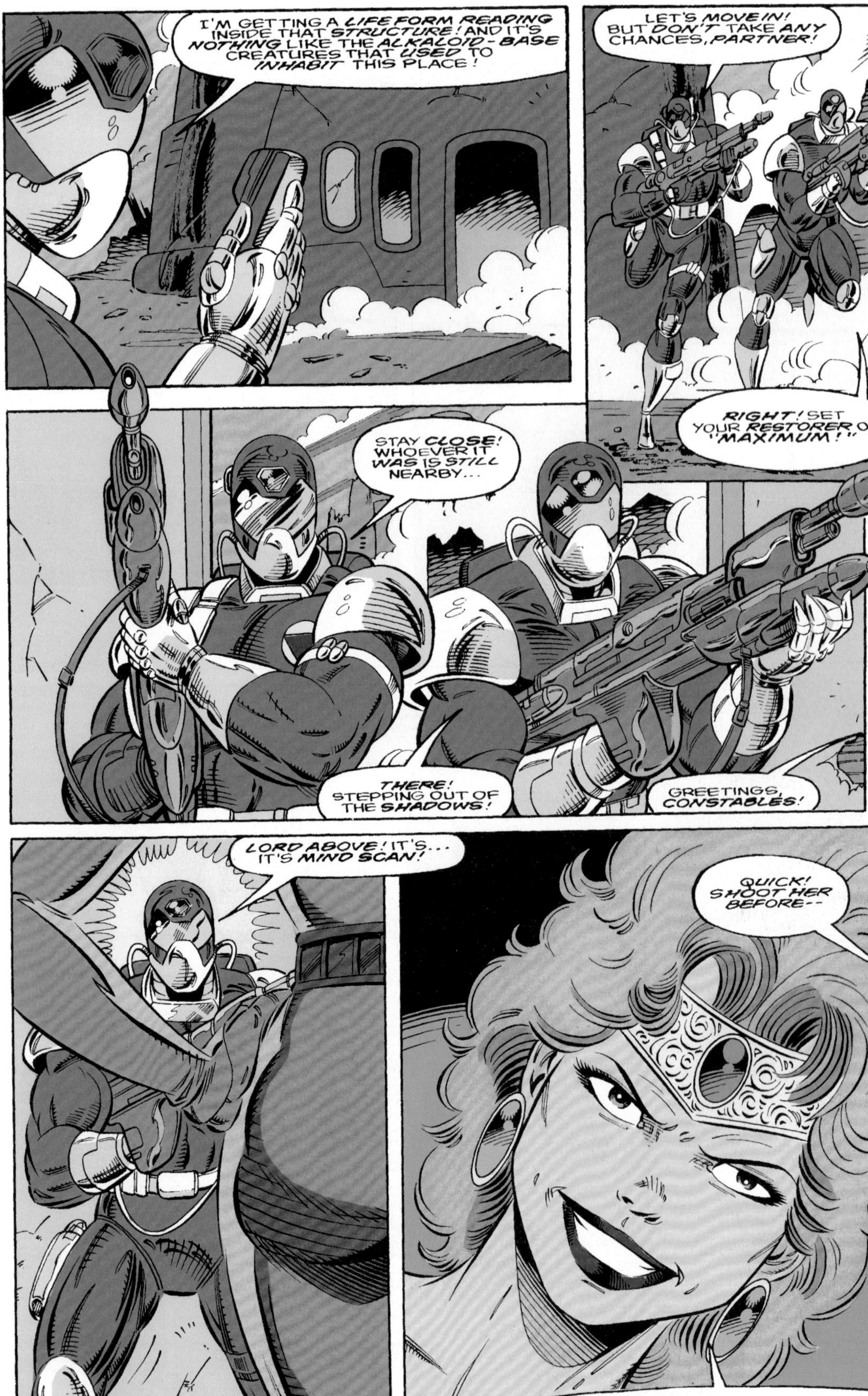
I'M GETTING A LIFE FORM READING INSIDE THAT STRUCTURE! AND IT'S NOTHING LIKE THE ALKALOID-BASE CREATURES THAT USED TO INHABIT THIS PLACE!
LET'S MOVE IN! BUT DON'T TAKE ANY CHANCES, PARTNER!
RIGHT! SET YOUR RESTORER ON "MAXIMUM!"
STAY CLOSE! WHOEVER IT WAS IS STILL NEARBY...
THERE! STEPPING OUT OF THE SHADOWS!
GREETINGS, CONSTABLES!
LORD ABOVE! IT'S... IT'S MIND SCAN!
QUICK! SHOOT HER BEFORE--
YOU DON'T WANT TO DO THAT, BOYS!

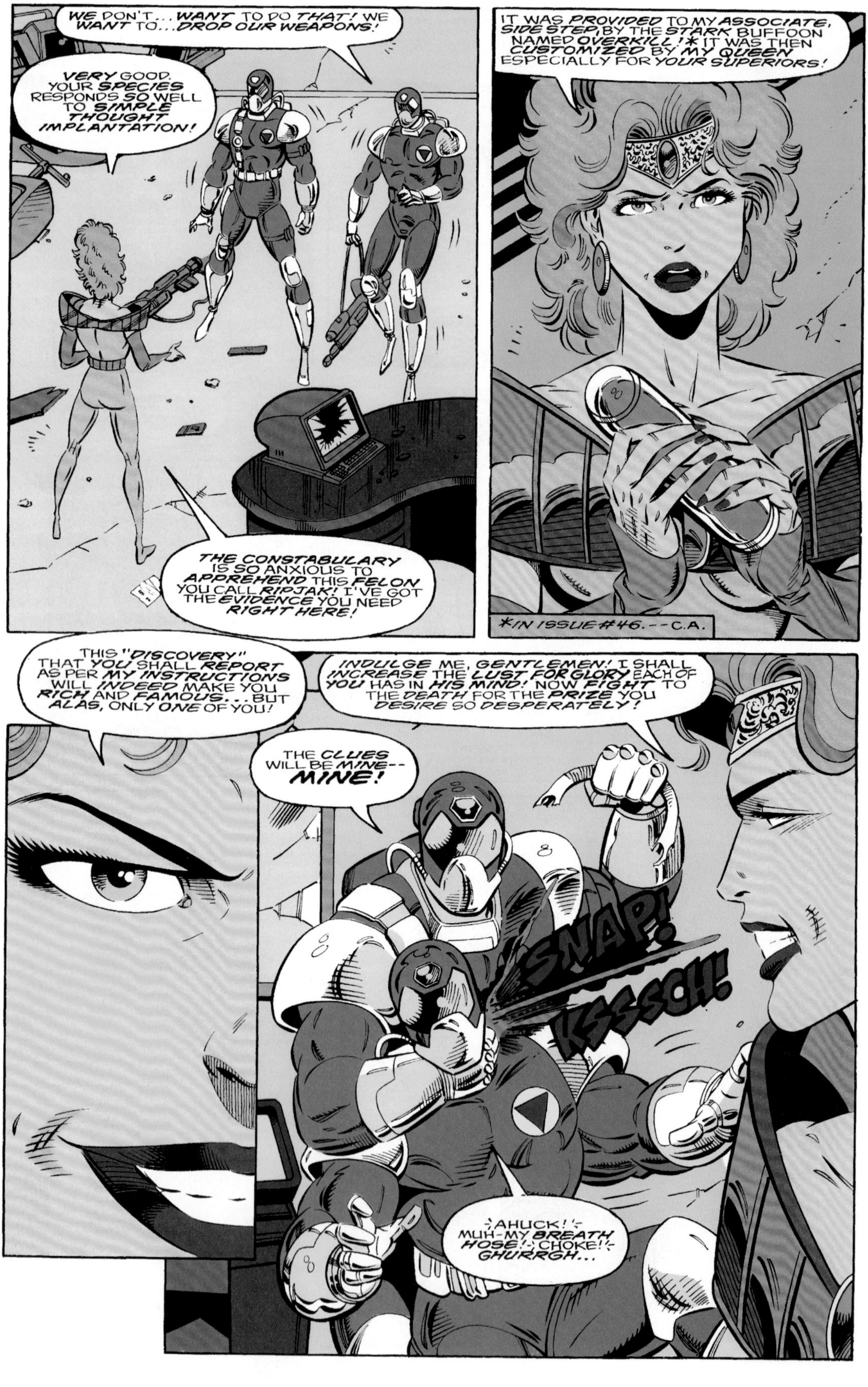

WE DON'T... WANT TO DO THAT! WE WANT TO... DROP OUR WEAPONS!
VERY GOOD. YOUR SPECIES RESPONDS SO WELL TO SIMPLE THOUGHT IMPLANTATION!
THE CONSTABULARY IS SO ANXIOUS TO APPREHEND THIS FELON YOU CALL RIPJAK! I'VE GOT THE EVIDENCE YOU NEED RIGHT HERE!
IT WAS PROVIDED TO MY ASSOCIATE, SIDE STEP, BY THE STARK BUFFOON NAMED OVERKILL! * IT WAS THEN CUSTOMIZED BY MY QUEEN ESPECIALLY FOR YOUR SUPERIORS!
*IN ISSUE #46.--C.A.
THIS "DISCOVERY" THAT YOU SHALL REPORT AS PER MY INSTRUCTIONS WILL INDEED MAKE YOU RICH AND FAMOUS... BUT ALAS, ONLY ONE OF YOU!
INDULGE ME, GENTLEMEN! I SHALL INCREASE THE LUST FOR GLORY EACH OF YOU HAS IN HIS MIND! NOW FIGHT TO THE DEATH FOR THE PRIZE YOU DESIRE SO DESPERATELY!
THE CLUES WILL BE MINE-- MINE!
SNAP!
KSSSCH!
AHUCK! MUH-MY BREATH HOSE! CHOKE! GHURRGH...

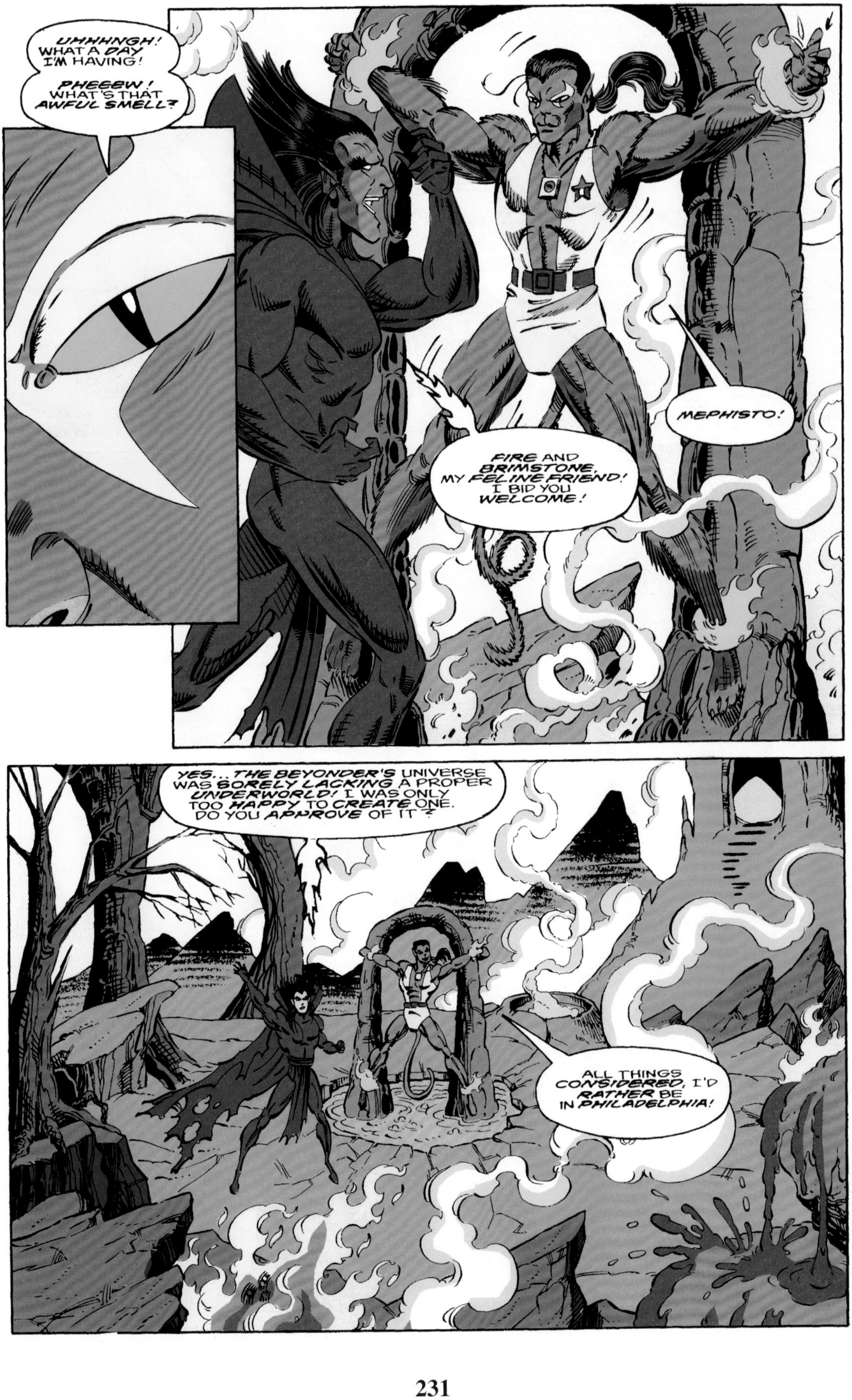
UHHHNGH! WHAT A DAY I'M HAVING!
PHEEEW! WHAT'S THAT AWFUL SMELL?
MEPHISTO!
FIRE AND BRIMSTONE, MY FELINE FRIEND! I BID YOU WELCOME!
YES... THE BEYONDER'S UNIVERSE WAS SORELY LACKING A PROPER UNDERWORLD! I WAS ONLY TOO HAPPY TO CREATE ONE. DO YOU APPROVE OF IT?
ALL THINGS CONSIDERED, I'D RATHER BE IN PHILADELPHIA!

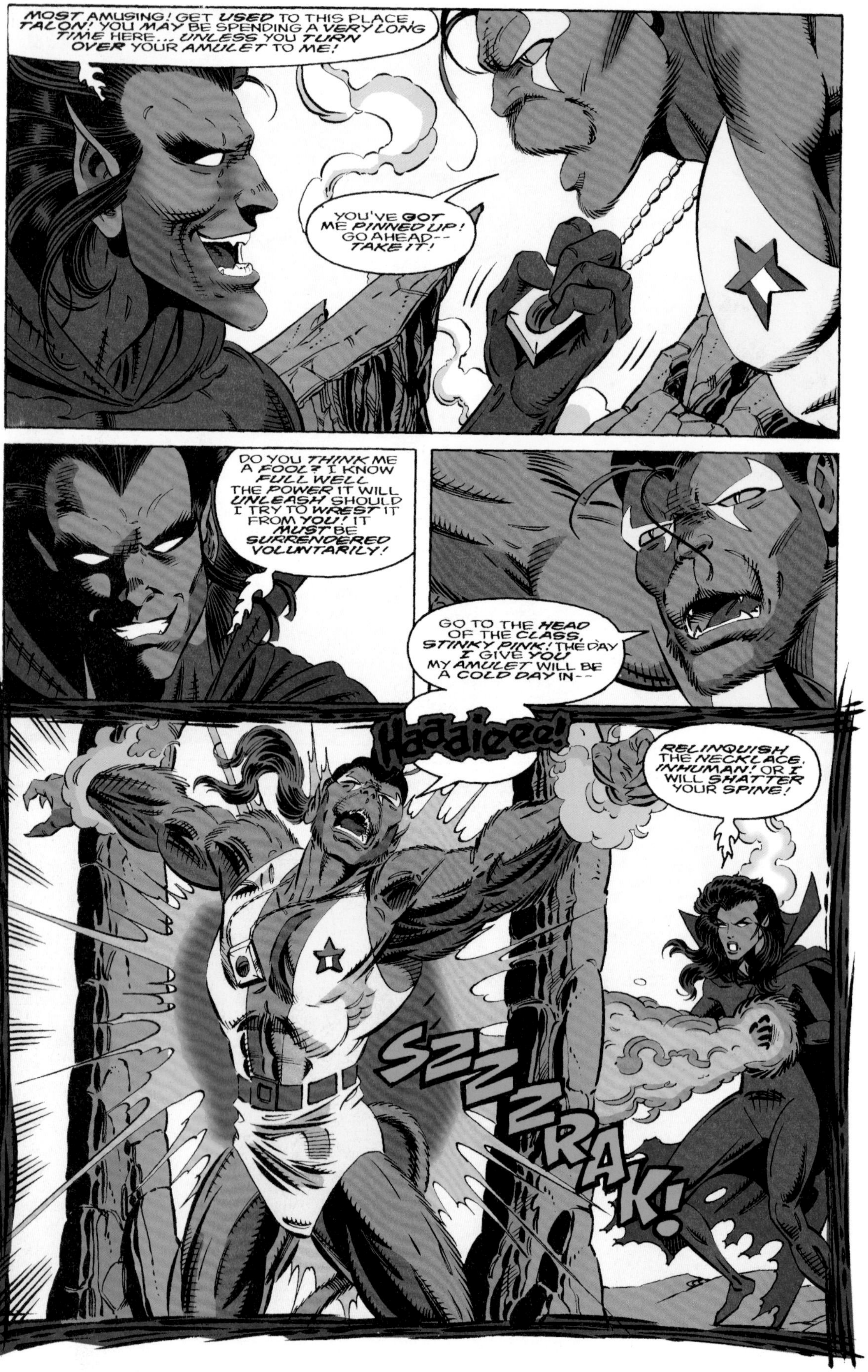
MOST AMUSING! GET USED TO THIS PLACE, TALON! YOU MAY BE SPENDING A VERY LONG TIME HERE... UNLESS YOU TURN OVER YOUR AMULET TO ME!
YOU'VE GOT ME PINNED UP! GO AHEAD-- TAKE IT!
DO YOU THINK ME A FOOL? I KNOW FULL WELL THE POWER IT WILL UNLEASH SHOULD I TRY TO WREST IT FROM YOU! IT MUST BE SURRENDERED VOLUNTARILY!
GO TO THE HEAD OF THE CLASS, STINKY PINK! THE DAY I GIVE YOU MY AMULET WILL BE A COLD DAY IN--
Haaaieee!
RELINQUISH THE NECKLACE, INHUMAN! OR I WILL SHATTER YOUR SPINE!
SZZZRAK!

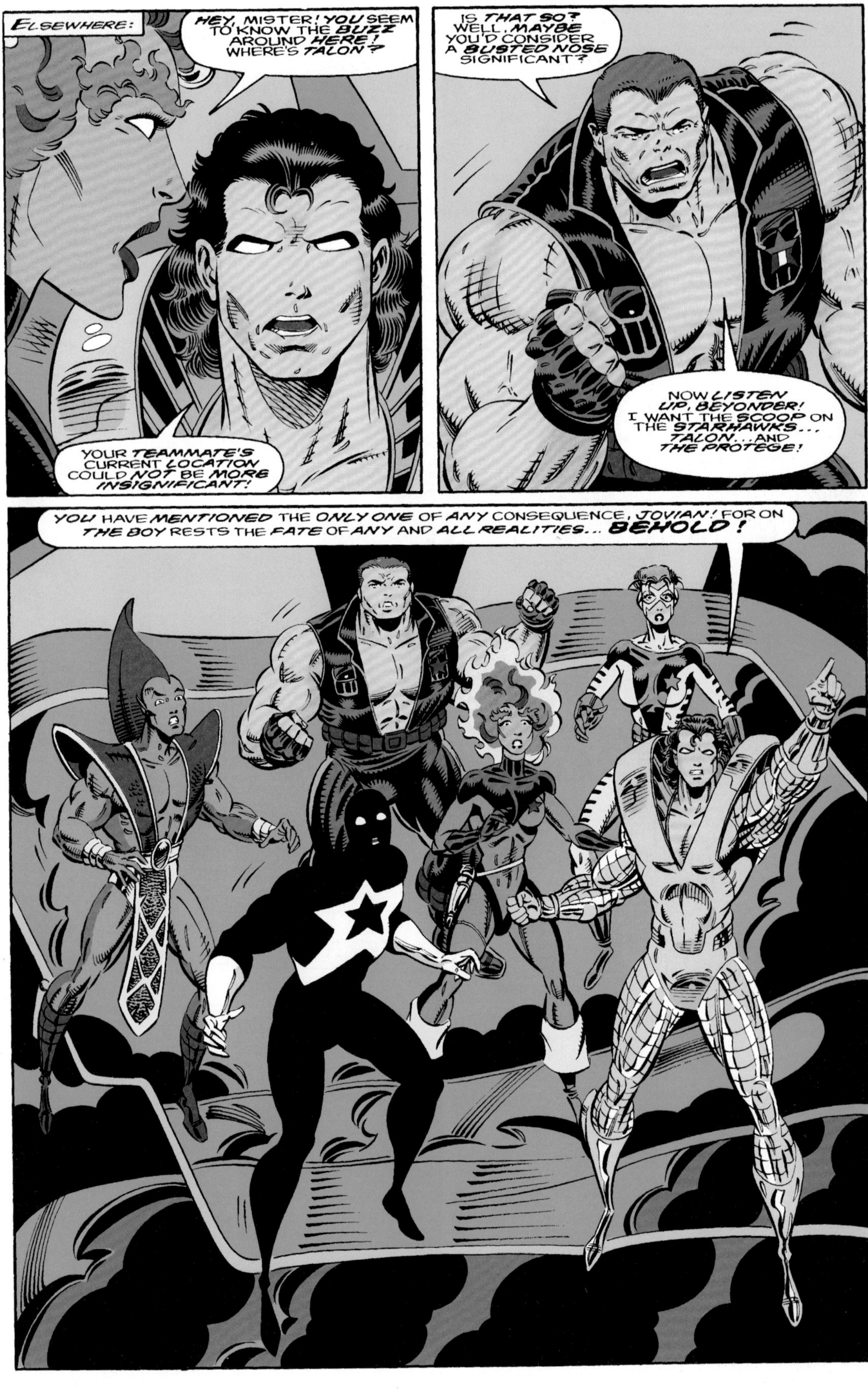
ELSEWHERE:
HEY, MISTER! YOU SEEM TO KNOW THE BUZZ AROUND HERE! WHERE'S TALON?
YOUR TEAMMATE'S CURRENT LOCATION COULD NOT BE MORE INSIGNIFICANT!
IS THAT SO? WELL, MAYBE YOU'D CONSIDER A BUSTED NOSE SIGNIFICANT?
NOW LISTEN UP, BEYONDER! I WANT THE SCOOP ON THE STARHAWKS... TALON... AND THE PROTEGE!
YOU HAVE MENTIONED THE ONLY ONE OF ANY CONSEQUENCE, JOVIAN! FOR ON THE BOY RESTS THE FATE OF ANY AND ALL REALITIES... BEHOLD!

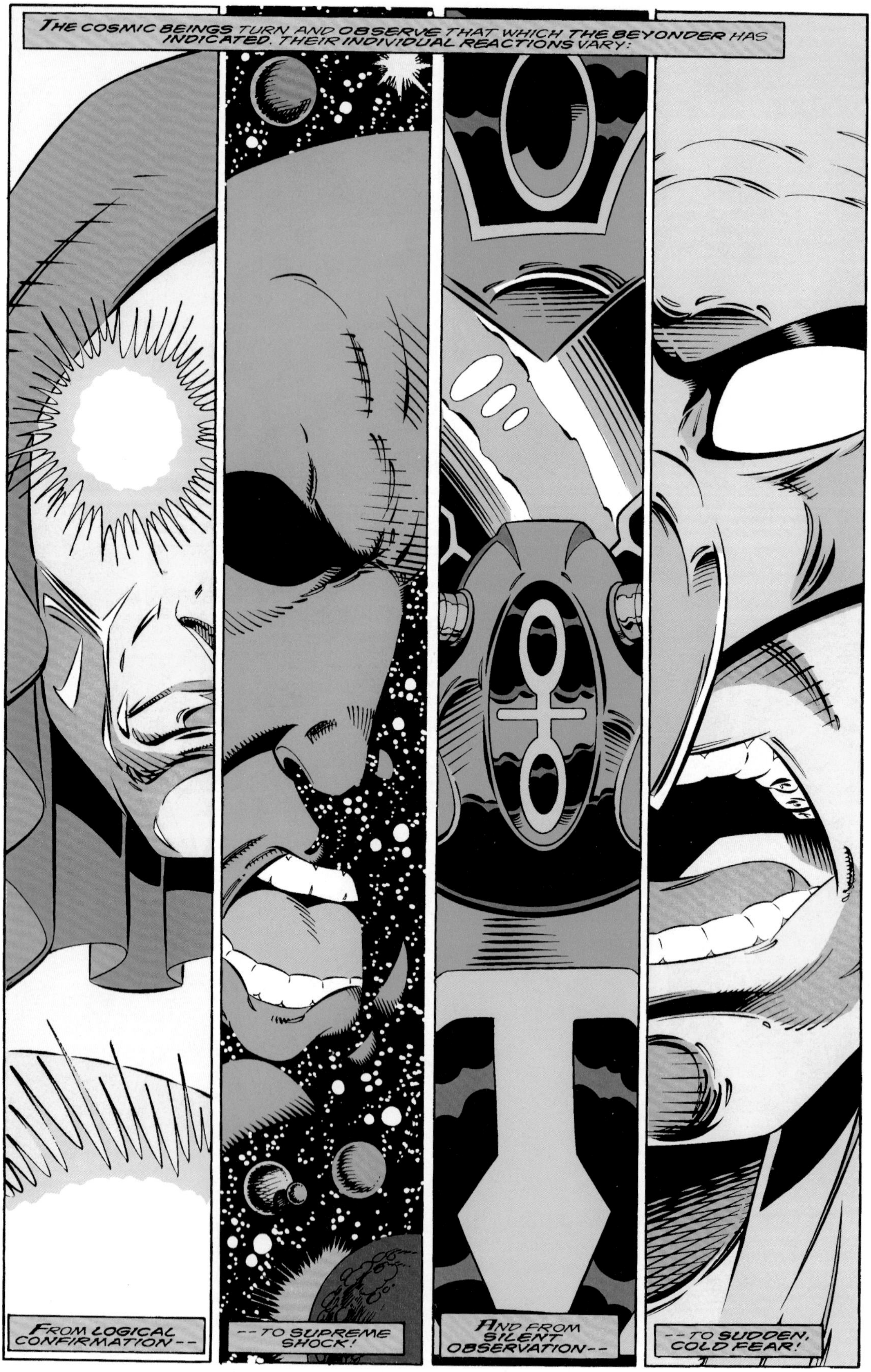
THE COSMIC BEINGS TURN AND OBSERVE THAT WHICH THE BEYONDER HAS INDICATED. THEIR INDIVIDUAL REACTIONS VARY:
FROM LOGICAL CONFIRMATION--
--TO SUPREME SHOCK!
AND FROM SILENT OBSERVATION--
--TO SUDDEN, COLD FEAR!

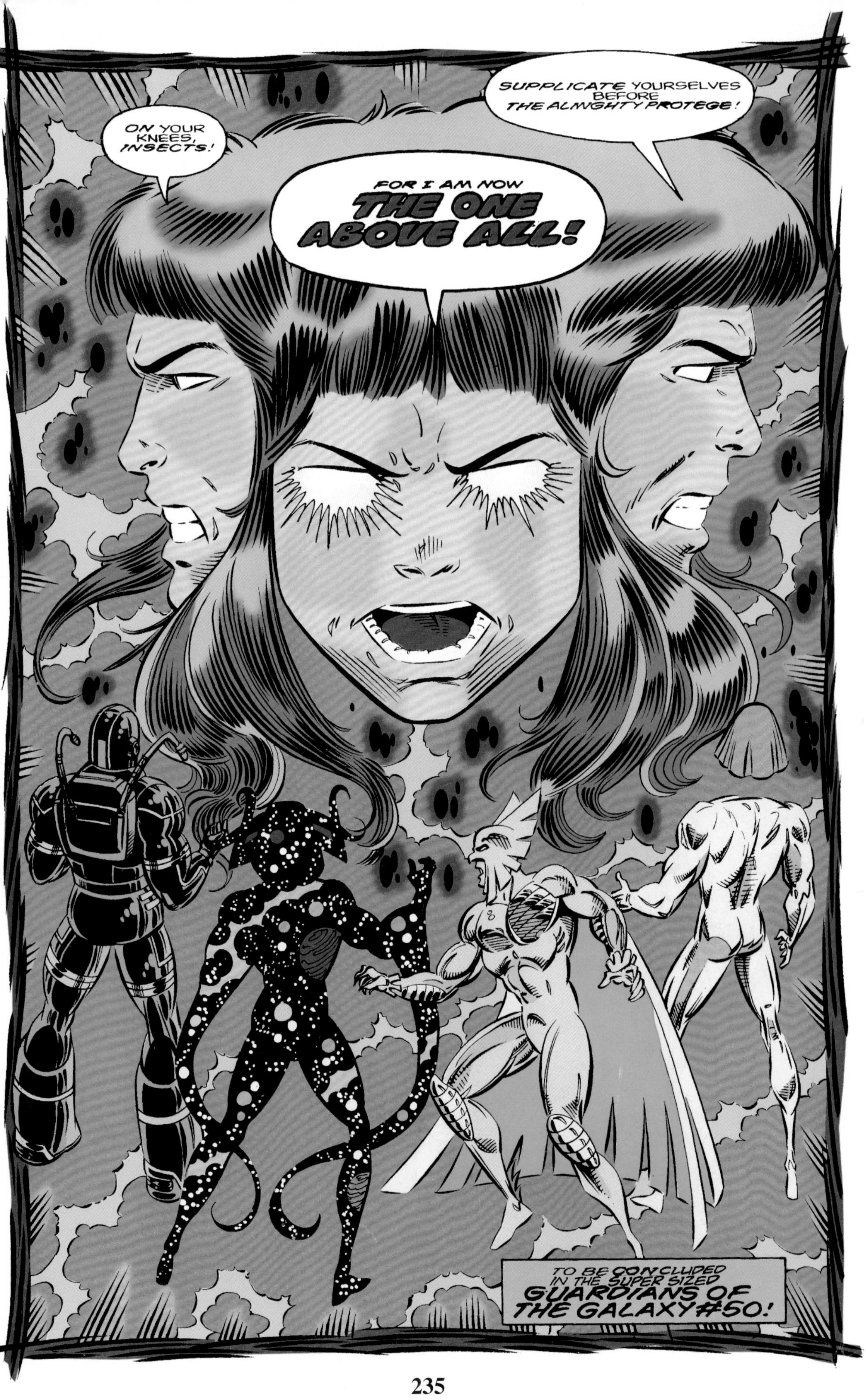
ON YOUR KNEES, INSECTS!
FOR I AM NOW THE ONE ABOVE ALL!
SUPPLICATE YOURSELVES BEFORE THE ALMIGHTY PROTEGE!
TO BE CONCLUDED IN THE SUPER SIZED GUARDIANS OF THE GALAXY #50!

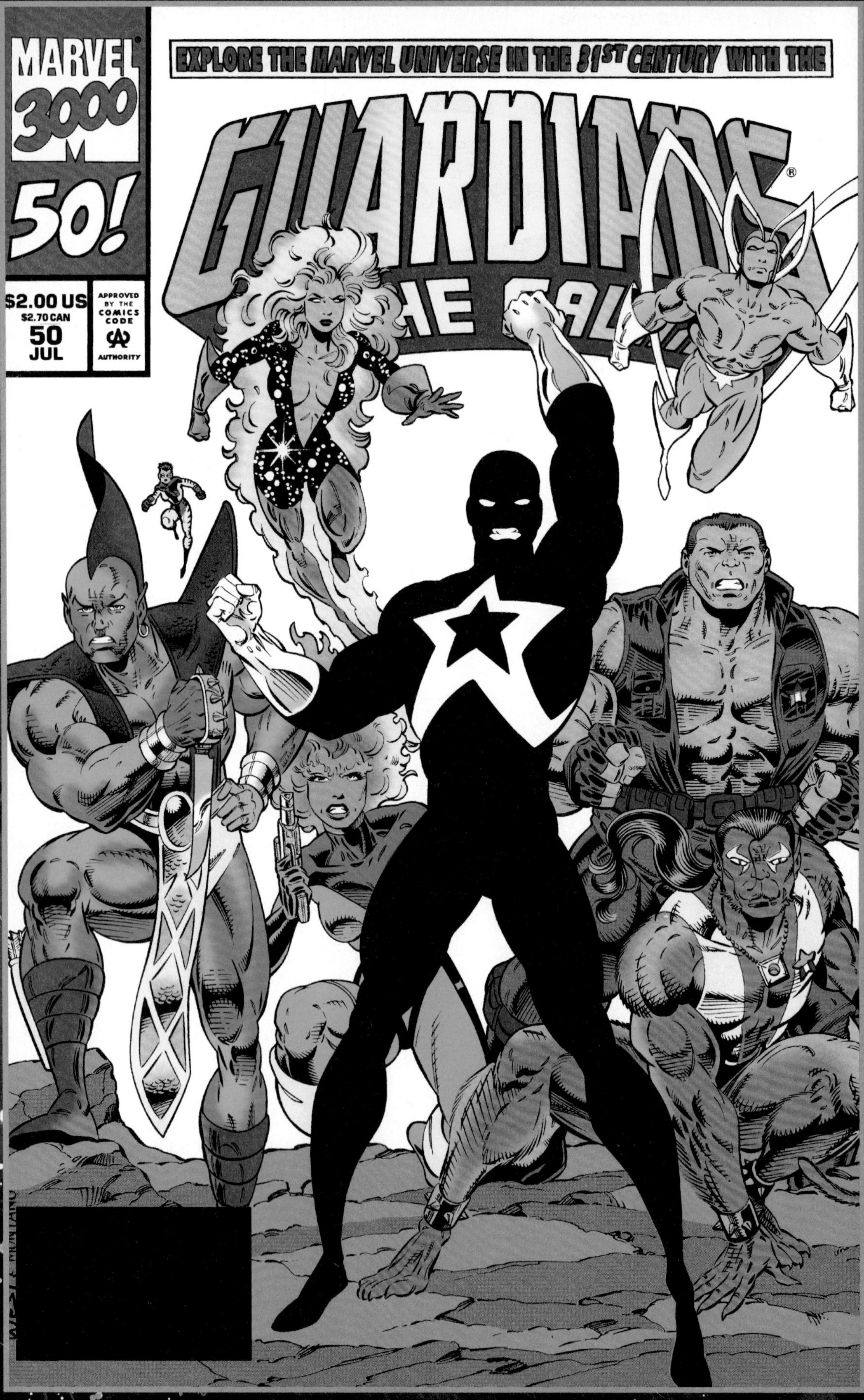
MARVEL
3000
50!
$2.00 US
$2.70 CAN
50
JUL
APPROVED BY THE COMICS CODE AUTHORITY
EXPLORE THE MARVEL UNIVERSE IN THE 31ST CENTURY WITH THE
GUARDIANS

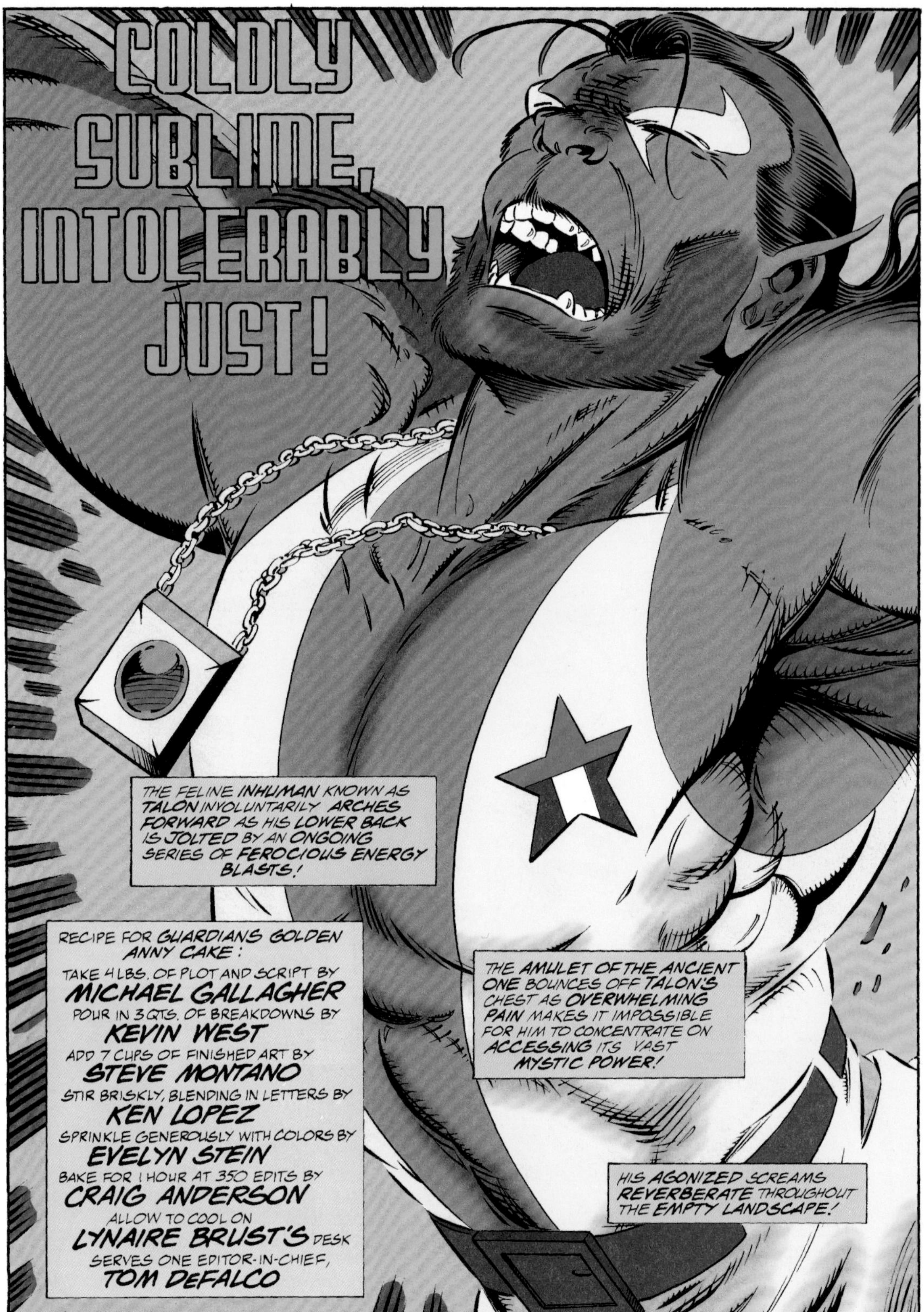
COLDLY SUBLIME, INTOLERABLY JUST!
THE FELINE INHUMAN KNOWN AS TALON INVOLUNTARILY ARCHES FORWARD AS HIS LOWER BACK IS JOLTED BY AN ONGOING SERIES OF FEROCIOUS ENERGY BLASTS!
RECIPE FOR GUARDIANS GOLDEN ANNY CAKE: TAKE 4 LBS. OF PLOT AND SCRIPT BY MICHAEL GALLAGHER POUR IN 3 QTS. OF BREAKDOWNS BY KEVIN WEST ADD 7 CUPS OF FINISHED ART BY STEVE MONTANO STIR BRISKLY, BLENDING IN LETTERS BY KEN LOPEZ SPRINKLE GENEROUSLY WITH COLORS BY EVELYN STEIN BAKE FOR 1 HOUR AT 350 EDITS BY CRAIG ANDERSON ALLOW TO COOL ON LYNAIRE BRUST'S DESK SERVES ONE EDITOR-IN-CHIEF, TOM DeFALCO
THE AMULET OF THE ANCIENT ONE BOUNCES OFF TALON'S CHEST AS OVERWHELMING PAIN MAKES IT IMPOSSIBLE FOR HIM TO CONCENTRATE ON ACCESSING ITS VAST MYSTIC POWER!
HIS AGONIZED SCREAMS REVERBERATE THROUGHOUT THE EMPTY LANDSCAPE!

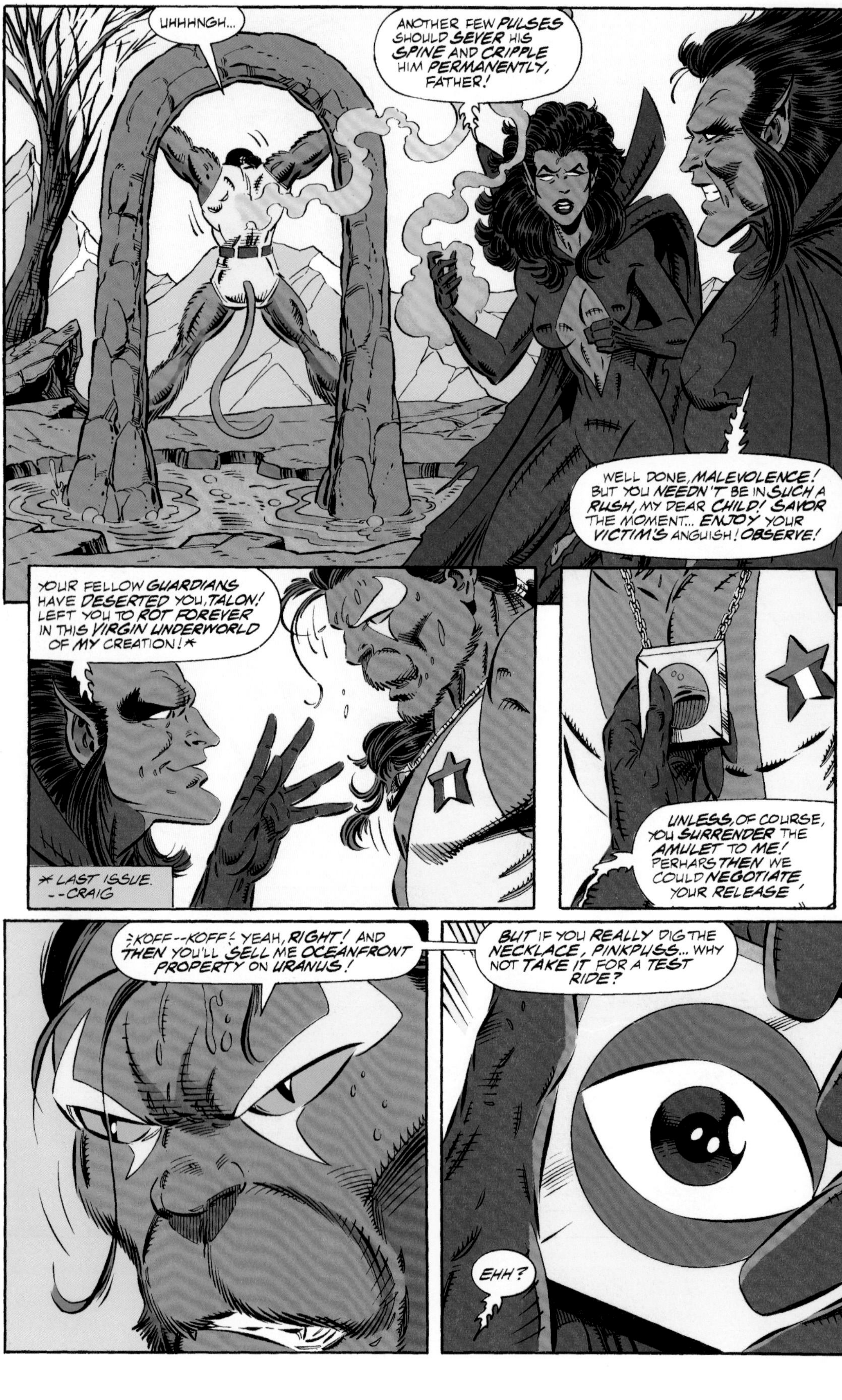
UHHHNGH...
ANOTHER FEW PULSES SHOULD SEVER HIS SPINE AND CRIPPLE HIM PERMANENTLY, FATHER!
WELL DONE, MALEVOLENCE! BUT YOU NEEDN'T BE IN SUCH A RUSH, MY DEAR CHILD! SAVOR THE MOMENT... ENJOY YOUR VICTIM'S ANGUISH! OBSERVE!
YOUR FELLOW GUARDIANS HAVE DESERTED YOU, TALON! LEFT YOU TO ROT FOREVER IN THIS VIRGIN UNDERWORLD OF MY CREATION! *
* LAST ISSUE. --CRAIG
UNLESS, OF COURSE, YOU SURRENDER THE AMULET TO ME! PERHAPS THEN WE COULD NEGOTIATE YOUR RELEASE
KOFF--KOFF YEAH, RIGHT! AND THEN YOU'LL SELL ME OCEANFRONT PROPERTY ON URANUS!
BUT IF YOU REALLY DIG THE NECKLACE, PINKPUSS... WHY NOT TAKE IT FOR A TEST RIDE?
EHH?

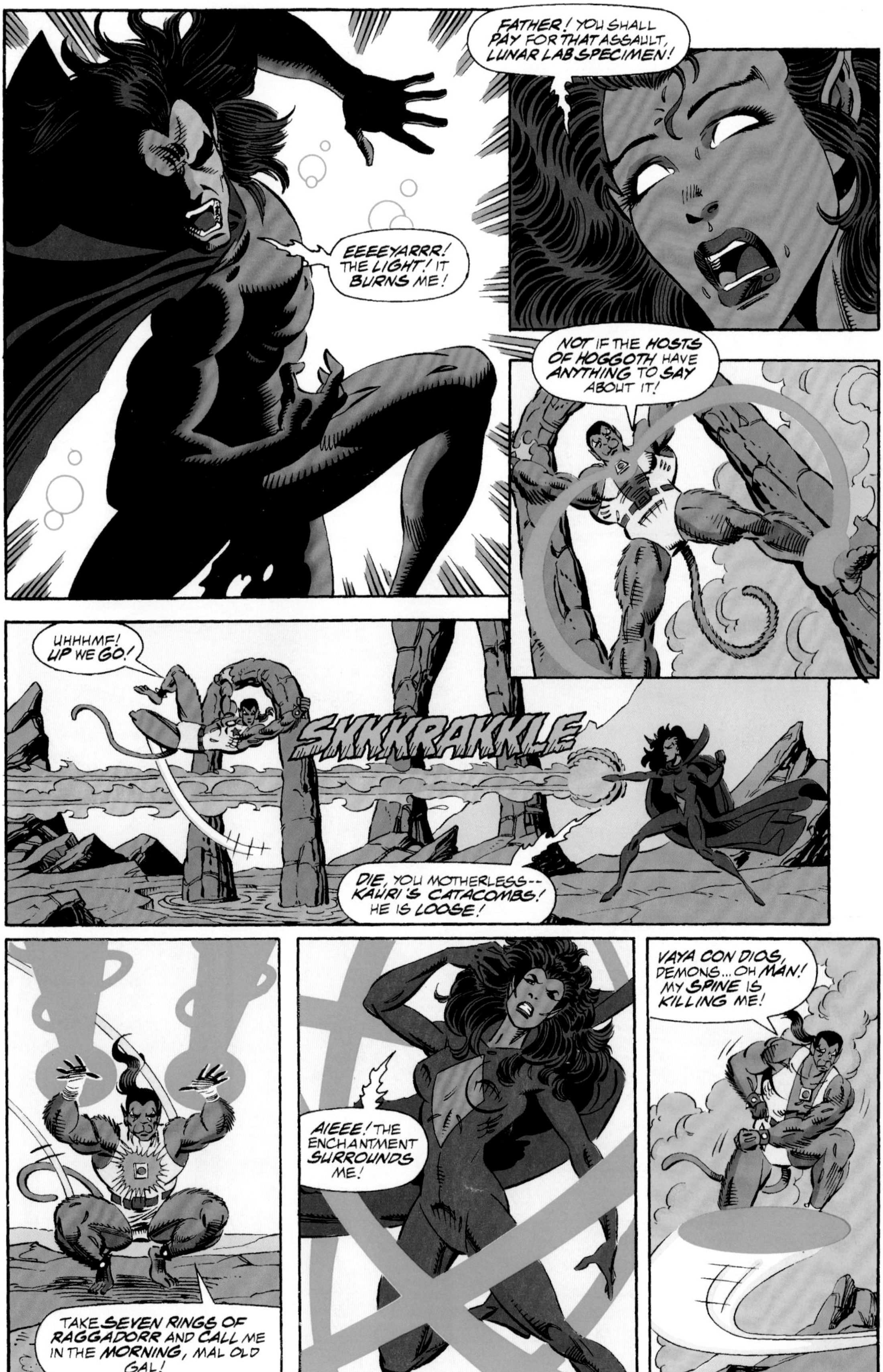
FATHER! YOU SHALL PAY FOR THAT ASSAULT, LUNAR LAB SPECIMEN!
EEEEYARRR! THE LIGHT! IT BURNS ME!
NOT IF THE HOSTS OF HOGGOTH HAVE ANYTHING TO SAY ABOUT IT!
UHHHMF! UP WE GO!
SKKKRAKKLE
DIE, YOU MOTHERLESS-- KAURI'S CATACOMBS! HE IS LOOSE!
TAKE SEVEN RINGS OF RAGGADORR AND CALL ME IN THE MORNING, MAL OLD GAL!
AIEEE! THE ENCHANTMENT SURROUNDS ME!
VAYA CON DIOS, DEMONS... OH MAN! MY SPINE IS KILLING ME!

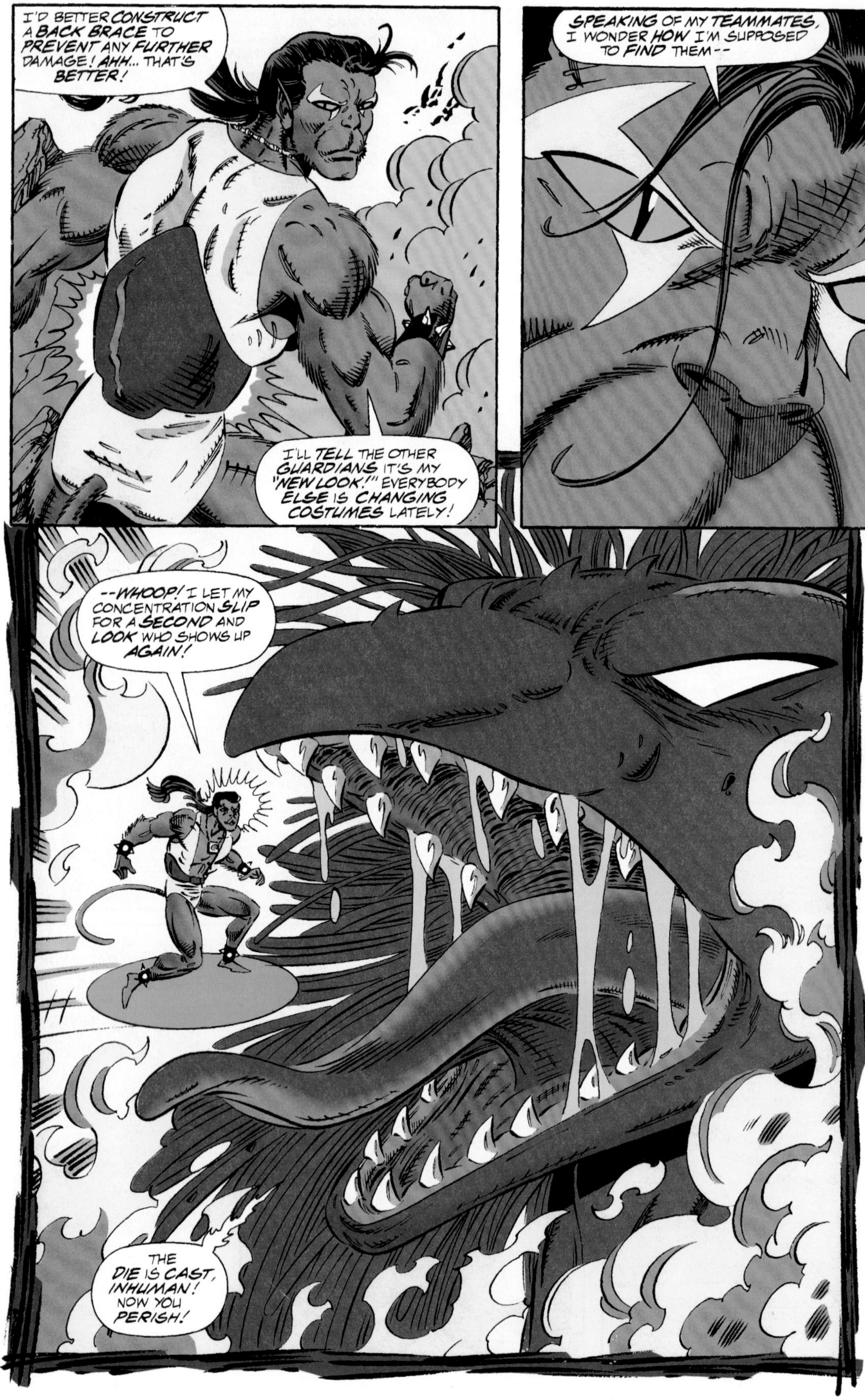
I'D BETTER CONSTRUCT A BACK BRACE TO PREVENT ANY FURTHER DAMAGE! AHH... THAT'S BETTER!
I'LL TELL THE OTHER GUARDIANS IT'S MY "NEW LOOK!" EVERYBODY ELSE IS CHANGING COSTUMES LATELY!
SPEAKING OF MY TEAMMATES, I WONDER HOW I'M SUPPOSED TO FIND THEM--
--WHOOP! I LET MY CONCENTRATION SLIP FOR A SECOND AND LOOK WHO SHOWS UP AGAIN!
THE DIE IS CAST, INHUMAN! NOW YOU PERISH!

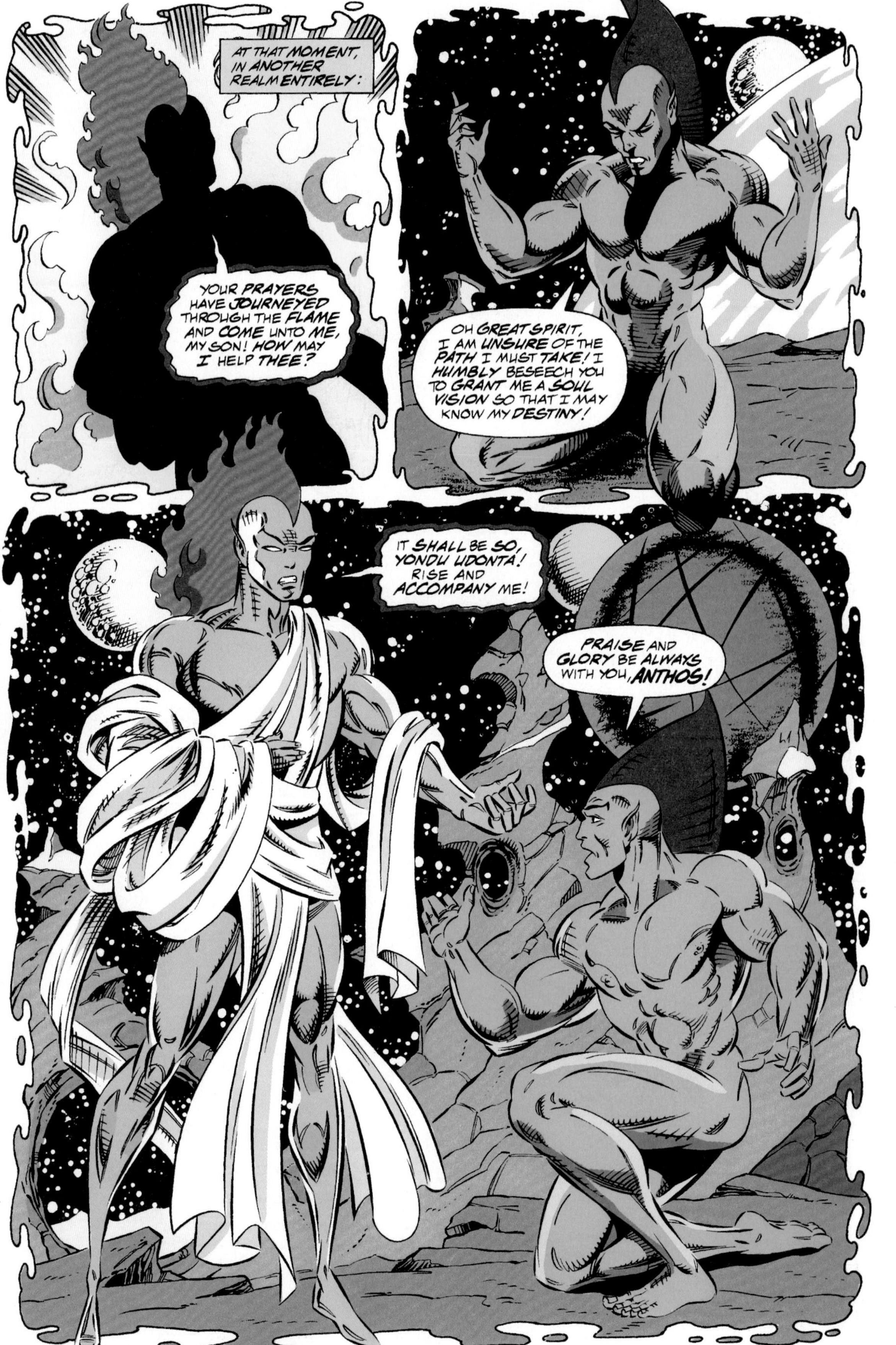
AT THAT MOMENT, IN ANOTHER REALM ENTIRELY:
YOUR PRAYERS HAVE JOURNEYED THROUGH THE FLAME AND COME UNTO ME, MY SON! HOW MAY I HELP THEE?
OH GREAT SPIRIT, I AM UNSURE OF THE PATH I MUST TAKE! I HUMBLY BESEECH YOU TO GRANT ME A SOUL VISION SO THAT I MAY KNOW MY DESTINY!
IT SHALL BE SO, YONDU UDONTA! RISE AND ACCOMPANY ME!
PRAISE AND GLORY BE ALWAYS WITH YOU, ANTHOS!

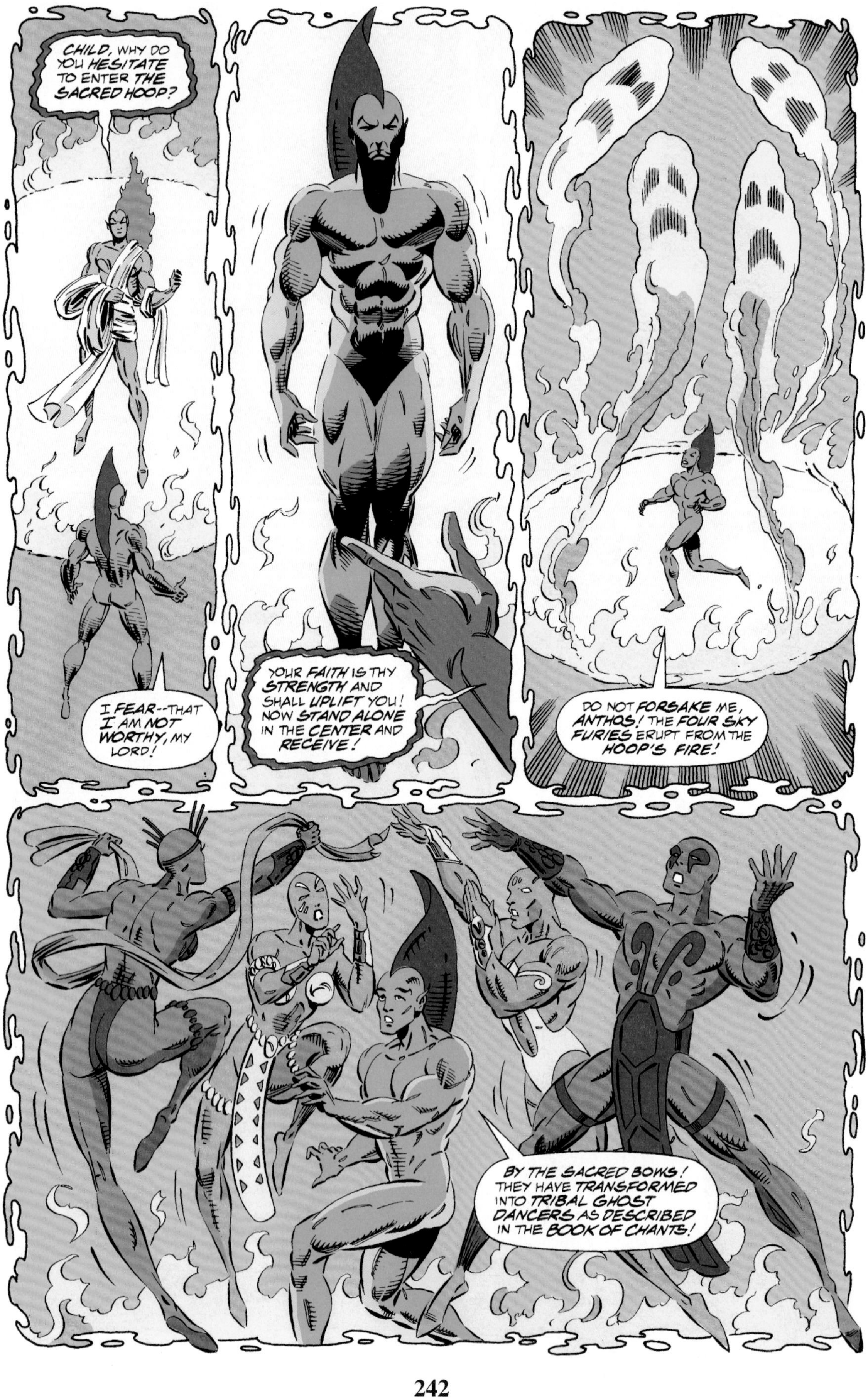
CHILD, WHY DO YOU HESITATE TO ENTER THE SACRED HOOP?
I FEAR--THAT I AM NOT WORTHY, MY LORD!
YOUR FAITH IS THY STRENGTH AND SHALL UPLIFT YOU! NOW STAND ALONE IN THE CENTER AND RECEIVE!
DO NOT FORSAKE ME, ANTHOS! THE FOUR SKY FURIES ERUPT FROM THE HOOP'S FIRE!
BY THE SACRED BOWS! THEY HAVE TRANSFORMED INTO TRIBAL GHOST DANCERS AS DESCRIBED IN THE BOOK OF CHANTS!

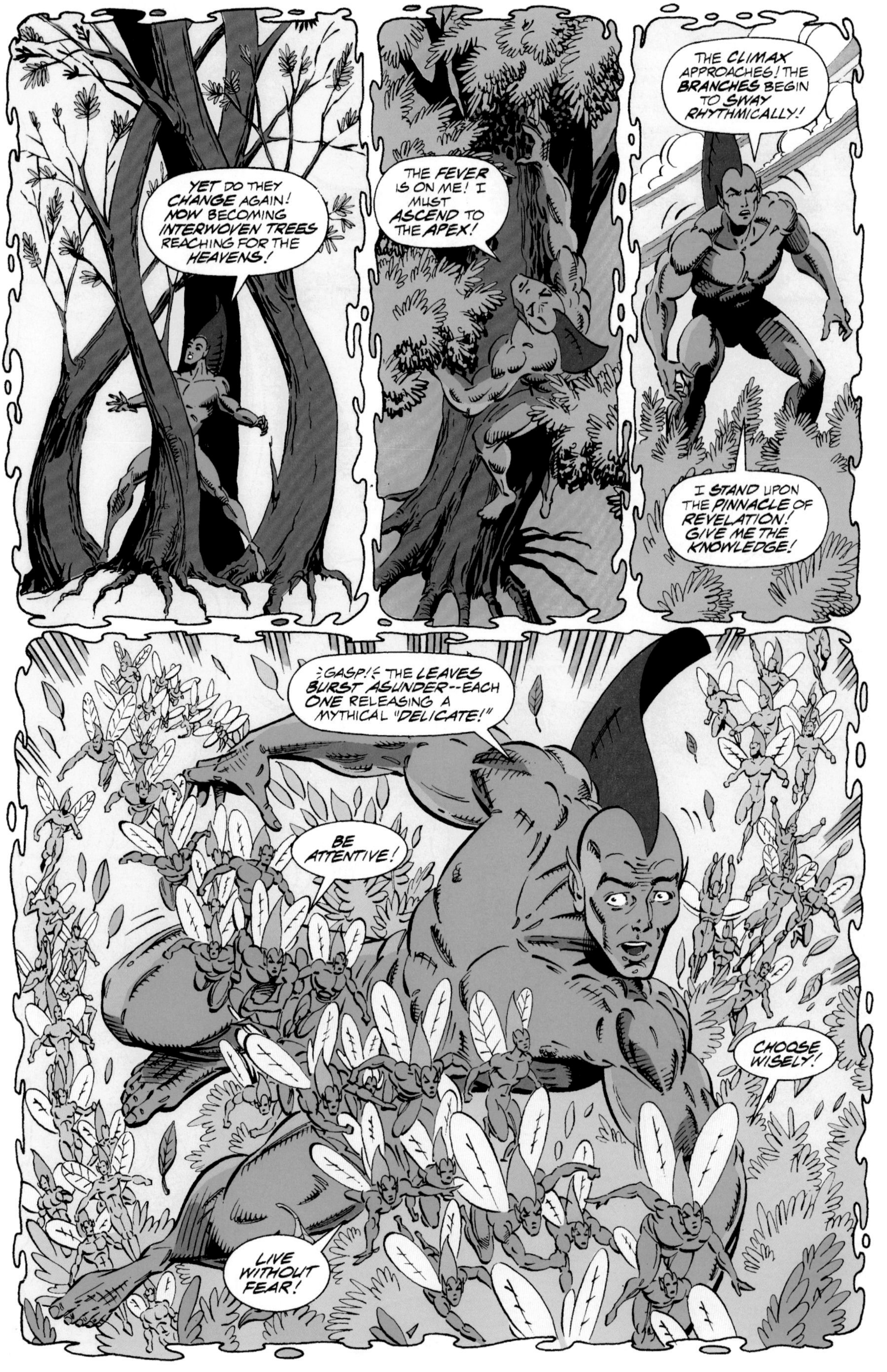
YET DO THEY CHANGE AGAIN! NOW BECOMING INTERWOVEN TREES REACHING FOR THE HEAVENS!
THE FEVER IS ON ME! I MUST ASCEND TO THE APEX!
THE CLIMAX APPROACHES! THE BRANCHES BEGIN TO SWAY RHYTHMICALLY!
I STAND UPON THE PINNACLE OF REVELATION! GIVE ME THE KNOWLEDGE!
GASP! THE LEAVES BURST ASUNDER--EACH ONE RELEASING A MYTHICAL "DELICATE!"
BE ATTENTIVE!
CHOOSE WISELY!
LIVE WITHOUT FEAR!

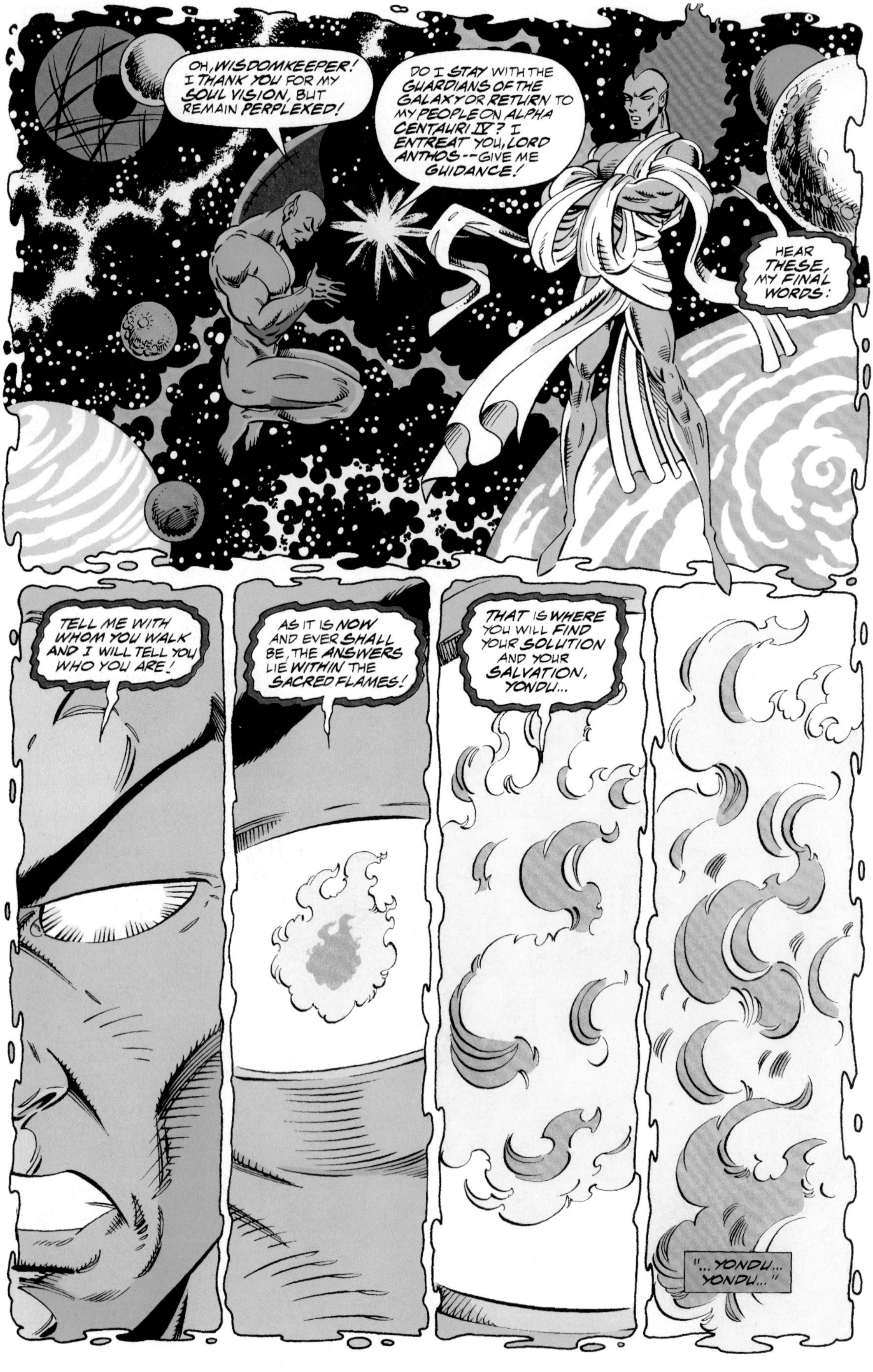
OH, WISDOMKEEPER! I THANK YOU FOR MY SOUL VISION, BUT REMAIN PERPLEXED!
DO I STAY WITH THE GUARDIANS OF THE GALAXY OR RETURN TO MY PEOPLE ON ALPHA CENTAURI IV? I ENTREAT YOU, LORD ANTHOS--GIVE ME GUIDANCE!
HEAR THESE, MY FINAL WORDS:
TELL ME WITH WHOM YOU WALK AND I WILL TELL YOU WHO YOU ARE!
AS IT IS NOW AND EVER SHALL BE, THE ANSWERS LIE WITHIN THE SACRED FLAMES!
THAT IS WHERE YOU WILL FIND YOUR SOLUTION AND YOUR SALVATION, YONDU...
"...YONDU... YONDU..."

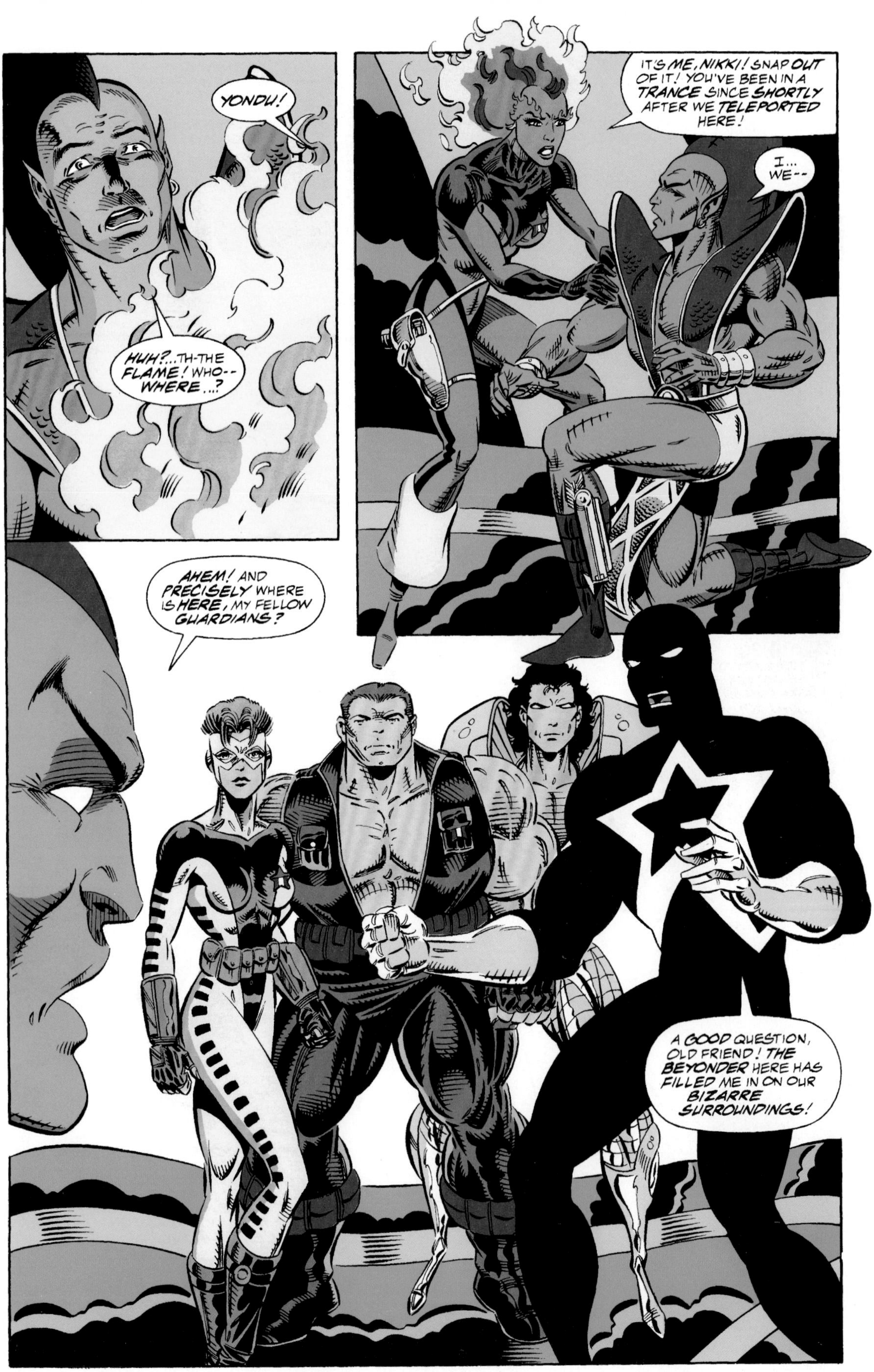
YONDU!
HUH?...TH-THE FLAME! WHO--WHERE...?
IT'S ME, NIKKI! SNAP OUT OF IT! YOU'VE BEEN IN A TRANCE SINCE SHORTLY AFTER WE TELEPORTED HERE!
I... WE--
AHEM! AND PRECISELY WHERE IS HERE, MY FELLOW GUARDIANS?
A GOOD QUESTION, OLD FRIEND! THE BEYONDER HERE HAS FILLED ME IN ON OUR BIZARRE SURROUNDINGS!

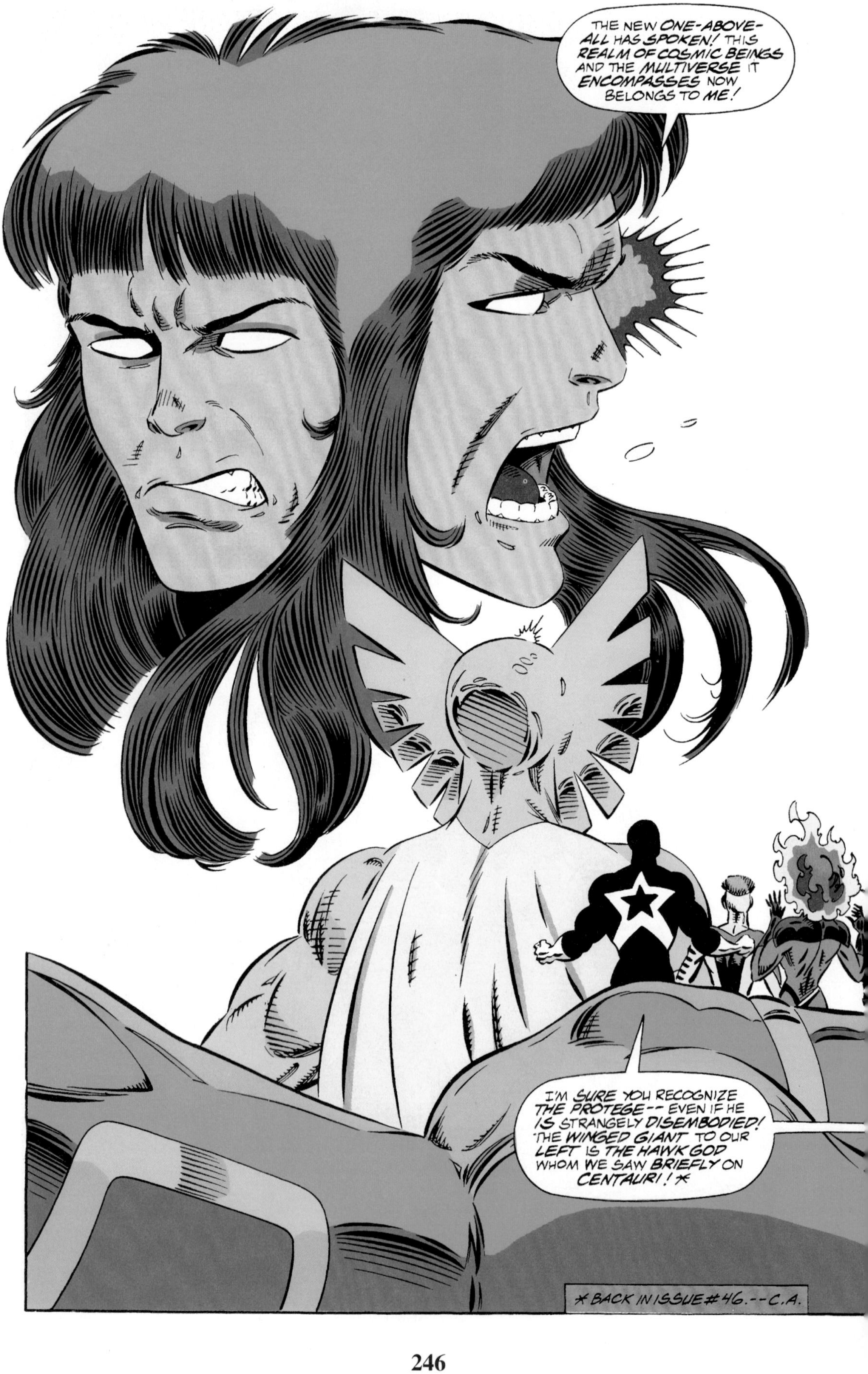
THE NEW ONE-ABOVE-ALL HAS SPOKEN! THIS REALM OF COSMIC BEINGS AND THE MULTIVERSE IT ENCOMPASSES NOW BELONGS TO ME!
I'M SURE YOU RECOGNIZE THE PROTEGE-- EVEN IF HE IS STRANGELY DISEMBODIED! THE WINGED GIANT TO OUR LEFT IS THE HAWK GOD WHOM WE SAW BRIEFLY ON CENTAURI! *
* BACK IN ISSUE #46.--C.A.

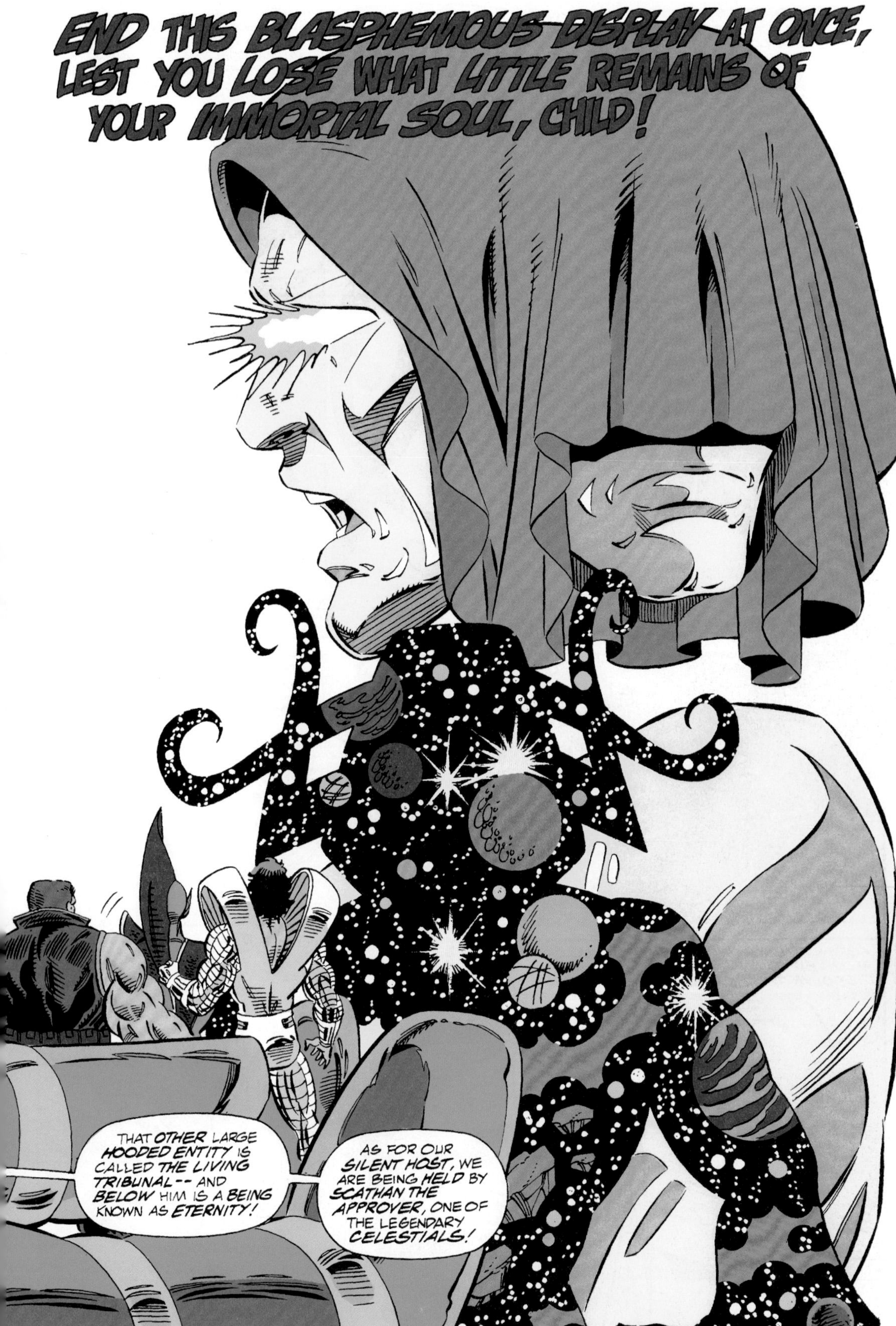
END THIS BLASPHEMOUS DISPLAY AT ONCE, LEST YOU LOSE WHAT LITTLE REMAINS OF YOUR IMMORTAL SOUL, CHILD!
THAT OTHER LARGE HOODED ENTITY IS CALLED THE LIVING TRIBUNAL-- AND BELOW HIM IS A BEING KNOWN AS ETERNITY!
AS FOR OUR SILENT HOST, WE ARE BEING HELD BY SCATHAN THE APPROVER, ONE OF THE LEGENDARY CELESTIALS!

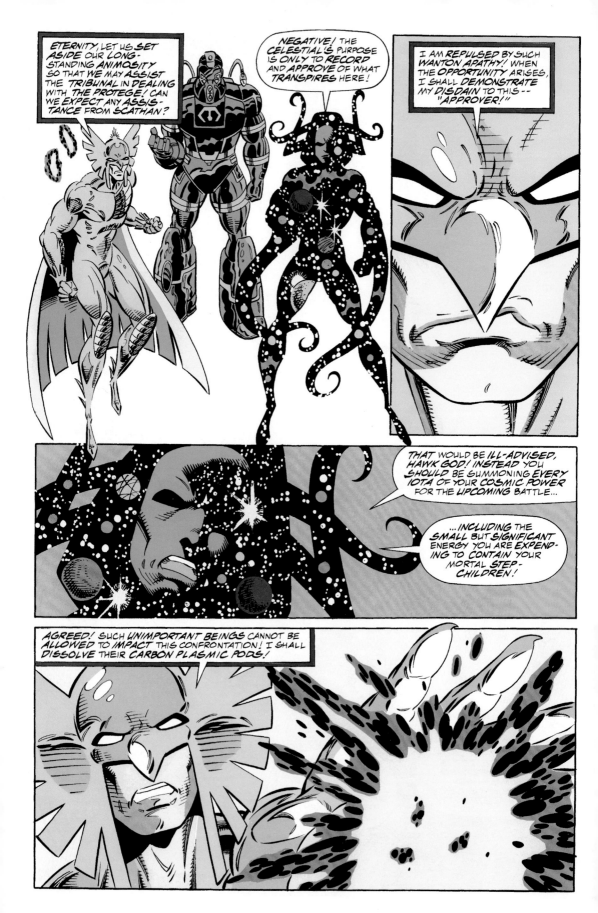

ETERNITY, LET US *SET ASIDE* OUR *LONG-STANDING ANIMOSITY* SO THAT WE MAY *ASSIST* THE *TRIBUNAL* IN DEALING WITH *THE PROTEGE!* CAN WE EXPECT ANY *ASSISTANCE* FROM *SCATHAN?*

NEGATIVE! THE *CELESTIAL'S* PURPOSE IS ONLY TO *RECORD* AND *APPROVE* OF WHAT *TRANSPIRES* HERE!

I AM *REPULSED* BY SUCH *WANTON APATHY!* WHEN THE *OPPORTUNITY* ARISES, I SHALL *DEMONSTRATE* MY *DISDAIN* TO THIS -- "*APPROVER!*"

THAT WOULD BE *ILL-ADVISED,* HAWK GOD! INSTEAD YOU *SHOULD* BE *SUMMONING* EVERY *IOTA* OF YOUR *COSMIC POWER* FOR THE *UPCOMING* BATTLE...

...INCLUDING THE *SMALL* BUT *SIGNIFICANT* ENERGY YOU ARE EXPENDING TO *CONTAIN* YOUR *MORTAL STEP-CHILDREN!*

AGREED! SUCH *UNIMPORTANT BEINGS* CANNOT BE ALLOWED TO *IMPACT* THIS CONFRONTATION! I SHALL *DISSOLVE* THEIR *CARBON PLASMIC PODS!*

248

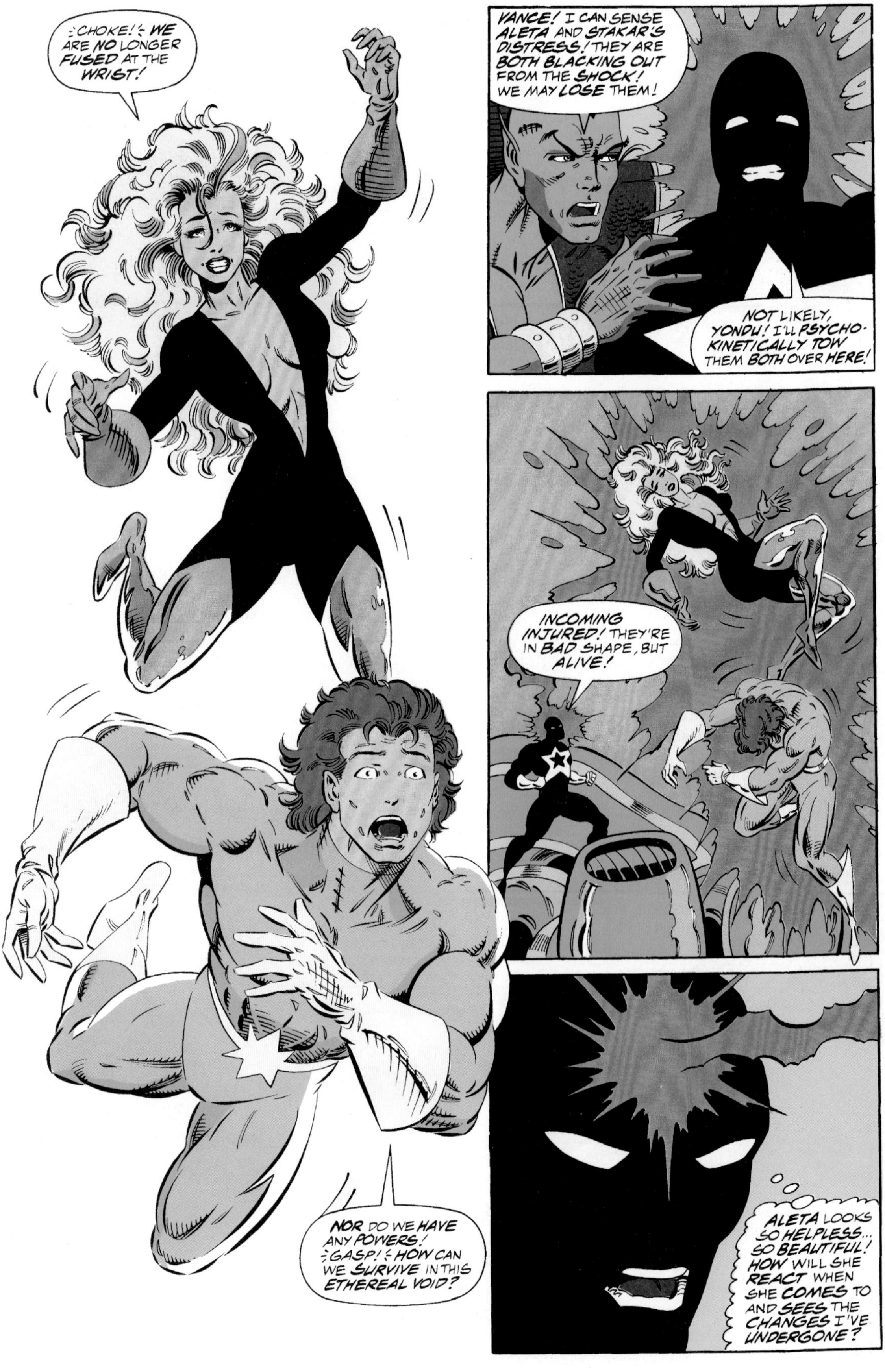
:CHOKE!: WE ARE NO LONGER FUSED AT THE WRIST!
VANCE! I CAN SENSE ALETA AND STAKAR'S DISTRESS! THEY ARE BOTH BLACKING OUT FROM THE SHOCK! WE MAY LOSE THEM!
NOT LIKELY, YONDU! I'LL PSYCHO-KINETICALLY TOW THEM BOTH OVER HERE!
INCOMING INJURED! THEY'RE IN BAD SHAPE, BUT ALIVE!
NOR DO WE HAVE ANY POWERS! :GASP!: HOW CAN WE SURVIVE IN THIS ETHEREAL VOID?
ALETA LOOKS SO HELPLESS... SO BEAUTIFUL! HOW WILL SHE REACT WHEN SHE COMES TO AND SEES THE CHANGES I'VE UNDERGONE?

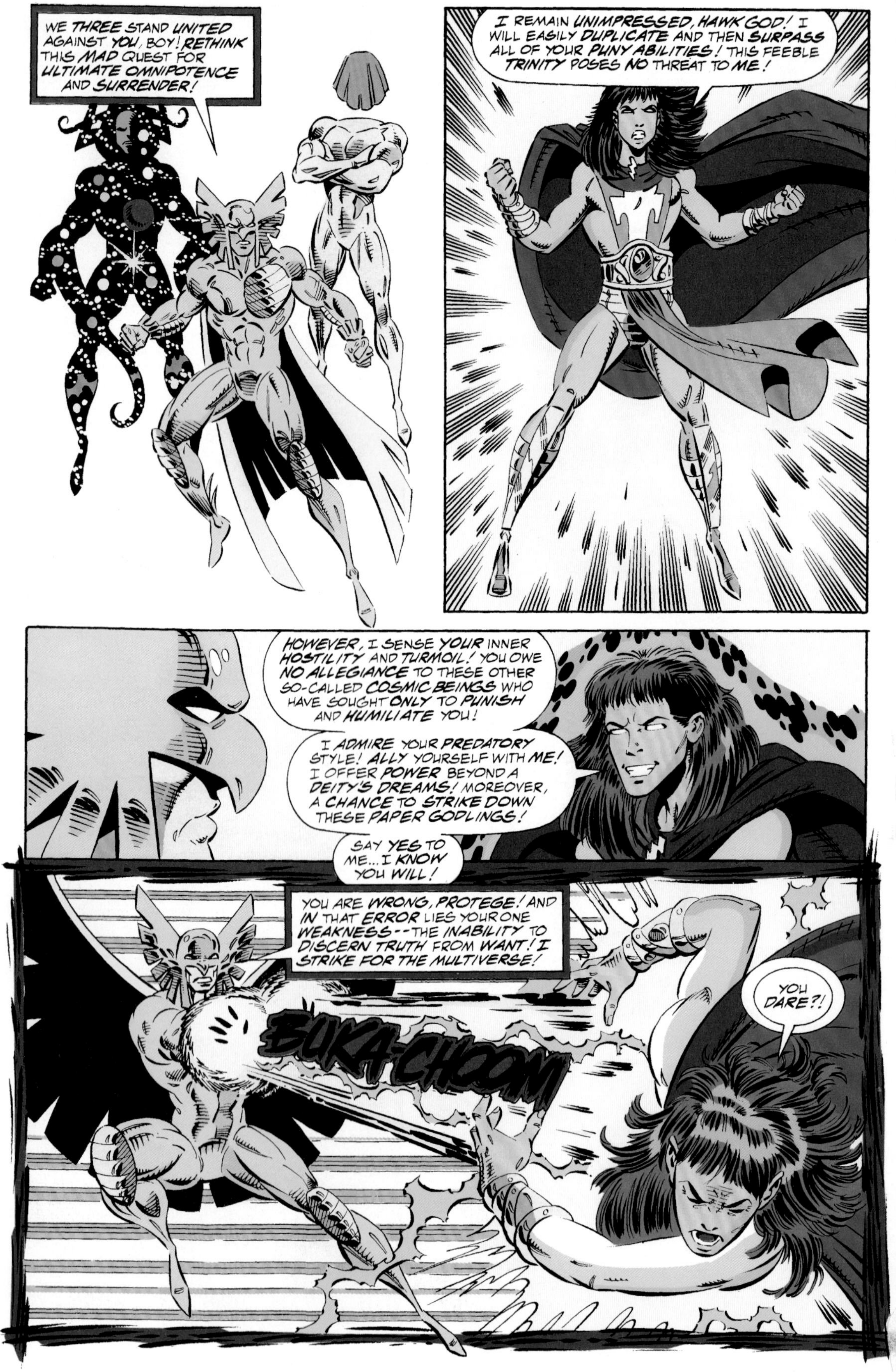

WE THREE STAND UNITED AGAINST YOU, BOY! RETHINK THIS MAD QUEST FOR ULTIMATE OMNIPOTENCE AND SURRENDER!
I REMAIN UNIMPRESSED, HAWK GOD! I WILL EASILY DUPLICATE AND THEN SURPASS ALL OF YOUR PUNY ABILITIES! THIS FEEBLE TRINITY POSES NO THREAT TO ME!
HOWEVER, I SENSE YOUR INNER HOSTILITY AND TURMOIL! YOU OWE NO ALLEGIANCE TO THESE OTHER SO-CALLED COSMIC BEINGS WHO HAVE SOUGHT ONLY TO PUNISH AND HUMILIATE YOU!
I ADMIRE YOUR PREDATORY STYLE! ALLY YOURSELF WITH ME! I OFFER POWER BEYOND A DEITY'S DREAMS! MOREOVER, A CHANCE TO STRIKE DOWN THESE PAPER GODLINGS!
SAY YES TO ME...I KNOW YOU WILL!
YOU ARE WRONG, PROTEGE! AND IN THAT ERROR LIES YOUR ONE WEAKNESS--THE INABILITY TO DISCERN TRUTH FROM WANT! I STRIKE FOR THE MULTIVERSE!
BUKA-CHOOOM
YOU DARE?!

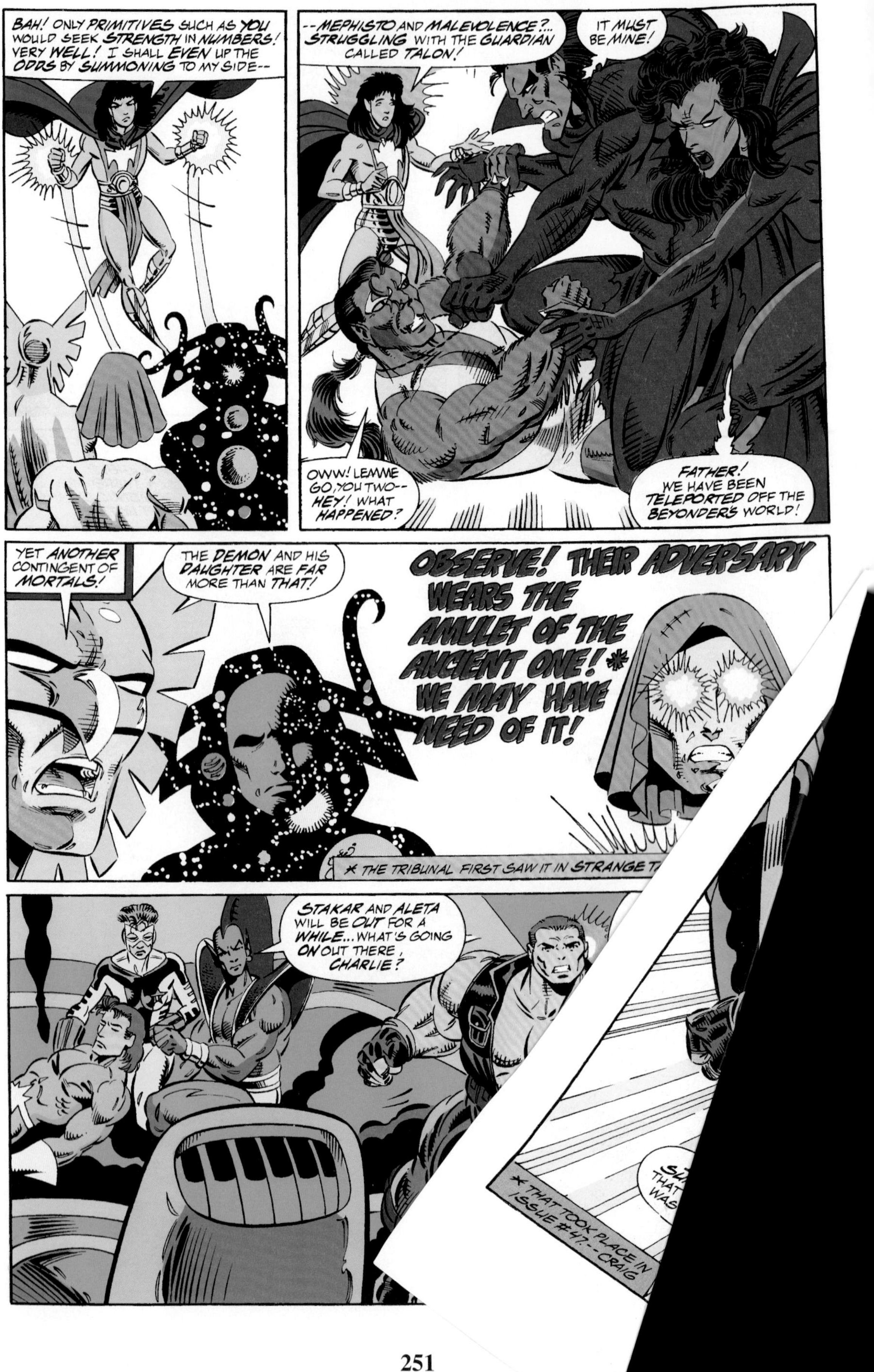
BAH! ONLY PRIMITIVES SUCH AS YOU WOULD SEEK STRENGTH IN NUMBERS! VERY WELL! I SHALL EVEN UP THE ODDS BY SUMMONING TO MY SIDE--
--MEPHISTO AND MALEVOLENCE?... STRUGGLING WITH THE GUARDIAN CALLED TALON!
IT MUST BE MINE!
OWW! LEMME GO, YOU TWO-- HEY! WHAT HAPPENED?
FATHER! WE HAVE BEEN TELEPORTED OFF THE BEYONDER'S WORLD!
YET ANOTHER CONTINGENT OF MORTALS!
THE DEMON AND HIS DAUGHTER ARE FAR MORE THAN THAT!
OBSERVE! THEIR ADVERSARY WEARS THE AMULET OF THE ANCIENT ONE!* WE MAY HAVE NEED OF IT!
* THE TRIBUNAL FIRST SAW IT IN STRANGE
STAKAR AND ALETA WILL BE OUT FOR A WHILE... WHAT'S GOING ON OUT THERE, CHARLIE?
* THAT TOOK PLACE IN ISSUE #47. -CRAIG

BY THE *RED SPOT!* I'M *SICK* AND *TIRED* OF *STANDING* ON THE *SIDELINES!* TALON *NEEDS* US AND WE *STAND* HERE LIKE *FLEAS* WATCHING A *DOGFIGHT!*

I ALSO GROW *WEARY* OF THIS *ONGOING SCENARIO!* WILL YOU *JOIN* ME, *GUARDIANS?*

WE WILL... *ASSIST* YOU, *BEYONDER!* GIVE US THE *SIZE* AND LET US GET *BUSY!*

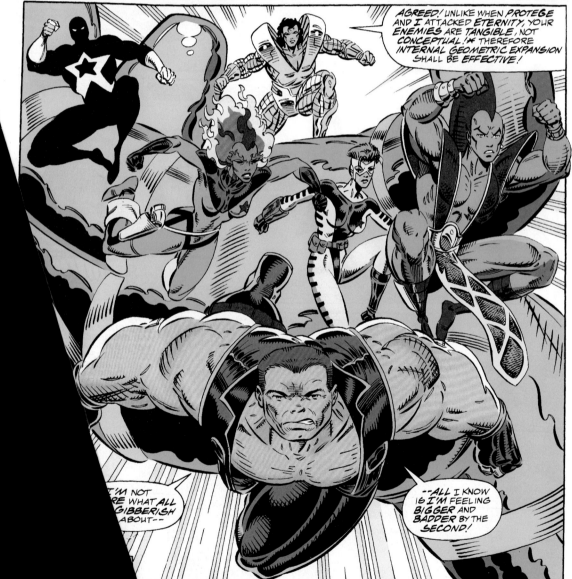

AGREED! UNLIKE WHEN *PROTÉGÉ* AND I ATTACKED *ETERNITY,* YOUR *ENEMIES* ARE TANGIBLE, NOT *CONCEPTUAL!* THEREFORE *INTERNAL GEOMETRIC EXPANSION* SHALL BE *EFFECTIVE!*

I'M NOT [SU]RE WHAT ALL [THE] GIBBERISH [IS] ABOUT--

--ALL I KNOW IS I'M FEELING *BIGGER* AND *BADDER* BY THE *SECOND!*

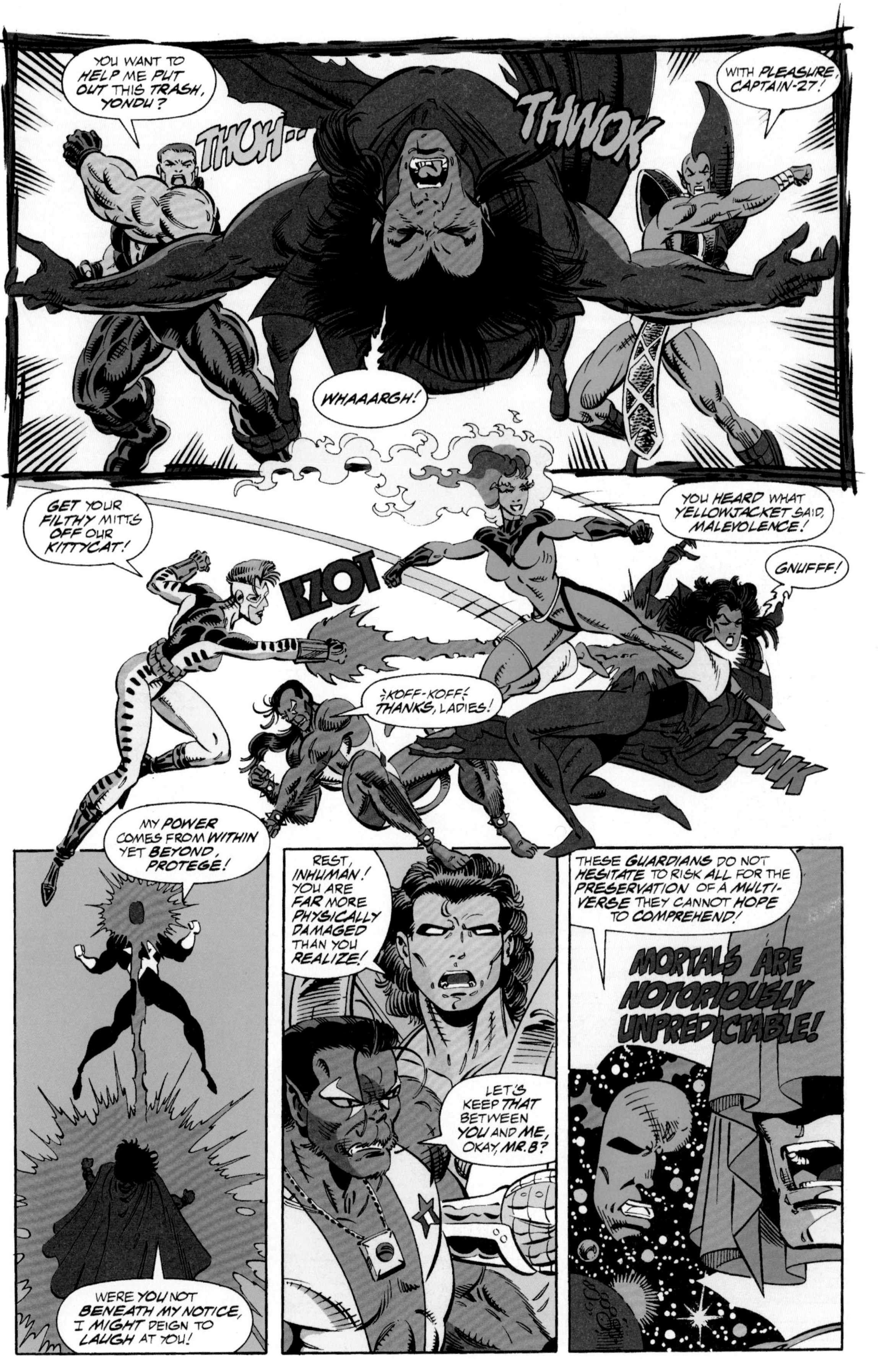

YOU WANT TO HELP ME PUT OUT THIS TRASH, YONDU?
THUH--
THWOK
WITH PLEASURE, CAPTAIN-27!
WHAAARGH!
GET YOUR FILTHY MITTS OFF OUR KITTYCAT!
YOU HEARD WHAT YELLOWJACKET SAID, MALEVOLENCE!
GNUFFF!
KZOT
-KOFF-KOFF- THANKS, LADIES!
FTUNK
MY POWER COMES FROM WITHIN YET BEYOND, PROTEGE!
WERE YOU NOT BENEATH MY NOTICE, I MIGHT DEIGN TO LAUGH AT YOU!
REST, INHUMAN! YOU ARE FAR MORE PHYSICALLY DAMAGED THAN YOU REALIZE!
LET'S KEEP THAT BETWEEN YOU AND ME, OKAY, MR. 8?
THESE GUARDIANS DO NOT HESITATE TO RISK ALL FOR THE PRESERVATION OF A MULTI-VERSE THEY CANNOT HOPE TO COMPREHEND!
MORTALS ARE NOTORIOUSLY UNPREDICTABLE!

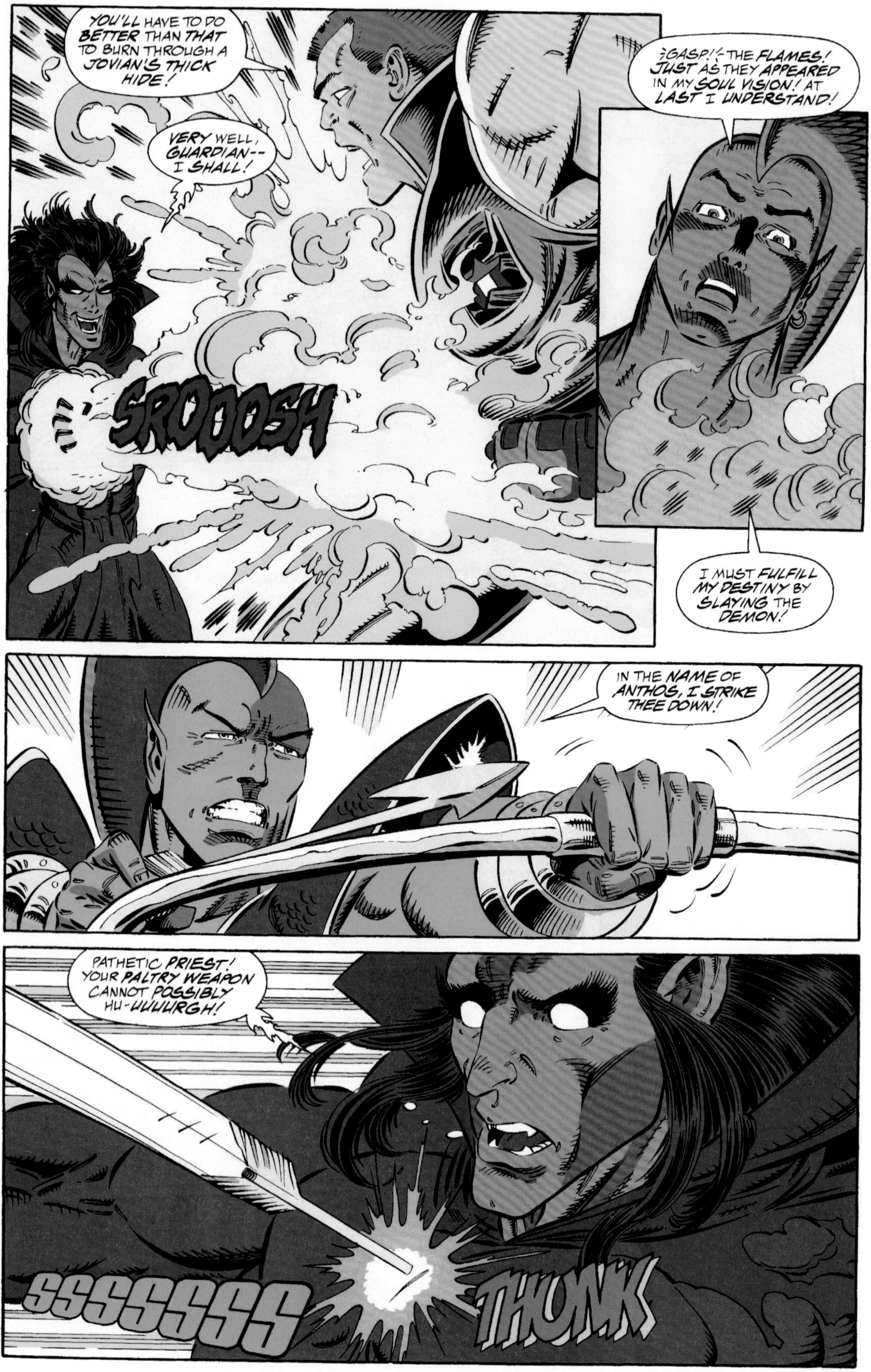
YOU'LL HAVE TO DO BETTER THAN THAT TO BURN THROUGH A JOVIAN'S THICK HIDE!
VERY WELL, GUARDIAN-- I SHALL!
SROOOSH
-GASP!- THE FLAMES! JUST AS THEY APPEARED IN MY SOUL VISION! AT LAST I UNDERSTAND!
I MUST FULFILL MY DESTINY BY SLAYING THE DEMON!
IN THE NAME OF ANTHOS, I STRIKE THEE DOWN!
PATHETIC PRIEST! YOUR PALTRY WEAPON CANNOT POSSIBLY HU-UUUURGH!
SSSSSSSS
THUNK

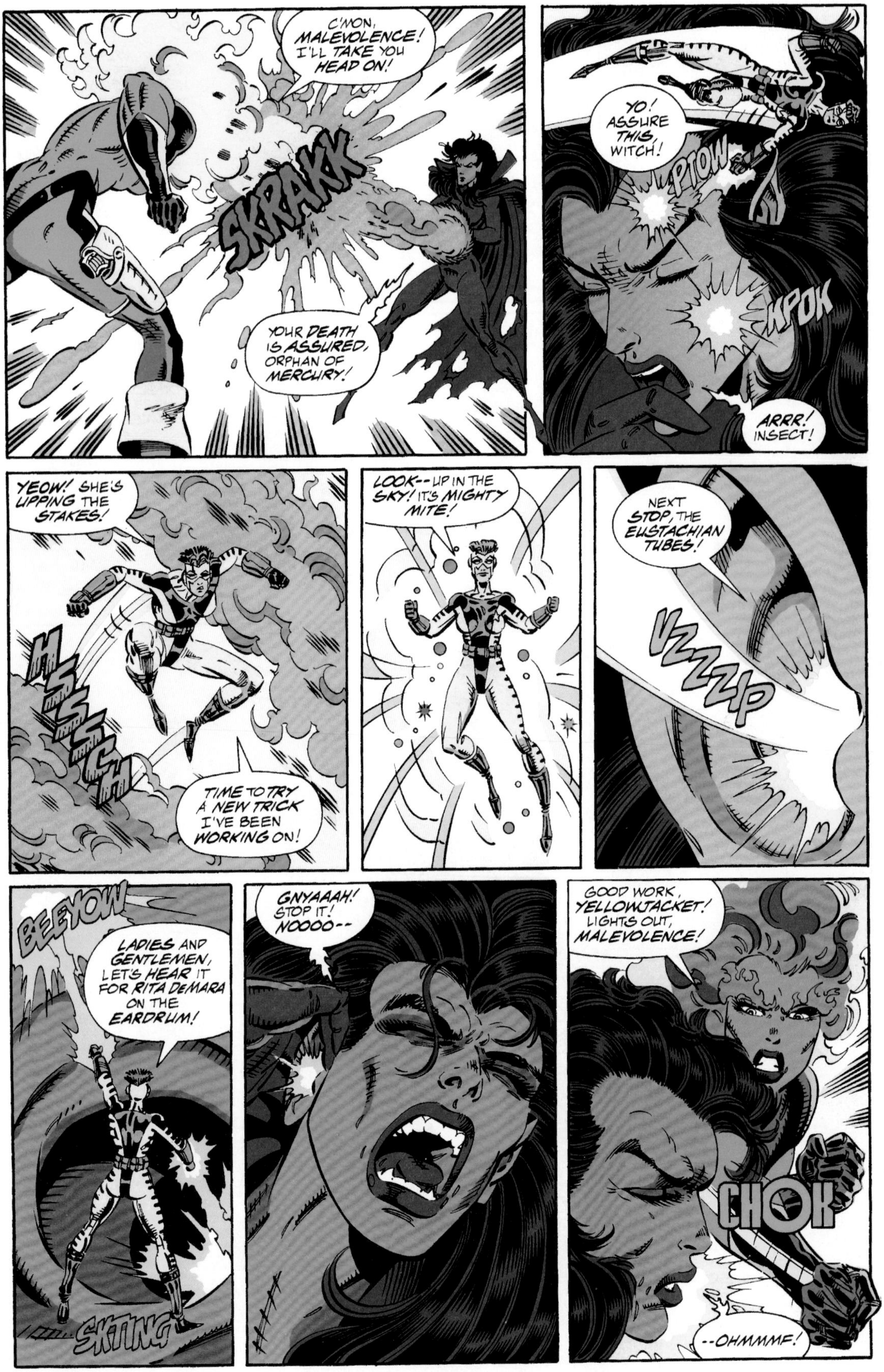
C'MON, MALEVOLENCE! I'LL TAKE YOU HEAD ON!
SKRAKK
YOUR DEATH IS ASSURED, ORPHAN OF MERCURY!
YO! ASSURE THIS, WITCH!
PTOW
KPOK
ARRR! INSECT!
YEOW! SHE'S UPPING THE STAKES!
HSSSCH
TIME TO TRY A NEW TRICK I'VE BEEN WORKING ON!
LOOK-- UP IN THE SKY! IT'S MIGHTY MITE!
NEXT STOP, THE EUSTACHIAN TUBES!
VZZZIP
BEEYOW
LADIES AND GENTLEMEN, LET'S HEAR IT FOR RITA DEMARA ON THE EARDRUM!
SKTING
GNYAAAH! STOP IT! NOOOO--
GOOD WORK, YELLOWJACKET! LIGHTS OUT, MALEVOLENCE!
CHOK
--OHMMMF!

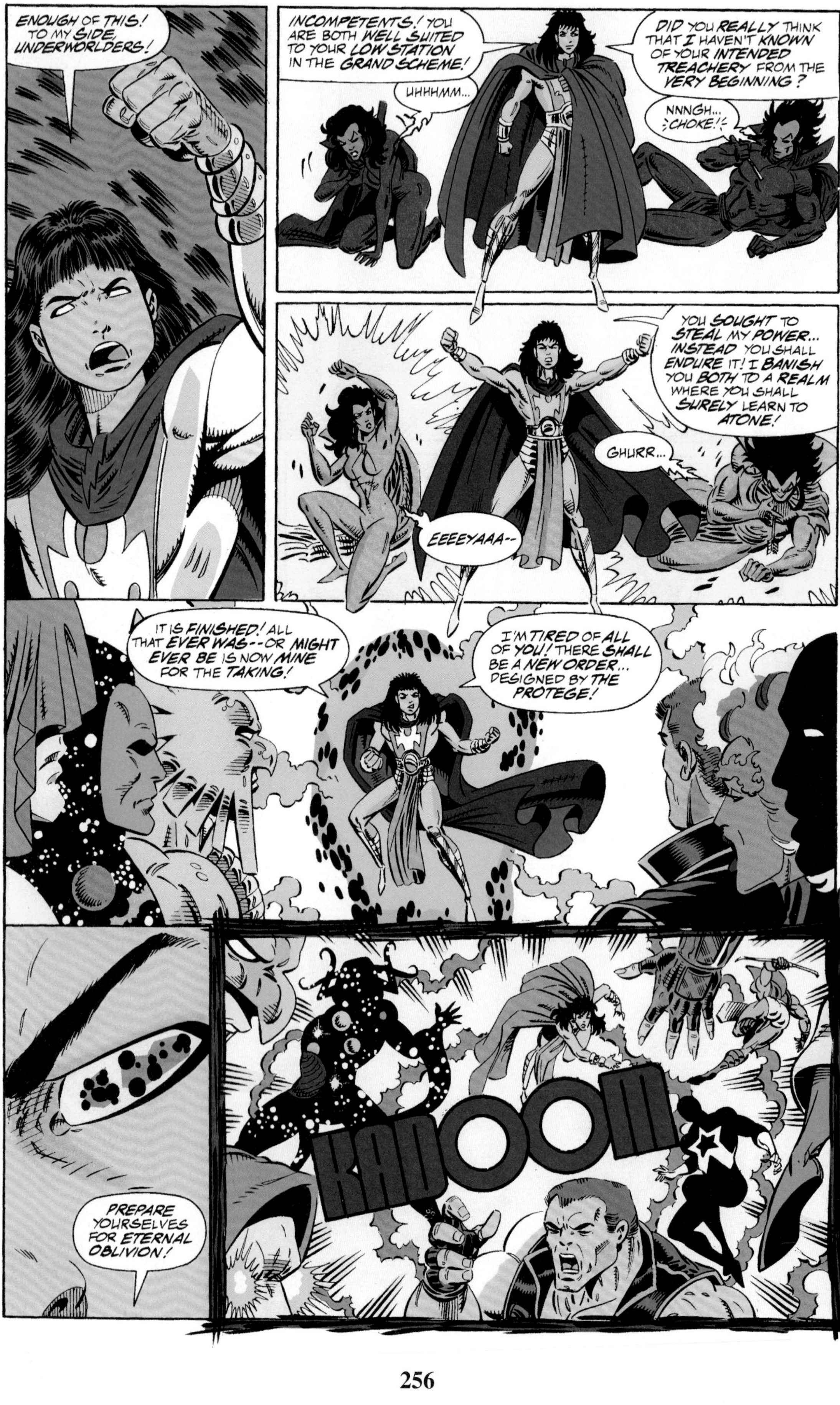
ENOUGH OF THIS! TO MY SIDE, UNDERWORLDERS!
INCOMPETENTS! YOU ARE BOTH WELL SUITED TO YOUR LOW STATION IN THE GRAND SCHEME!
DID YOU REALLY THINK THAT I HAVEN'T KNOWN OF YOUR INTENDED TREACHERY FROM THE VERY BEGINNING?
UHHHMM...
NNNGH... CHOKE!
YOU SOUGHT TO STEAL MY POWER... INSTEAD YOU SHALL ENDURE IT! I BANISH YOU BOTH TO A REALM WHERE YOU SHALL SURELY LEARN TO ATONE!
GHURR...
EEEEYAAA--
IT IS FINISHED! ALL THAT EVER WAS--OR MIGHT EVER BE IS NOW MINE FOR THE TAKING!
I'M TIRED OF ALL OF YOU! THERE SHALL BE A NEW ORDER... DESIGNED BY THE PROTEGE!
PREPARE YOURSELVES FOR ETERNAL OBLIVION!
KADOOOM

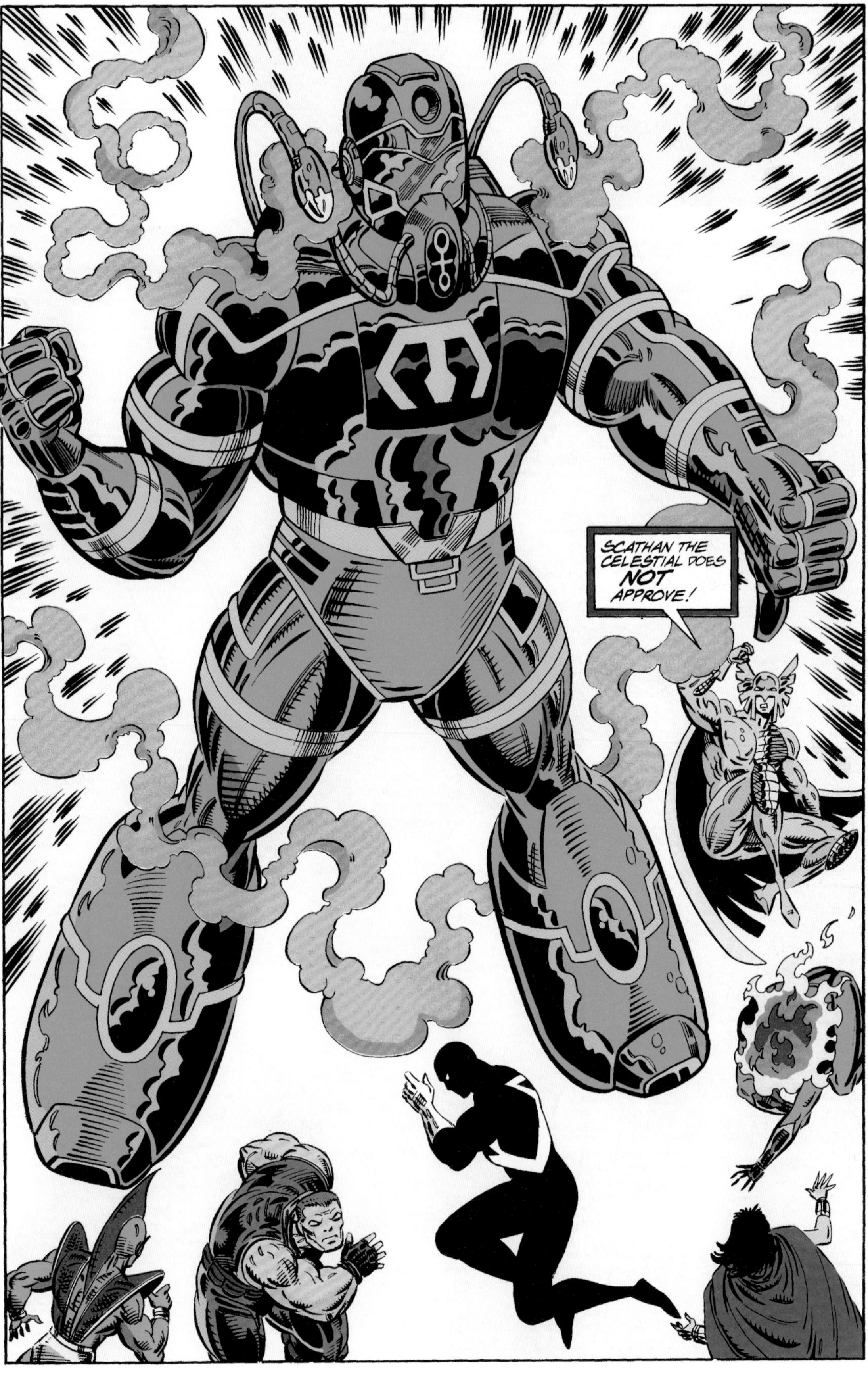
SCATHAN THE CELESTIAL DOES NOT APPROVE!

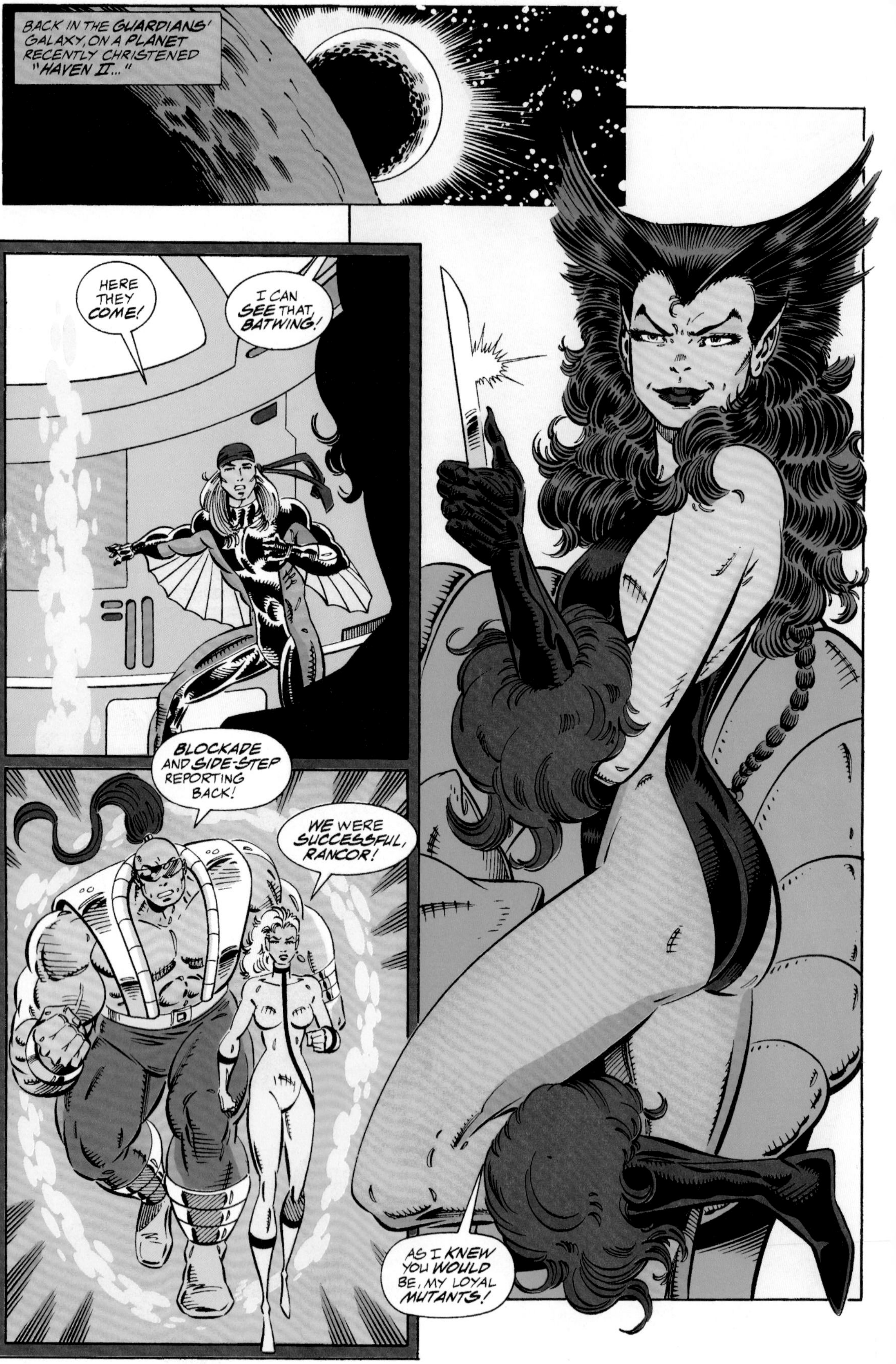
BACK IN THE GUARDIANS' GALAXY, ON A PLANET RECENTLY CHRISTENED "HAVEN II..."
HERE THEY COME!
I CAN SEE THAT, BATWING!
BLOCKADE AND SIDE-STEP REPORTING BACK!
WE WERE SUCCESSFUL, RANCOR!
AS I KNEW YOU WOULD BE, MY LOYAL MUTANTS!

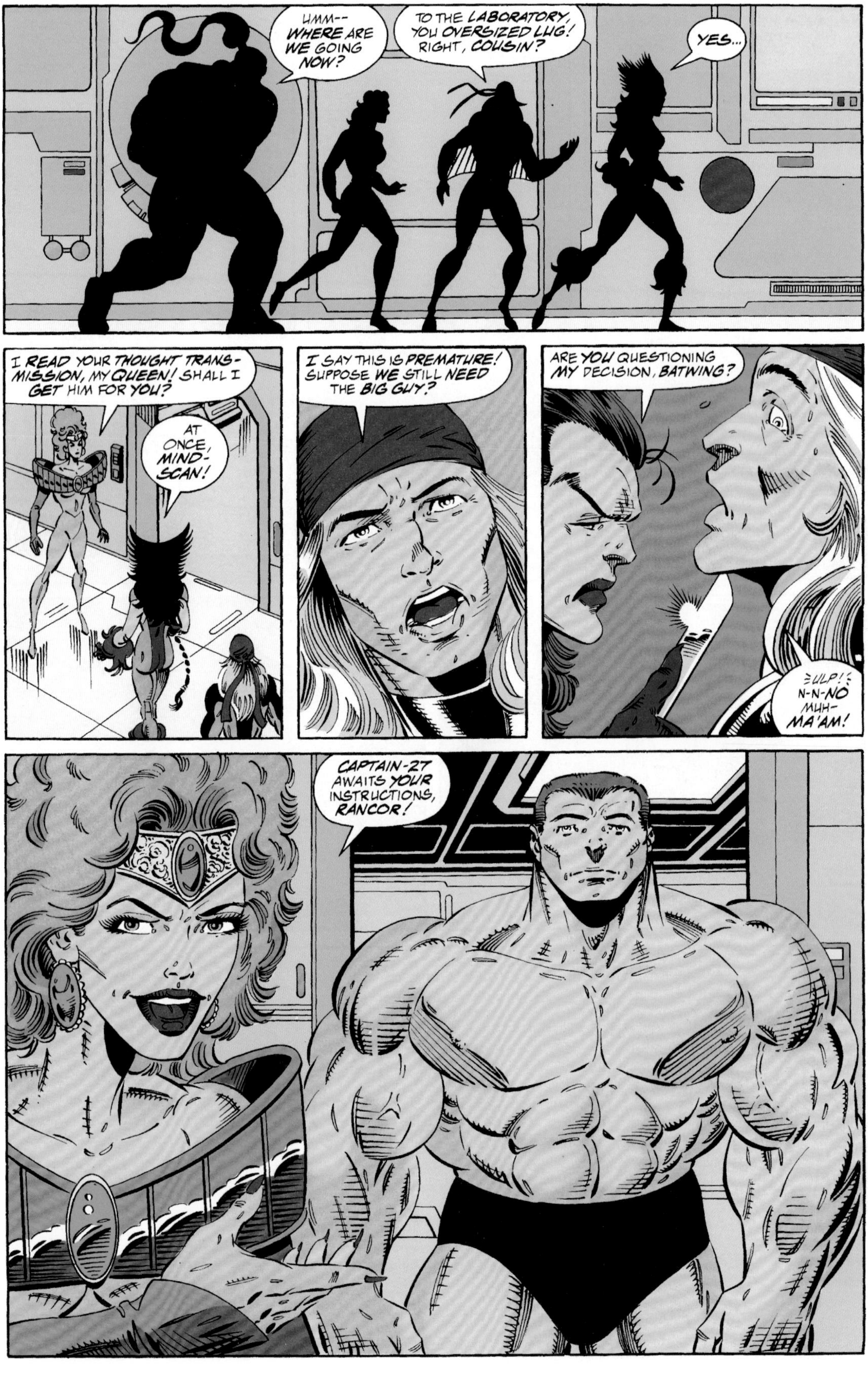
UMM-- WHERE ARE WE GOING NOW?
TO THE LABORATORY, YOU OVERSIZED LUG! RIGHT, COUSIN?
YES...
I READ YOUR THOUGHT TRANSMISSION, MY QUEEN! SHALL I GET HIM FOR YOU?
AT ONCE, MIND-SCAN!
I SAY THIS IS PREMATURE! SUPPOSE WE STILL NEED THE BIG GUY?
ARE YOU QUESTIONING MY DECISION, BATWING?
GULP! N-N-NO MUH-MA'AM!
CAPTAIN-27 AWAITS YOUR INSTRUCTIONS, RANCOR!

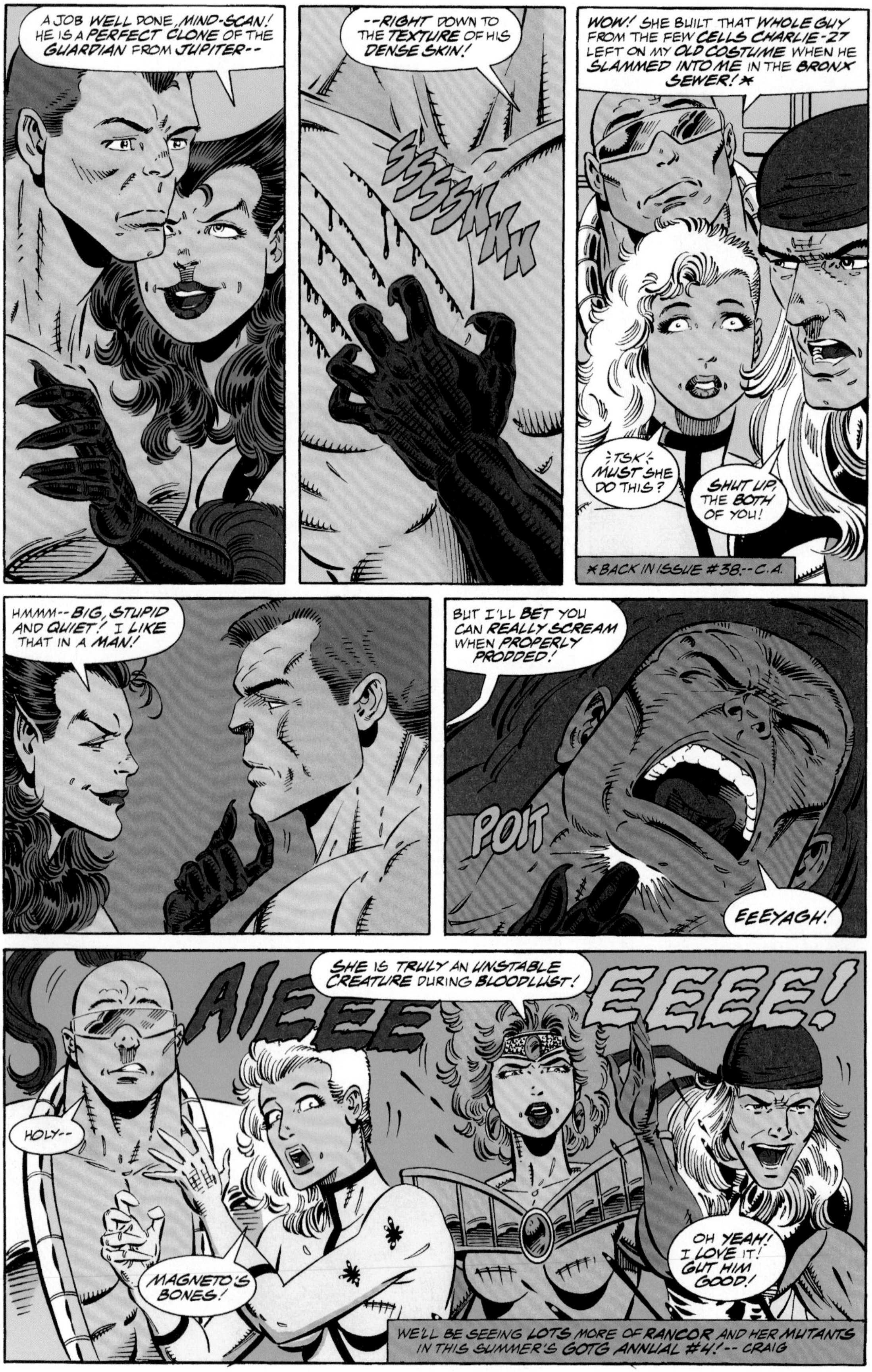
A JOB WELL DONE, MIND-SCAN! HE IS A PERFECT CLONE OF THE GUARDIAN FROM JUPITER--
--RIGHT DOWN TO THE TEXTURE OF HIS DENSE SKIN!
SSSSKKK
WOW! SHE BUILT THAT WHOLE GUY FROM THE FEW CELLS CHARLIE-27 LEFT ON MY OLD COSTUME WHEN HE SLAMMED INTO ME IN THE BRONX SEWER! *
TSK MUST SHE DO THIS?
SHUT UP, THE BOTH OF YOU!
* BACK IN ISSUE #38.-- C.A.
HMMM--BIG, STUPID AND QUIET! I LIKE THAT IN A MAN!
BUT I'LL BET YOU CAN REALLY SCREAM WHEN PROPERLY PRODDED!
POIT
EEEYAGH!
AIEEE
SHE IS TRULY AN UNSTABLE CREATURE DURING BLOODLUST!
EEEE!
HOLY--
MAGNETO'S BONES!
OH YEAH! I LOVE IT! GUT HIM GOOD!
WE'LL BE SEEING LOTS MORE OF RANCOR AND HER MUTANTS IN THIS SUMMER'S GOTG ANNUAL #4! -- CRAIG

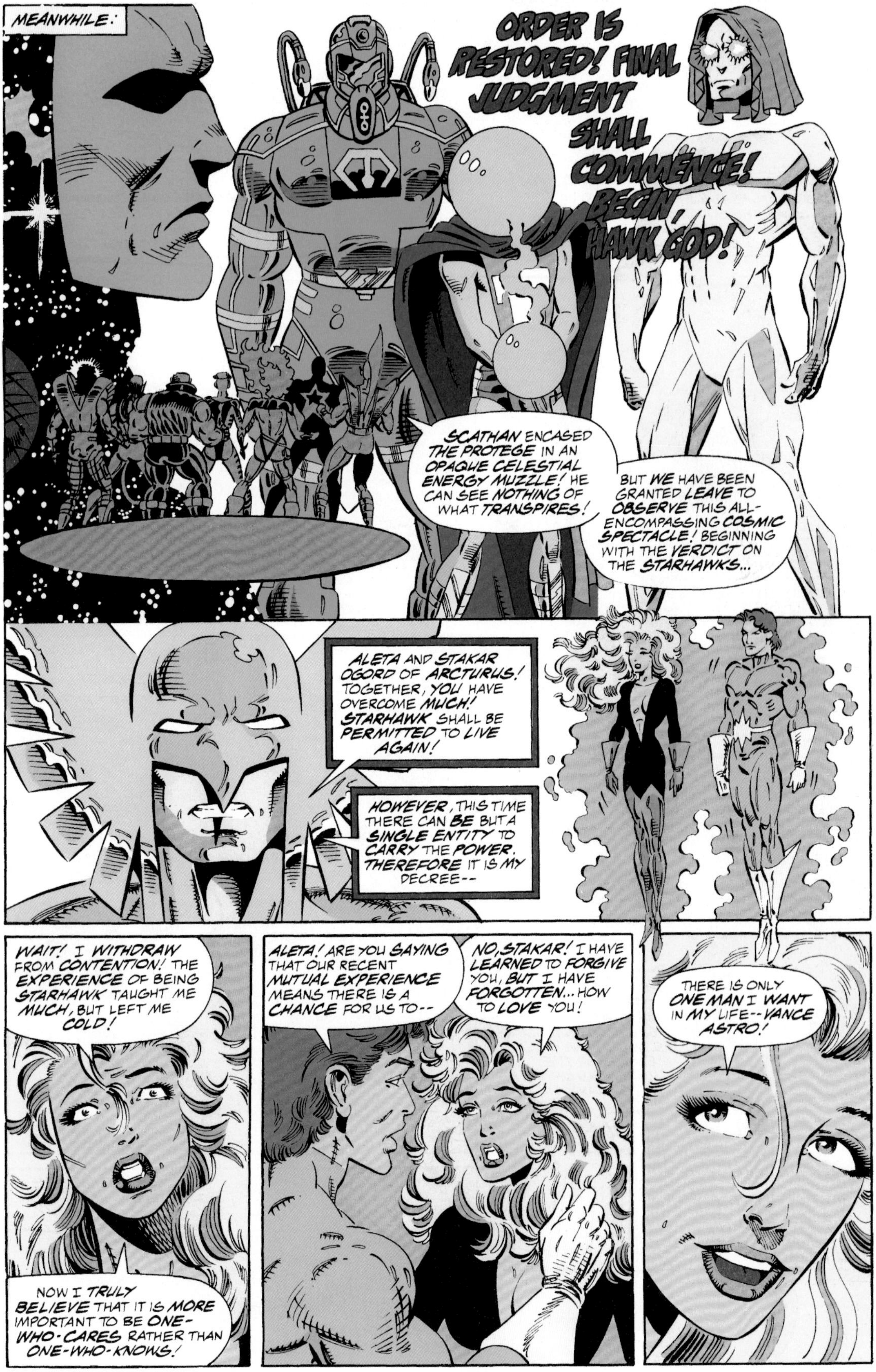
MEANWHILE:
ORDER IS RESTORED! FINAL JUDGMENT SHALL COMMENCE! BEGIN, HAWK GOD!
SCATHAN ENCASED THE PROTEGE IN AN OPAQUE CELESTIAL ENERGY MUZZLE! HE CAN SEE NOTHING OF WHAT TRANSPIRES!
BUT WE HAVE BEEN GRANTED LEAVE TO OBSERVE THIS ALL-ENCOMPASSING COSMIC SPECTACLE! BEGINNING WITH THE VERDICT ON THE STARHAWKS...
ALETA AND STAKAR OGORD OF ARCTURUS! TOGETHER, YOU HAVE OVERCOME MUCH! STARHAWK SHALL BE PERMITTED TO LIVE AGAIN!
HOWEVER, THIS TIME THERE CAN BE BUT A SINGLE ENTITY TO CARRY THE POWER. THEREFORE IT IS MY DECREE--
WAIT! I WITHDRAW FROM CONTENTION! THE EXPERIENCE OF BEING STARHAWK TAUGHT ME MUCH, BUT LEFT ME COLD!
NOW I TRULY BELIEVE THAT IT IS MORE IMPORTANT TO BE ONE-WHO-CARES RATHER THAN ONE-WHO-KNOWS!
ALETA! ARE YOU SAYING THAT OUR RECENT MUTUAL EXPERIENCE MEANS THERE IS A CHANCE FOR US TO--
NO, STAKAR! I HAVE LEARNED TO FORGIVE YOU, BUT I HAVE FORGOTTEN... HOW TO LOVE YOU!
THERE IS ONLY ONE MAN I WANT IN MY LIFE--VANCE ASTRO!

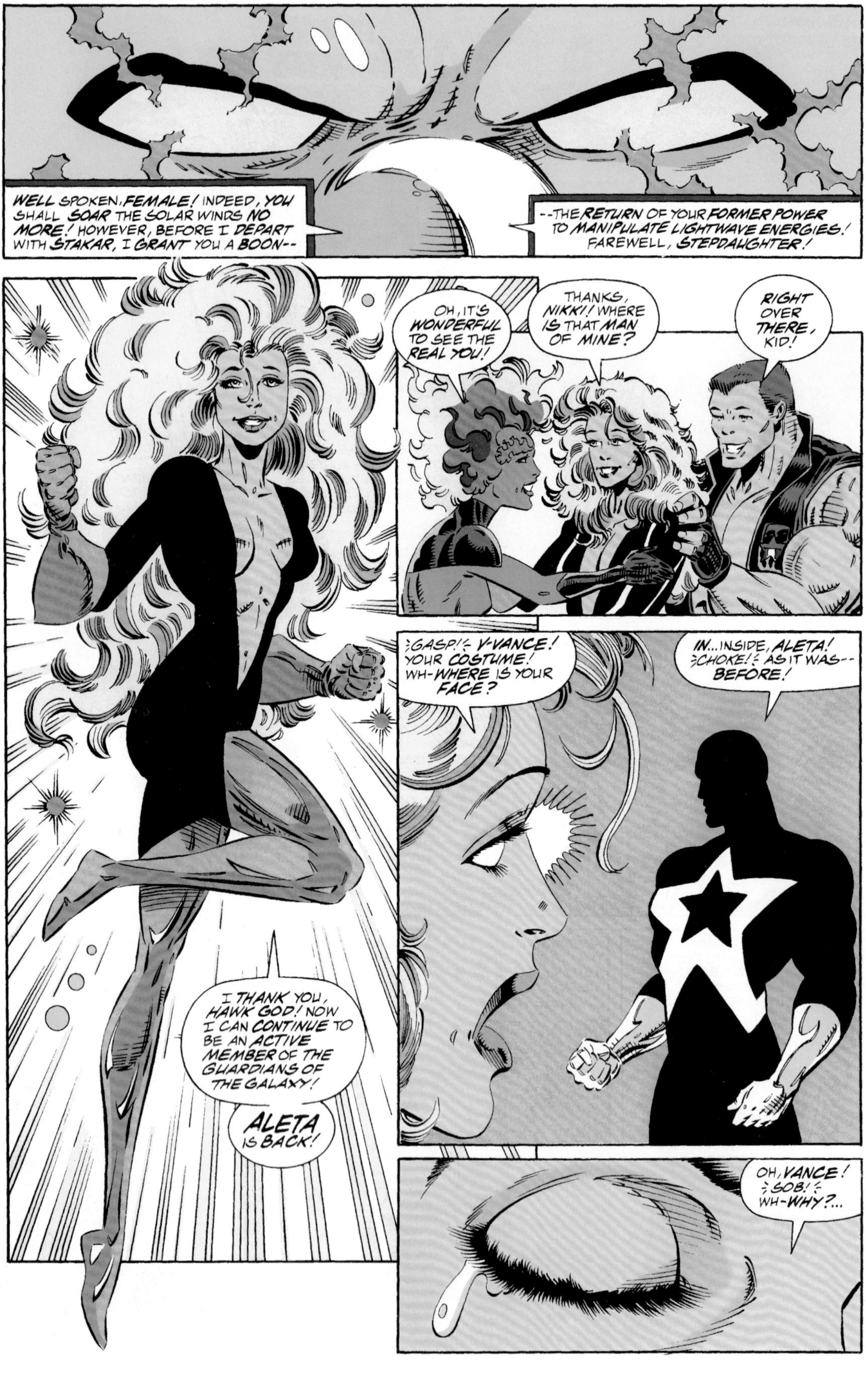
WELL SPOKEN, FEMALE! INDEED, YOU SHALL SOAR THE SOLAR WINDS NO MORE! HOWEVER, BEFORE I DEPART WITH STAKAR, I GRANT YOU A BOON--
--THE RETURN OF YOUR FORMER POWER TO MANIPULATE LIGHTWAVE ENERGIES! FAREWELL, STEPDAUGHTER!
I THANK YOU, HAWK GOD! NOW I CAN CONTINUE TO BE AN ACTIVE MEMBER OF THE GUARDIANS OF THE GALAXY!
ALETA IS BACK!
OH, IT'S WONDERFUL TO SEE THE REAL YOU!
THANKS, NIKKI! WHERE IS THAT MAN OF MINE?
RIGHT OVER THERE, KID!
:GASP!: V-VANCE! YOUR COSTUME! WH-WHERE IS YOUR FACE?
IN... INSIDE, ALETA! :CHOKE!: AS IT WAS--BEFORE!
OH, VANCE! :SOB!: WH-WHY?...

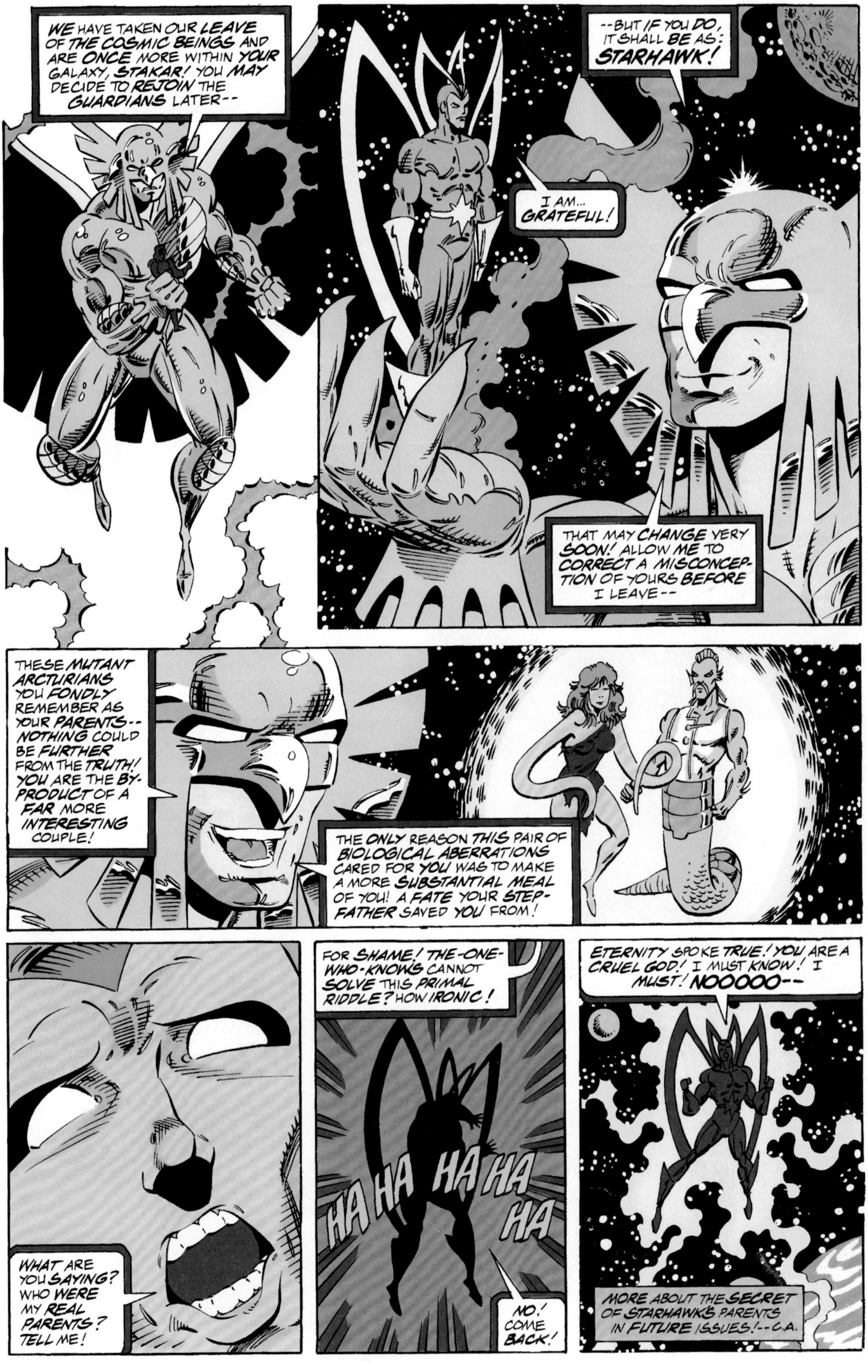
WE HAVE TAKEN OUR LEAVE OF THE COSMIC BEINGS AND ARE ONCE MORE WITHIN YOUR GALAXY, STAKAR! YOU MAY DECIDE TO REJOIN THE GUARDIANS LATER--
--BUT IF YOU DO, IT SHALL BE AS: STARHAWK!
I AM... GRATEFUL!
THAT MAY CHANGE VERY SOON! ALLOW ME TO CORRECT A MISCONCEPTION OF YOURS BEFORE I LEAVE--
THESE MUTANT ARCTURIANS YOU FONDLY REMEMBER AS YOUR PARENTS-- NOTHING COULD BE FURTHER FROM THE TRUTH! YOU ARE THE BY-PRODUCT OF A FAR MORE INTERESTING COUPLE!
THE ONLY REASON THIS PAIR OF BIOLOGICAL ABERRATIONS CARED FOR YOU WAS TO MAKE A MORE SUBSTANTIAL MEAL OF YOU! A FATE YOUR STEP-FATHER SAVED YOU FROM!
WHAT ARE YOU SAYING? WHO WERE MY REAL PARENTS? TELL ME!
FOR SHAME! THE-ONE-WHO-KNOWS CANNOT SOLVE THIS PRIMAL RIDDLE? HOW IRONIC!
HA HA HA HA HA HA
NO! COME BACK!
ETERNITY SPOKE TRUE! YOU ARE A CRUEL GOD! I MUST KNOW! I MUST! NOOOOO--
MORE ABOUT THE SECRET OF STARHAWK'S PARENTS IN FUTURE ISSUES!--C.A.

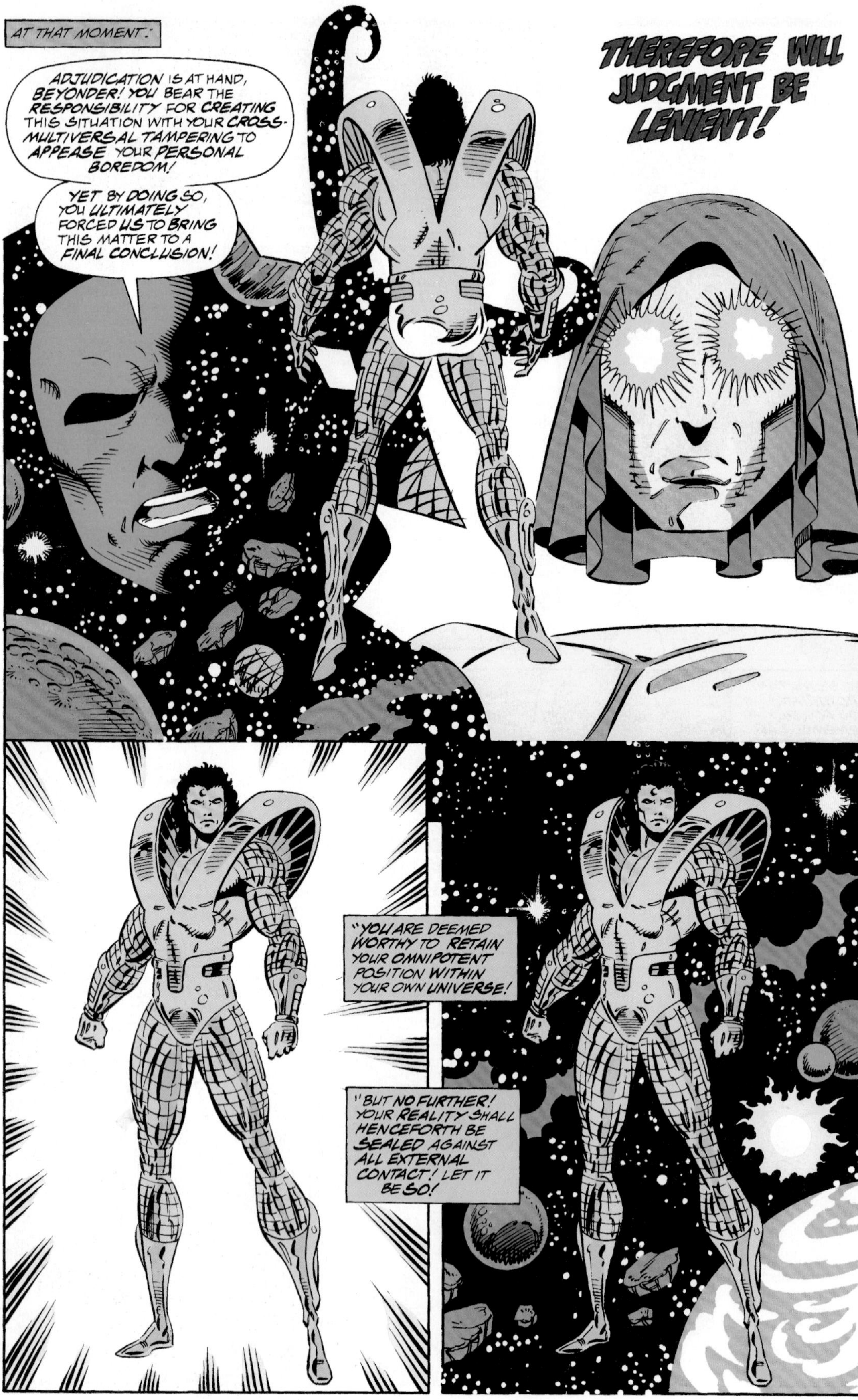
AT THAT MOMENT:
ADJUDICATION IS AT HAND, BEYONDER! YOU BEAR THE RESPONSIBILITY FOR CREATING THIS SITUATION WITH YOUR CROSS-MULTIVERSAL TAMPERING TO APPEASE YOUR PERSONAL BOREDOM!
YET BY DOING SO, YOU ULTIMATELY FORCED US TO BRING THIS MATTER TO A FINAL CONCLUSION!
THEREFORE WILL JUDGMENT BE LENIENT!
"YOU ARE DEEMED WORTHY TO RETAIN YOUR OMNIPOTENT POSITION WITHIN YOUR OWN UNIVERSE!
"BUT NO FURTHER! YOUR REALITY SHALL HENCEFORTH BE SEALED AGAINST ALL EXTERNAL CONTACT! LET IT BE SO!

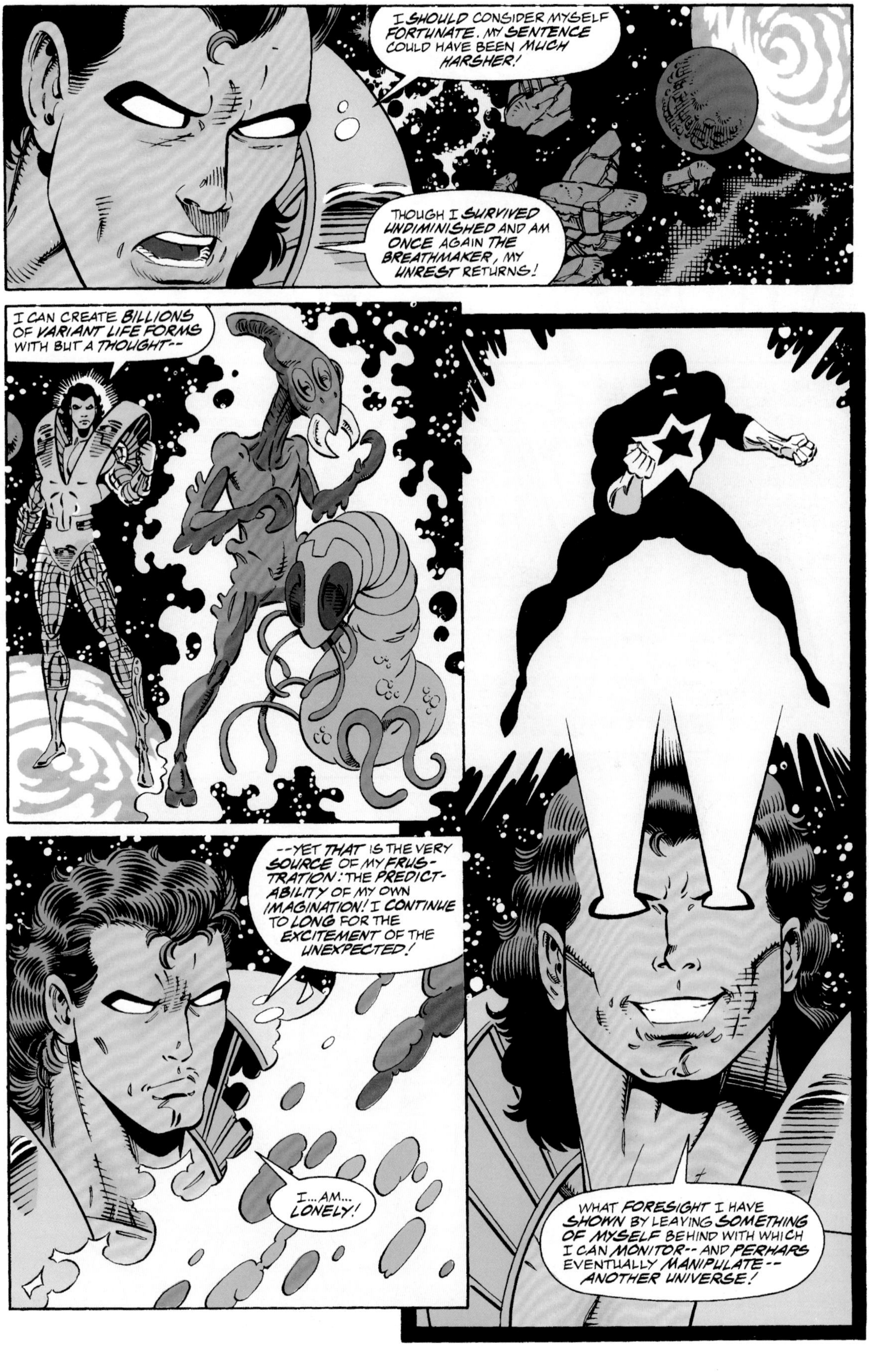
I SHOULD CONSIDER MYSELF FORTUNATE. MY SENTENCE COULD HAVE BEEN MUCH HARSHER!
THOUGH I SURVIVED UNDIMINISHED AND AM ONCE AGAIN THE BREATHMAKER, MY UNREST RETURNS!
I CAN CREATE BILLIONS OF VARIANT LIFE FORMS WITH BUT A THOUGHT--
--YET THAT IS THE VERY SOURCE OF MY FRUSTRATION: THE PREDICTABILITY OF MY OWN IMAGINATION! I CONTINUE TO LONG FOR THE EXCITEMENT OF THE UNEXPECTED!
I...AM... LONELY!
WHAT FORESIGHT I HAVE SHOWN BY LEAVING SOMETHING OF MYSELF BEHIND WITH WHICH I CAN MONITOR-- AND PERHAPS EVENTUALLY MANIPULATE-- ANOTHER UNIVERSE!

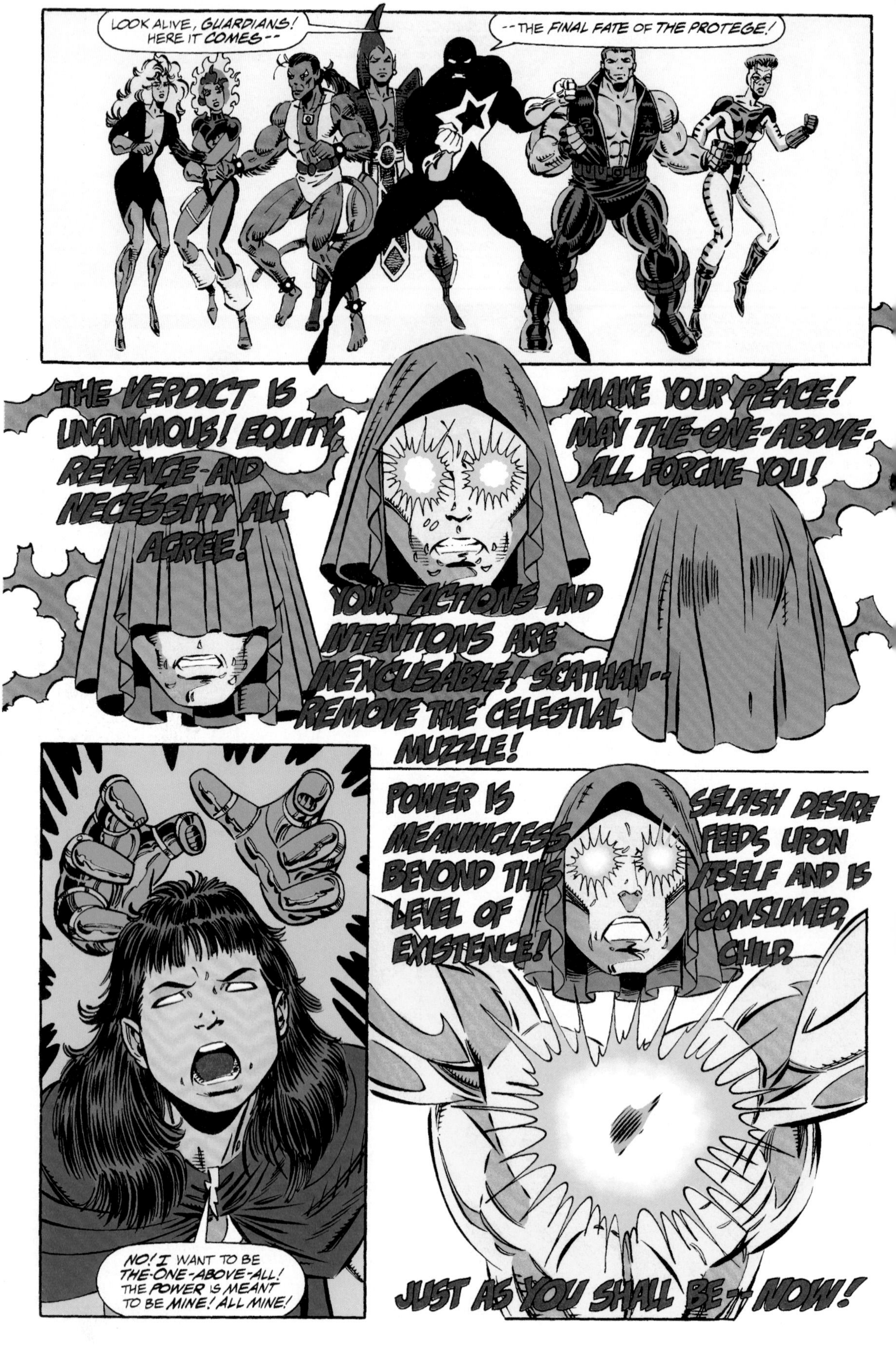
LOOK ALIVE, GUARDIANS! HERE IT COMES--
--THE FINAL FATE OF THE PROTEGE!
THE VERDICT IS UNANIMOUS! EQUITY, REVENGE--AND NECESSITY ALL AGREE!
MAKE YOUR PEACE! MAY THE-ONE-ABOVE-ALL FORGIVE YOU!
YOUR ACTIONS AND INTENTIONS ARE INEXCUSABLE! SCATHAN--REMOVE THE CELESTIAL MUZZLE!
NO! I WANT TO BE THE-ONE-ABOVE-ALL! THE POWER IS MEANT TO BE MINE! ALL MINE!
POWER IS MEANINGLESS BEYOND THIS LEVEL OF EXISTENCE!
SELFISH DESIRE FEEDS UPON ITSELF AND IS CONSUMED, CHILD.
JUST AS YOU SHALL BE--NOW!

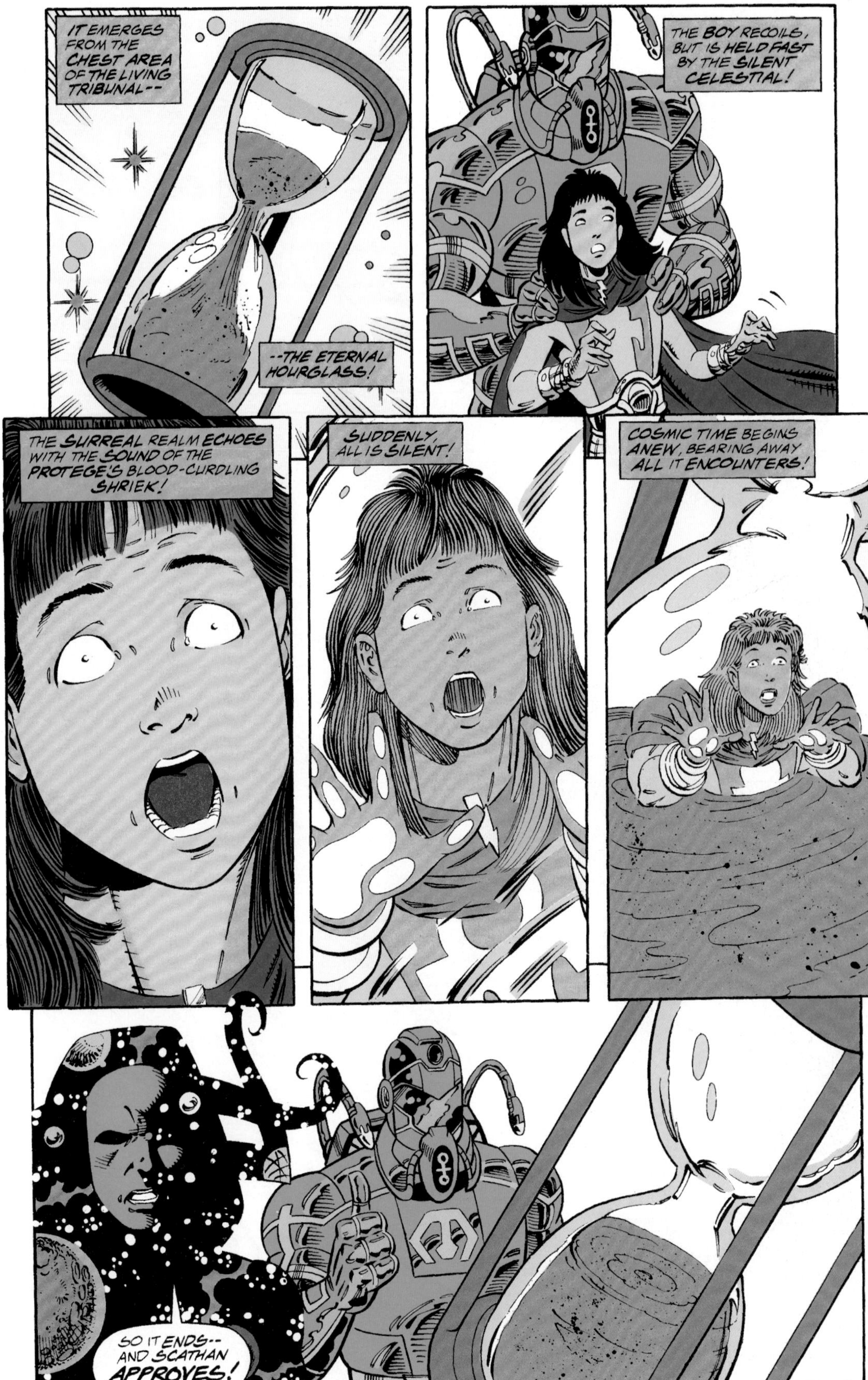
IT EMERGES FROM THE CHEST AREA OF THE LIVING TRIBUNAL--
--THE ETERNAL HOURGLASS!
THE BOY RECOILS, BUT IS HELD FAST BY THE SILENT CELESTIAL!
THE SURREAL REALM ECHOES WITH THE SOUND OF THE PROTEGE'S BLOOD-CURDLING SHRIEK!
SUDDENLY, ALL IS SILENT!
COSMIC TIME BEGINS ANEW, BEARING AWAY ALL IT ENCOUNTERS!
SO IT ENDS-- AND SCATHAN APPROVES!

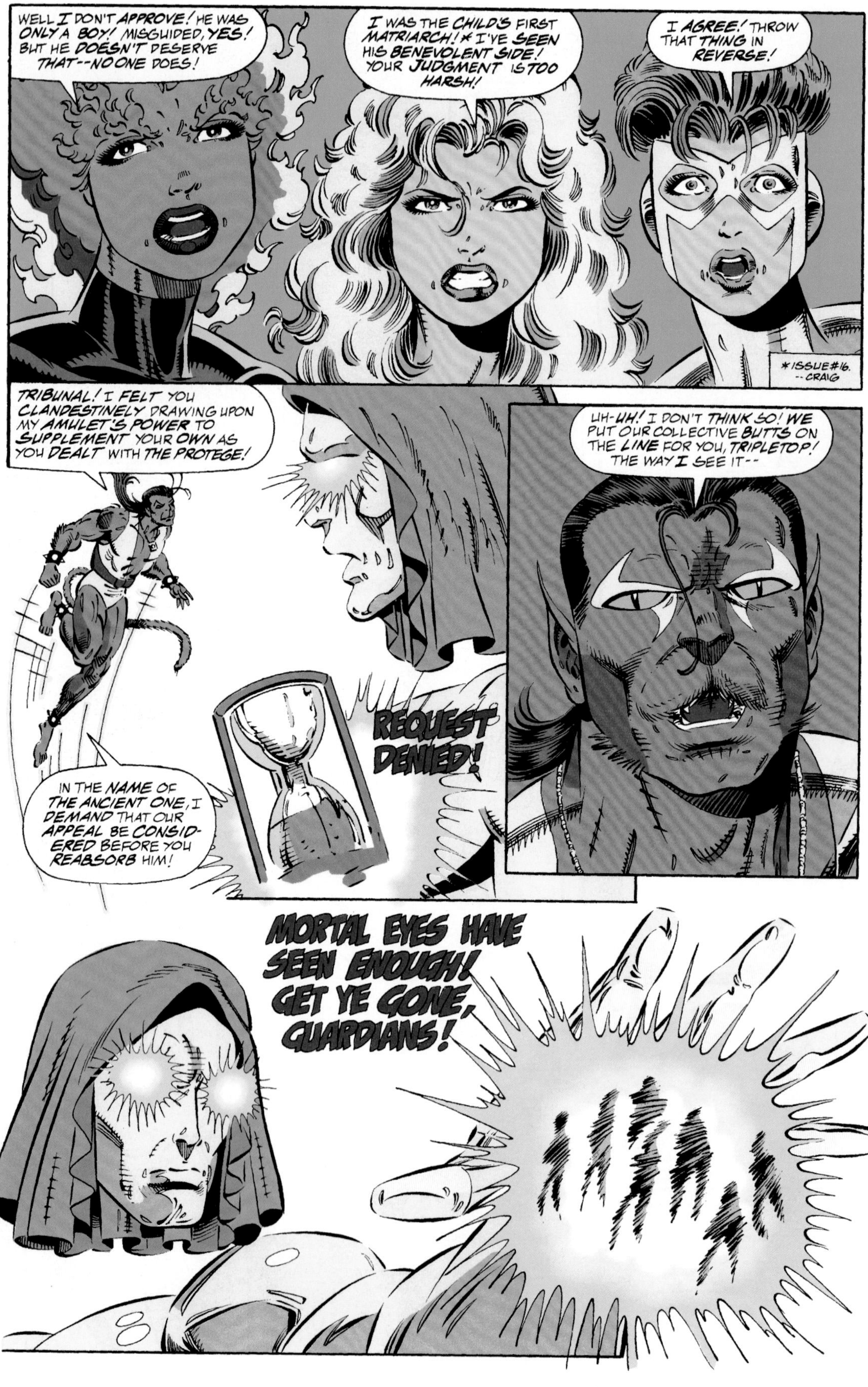
WELL I DON'T APPROVE! HE WAS ONLY A BOY! MISGUIDED, YES! BUT HE DOESN'T DESERVE THAT--NO ONE DOES!
I WAS THE CHILD'S FIRST MATRIARCH! * I'VE SEEN HIS BENEVOLENT SIDE! YOUR JUDGMENT IS TOO HARSH!
I AGREE! THROW THAT THING IN REVERSE!
* ISSUE #16. --CRAIG
TRIBUNAL! I FELT YOU CLANDESTINELY DRAWING UPON MY AMULET'S POWER TO SUPPLEMENT YOUR OWN AS YOU DEALT WITH THE PROTEGE!
UH-UH! I DON'T THINK SO! WE PUT OUR COLLECTIVE BUTTS ON THE LINE FOR YOU, TRIPLETOP! THE WAY I SEE IT--
IN THE NAME OF THE ANCIENT ONE, I DEMAND THAT OUR APPEAL BE CONSIDERED BEFORE YOU REABSORB HIM!
REQUEST DENIED!
MORTAL EYES HAVE SEEN ENOUGH! GET YE GONE, GUARDIANS!

INSTANTANEOUSLY:

HARKOV'S *ASHES!* WE'RE *BACK* ON BOARD *ICARUS!*

JUST LIKE *THAT!* THOSE *STAND-UP COSMICS* DON'T BELIEVE IN *LONG GOODBYES!*

BE *GRATEFUL* THAT *THEY* HAVE *ALLOWED* US TO *RETAIN* THE *MEMORY* OF WHAT WE WERE *PRIVILEGED* TO *OBSERVE!*

CHUNKY...THAT *WHOLE* EXPERIENCE *CREEPED ME OUT!*

ME *TOO,NICHOLETTE!* THE *SOONER* WE GET *BACK* TO *GUARDING* OUR *LITTLE GALAXY,* THE *BETTER!*

AGREED, CAPTAIN-27! AND THE *FIRST* ORDER OF *BUSINESS* IS TO *DETERMINE* WHETHER WE ARE A *TEAM* OF *SIX* OR *SEVEN* MEMBERS.

HOW *ABOUT* IT, *YONDU?*

I HAVE *MADE* MY *DECISION,* MAJOR *ASTRO*--

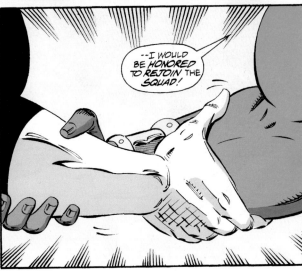

--I WOULD BE *HONORED* TO *REJOIN* THE *SQUAD!*

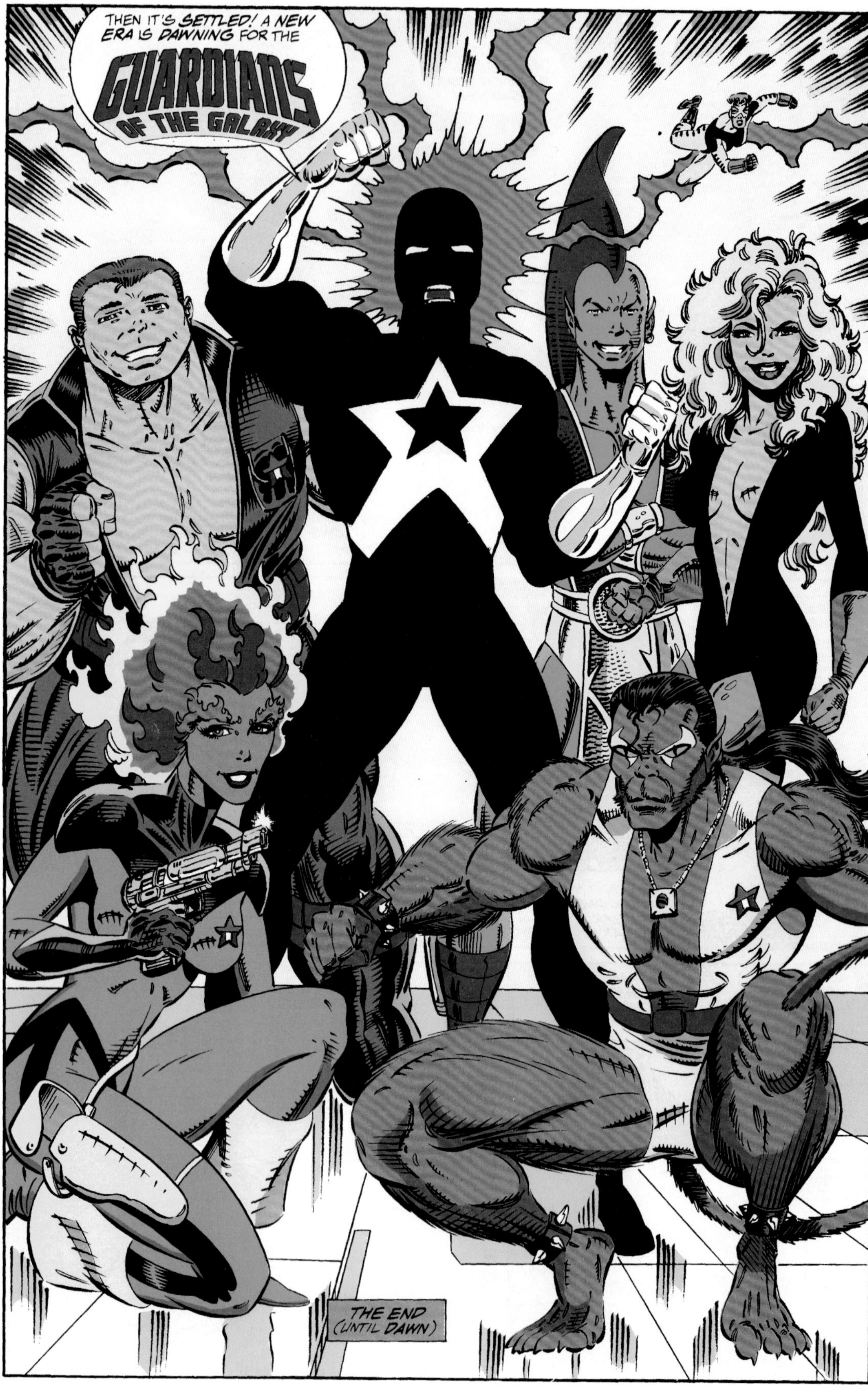
THEN IT'S SETTLED! A NEW ERA IS DAWNING FOR THE GUARDIANS OF THE GALAXY
THE END (UNTIL DAWN)

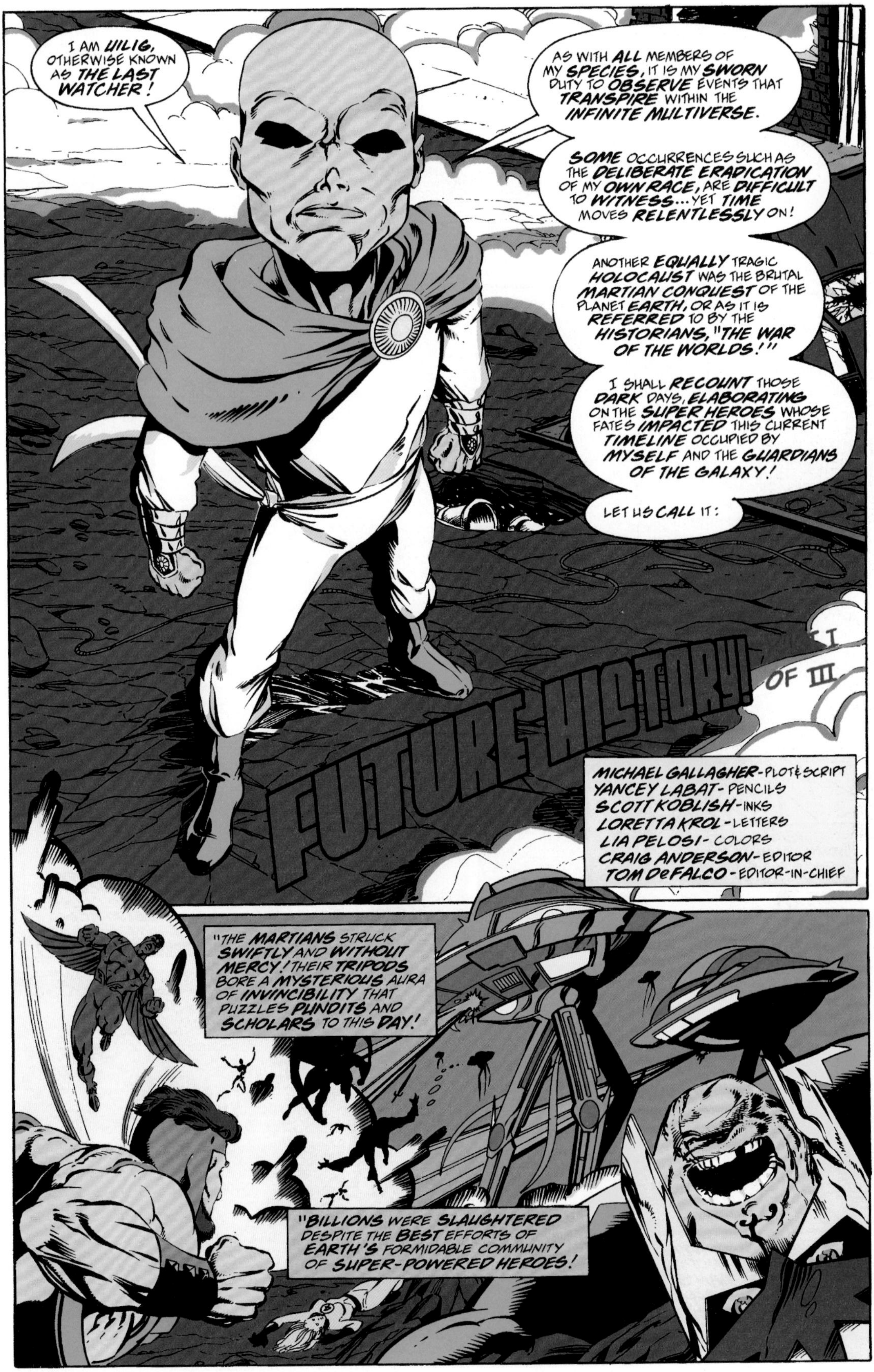
I AM UILIG, OTHERWISE KNOWN AS THE LAST WATCHER!
AS WITH ALL MEMBERS OF MY SPECIES, IT IS MY SWORN DUTY TO OBSERVE EVENTS THAT TRANSPIRE WITHIN THE INFINITE MULTIVERSE.
SOME OCCURRENCES SUCH AS THE DELIBERATE ERADICATION OF MY OWN RACE, ARE DIFFICULT TO WITNESS... YET TIME MOVES RELENTLESSLY ON!
ANOTHER EQUALLY TRAGIC HOLOCAUST WAS THE BRUTAL MARTIAN CONQUEST OF THE PLANET EARTH, OR AS IT IS REFERRED TO BY THE HISTORIANS, "THE WAR OF THE WORLDS!"
I SHALL RECOUNT THOSE DARK DAYS, ELABORATING ON THE SUPER HEROES WHOSE FATES IMPACTED THIS CURRENT TIMELINE OCCUPIED BY MYSELF AND THE GUARDIANS OF THE GALAXY!
LET US CALL IT:
FUTURE-HISTORY!
I OF III
MICHAEL GALLAGHER - PLOT & SCRIPT
YANCEY LABAT - PENCILS
SCOTT KOBLISH - INKS
LORETTA KROL - LETTERS
LIA PELOSI - COLORS
CRAIG ANDERSON - EDITOR
TOM DeFALCO - EDITOR-IN-CHIEF
"THE MARTIANS STRUCK SWIFTLY AND WITHOUT MERCY! THEIR TRIPODS BORE A MYSTERIOUS AURA OF INVINCIBILITY THAT PUZZLES PUNDITS AND SCHOLARS TO THIS DAY!
"BILLIONS WERE SLAUGHTERED DESPITE THE BEST EFFORTS OF EARTH'S FORMIDABLE COMMUNITY OF SUPER-POWERED HEROES!

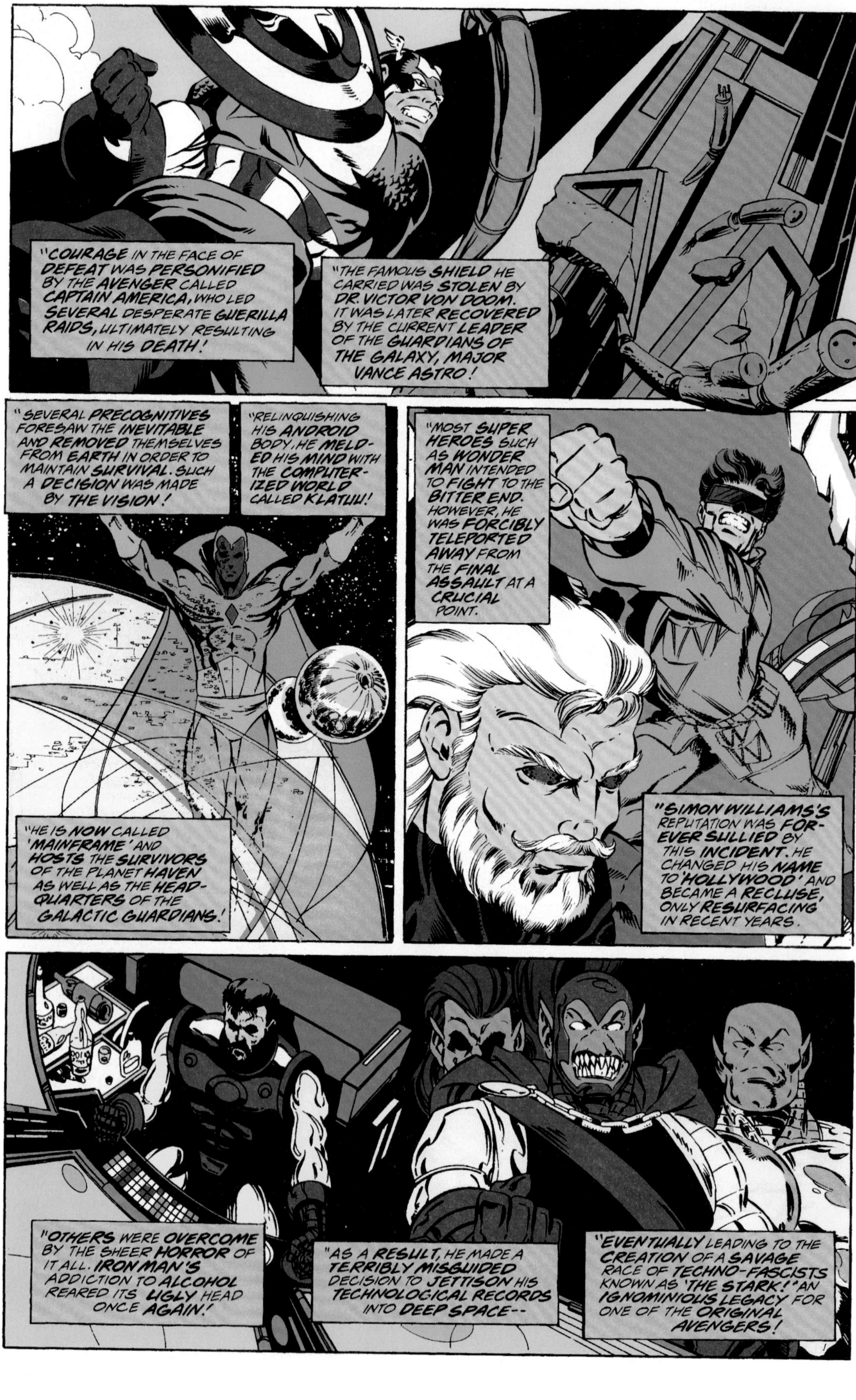
"COURAGE IN THE FACE OF DEFEAT WAS PERSONIFIED BY THE AVENGER CALLED CAPTAIN AMERICA, WHO LED SEVERAL DESPERATE GUERILLA RAIDS, ULTIMATELY RESULTING IN HIS DEATH!
"THE FAMOUS SHIELD HE CARRIED WAS STOLEN BY DR. VICTOR VON DOOM. IT WAS LATER RECOVERED BY THE CURRENT LEADER OF THE GUARDIANS OF THE GALAXY, MAJOR VANCE ASTRO!
"SEVERAL PRECOGNITIVES FORESAW THE INEVITABLE AND REMOVED THEMSELVES FROM EARTH IN ORDER TO MAINTAIN SURVIVAL. SUCH A DECISION WAS MADE BY THE VISION!
"RELINQUISHING HIS ANDROID BODY, HE MELDED HIS MIND WITH THE COMPUTERIZED WORLD CALLED KLATUU!
"HE IS NOW CALLED 'MAINFRAME' AND HOSTS THE SURVIVORS OF THE PLANET HAVEN AS WELL AS THE HEADQUARTERS OF THE GALACTIC GUARDIANS!
"MOST SUPER HEROES SUCH AS WONDER MAN INTENDED TO FIGHT TO THE BITTER END. HOWEVER, HE WAS FORCIBLY TELEPORTED AWAY FROM THE FINAL ASSAULT AT A CRUCIAL POINT.
"SIMON WILLIAMS'S REPUTATION WAS FOREVER SULLIED BY THIS INCIDENT. HE CHANGED HIS NAME TO 'HOLLYWOOD' AND BECAME A RECLUSE, ONLY RESURFACING IN RECENT YEARS.
"OTHERS WERE OVERCOME BY THE SHEER HORROR OF IT ALL. IRON MAN'S ADDICTION TO ALCOHOL REARED ITS UGLY HEAD ONCE AGAIN!
"AS A RESULT, HE MADE A TERRIBLY MISGUIDED DECISION TO JETTISON HIS TECHNOLOGICAL RECORDS INTO DEEP SPACE--
"EVENTUALLY LEADING TO THE CREATION OF A SAVAGE RACE OF TECHNO-FASCISTS KNOWN AS 'THE STARK!' AN IGNOMINIOUS LEGACY FOR ONE OF THE ORIGINAL AVENGERS!

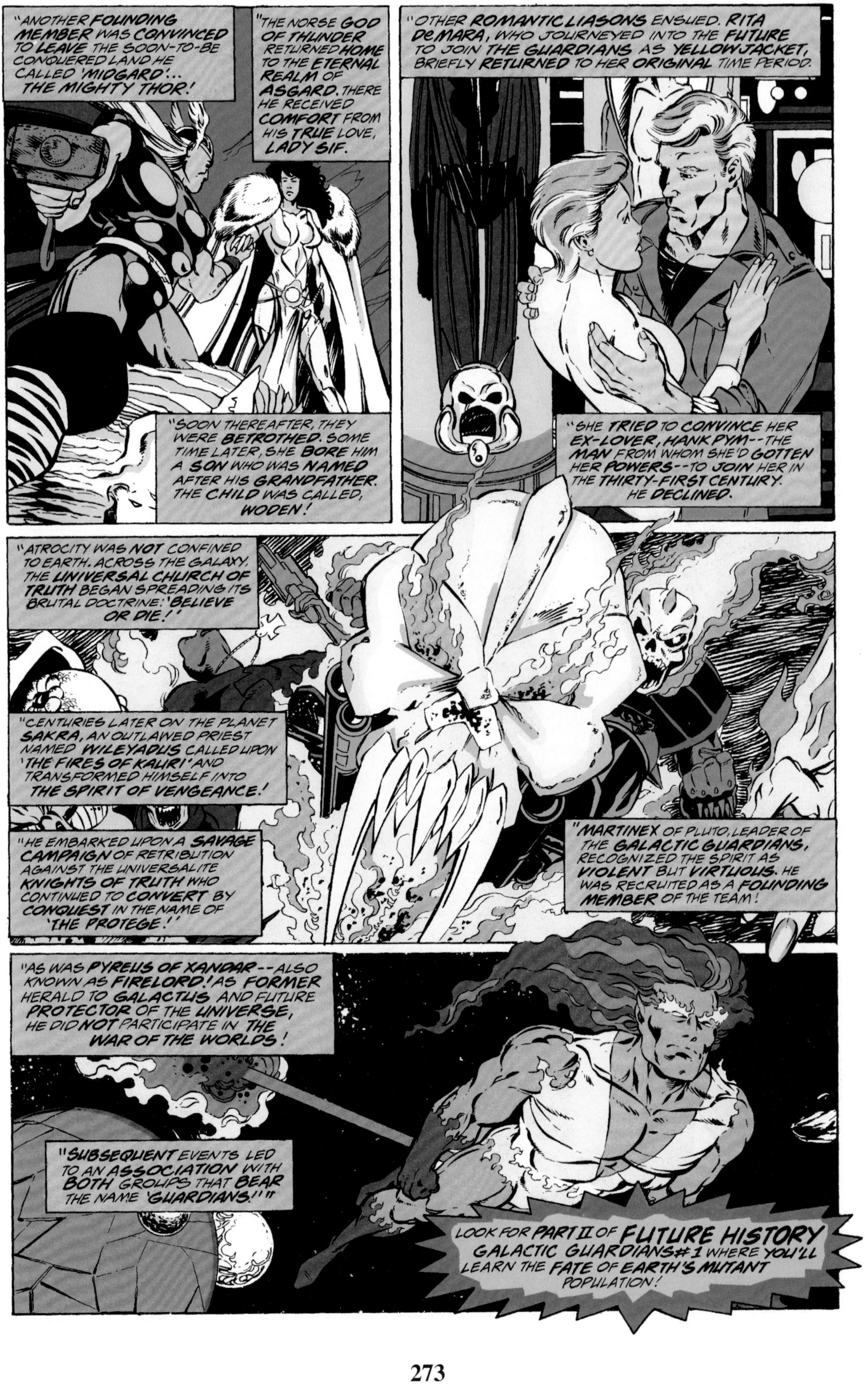
"ANOTHER FOUNDING MEMBER WAS CONVINCED TO LEAVE THE SOON-TO-BE CONQUERED LAND HE CALLED 'MIDGARD'... THE MIGHTY THOR!
"THE NORSE GOD OF THUNDER RETURNED HOME TO THE ETERNAL REALM OF ASGARD. THERE HE RECEIVED COMFORT FROM HIS TRUE LOVE, LADY SIF.
"SOON THEREAFTER, THEY WERE BETROTHED. SOME TIME LATER, SHE BORE HIM A SON WHO WAS NAMED AFTER HIS GRANDFATHER. THE CHILD WAS CALLED, WODEN!
"OTHER ROMANTIC LIASONS ENSUED. RITA DeMARA, WHO JOURNEYED INTO THE FUTURE TO JOIN THE GUARDIANS AS YELLOWJACKET, BRIEFLY RETURNED TO HER ORIGINAL TIME PERIOD.
"SHE TRIED TO CONVINCE HER EX-LOVER, HANK PYM--THE MAN FROM WHOM SHE'D GOTTEN HER POWERS--TO JOIN HER IN THE THIRTY-FIRST CENTURY. HE DECLINED.
"ATROCITY WAS NOT CONFINED TO EARTH. ACROSS THE GALAXY, THE UNIVERSAL CHURCH OF TRUTH BEGAN SPREADING ITS BRUTAL DOCTRINE: 'BELIEVE OR DIE!'
"CENTURIES LATER ON THE PLANET SAKRA, AN OUTLAWED PRIEST NAMED WILEYADUS CALLED UPON 'THE FIRES OF KAURI' AND TRANSFORMED HIMSELF INTO THE SPIRIT OF VENGEANCE!
"HE EMBARKED UPON A SAVAGE CAMPAIGN OF RETRIBUTION AGAINST THE UNIVERSALITE KNIGHTS OF TRUTH WHO CONTINUED TO CONVERT BY CONQUEST IN THE NAME OF 'THE PROTEGE!'
"MARTINEX OF PLUTO, LEADER OF THE GALACTIC GUARDIANS, RECOGNIZED THE SPIRIT AS VIOLENT BUT VIRTUOUS. HE WAS RECRUITED AS A FOUNDING MEMBER OF THE TEAM!
"AS WAS PYREUS OF XANDAR--ALSO KNOWN AS FIRELORD! AS FORMER HERALD TO GALACTUS AND FUTURE PROTECTOR OF THE UNIVERSE, HE DID NOT PARTICIPATE IN THE WAR OF THE WORLDS!
"SUBSEQUENT EVENTS LED TO AN ASSOCIATION WITH BOTH GROUPS THAT BEAR THE NAME 'GUARDIANS!'"
LOOK FOR PART II OF FUTURE HISTORY GALACTIC GUARDIANS #1 WHERE YOU'LL LEARN THE FATE OF EARTH'S MUTANT POPULATION!

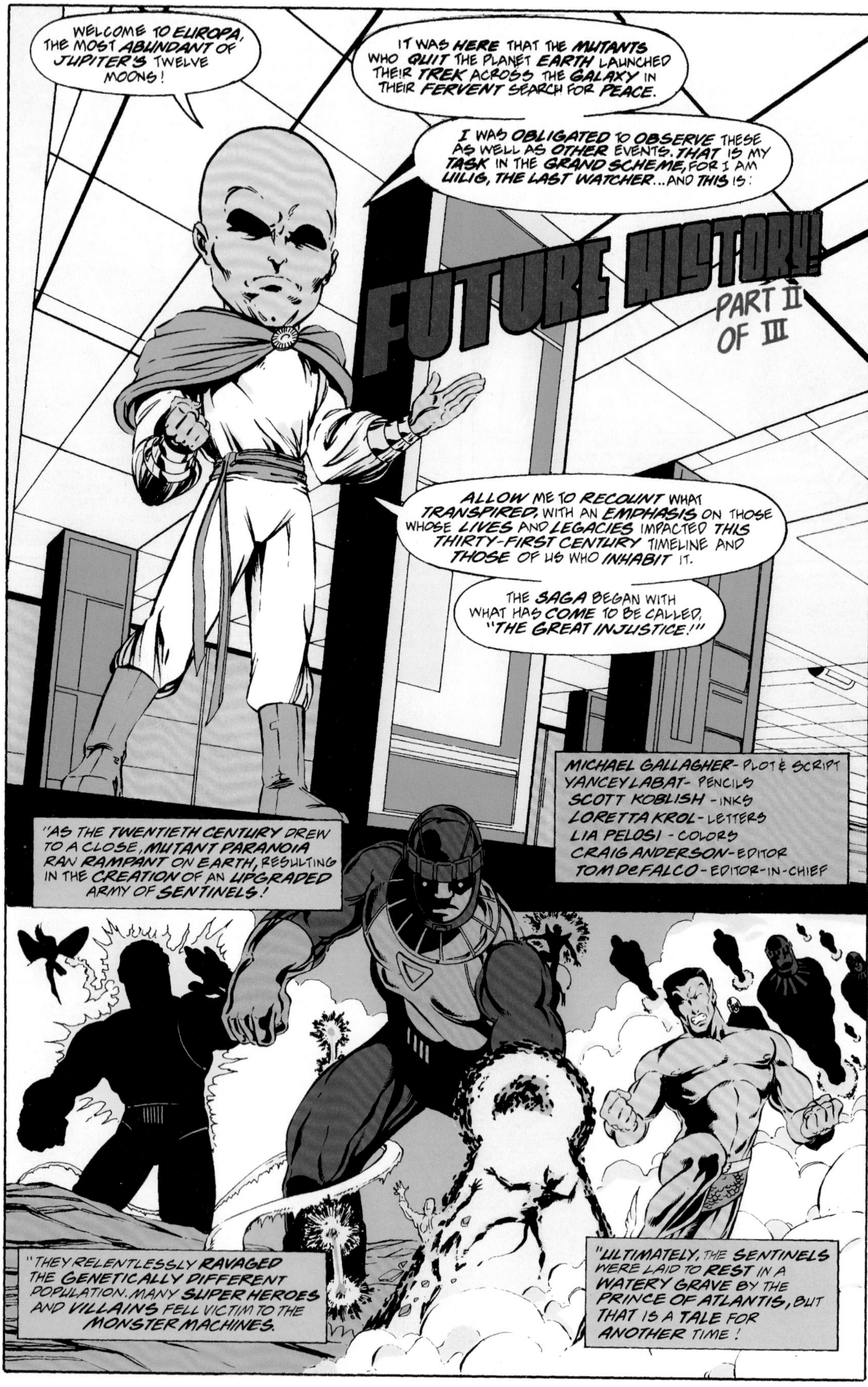

WELCOME TO EUROPA, THE MOST ABUNDANT OF JUPITER'S TWELVE MOONS!
IT WAS HERE THAT THE MUTANTS WHO QUIT THE PLANET EARTH LAUNCHED THEIR TREK ACROSS THE GALAXY IN THEIR FERVENT SEARCH FOR PEACE.
I WAS OBLIGATED TO OBSERVE THESE AS WELL AS OTHER EVENTS. THAT IS MY TASK IN THE GRAND SCHEME, FOR I AM UILIG, THE LAST WATCHER...AND THIS IS:
FUTURE HISTORY!
PART II OF III
ALLOW ME TO RECOUNT WHAT TRANSPIRED, WITH AN EMPHASIS ON THOSE WHOSE LIVES AND LEGACIES IMPACTED THIS THIRTY-FIRST CENTURY TIMELINE AND THOSE OF US WHO INHABIT IT.
THE SAGA BEGAN WITH WHAT HAS COME TO BE CALLED, "THE GREAT INJUSTICE!"
MICHAEL GALLAGHER- PLOT & SCRIPT
YANCEY LABAT- PENCILS
SCOTT KOBLISH - INKS
LORETTA KROL- LETTERS
LIA PELOSI - COLORS
CRAIG ANDERSON- EDITOR
TOM DeFALCO- EDITOR-IN-CHIEF
"AS THE TWENTIETH CENTURY DREW TO A CLOSE, MUTANT PARANOIA RAN RAMPANT ON EARTH, RESULTING IN THE CREATION OF AN UPGRADED ARMY OF SENTINELS!
"THEY RELENTLESSLY RAVAGED THE GENETICALLY DIFFERENT POPULATION. MANY SUPER HEROES AND VILLAINS FELL VICTIM TO THE MONSTER MACHINES.
"ULTIMATELY, THE SENTINELS WERE LAID TO REST IN A WATERY GRAVE BY THE PRINCE OF ATLANTIS, BUT THAT IS A TALE FOR ANOTHER TIME!

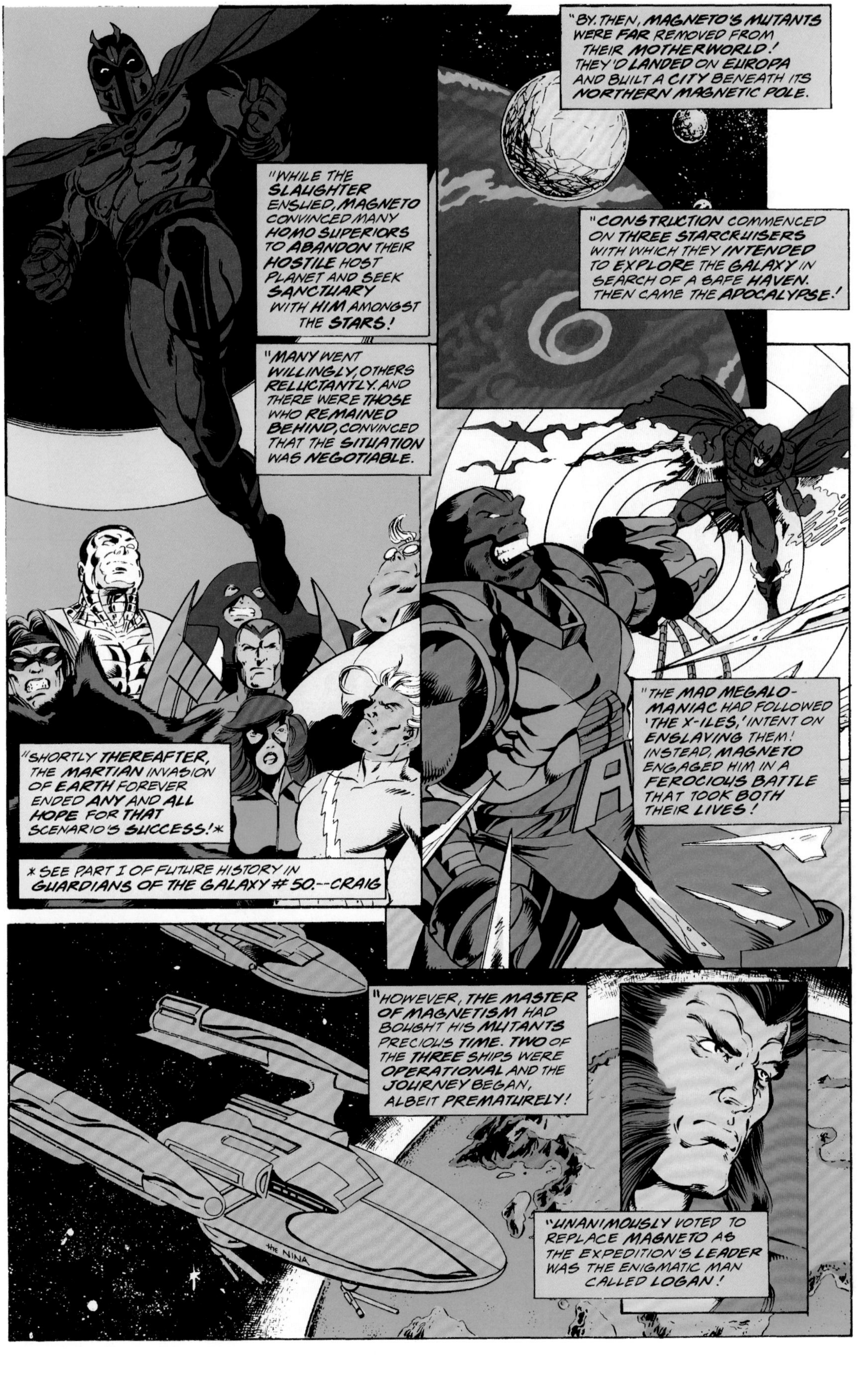

"BY THEN, MAGNETO'S MUTANTS WERE FAR REMOVED FROM THEIR MOTHERWORLD! THEY'D LANDED ON EUROPA AND BUILT A CITY BENEATH ITS NORTHERN MAGNETIC POLE.
"WHILE THE SLAUGHTER ENSUED, MAGNETO CONVINCED MANY HOMO SUPERIORS TO ABANDON THEIR HOSTILE HOST PLANET AND SEEK SANCTUARY WITH HIM AMONGST THE STARS!
"CONSTRUCTION COMMENCED ON THREE STARCRUISERS WITH WHICH THEY INTENDED TO EXPLORE THE GALAXY IN SEARCH OF A SAFE HAVEN. THEN CAME THE APOCALYPSE!
"MANY WENT WILLINGLY, OTHERS RELUCTANTLY. AND THERE WERE THOSE WHO REMAINED BEHIND, CONVINCED THAT THE SITUATION WAS NEGOTIABLE.
"THE MAD MEGALO-MANIAC HAD FOLLOWED 'THE X-ILES,' INTENT ON ENSLAVING THEM! INSTEAD, MAGNETO ENGAGED HIM IN A FEROCIOUS BATTLE THAT TOOK BOTH THEIR LIVES!
"SHORTLY THEREAFTER, THE MARTIAN INVASION OF EARTH FOREVER ENDED ANY AND ALL HOPE FOR THAT SCENARIO'S SUCCESS!*
* SEE PART I OF FUTURE HISTORY IN GUARDIANS OF THE GALAXY # 50.--CRAIG
"HOWEVER, THE MASTER OF MAGNETISM HAD BOUGHT HIS MUTANTS PRECIOUS TIME. TWO OF THE THREE SHIPS WERE OPERATIONAL AND THE JOURNEY BEGAN, ALBEIT PREMATURELY!
"UNANIMOUSLY VOTED TO REPLACE MAGNETO AS THE EXPEDITION'S LEADER WAS THE ENIGMATIC MAN CALLED LOGAN!

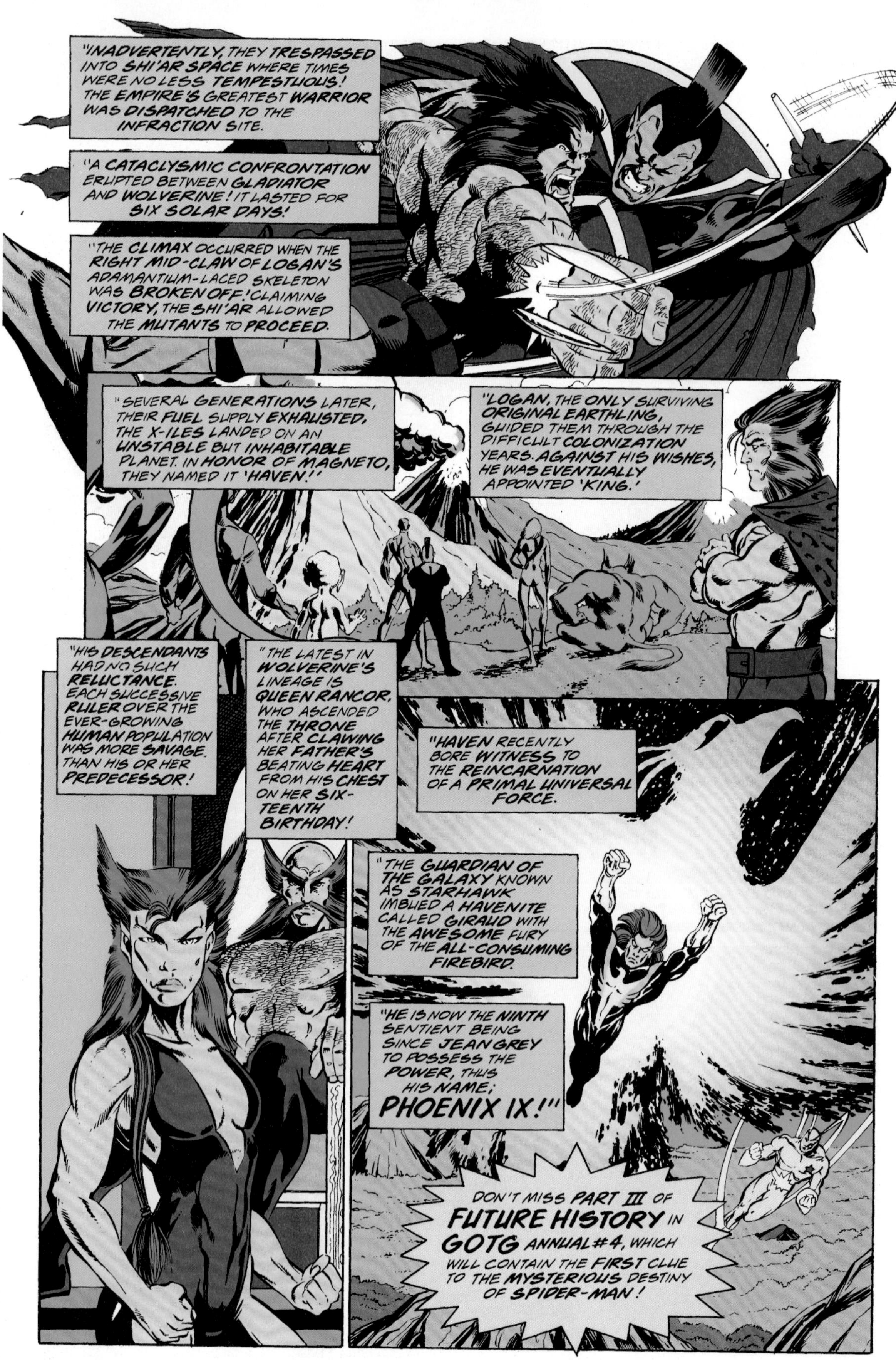
"INADVERTENTLY, THEY TRESPASSED INTO SHI'AR SPACE WHERE TIMES WERE NO LESS TEMPESTUOUS! THE EMPIRE'S GREATEST WARRIOR WAS DISPATCHED TO THE INFRACTION SITE.
"A CATACLYSMIC CONFRONTATION ERUPTED BETWEEN GLADIATOR AND WOLVERINE! IT LASTED FOR SIX SOLAR DAYS!
"THE CLIMAX OCCURRED WHEN THE RIGHT MID-CLAW OF LOGAN'S ADAMANTIUM-LACED SKELETON WAS BROKEN OFF! CLAIMING VICTORY, THE SHI'AR ALLOWED THE MUTANTS TO PROCEED.
"SEVERAL GENERATIONS LATER, THEIR FUEL SUPPLY EXHAUSTED, THE X-ILES LANDED ON AN UNSTABLE BUT INHABITABLE PLANET. IN HONOR OF MAGNETO, THEY NAMED IT 'HAVEN.'
"LOGAN, THE ONLY SURVIVING ORIGINAL EARTHLING, GUIDED THEM THROUGH THE DIFFICULT COLONIZATION YEARS. AGAINST HIS WISHES, HE WAS EVENTUALLY APPOINTED 'KING.'
"HIS DESCENDANTS HAD NO SUCH RELUCTANCE. EACH SUCCESSIVE RULER OVER THE EVER-GROWING HUMAN POPULATION WAS MORE SAVAGE THAN HIS OR HER PREDECESSOR!
"THE LATEST IN WOLVERINE'S LINEAGE IS QUEEN RANCOR, WHO ASCENDED THE THRONE AFTER CLAWING HER FATHER'S BEATING HEART FROM HIS CHEST ON HER SIXTEENTH BIRTHDAY!
"HAVEN RECENTLY BORE WITNESS TO THE REINCARNATION OF A PRIMAL UNIVERSAL FORCE.
"THE GUARDIAN OF THE GALAXY KNOWN AS STARHAWK IMBUED A HAVENITE CALLED GIRAUD WITH THE AWESOME FURY OF THE ALL-CONSUMING FIREBIRD.
"HE IS NOW THE NINTH SENTIENT BEING SINCE JEAN GREY TO POSSESS THE POWER, THUS HIS NAME; PHOENIX IX!"
DON'T MISS PART III OF FUTURE HISTORY IN GOTG ANNUAL #4, WHICH WILL CONTAIN THE FIRST CLUE TO THE MYSTERIOUS DESTINY OF SPIDER-MAN!

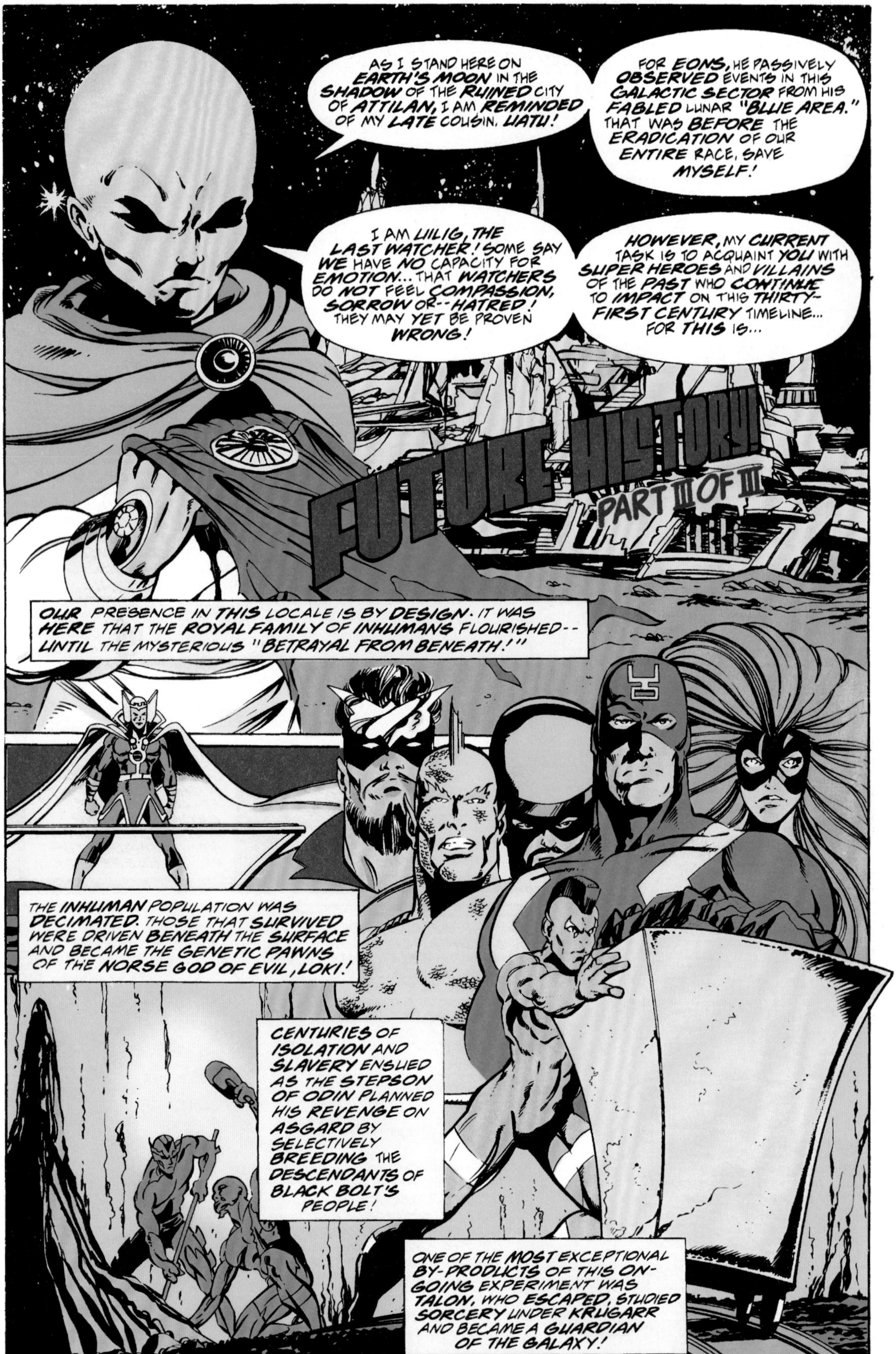
AS I STAND HERE ON EARTH'S MOON IN THE SHADOW OF THE RUINED CITY OF ATTILAN, I AM REMINDED OF MY LATE COUSIN, UATU!
FOR EONS, HE PASSIVELY OBSERVED EVENTS IN THIS GALACTIC SECTOR FROM HIS FABLED LUNAR "BLUE AREA." THAT WAS BEFORE THE ERADICATION OF OUR ENTIRE RACE, SAVE MYSELF!
I AM ULIG, THE LAST WATCHER! SOME SAY WE HAVE NO CAPACITY FOR EMOTION... THAT WATCHERS DO NOT FEEL COMPASSION, SORROW OR--HATRED! THEY MAY YET BE PROVEN WRONG!
HOWEVER, MY CURRENT TASK IS TO ACQUAINT YOU WITH SUPER HEROES AND VILLAINS OF THE PAST WHO CONTINUE TO IMPACT ON THIS THIRTY-FIRST CENTURY TIMELINE... FOR THIS IS...
FUTURE HISTORY!
PART III OF III
OUR PRESENCE IN THIS LOCALE IS BY DESIGN. IT WAS HERE THAT THE ROYAL FAMILY OF INHUMANS FLOURISHED--UNTIL THE MYSTERIOUS "BETRAYAL FROM BENEATH!"
THE INHUMAN POPULATION WAS DECIMATED. THOSE THAT SURVIVED WERE DRIVEN BENEATH THE SURFACE AND BECAME THE GENETIC PAWNS OF THE NORSE GOD OF EVIL, LOKI!
CENTURIES OF ISOLATION AND SLAVERY ENSUED AS THE STEPSON OF ODIN PLANNED HIS REVENGE ON ASGARD BY SELECTIVELY BREEDING THE DESCENDANTS OF BLACK BOLT'S PEOPLE!
ONE OF THE MOST EXCEPTIONAL BY-PRODUCTS OF THIS ON-GOING EXPERIMENT WAS TALON, WHO ESCAPED, STUDIED SORCERY UNDER KRUGARR AND BECAME A GUARDIAN OF THE GALAXY!

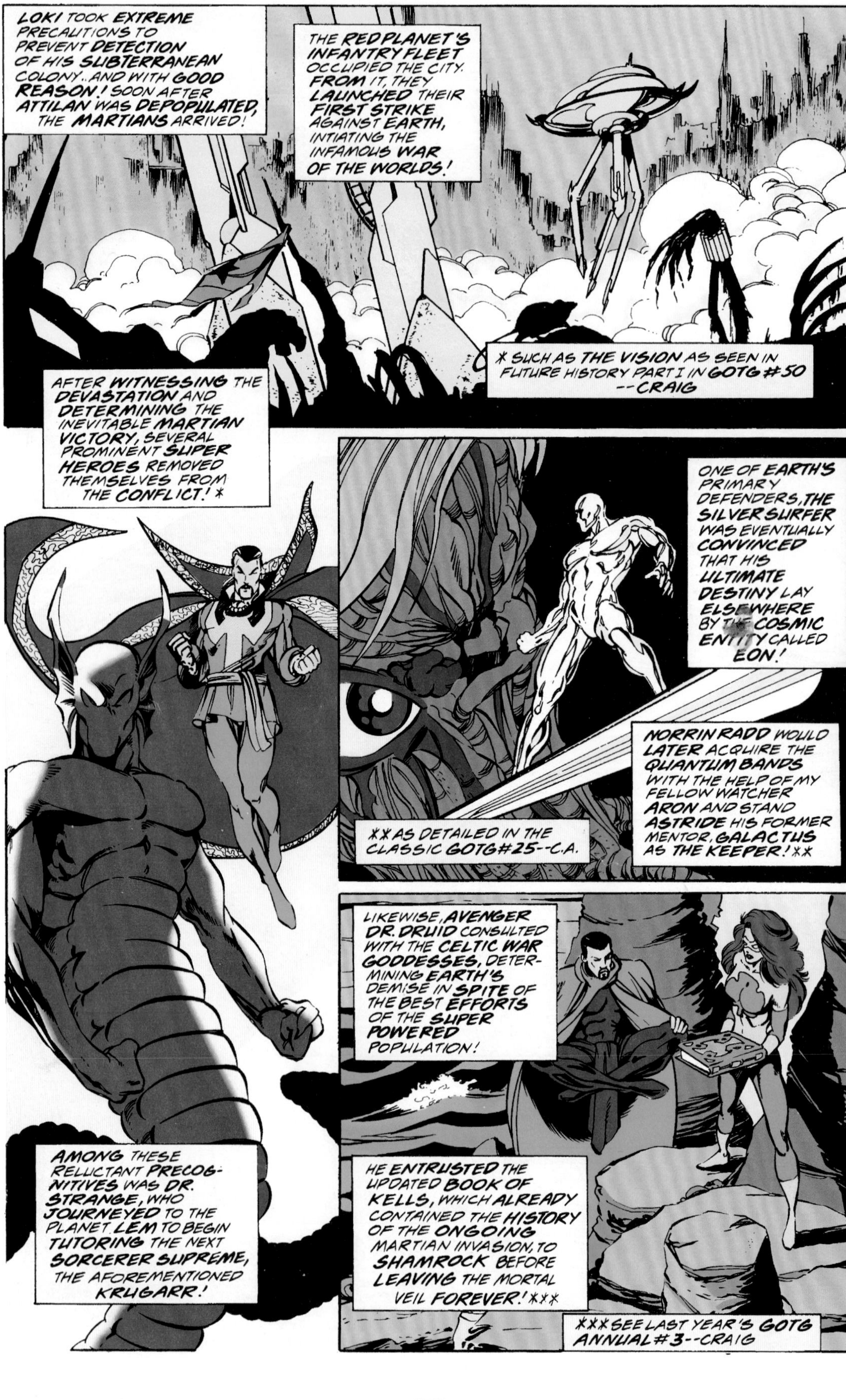
LOKI TOOK EXTREME PRECAUTIONS TO PREVENT DETECTION OF HIS SUBTERRANEAN COLONY...AND WITH GOOD REASON! SOON AFTER ATTILAN WAS DEPOPULATED, THE MARTIANS ARRIVED!
THE RED PLANET'S INFANTRY FLEET OCCUPIED THE CITY. FROM IT, THEY LAUNCHED THEIR FIRST STRIKE AGAINST EARTH, INTIATING THE INFAMOUS WAR OF THE WORLDS!
* SUCH AS THE VISION AS SEEN IN FUTURE HISTORY PART I IN GOTG #50 --CRAIG
AFTER WITNESSING THE DEVASTATION AND DETERMINING THE INEVITABLE MARTIAN VICTORY, SEVERAL PROMINENT SUPER HEROES REMOVED THEMSELVES FROM THE CONFLICT! *
ONE OF EARTH'S PRIMARY DEFENDERS, THE SILVER SURFER WAS EVENTUALLY CONVINCED THAT HIS ULTIMATE DESTINY LAY ELSEWHERE BY THE COSMIC ENTITY CALLED EON!
NORRIN RADD WOULD LATER ACQUIRE THE QUANTUM BANDS WITH THE HELP OF MY FELLOW WATCHER ARON AND STAND ASTRIDE HIS FORMER MENTOR, GALACTUS AS THE KEEPER! **
** AS DETAILED IN THE CLASSIC GOTG #25--C.A.
AMONG THESE RELUCTANT PRECOGNITIVES WAS DR. STRANGE, WHO JOURNEYED TO THE PLANET LEM TO BEGIN TUTORING THE NEXT SORCERER SUPREME, THE AFOREMENTIONED KRUGARR!
LIKEWISE, AVENGER DR. DRUID CONSULTED WITH THE CELTIC WAR GODDESSES, DETERMINING EARTH'S DEMISE IN SPITE OF THE BEST EFFORTS OF THE SUPER POWERED POPULATION!
HE ENTRUSTED THE UPDATED BOOK OF KELLS, WHICH ALREADY CONTAINED THE HISTORY OF THE ONGOING MARTIAN INVASION, TO SHAMROCK BEFORE LEAVING THE MORTAL VEIL FOREVER! ***
*** SEE LAST YEAR'S GOTG ANNUAL #3--CRAIG

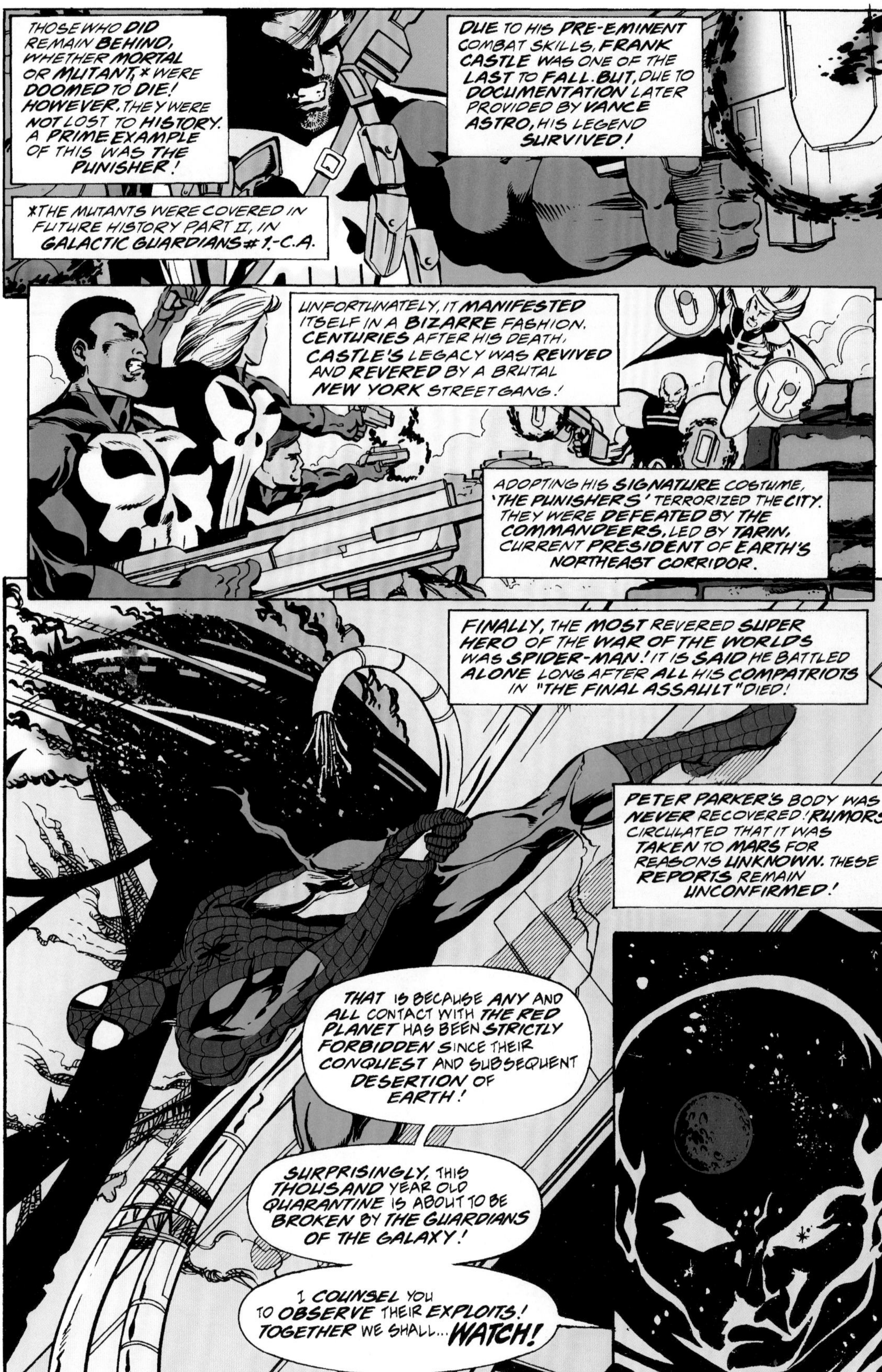
THOSE WHO DID REMAIN BEHIND, WHETHER MORTAL OR MUTANT,* WERE DOOMED TO DIE! HOWEVER, THEY WERE NOT LOST TO HISTORY. A PRIME EXAMPLE OF THIS WAS THE PUNISHER!
DUE TO HIS PRE-EMINENT COMBAT SKILLS, FRANK CASTLE WAS ONE OF THE LAST TO FALL. BUT, DUE TO DOCUMENTATION LATER PROVIDED BY VANCE ASTRO, HIS LEGEND SURVIVED!
*THE MUTANTS WERE COVERED IN FUTURE HISTORY PART II, IN GALACTIC GUARDIANS #1.-C.A.
UNFORTUNATELY, IT MANIFESTED ITSELF IN A BIZARRE FASHION. CENTURIES AFTER HIS DEATH, CASTLE'S LEGACY WAS REVIVED AND REVERED BY A BRUTAL NEW YORK STREET GANG!
ADOPTING HIS SIGNATURE COSTUME, 'THE PUNISHERS' TERRORIZED THE CITY. THEY WERE DEFEATED BY THE COMMANDEERS, LED BY TARIN, CURRENT PRESIDENT OF EARTH'S NORTHEAST CORRIDOR.
FINALLY, THE MOST REVERED SUPER HERO OF THE WAR OF THE WORLDS WAS SPIDER-MAN! IT IS SAID HE BATTLED ALONE LONG AFTER ALL HIS COMPATRIOTS IN "THE FINAL ASSAULT" DIED!
PETER PARKER'S BODY WAS NEVER RECOVERED! RUMORS CIRCULATED THAT IT WAS TAKEN TO MARS FOR REASONS UNKNOWN. THESE REPORTS REMAIN UNCONFIRMED!
THAT IS BECAUSE ANY AND ALL CONTACT WITH THE RED PLANET HAS BEEN STRICTLY FORBIDDEN SINCE THEIR CONQUEST AND SUBSEQUENT DESERTION OF EARTH!
SURPRISINGLY, THIS THOUSAND YEAR OLD QUARANTINE IS ABOUT TO BE BROKEN BY THE GUARDIANS OF THE GALAXY!
I COUNSEL YOU TO OBSERVE THEIR EXPLOITS! TOGETHER WE SHALL... WATCH!

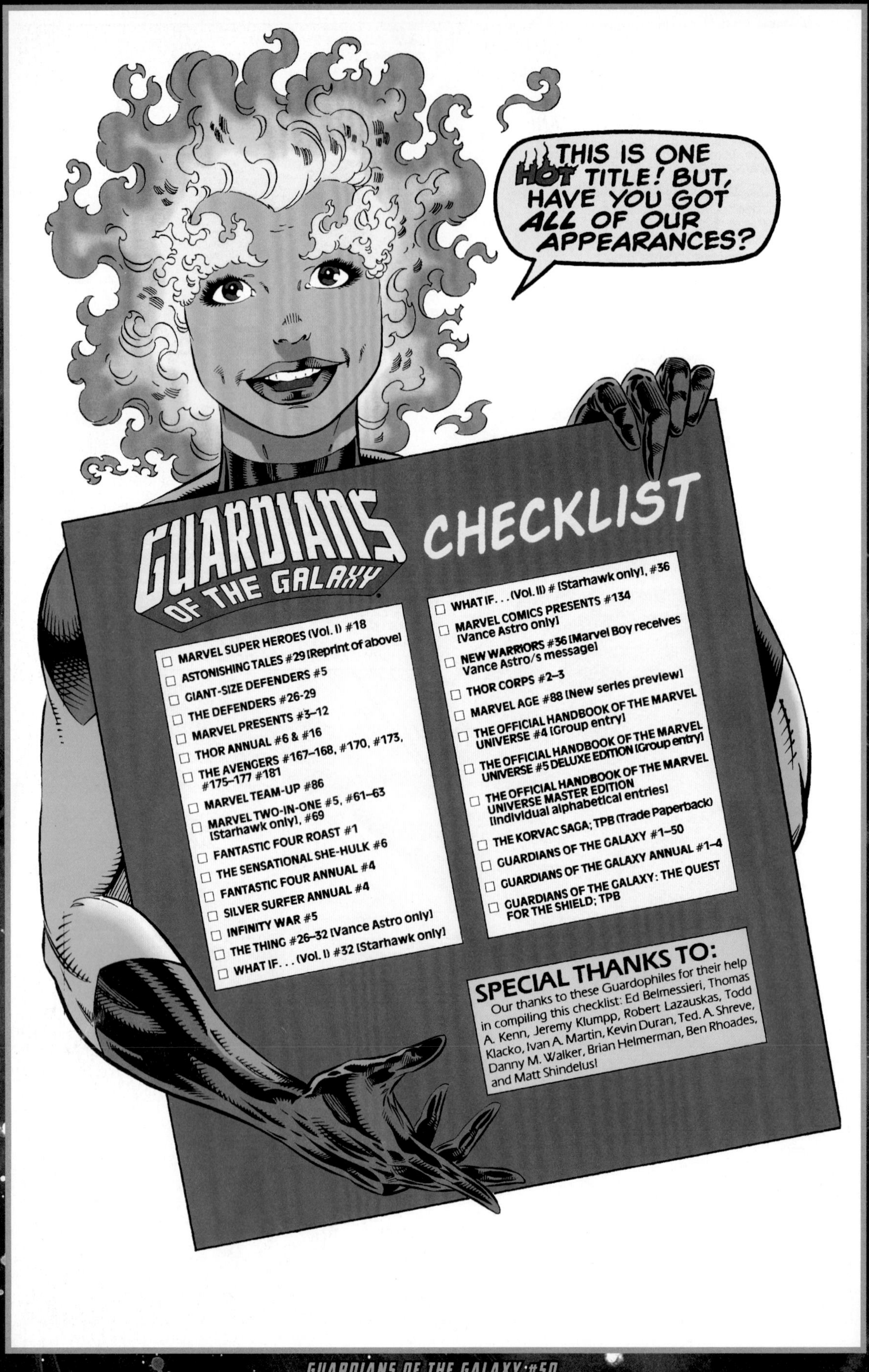
THIS IS ONE HOT TITLE! BUT, HAVE YOU GOT ALL OF OUR APPEARANCES?
GUARDIANS OF THE GALAXY
CHECKLIST
☐ MARVEL SUPER HEROES (Vol. I) #18
☐ ASTONISHING TALES #29 [Reprint of above]
☐ GIANT-SIZE DEFENDERS #5
☐ THE DEFENDERS #26-29
☐ MARVEL PRESENTS #3–12
☐ THOR ANNUAL #6 & #16
☐ THE AVENGERS #167–168, #170, #173, #175–177 #181
☐ MARVEL TEAM-UP #86
☐ MARVEL TWO-IN-ONE #5, #61–63 [Starhawk only], #69
☐ FANTASTIC FOUR ROAST #1
☐ THE SENSATIONAL SHE-HULK #6
☐ FANTASTIC FOUR ANNUAL #4
☐ SILVER SURFER ANNUAL #4
☐ INFINITY WAR #5
☐ THE THING #26–32 [Vance Astro only]
☐ WHAT IF. . . (Vol. I) #32 [Starhawk only]
☐ WHAT IF. . . (Vol. II) # [Starhawk only], #36
☐ MARVEL COMICS PRESENTS #134 [Vance Astro only]
☐ NEW WARRIORS #36 [Marvel Boy receives Vance Astro/s message]
☐ THOR CORPS #2–3
☐ MARVEL AGE #88 [New series preview]
☐ THE OFFICIAL HANDBOOK OF THE MARVEL UNIVERSE #4 [Group entry]
☐ THE OFFICIAL HANDBOOK OF THE MARVEL UNIVERSE #5 DELUXE EDITION [Group entry]
☐ THE OFFICIAL HANDBOOK OF THE MARVEL UNIVERSE MASTER EDITION [individual alphabetical entries]
☐ THE KORVAC SAGA; TPB (Trade Paperback)
☐ GUARDIANS OF THE GALAXY #1–50
☐ GUARDIANS OF THE GALAXY ANNUAL #1–4
☐ GUARDIANS OF THE GALAXY: THE QUEST FOR THE SHIELD; TPB
SPECIAL THANKS TO:
Our thanks to these Guardophiles for their help in compiling this checklist: Ed Belmessieri, Thomas A. Kenn, Jeremy Klumpp, Robert Lazauskas, Todd Klacko, Ivan A. Martin, Kevin Duran, Ted. A. Shreve, Danny M. Walker, Brian Helmerman, Ben Rhoades, and Matt Shindelus!

GUARDIANS OF THE GALAXY #50
CHECKLIST PINUP BY KEVIN WEST

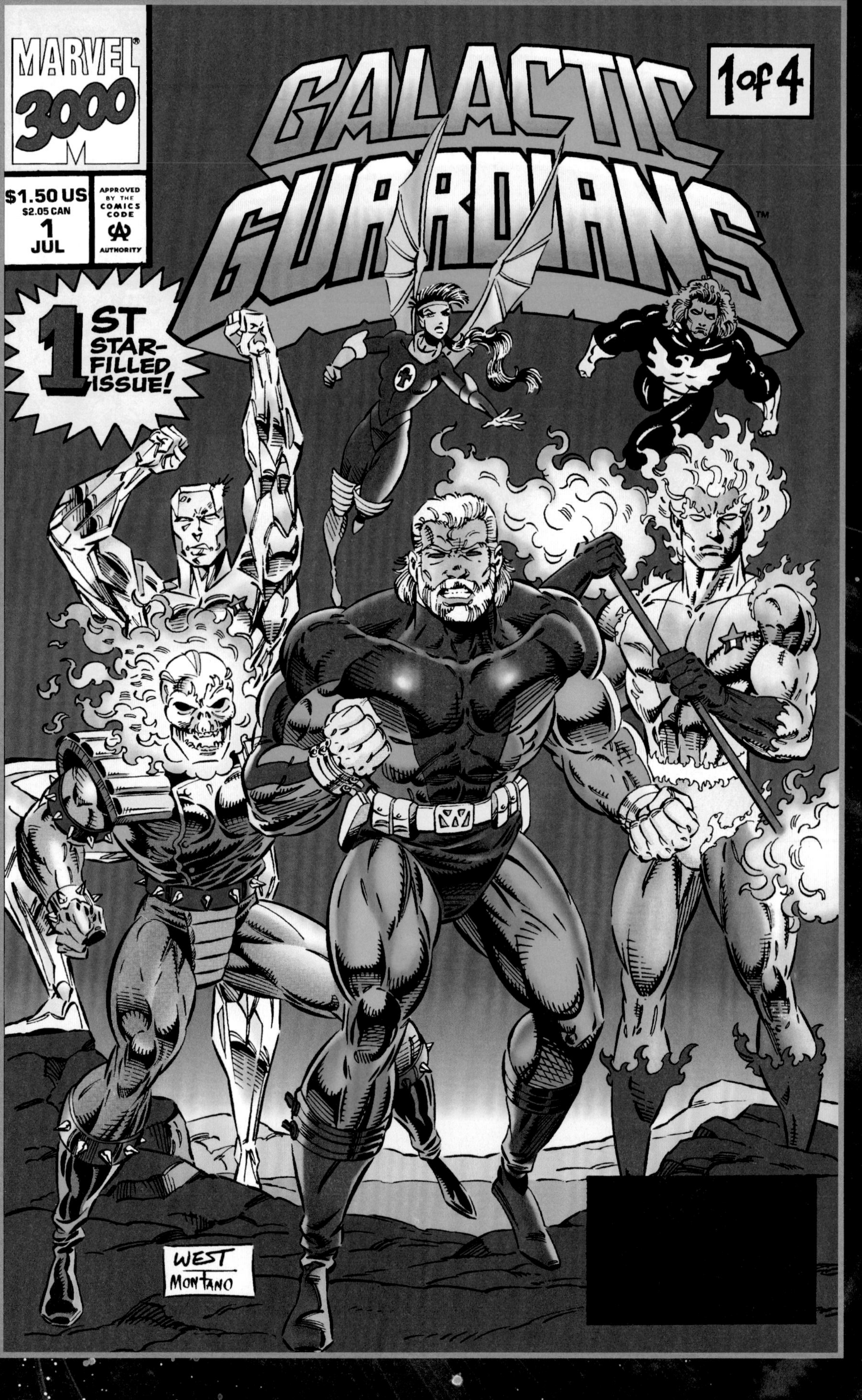
MARVEL®
3000
M
$1.50 US
$2.05 CAN
1
JUL
APPROVED BY THE COMICS CODE AUTHORITY
GALACTIC GUARDIANS™
1 of 4
1ST STAR-FILLED ISSUE!
WEST
MONTANO

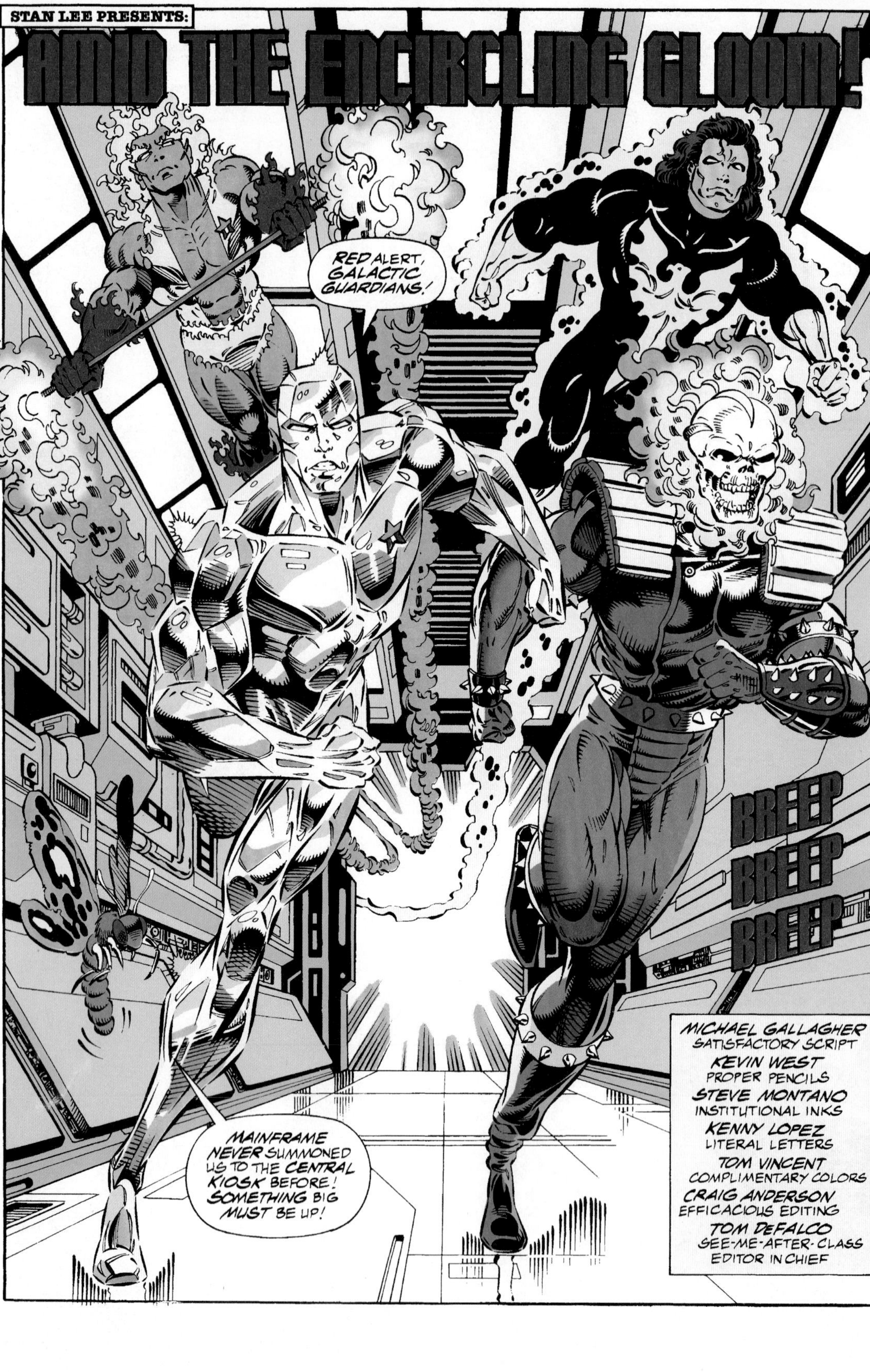
STAN LEE PRESENTS:
AMID THE ENCIRCLING GLOOM!
RED ALERT, GALACTIC GUARDIANS!
BREEP BREEP BREEP
MAINFRAME NEVER SUMMONED US TO THE CENTRAL KIOSK BEFORE! SOMETHING BIG MUST BE UP!
MICHAEL GALLAGHER SATISFACTORY SCRIPT
KEVIN WEST PROPER PENCILS
STEVE MONTANO INSTITUTIONAL INKS
KENNY LOPEZ LITERAL LETTERS
TOM VINCENT COMPLIMENTARY COLORS
CRAIG ANDERSON EFFICACIOUS EDITING
TOM DEFALCO SEE-ME-AFTER-CLASS EDITOR IN CHIEF

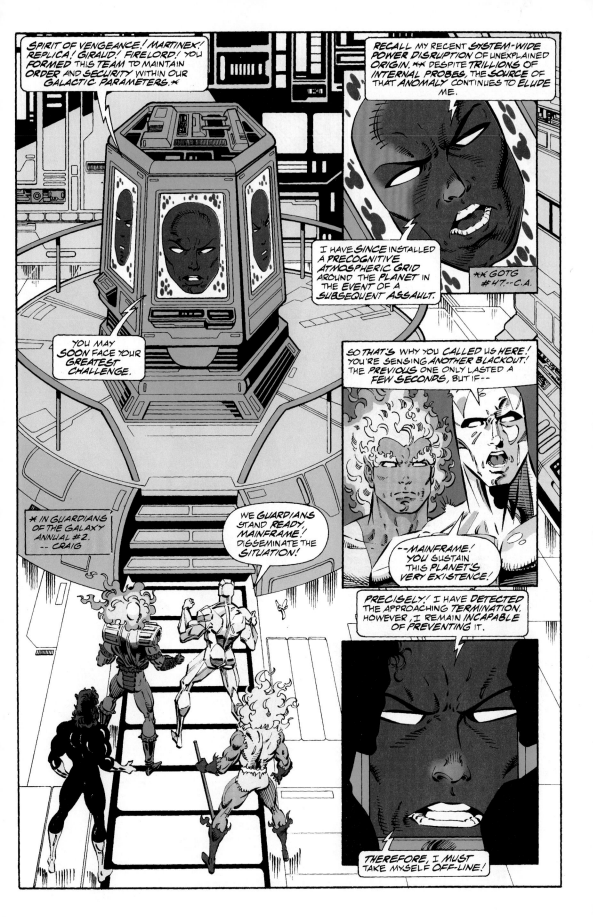

SPIRIT OF VENGEANCE! MARTINEX! REPLICA! GIRAUD! FIRELORD! YOU FORMED THIS TEAM TO MAINTAIN ORDER AND SECURITY WITHIN OUR GALACTIC PARAMETERS.*

RECALL MY RECENT SYSTEM-WIDE POWER DISRUPTION OF UNEXPLAINED ORIGIN.** DESPITE TRILLIONS OF INTERNAL PROBES, THE SOURCE OF THAT ANOMALY CONTINUES TO ELUDE ME.

I HAVE SINCE INSTALLED A PRECOGNITIVE ATMOSPHERIC GRID AROUND THE PLANET IN THE EVENT OF A SUBSEQUENT ASSAULT.

** GOTG #47.--C.A.

YOU MAY SOON FACE YOUR GREATEST CHALLENGE.

SO THAT'S WHY YOU CALLED US HERE! YOU'RE SENSING ANOTHER BLACKOUT! THE PREVIOUS ONE ONLY LASTED A FEW SECONDS, BUT IF--

* IN GUARDIANS OF THE GALAXY ANNUAL #2. --CRAIG

WE GUARDIANS STAND READY, MAINFRAME! DISSEMINATE THE SITUATION!

--MAINFRAME! YOU SUSTAIN THIS PLANET'S VERY EXISTENCE!

PRECISELY! I HAVE DETECTED THE APPROACHING TERMINATION. HOWEVER, I REMAIN INCAPABLE OF PREVENTING IT.

THEREFORE, I MUST TAKE MYSELF OFF-LINE!

283

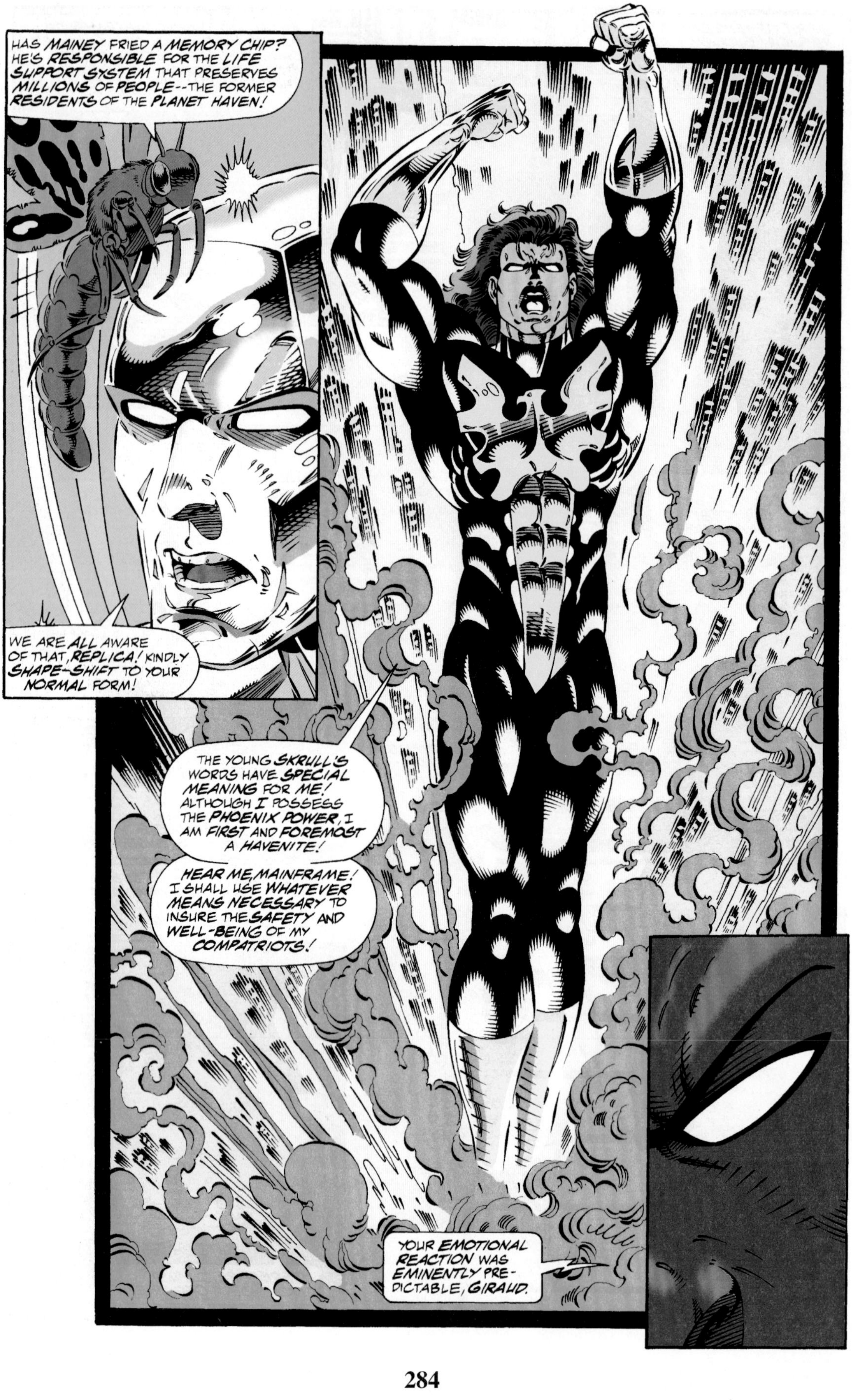
HAS MAINEY FRIED A MEMORY CHIP? HE'S RESPONSIBLE FOR THE LIFE SUPPORT SYSTEM THAT PRESERVES MILLIONS OF PEOPLE--THE FORMER RESIDENTS OF THE PLANET HAVEN!
WE ARE ALL AWARE OF THAT, REPLICA! KINDLY SHAPE-SHIFT TO YOUR NORMAL FORM!
THE YOUNG SKRULL'S WORDS HAVE SPECIAL MEANING FOR ME! ALTHOUGH I POSSESS THE PHOENIX POWER, I AM FIRST AND FOREMOST A HAVENITE!
HEAR ME, MAINFRAME! I SHALL USE WHATEVER MEANS NECESSARY TO INSURE THE SAFETY AND WELL-BEING OF MY COMPATRIOTS!
YOUR EMOTIONAL REACTION WAS EMINENTLY PRE-DICTABLE, GIRAUD.

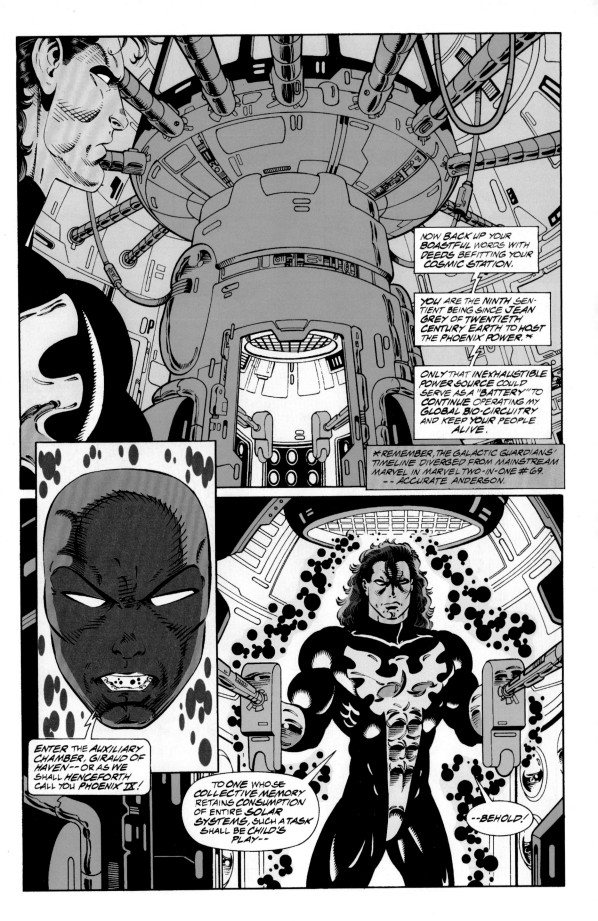

NOW *BACK UP* YOUR *BOASTFUL* WORDS WITH *DEEDS* BEFITTING YOUR *COSMIC STATION.*

YOU ARE THE *NINTH* SEN-TIENT BEING SINCE *JEAN GREY* OF TWENTIETH CENTURY EARTH TO HOST THE *PHOENIX POWER.* ✶

ONLY THAT *INEXHAUSTIBLE* POWER SOURCE COULD SERVE AS A *"BATTERY"* TO *CONTINUE* OPERATING MY *GLOBAL* BIO-CIRCUITRY AND KEEP *YOUR* PEOPLE *ALIVE.*

✶REMEMBER, THE GALACTIC GUARDIANS' TIMELINE DIVERGED FROM MAINSTREAM MARVEL IN *MARVEL TWO-IN-ONE* # 69. -- ACCURATE ANDERSON.

ENTER THE *AUXILIARY CHAMBER,* GIRAUD OF HAVEN -- OR AS WE SHALL *HENCEFORTH* CALL YOU *PHOENIX IX* !

TO ONE WHOSE *COLLECTIVE* MEMORY RETAINS *CONSUMPTION* OF ENTIRE *SOLAR SYSTEMS,* SUCH A TASK SHALL BE *CHILD'S PLAY* --

--*BEHOLD!*

285

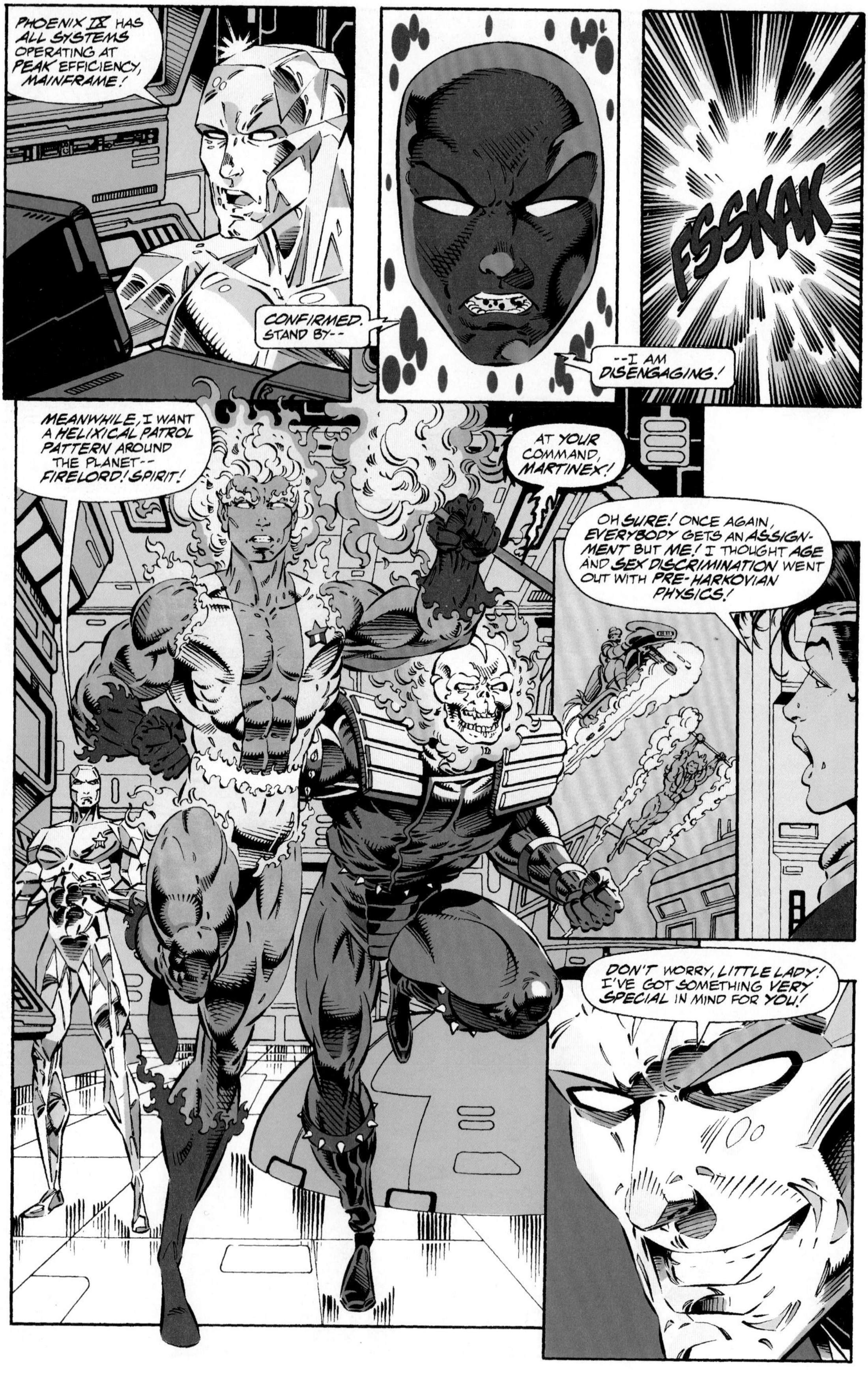
PHOENIX IX HAS ALL SYSTEMS OPERATING AT PEAK EFFICIENCY, MAINFRAME!
CONFIRMED. STAND BY--
--I AM DISENGAGING!
FSSKAK
MEANWHILE, I WANT A HELIXICAL PATROL PATTERN AROUND THE PLANET-- FIRELORD! SPIRIT!
AT YOUR COMMAND, MARTINEX!
OH SURE! ONCE AGAIN, EVERYBODY GETS AN ASSIGNMENT BUT ME! I THOUGHT AGE AND SEX DISCRIMINATION WENT OUT WITH PRE-HARKOVIAN PHYSICS!
DON'T WORRY, LITTLE LADY! I'VE GOT SOMETHING VERY SPECIAL IN MIND FOR YOU!

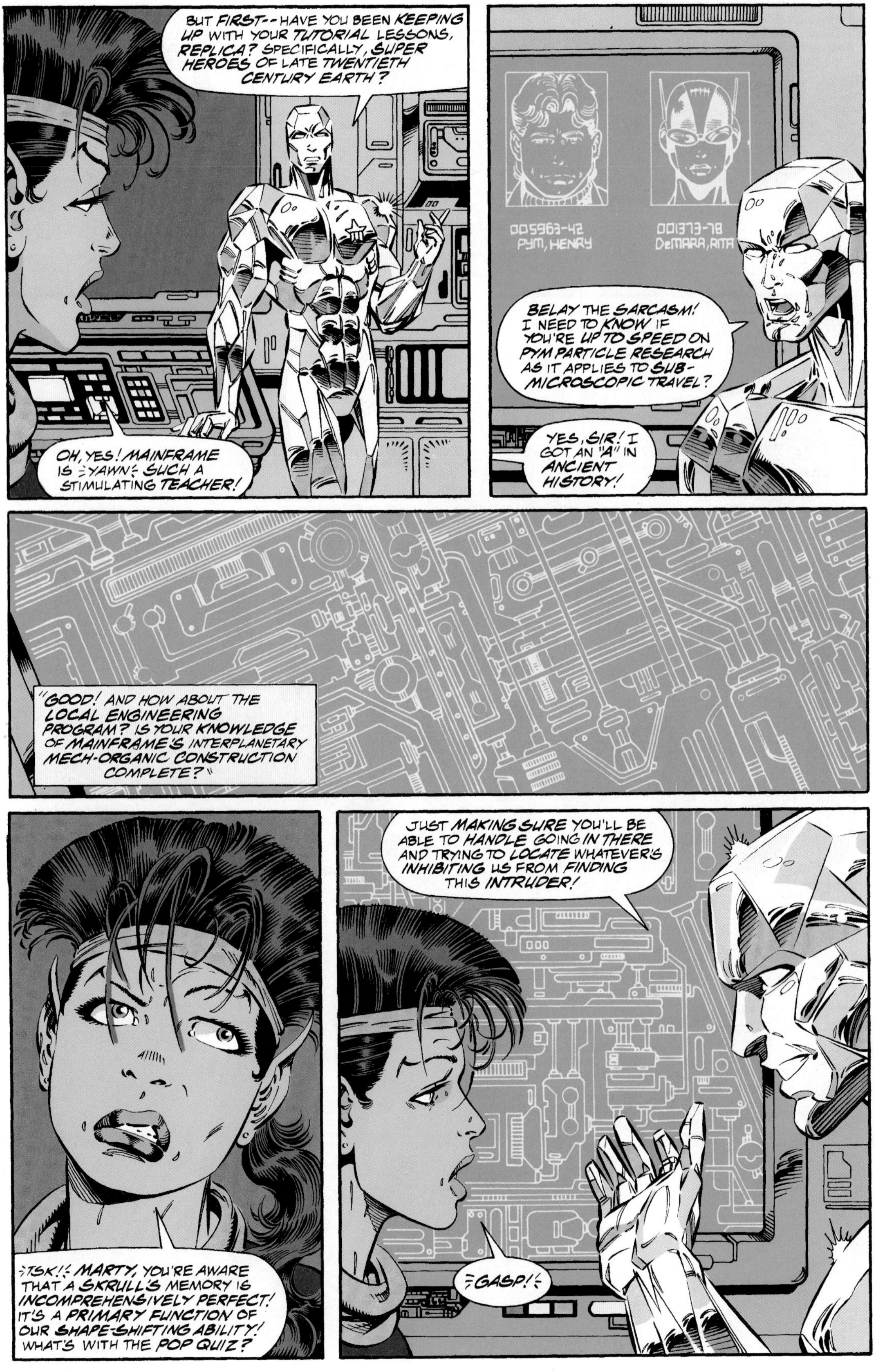
BUT FIRST--HAVE YOU BEEN KEEPING UP WITH YOUR TUTORIAL LESSONS, REPLICA? SPECIFICALLY, SUPER HEROES OF LATE TWENTIETH CENTURY EARTH?
OH, YES! MAINFRAME IS =YAWN= SUCH A STIMULATING TEACHER!
005963-42 PYM, HENRY
001373-78 DeMARA, RITA
BELAY THE SARCASM! I NEED TO KNOW IF YOU'RE UP TO SPEED ON PYM PARTICLE RESEARCH AS IT APPLIES TO SUB-MICROSCOPIC TRAVEL?
YES, SIR! I GOT AN "A" IN ANCIENT HISTORY!
"GOOD! AND HOW ABOUT THE LOCAL ENGINEERING PROGRAM? IS YOUR KNOWLEDGE OF MAINFRAME'S INTERPLANETARY MECH-ORGANIC CONSTRUCTION COMPLETE?"
=TSK!= MARTY, YOU'RE AWARE THAT A SKRULL'S MEMORY IS INCOMPREHENSIVELY PERFECT! IT'S A PRIMARY FUNCTION OF OUR SHAPE-SHIFTING ABILITY! WHAT'S WITH THE POP QUIZ?
JUST MAKING SURE YOU'LL BE ABLE TO HANDLE GOING IN THERE AND TRYING TO LOCATE WHATEVER'S INHIBITING US FROM FINDING THIS INTRUDER!
=GASP!=

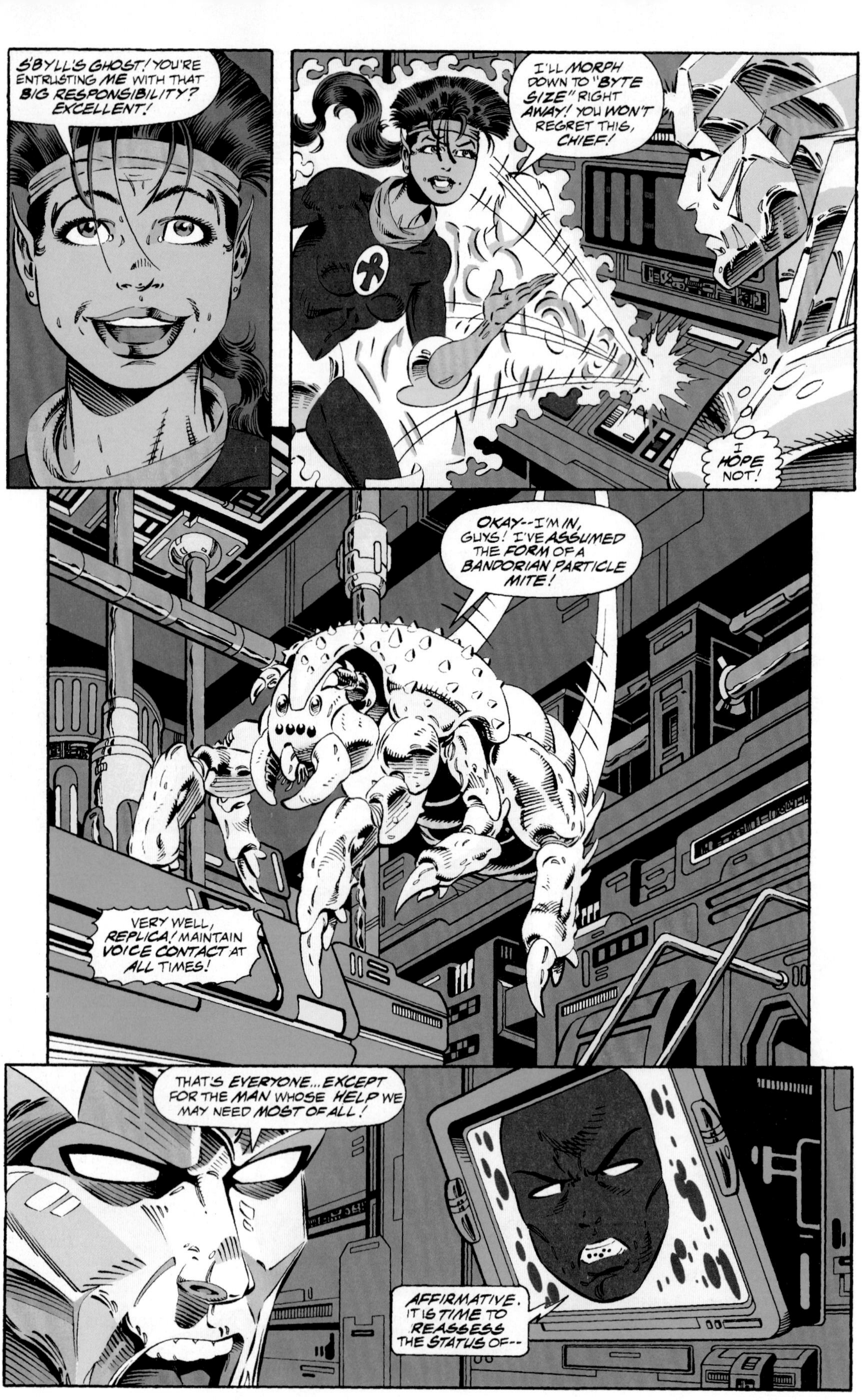
S'BYLL'S GHOST! YOU'RE ENTRUSTING ME WITH THAT BIG RESPONSIBILITY? EXCELLENT!
I'LL MORPH DOWN TO "BYTE SIZE" RIGHT AWAY! YOU WON'T REGRET THIS, CHIEF!
I HOPE NOT!
OKAY--I'M IN, GUYS! I'VE ASSUMED THE FORM OF A BANDORIAN PARTICLE MITE!
VERY WELL, REPLICA! MAINTAIN VOICE CONTACT AT ALL TIMES!
THAT'S EVERYONE... EXCEPT FOR THE MAN WHOSE HELP WE MAY NEED MOST OF ALL!
AFFIRMATIVE. IT IS TIME TO REASSESS THE STATUS OF--

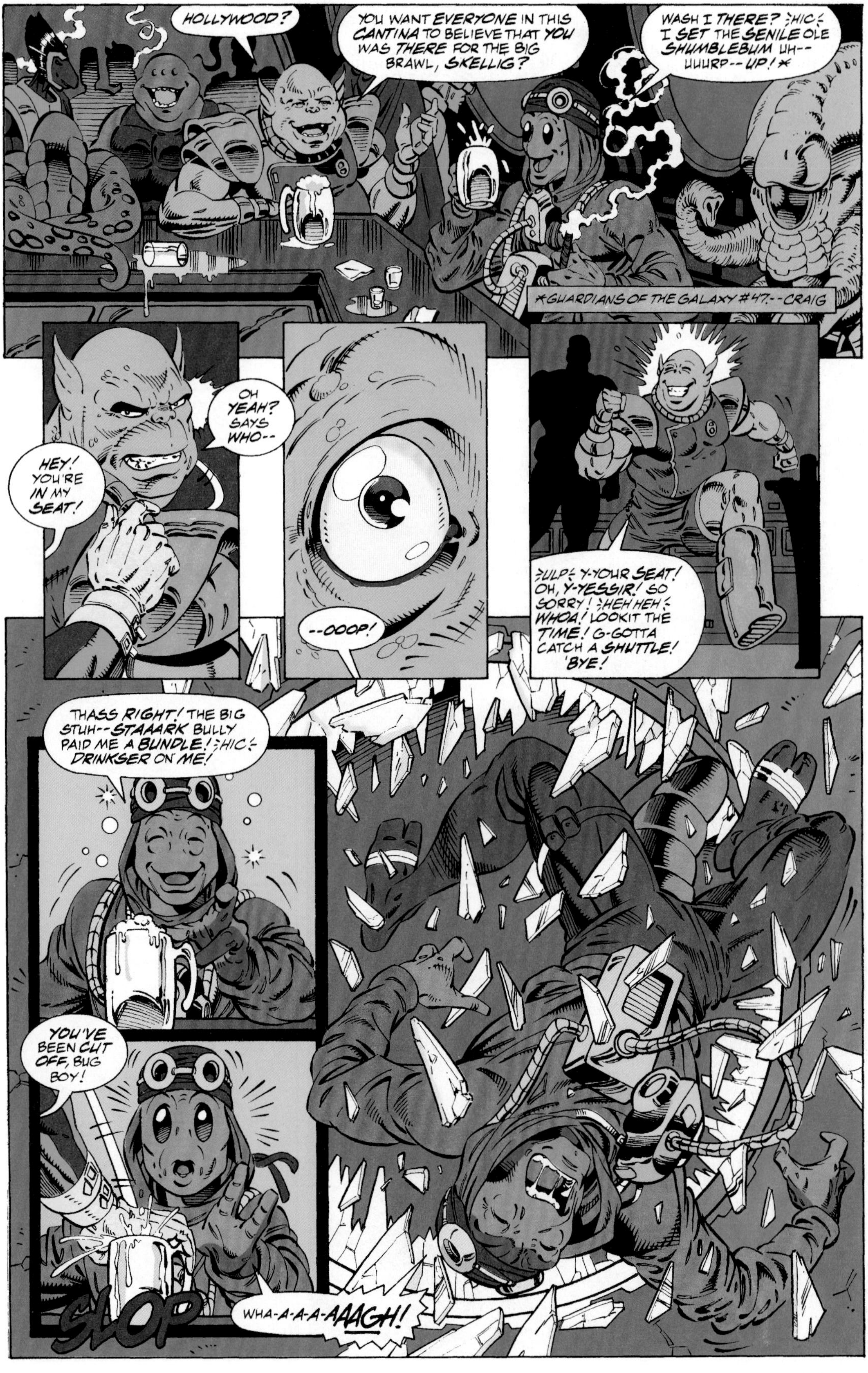
HOLLYWOOD?
YOU WANT EVERYONE IN THIS CANTINA TO BELIEVE THAT YOU WAS THERE FOR THE BIG BRAWL, SKELLIG?
WASH I THERE? ‹HIC› I SET THE SENILE OLE SHUMBLEBUM UH-- UUURP-- UP! *
*GUARDIANS OF THE GALAXY #47.--CRAIG
HEY! YOU'RE IN MY SEAT!
OH YEAH? SAYS WHO--
--OOOP!
‹ULP› Y-YOUR SEAT! OH, Y-YESSIR! SO SORRY! ‹HEH HEH› WHOA! LOOKIT THE TIME! G-GOTTA CATCH A SHUTTLE! 'BYE!
THASS RIGHT! THE BIG STUH--STAAARK BULLY PAID ME A BUNDLE! ‹HIC› DRINKSER ON' ME!
YOU'VE BEEN CUT OFF, BUG BOY!
SLOP
WHA-A-A-A-AAAGH!

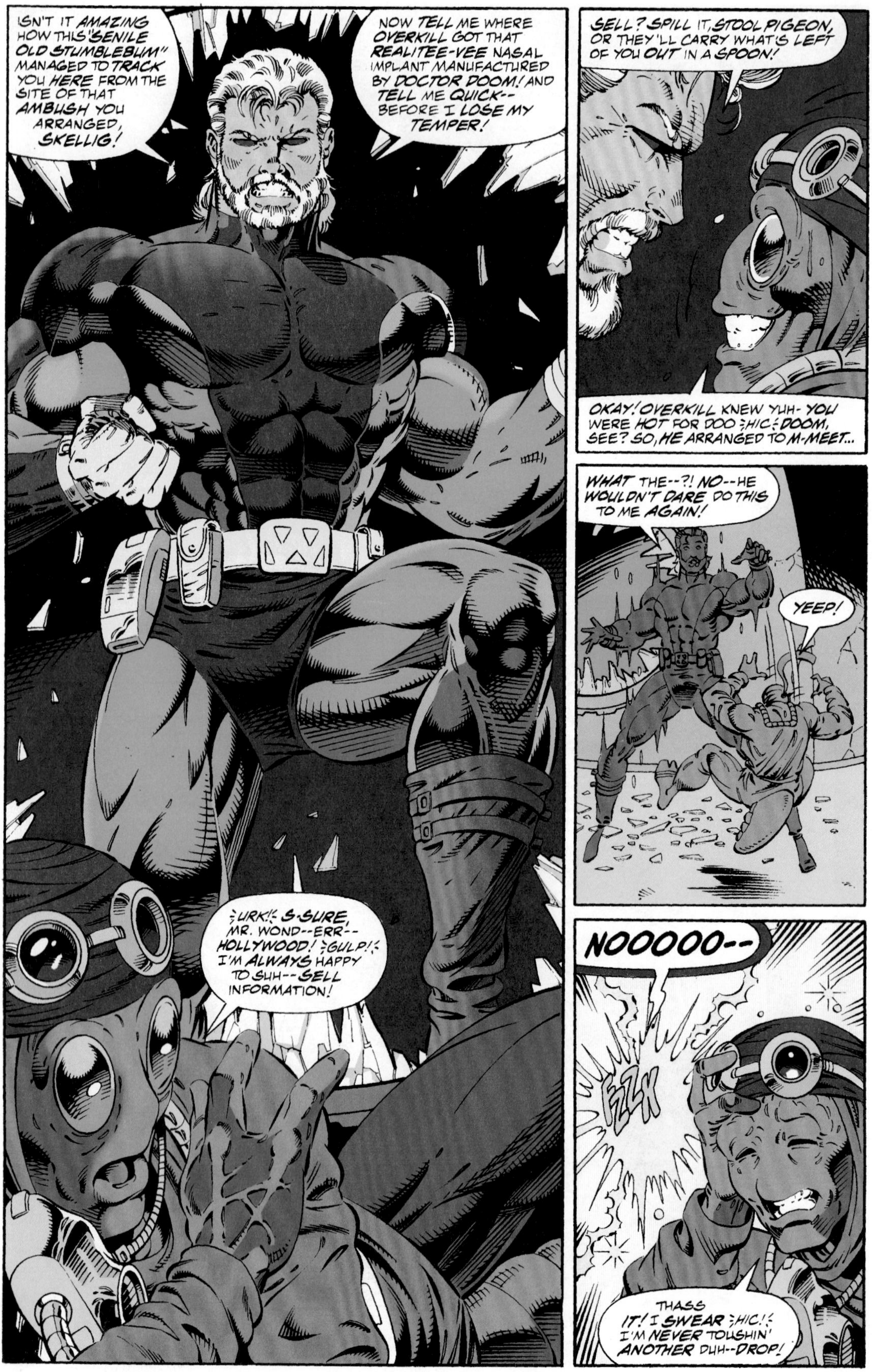

ISN'T IT AMAZING HOW THIS "SENILE OLD STUMBLEBUM" MANAGED TO TRACK YOU HERE FROM THE SITE OF THAT AMBUSH YOU ARRANGED, SKELLIG!
NOW TELL ME WHERE OVERKILL GOT THAT REALITEE-VEE NASAL IMPLANT MANUFACTURED BY DOCTOR DOOM! AND TELL ME QUICK-- BEFORE I LOSE MY TEMPER!
¡URK!¡ S-SURE, MR. WOND--ERR-- HOLLYWOOD! ¡GULP!¡ I'M ALWAYS HAPPY TO SUH--SELL INFORMATION!
SELL? SPILL IT, STOOL PIGEON, OR THEY'LL CARRY WHAT'S LEFT OF YOU OUT IN A SPOON!
OKAY! OVERKILL KNEW YUH- YOU WERE HOT FOR DOO ¡HIC¡ DOOM, SEE? SO, HE ARRANGED TO M-MEET...
WHAT THE--?! NO--HE WOULDN'T DARE DO THIS TO ME AGAIN!
YEEP!
NOOOOO--
FZZK
THASS IT! I SWEAR ¡HIC!¡ I'M NEVER TOUSHIN' ANOTHER DUH--DROP!

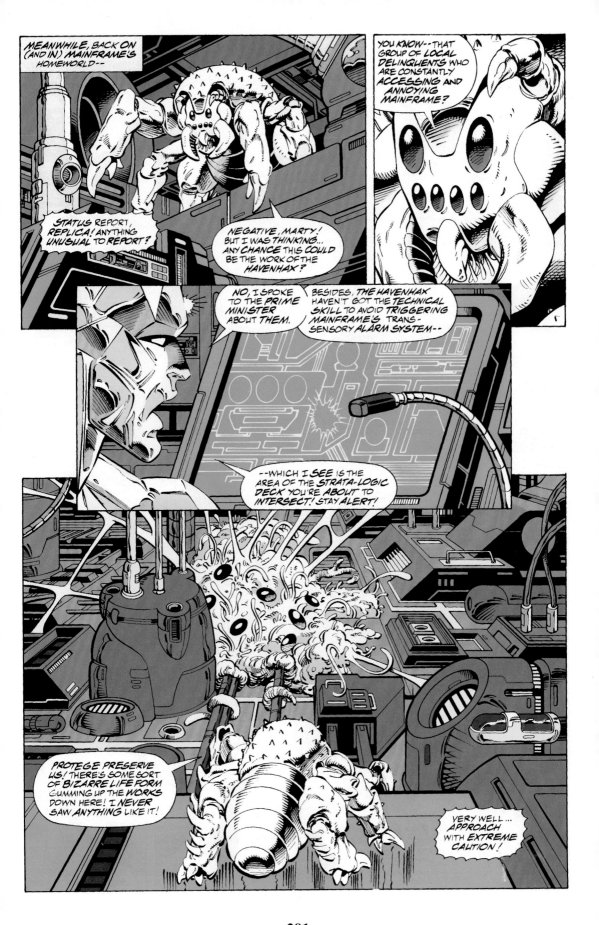

MEANWHILE, BACK ON (AND IN) MAINFRAME'S HOMEWORLD--

STATUS REPORT, REPLICA! ANYTHING UNUSUAL TO REPORT?

NEGATIVE, MARTY! BUT I WAS THINKING... ANY CHANCE THIS COULD BE THE WORK OF THE HAVENHAX?

YOU KNOW--THAT GROUP OF LOCAL DELINQUENTS WHO ARE CONSTANTLY ACCESSING AND ANNOYING MAINFRAME?

NO, I SPOKE TO THE PRIME MINISTER ABOUT THEM.

BESIDES, THE HAVENHAX HAVEN'T GOT THE TECHNICAL SKILL TO AVOID TRIGGERING MAINFRAME'S TRANS-SENSORY ALARM SYSTEM--

--WHICH I SEE IS THE AREA OF THE STRATA-LOGIC DECK YOU'RE ABOUT TO INTERSECT! STAY ALERT!

PROTEGE PRESERVE US! THERE'S SOME SORT OF BIZARRE LIFE FORM GUMMING UP THE WORKS DOWN HERE! I NEVER SAW ANYTHING LIKE IT!

VERY WELL... APPROACH WITH EXTREME CAUTION!

291

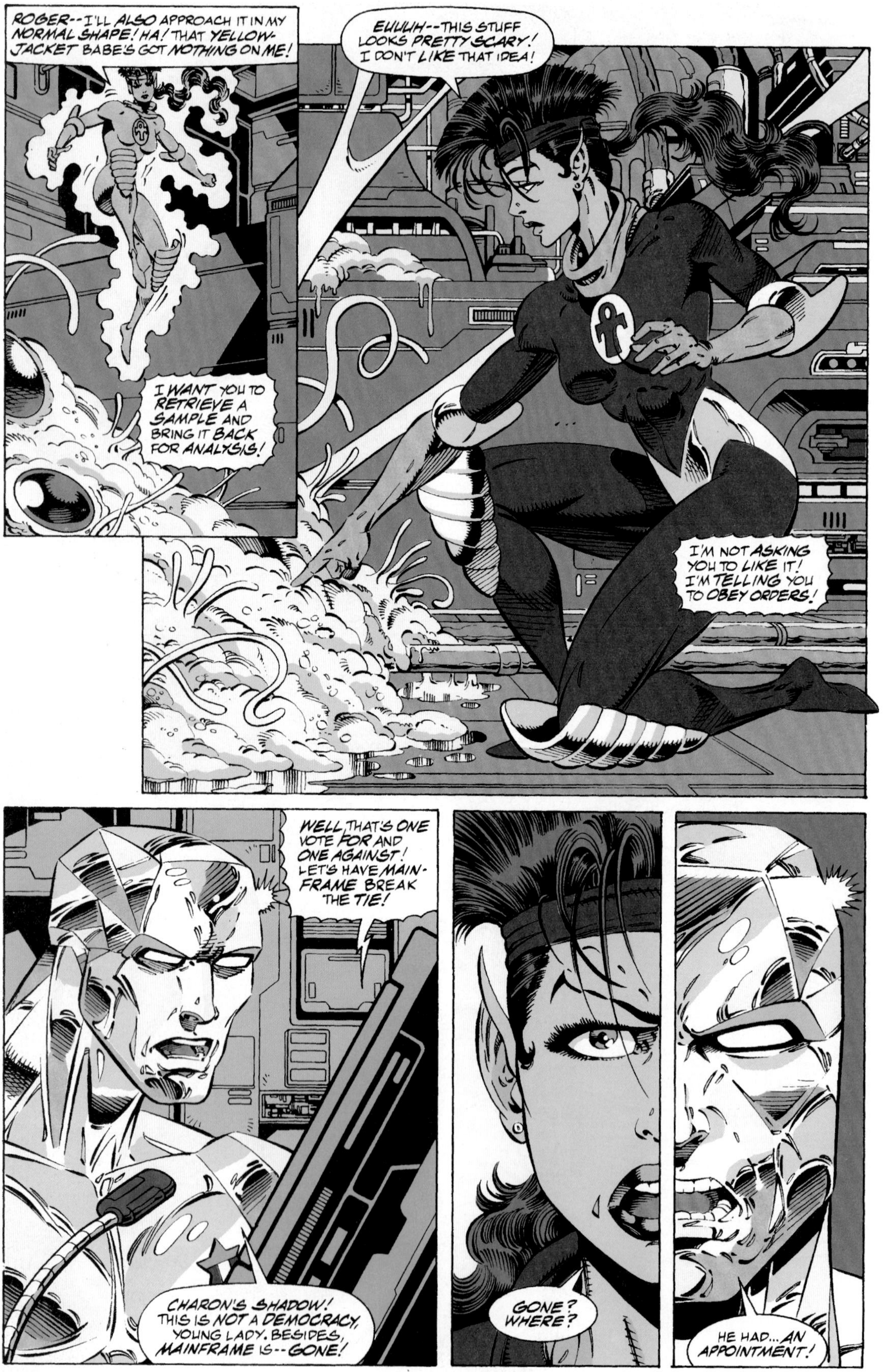
ROGER--I'LL ALSO APPROACH IT IN MY NORMAL SHAPE! HA! THAT YELLOW-JACKET BABE'S GOT NOTHING ON ME!
EUULLH--THIS STUFF LOOKS PRETTY SCARY! I DON'T LIKE THAT IDEA!
I WANT YOU TO RETRIEVE A SAMPLE AND BRING IT BACK FOR ANALYSIS!
I'M NOT ASKING YOU TO LIKE IT! I'M TELLING YOU TO OBEY ORDERS!
WELL, THAT'S ONE VOTE FOR AND ONE AGAINST! LET'S HAVE MAIN-FRAME BREAK THE TIE!
CHARON'S SHADOW! THIS IS NOT A DEMOCRACY, YOUNG LADY. BESIDES, MAINFRAME IS--GONE!
GONE? WHERE?
HE HAD... AN APPOINTMENT!

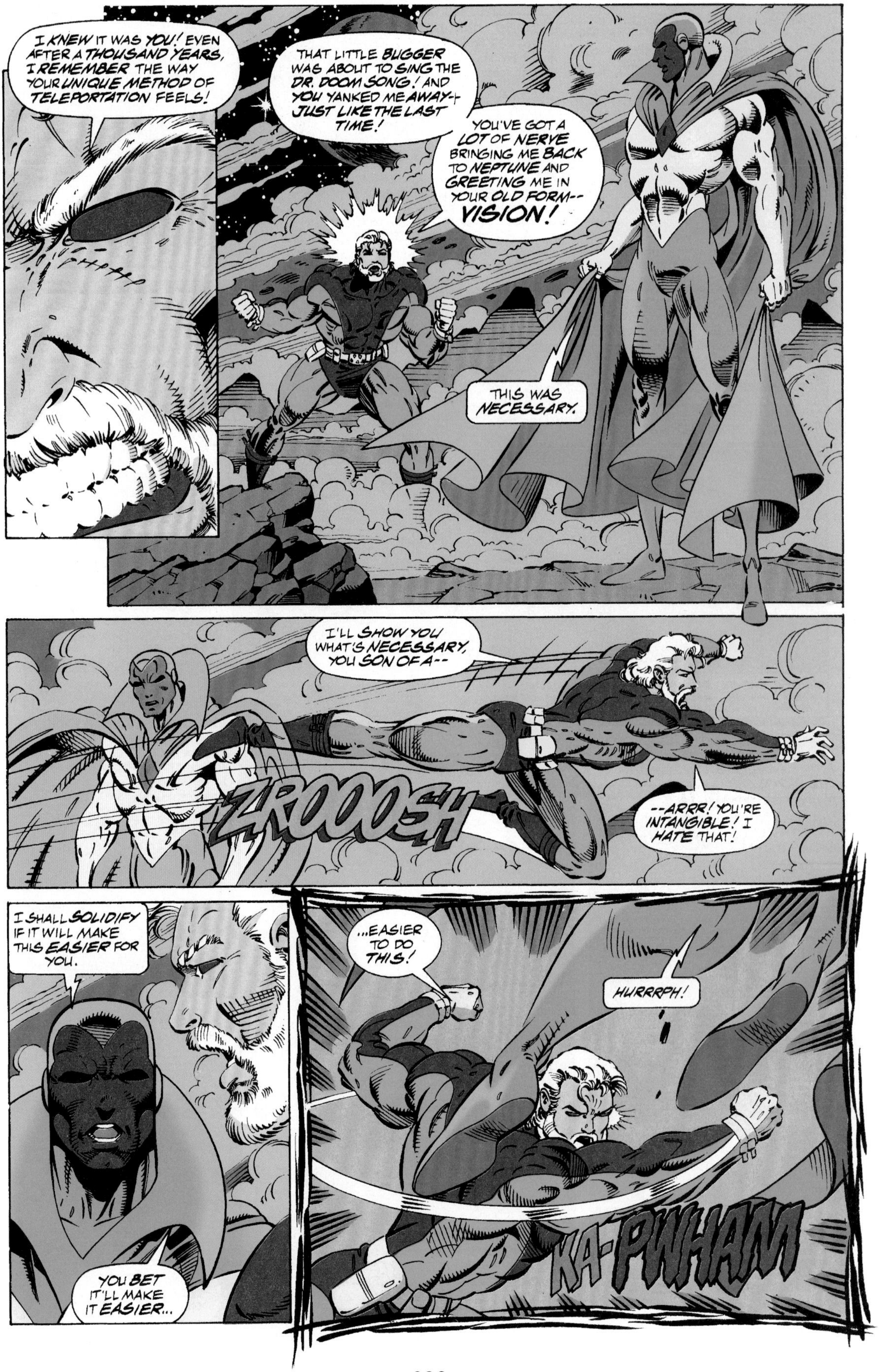
I KNEW IT WAS YOU! EVEN AFTER A THOUSAND YEARS, I REMEMBER THE WAY YOUR UNIQUE METHOD OF TELEPORTATION FEELS!
THAT LITTLE BUGGER WAS ABOUT TO SING THE DR. DOOM SONG! AND YOU YANKED ME AWAY-- JUST LIKE THE LAST TIME!
YOU'VE GOT A LOT OF NERVE BRINGING ME BACK TO NEPTUNE AND GREETING ME IN YOUR OLD FORM-- VISION!
THIS WAS NECESSARY.
I'LL SHOW YOU WHAT'S NECESSARY, YOU SON OF A--
ZROOOOSH
--ARRR! YOU'RE INTANGIBLE! I HATE THAT!
I SHALL SOLIDIFY IF IT WILL MAKE THIS EASIER FOR YOU.
YOU BET IT'LL MAKE IT EASIER...
...EASIER TO DO THIS!
HURRRPH!
KA-PWHAM

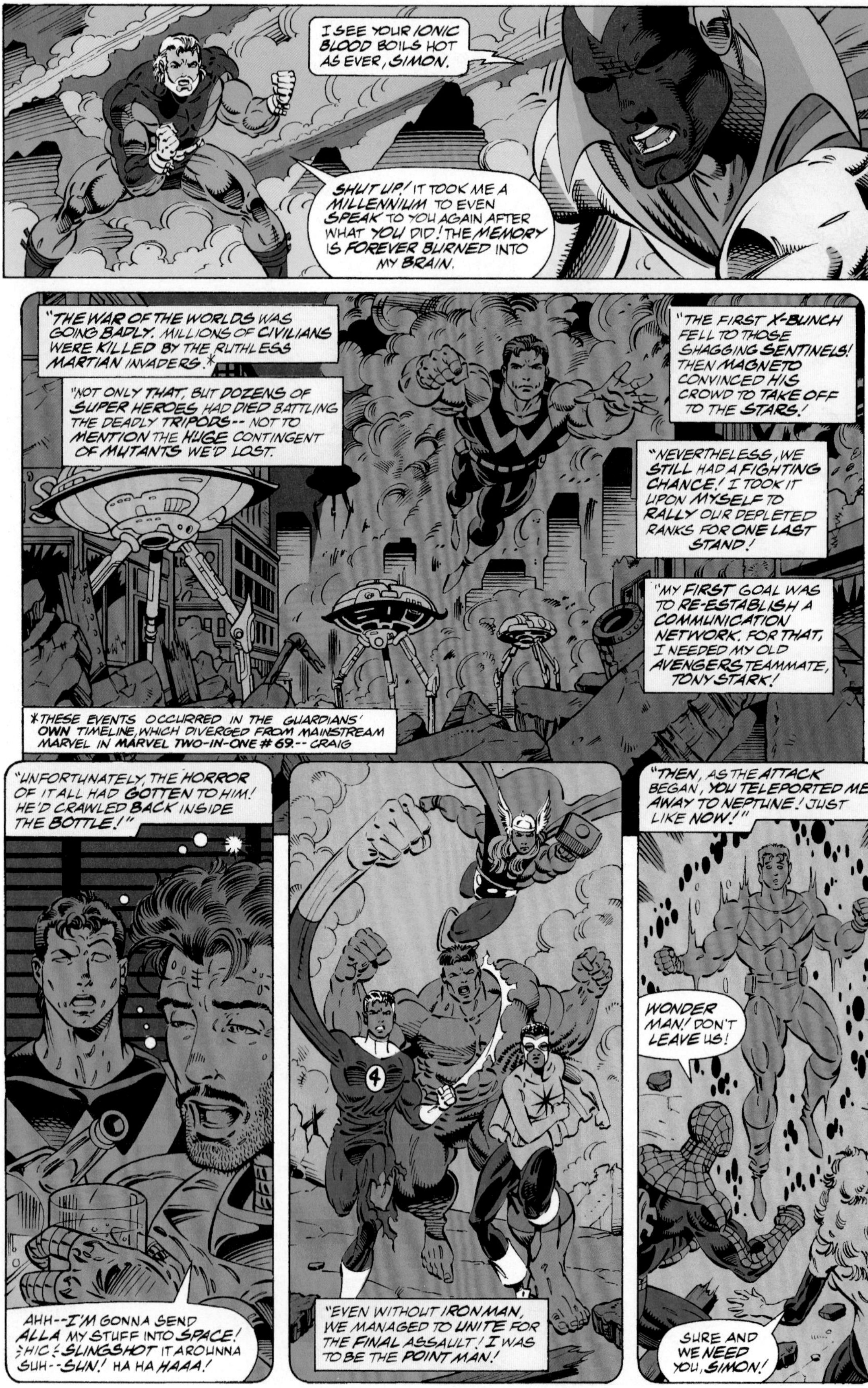
I SEE YOUR IONIC BLOOD BOILS HOT AS EVER, SIMON.
SHUT UP! IT TOOK ME A MILLENNIUM TO EVEN SPEAK TO YOU AGAIN AFTER WHAT YOU DID! THE MEMORY IS FOREVER BURNED INTO MY BRAIN.
"THE WAR OF THE WORLDS WAS GOING BADLY. MILLIONS OF CIVILIANS WERE KILLED BY THE RUTHLESS MARTIAN INVADERS.*
"NOT ONLY THAT, BUT DOZENS OF SUPER HEROES HAD DIED BATTLING THE DEADLY TRIPODS-- NOT TO MENTION THE HUGE CONTINGENT OF MUTANTS WE'D LOST.
"THE FIRST X-BUNCH FELL TO THOSE SHAGGING SENTINELS! THEN MAGNETO CONVINCED HIS CROWD TO TAKE OFF TO THE STARS!
"NEVERTHELESS, WE STILL HAD A FIGHTING CHANCE! I TOOK IT UPON MYSELF TO RALLY OUR DEPLETED RANKS FOR ONE LAST STAND!
"MY FIRST GOAL WAS TO RE-ESTABLISH A COMMUNICATION NETWORK. FOR THAT, I NEEDED MY OLD AVENGERS TEAMMATE, TONY STARK!
*THESE EVENTS OCCURRED IN THE GUARDIANS' OWN TIMELINE, WHICH DIVERGED FROM MAINSTREAM MARVEL IN MARVEL TWO-IN-ONE #69.-- CRAIG
"UNFORTUNATELY, THE HORROR OF IT ALL HAD GOTTEN TO HIM! HE'D CRAWLED BACK INSIDE THE BOTTLE!"
AHH--I'M GONNA SEND ALLA MY STUFF INTO SPACE! ≷HIC≷ SLINGSHOT IT AROUNNA SUH--SUN! HA HA HAAA!
"EVEN WITHOUT IRON MAN, WE MANAGED TO UNITE FOR THE FINAL ASSAULT! I WAS TO BE THE POINT MAN!
"THEN, AS THE ATTACK BEGAN, YOU TELEPORTED ME AWAY TO NEPTUNE! JUST LIKE NOW!"
WONDER MAN! DON'T LEAVE US!
SURE AND WE NEED YOU, SIMON!

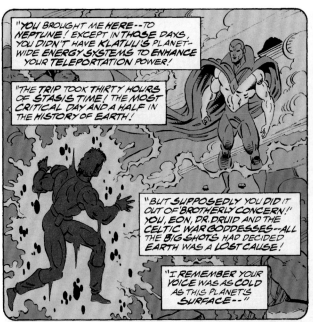

"YOU BROUGHT ME HERE--TO NEPTUNE! EXCEPT IN THOSE DAYS, YOU DIDN'T HAVE KLATHU'S PLANET-WIDE ENERGY SYSTEMS TO ENHANCE YOUR TELEPORTATION POWER!

"THE TRIP TOOK THIRTY HOURS OF STASIS TIME! THE MOST CRITICAL DAY AND A HALF IN THE HISTORY OF EARTH!

"BUT SUPPOSEDLY YOU DID IT OUT OF 'BROTHERLY CONCERN!' YOU, EON, DR. DRUID AND THE CELTIC WAR GODDESSES--ALL THE BIG SHOTS HAD DECIDED EARTH WAS A LOST CAUSE!

"I REMEMBER YOUR VOICE WAS AS COLD AS THIS PLANET'S SURFACE--"

SIMON, I SHALL EXPLAIN THE LOGIC OF MY DECISION TO EXTRICATE YOU.

LOGIC?! OUR PEOPLE ARE GETTING BUTCHERED! EXPLAIN IT TO ME LATER! SEND ME BACK NOW! DO YOU HEAR ME? NOW!

"WHICH YOU DID--WITH ME CURSING YOUR EXISTENCE ALL THE WAY! THOSE NEXT THIRTY HOURS IN TRANSIT WERE TORTURE! BUT I MADE IT HOME...

"...BY THEN, IT WAS ALL OVER!"

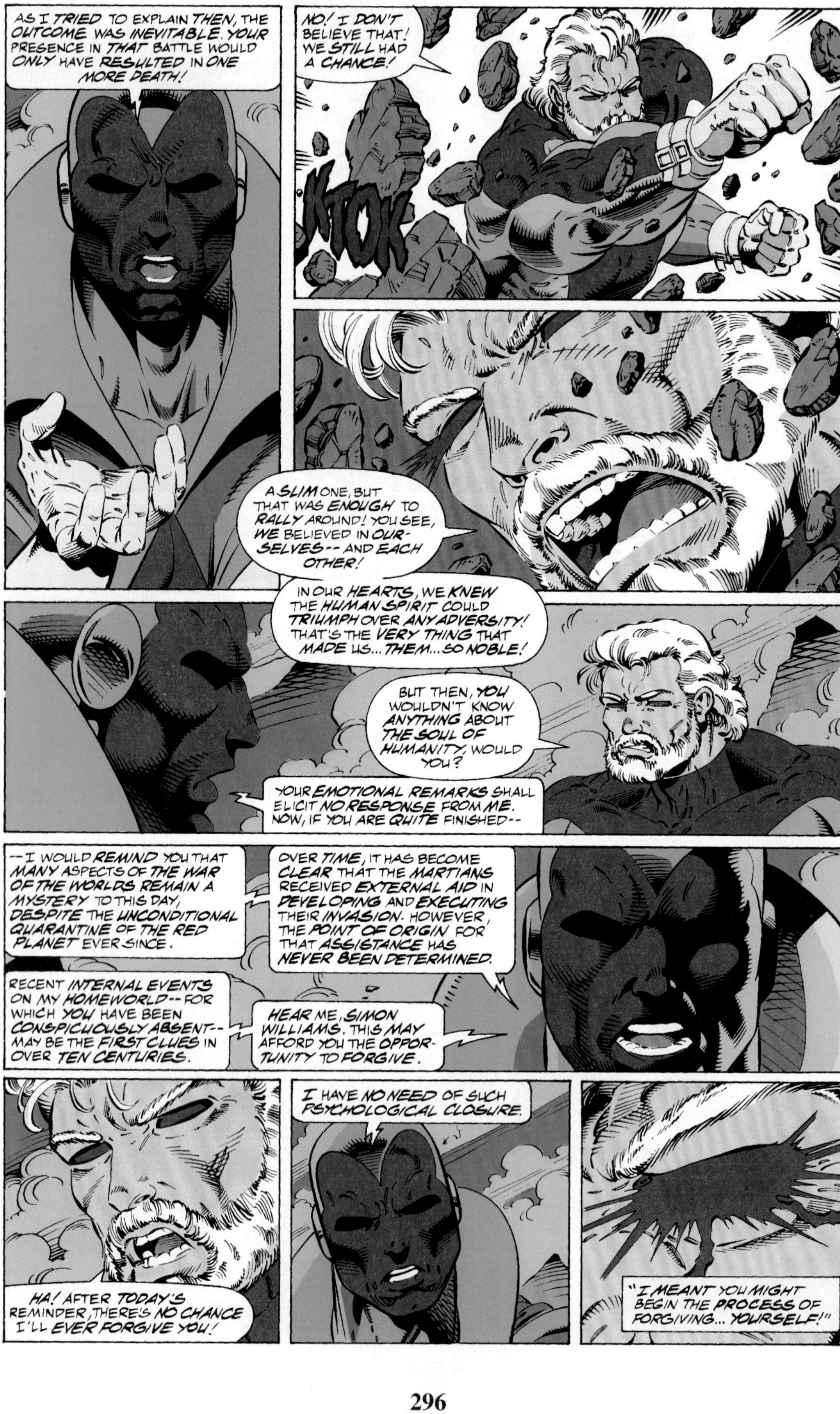
AS I TRIED TO EXPLAIN THEN, THE OUTCOME WAS INEVITABLE. YOUR PRESENCE IN THAT BATTLE WOULD ONLY HAVE RESULTED IN ONE MORE DEATH!
NO! I DON'T BELIEVE THAT! WE STILL HAD A CHANCE!
KTOK
A SLIM ONE, BUT THAT WAS ENOUGH TO RALLY AROUND! YOU SEE, WE BELIEVED IN OURSELVES -- AND EACH OTHER!
IN OUR HEARTS, WE KNEW THE HUMAN SPIRIT COULD TRIUMPH OVER ANY ADVERSITY! THAT'S THE VERY THING THAT MADE US... THEM... SO NOBLE!
BUT THEN, YOU WOULDN'T KNOW ANYTHING ABOUT THE SOUL OF HUMANITY, WOULD YOU?
YOUR EMOTIONAL REMARKS SHALL ELICIT NO RESPONSE FROM ME. NOW, IF YOU ARE QUITE FINISHED--
--I WOULD REMIND YOU THAT MANY ASPECTS OF THE WAR OF THE WORLDS REMAIN A MYSTERY TO THIS DAY, DESPITE THE UNCONDITIONAL QUARANTINE OF THE RED PLANET EVER SINCE.
OVER TIME, IT HAS BECOME CLEAR THAT THE MARTIANS RECEIVED EXTERNAL AID IN DEVELOPING AND EXECUTING THEIR INVASION. HOWEVER, THE POINT OF ORIGIN FOR THAT ASSISTANCE HAS NEVER BEEN DETERMINED.
RECENT INTERNAL EVENTS ON MY HOMEWORLD -- FOR WHICH YOU HAVE BEEN CONSPICUOUSLY ABSENT -- MAY BE THE FIRST CLUES IN OVER TEN CENTURIES.
HEAR ME, SIMON WILLIAMS. THIS MAY AFFORD YOU THE OPPORTUNITY TO FORGIVE.
HA! AFTER TODAY'S REMINDER, THERE'S NO CHANCE I'LL EVER FORGIVE YOU!
I HAVE NO NEED OF SUCH PSYCHOLOGICAL CLOSURE.
"I MEANT YOU MIGHT BEGIN THE PROCESS OF FORGIVING... YOURSELF!"

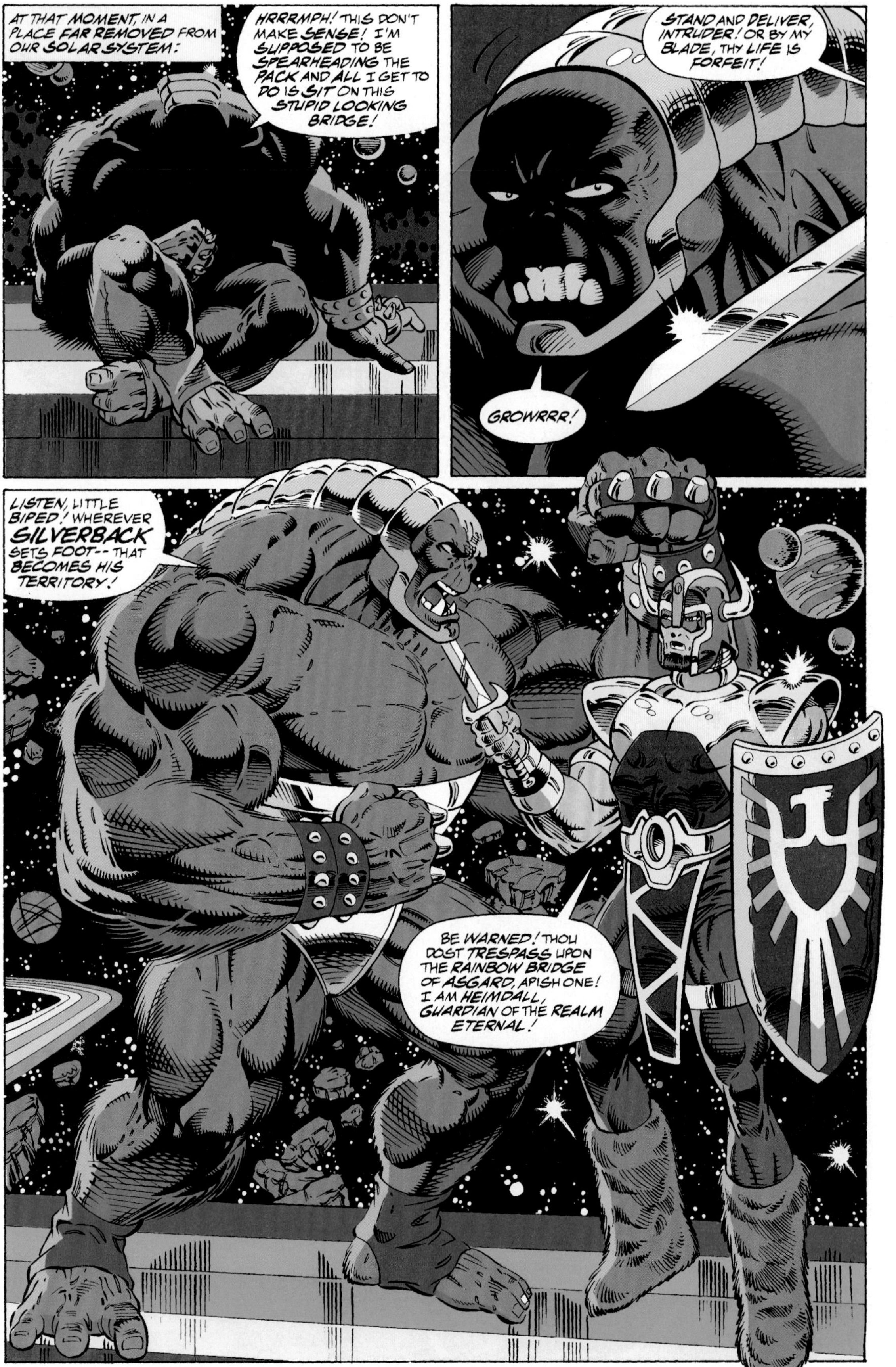
AT THAT MOMENT, IN A PLACE FAR REMOVED FROM OUR SOLAR SYSTEM:
HRRRMPH! THIS DON'T MAKE SENSE! I'M SUPPOSED TO BE SPEARHEADING THE PACK AND ALL I GET TO DO IS SIT ON THIS STUPID LOOKING BRIDGE!
STAND AND DELIVER, INTRUDER! OR BY MY BLADE, THY LIFE IS FORFEIT!
GROWRRR!
LISTEN, LITTLE BIPED! WHEREVER SILVERBACK SETS FOOT-- THAT BECOMES HIS TERRITORY!
BE WARNED! THOU DOST TRESPASS UPON THE RAINBOW BRIDGE OF ASGARD, APISH ONE! I AM HEIMDALL, GUARDIAN OF THE REALM ETERNAL!

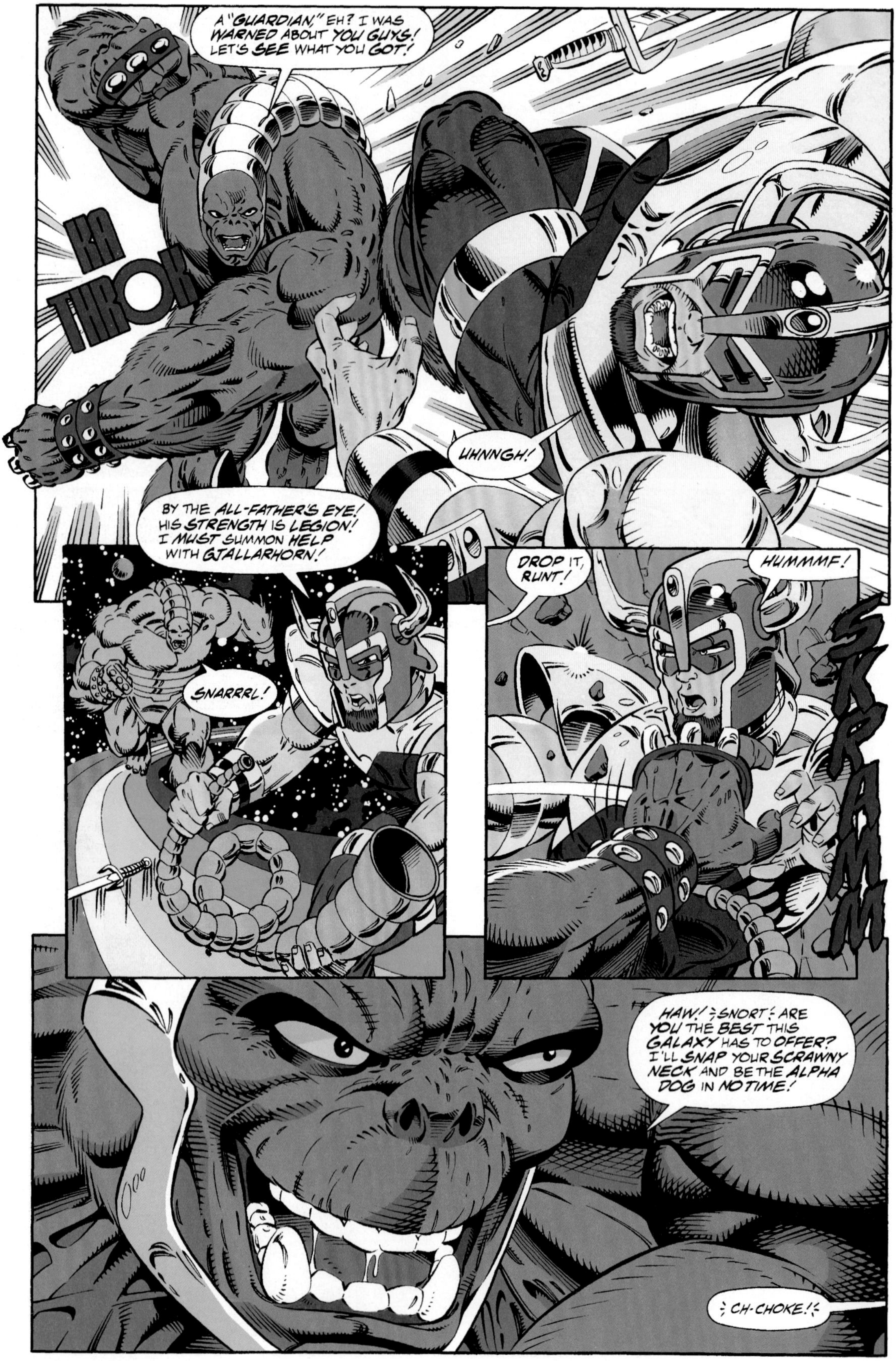

A "GUARDIAN," EH? I WAS WARNED ABOUT YOU GUYS! LET'S SEE WHAT YOU GOT!
KA THROK
UHNNGH!
BY THE ALL-FATHER'S EYE! HIS STRENGTH IS LEGION! I MUST SUMMON HELP WITH GJALLARHORN!
SNARRRL!
DROP IT, RUNT!
HUMMMF!
SKRAM
HAW! ;SNORT; ARE YOU THE BEST THIS GALAXY HAS TO OFFER? I'LL SNAP YOUR SCRAWNY NECK AND BE THE ALPHA DOG IN NO TIME!
;CH-CHOKE!;

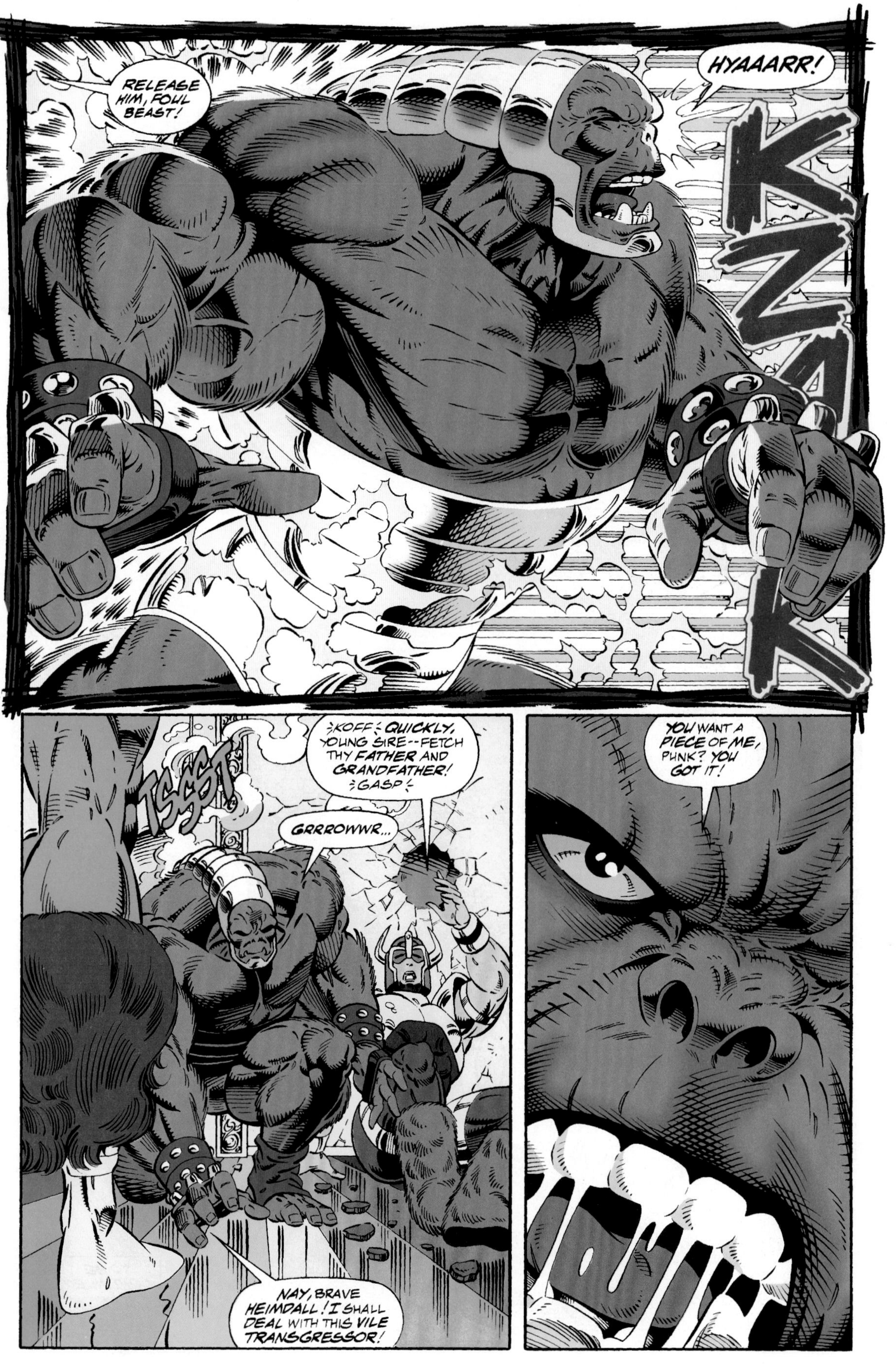
RELEASE HIM, FOUL BEAST!
HYAAARR!
KNAK
TSSST
KOFF QUICKLY, YOUNG SIRE--FETCH THY FATHER AND GRANDFATHER! GASP
GRRROWWR...
NAY, BRAVE HEIMDALL! I SHALL DEAL WITH THIS VILE TRANSGRESSOR!
YOU WANT A PIECE OF ME, PUNK? YOU GOT IT!

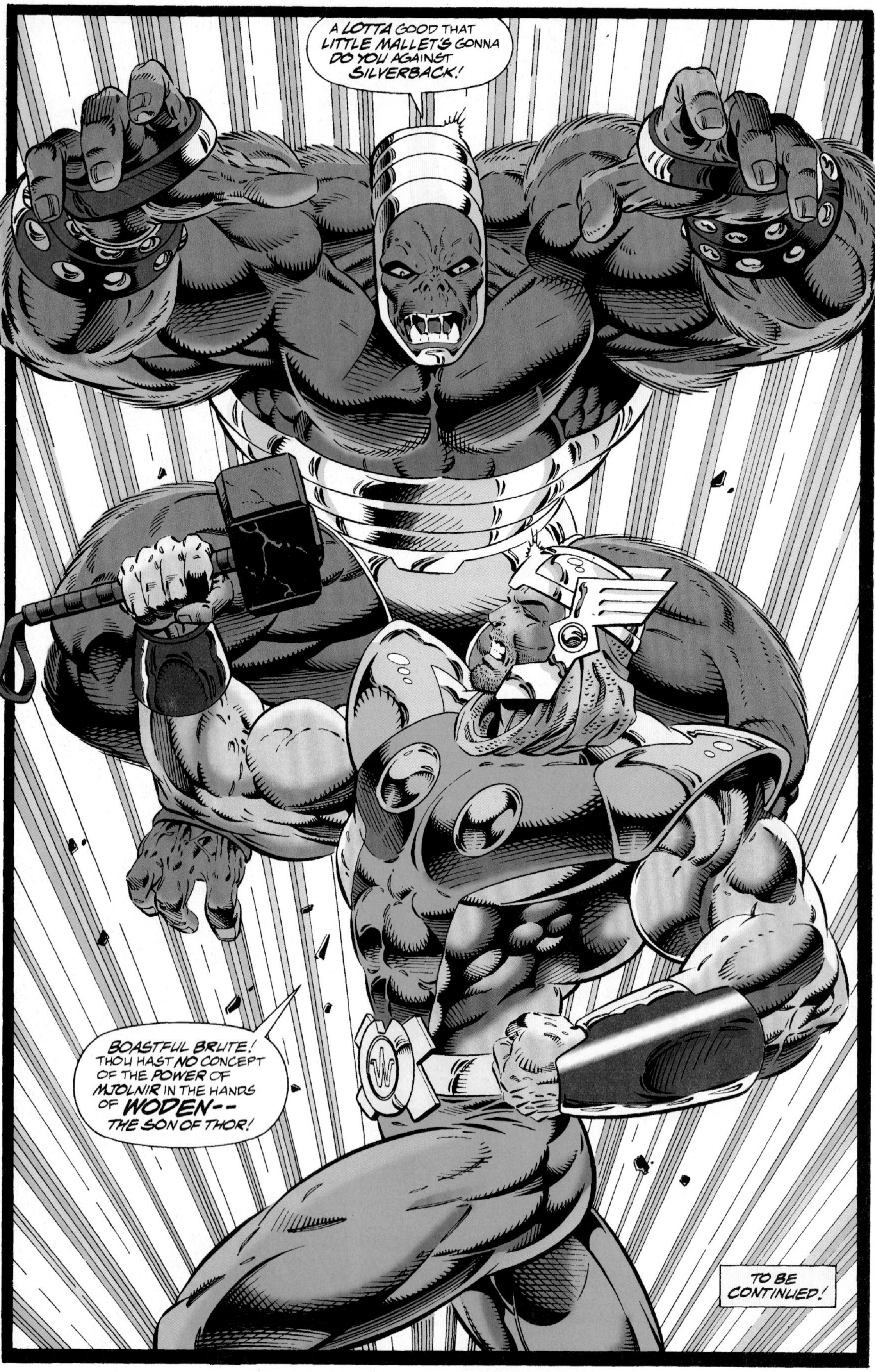
A LOTTA GOOD THAT LITTLE MALLET'S GONNA DO YOU AGAINST SILVERBACK!
BOASTFUL BRUTE! THOU HAST NO CONCEPT OF THE POWER OF MJOLNIR IN THE HANDS OF WODEN-- THE SON OF THOR!
TO BE CONTINUED!

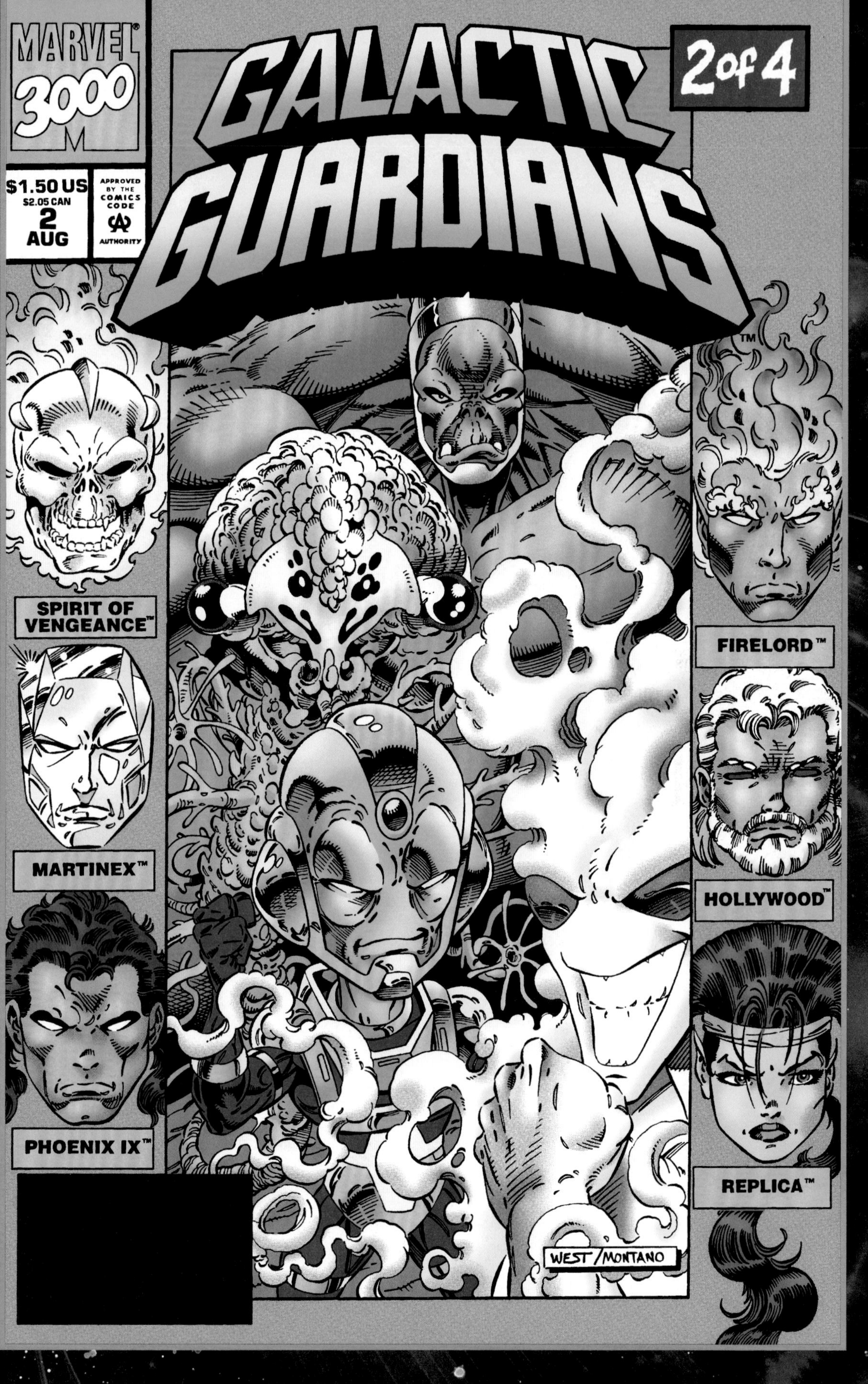

MARVEL 3000
GALACTIC GUARDIANS
2 of 4
$1.50 US
$2.05 CAN
2
AUG
APPROVED BY THE COMICS CODE AUTHORITY
SPIRIT OF VENGEANCE™
MARTINEX™
PHOENIX IX™
FIRELORD™
HOLLYWOOD™
REPLICA™
WEST/MONTANO

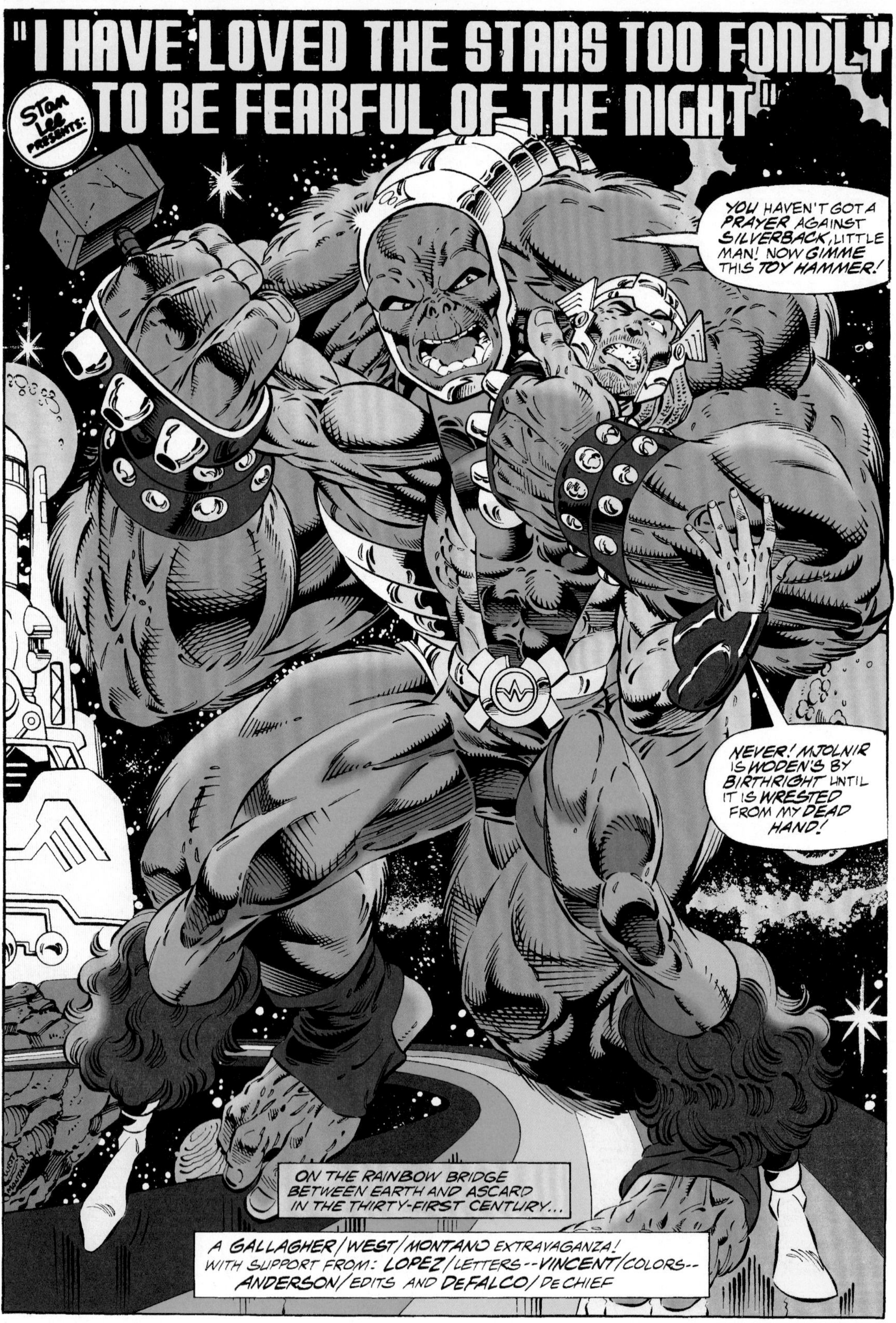
"I HAVE LOVED THE STARS TOO FONDLY TO BE FEARFUL OF THE NIGHT"
STAN LEE PRESENTS:
YOU HAVEN'T GOT A PRAYER AGAINST SILVERBACK, LITTLE MAN! NOW GIMME THIS TOY HAMMER!
NEVER! MJOLNIR IS WODEN'S BY BIRTHRIGHT UNTIL IT IS WRESTED FROM MY DEAD HAND!
ON THE RAINBOW BRIDGE BETWEEN EARTH AND ASGARD IN THE THIRTY-FIRST CENTURY...
A GALLAGHER/WEST/MONTANO EXTRAVAGANZA!
WITH SUPPORT FROM: LOPEZ/LETTERS--VINCENT/COLORS--
ANDERSON/EDITS AND DEFALCO/DE CHIEF

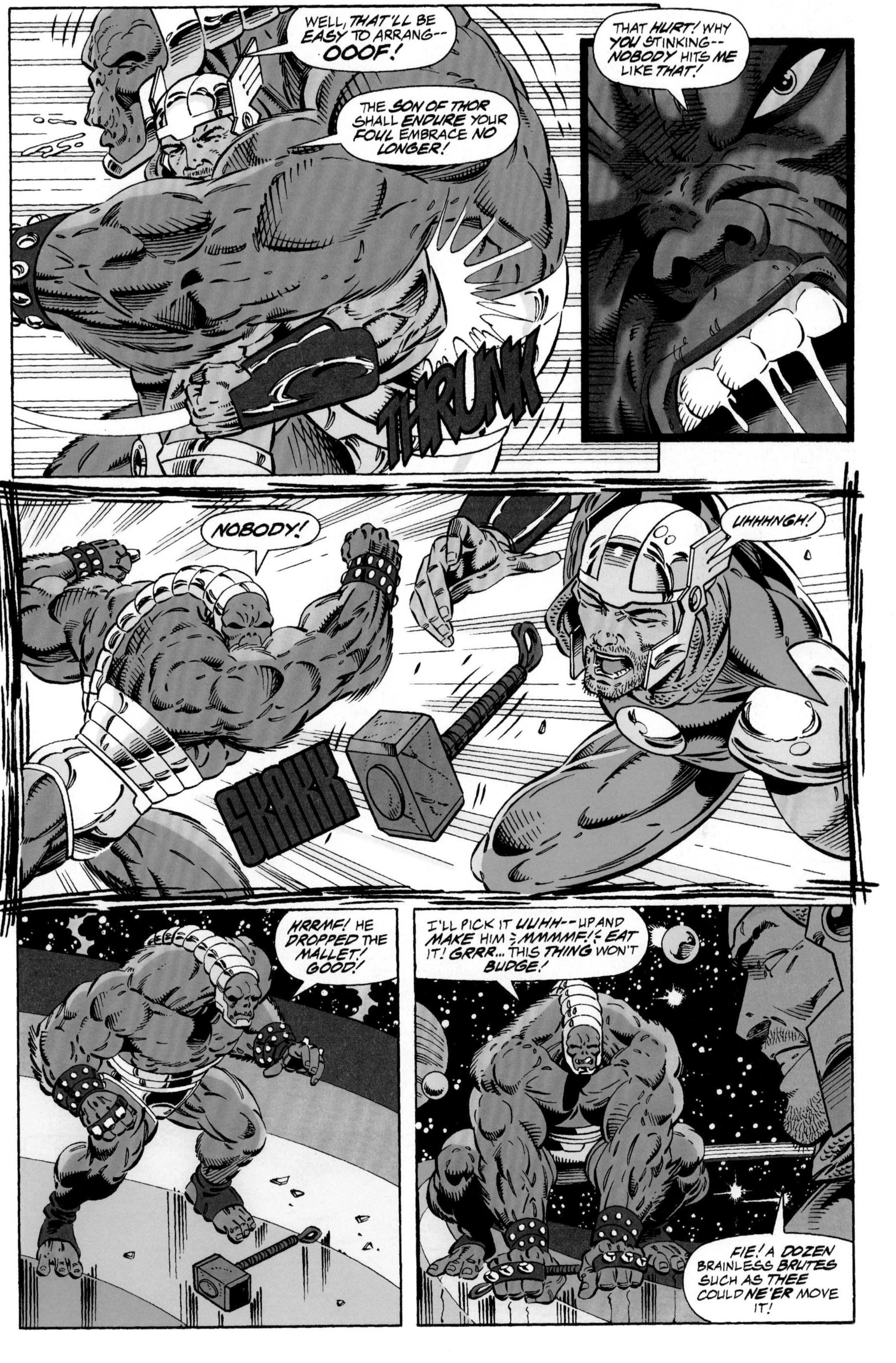

WELL, THAT'LL BE EASY TO ARRANG-- OOOF!
THE SON OF THOR SHALL ENDURE YOUR FOUL EMBRACE NO LONGER!
THRUNK
THAT HURT! WHY YOU STINKING-- NOBODY HITS ME LIKE THAT!
NOBODY!
UHHHNGH!
SKAKK
HRRMF! HE DROPPED THE MALLET! GOOD!
I'LL PICK IT UUHH--UP AND MAKE HIM ≷MMMMF!≶ EAT IT! GRRR... THIS THING WON'T BUDGE!
FIE! A DOZEN BRAINLESS BRUTES SUCH AS THEE COULD NE'ER MOVE IT!

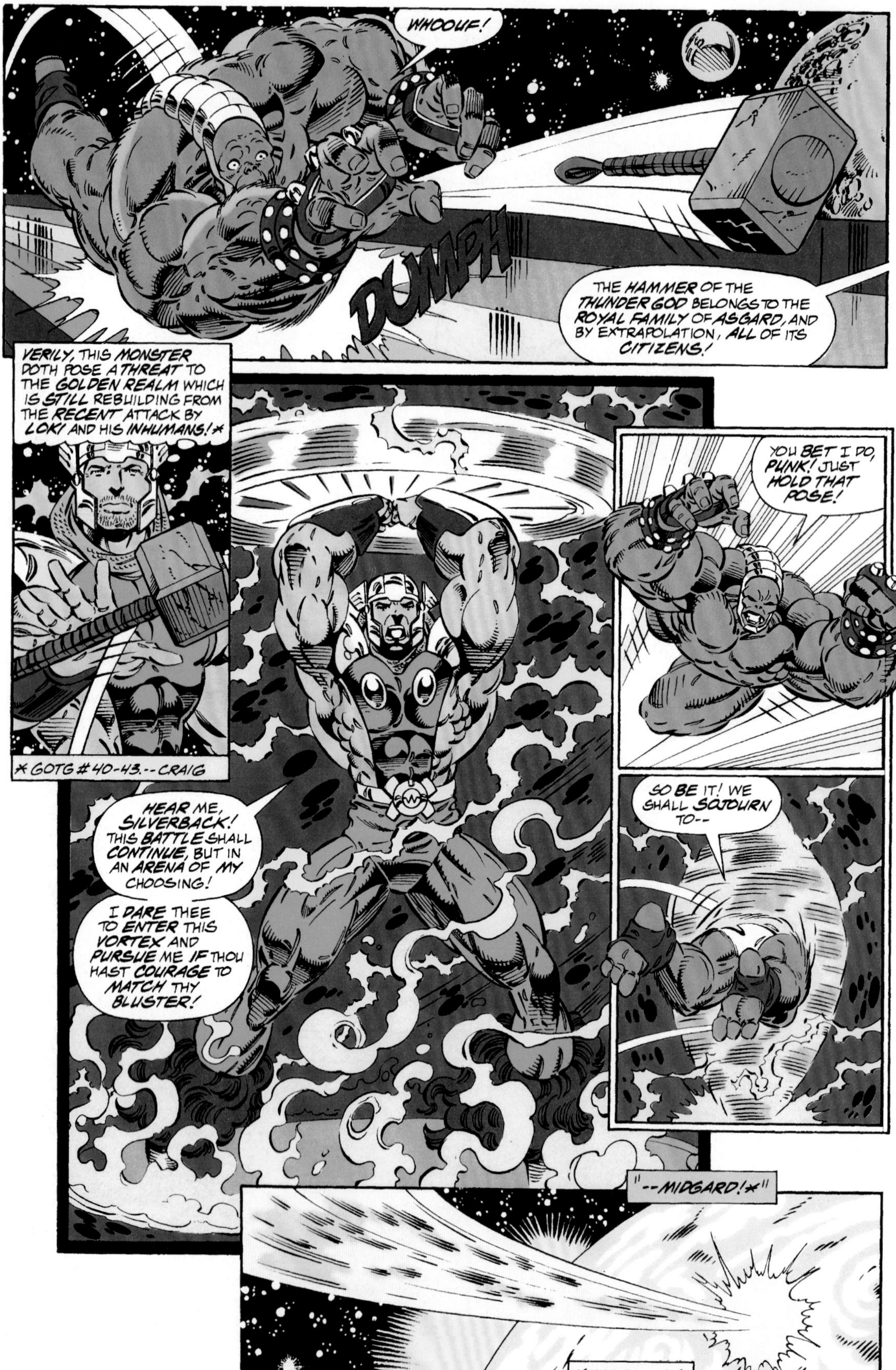
WHOOUF!
DUMPH
THE HAMMER OF THE THUNDER GOD BELONGS TO THE ROYAL FAMILY OF ASGARD, AND BY EXTRAPOLATION, ALL OF ITS CITIZENS!
VERILY, THIS MONSTER DOTH POSE A THREAT TO THE GOLDEN REALM WHICH IS STILL REBUILDING FROM THE RECENT ATTACK BY LOKI AND HIS INHUMANS!*
*GOTG #40-43.--CRAIG
HEAR ME, SILVERBACK! THIS BATTLE SHALL CONTINUE, BUT IN AN ARENA OF MY CHOOSING!
I DARE THEE TO ENTER THIS VORTEX AND PURSUE ME IF THOU HAST COURAGE TO MATCH THY BLUSTER!
YOU BET I DO, PUNK! JUST HOLD THAT POSE!
SO BE IT! WE SHALL SOJOURN TO--
"--MIDGARD!*"
*EARTH.--C.A.

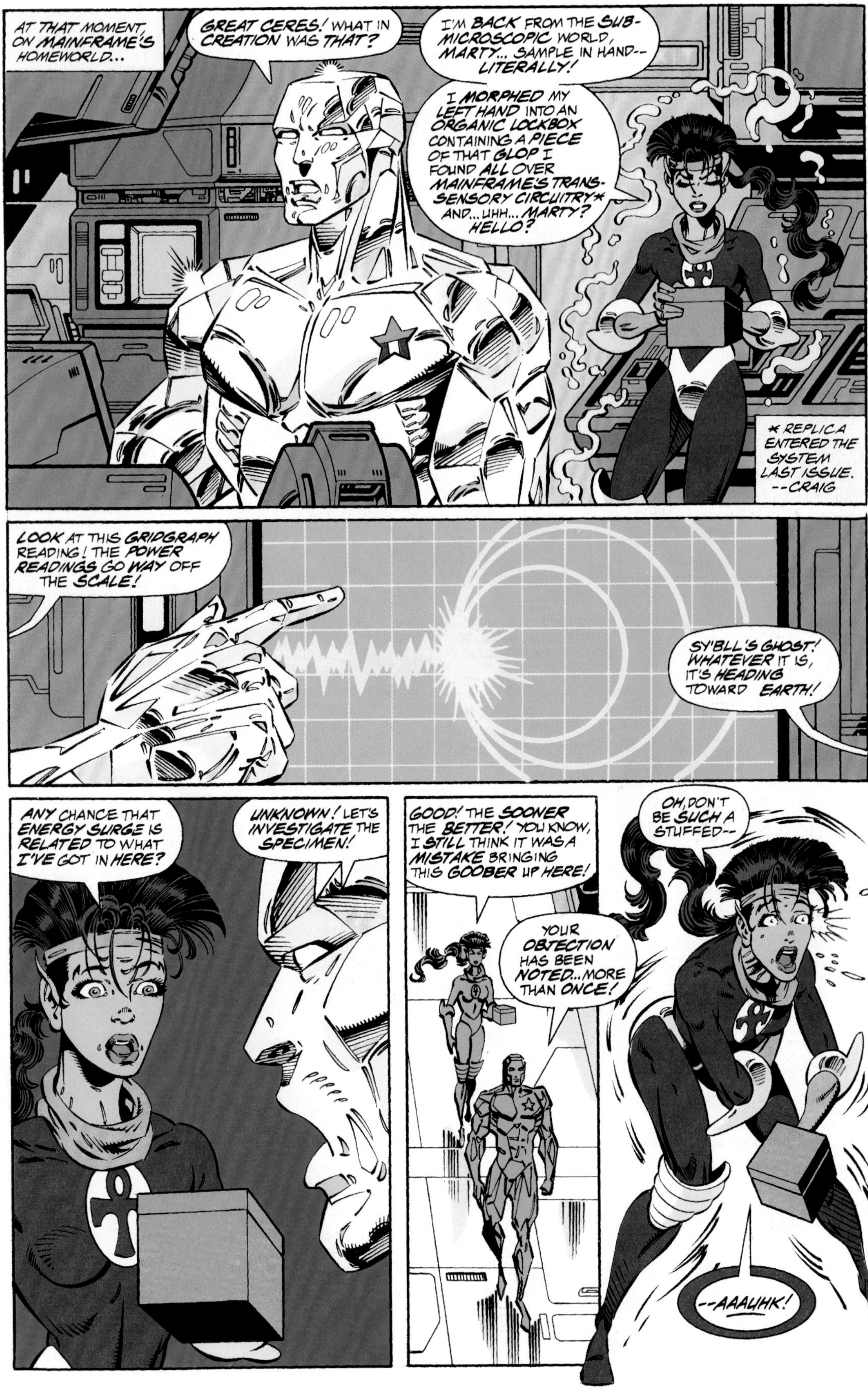

AT THAT MOMENT, ON MAINFRAME'S HOMEWORLD...
GREAT CERES! WHAT IN CREATION WAS THAT?
I'M BACK FROM THE SUB-MICROSCOPIC WORLD, MARTY... SAMPLE IN HAND-- LITERALLY!
I MORPHED MY LEFT HAND INTO AN ORGANIC LOCKBOX CONTAINING A PIECE OF THAT GLOP I FOUND ALL OVER MAINFRAME'S TRANS-SENSORY CIRCUITRY* AND... UHH... MARTY? HELLO?
* REPLICA ENTERED THE SYSTEM LAST ISSUE. --CRAIG
LOOK AT THIS GRIDGRAPH READING! THE POWER READINGS GO WAY OFF THE SCALE!
SY'BLL'S GHOST! WHATEVER IT IS, IT'S HEADING TOWARD EARTH!
ANY CHANCE THAT ENERGY SURGE IS RELATED TO WHAT I'VE GOT IN HERE?
UNKNOWN! LET'S INVESTIGATE THE SPECIMEN!
GOOD! THE SOONER THE BETTER! YOU KNOW, I STILL THINK IT WAS A MISTAKE BRINGING THIS GOOBER UP HERE!
YOUR OBJECTION HAS BEEN NOTED... MORE THAN ONCE!
OH, DON'T BE SUCH A STUFFED--
--AAAUHK!

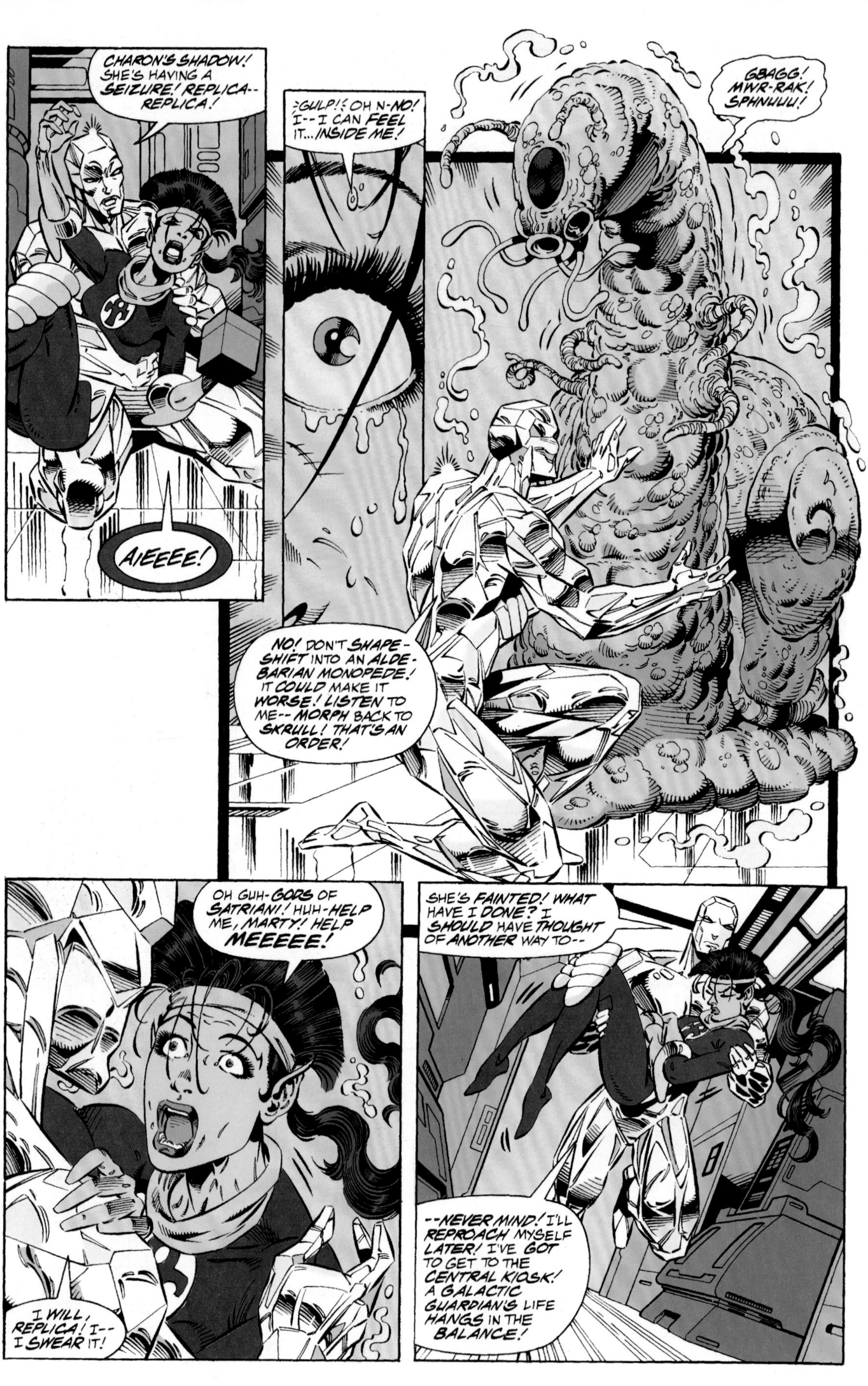
CHARON'S SHADOW! SHE'S HAVING A SEIZURE! REPLICA-- REPLICA!
AIEEEE!
GULP! OH N-NO! I--I CAN FEEL IT...INSIDE ME!
GBAGG! MWR-RAK! SPHNUUU!
NO! DON'T SHAPE-SHIFT INTO AN ALDEBARIAN MONOPEDE! IT COULD MAKE IT WORSE! LISTEN TO ME-- MORPH BACK TO SKRULL! THAT'S AN ORDER!
OH GUH-GODS OF SATRIANI! HUH-HELP ME, MARTY! HELP MEEEEE!
I WILL, REPLICA! I-- I SWEAR IT!
SHE'S FAINTED! WHAT HAVE I DONE? I SHOULD HAVE THOUGHT OF ANOTHER WAY TO--
--NEVER MIND! I'LL REPROACH MYSELF LATER! I'VE GOT TO GET TO THE CENTRAL KIOSK! A GALACTIC GUARDIAN'S LIFE HANGS IN THE BALANCE!

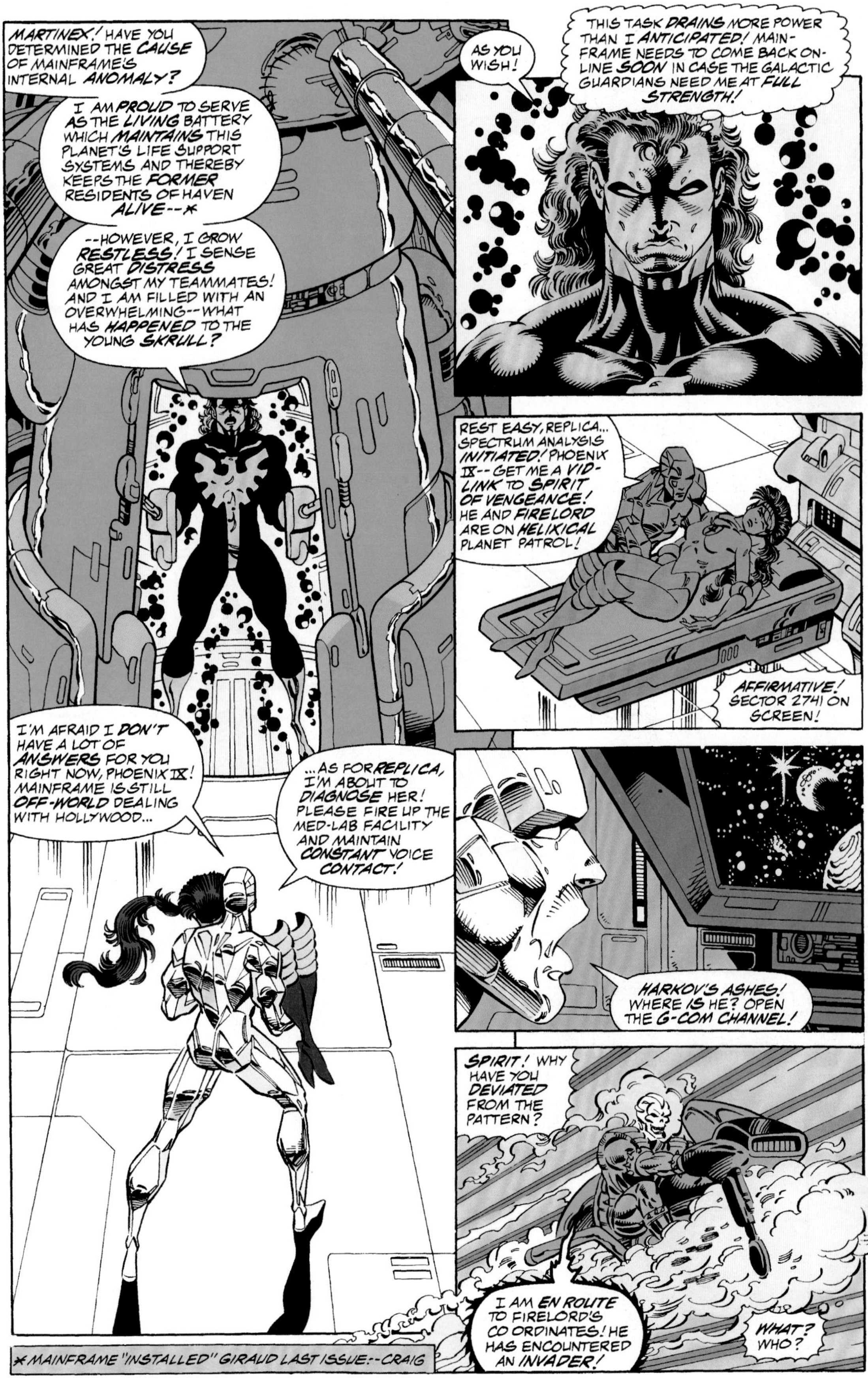

MARTINEX! HAVE YOU DETERMINED THE CAUSE OF MAINFRAME'S INTERNAL ANOMALY?
AS YOU WISH!
THIS TASK DRAINS MORE POWER THAN I ANTICIPATED! MAINFRAME NEEDS TO COME BACK ON-LINE SOON IN CASE THE GALACTIC GUARDIANS NEED ME AT FULL STRENGTH!
I AM PROUD TO SERVE AS THE LIVING BATTERY WHICH MAINTAINS THIS PLANET'S LIFE SUPPORT SYSTEMS AND THEREBY KEEPS THE FORMER RESIDENTS OF HAVEN ALIVE--*
--HOWEVER, I GROW RESTLESS! I SENSE GREAT DISTRESS AMONGST MY TEAMMATES! AND I AM FILLED WITH AN OVERWHELMING--WHAT HAS HAPPENED TO THE YOUNG SKRULL?
REST EASY, REPLICA... SPECTRUM ANALYSIS INITIATED! PHOENIX IX-- GET ME A VID-LINK TO SPIRIT OF VENGEANCE! HE AND FIRELORD ARE ON HELIXICAL PLANET PATROL!
AFFIRMATIVE! SECTOR 2741 ON SCREEN!
I'M AFRAID I DON'T HAVE A LOT OF ANSWERS FOR YOU RIGHT NOW, PHOENIX IX! MAINFRAME IS STILL OFF-WORLD DEALING WITH HOLLYWOOD...
...AS FOR REPLICA, I'M ABOUT TO DIAGNOSE HER! PLEASE FIRE UP THE MED-LAB FACILITY AND MAINTAIN CONSTANT VOICE CONTACT!
HARKOV'S ASHES! WHERE IS HE? OPEN THE G-COM CHANNEL!
SPIRIT! WHY HAVE YOU DEVIATED FROM THE PATTERN?
I AM EN ROUTE TO FIRELORD'S CO ORDINATES! HE HAS ENCOUNTERED AN INVADER!
WHAT? WHO?
*MAINFRAME "INSTALLED" GIRAUD LAST ISSUE.--CRAIG

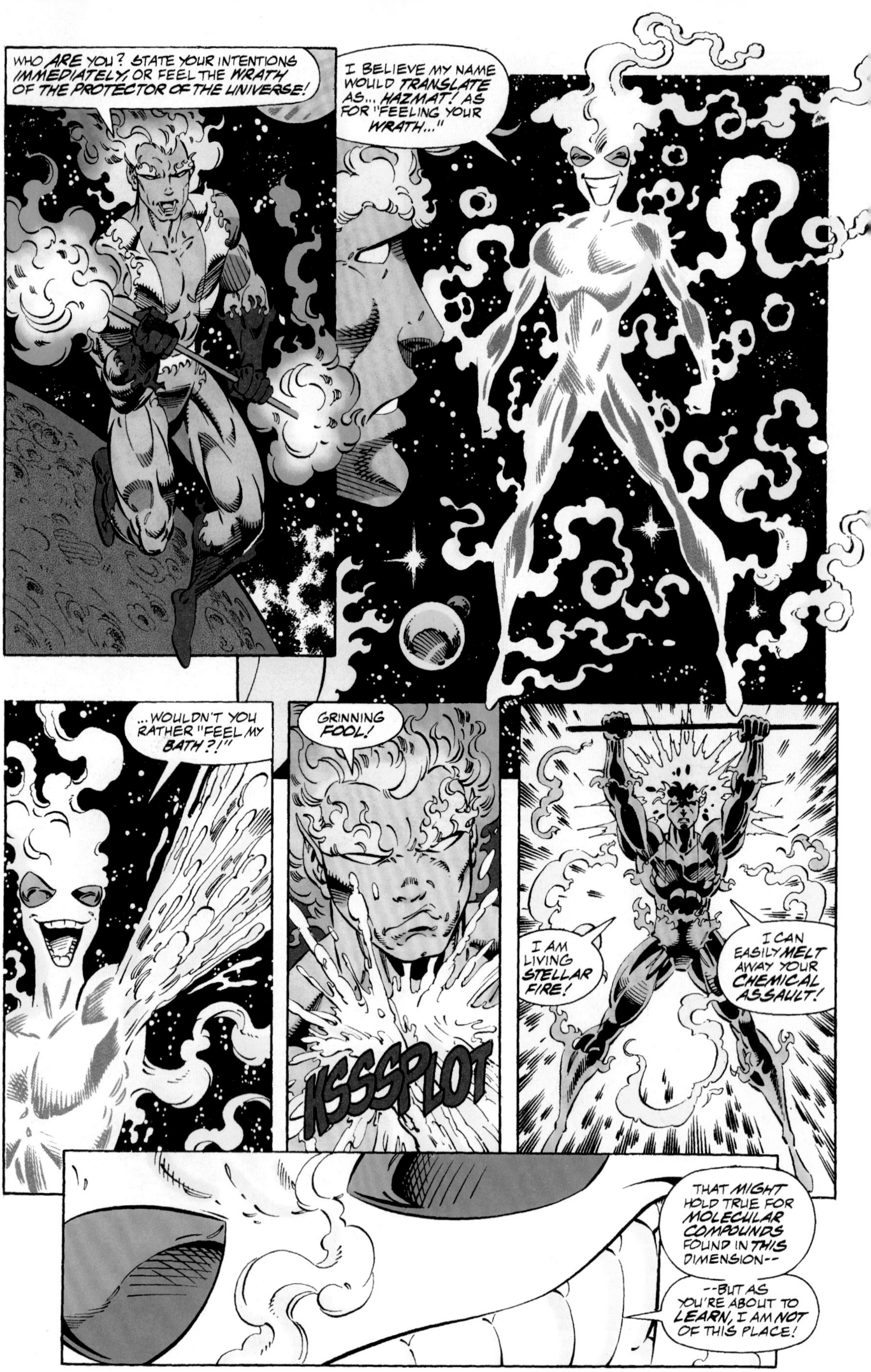
WHO ARE YOU? STATE YOUR INTENTIONS IMMEDIATELY, OR FEEL THE WRATH OF THE PROTECTOR OF THE UNIVERSE!
I BELIEVE MY NAME WOULD TRANSLATE AS... HAZMAT! AS FOR "FEELING YOUR WRATH..."
...WOULDN'T YOU RATHER "FEEL MY BATH?!"
GRINNING FOOL!
KSSSPLOT
I AM LIVING STELLAR FIRE!
I CAN EASILY MELT AWAY YOUR CHEMICAL ASSAULT!
THAT MIGHT HOLD TRUE FOR MOLECULAR COMPOUNDS FOUND IN THIS DIMENSION--
--BUT AS YOU'RE ABOUT TO LEARN, I AM NOT OF THIS PLACE!

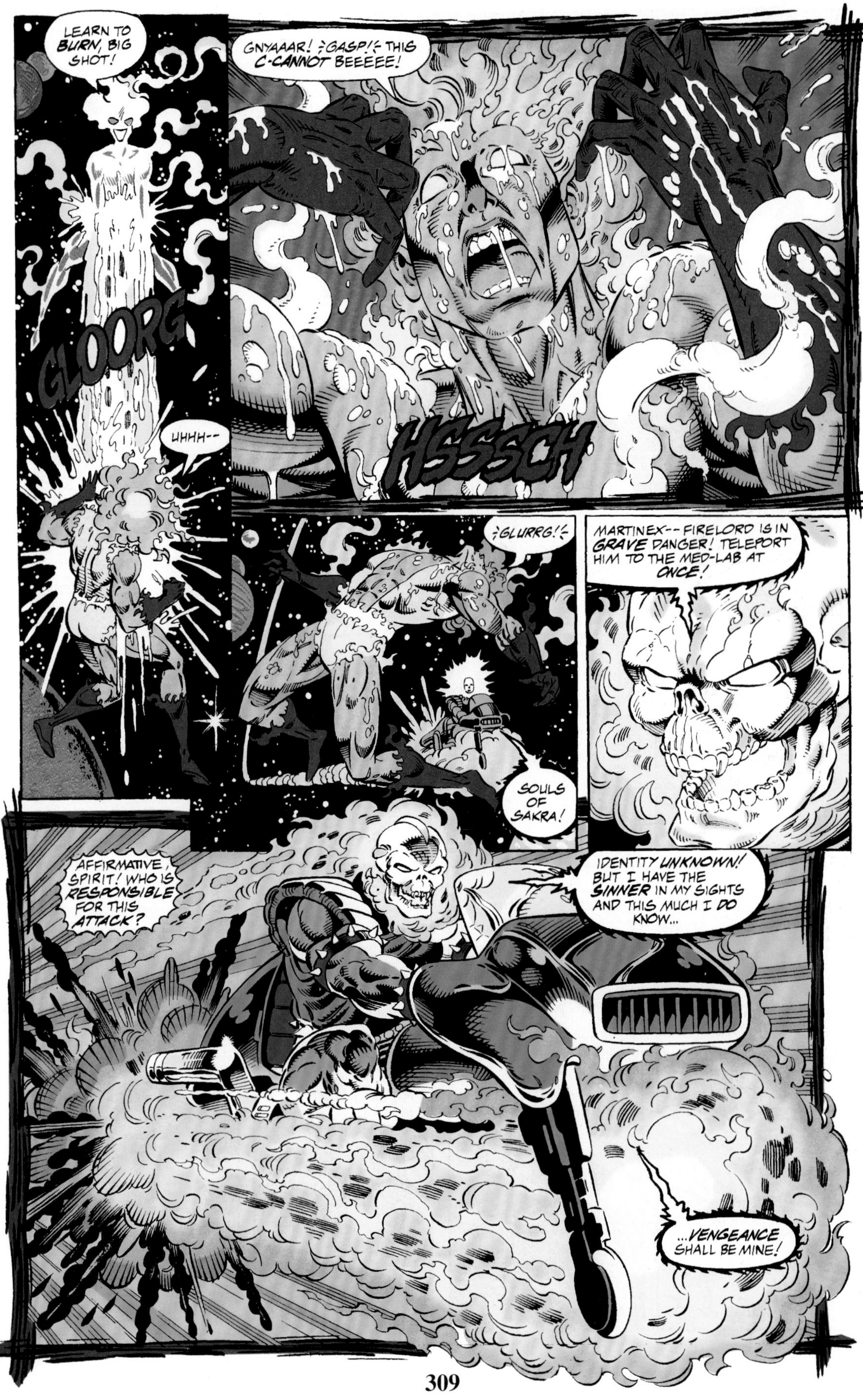
LEARN TO BURN, BIG SHOT!
GNYAAAR! ¡GASP!¡ THIS C-CANNOT BEEEEE!
GLOORG
HSSSCH
UHHH--
¡GLURRG!¡
MARTINEX--FIRELORD IS IN GRAVE DANGER! TELEPORT HIM TO THE MED-LAB AT ONCE!
SOULS OF SAKRA!
AFFIRMATIVE, SPIRIT! WHO IS RESPONSIBLE FOR THIS ATTACK?
IDENTITY UNKNOWN! BUT I HAVE THE SINNER IN MY SIGHTS AND THIS MUCH I DO KNOW...
...VENGEANCE SHALL BE MINE!

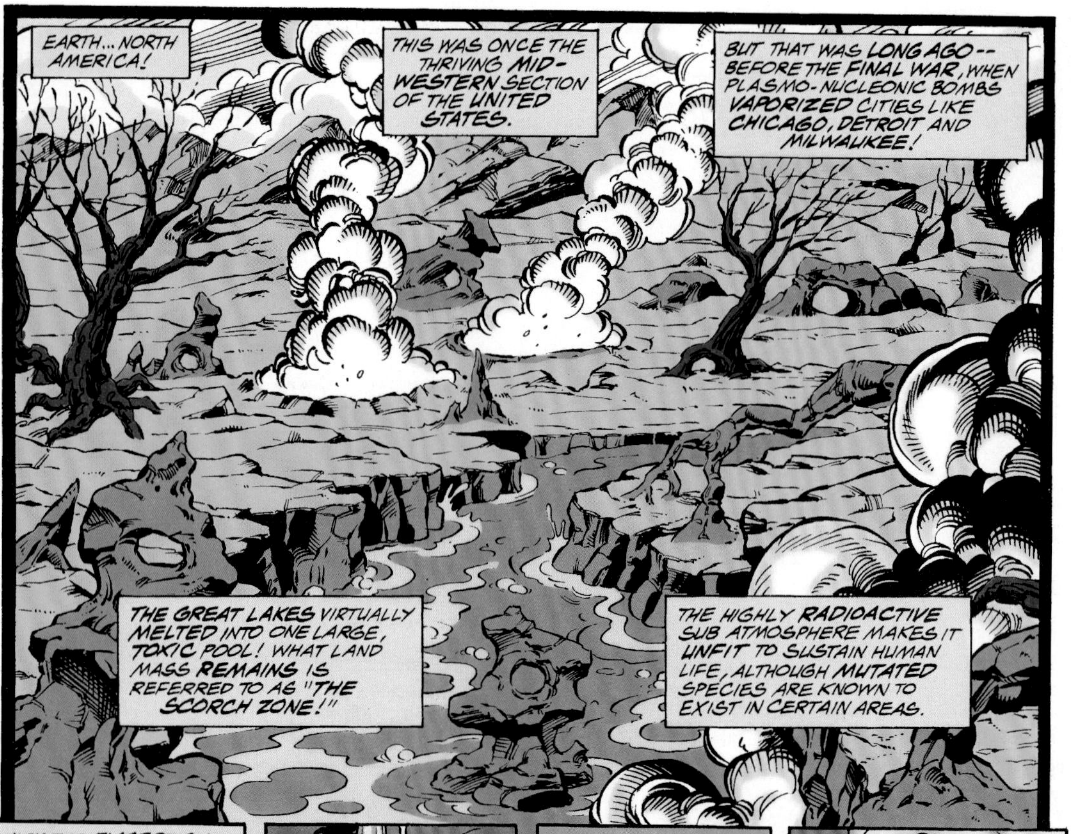
EARTH... NORTH AMERICA!
THIS WAS ONCE THE THRIVING MID-WESTERN SECTION OF THE UNITED STATES.
BUT THAT WAS LONG AGO-- BEFORE THE FINAL WAR, WHEN PLASMO-NUCLEONIC BOMBS VAPORIZED CITIES LIKE CHICAGO, DETROIT AND MILWAUKEE!
THE GREAT LAKES VIRTUALLY MELTED INTO ONE LARGE, TOXIC POOL! WHAT LAND MASS REMAINS IS REFERRED TO AS "THE SCORCH ZONE!"
THE HIGHLY RADIOACTIVE SUB ATMOSPHERE MAKES IT UNFIT TO SUSTAIN HUMAN LIFE, ALTHOUGH MUTATED SPECIES ARE KNOWN TO EXIST IN CERTAIN AREAS.

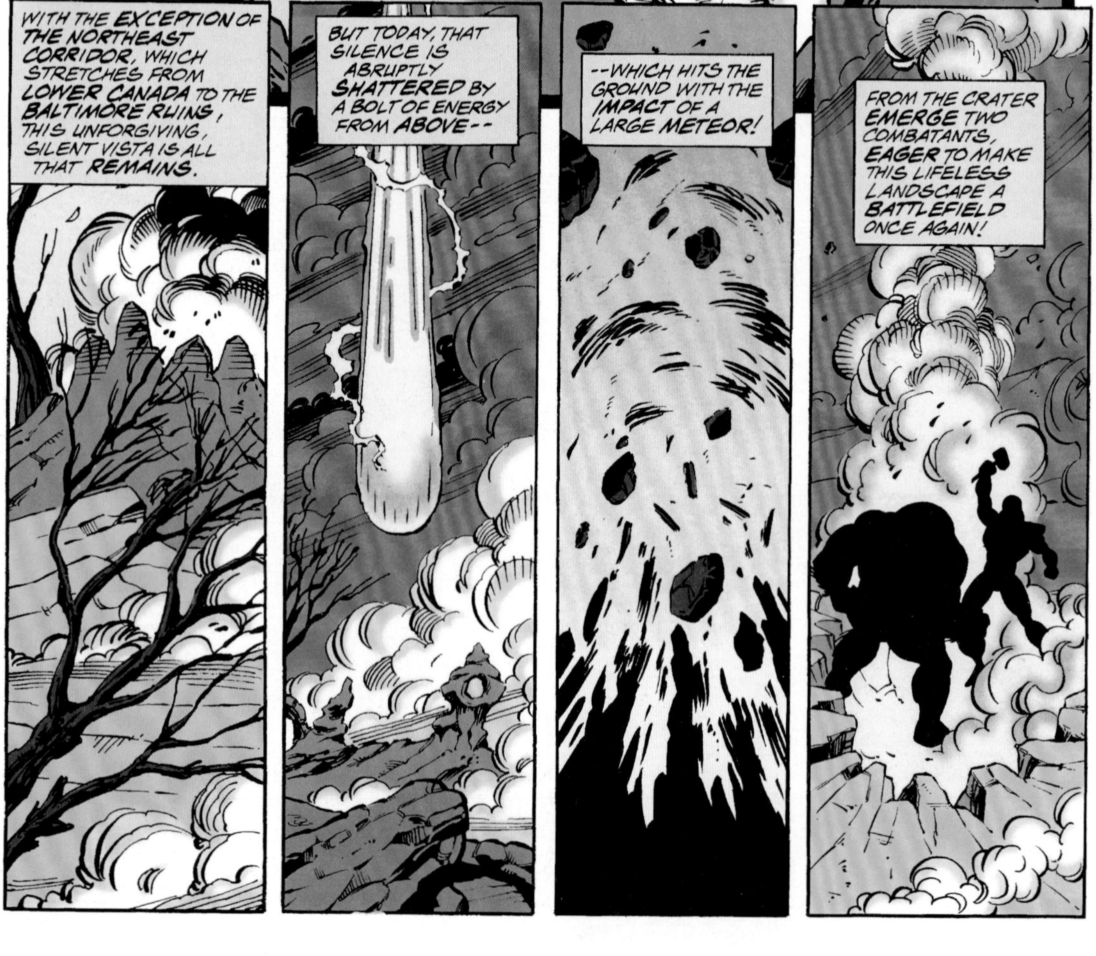
WITH THE EXCEPTION OF THE NORTHEAST CORRIDOR, WHICH STRETCHES FROM LOWER CANADA TO THE BALTIMORE RUINS, THIS UNFORGIVING, SILENT VISTA IS ALL THAT REMAINS.
BUT TODAY, THAT SILENCE IS ABRUPTLY SHATTERED BY A BOLT OF ENERGY FROM ABOVE--
--WHICH HITS THE GROUND WITH THE IMPACT OF A LARGE METEOR!
FROM THE CRATER EMERGE TWO COMBATANTS, EAGER TO MAKE THIS LIFELESS LANDSCAPE A BATTLEFIELD ONCE AGAIN!

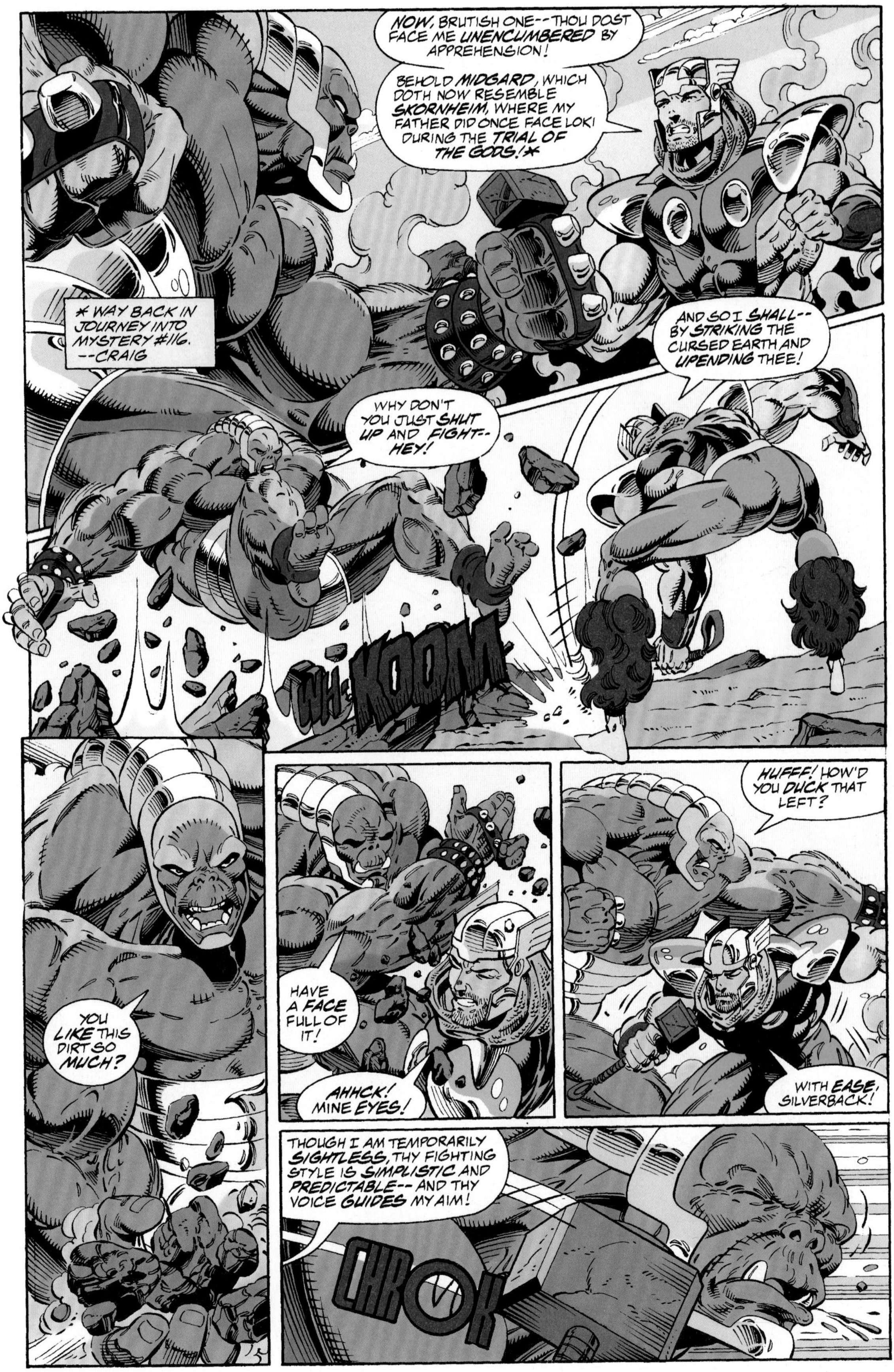
NOW, BRUTISH ONE--THOU DOST FACE ME UNENCUMBERED BY APPREHENSION!
BEHOLD MIDGARD, WHICH DOTH NOW RESEMBLE SKORNHEIM, WHERE MY FATHER DID ONCE FACE LOKI DURING THE TRIAL OF THE GODS!*
* WAY BACK IN JOURNEY INTO MYSTERY #116. --CRAIG
AND SO I SHALL--BY STRIKING THE CURSED EARTH AND UPENDING THEE!
WHY DON'T YOU JUST SHUT UP AND FIGHT--HEY!
WH-KOOM
YOU LIKE THIS DIRT SO MUCH?
HAVE A FACE FULL OF IT!
AHHCK! MINE EYES!
HUFFF! HOW'D YOU DUCK THAT LEFT?
WITH EASE, SILVERBACK!
THOUGH I AM TEMPORARILY SIGHTLESS, THY FIGHTING STYLE IS SIMPLISTIC AND PREDICTABLE--AND THY VOICE GUIDES MY AIM!
CHROK

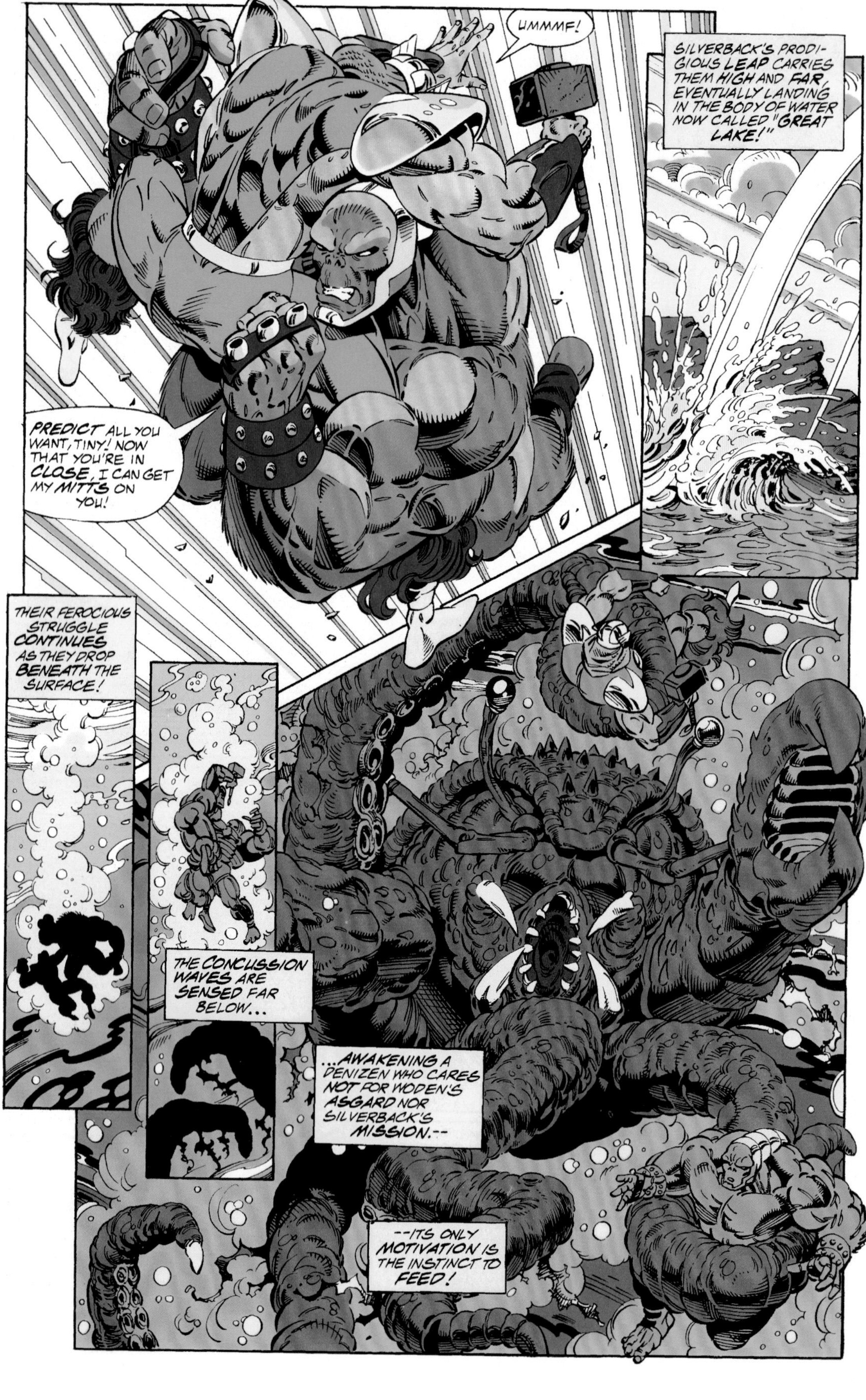
UMMMF!
SILVERBACK'S PRODIGIOUS LEAP CARRIES THEM HIGH AND FAR, EVENTUALLY LANDING IN THE BODY OF WATER NOW CALLED "GREAT LAKE!"
PREDICT ALL YOU WANT, TINY! NOW THAT YOU'RE IN CLOSE, I CAN GET MY MITTS ON YOU!
THEIR FEROCIOUS STRUGGLE CONTINUES AS THEY DROP BENEATH THE SURFACE!
THE CONCUSSION WAVES ARE SENSED FAR BELOW...
...AWAKENING A DENIZEN WHO CARES NOT FOR WODEN'S ASGARD NOR SILVERBACK'S MISSION.--
--ITS ONLY MOTIVATION IS THE INSTINCT TO FEED!

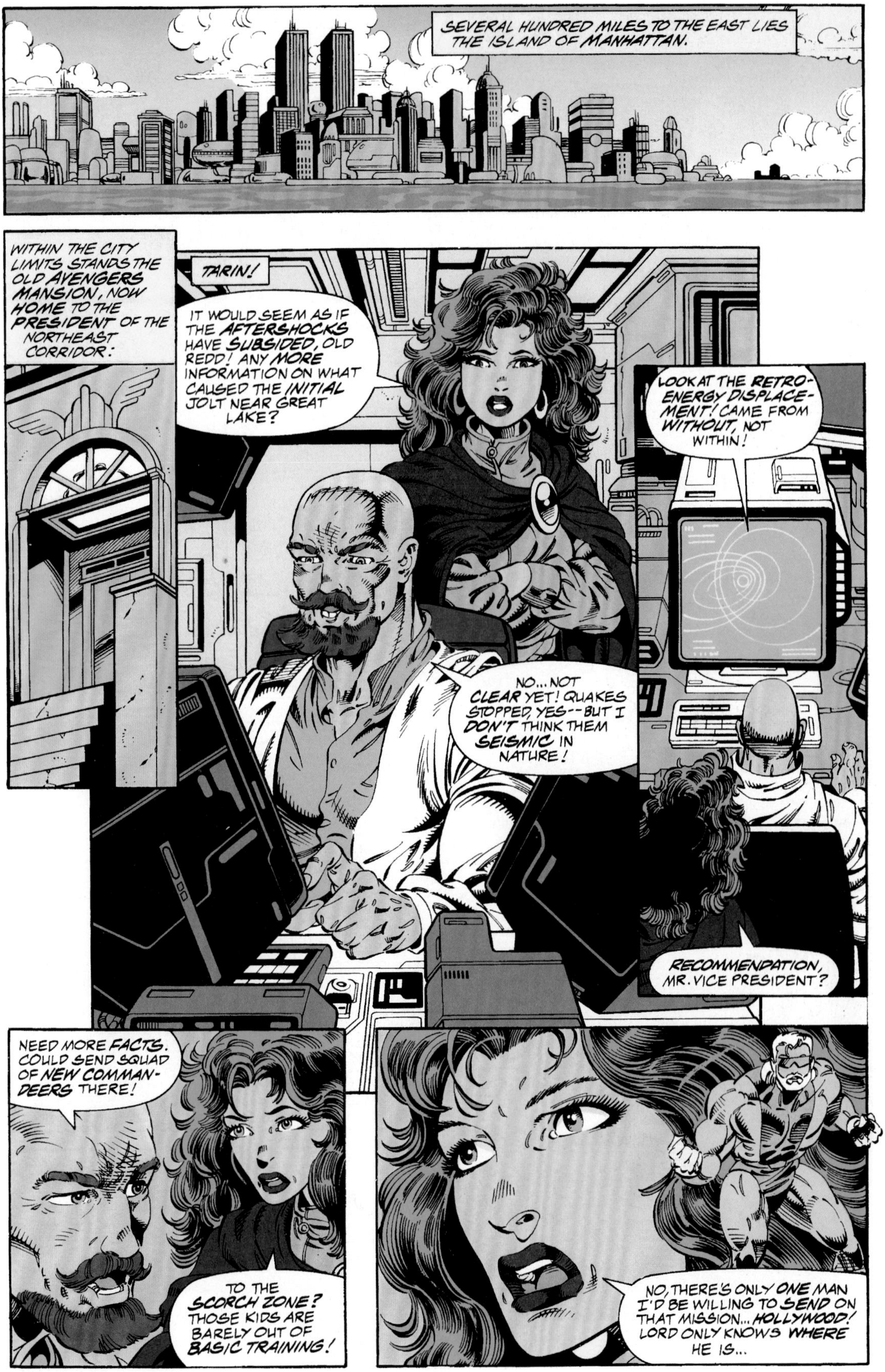
SEVERAL HUNDRED MILES TO THE EAST LIES THE ISLAND OF MANHATTAN.
WITHIN THE CITY LIMITS STANDS THE OLD AVENGERS MANSION, NOW HOME TO THE PRESIDENT OF THE NORTHEAST CORRIDOR:
TARIN!
IT WOULD SEEM AS IF THE AFTERSHOCKS HAVE SUBSIDED, OLD REDD! ANY MORE INFORMATION ON WHAT CAUSED THE INITIAL JOLT NEAR GREAT LAKE?
NO... NOT CLEAR YET! QUAKES STOPPED, YES--BUT I DON'T THINK THEM SEISMIC IN NATURE!
LOOK AT THE RETRO-ENERGY DISPLACEMENT! CAME FROM WITHOUT, NOT WITHIN!
RECOMMENDATION, MR. VICE PRESIDENT?
NEED MORE FACTS. COULD SEND SQUAD OF NEW COMMANDEERS THERE!
TO THE SCORCH ZONE? THOSE KIDS ARE BARELY OUT OF BASIC TRAINING!
NO, THERE'S ONLY ONE MAN I'D BE WILLING TO SEND ON THAT MISSION... HOLLYWOOD! LORD ONLY KNOWS WHERE HE IS...

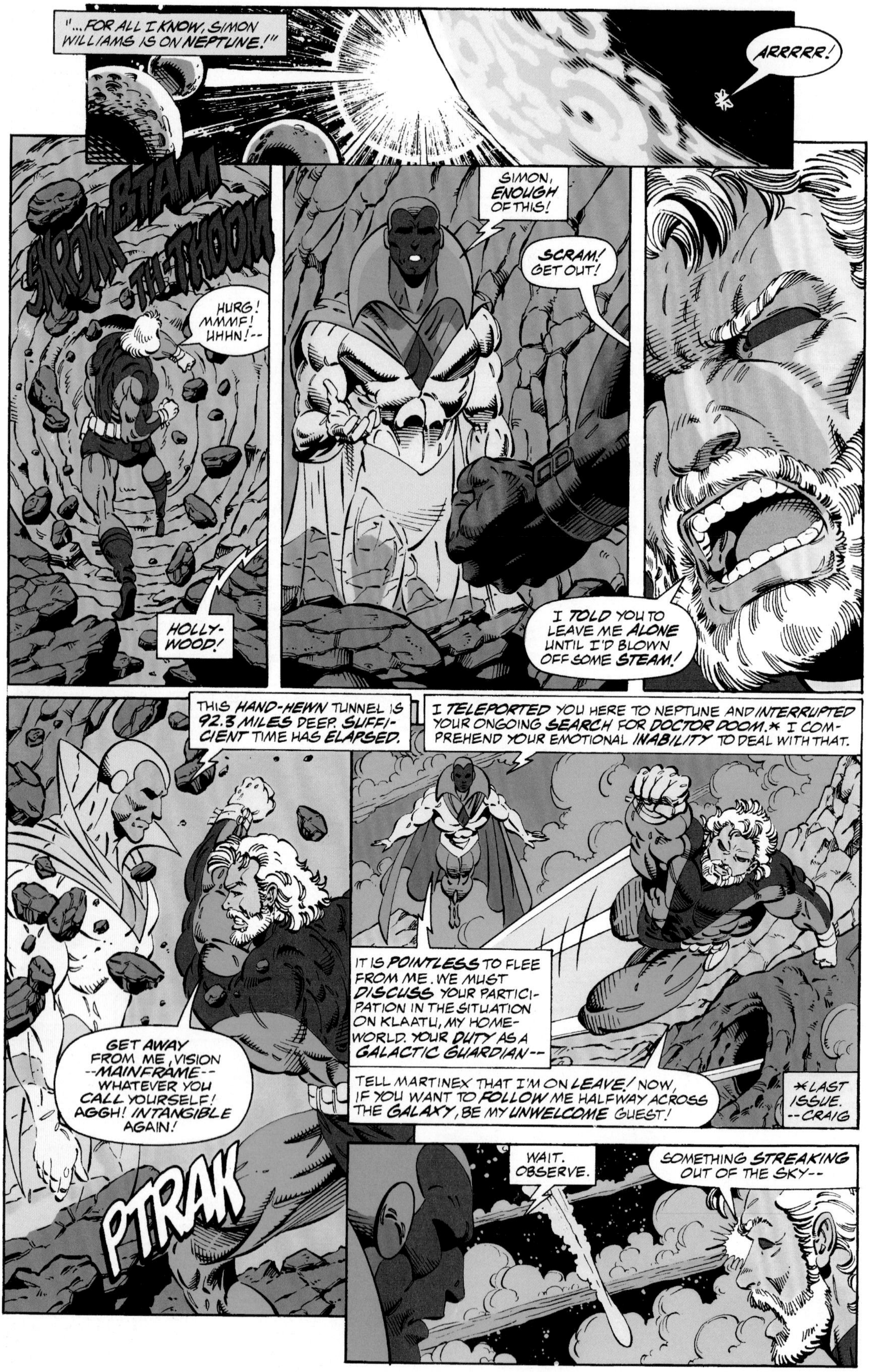

"...FOR ALL I KNOW, SIMON WILLIAMS IS ON NEPTUNE!"
ARRRRR!
SKROKK BTAM TH THOOM
HURG! MMMF! UHHN!--
HOLLY-WOOD!
SIMON, ENOUGH OF THIS!
SCRAM! GET OUT!
I TOLD YOU TO LEAVE ME ALONE UNTIL I'D BLOWN OFF SOME STEAM!
THIS HAND-HEWN TUNNEL IS 92.3 MILES DEEP. SUFFICIENT TIME HAS ELAPSED.
GET AWAY FROM ME, VISION --MAINFRAME-- WHATEVER YOU CALL YOURSELF! AGGH! INTANGIBLE AGAIN!
PTRAK
I TELEPORTED YOU HERE TO NEPTUNE AND INTERRUPTED YOUR ONGOING SEARCH FOR DOCTOR DOOM.* I COMPREHEND YOUR EMOTIONAL INABILITY TO DEAL WITH THAT.
IT IS POINTLESS TO FLEE FROM ME. WE MUST DISCUSS YOUR PARTICIPATION IN THE SITUATION ON KLAATU, MY HOMEWORLD. YOUR DUTY AS A GALACTIC GUARDIAN--
TELL MARTINEX THAT I'M ON LEAVE! NOW, IF YOU WANT TO FOLLOW ME HALFWAY ACROSS THE GALAXY, BE MY UNWELCOME GUEST!
*LAST ISSUE. --CRAIG
WAIT. OBSERVE.
SOMETHING STREAKING OUT OF THE SKY--

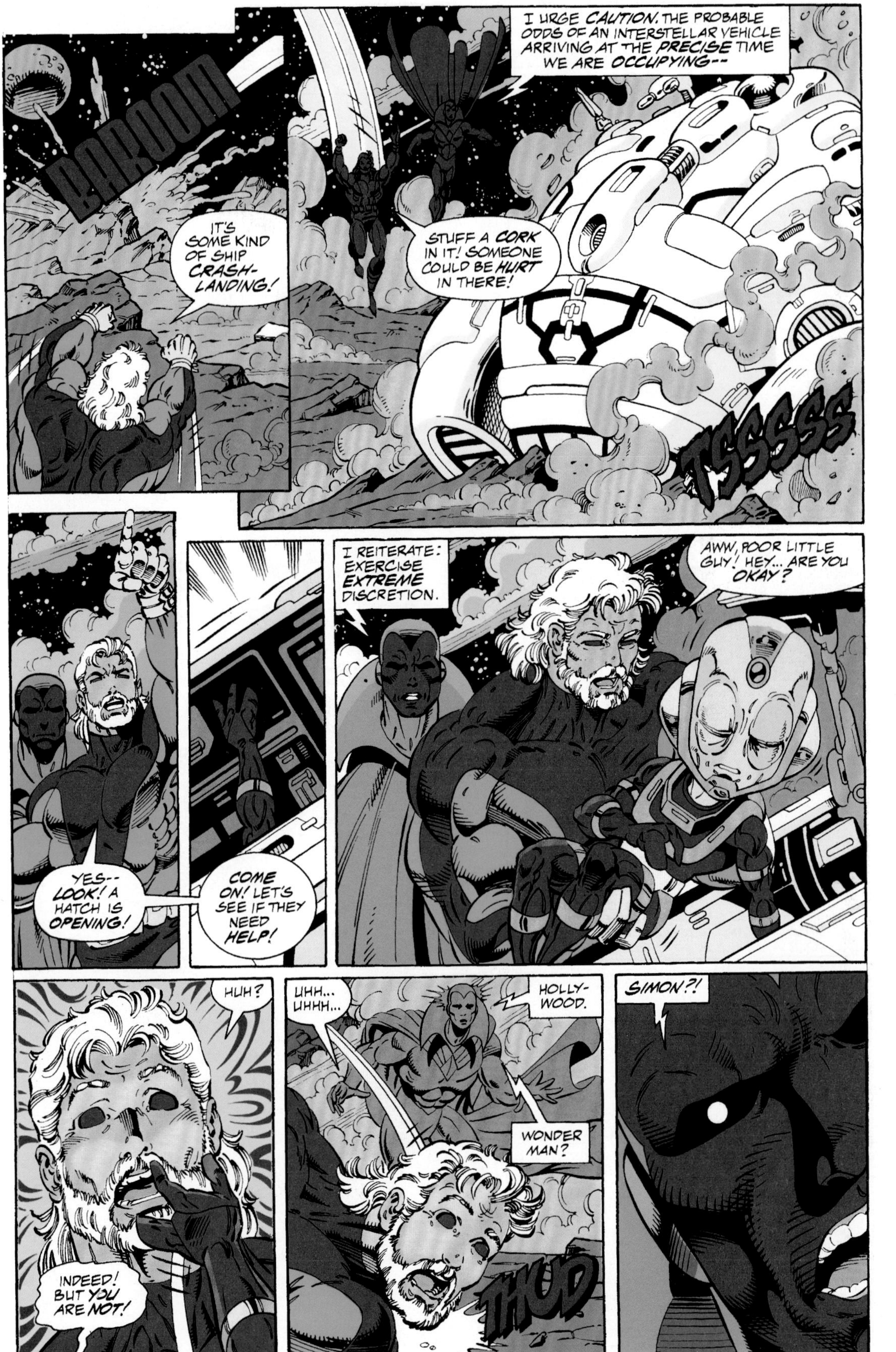
BAROOM
IT'S SOME KIND OF SHIP CRASH-LANDING!
I URGE CAUTION. THE PROBABLE ODDS OF AN INTERSTELLAR VEHICLE ARRIVING AT THE PRECISE TIME WE ARE OCCUPYING--
STUFF A CORK IN IT! SOMEONE COULD BE HURT IN THERE!
TSSSSS
YES-- LOOK! A HATCH IS OPENING!
COME ON! LET'S SEE IF THEY NEED HELP!
I REITERATE: EXERCISE EXTREME DISCRETION.
AWW, POOR LITTLE GUY! HEY... ARE YOU OKAY?
HUH?
INDEED! BUT YOU ARE NOT!
UHH... UHHH...
HOLLY-WOOD.
WONDER MAN?
THUD
SIMON?!

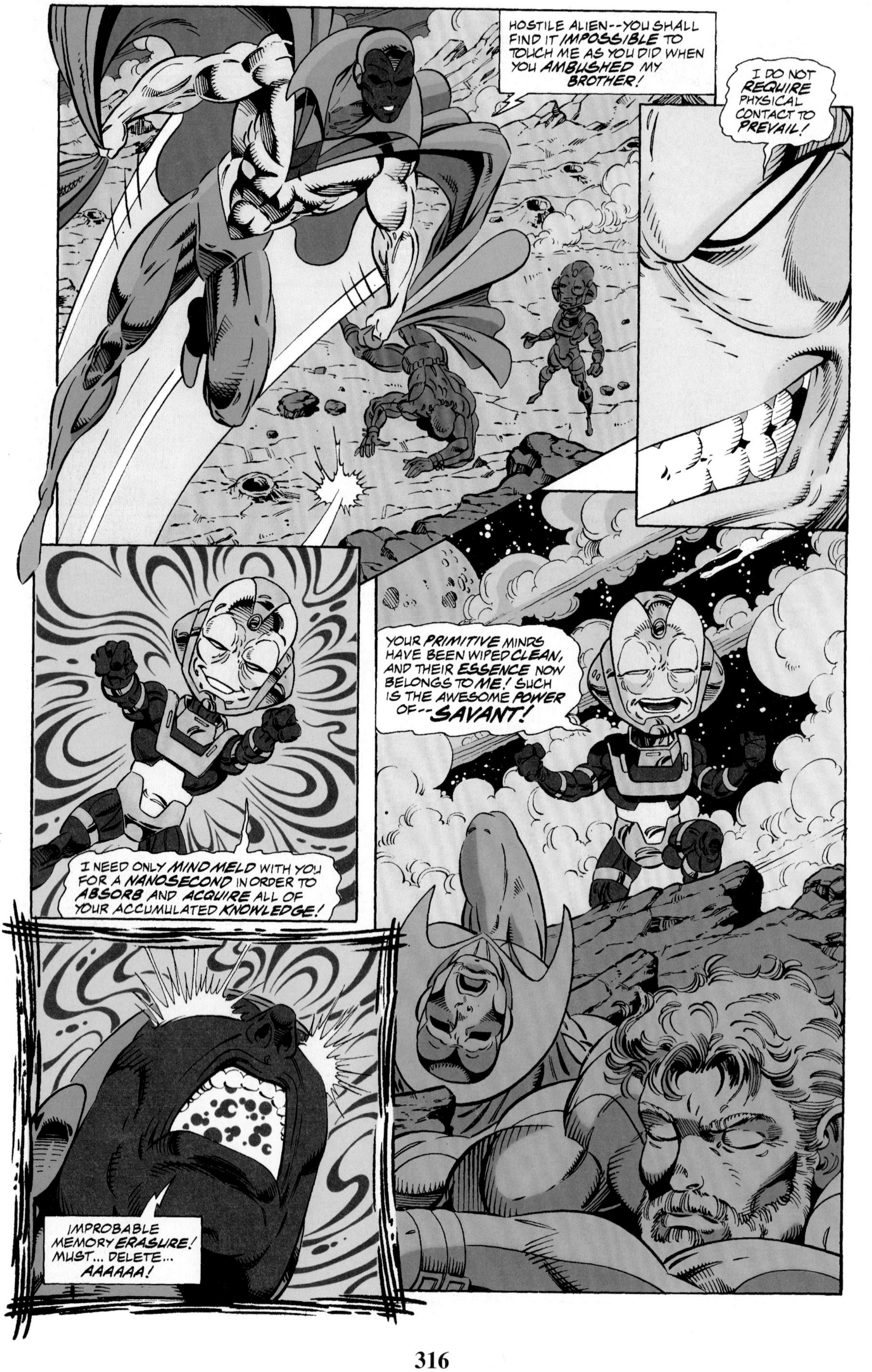
HOSTILE ALIEN--YOU SHALL FIND IT IMPOSSIBLE TO TOUCH ME AS YOU DID WHEN YOU AMBUSHED MY BROTHER!
I DO NOT REQUIRE PHYSICAL CONTACT TO PREVAIL!
I NEED ONLY MIND MELD WITH YOU FOR A NANOSECOND IN ORDER TO ABSORB AND ACQUIRE ALL OF YOUR ACCUMULATED KNOWLEDGE!
YOUR PRIMITIVE MINDS HAVE BEEN WIPED CLEAN, AND THEIR ESSENCE NOW BELONGS TO ME! SUCH IS THE AWESOME POWER OF--SAVANT!
IMPROBABLE MEMORY ERASURE! MUST... DELETE... AAAAAA!

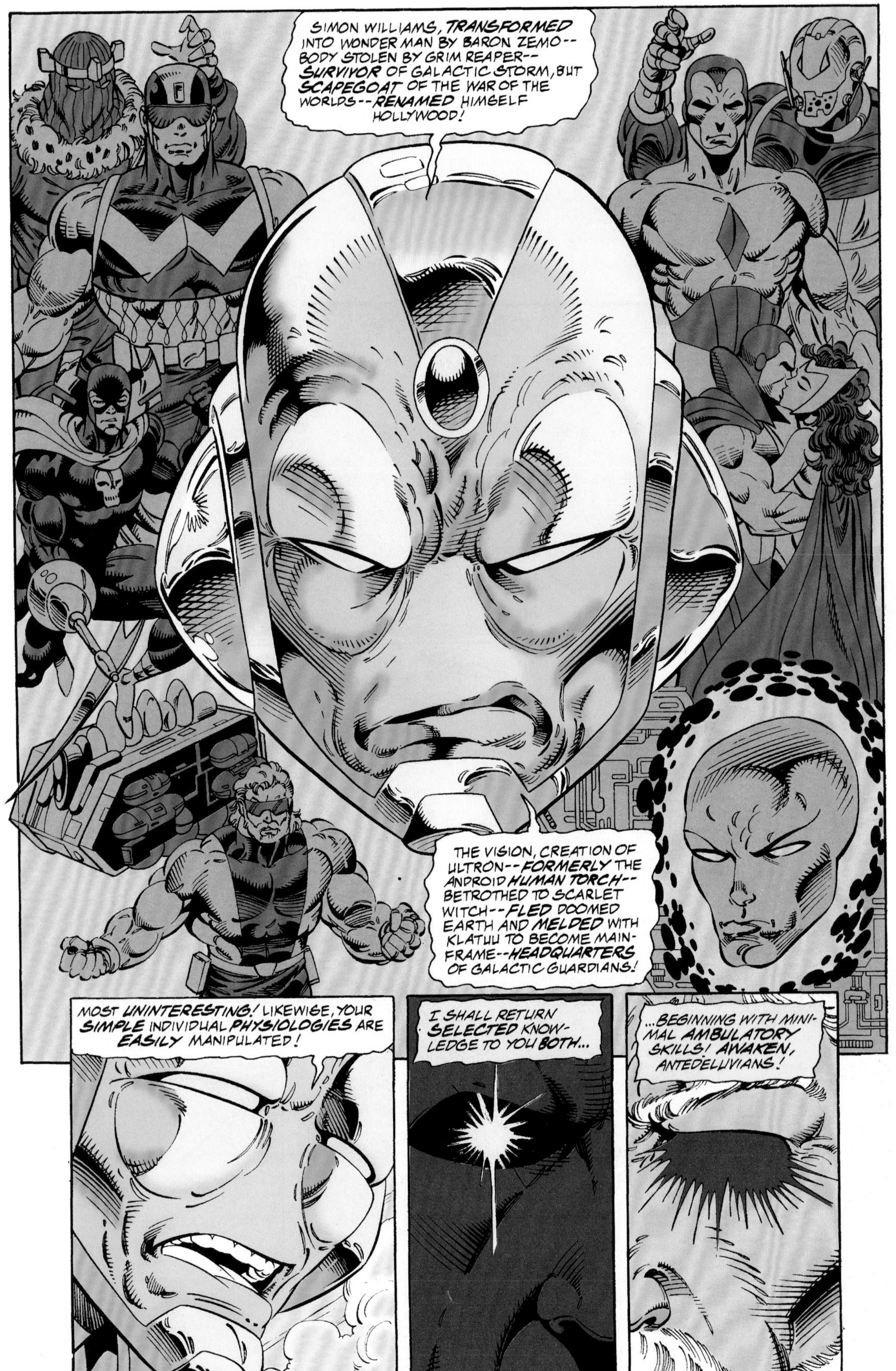
SIMON WILLIAMS, TRANSFORMED INTO WONDER MAN BY BARON ZEMO--BODY STOLEN BY GRIM REAPER--SURVIVOR OF GALACTIC STORM, BUT SCAPEGOAT OF THE WAR OF THE WORLDS--RENAMED HIMSELF HOLLYWOOD!
THE VISION, CREATION OF ULTRON--FORMERLY THE ANDROID HUMAN TORCH--BETROTHED TO SCARLET WITCH--FLED DOOMED EARTH AND MELDED WITH KLATUU TO BECOME MAIN-FRAME--HEADQUARTERS OF GALACTIC GUARDIANS!
MOST UNINTERESTING! LIKEWISE, YOUR SIMPLE INDIVIDUAL PHYSIOLOGIES ARE EASILY MANIPULATED!
I SHALL RETURN SELECTED KNOWLEDGE TO YOU BOTH...
...BEGINNING WITH MINIMAL AMBULATORY SKILLS! AWAKEN, ANTEDELUVIANS!

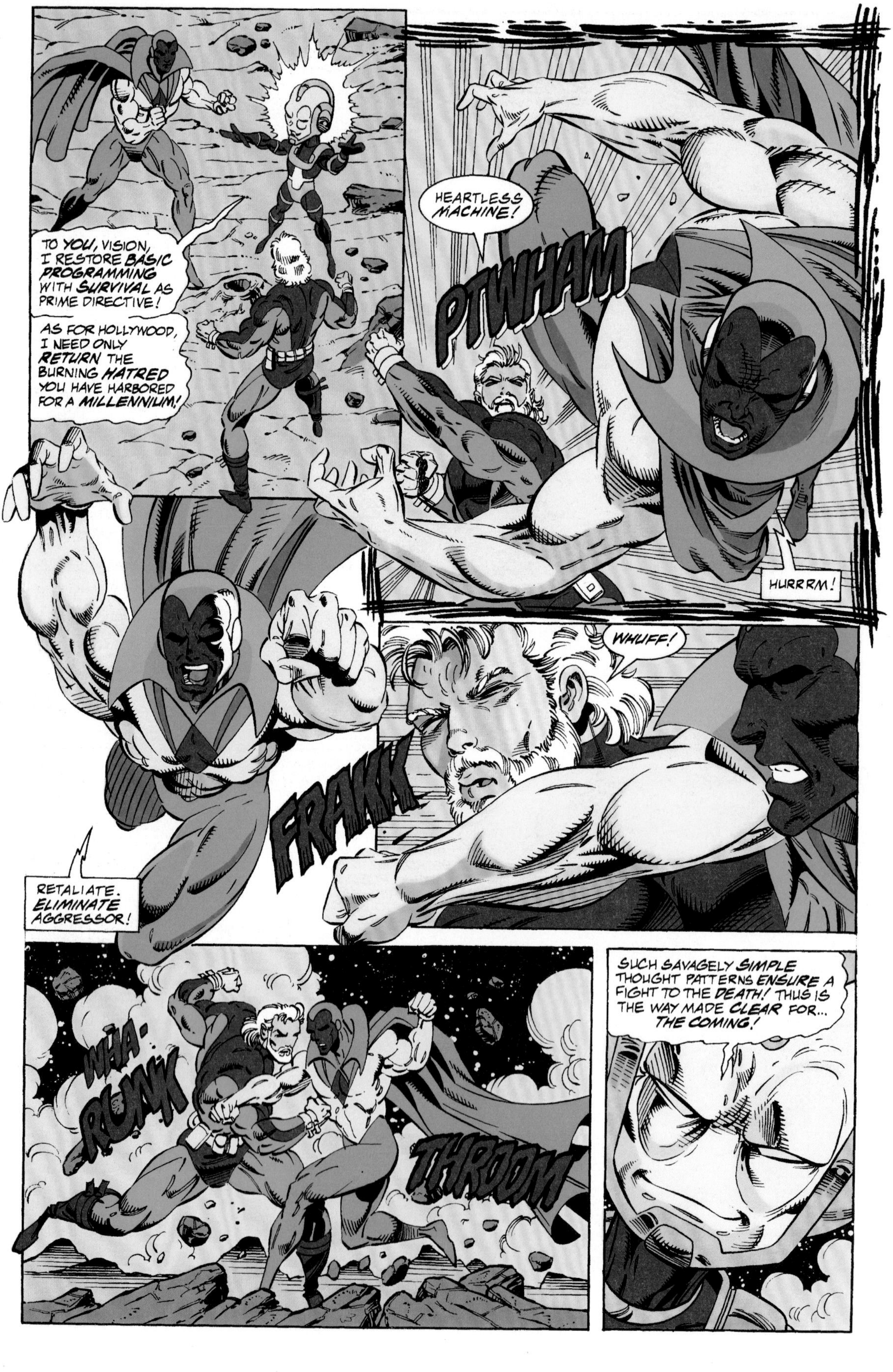
TO YOU, VISION, I RESTORE BASIC PROGRAMMING WITH SURVIVAL AS PRIME DIRECTIVE!
AS FOR HOLLYWOOD, I NEED ONLY RETURN THE BURNING HATRED YOU HAVE HARBORED FOR A MILLENNIUM!
HEARTLESS MACHINE!
PTWHAM
HURRRM!
WHUFF!
FRAKK
RETALIATE. ELIMINATE AGGRESSOR!
WHA-RUNK
THROOM
SUCH SAVAGELY SIMPLE THOUGHT PATTERNS ENSURE A FIGHT TO THE DEATH! THUS IS THE WAY MADE CLEAR FOR... THE COMING!

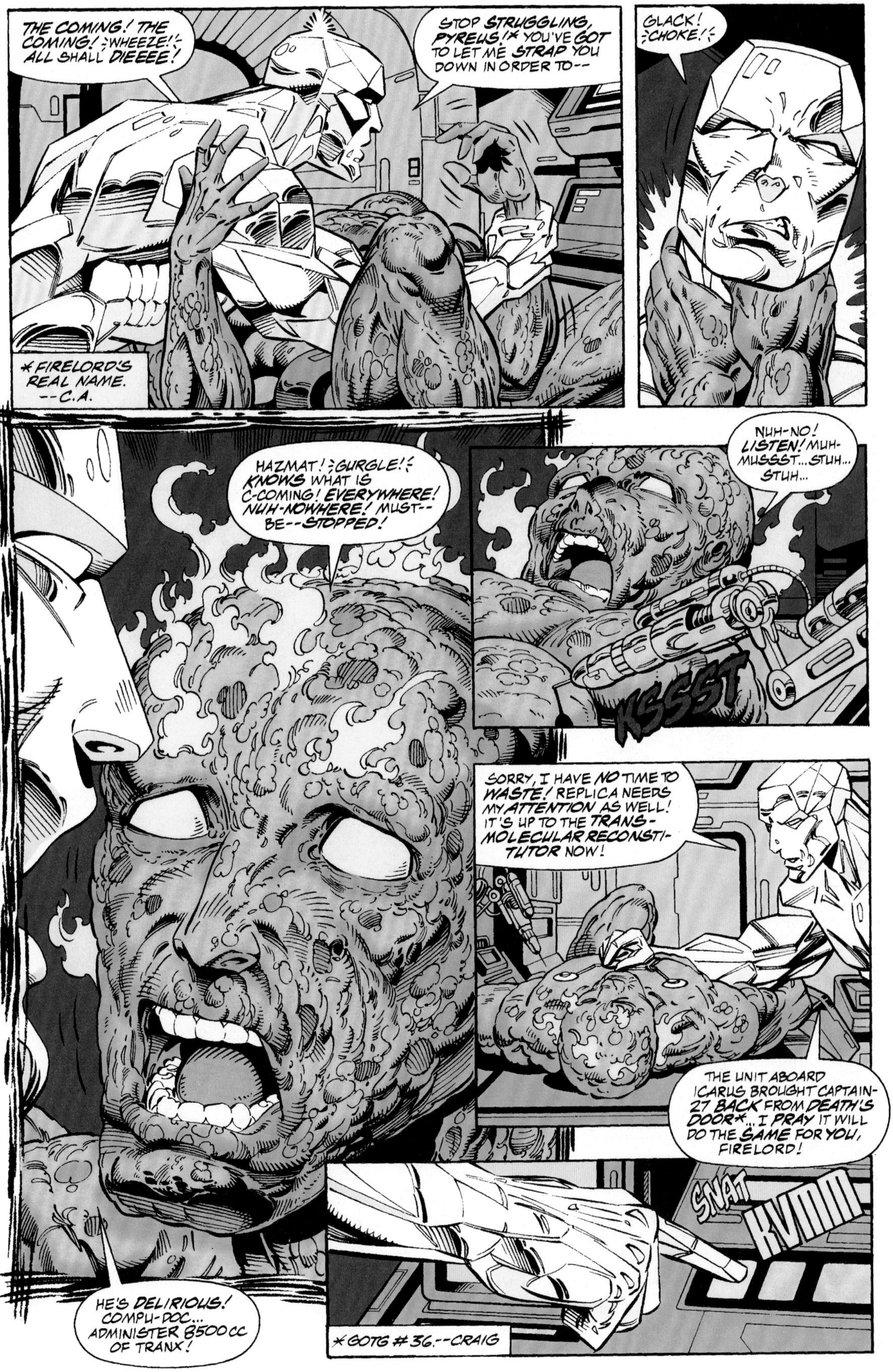
THE COMING! THE COMING! :WHEEZE!: ALL SHALL DIEEEE!
STOP STRUGGLING, PYREUS!* YOU'VE GOT TO LET ME STRAP YOU DOWN IN ORDER TO--
*FIRELORD'S REAL NAME. --C.A.
GLACK! :CHOKE!:
HAZMAT! :GURGLE!: KNOWS WHAT IS C-COMING! EVERYWHERE! NUH-NOWHERE! MUST--BE--STOPPED!
NUH-NO! LISTEN! MUH-MUSSST...STUH... STUH...
KSSST
SORRY, I HAVE NO TIME TO WASTE! REPLICA NEEDS MY ATTENTION AS WELL! IT'S UP TO THE TRANS-MOLECULAR RECONSTITUTOR NOW!
THE UNIT ABOARD ICARUS BROUGHT CAPTAIN-27 BACK FROM DEATH'S DOOR*...I PRAY IT WILL DO THE SAME FOR YOU, FIRELORD!
SNAT
KVMM
*GOTG #36.--CRAIG
HE'S DELIRIOUS! COMPU-DOC... ADMINISTER 8500 CC OF TRANX!

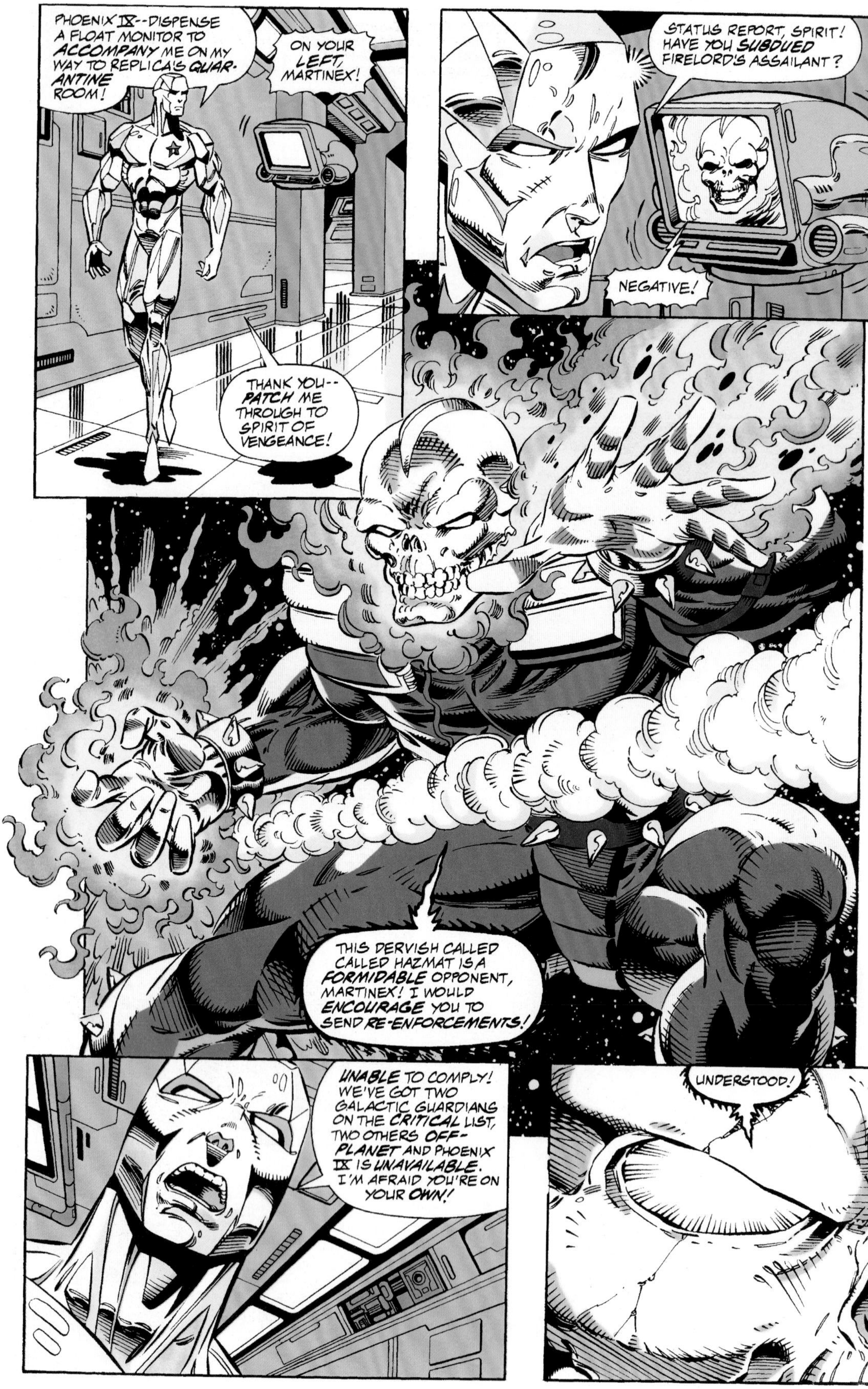

PHOENIX IX--DISPENSE A FLOAT MONITOR TO ACCOMPANY ME ON MY WAY TO REPLICA'S QUARANTINE ROOM!
ON YOUR LEFT, MARTINEX!
THANK YOU-- PATCH ME THROUGH TO SPIRIT OF VENGEANCE!
STATUS REPORT, SPIRIT! HAVE YOU SUBDUED FIRELORD'S ASSAILANT?
NEGATIVE!
THIS DERVISH CALLED CALLED HAZMAT IS A FORMIDABLE OPPONENT, MARTINEX! I WOULD ENCOURAGE YOU TO SEND RE-ENFORCEMENTS!
UNABLE TO COMPLY! WE'VE GOT TWO GALACTIC GUARDIANS ON THE CRITICAL LIST, TWO OTHERS OFF-PLANET AND PHOENIX IX IS UNAVAILABLE. I'M AFRAID YOU'RE ON YOUR OWN!
UNDERSTOOD!

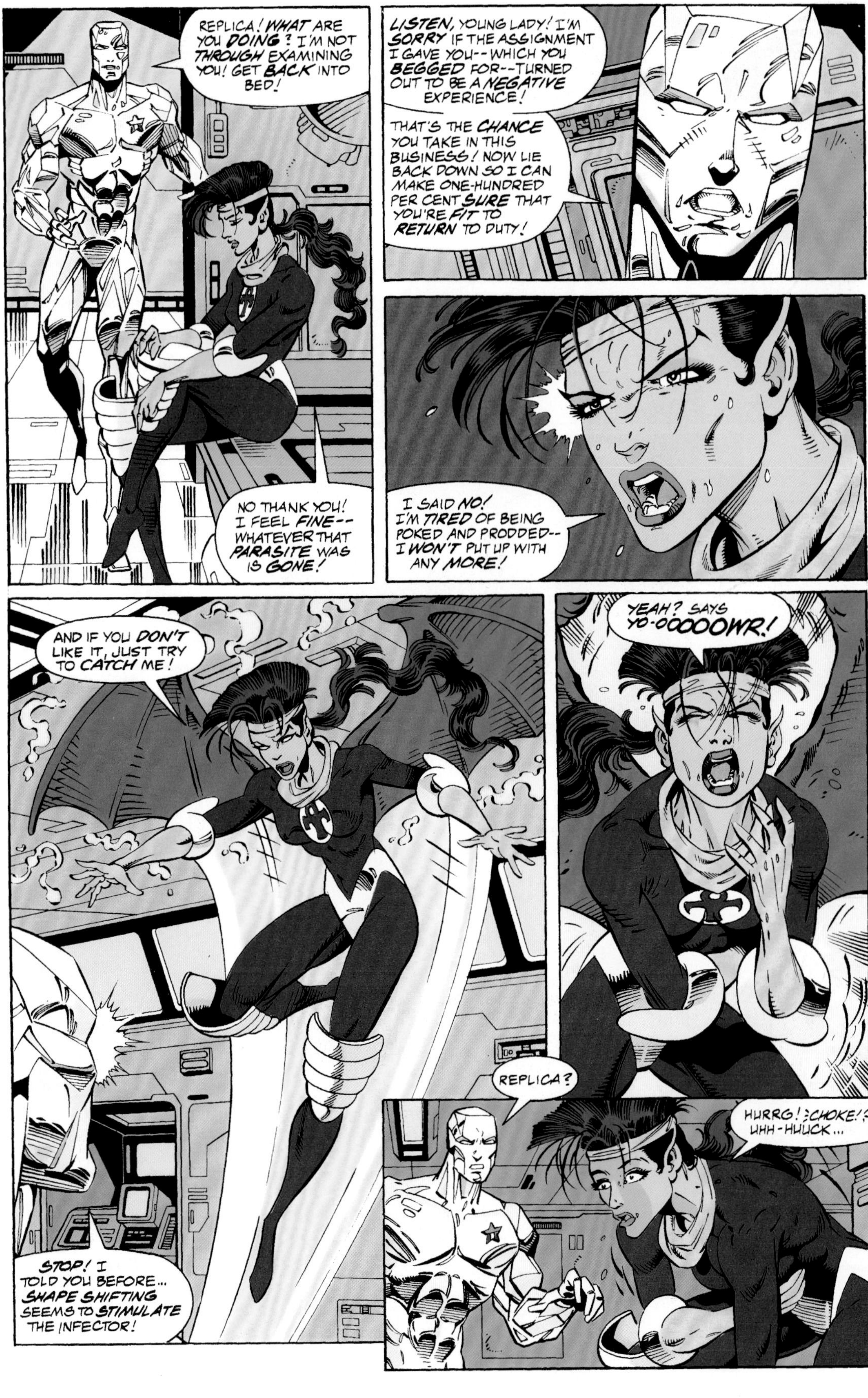
REPLICA! WHAT ARE YOU DOING? I'M NOT THROUGH EXAMINING YOU! GET BACK INTO BED!
NO THANK YOU! I FEEL FINE-- WHATEVER THAT PARASITE WAS IS GONE!
LISTEN, YOUNG LADY! I'M SORRY IF THE ASSIGNMENT I GAVE YOU--WHICH YOU BEGGED FOR--TURNED OUT TO BE A NEGATIVE EXPERIENCE!
THAT'S THE CHANCE YOU TAKE IN THIS BUSINESS! NOW LIE BACK DOWN SO I CAN MAKE ONE-HUNDRED PER CENT SURE THAT YOU'RE FIT TO RETURN TO DUTY!
I SAID NO! I'M TIRED OF BEING POKED AND PRODDED-- I WON'T PUT UP WITH ANY MORE!
AND IF YOU DON'T LIKE IT, JUST TRY TO CATCH ME!
STOP! I TOLD YOU BEFORE... SHAPE SHIFTING SEEMS TO STIMULATE THE INFECTOR!
YEAH? SAYS YO-OOOOOWR!
REPLICA?
HURRG! :CHOKE!: UHH-HUUCK...

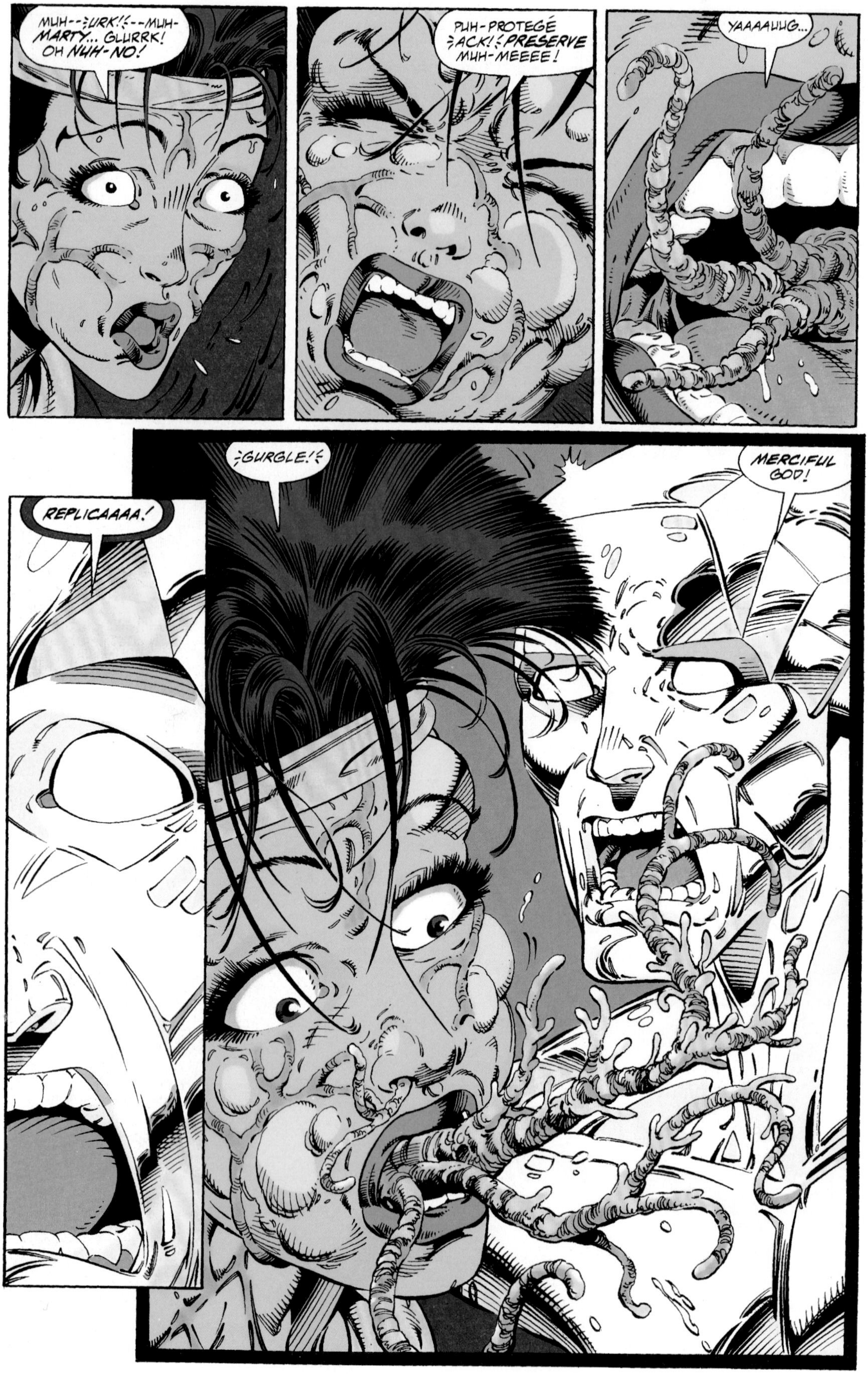
MUH--URK!--MUH-MARTY... GLURRK! OH NUH-NO!
PUH-PROTEGÉ ACK! PRESERVE MUH-MEEEE!
YAAAAUUG...
GURGLE!
MERCIFUL GOD!
REPLICAAAA!

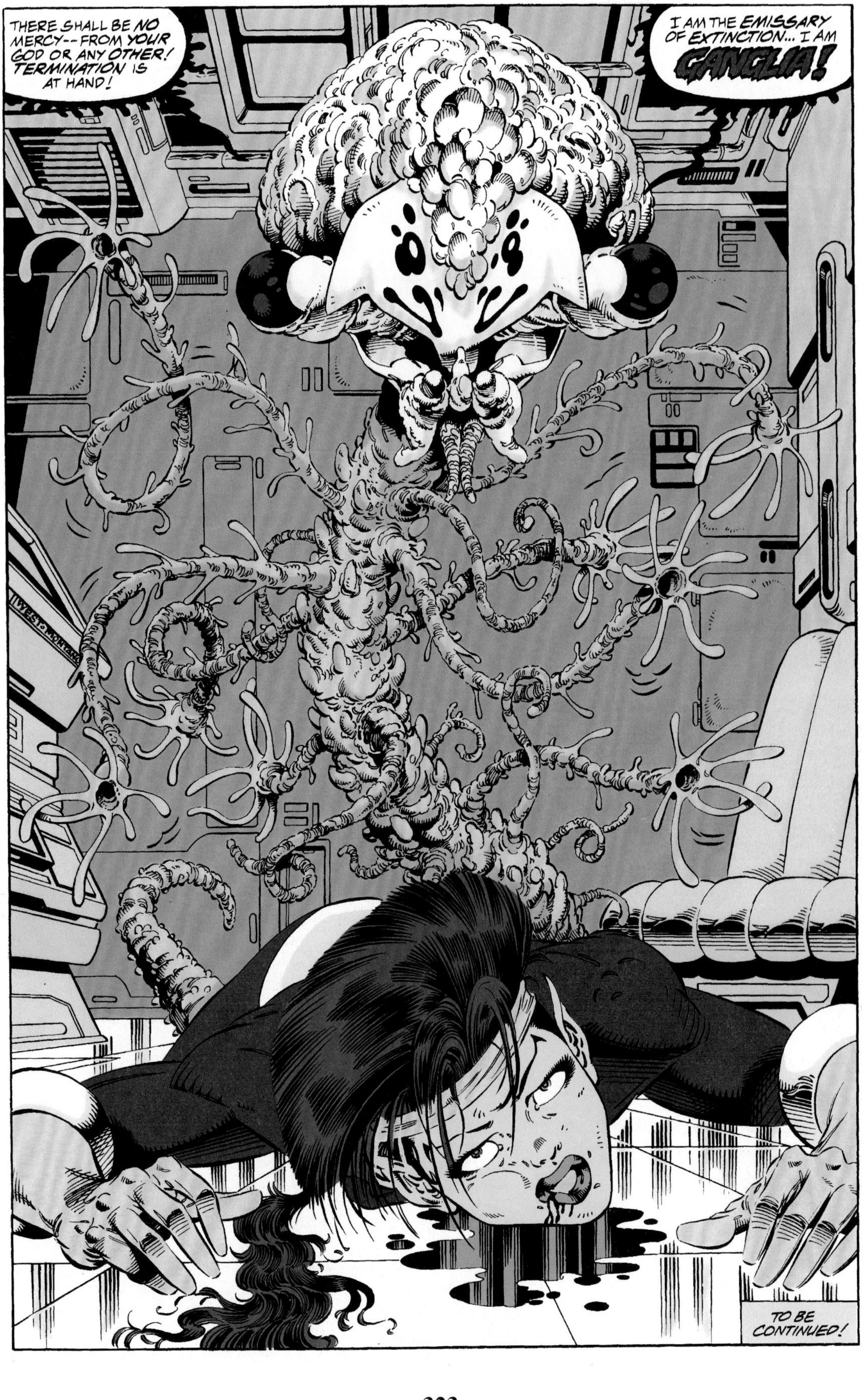
THERE SHALL BE NO MERCY--FROM YOUR GOD OR ANY OTHER! TERMINATION IS AT HAND!
I AM THE EMISSARY OF EXTINCTION... I AM GANGLIA!
TO BE CONTINUED!

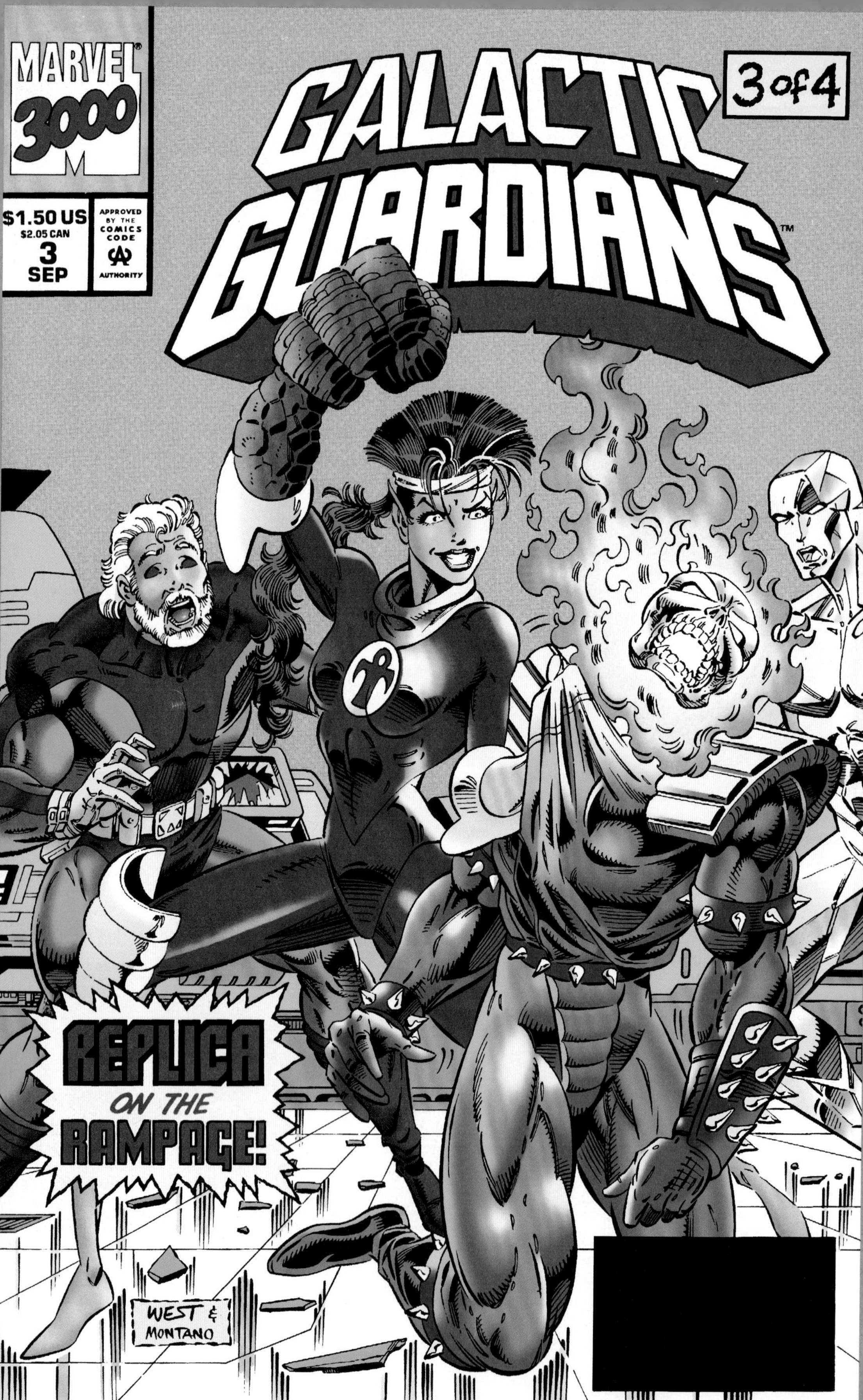
MARVEL 3000
GALACTIC GUARDIANS™
3 of 4
$1.50 US
$2.05 CAN
3
SEP
APPROVED BY THE COMICS CODE AUTHORITY
REPLICA ON THE RAMPAGE!
WEST & MONTANO

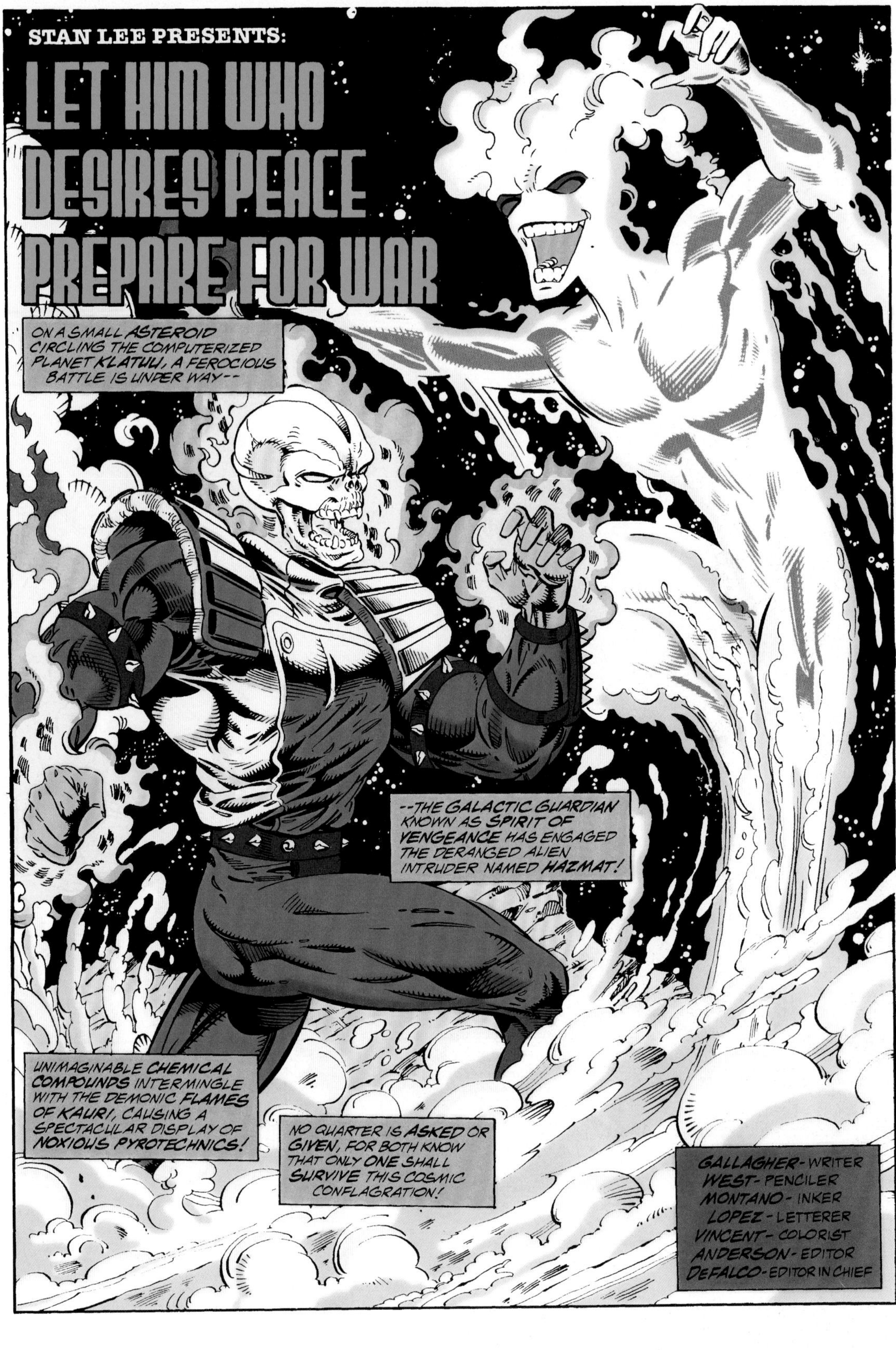
STAN LEE PRESENTS:
LET HIM WHO DESIRES PEACE PREPARE FOR WAR
ON A SMALL ASTEROID CIRCLING THE COMPUTERIZED PLANET KLATULI, A FEROCIOUS BATTLE IS UNDER WAY--
--THE GALACTIC GUARDIAN KNOWN AS SPIRIT OF VENGEANCE HAS ENGAGED THE DERANGED ALIEN INTRUDER NAMED HAZMAT!
UNIMAGINABLE CHEMICAL COMPOUNDS INTERMINGLE WITH THE DEMONIC FLAMES OF KAURI, CAUSING A SPECTACULAR DISPLAY OF NOXIOUS PYROTECHNICS!
NO QUARTER IS ASKED OR GIVEN, FOR BOTH KNOW THAT ONLY ONE SHALL SURVIVE THIS COSMIC CONFLAGRATION!
GALLAGHER- WRITER
WEST- PENCILER
MONTANO- INKER
LOPEZ- LETTERER
VINCENT- COLORIST
ANDERSON- EDITOR
DEFALCO- EDITOR IN CHIEF

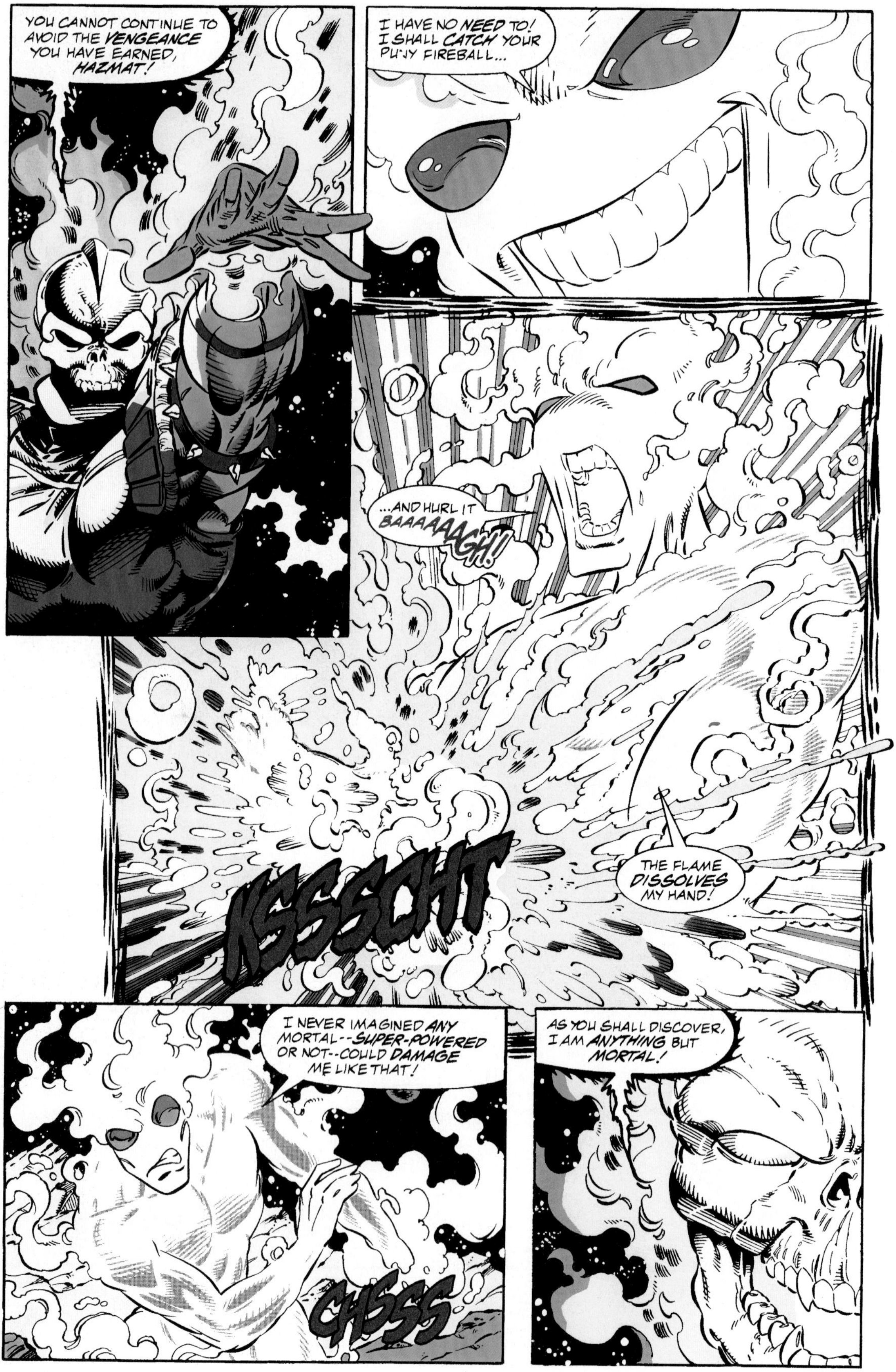

YOU CANNOT CONTINUE TO AVOID THE VENGEANCE YOU HAVE EARNED, HAZMAT!
I HAVE NO NEED TO! I SHALL CATCH YOUR PUNY FIREBALL...
...AND HURL IT BAAAAAAGH!
KSSSCHT
THE FLAME DISSOLVES MY HAND!
I NEVER IMAGINED ANY MORTAL--SUPER-POWERED OR NOT--COULD DAMAGE ME LIKE THAT!
CHSSS
AS YOU SHALL DISCOVER, I AM ANYTHING BUT MORTAL!

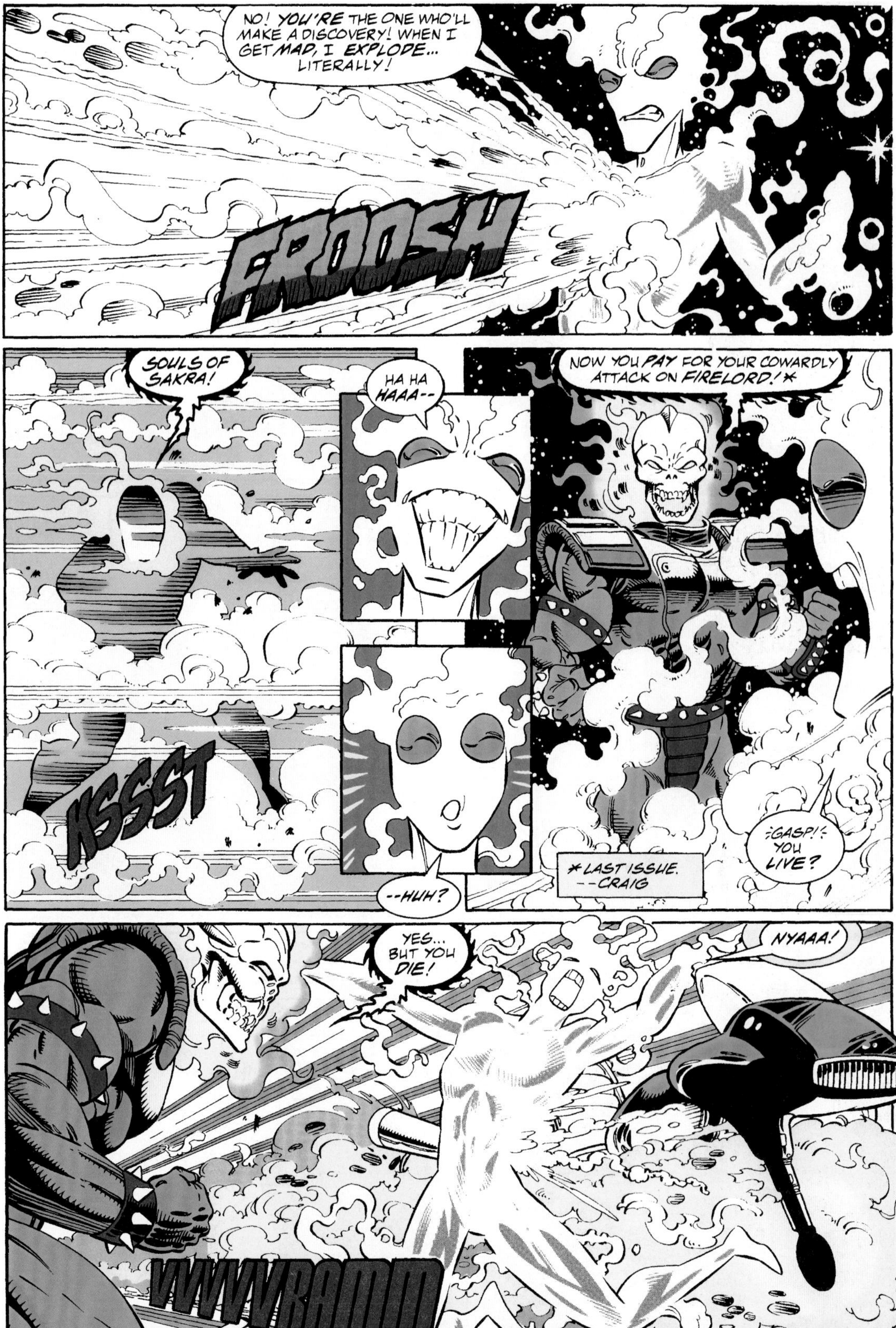
NO! YOU'RE THE ONE WHO'LL MAKE A DISCOVERY! WHEN I GET MAD, I EXPLODE... LITERALLY!
FROOSH
SOULS OF SAKRA!
KSSST
HA HA HAAA--
--HUH?
NOW YOU PAY FOR YOUR COWARDLY ATTACK ON FIRELORD! *
:GASP!: YOU LIVE?
* LAST ISSUE. --CRAIG
YES... BUT YOU DIE!
NYAAA!
VVVVVRAMM

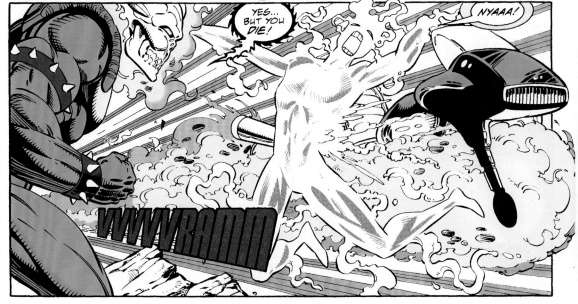

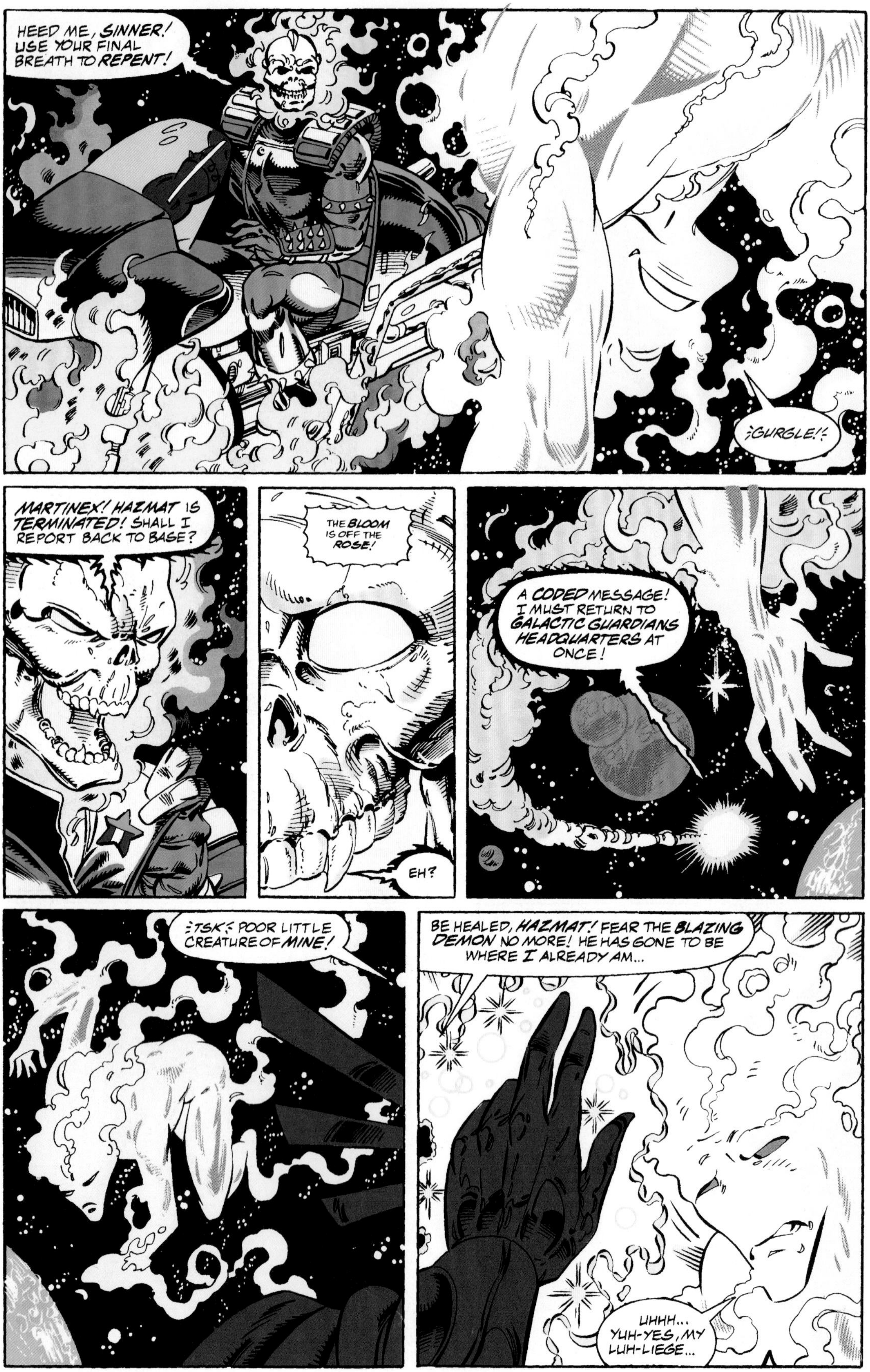

HEED ME, SINNER! USE YOUR FINAL BREATH TO REPENT!
¡GURGLE!¡
MARTINEX! HAZMAT IS TERMINATED! SHALL I REPORT BACK TO BASE?
THE BLOOM IS OFF THE ROSE!
EH?
A CODED MESSAGE! I MUST RETURN TO GALACTIC GUARDIANS HEADQUARTERS AT ONCE!
¡TSK¡ POOR LITTLE CREATURE OF MINE!
BE HEALED, HAZMAT! FEAR THE BLAZING DEMON NO MORE! HE HAS GONE TO BE WHERE I ALREADY AM...
UHHH... YUH-YES, MY LUH-LIEGE...

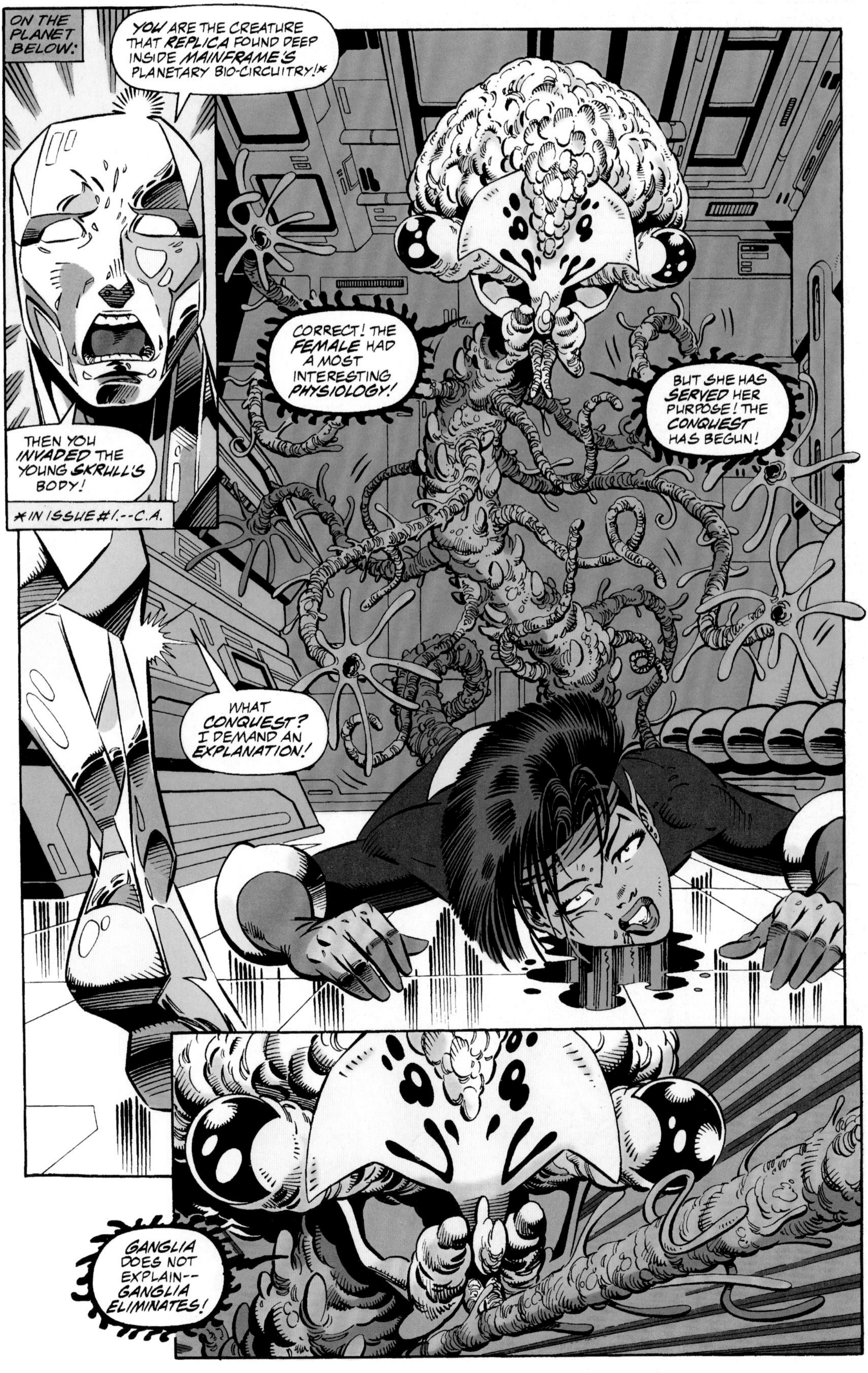

ON THE PLANET BELOW:
YOU ARE THE CREATURE THAT REPLICA FOUND DEEP INSIDE MAINFRAME'S PLANETARY BIO-CIRCUITRY!*
THEN YOU INVADED THE YOUNG SKRULL'S BODY!
*IN ISSUE #1.--C.A.
CORRECT! THE FEMALE HAD A MOST INTERESTING PHYSIOLOGY!
BUT SHE HAS SERVED HER PURPOSE! THE CONQUEST HAS BEGUN!
WHAT CONQUEST? I DEMAND AN EXPLANATION!
GANGLIA DOES NOT EXPLAIN-- GANGLIA ELIMINATES!

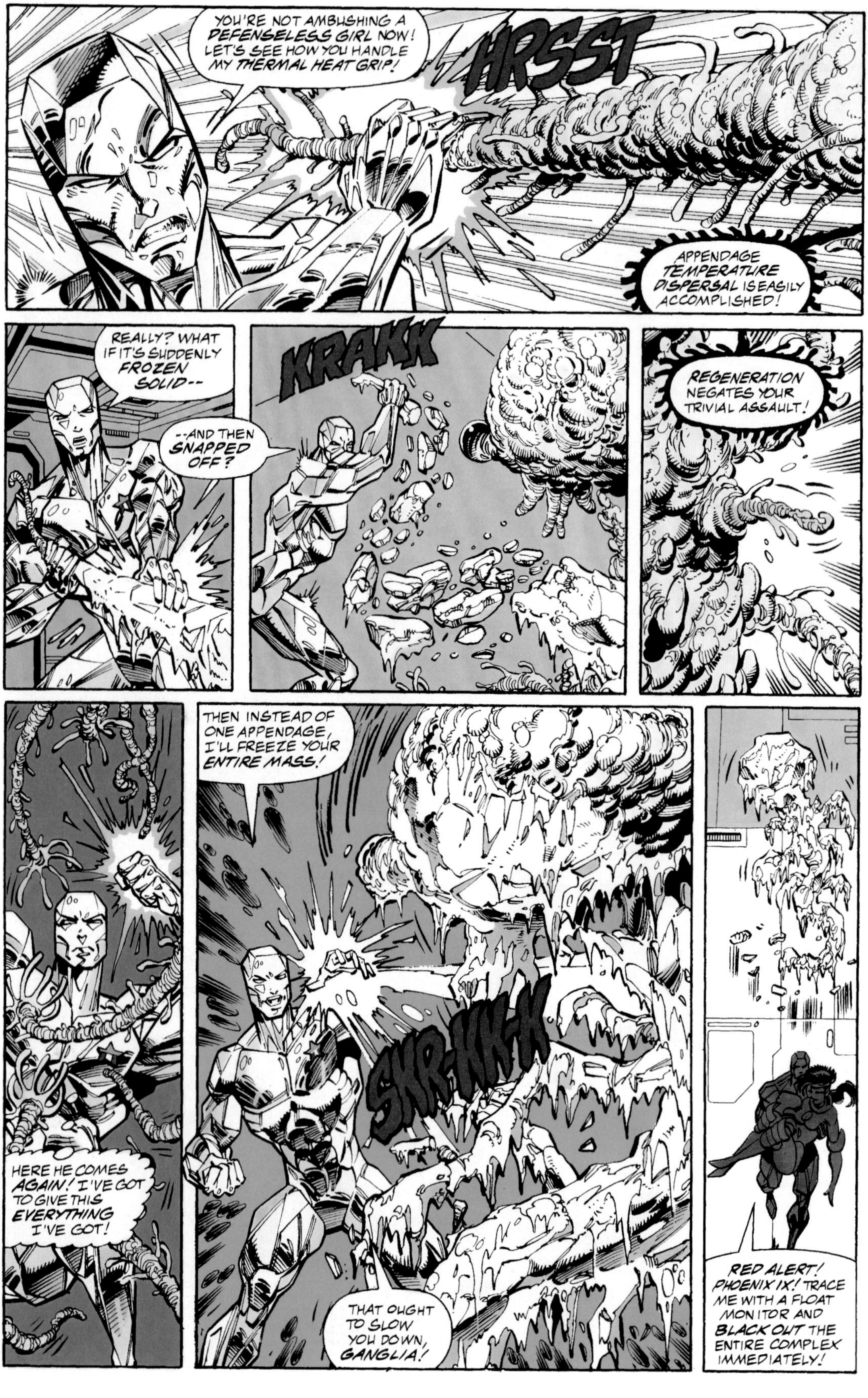
YOU'RE NOT AMBUSHING A DEFENSELESS GIRL NOW! LET'S SEE HOW YOU HANDLE MY THERMAL HEAT GRIP!
HRSST
APPENDAGE TEMPERATURE DISPERSAL IS EASILY ACCOMPLISHED!
REALLY? WHAT IF IT'S SUDDENLY FROZEN SOLID--
--AND THEN SNAPPED OFF?
KRAKK
REGENERATION NEGATES YOUR TRIVIAL ASSAULT!
HERE HE COMES AGAIN! I'VE GOT TO GIVE THIS EVERYTHING I'VE GOT!
THEN INSTEAD OF ONE APPENDAGE, I'LL FREEZE YOUR ENTIRE MASS!
SHR-KK-K
THAT OUGHT TO SLOW YOU DOWN, GANGLIA!
RED ALERT! PHOENIX IX! TRACE ME WITH A FLOAT MONITOR AND BLACK OUT THE ENTIRE COMPLEX IMMEDIATELY!

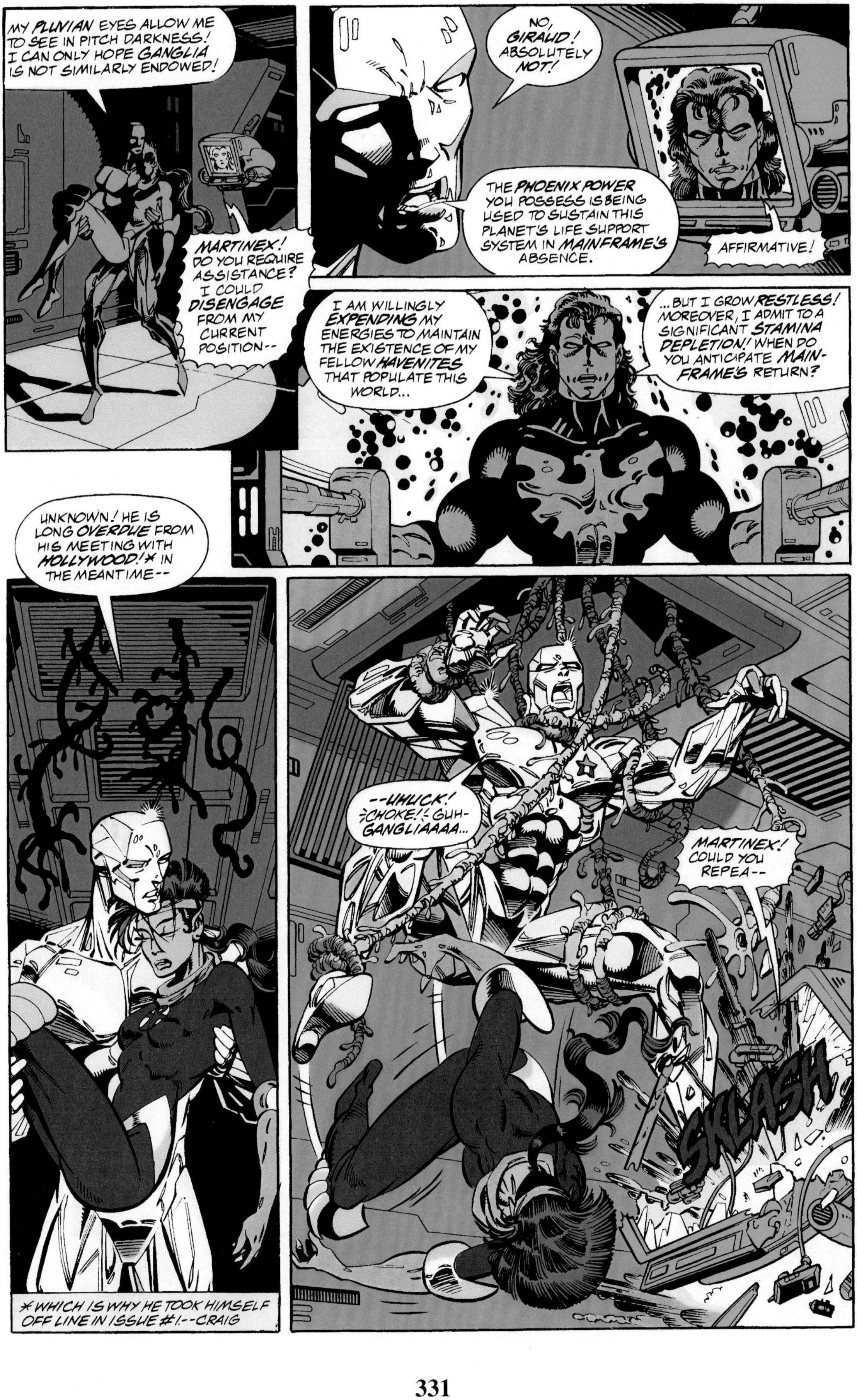
MY PLUVIAN EYES ALLOW ME TO SEE IN PITCH DARKNESS! I CAN ONLY HOPE GANGLIA IS NOT SIMILARLY ENDOWED!
MARTINEX! DO YOU REQUIRE ASSISTANCE? I COULD DISENGAGE FROM MY CURRENT POSITION--
NO, GIRAUD! ABSOLUTELY NOT!
THE PHOENIX POWER YOU POSSESS IS BEING USED TO SUSTAIN THIS PLANET'S LIFE SUPPORT SYSTEM IN MAINFRAME'S ABSENCE.
AFFIRMATIVE!
I AM WILLINGLY EXPENDING MY ENERGIES TO MAINTAIN THE EXISTENCE OF MY FELLOW HAVENITES THAT POPULATE THIS WORLD...
...BUT I GROW RESTLESS! MOREOVER, I ADMIT TO A SIGNIFICANT STAMINA DEPLETION! WHEN DO YOU ANTICIPATE MAIN-FRAME'S RETURN?
UNKNOWN! HE IS LONG OVERDUE FROM HIS MEETING WITH HOLLYWOOD!* IN THE MEANTIME--
*WHICH IS WHY HE TOOK HIMSELF OFF LINE IN ISSUE #1.--CRAIG
--UHUCK! ;CHOKE!; GUH-GANGLIAAAA...
MARTINEX! COULD YOU REPEA--
SKLASH

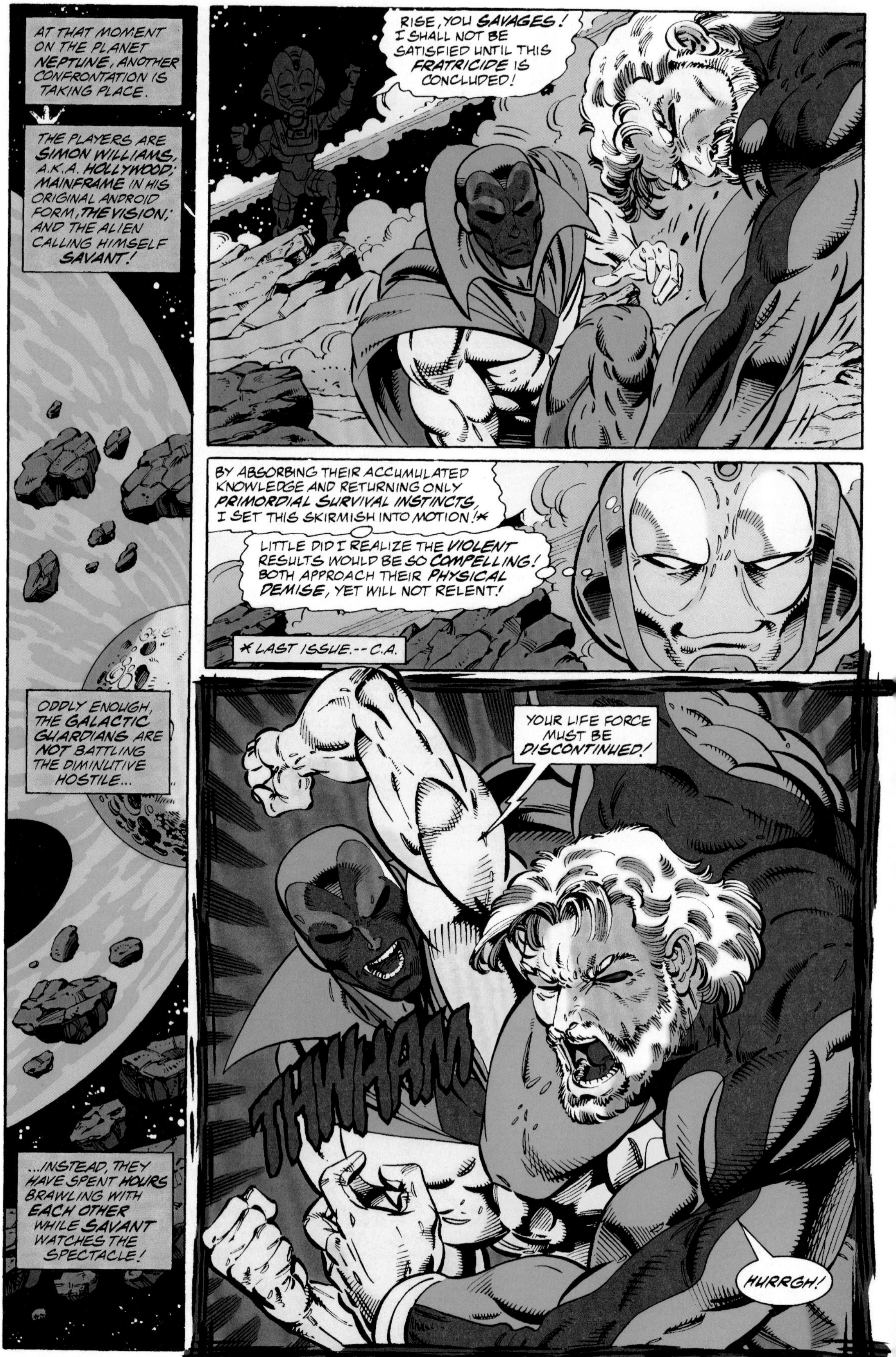
AT THAT MOMENT ON THE PLANET NEPTUNE, ANOTHER CONFRONTATION IS TAKING PLACE.
THE PLAYERS ARE SIMON WILLIAMS, A.K.A. HOLLYWOOD; MAINFRAME IN HIS ORIGINAL ANDROID FORM, THE VISION; AND THE ALIEN CALLING HIMSELF SAVANT!
RISE, YOU SAVAGES! I SHALL NOT BE SATISFIED UNTIL THIS FRATRICIDE IS CONCLUDED!
BY ABSORBING THEIR ACCUMULATED KNOWLEDGE AND RETURNING ONLY PRIMORDIAL SURVIVAL INSTINCTS, I SET THIS SKIRMISH INTO MOTION!*
LITTLE DID I REALIZE THE VIOLENT RESULTS WOULD BE SO COMPELLING! BOTH APPROACH THEIR PHYSICAL DEMISE, YET WILL NOT RELENT!
*LAST ISSUE.--C.A.
ODDLY ENOUGH, THE GALACTIC GUARDIANS ARE NOT BATTLING THE DIMINUTIVE HOSTILE...
YOUR LIFE FORCE MUST BE DISCONTINUED!
THWHAM
...INSTEAD, THEY HAVE SPENT HOURS BRAWLING WITH EACH OTHER WHILE SAVANT WATCHES THE SPECTACLE!
HURRGH!

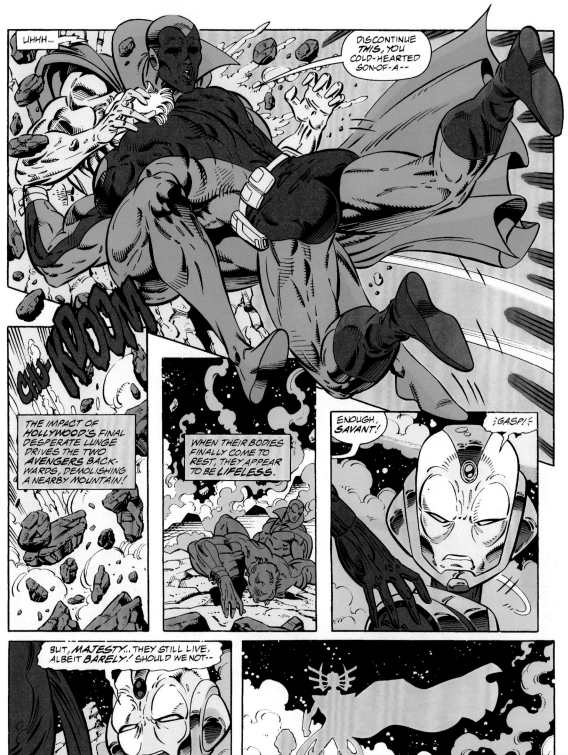

UHHH...

DISCONTINUE *THIS*, YOU COLD-HEARTED SON-OF-A--

KA-KRROOM

THE IMPACT OF *HOLLYWOOD'S* FINAL DESPERATE LUNGE DRIVES THE TWO *AVENGERS* BACKWARDS, DEMOLISHING A NEARBY MOUNTAIN!

WHEN THEIR BODIES FINALLY COME TO REST, THEY APPEAR TO BE *LIFELESS*.

ENOUGH, *SAVANT!*

¡GASP!¡

BUT, *MAJESTY*... THEY STILL LIVE, ALBEIT *BARELY!* SHOULD WE NOT--

YOUR PRESENCE IS REQUIRED AT *MY* SIDE ELSEWHERE!

AS YOU WISH! WHAT OF THEIR *ACQUIRED ERUDITION?* IT IS CRUDE AND *DISTASTEFUL* TO BEAR!

DISSEMINATE IT AMONGST THE *NATIVE ROCK* AND LET US AWAY!

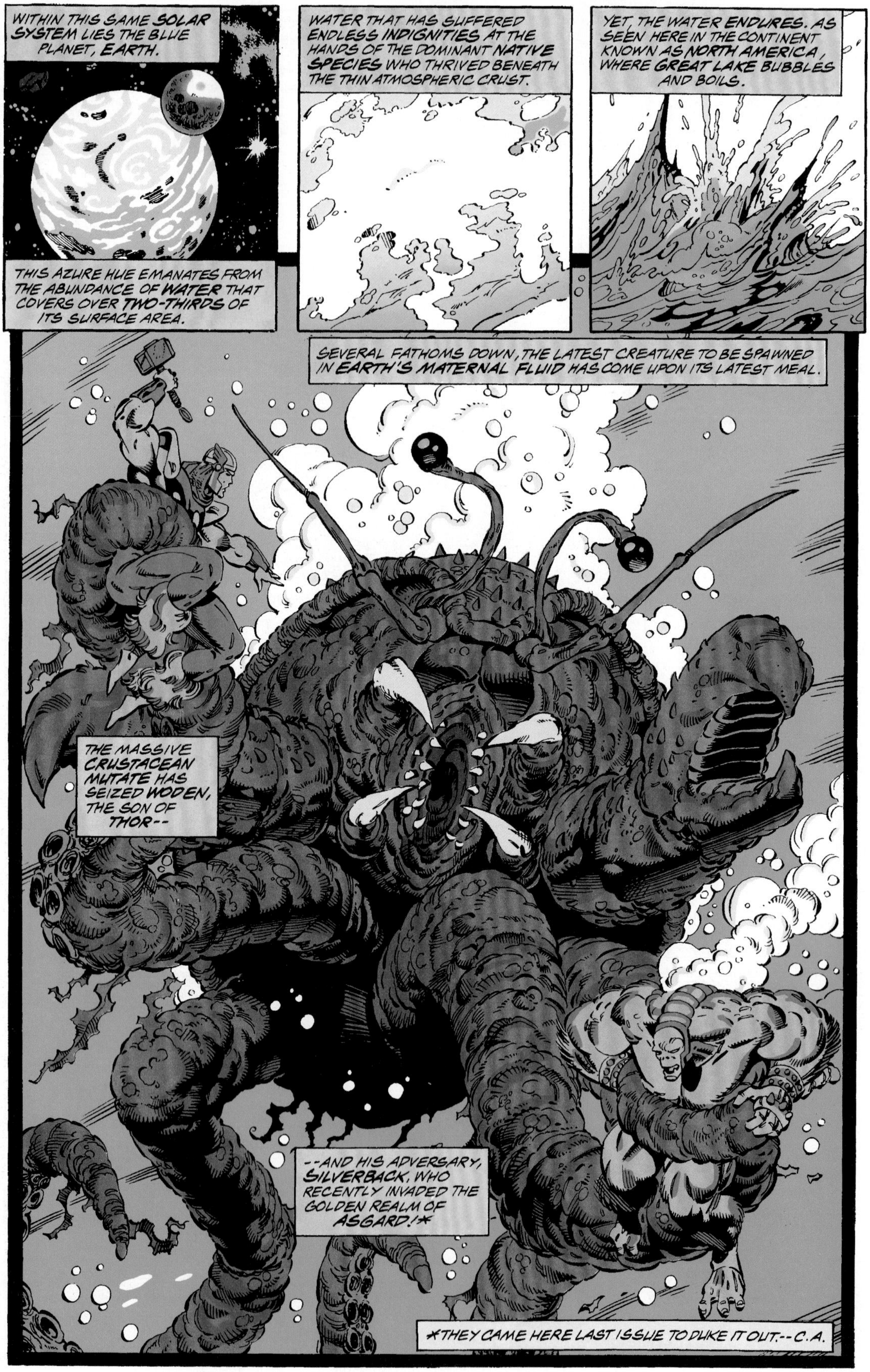
WITHIN THIS SAME SOLAR SYSTEM LIES THE BLUE PLANET, EARTH.
THIS AZURE HUE EMANATES FROM THE ABUNDANCE OF WATER THAT COVERS OVER TWO-THIRDS OF ITS SURFACE AREA.
WATER THAT HAS SUFFERED ENDLESS INDIGNITIES AT THE HANDS OF THE DOMINANT NATIVE SPECIES WHO THRIVED BENEATH THE THIN ATMOSPHERIC CRUST.
YET, THE WATER ENDURES. AS SEEN HERE IN THE CONTINENT KNOWN AS NORTH AMERICA, WHERE GREAT LAKE BUBBLES AND BOILS.
SEVERAL FATHOMS DOWN, THE LATEST CREATURE TO BE SPAWNED IN EARTH'S MATERNAL FLUID HAS COME UPON ITS LATEST MEAL.
THE MASSIVE CRUSTACEAN MUTATE HAS SEIZED WODEN, THE SON OF THOR--
--AND HIS ADVERSARY, SILVERBACK, WHO RECENTLY INVADED THE GOLDEN REALM OF ASGARD!*
*THEY CAME HERE LAST ISSUE TO DUKE IT OUT.-- C.A.

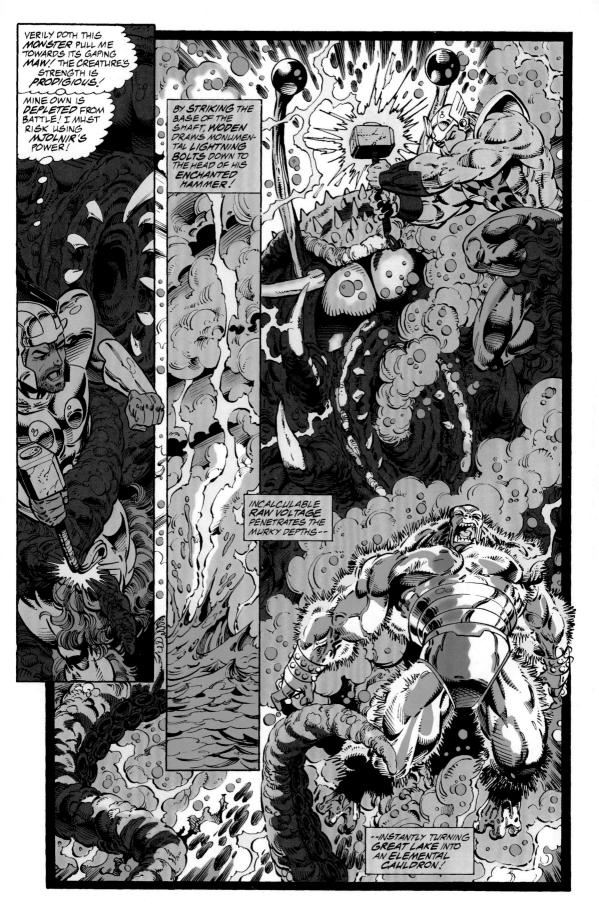

VERILY DOTH THIS *MONSTER* PULL ME TOWARDS ITS GAPING *MAW!* THE CREATURE'S STRENGTH IS *PRODIGIOUS!*

MINE OWN IS *DEPLETED* FROM BATTLE! I MUST RISK USING *MJOLNIR'S* POWER!

BY *STRIKING* THE BASE OF THE SHAFT, *WODEN* DRAWS MONUMENTAL *LIGHTNING BOLTS* DOWN TO THE HEAD OF HIS *ENCHANTED HAMMER!*

INCALCULABLE *RAW VOLTAGE* PENETRATES THE *MURKY DEPTHS--*

--INSTANTLY TURNING *GREAT LAKE* INTO AN *ELEMENTAL CAULDRON!*

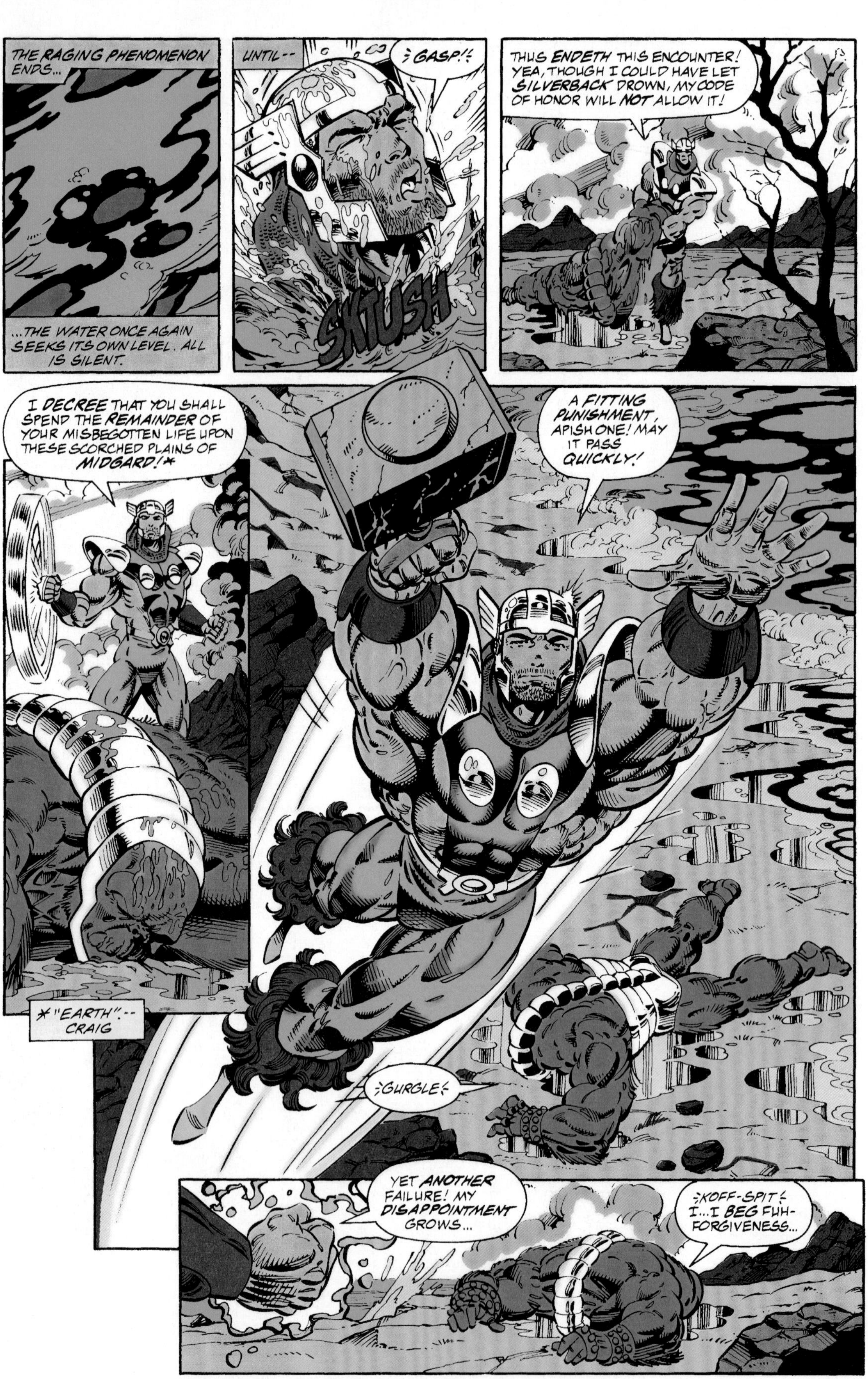
THE RAGING PHENOMENON ENDS...
...THE WATER ONCE AGAIN SEEKS ITS OWN LEVEL. ALL IS SILENT.
UNTIL--
GASP!
SKTUSH
THUS ENDETH THIS ENCOUNTER! YEA, THOUGH I COULD HAVE LET SILVERBACK DROWN, MY CODE OF HONOR WILL NOT ALLOW IT!
I DECREE THAT YOU SHALL SPEND THE REMAINDER OF YOUR MISBEGOTTEN LIFE UPON THESE SCORCHED PLAINS OF MIDGARD!*
A FITTING PUNISHMENT, APISH ONE! MAY IT PASS QUICKLY!
*"EARTH".-- CRAIG
GURGLE
YET ANOTHER FAILURE! MY DISAPPOINTMENT GROWS...
KOFF-SPIT! I...I BEG FUH-FORGIVENESS...

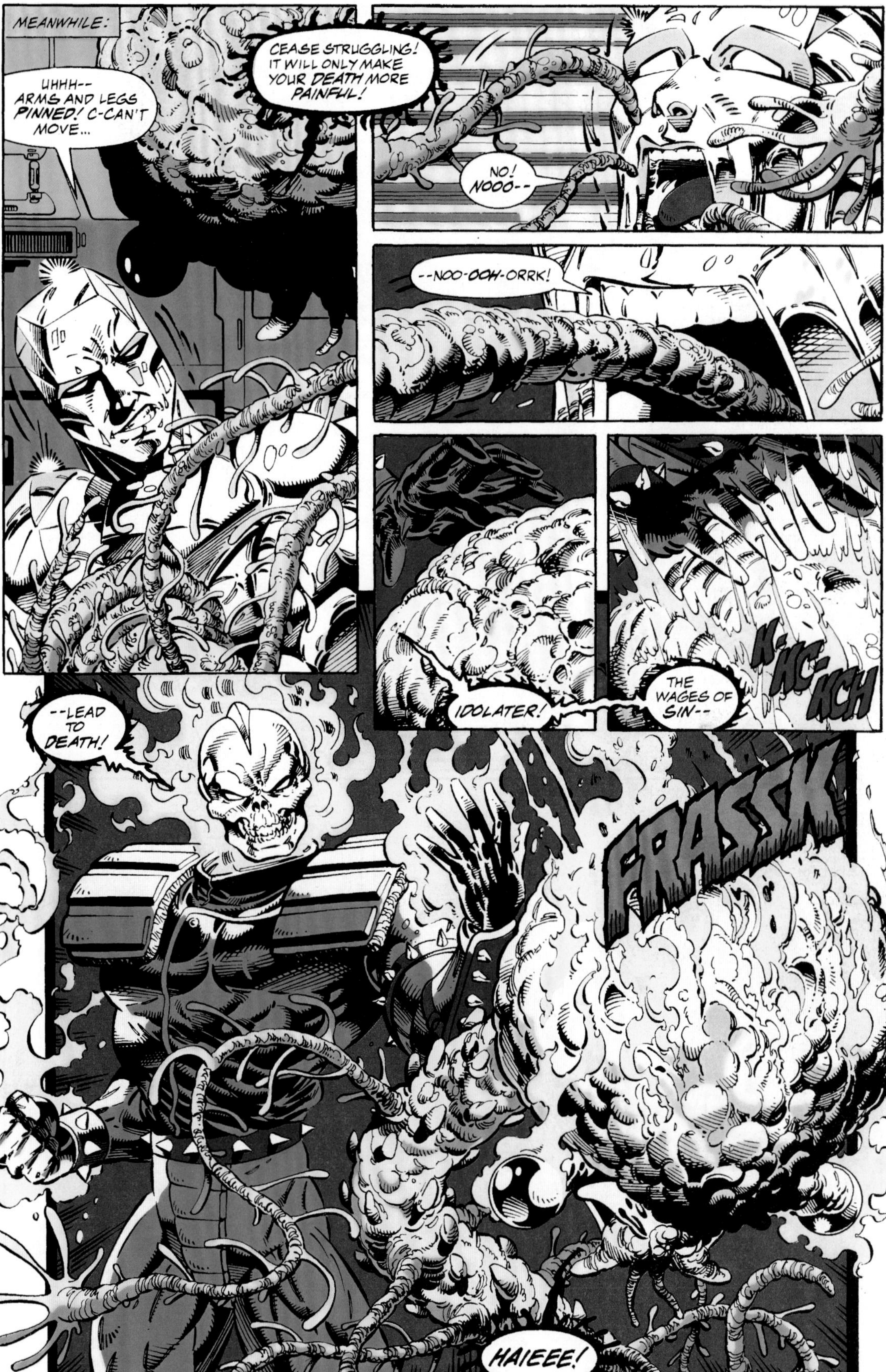
MEANWHILE:
UHHH-- ARMS AND LEGS PINNED! C-CAN'T MOVE...
CEASE STRUGGLING! IT WILL ONLY MAKE YOUR DEATH MORE PAINFUL!
NO! NOOO--
--NOO-OOH-ORRK!
IDOLATER!
THE WAGES OF SIN--
K-KC-KCH
--LEAD TO DEATH!
FRASSK
HAIEEE!

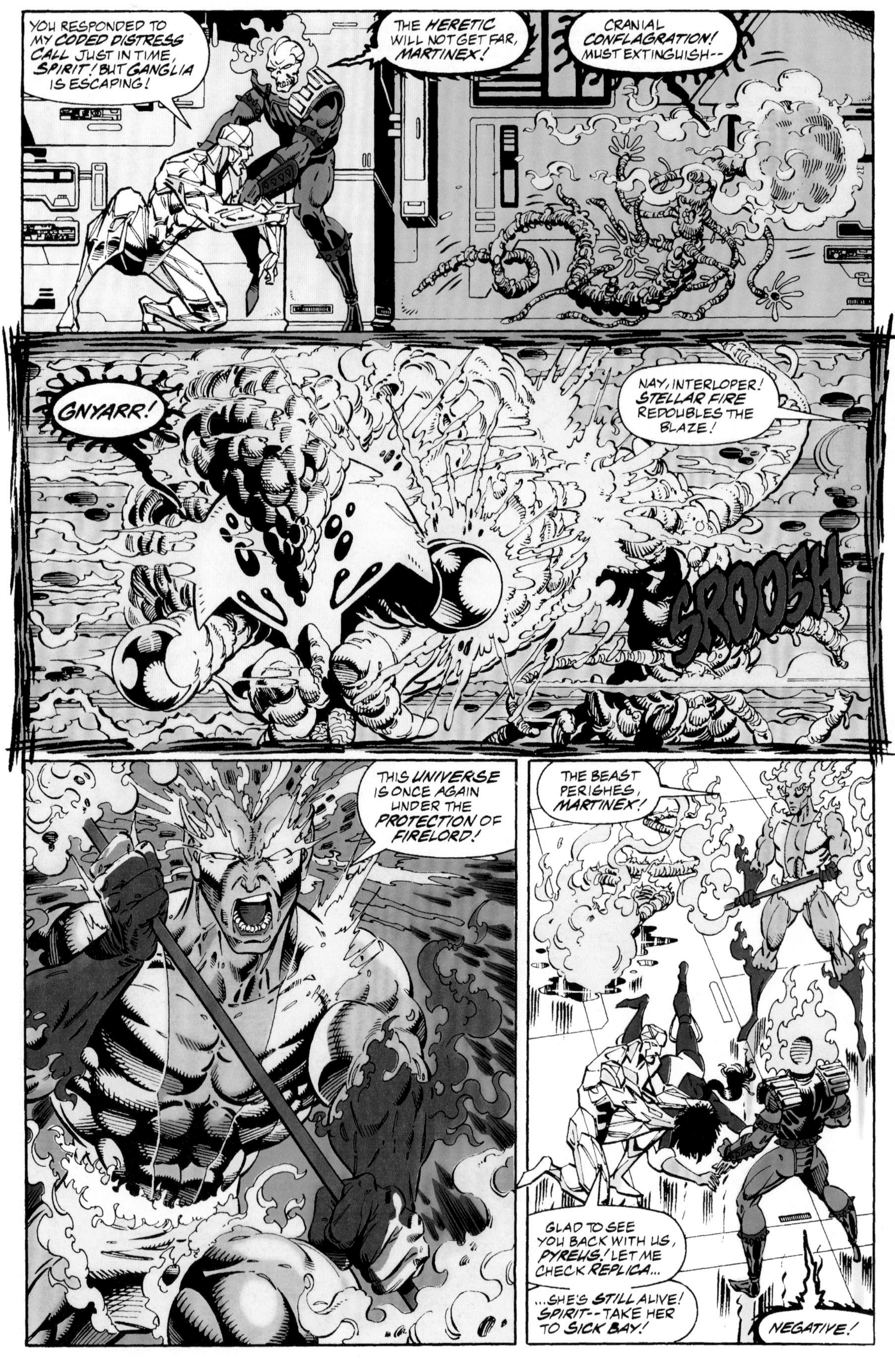
YOU RESPONDED TO MY CODED DISTRESS CALL JUST IN TIME, SPIRIT! BUT GANGLIA IS ESCAPING!
THE HERETIC WILL NOT GET FAR, MARTINEX!
CRANIAL CONFLAGRATION! MUST EXTINGUISH--
GNYARR!
NAY, INTERLOPER! STELLAR FIRE REDOUBLES THE BLAZE!
SROOSH
THIS UNIVERSE IS ONCE AGAIN UNDER THE PROTECTION OF FIRELORD!
THE BEAST PERISHES, MARTINEX!
GLAD TO SEE YOU BACK WITH US, PYREUS! LET ME CHECK REPLICA...
...SHE'S STILL ALIVE! SPIRIT--TAKE HER TO SICK BAY!
NEGATIVE!

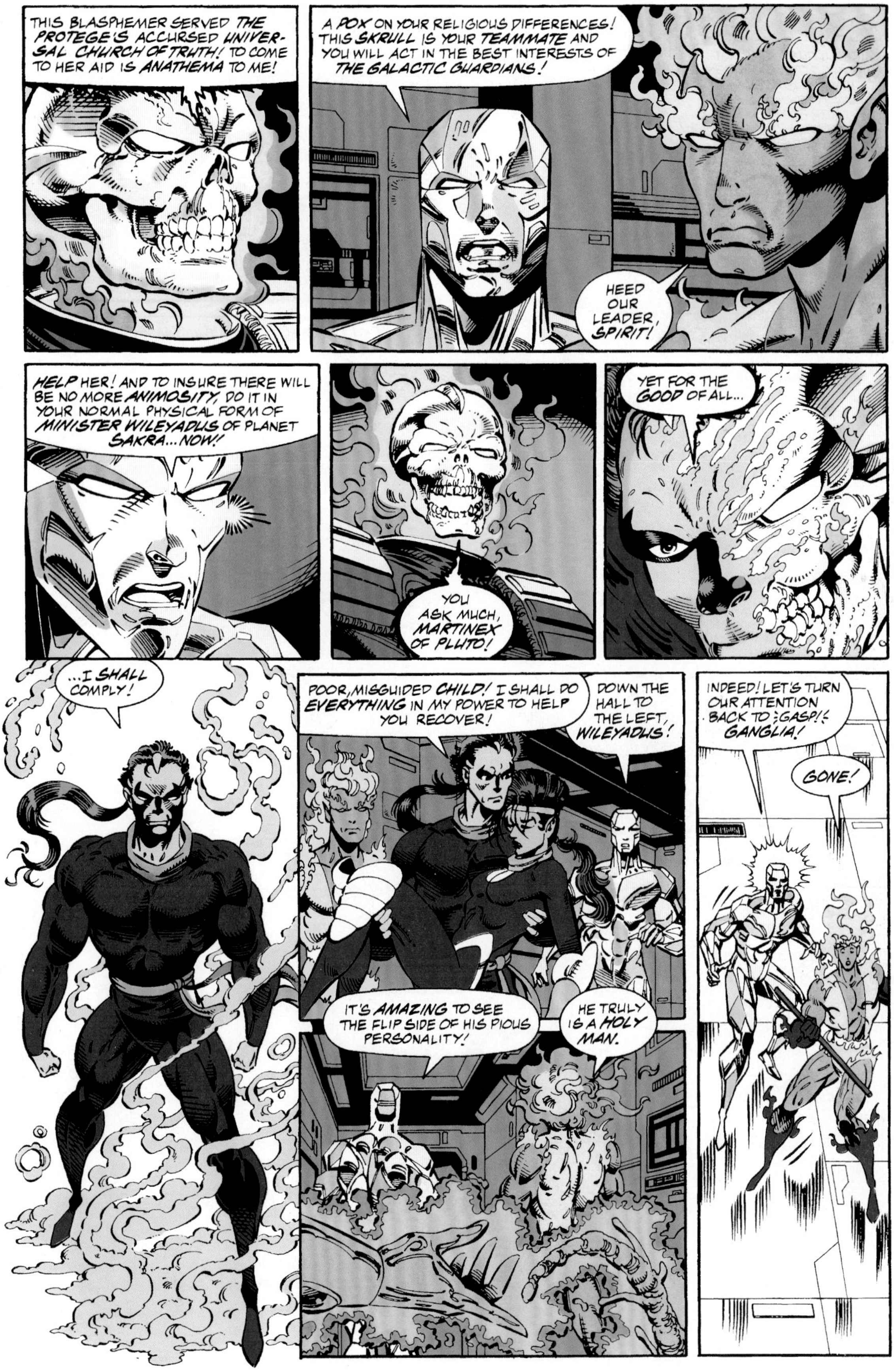
THIS BLASPHEMER SERVED THE PROTEGE'S ACCURSED UNIVERSAL CHURCH OF TRUTH! TO COME TO HER AID IS ANATHEMA TO ME!
A POX ON YOUR RELIGIOUS DIFFERENCES! THIS SKRULL IS YOUR TEAMMATE AND YOU WILL ACT IN THE BEST INTERESTS OF THE GALACTIC GUARDIANS!
HEED OUR LEADER, SPIRIT!
HELP HER! AND TO INSURE THERE WILL BE NO MORE ANIMOSITY, DO IT IN YOUR NORMAL PHYSICAL FORM OF MINISTER WILEYADUS OF PLANET SAKRA... NOW!
YOU ASK MUCH, MARTINEX OF PLUTO!
YET FOR THE GOOD OF ALL...
...I SHALL COMPLY!
POOR, MISGUIDED CHILD! I SHALL DO EVERYTHING IN MY POWER TO HELP YOU RECOVER!
DOWN THE HALL TO THE LEFT, WILEYADUS!
IT'S AMAZING TO SEE THE FLIP SIDE OF HIS PIOUS PERSONALITY!
HE TRULY IS A HOLY MAN.
INDEED! LET'S TURN OUR ATTENTION BACK TO -GASP!- GANGLIA!
GONE!

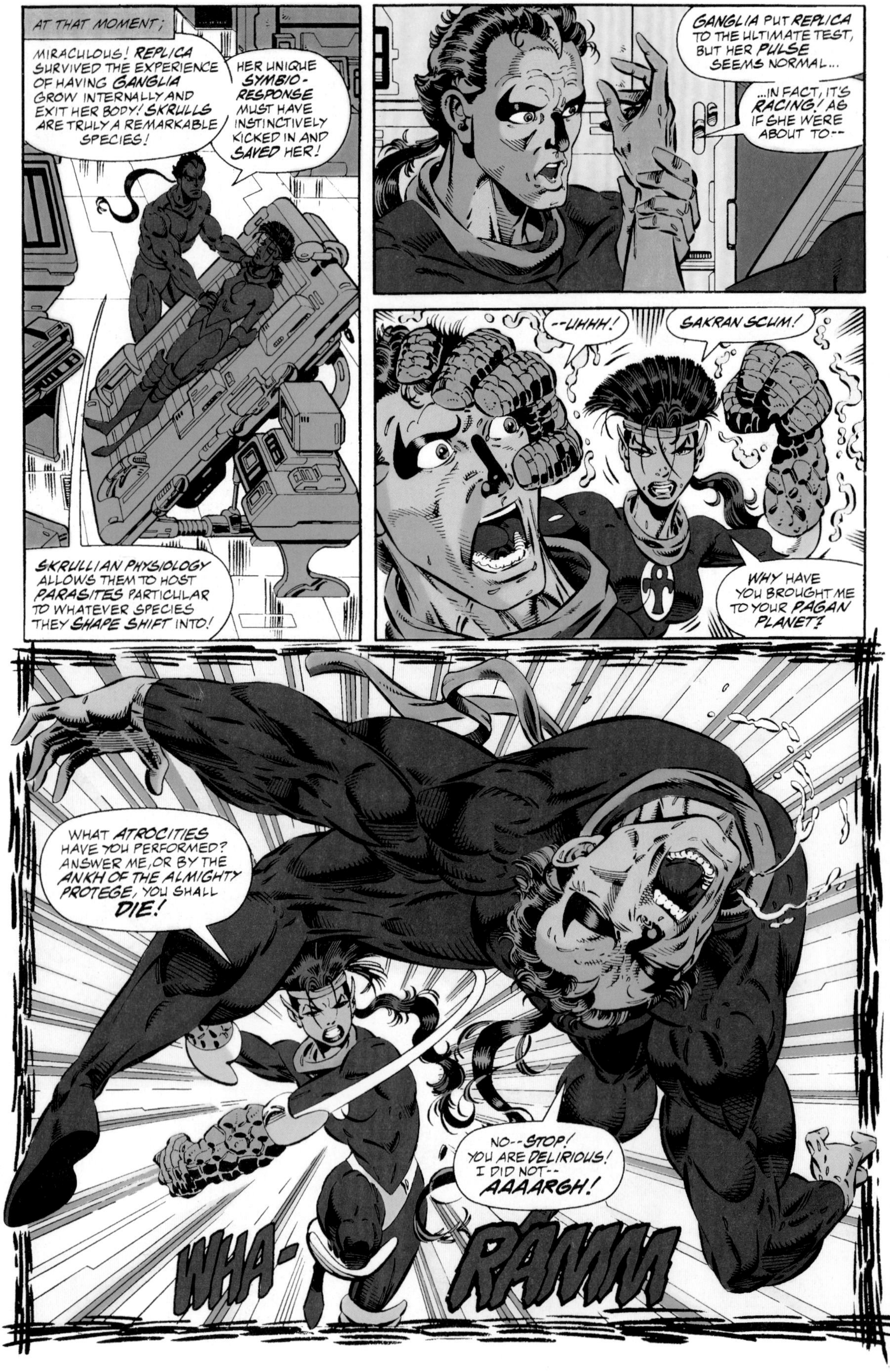
AT THAT MOMENT;
MIRACULOUS! REPLICA SURVIVED THE EXPERIENCE OF HAVING GANGLIA GROW INTERNALLY AND EXIT HER BODY! SKRULLS ARE TRULY A REMARKABLE SPECIES!
HER UNIQUE SYMBIO-RESPONSE MUST HAVE INSTINCTIVELY KICKED IN AND SAVED HER!
SKRULLIAN PHYSIOLOGY ALLOWS THEM TO HOST PARASITES PARTICULAR TO WHATEVER SPECIES THEY SHAPE SHIFT INTO!
GANGLIA PUT REPLICA TO THE ULTIMATE TEST, BUT HER PULSE SEEMS NORMAL...
...IN FACT, IT'S RACING! AS IF SHE WERE ABOUT TO--
--UHHH!
SAKRAN SCUM!
WHY HAVE YOU BROUGHT ME TO YOUR PAGAN PLANET?
WHAT ATROCITIES HAVE YOU PERFORMED? ANSWER ME, OR BY THE ANKH OF THE ALMIGHTY PROTEGE, YOU SHALL DIE!
NO--STOP! YOU ARE DELIRIOUS! I DID NOT-- AAAARGH!
WHA-RAMM

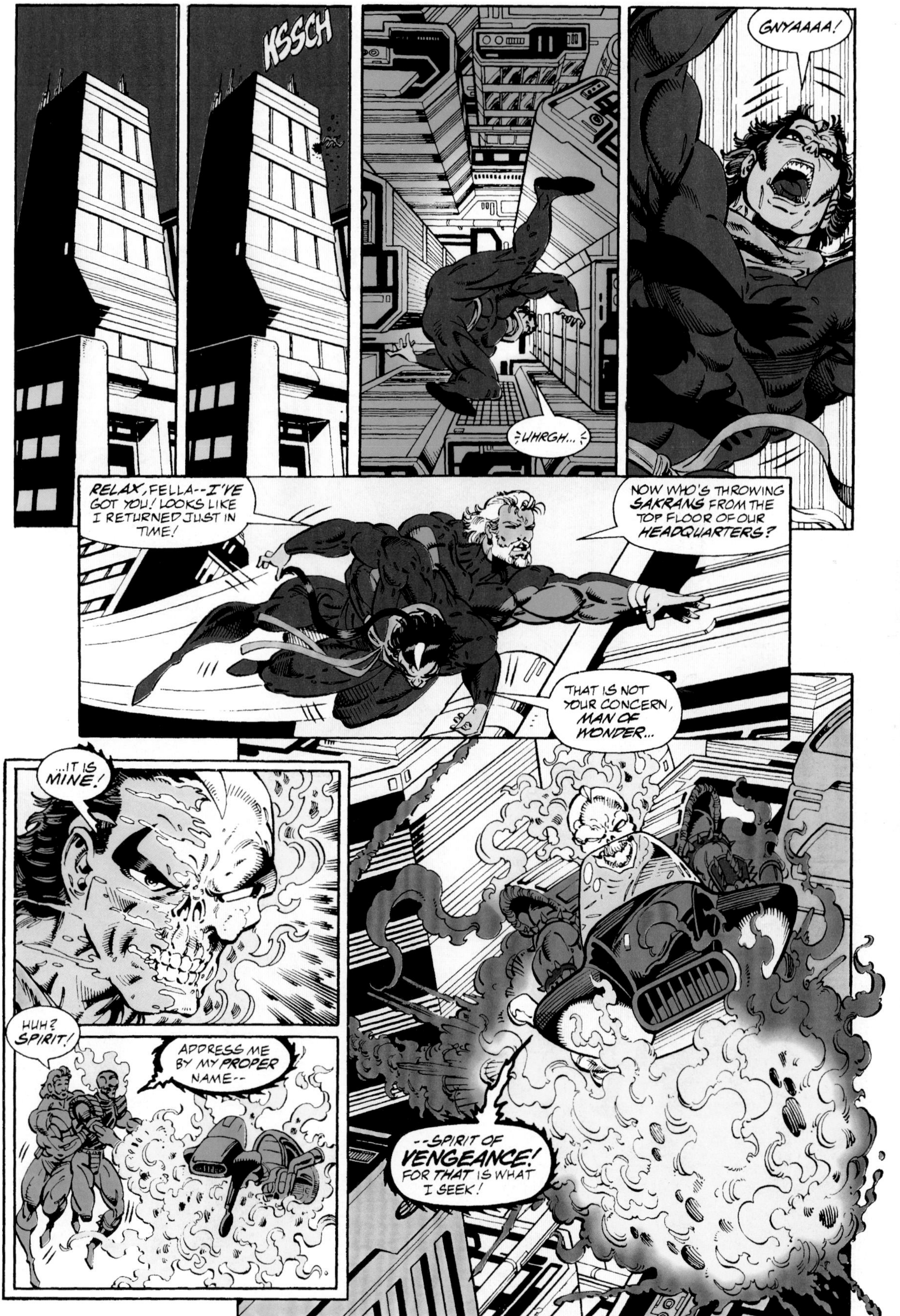
KSSCH
UHRGH...
GNYAAAA!
RELAX, FELLA--I'VE GOT YOU! LOOKS LIKE I RETURNED JUST IN TIME!
NOW WHO'S THROWING SAKRANS FROM THE TOP FLOOR OF OUR HEADQUARTERS?
THAT IS NOT YOUR CONCERN, MAN OF WONDER...
...IT IS MINE!
HUH? SPIRIT!
ADDRESS ME BY MY PROPER NAME--
--SPIRIT OF VENGEANCE! FOR THAT IS WHAT I SEEK!

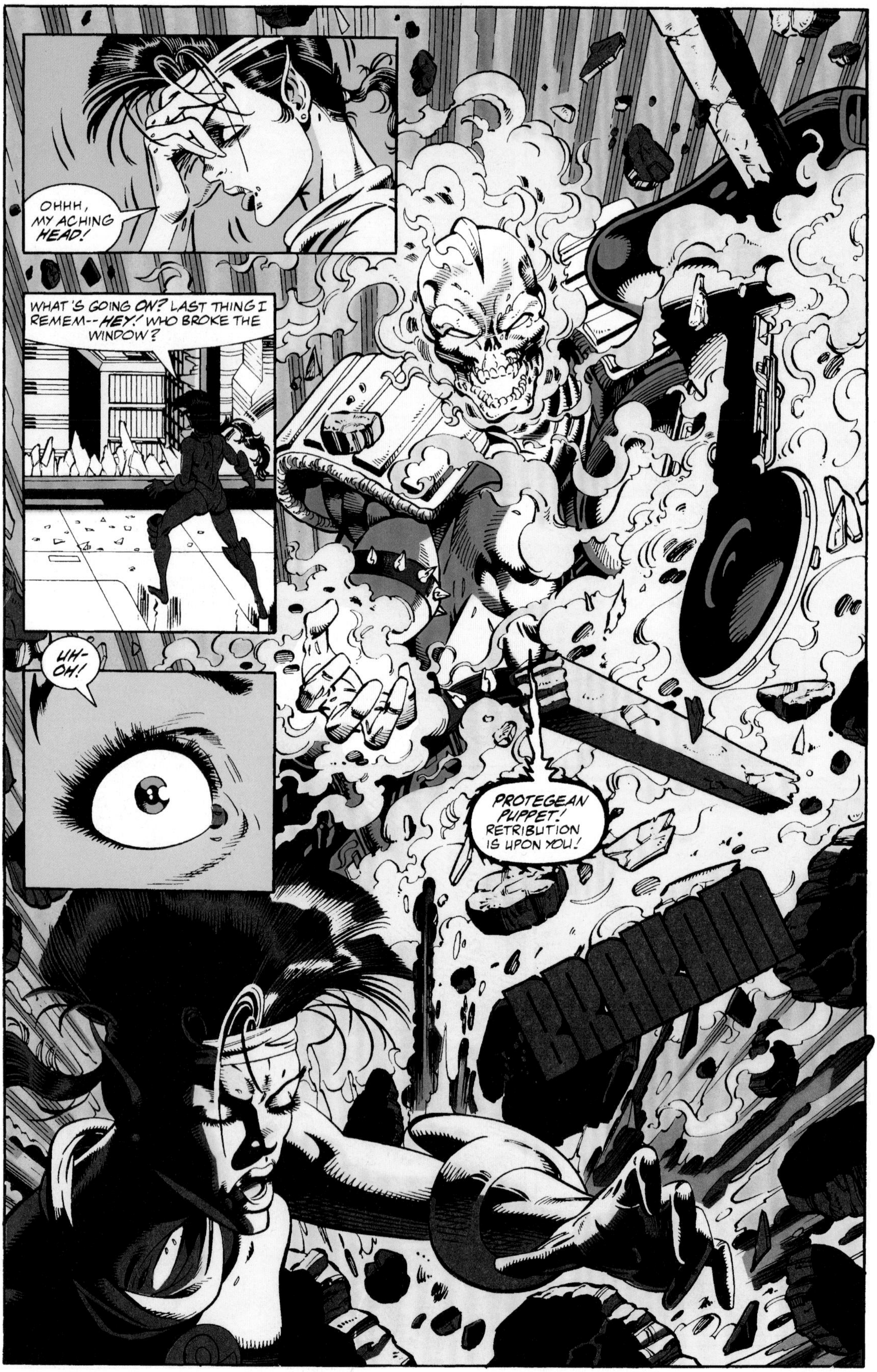

OHHH, MY ACHING HEAD!
WHAT'S GOING ON? LAST THING I REMEM--HEY! WHO BROKE THE WINDOW?
UH-OH!
PROTEGEAN PUPPET! RETRIBUTION IS UPON YOU!
BRAKAM

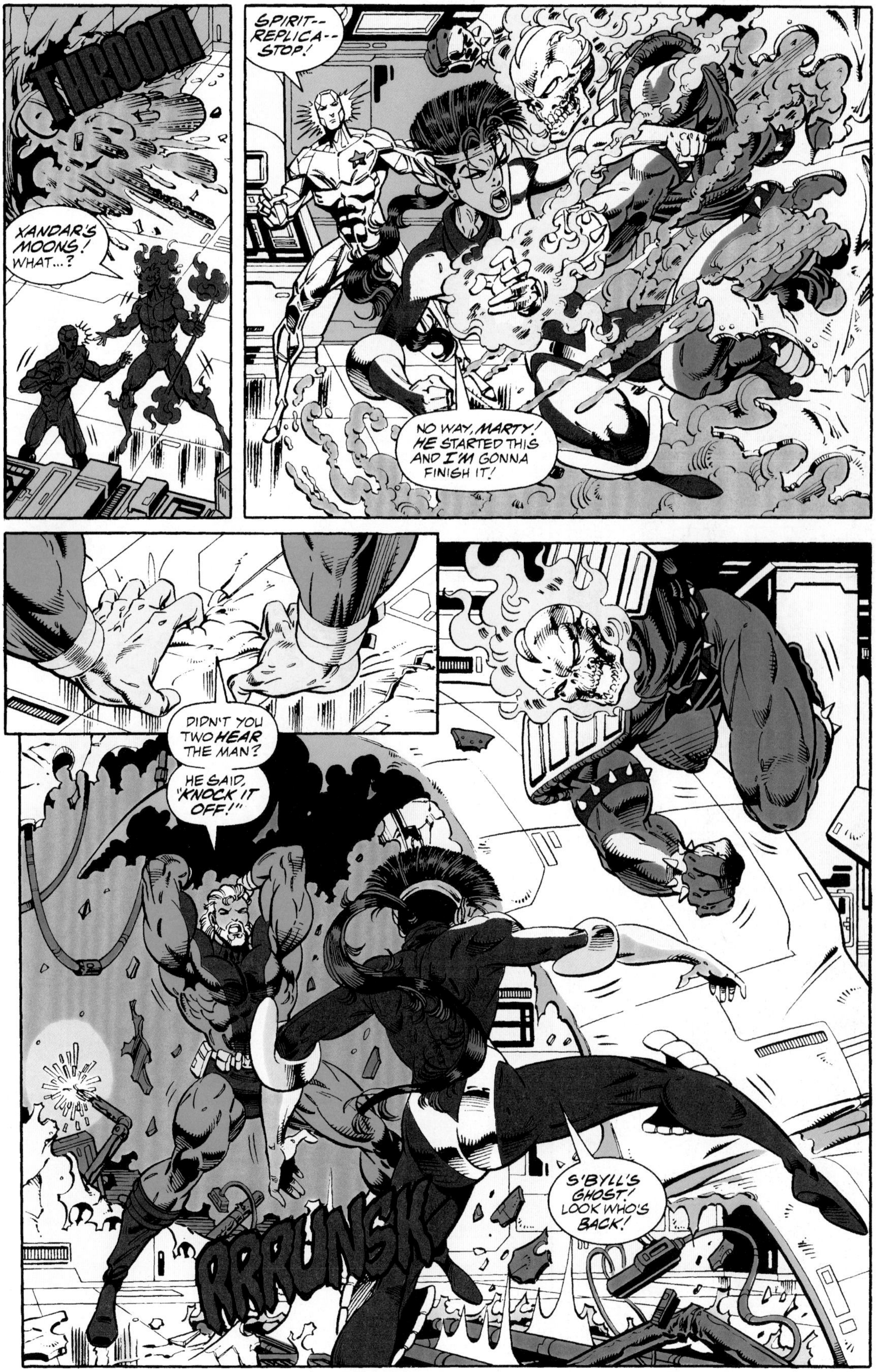
THROOM
XANDAR'S MOONS! WHAT...?
SPIRIT-- REPLICA-- STOP!
NO WAY, MARTY! HE STARTED THIS AND I'M GONNA FINISH IT!
DIDN'T YOU TWO HEAR THE MAN?
HE SAID, "KNOCK IT OFF!"
S'BYLL'S GHOST! LOOK WHO'S BACK!
RRRUNSK!

CEASE HOSTILITIES!

HOLLYWOOD! AM I GLAD TO SEE YOU! AND IF *YOU'RE* HERE, THEN THAT MEANS --

AFFIRMITIVE, *MARTINEX.* I AM BACK ON LINE.

EXCELLENT, *MAINFRAME!*

I'LL BE ANXIOUS TO HEAR THE EXPLANATION... LATER.

NOW, HOW SOON CAN *PHOENIX IX* DISENGAGE AND REJOIN US?

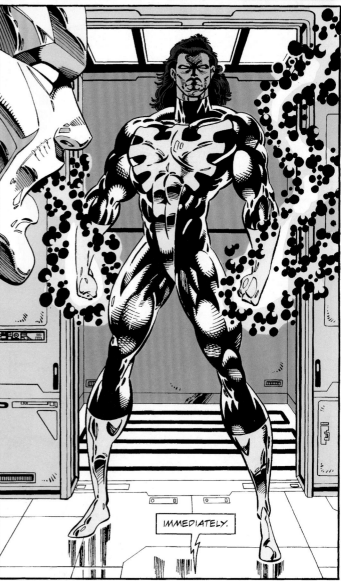

IMMEDIATELY.

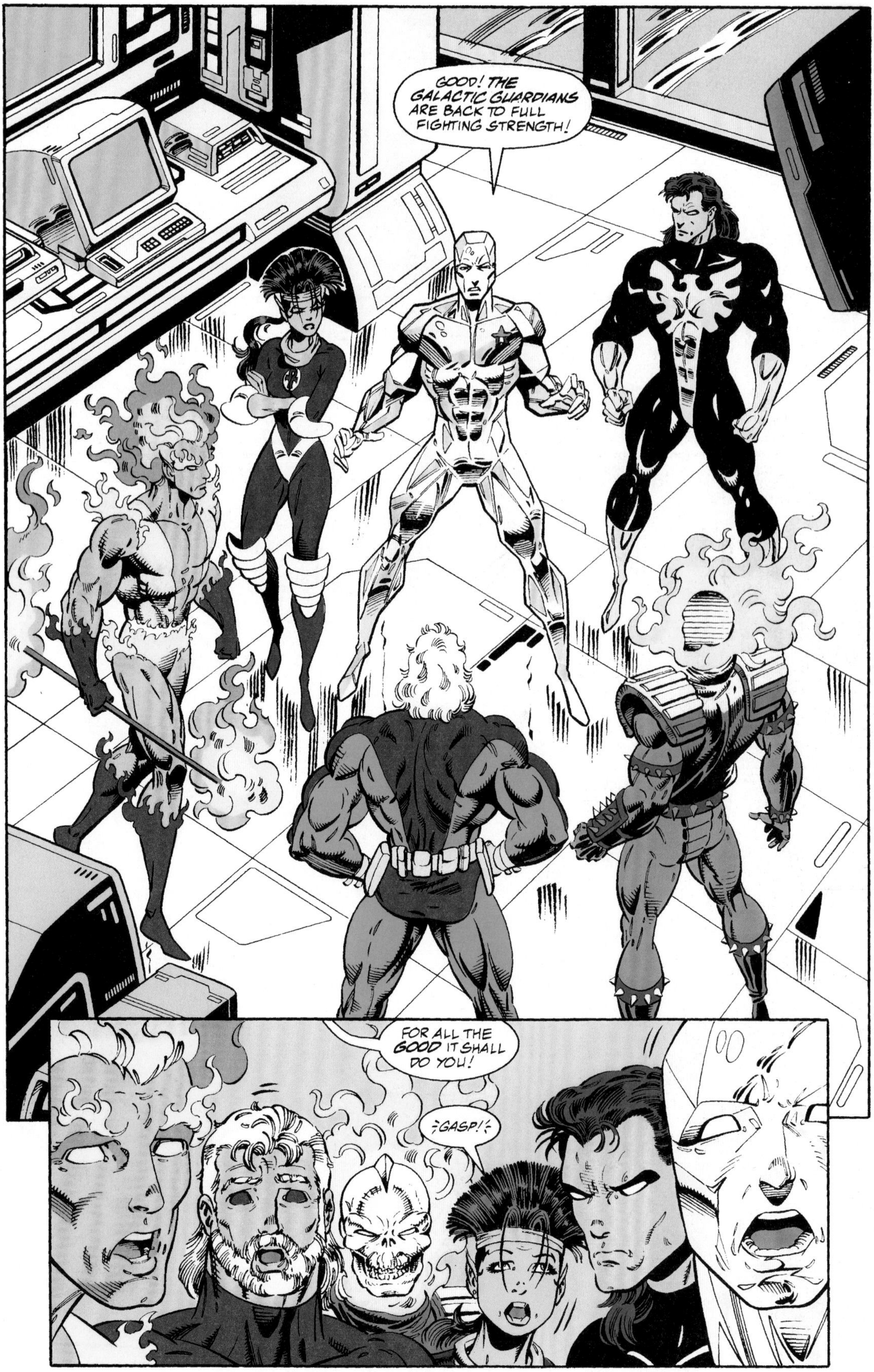
GOOD! THE GALACTIC GUARDIANS ARE BACK TO FULL FIGHTING STRENGTH!
FOR ALL THE GOOD IT SHALL DO YOU!
GASP!

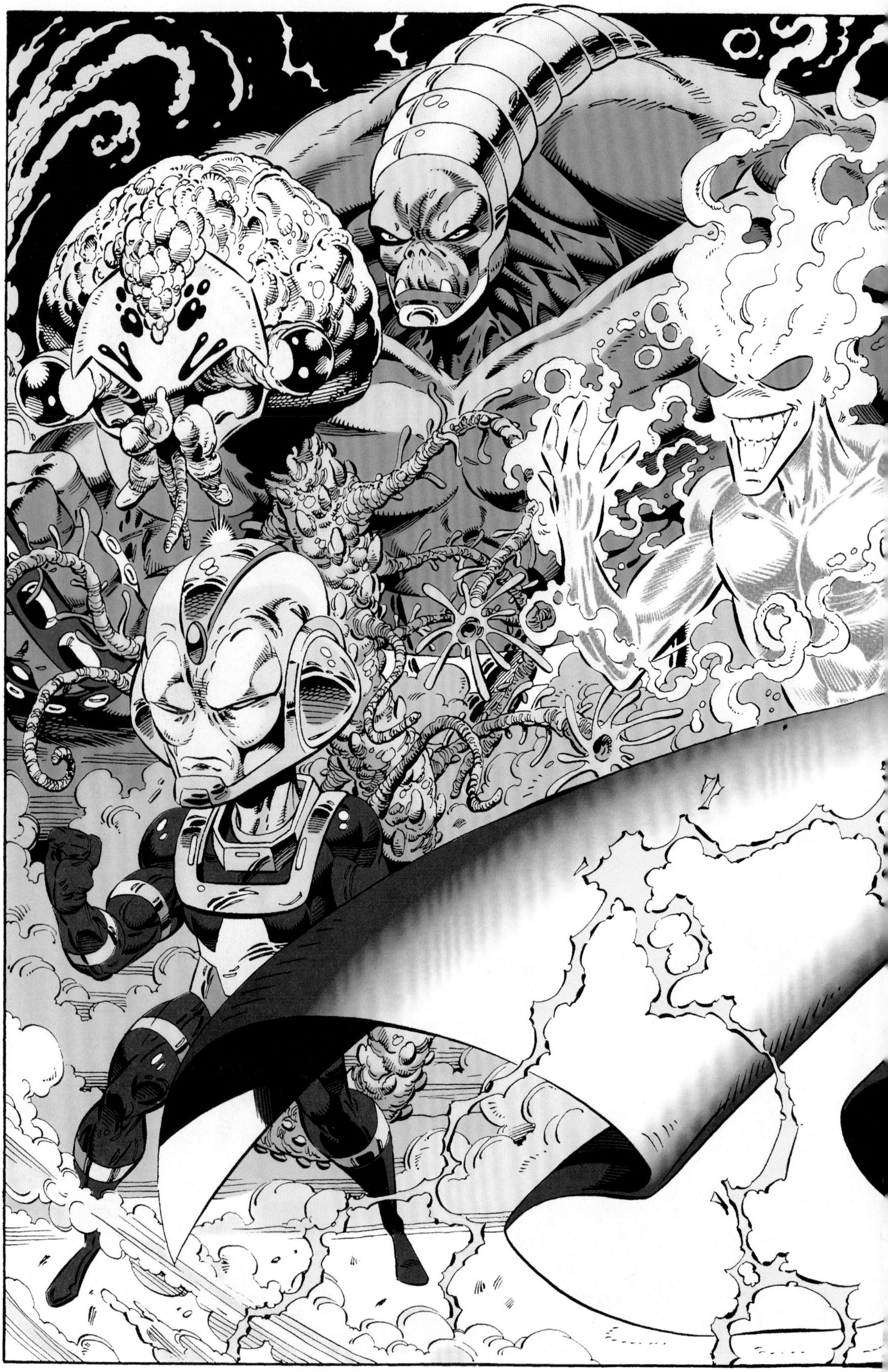

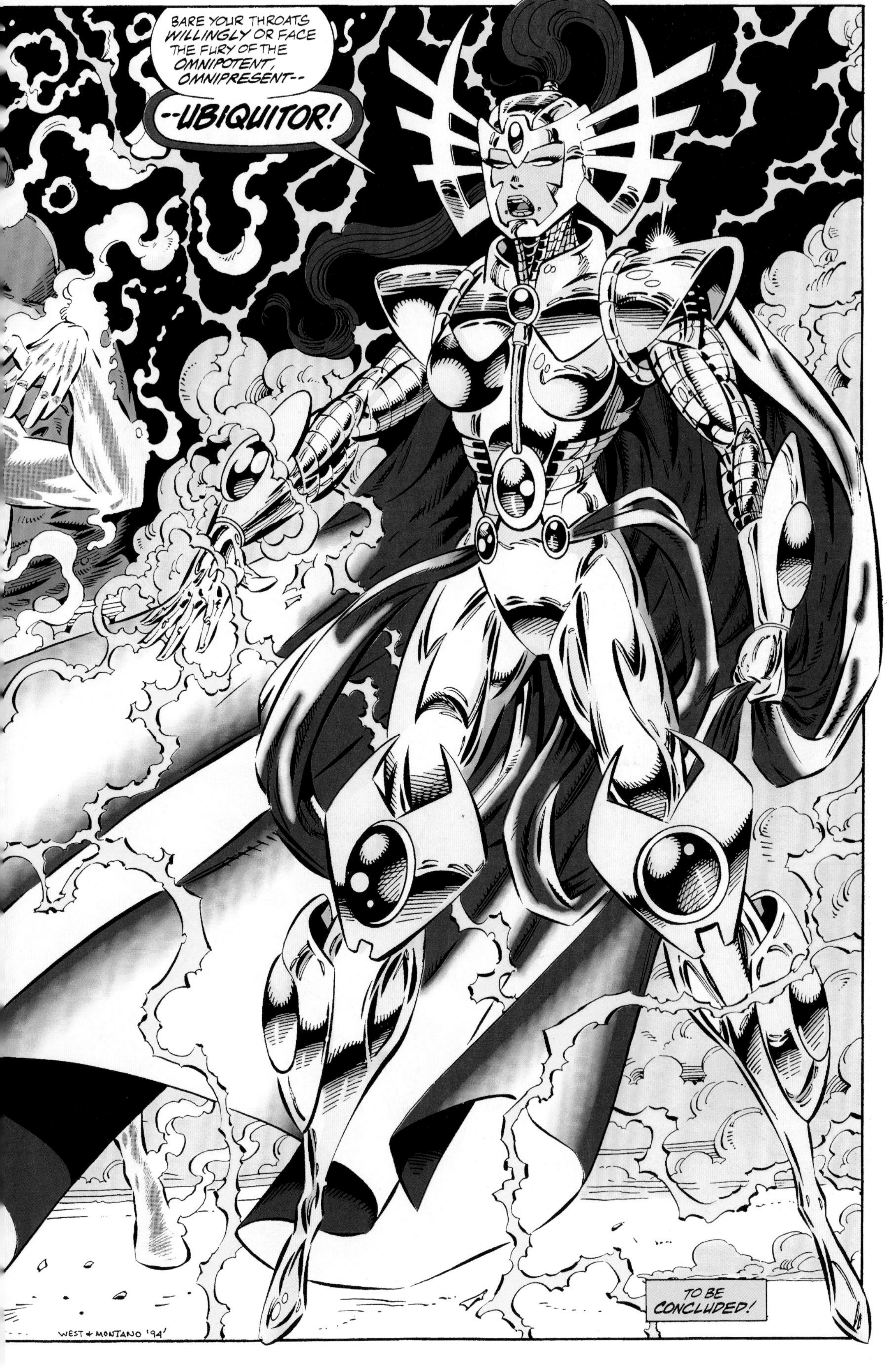
BARE YOUR THROATS WILLINGLY OR FACE THE FURY OF THE OMNIPOTENT, OMNIPRESENT--
--UBIQUITOR!
TO BE CONCLUDED!
WEST + MONTANO '94'

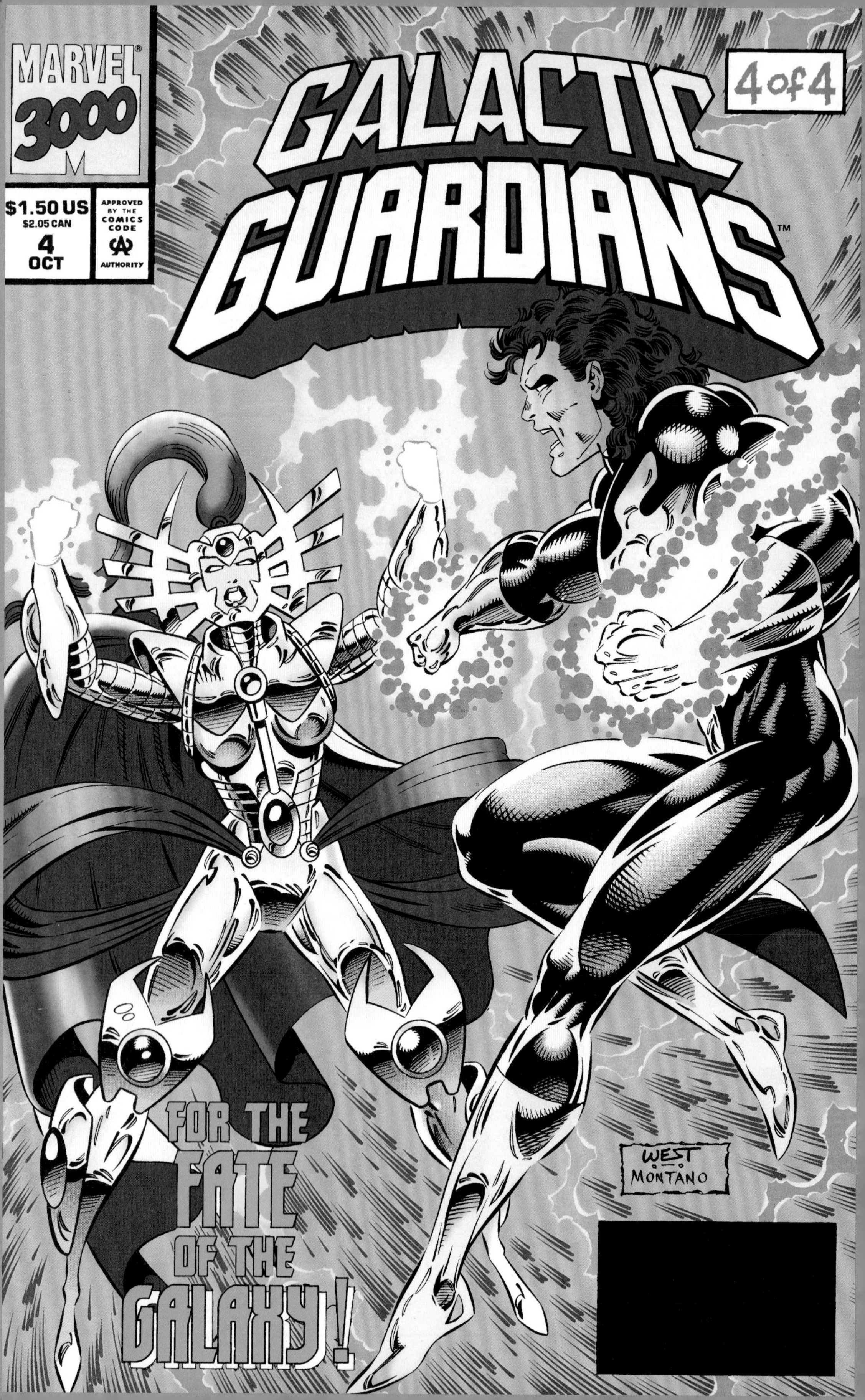
MARVEL® 3000
$1.50 US
$2.05 CAN
4
OCT
APPROVED BY THE COMICS CODE AUTHORITY
GALACTIC GUARDIANS™
4 of 4
FOR THE FATE OF THE GALAXY!
WEST MONTANO

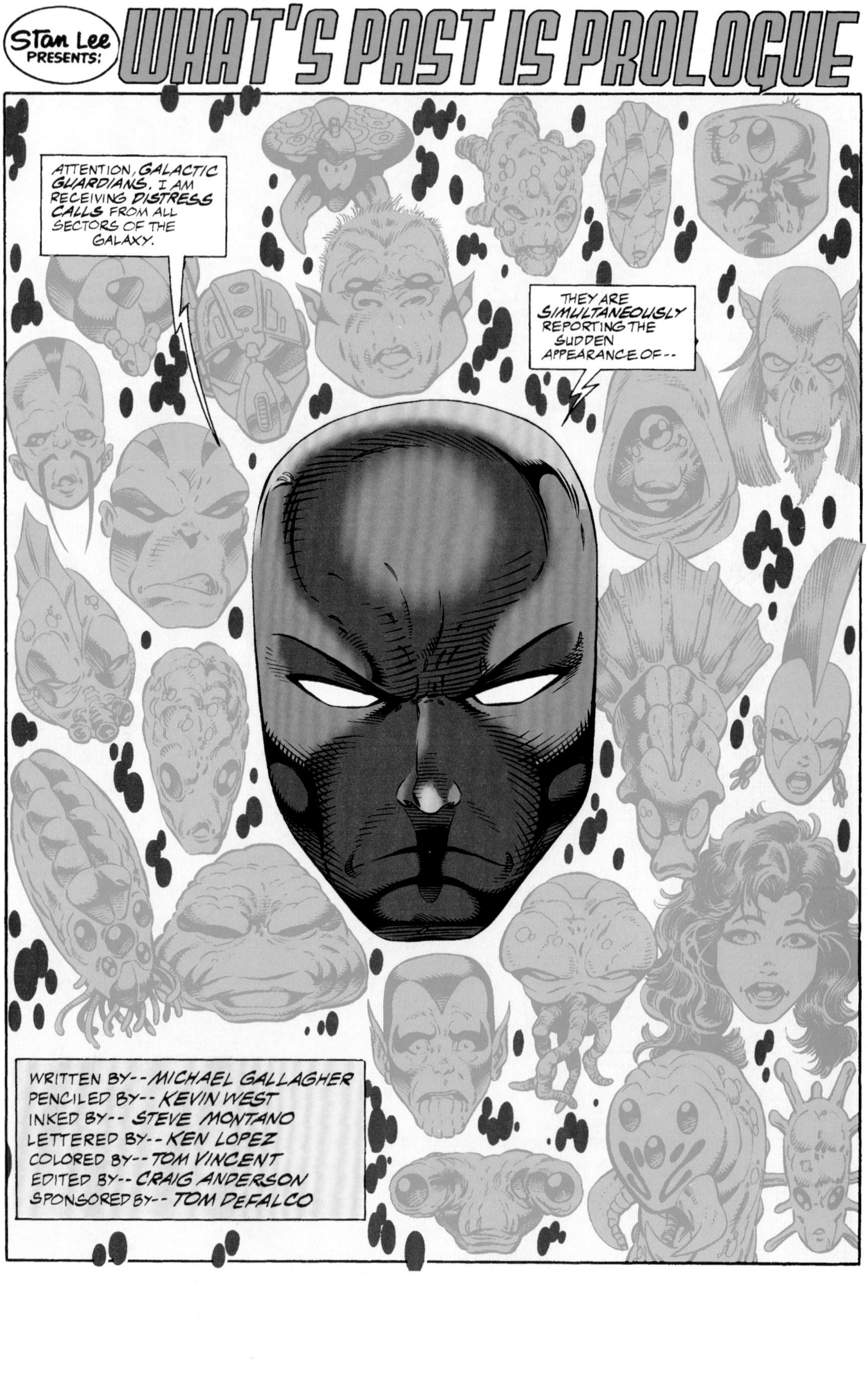
Stan Lee PRESENTS:
WHAT'S PAST IS PROLOGUE
ATTENTION, GALACTIC GUARDIANS. I AM RECEIVING DISTRESS CALLS FROM ALL SECTORS OF THE GALAXY.
THEY ARE SIMULTANEOUSLY REPORTING THE SUDDEN APPEARANCE OF--
WRITTEN BY--MICHAEL GALLAGHER
PENCILED BY--KEVIN WEST
INKED BY--STEVE MONTANO
LETTERED BY--KEN LOPEZ
COLORED BY--TOM VINCENT
EDITED BY--CRAIG ANDERSON
SPONSORED BY--TOM DEFALCO

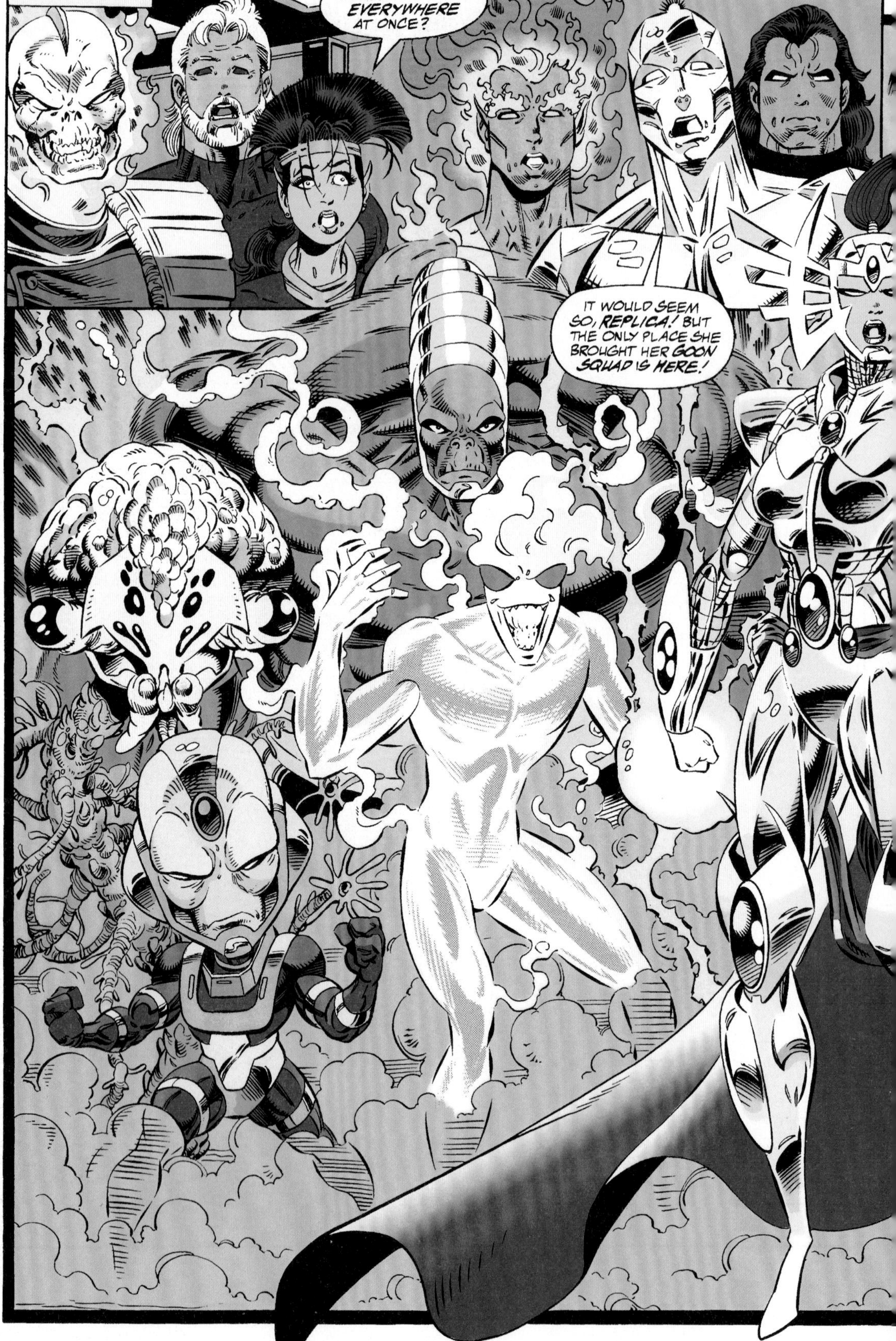
"--UBIQUITOR!"
M-MARTINE IS SHE EVERYWHERE AT ONCE?
IT WOULD SEEM SO, REPLICA! BUT THE ONLY PLACE SHE BROUGHT HER GOON SQUAD IS HERE!

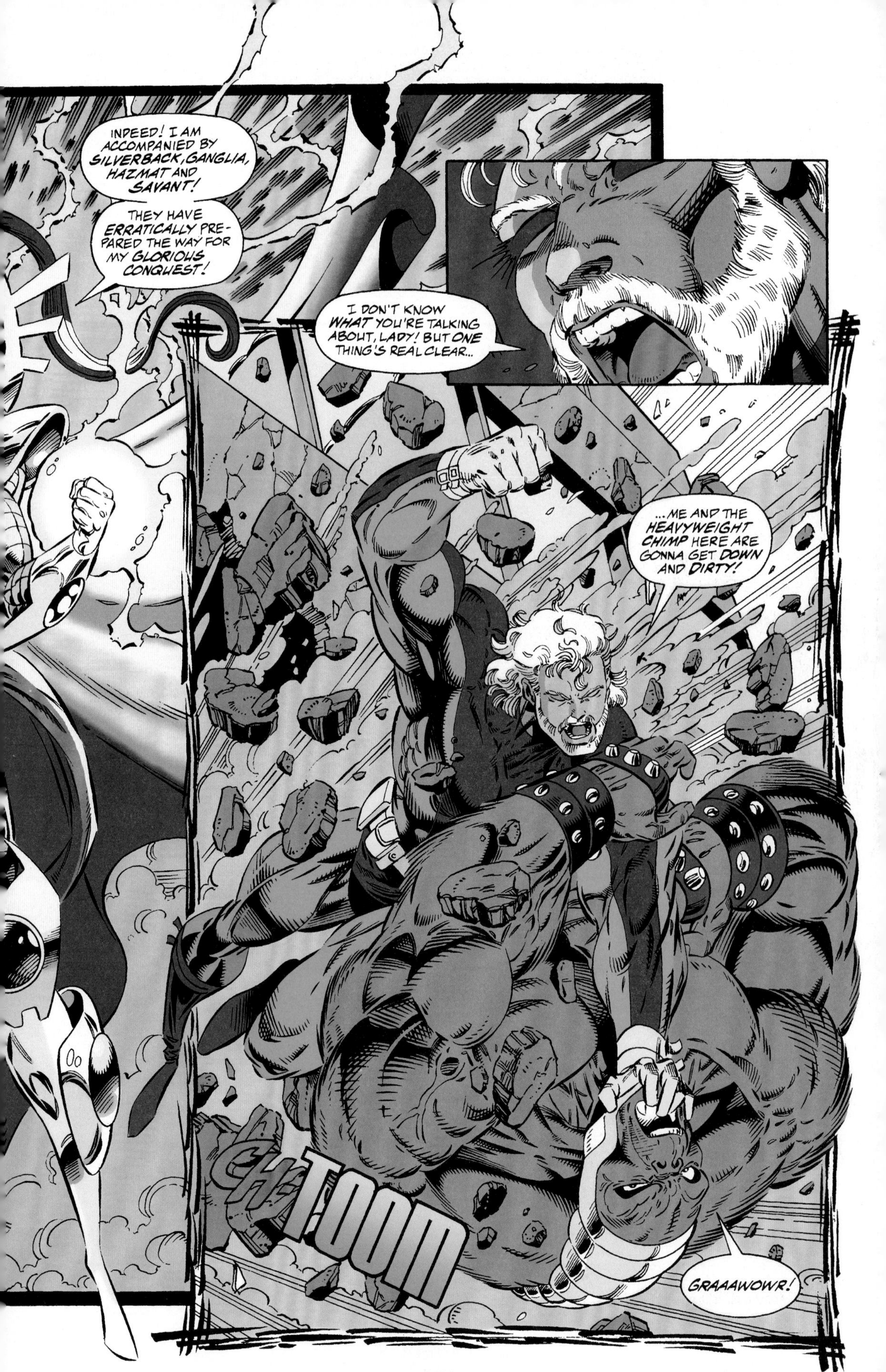
INDEED! I AM ACCOMPANIED BY SILVERBACK, GANGLIA, HAZMAT AND SAVANT!
THEY HAVE ERRATICALLY PREPARED THE WAY FOR MY GLORIOUS CONQUEST!
I DON'T KNOW WHAT YOU'RE TALKING ABOUT, LADY! BUT ONE THING'S REAL CLEAR...
...ME AND THE HEAVYWEIGHT CHIMP HERE ARE GONNA GET DOWN AND DIRTY!
CH-TOOM
GRAAAWOWR!

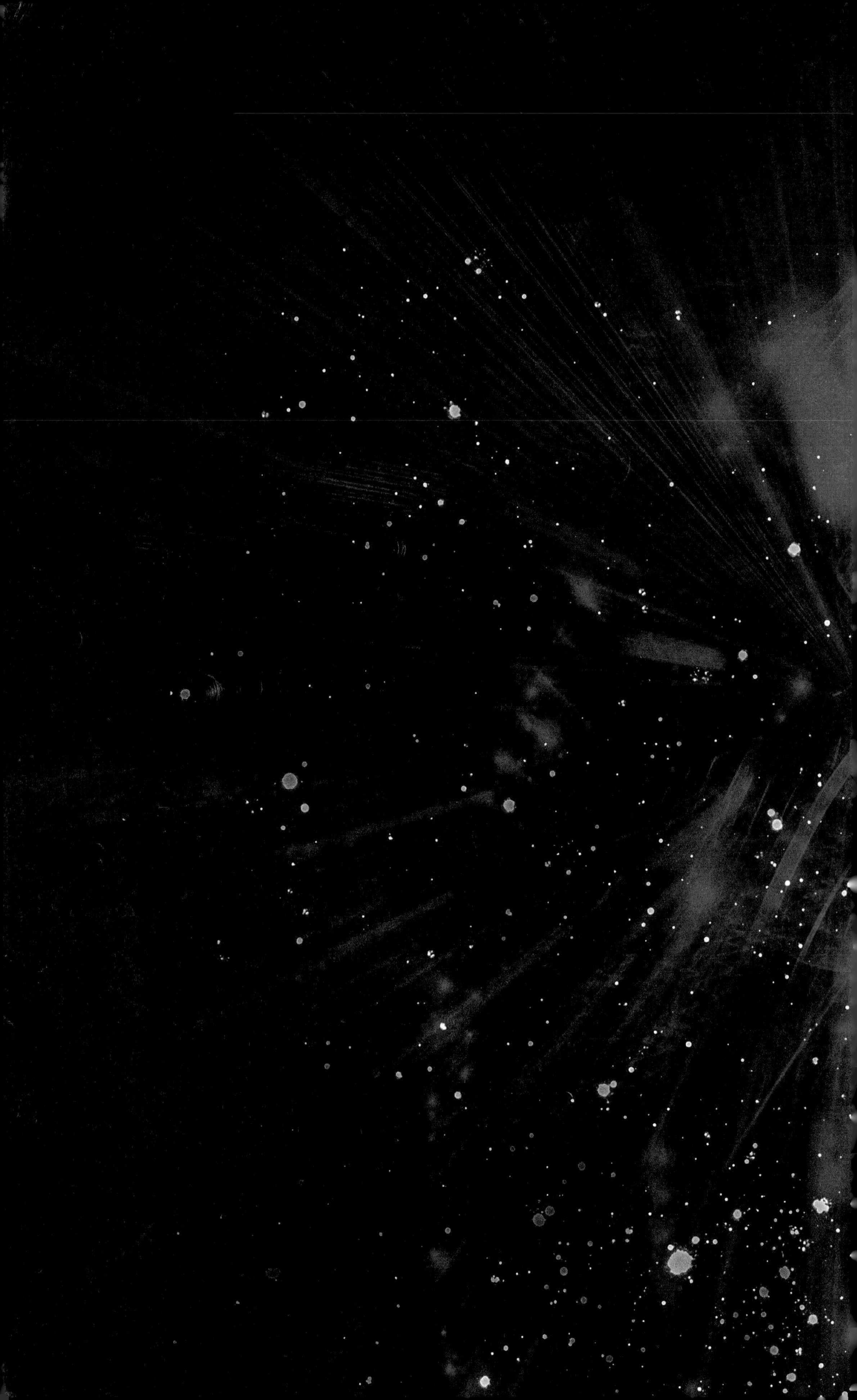

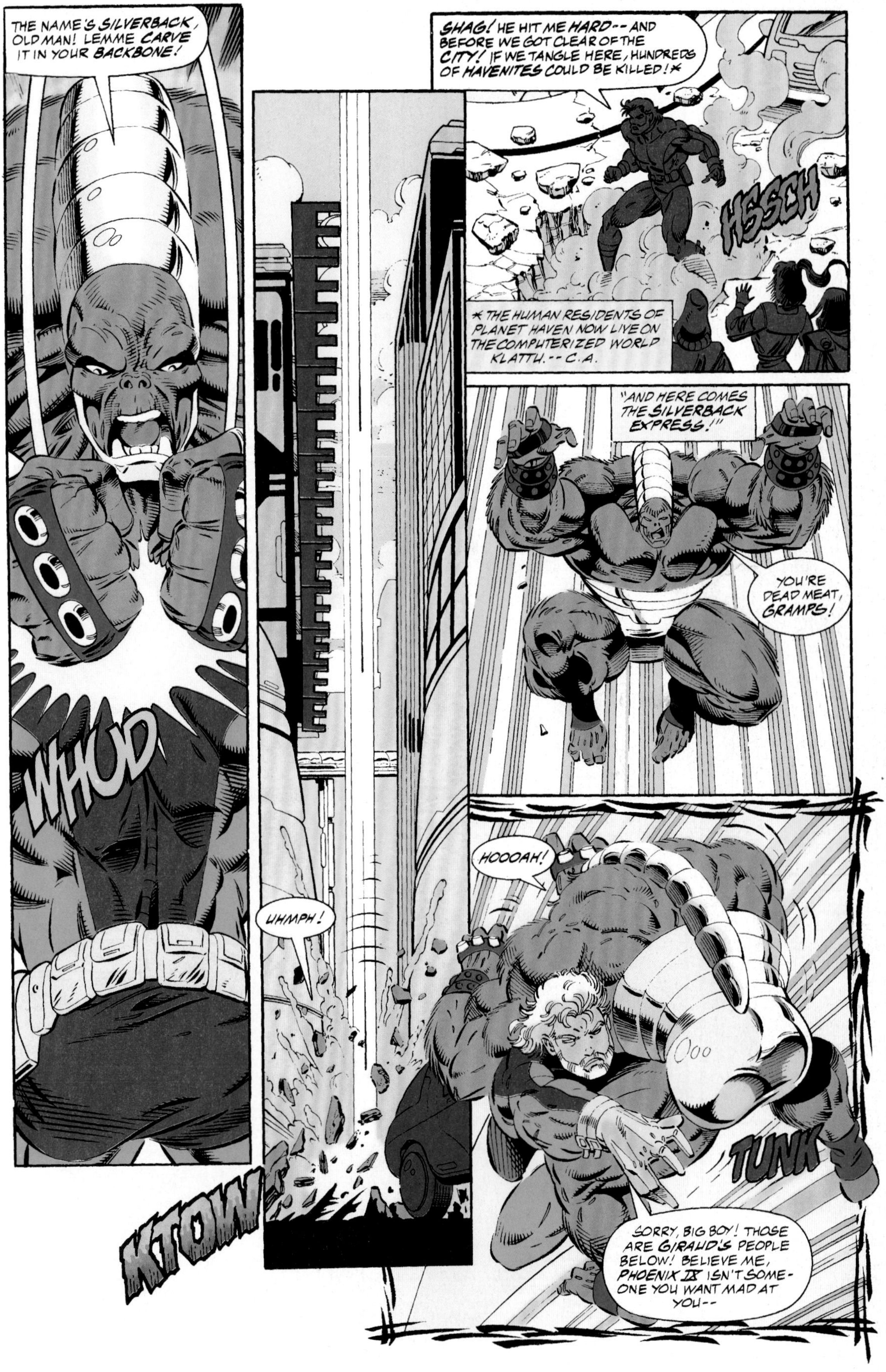
THE NAME'S SILVERBACK, OLD MAN! LEMME CARVE IT IN YOUR BACKBONE!
WHUD
KTOW
UHMPH!
SHAG! HE HIT ME HARD-- AND BEFORE WE GOT CLEAR OF THE CITY! IF WE TANGLE HERE, HUNDREDS OF HAVENITES COULD BE KILLED!*
HSSCH
*THE HUMAN RESIDENTS OF PLANET HAVEN NOW LIVE ON THE COMPUTERIZED WORLD KLATTU. --C.A.
"AND HERE COMES THE SILVERBACK EXPRESS!"
YOU'RE DEAD MEAT, GRAMPS!
HOOOAH!
TUNK
SORRY, BIG BOY! THOSE ARE GIRAUD'S PEOPLE BELOW! BELIEVE ME, PHOENIX IX ISN'T SOME-ONE YOU WANT MAD AT YOU--

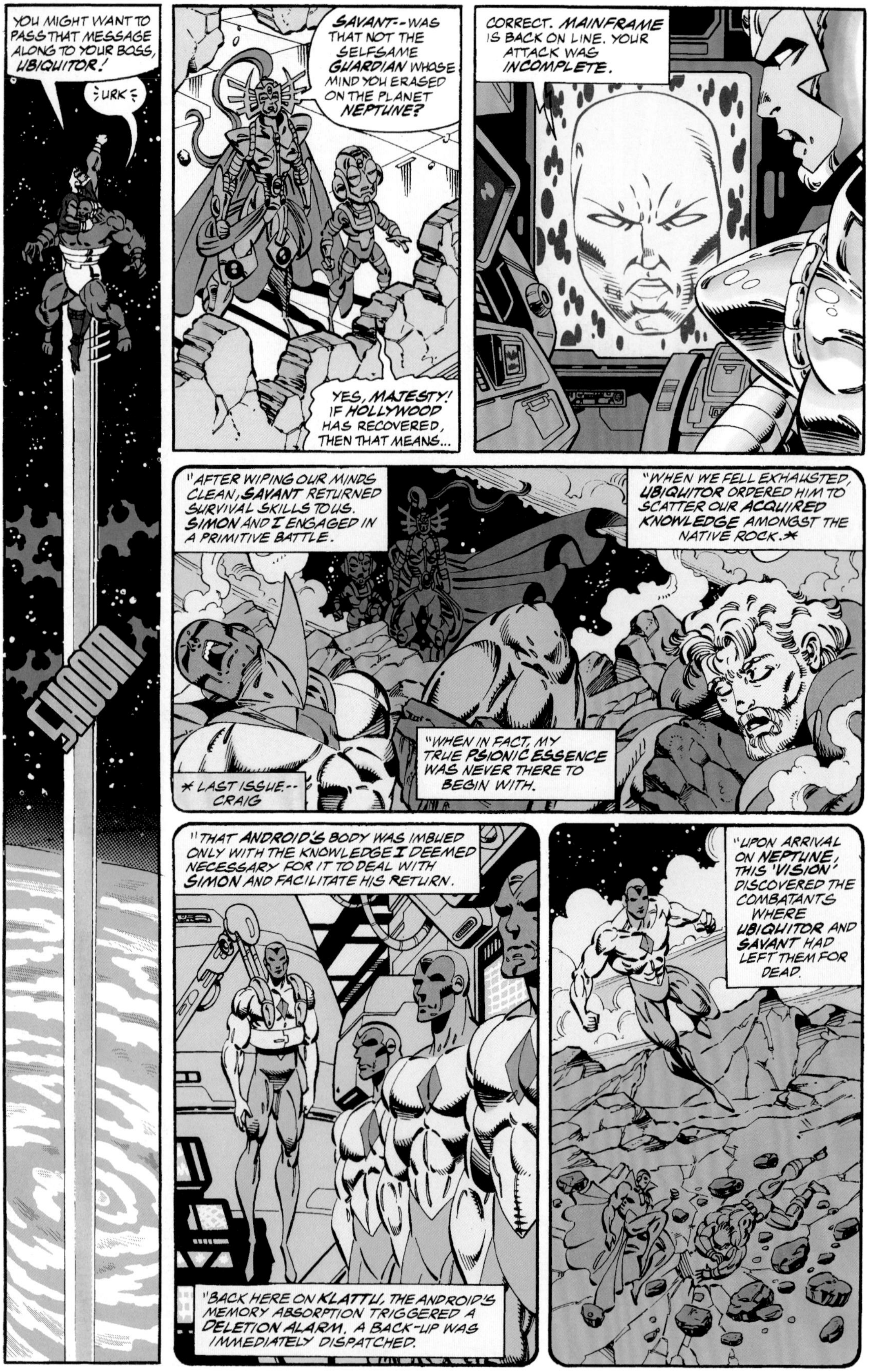

YOU MIGHT WANT TO PASS THAT MESSAGE ALONG TO YOUR BOSS, UBIQUITOR!
URK
SHOOM
SAVANT--WAS THAT NOT THE SELFSAME GUARDIAN WHOSE MIND YOU ERASED ON THE PLANET NEPTUNE?
YES, MAJESTY! IF HOLLYWOOD HAS RECOVERED, THEN THAT MEANS...
CORRECT. MAINFRAME IS BACK ON LINE. YOUR ATTACK WAS INCOMPLETE.
"AFTER WIPING OUR MINDS CLEAN, SAVANT RETURNED SURVIVAL SKILLS TO US. SIMON AND I ENGAGED IN A PRIMITIVE BATTLE.
"WHEN WE FELL EXHAUSTED, UBIQUITOR ORDERED HIM TO SCATTER OUR ACQUIRED KNOWLEDGE AMONGST THE NATIVE ROCK.*
"WHEN IN FACT, MY TRUE PSIONIC ESSENCE WAS NEVER THERE TO BEGIN WITH.
* LAST ISSUE.-- CRAIG
"THAT ANDROID'S BODY WAS IMBUED ONLY WITH THE KNOWLEDGE I DEEMED NECESSARY FOR IT TO DEAL WITH SIMON AND FACILITATE HIS RETURN.
"BACK HERE ON KLATTU, THE ANDROID'S MEMORY ABSORPTION TRIGGERED A DELETION ALARM. A BACK-UP WAS IMMEDIATELY DISPATCHED.
"UPON ARRIVAL ON NEPTUNE, THIS 'VISION' DISCOVERED THE COMBATANTS WHERE UBIQUITOR AND SAVANT HAD LEFT THEM FOR DEAD.

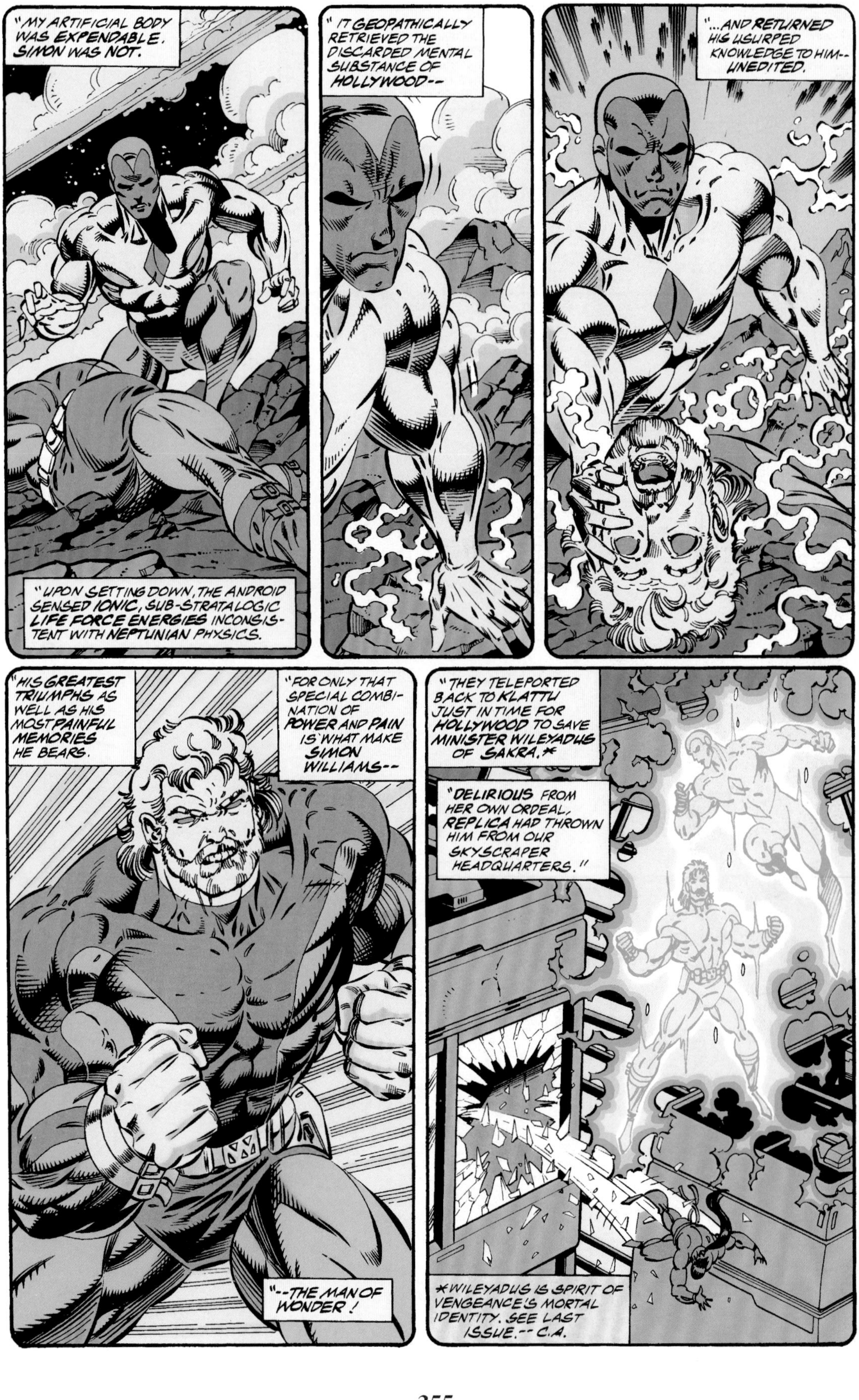
"MY ARTIFICIAL BODY WAS EXPENDABLE. SIMON WAS NOT.
"UPON SETTING DOWN, THE ANDROID SENSED IONIC, SUB-STRATALOGIC LIFE FORCE ENERGIES INCONSISTENT WITH NEPTUNIAN PHYSICS.
"IT GEOPATHICALLY RETRIEVED THE DISCARDED MENTAL SUBSTANCE OF HOLLYWOOD--
"...AND RETURNED HIS USURPED KNOWLEDGE TO HIM--UNEDITED.
"HIS GREATEST TRIUMPHS AS WELL AS HIS MOST PAINFUL MEMORIES HE BEARS.
"FOR ONLY THAT SPECIAL COMBINATION OF POWER AND PAIN IS WHAT MAKE SIMON WILLIAMS--
"--THE MAN OF WONDER!
"THEY TELEPORTED BACK TO KLATTU JUST IN TIME FOR HOLLYWOOD TO SAVE MINISTER WILEYADUS OF SAKRA.*
"DELIRIOUS FROM HER OWN ORDEAL, REPLICA HAD THROWN HIM FROM OUR SKYSCRAPER HEADQUARTERS."
*WILEYADUS IS SPIRIT OF VENGEANCE'S MORTAL IDENTITY. SEE LAST ISSUE. --C.A.

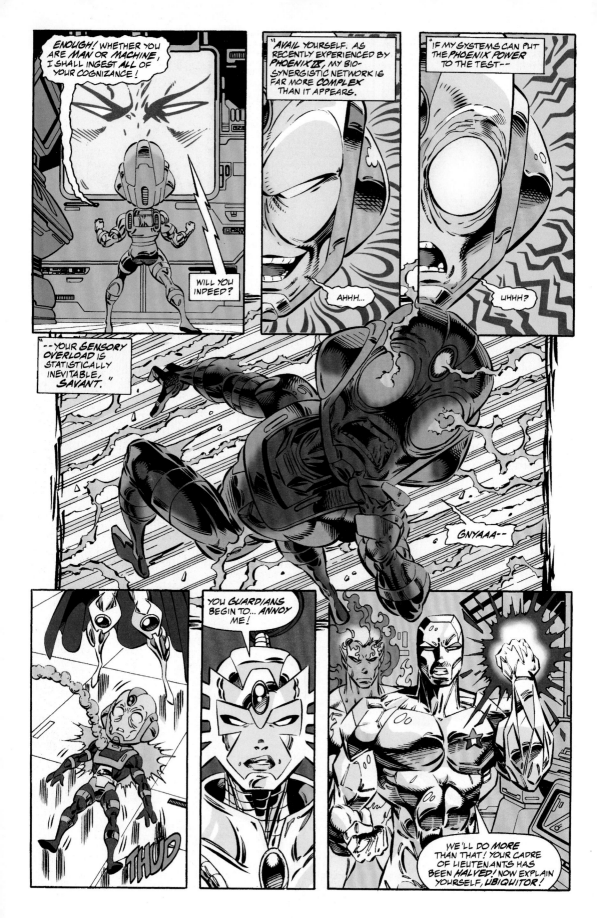

ENOUGH! WHETHER YOU ARE *MAN* OR *MACHINE*, I SHALL INGEST *ALL* OF YOUR COGNIZANCE!

WILL YOU INDEED?

"AVAIL YOURSELF. AS RECENTLY EXPERIENCED BY *PHOENIX IX*, MY BIO-SYNERGISTIC NETWORK IS FAR MORE *COMPLEX* THAN IT APPEARS.

AHHH...

"IF MY SYSTEMS CAN PUT THE *PHOENIX POWER* TO THE TEST--

UHHH?

"--YOUR *SENSORY OVERLOAD* IS STATISTICALLY INEVITABLE, SAVANT. "

GNYAAA--

YOU *GUARDIANS* BEGIN TO... *ANNOY* ME!

THUD

WE'LL DO *MORE* THAN THAT! YOUR CADRE OF LIEUTENANTS HAS BEEN *HALVED*! NOW EXPLAIN YOURSELF, *UBIQUITOR*!

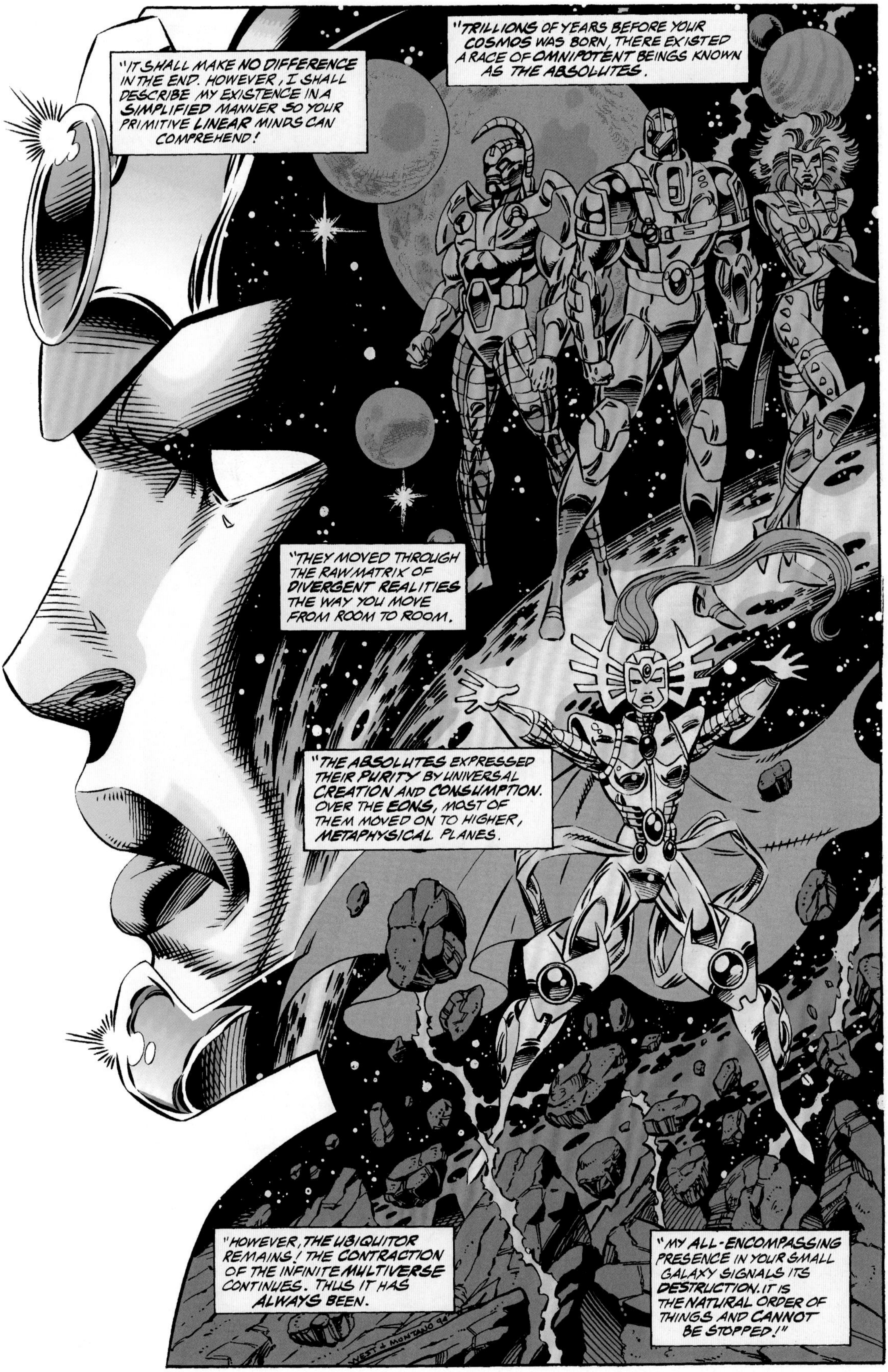
"IT SHALL MAKE NO DIFFERENCE IN THE END. HOWEVER, I SHALL DESCRIBE MY EXISTENCE IN A SIMPLIFIED MANNER SO YOUR PRIMITIVE LINEAR MINDS CAN COMPREHEND!
"TRILLIONS OF YEARS BEFORE YOUR COSMOS WAS BORN, THERE EXISTED A RACE OF OMNIPOTENT BEINGS KNOWN AS THE ABSOLUTES.
"THEY MOVED THROUGH THE RAW MATRIX OF DIVERGENT REALITIES THE WAY YOU MOVE FROM ROOM TO ROOM.
"THE ABSOLUTES EXPRESSED THEIR PURITY BY UNIVERSAL CREATION AND CONSUMPTION. OVER THE EONS, MOST OF THEM MOVED ON TO HIGHER, METAPHYSICAL PLANES.
"HOWEVER, THE UBIQUITOR REMAINS! THE CONTRACTION OF THE INFINITE MULTIVERSE CONTINUES. THUS IT HAS ALWAYS BEEN.
"MY ALL-ENCOMPASSING PRESENCE IN YOUR SMALL GALAXY SIGNALS ITS DESTRUCTION. IT IS THE NATURAL ORDER OF THINGS AND CANNOT BE STOPPED!"

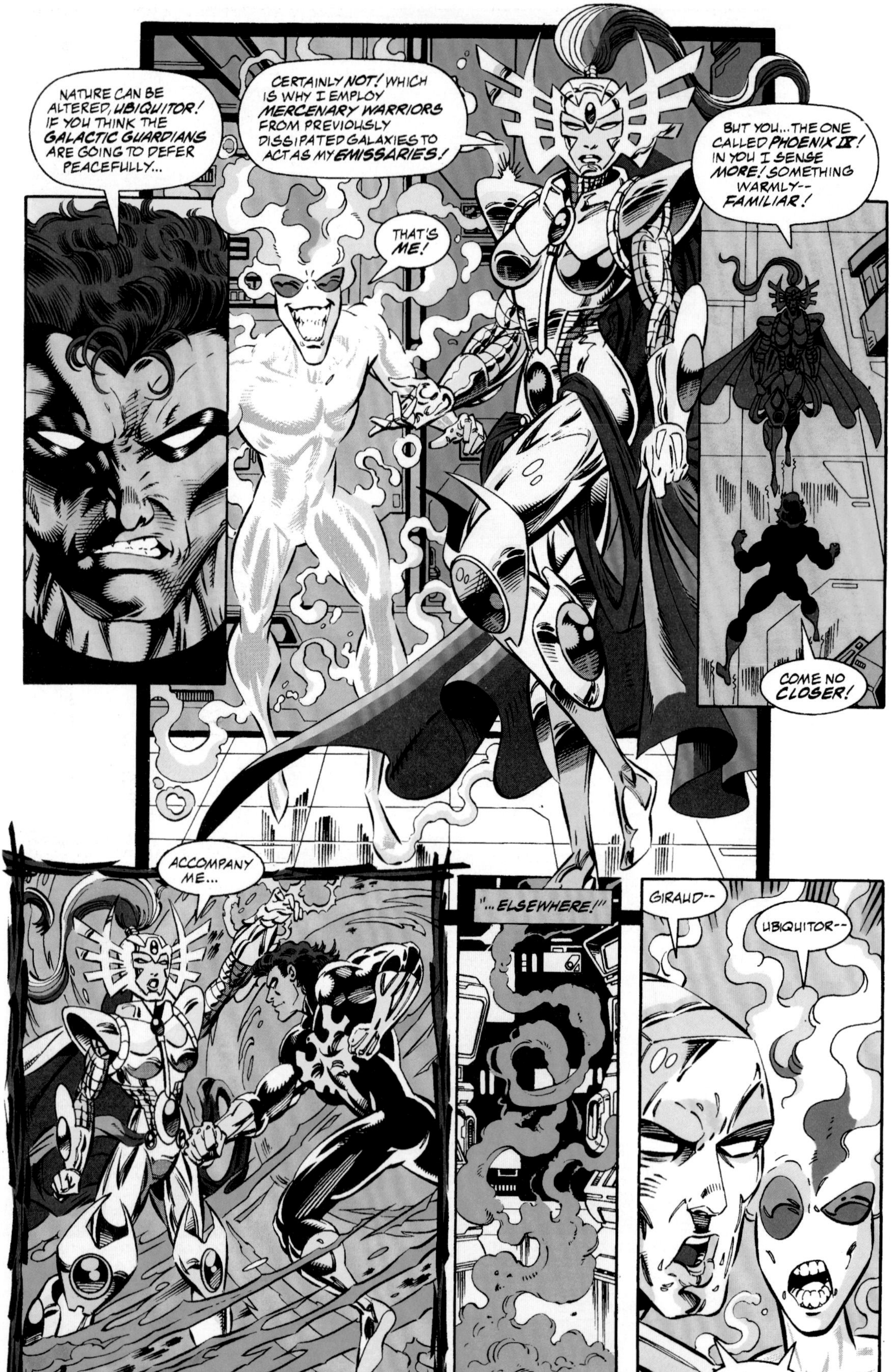
NATURE CAN BE ALTERED, UBIQUITOR! IF YOU THINK THE GALACTIC GUARDIANS ARE GOING TO DEFER PEACEFULLY...
CERTAINLY NOT! WHICH IS WHY I EMPLOY MERCENARY WARRIORS FROM PREVIOUSLY DISSIPATED GALAXIES TO ACT AS MY EMISSARIES!
THAT'S ME!
BUT YOU... THE ONE CALLED PHOENIX IX! IN YOU I SENSE MORE! SOMETHING WARMLY-- FAMILIAR!
COME NO CLOSER!
ACCOMPANY ME...
"...ELSEWHERE!"
GIRAUD--
UBIQUITOR--
--GONE!

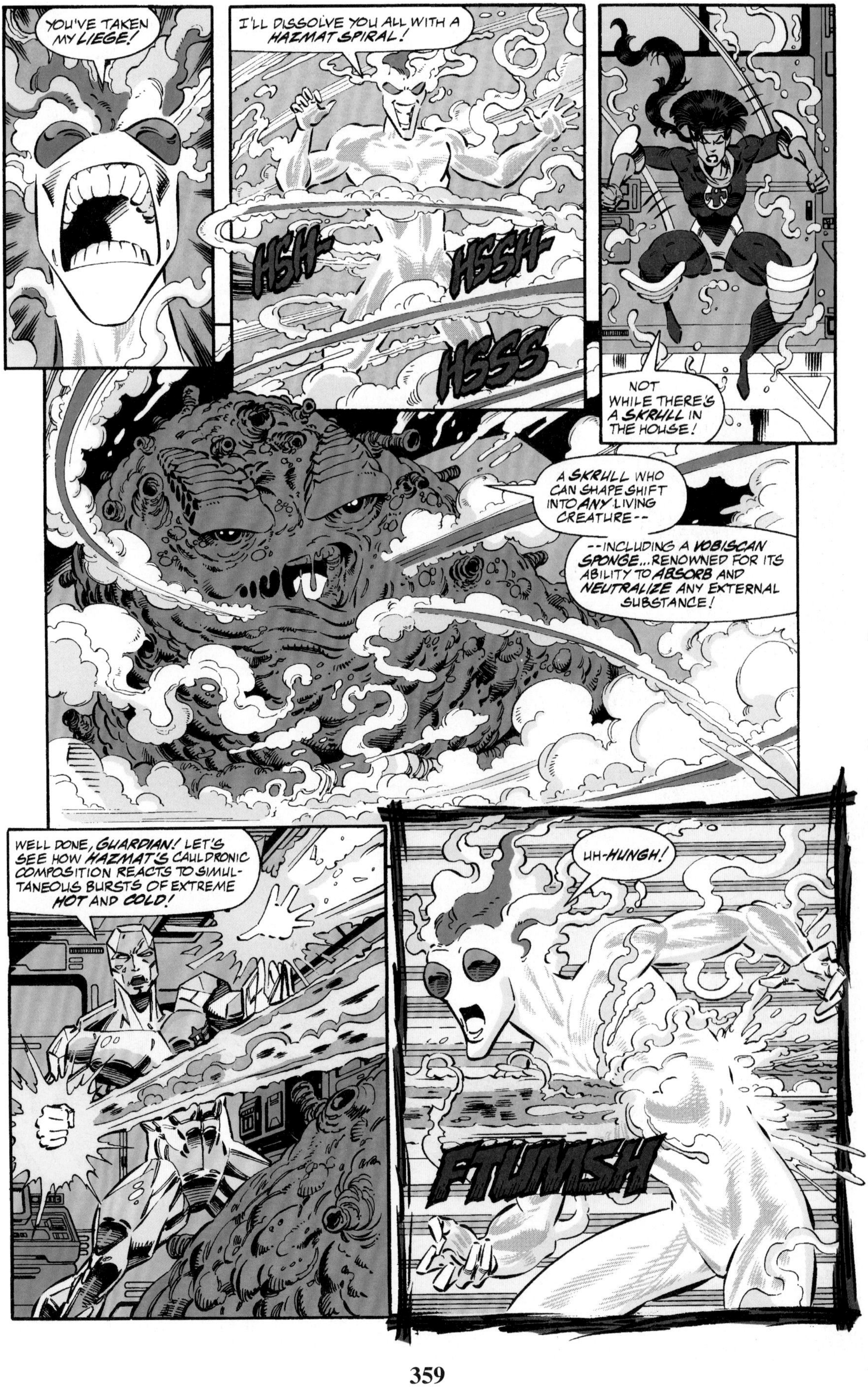
YOU'VE TAKEN MY LIEGE!
I'LL DISSOLVE YOU ALL WITH A HAZMAT SPIRAL!
HSH-
HSSH-
HSSS
NOT WHILE THERE'S A SKRULL IN THE HOUSE!
A SKRULL WHO CAN SHAPE SHIFT INTO ANY LIVING CREATURE--
--INCLUDING A VOBISCAN SPONGE...RENOWNED FOR ITS ABILITY TO ABSORB AND NEUTRALIZE ANY EXTERNAL SUBSTANCE!
WELL DONE, GUARDIAN! LET'S SEE HOW HAZMAT'S CAULDRONIC COMPOSITION REACTS TO SIMULTANEOUS BURSTS OF EXTREME HOT AND COLD!
UH-HUNGH!
FTUMSH

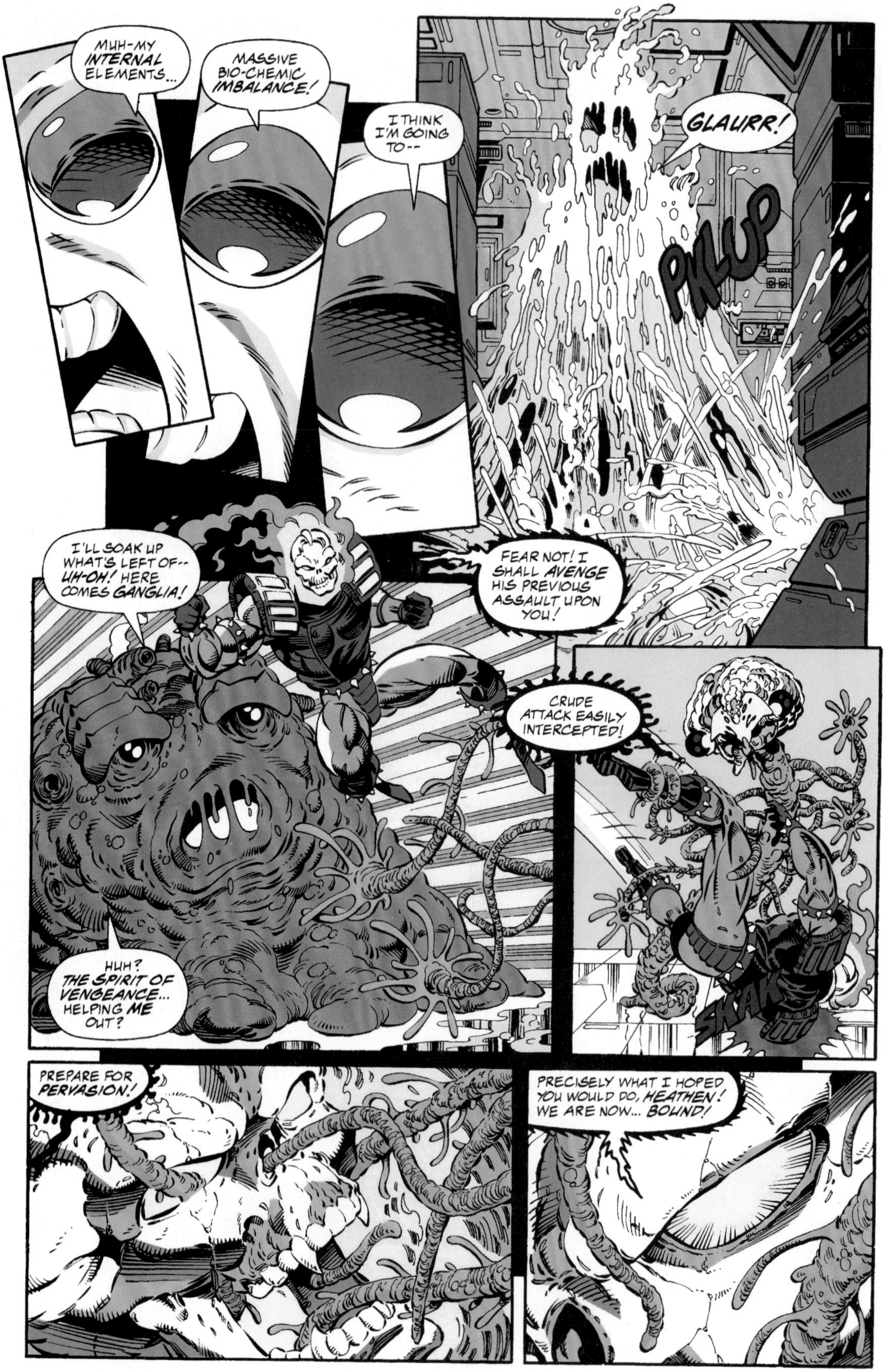
MUH-MY INTERNAL ELEMENTS...
MASSIVE BIO-CHEMIC IMBALANCE!
I THINK I'M GOING TO--
GLAURR!
PKLUP
I'LL SOAK UP WHAT'S LEFT OF-- UH-OH! HERE COMES GANGLIA!
FEAR NOT! I SHALL AVENGE HIS PREVIOUS ASSAULT UPON YOU!
CRUDE ATTACK EASILY INTERCEPTED!
HUH? THE SPIRIT OF VENGEANCE... HELPING ME OUT?
SKAK
PREPARE FOR PERVASION!
PRECISELY WHAT I HOPED YOU WOULD DO, HEATHEN! WE ARE NOW... BOUND!

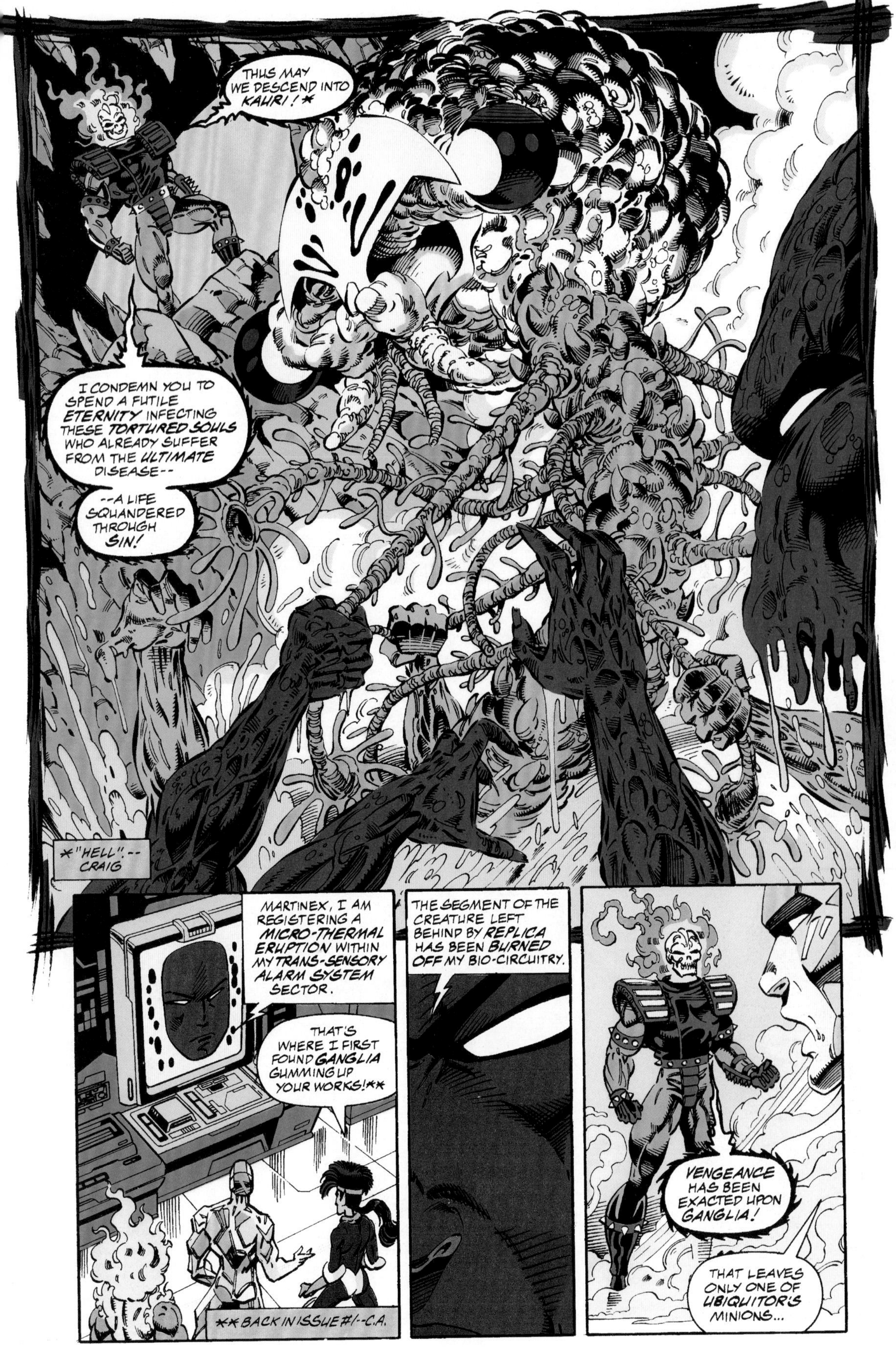
THUS MAY WE DESCEND INTO KAURI! *
I CONDEMN YOU TO SPEND A FUTILE ETERNITY INFECTING THESE TORTURED SOULS WHO ALREADY SUFFER FROM THE ULTIMATE DISEASE--
--A LIFE SQUANDERED THROUGH SIN!
* "HELL".-- CRAIG
MARTINEX, I AM REGISTERING A MICRO-THERMAL ERUPTION WITHIN MY TRANS-SENSORY ALARM SYSTEM SECTOR.
THAT'S WHERE I FIRST FOUND GANGLIA GUMMING UP YOUR WORKS! **
** BACK IN ISSUE #1 --C.A.
THE SEGMENT OF THE CREATURE LEFT BEHIND BY REPLICA HAS BEEN BURNED OFF MY BIO-CIRCUITRY.
VENGEANCE HAS BEEN EXACTED UPON GANGLIA!
THAT LEAVES ONLY ONE OF UBIQUITOR'S MINIONS...

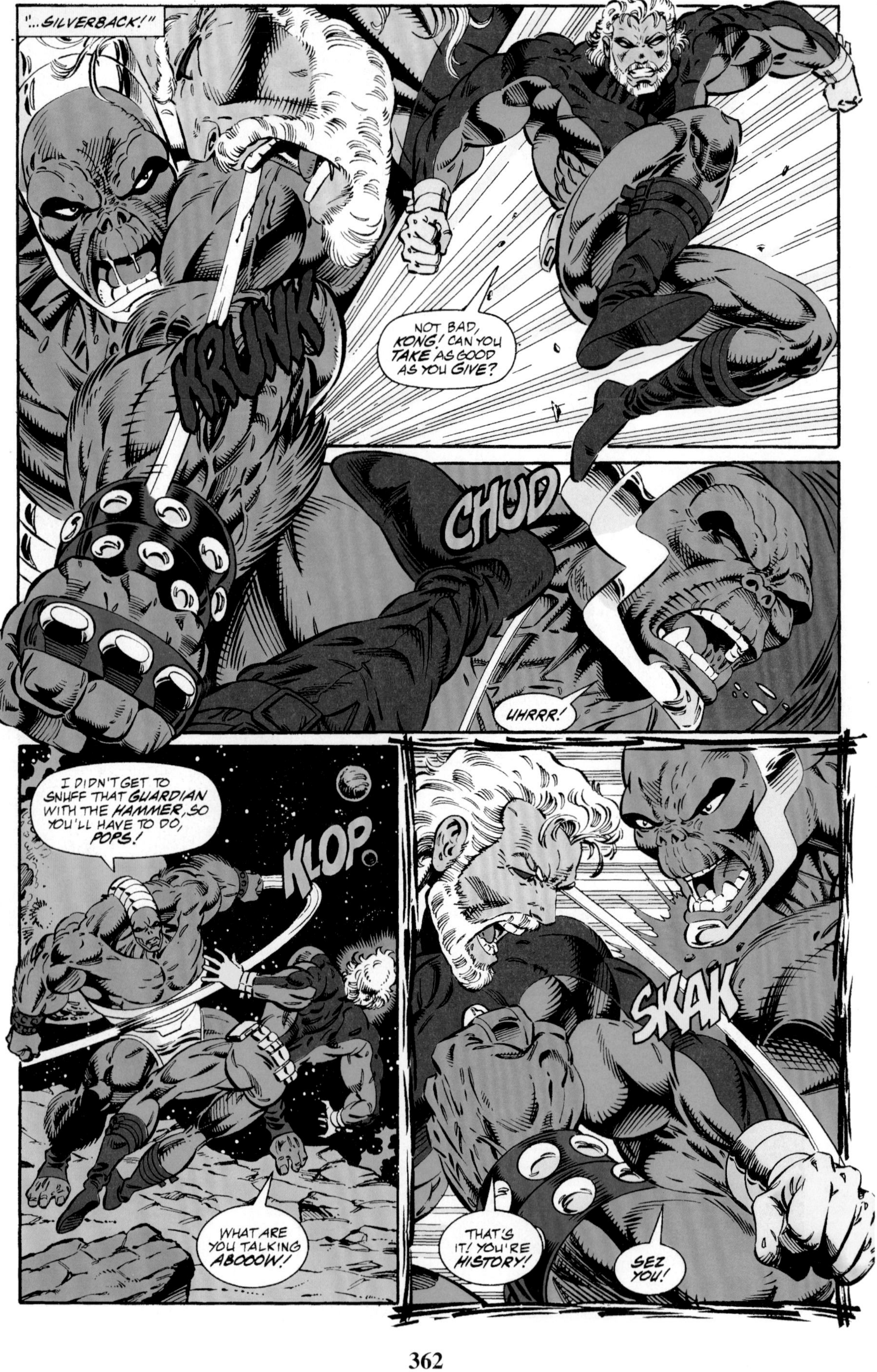
"...SILVERBACK!"
NOT BAD, KONG! CAN YOU TAKE AS GOOD AS YOU GIVE?
KRUNK
CHUD
UHRRR!
I DIDN'T GET TO SNUFF THAT GUARDIAN WITH THE HAMMER, SO YOU'LL HAVE TO DO, POPS!
KLOP
WHAT ARE YOU TALKING ABOOOW!
SKAK
THAT'S IT! YOU'RE HISTORY!
SEZ YOU!

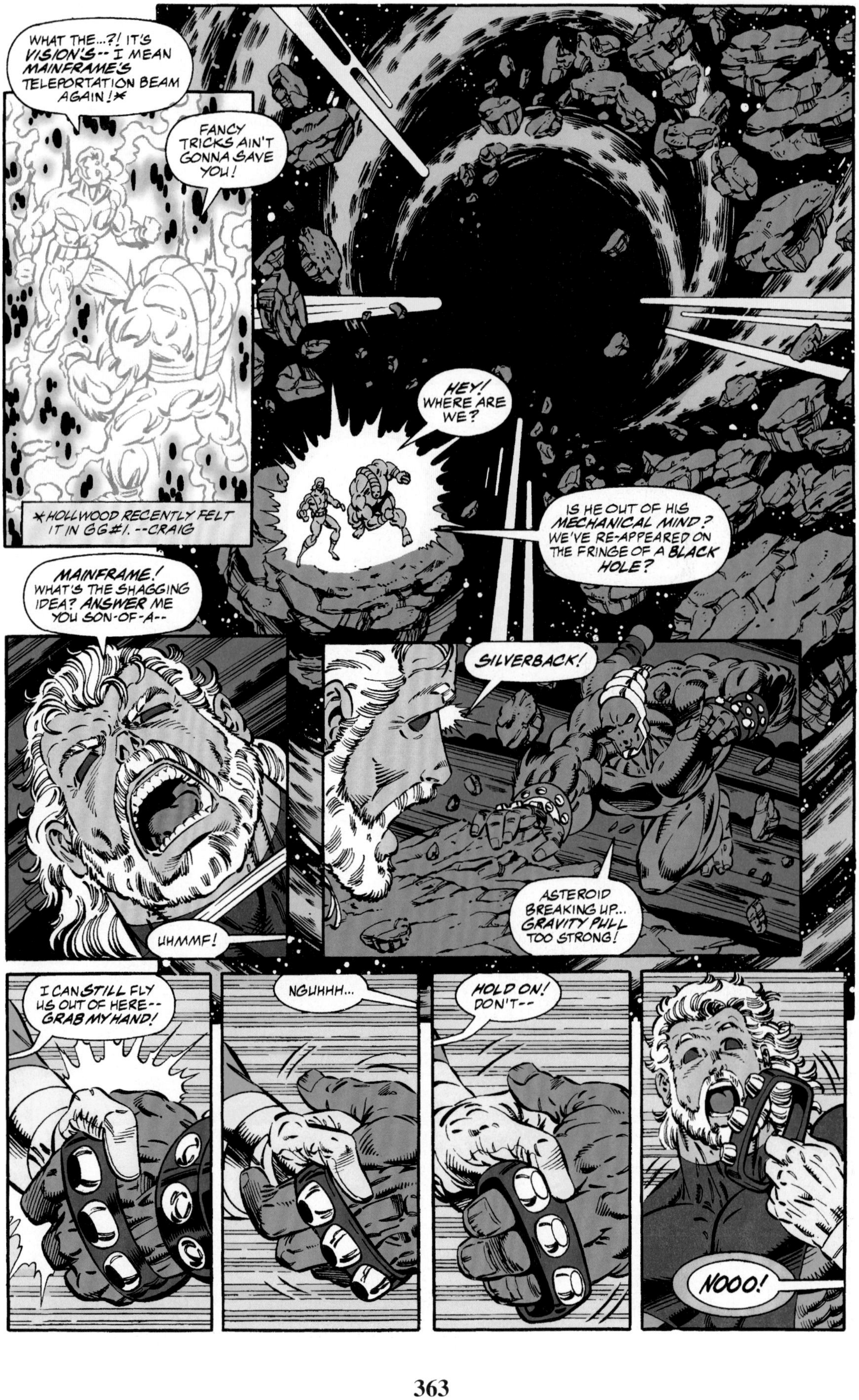
WHAT THE...?! IT'S VISION'S-- I MEAN MAINFRAME'S TELEPORTATION BEAM AGAIN!*
FANCY TRICKS AIN'T GONNA SAVE YOU!
*HOLLWOOD RECENTLY FELT IT IN GG#1. --CRAIG
HEY! WHERE ARE WE?
IS HE OUT OF HIS MECHANICAL MIND? WE'VE RE-APPEARED ON THE FRINGE OF A BLACK HOLE?
MAINFRAME! WHAT'S THE SHAGGING IDEA? ANSWER ME YOU SON-OF-A--
UHMMF!
SILVERBACK!
ASTEROID BREAKING UP... GRAVITY PULL TOO STRONG!
I CAN STILL FLY US OUT OF HERE-- GRAB MY HAND!
NGUHHH...
HOLD ON! DON'T--
NOOO!

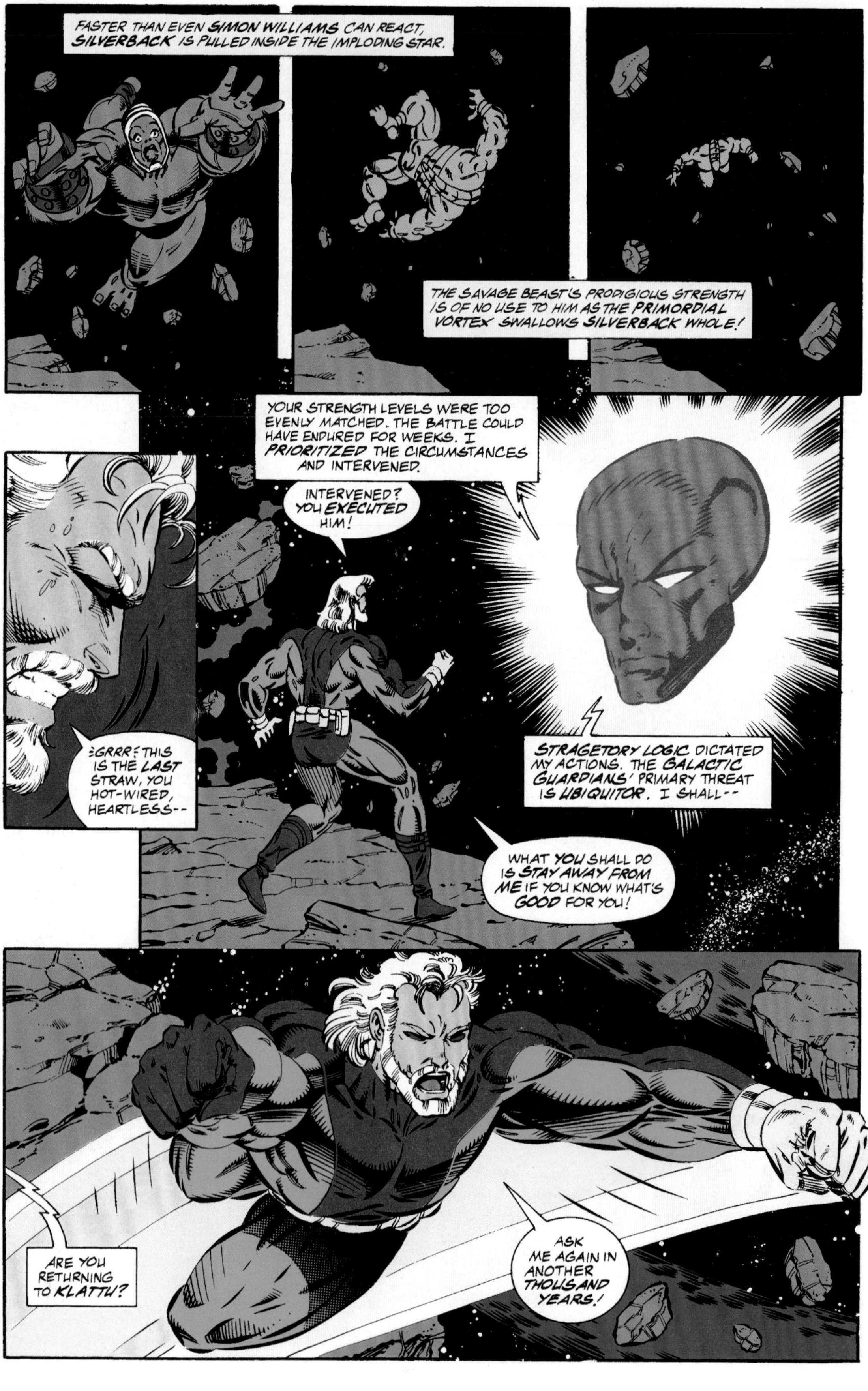
FASTER THAN EVEN SIMON WILLIAMS CAN REACT, SILVERBACK IS PULLED INSIDE THE IMPLODING STAR.
THE SAVAGE BEAST'S PRODIGIOUS STRENGTH IS OF NO USE TO HIM AS THE PRIMORDIAL VORTEX SWALLOWS SILVERBACK WHOLE!
YOUR STRENGTH LEVELS WERE TOO EVENLY MATCHED. THE BATTLE COULD HAVE ENDURED FOR WEEKS. I PRIORITIZED THE CIRCUMSTANCES AND INTERVENED.
INTERVENED? YOU EXECUTED HIM!
STRAGETORY LOGIC DICTATED MY ACTIONS. THE GALACTIC GUARDIANS' PRIMARY THREAT IS UBIQUITOR. I SHALL--
=GRRR= THIS IS THE LAST STRAW, YOU HOT-WIRED, HEARTLESS--
WHAT YOU SHALL DO IS STAY AWAY FROM ME IF YOU KNOW WHAT'S GOOD FOR YOU!
ARE YOU RETURNING TO KLATTU?
ASK ME AGAIN IN ANOTHER THOUSAND YEARS!

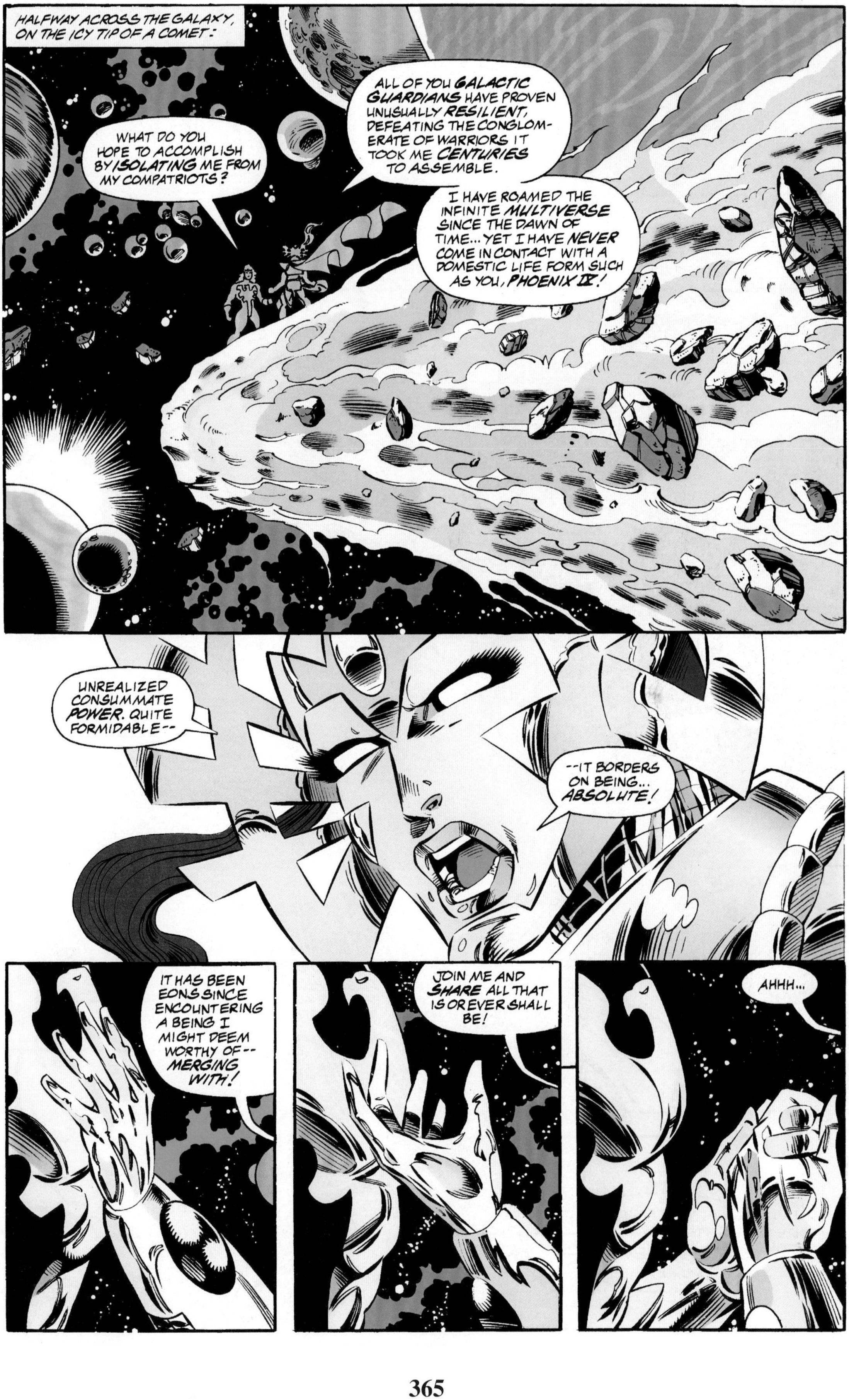
HALFWAY ACROSS THE GALAXY, ON THE ICY TIP OF A COMET:
WHAT DO YOU HOPE TO ACCOMPLISH BY ISOLATING ME FROM MY COMPATRIOTS?
ALL OF YOU GALACTIC GUARDIANS HAVE PROVEN UNUSUALLY RESILIENT, DEFEATING THE CONGLOMERATE OF WARRIORS IT TOOK ME CENTURIES TO ASSEMBLE.
I HAVE ROAMED THE INFINITE MULTIVERSE SINCE THE DAWN OF TIME... YET I HAVE NEVER COME IN CONTACT WITH A DOMESTIC LIFE FORM SUCH AS YOU, PHOENIX IV!
UNREALIZED CONSUMMATE POWER. QUITE FORMIDABLE--
--IT BORDERS ON BEING... ABSOLUTE!
IT HAS BEEN EONS SINCE ENCOUNTERING A BEING I MIGHT DEEM WORTHY OF-- MERGING WITH!
JOIN ME AND SHARE ALL THAT IS OR EVER SHALL BE!
AHHH...

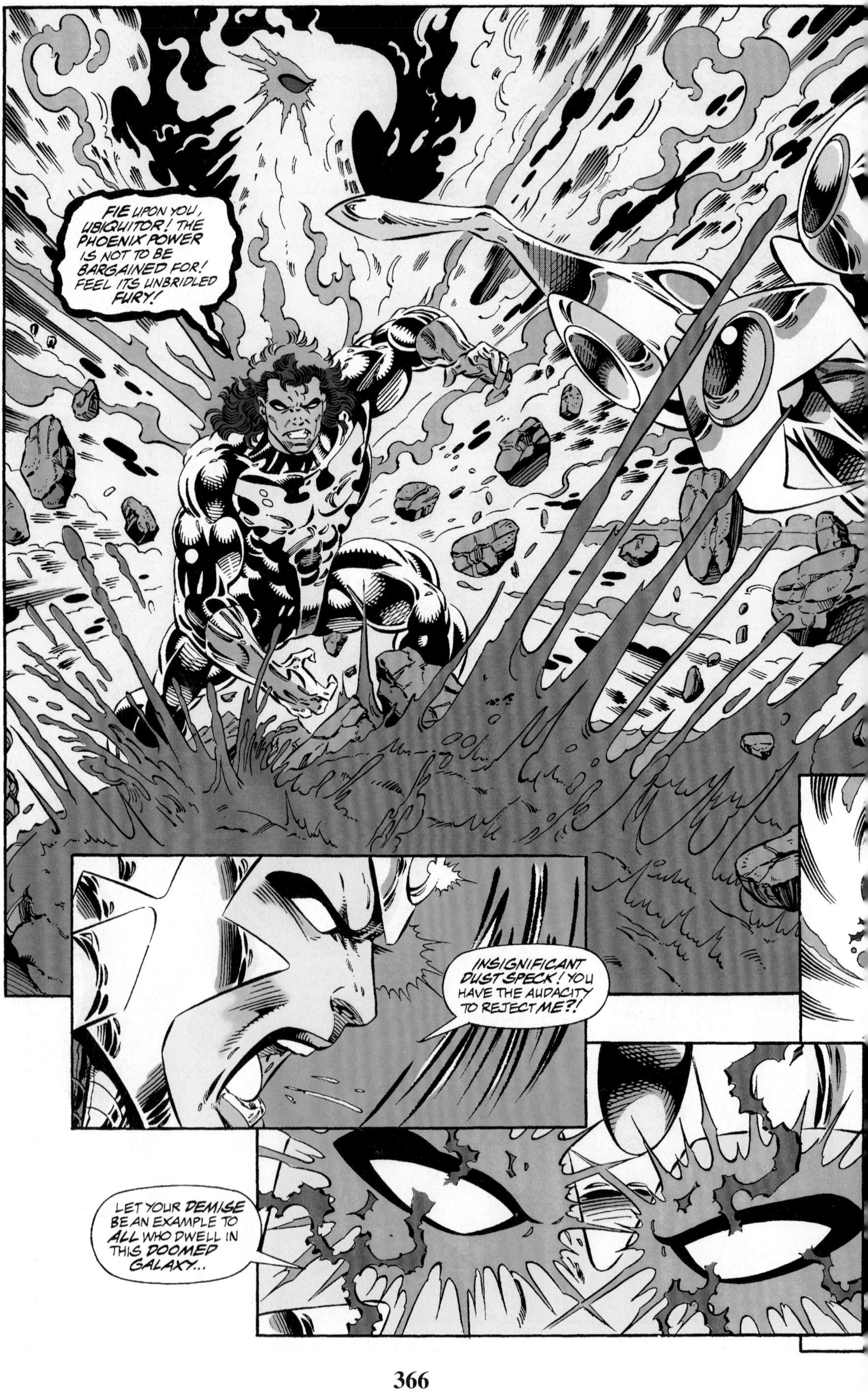
FIE UPON YOU, UBIQUITOR! THE PHOENIX POWER IS NOT TO BE BARGAINED FOR! FEEL ITS UNBRIDLED FURY!
INSIGNIFICANT DUST SPECK! YOU HAVE THE AUDACITY TO REJECT ME?!
LET YOUR DEMISE BE AN EXAMPLE TO ALL WHO DWELL IN THIS DOOMED GALAXY...

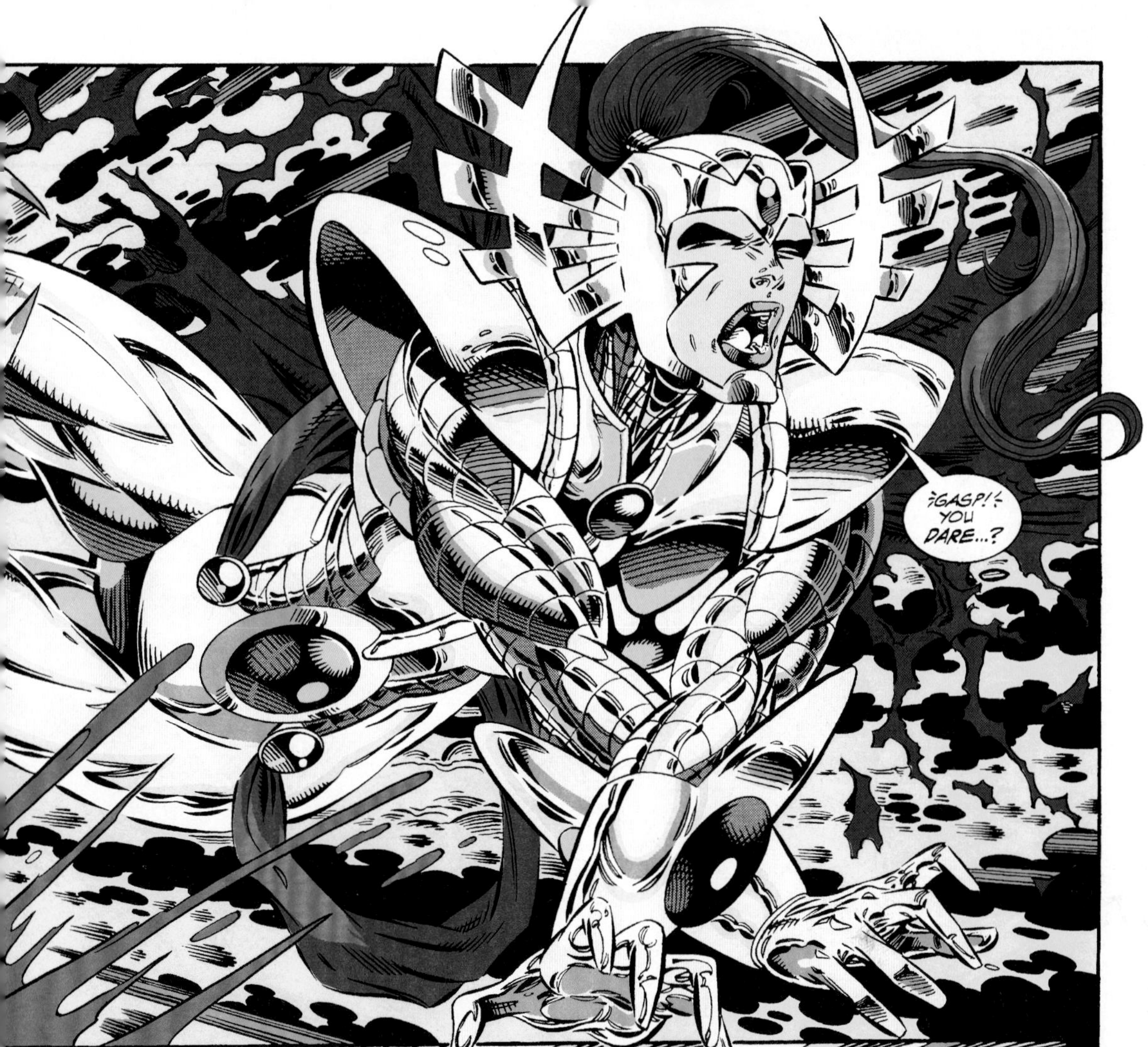
¡GASP! YOU DARE...?

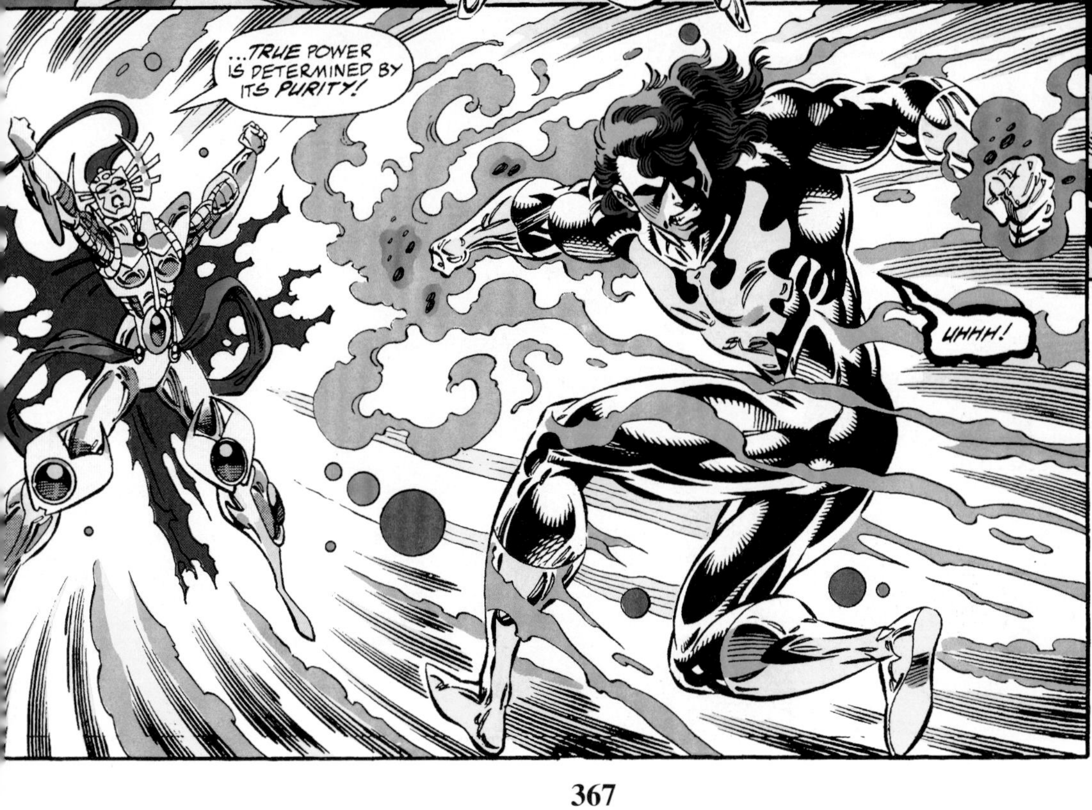
...TRUE POWER IS DETERMINED BY ITS PURITY!
UHHH!

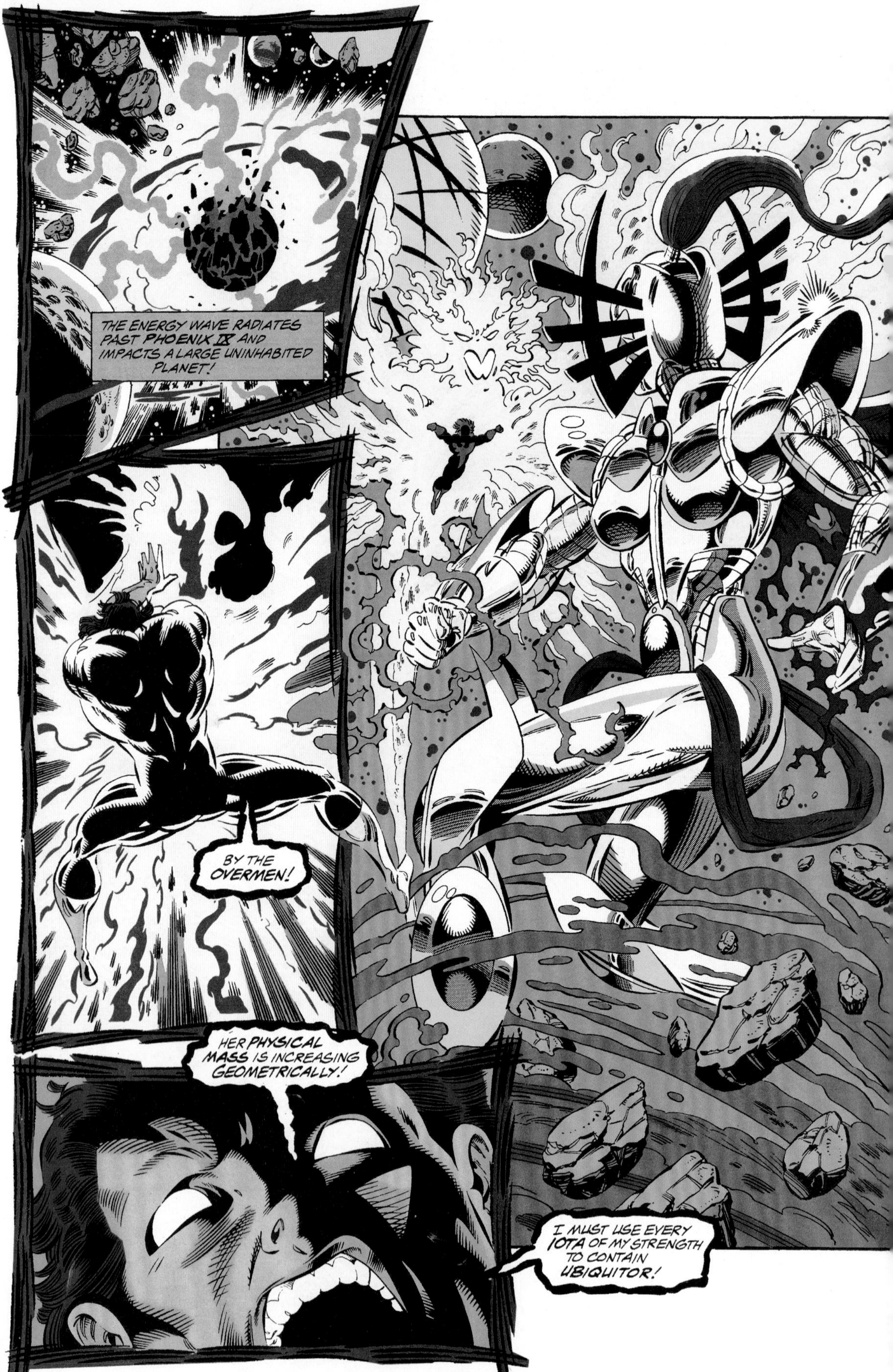
THE ENERGY WAVE RADIATES PAST PHOENIX IX AND IMPACTS A LARGE UNINHABITED PLANET!
BY THE OVERMEN!
HER PHYSICAL MASS IS INCREASING GEOMETRICALLY!
I MUST USE EVERY IOTA OF MY STRENGTH TO CONTAIN UBIQUITOR!

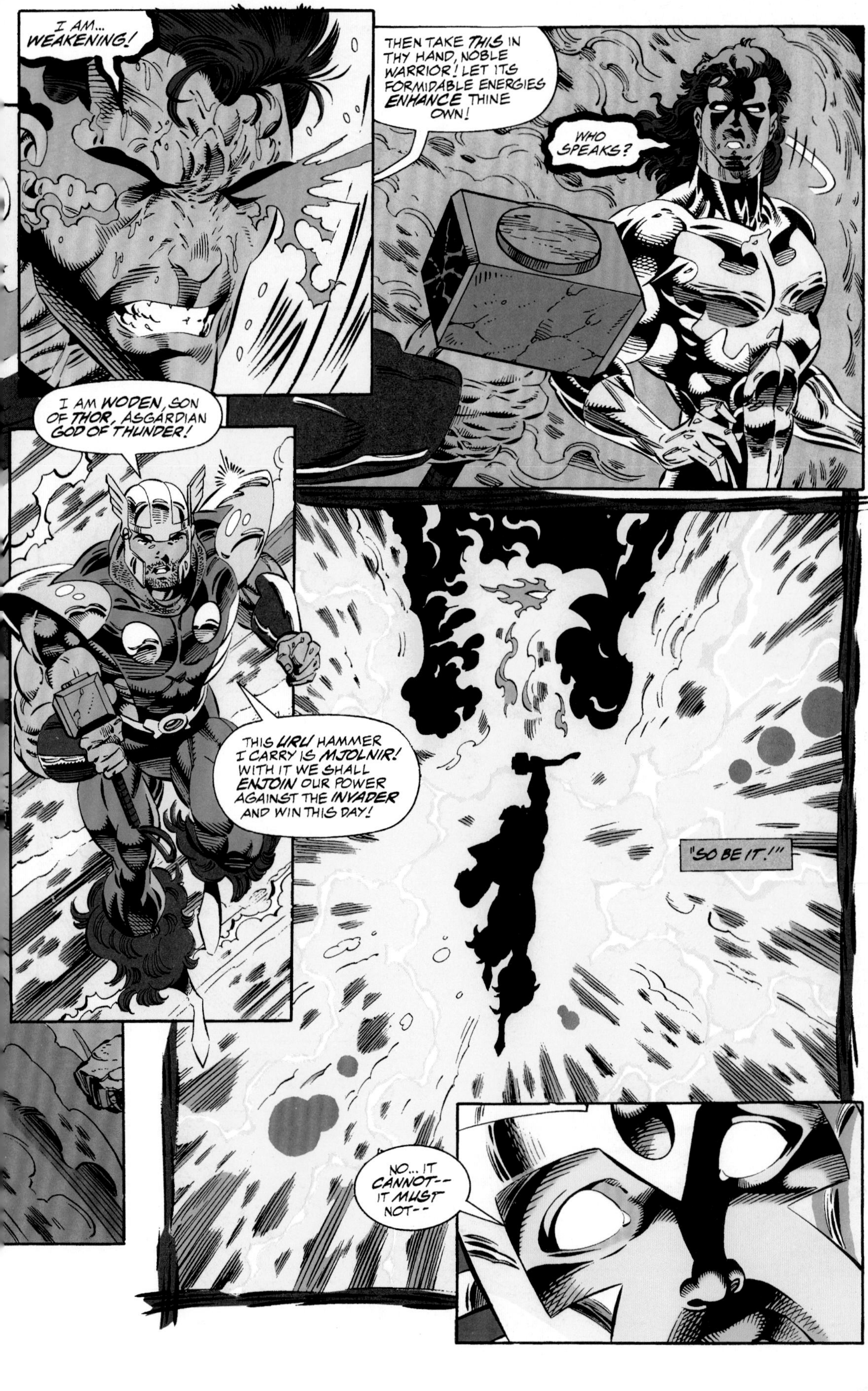
I AM... WEAKENING!
THEN TAKE THIS IN THY HAND, NOBLE WARRIOR! LET ITS FORMIDABLE ENERGIES ENHANCE THINE OWN!
WHO SPEAKS?
I AM WODEN, SON OF THOR, ASGARDIAN GOD OF THUNDER!
THIS URU HAMMER I CARRY IS MJOLNIR! WITH IT WE SHALL ENJOIN OUR POWER AGAINST THE INVADER AND WIN THIS DAY!
"SO BE IT!"
NO... IT CANNOT-- IT MUST NOT--

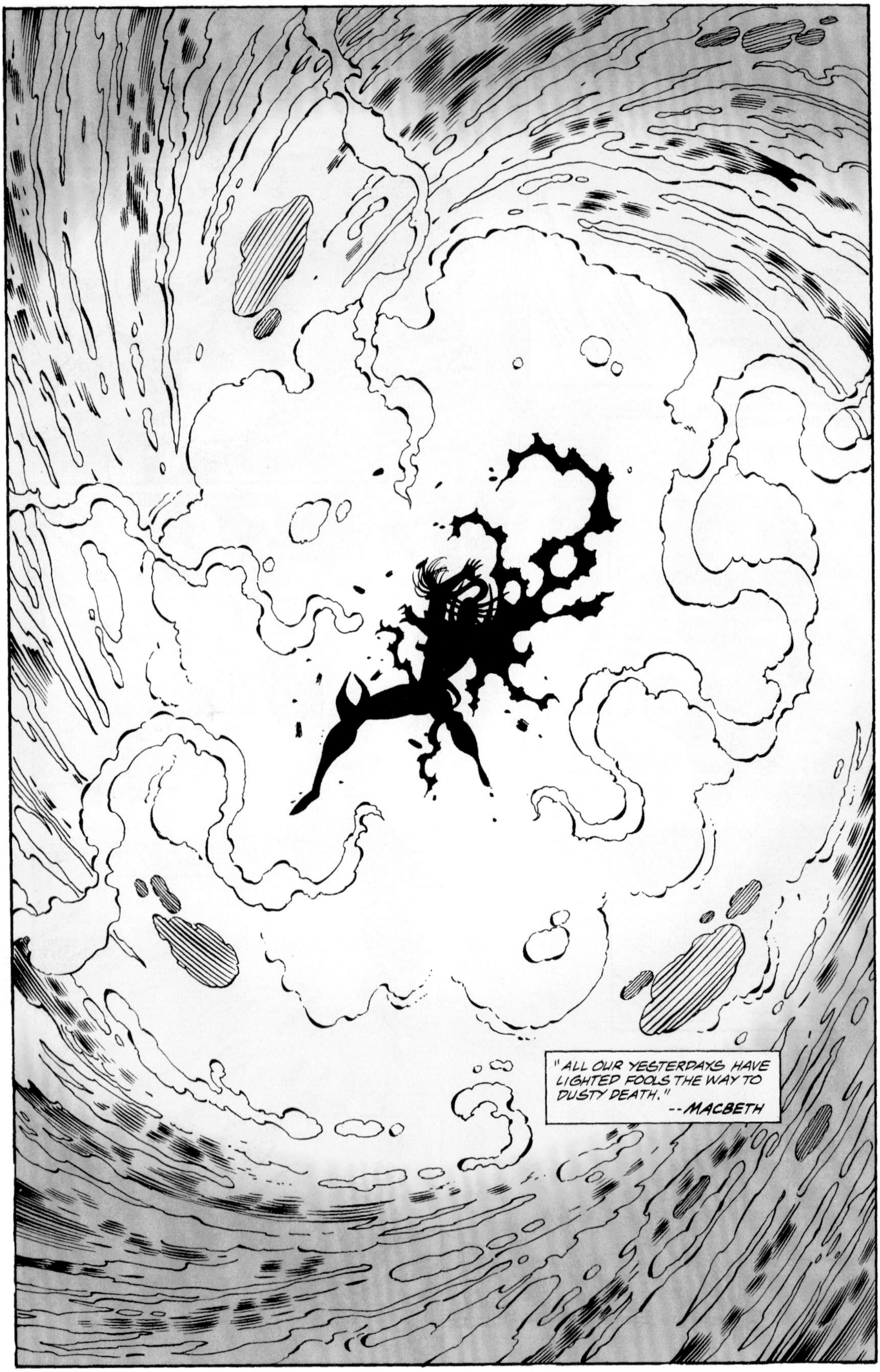
"ALL OUR YESTERDAYS HAVE LIGHTED FOOLS THE WAY TO DUSTY DEATH." --MACBETH

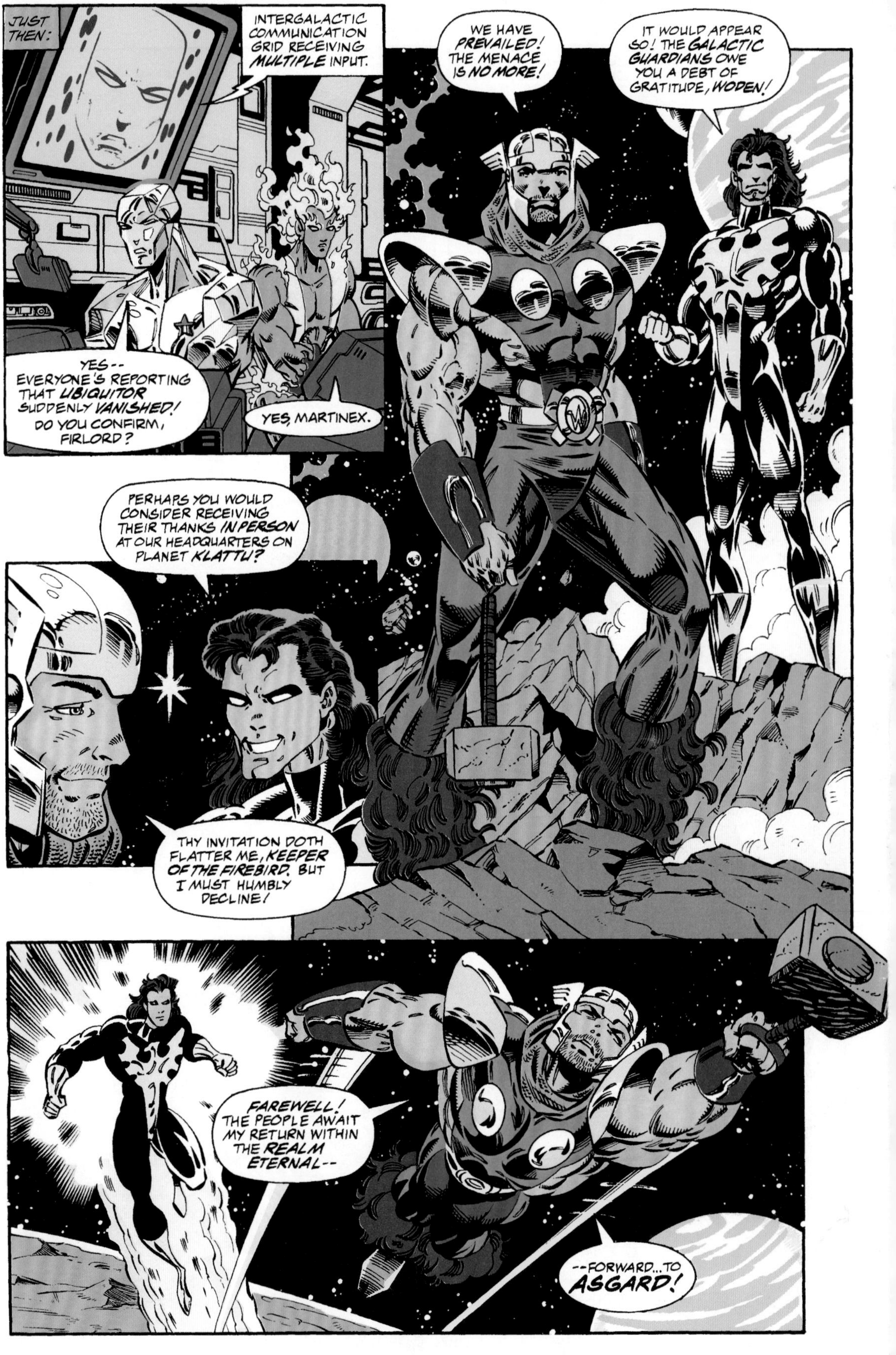
JUST THEN:
INTERGALACTIC COMMUNICATION GRID RECEIVING MULTIPLE INPUT.
YES-- EVERYONE'S REPORTING THAT UBIQUITOR SUDDENLY VANISHED! DO YOU CONFIRM, FIRLORD?
YES, MARTINEX.
WE HAVE PREVAILED! THE MENACE IS NO MORE!
IT WOULD APPEAR SO! THE GALACTIC GUARDIANS OWE YOU A DEBT OF GRATITUDE, WODEN!
PERHAPS YOU WOULD CONSIDER RECEIVING THEIR THANKS IN PERSON AT OUR HEADQUARTERS ON PLANET KLATTU?
THY INVITATION DOTH FLATTER ME, KEEPER OF THE FIREBIRD. BUT I MUST HUMBLY DECLINE!
FAREWELL! THE PEOPLE AWAIT MY RETURN WITHIN THE REALM ETERNAL--
--FORWARD...TO ASGARD!

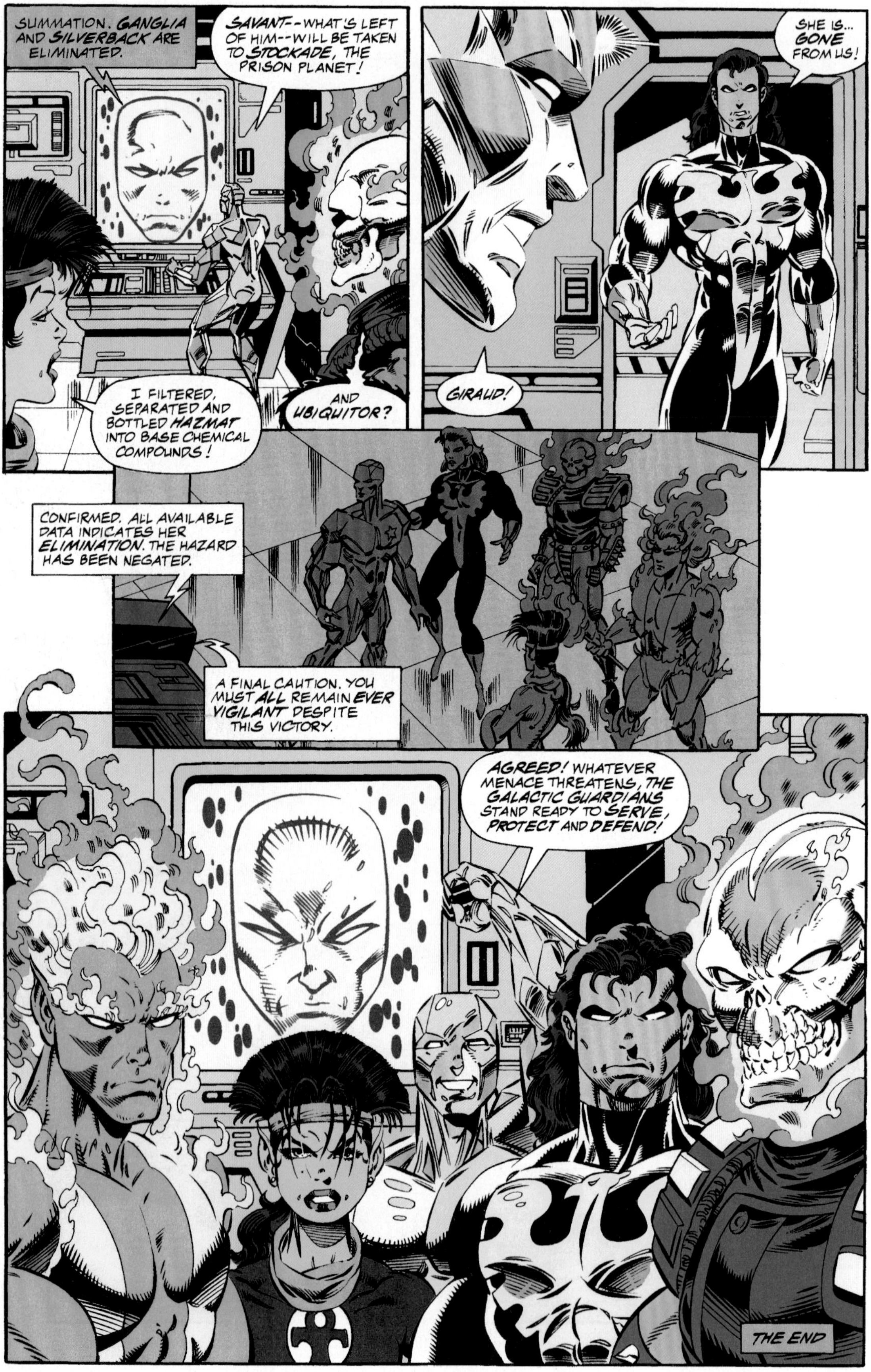
SUMMATION. GANGLIA AND SILVERBACK ARE ELIMINATED.
SAVANT--WHAT'S LEFT OF HIM--WILL BE TAKEN TO STOCKADE, THE PRISON PLANET!
I FILTERED, SEPARATED AND BOTTLED HAZMAT INTO BASE CHEMICAL COMPOUNDS!
AND UBIQUITOR?
SHE IS... GONE FROM US!
GIRAUD!
CONFIRMED. ALL AVAILABLE DATA INDICATES HER ELIMINATION. THE HAZARD HAS BEEN NEGATED.
A FINAL CAUTION. YOU MUST ALL REMAIN EVER VIGILANT DESPITE THIS VICTORY.
AGREED! WHATEVER MENACE THREATENS, THE GALACTIC GUARDIANS STAND READY TO SERVE, PROTECT AND DEFEND!
THE END

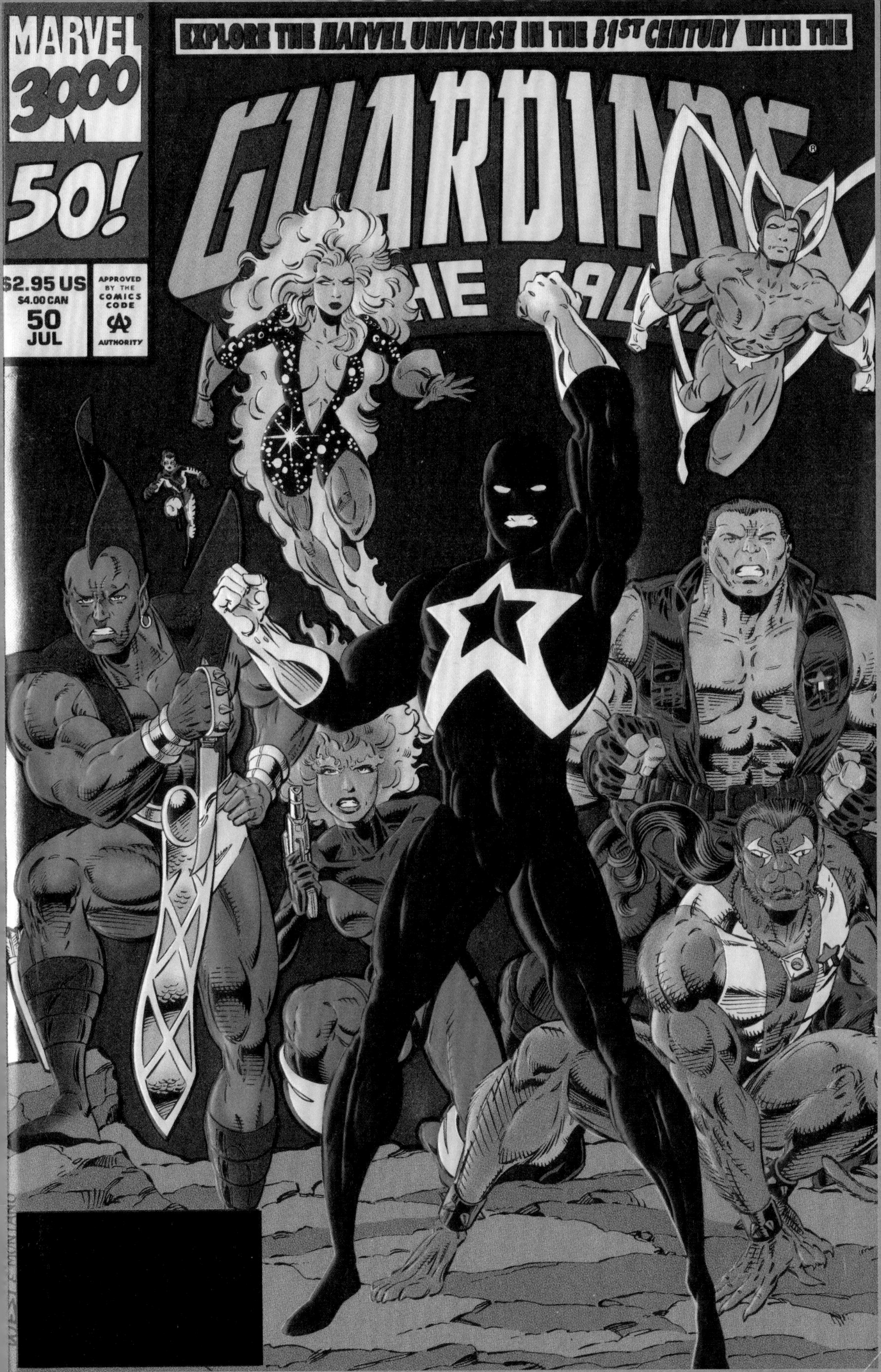
MARVEL
3000
50!
EXPLORE THE MARVEL UNIVERSE IN THE 31ST CENTURY WITH THE
GUARDIANS
$2.95 US
$4.00 CAN
50
JUL
APPROVED BY THE COMICS CODE AUTHORITY

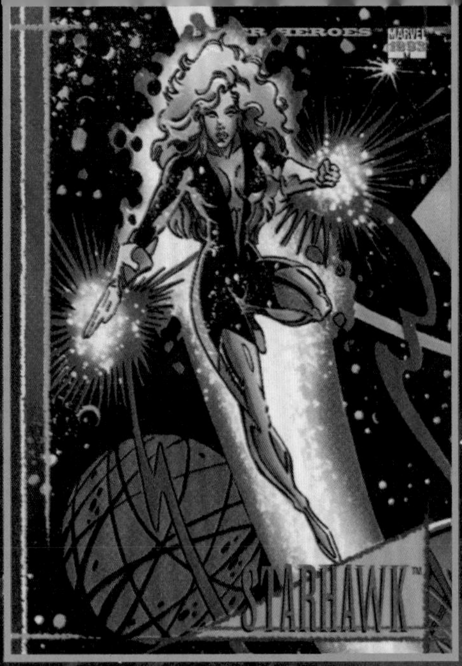
MARVEL
STARHAWK
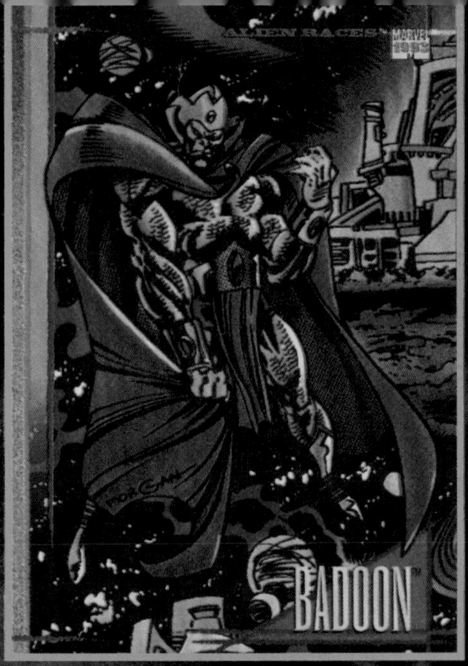
ALIEN RACES
MARVEL
BADOON

MARVEL UNIVERSE SERIES IV (1993) TRADING-CARD
ART BY RON LIM, TOM CHRISTOPHER, TOM MORGAN & PAUL MOUNTS

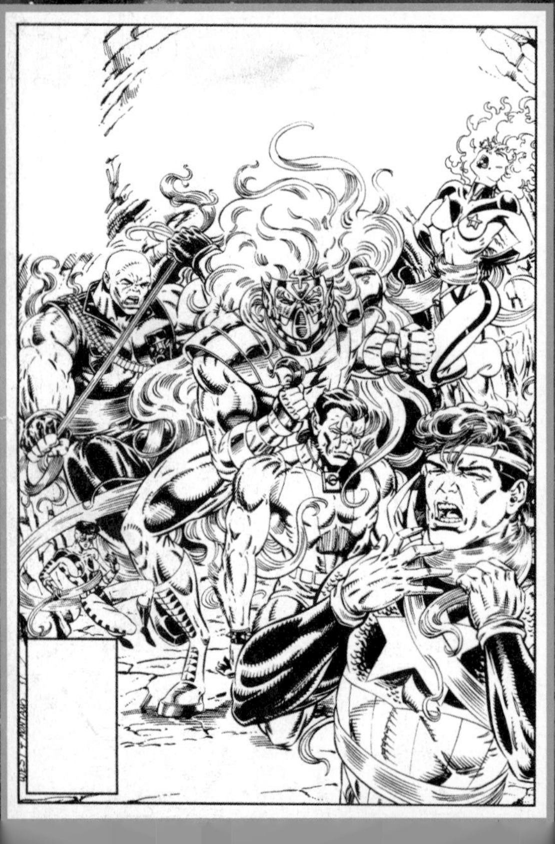
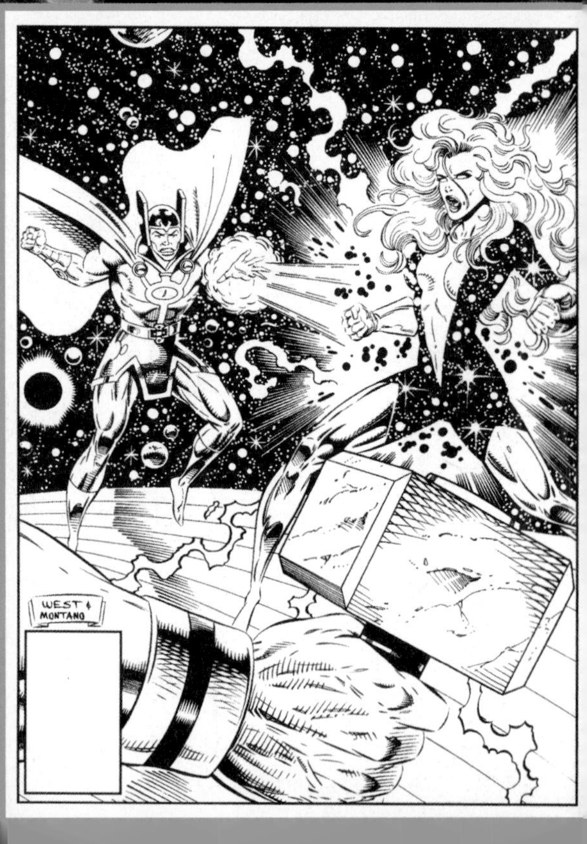
WEST &
MONTANO

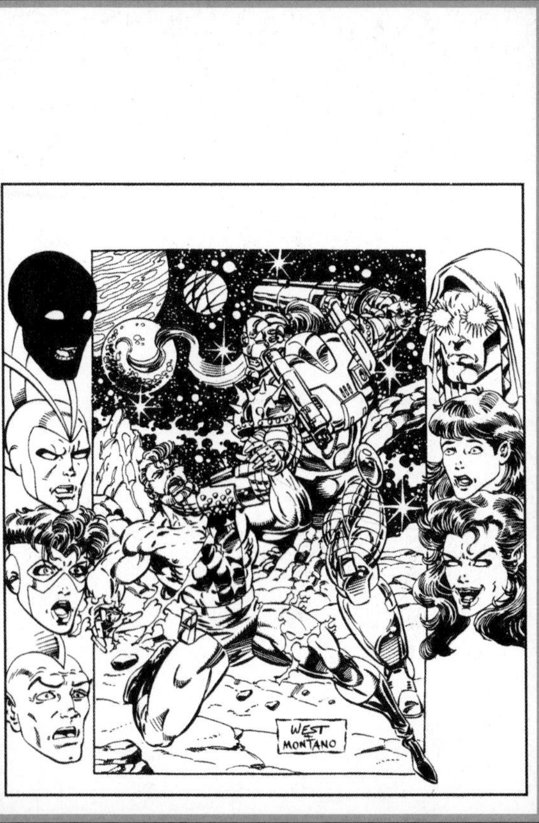
WEST
MONTANO

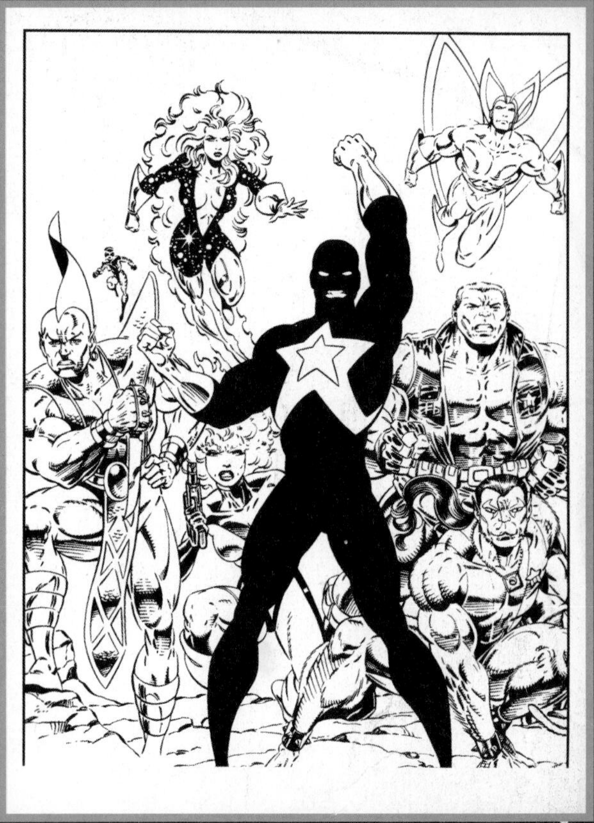

GUARDIANS OF THE GALAXY #48 & #50
COVER ART BY KEVIN WEST & STEVE MONTANO

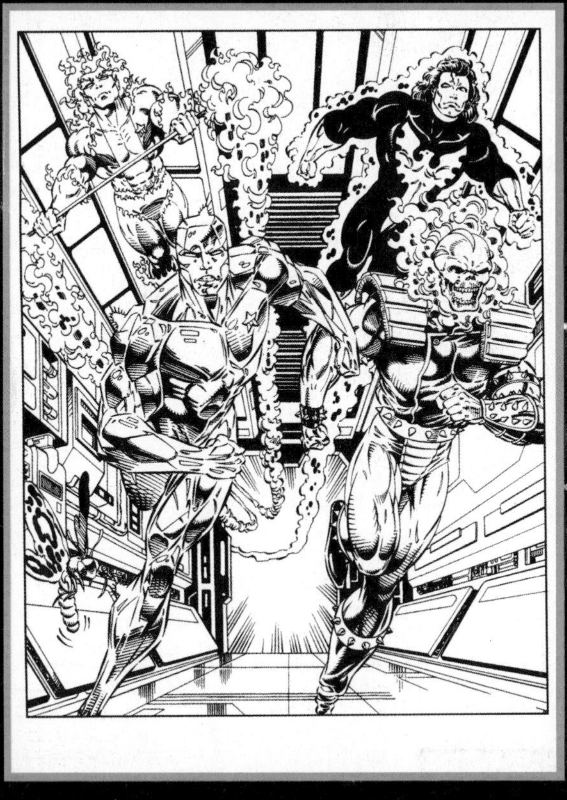

GALACTIC GUARDIANS #1, PAGE 1
ART BY KEVIN WEST & STEVE MONTANO

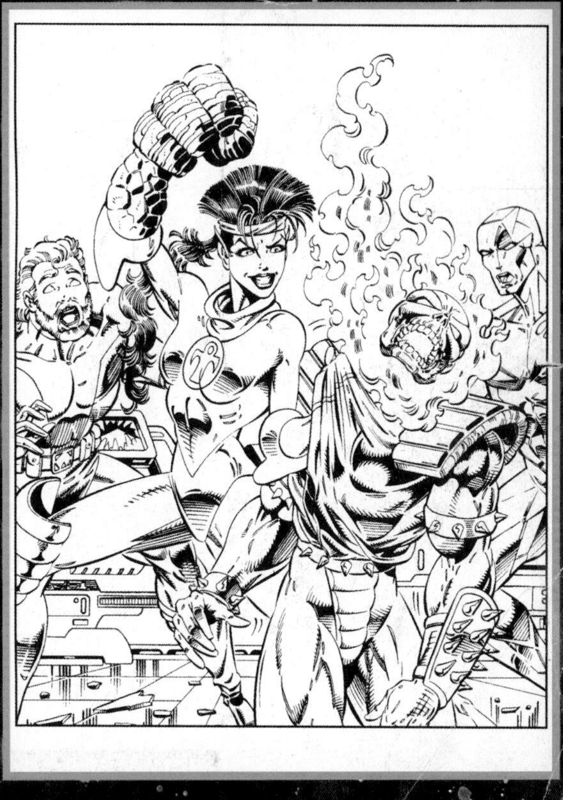

GALACTIC GUARDIANS #3
COVER ART BY KEVIN WEST & STEVE MONTANO

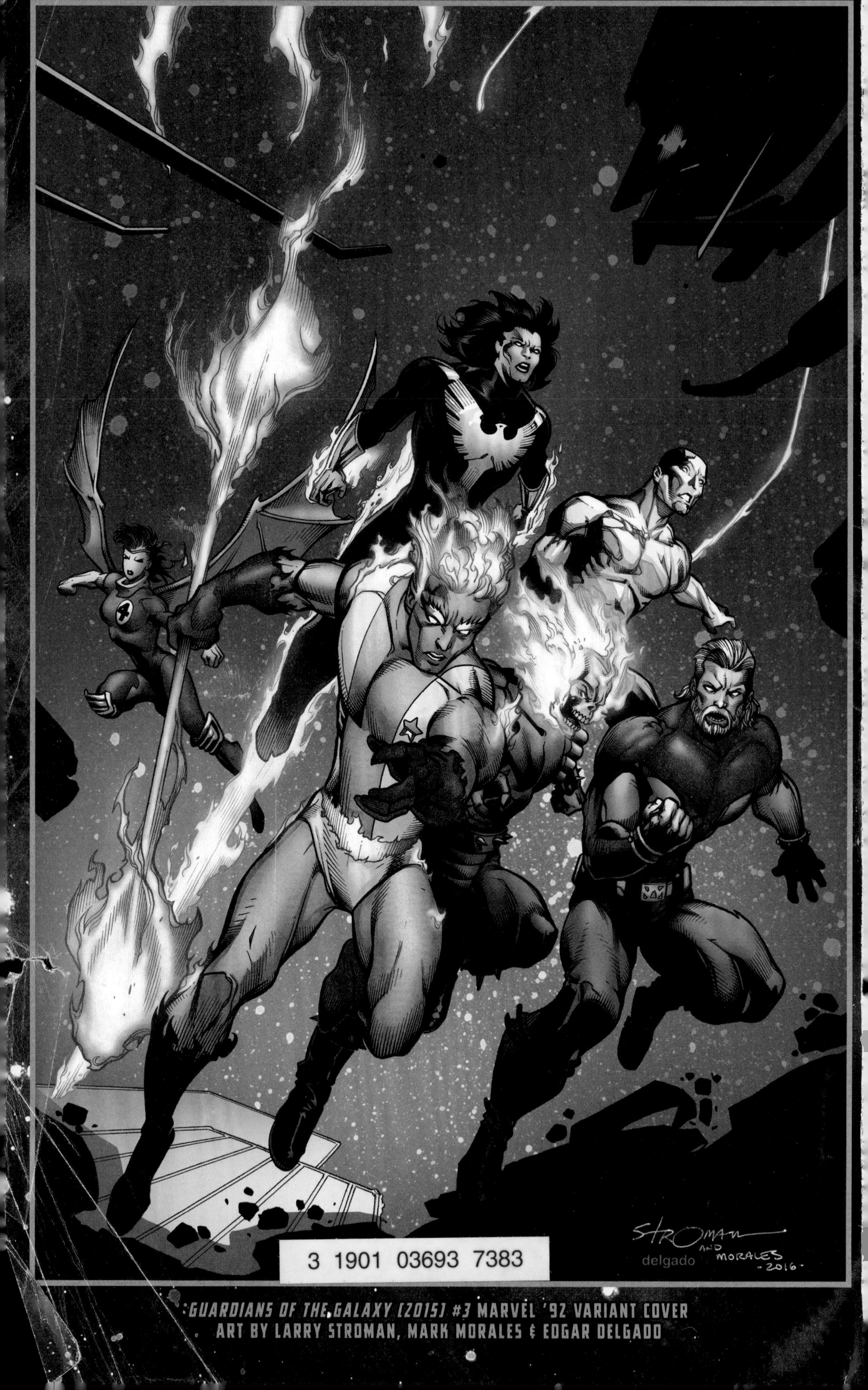
STROMAN AND MORALES -2016-
delgado

GUARDIANS OF THE GALAXY (2015) #3 MARVEL '92 VARIANT COVER
ART BY LARRY STROMAN, MARK MORALES & EDGAR DELGADO